Narrative, Apparatus, Ideology

Narrative, Apparatus, Ideology

A Film Theory Reader

Edited by Philip Rosen

Columbia University Press
New York   1986

Columbia University Press
New York   Guildford, Surrey
Copyright © 1986 Columbia University Press
All rights reserved

Printed in the United States of America

This book is Smyth-sewn.

Library of Congress Cataloging-in-Publication Data

Narrative, apparatus, ideology.

   Includes bibliographies.
   1. Moving-pictures—Philosophy—Addresses, essays,
lectures.   I. Rosen, Philip.
PN1995.N34   1986   791.43'01   86-2619
ISBN 0-231-05880-2
ISBN 0-231-05881-0 (pbk.)

Book design by Ken Venezio

Contents

Preface

Within two or three decades of the earliest public exhibitions of films, there appeared film theory. By now film theory is a tradition of thought with its own history. There have been especially fertile periods and movements in film theory (for example, the 1920s and the Soviet montage school), classic disputes (e.g., between followers of Bazin and of Eisenstein), and a number of standard types of argument which can be studied and discussed.[1]

Despite the interest of most film theoreticians in issues of aesthetics and criticism, major developments in classical film theory most often have not been presented as individualized responses to film, belletristic criticisms of taste, etc. Instead, they tended to be those which provided means for thinking of the cinematic experience in more systematic, therefore generalized terms. For example, Sergei Eisenstein often drew on disciplines such as social anthropology, psychology, and psycholinguistics to construct a concept of a properly aesthetic effect based on specific notions about regularities in human emotional processes. And André Bazin—best known for his thesis that cinema is a medium with a special capacity for conveying an experience of an ontologically ambiguous reality and that film art is therefore uniquely an art of reality—provided brilliant generalizations and hypotheses about the systematic parameters of film form and style during different historical periods.[2]

Now another major movement in film theory has occurred, centered in France, Great Britain, and the United States. Beginning in the 1960s, accelerating at the end of the decade, and exploding with full force during the 1970s, this "movement" is in fact difficult to label. It has partaken of and been strongly influenced by contemporaneous intellectual approaches in the humanities and cultural studies such as semiotics, structuralism, and post-structuralism. However, so many individuals of varying backgrounds have contributed significant work to it that to call it a "movement" already raises problems of definition. Perhaps it is better to consider what has happened as the emergence of a generation of thinkers about film who have in common a basic core bibliography regarding theories of culture and criticism and who, for the most part, are familiar with one another's work regarding the conceptualization of film and culture. Undoubtedly, the emergence of such a large group of important film theorists and analysts during a relatively limited historical period requires its own explanation. Such explanation would revolve around a conjuncture of factors, ranging from the cultural politics of the period to its sociointellectual history. It would also include both the kinds of filmmaking which were concurrent with their emergence, and the academic institutionalization of film studies which seems to have occurred most intensively (but not uniquely) in the United States through the 1960s and 1970s. It would, of course, have to take account of significant alternative approaches in film theory during these years; however, it might well identify what Russian Formalism labels a "dominant," that is, a constellation of issues, concerns, and arguments which served as an organizing matrix of discussion for the period, and to which even competing alternatives had to respond. As a shorthand, we can say that this dominant was composed of usually overlapping conceptualizations of narrative in film, of the cinematic apparatus, and of ideology—with all these often thought out in relation to a theory of the subject.

This anthology finds its rationale in the complicated tissue of cross-references and debates which flowered during the late 1960s and the 1970s. What requires repetition and emphasis is that it would be a distortion to hypostatize this discursive network into an easily unifiable theoretical entity. For example, it might be useful for the sake of convenience to label the body of work which this anthology seeks to exemplify as "post-structuralist cinema semiotics." But this label could be employed only with qualifications. Within the kinds of work with which this anthology is concerned, there is a good deal of heterogeneity; contributors include not only those who might label themselves semioticians or post-structuralists, but also psychoanalytic textual theorists, feminists, historical materialists, and neo-Formalists, to take a few of the most important strains. Furthermore, close scrutiny of the work of some of those most central to this "movement" can reveal a great deal of fracturing and rethinking. For example, to take two influential articles included in this volume, the work of Christian Metz in "The Imaginary Signifier" (1975) is in important respects distinct from his work in "Problems of Denotation in the Fiction Film" (1966–1967). Indeed, debate and disagreement among individual theorists and critics who work within some of its most significant conceptual parameters have made it clear that this "movement" is not monolithic.

Despite the difficulty of finding a label, however, the network of common theoretical argumentation and cross-references makes it difficult to avoid the impression that, in the last two decades, something important in the history of film theory has occurred and that it involves a large number of theorists who are aware of one another across national boundaries. Perhaps the best indication of this is the appearance of a group of interrelated issues with which a wide variety of the most important theoretical work of the period is concerned: is cinema as the production of signs best understood in the framework of linguistics and/or semiotics? What is the relation of narrative to cinematic signification? Why do certain parameters of narrative construction seem to define what most people would take as "normal" uses of cinematic images and sounds? How does film appeal to the spectator? Is film's appeal to the spectator founded on a sociocultural deployment of visual and sonic representation? Is that appeal inseparable from narrative? Does the signification of gender and sexuality have a central function for cinematic form and/or the technological apparatus of cinema? How do such questions inflect the way one conceives of cultural politics in cinema or conceives of film history?

The centrality and interrelation, by the 1970s, of such questions in so much significant and active film theory is the ultimate justification for this collection. The title of this anthology indicates three nodal points of interest throughout the period: the theorization of cinema as narrative (and the resulting issues raised by cinema with non-mainstream ways of organizing narrative, or cinema which is nonnarrative or at least seems "less" narrativized); the theorization of cinema as "apparatus" (the cultural determinations and effectivities of the cinematic machinery and of the disposition of production and exhibition technologies and techniques); and the theorization of cinema as ideology (the mass of representational entities and strategies social and cultural formations provide their agents for thinking about and experiencing the world). It is hoped that collecting so many of these articles together will help register the impact and importance of those questions and of the work that engages them.

The goal of this anthology, then, is to make available in one volume central samples of the crucial and/or exemplary work from this network of film-theoretical discourse. There are many ways to organize such a collection. The final decision was to organize them keeping in mind one general argument readable in the development of this network of film-theoretical writings. The argument can be schematized in a few statements, though every one of its elements requires elaboration. It goes as follows: "structuralist" analysis of signification has provided, in both its large-scale and its more microscopic assertions, powerful means of generalizing about narrative; and application of certain structuralist methods to film has been revelatory, in part because of the evident centrality of narrative to dominant film cultures (a centrality which itself needs to be explained). However, crucial aspects of the objects of analysis (narrative, film) are not accounted for by a structuralist approach. Therefore, other methodological tools, in some degree complementary to structuralism and in some degree opposed to it, are necessary in order to deal with that which exceeds structuralism. The version of this "post-structuralism" which has been strongest in the study of cinema has focused on a specific conception of the processes of human subjectivity. The consequent interest in the "theory of the subject" in cinema resulted in elaborations of certain interrelated and powerful (though often controversial) formulations which variously define the human subject as an epistemological category, a social category, and/or a psychoanalytic category, all of which are conceived in relation to processes of signification.

With some distortion and wrenching, all the selections in this anthology, though written at different times and places for different kinds of publications and occasions, could be placed in terms of this broadly sketched framework. The collection is divided into four parts. The break between structuralist-oriented studies and focusing on a theory of the subject comes between parts 1 and 2. Part 1 ("Structures of Filmic Narrative") includes articles which present and exemplify the tendency in cinema semiotics oriented toward a structuralism (sometimes in a loose sense of the term), especially as it relates to a privileged object of analysis variously called classical cinema, the classical text, and so forth; and articles which conceptualize opposition to this kind of filmmaking in ways that necessitate changes in the analytic model. (As will be noted in the introduction to part 1, however, virtually every article included in this part has an uneasy, most often critical, relation to structuralism strictly defined.)

The next three parts present arguments and analyses that deal with what a structuralist tendency is said to ignore or avoid dealing with. Part 2 ("Subject, Narrative, Cinema") includes articles which present one of the most important metalanguages in recent analyses of the relations of human subjectivity to filmic texts, one which seeks to join semiotic investigation of cinema and narrative to psychoanalytic categories in the study of how films address spectators. Part 3 ("Apparatus") presents essays in which such general concerns are worked out with respect to cinematic specificity and fundamental cinematic technology. Part 4 ("Textuality as Ideology") includes articles which summarize and return to issues encountered throughout the volume, but with a concern for problems of cultural politics and a historiography of filmic textuality.

In addition to the articles themselves, editorial introductions will fill out some of the terms and backgrounds of this structuring argument. The concerns of these introductions will not be to explain the twists and turns of every article in the anthology, but rather to prepare the way for some of the terminology and implicit premises on which the film theorists draw. These introductions, then, will gloss certain aspects of the work of individuals who were in fact not film theorists—such as the linguist Ferdinand de Saussure, the Marxist philosopher Louis Althusser, and the psychoanalytic theorist Jacques Lacan—whose writings have proven so important for the network of film theory covered in this collection. This is not to say that these are the only outside thinkers on whom the network of film-theoretical work of concern here has drawn. Nor is it to say that all the selections necessarily are based on the work of these particular thinkers. The points of concentration in the introductions are only organizational tools for necessarily brief presentations of a number of complex theses, acquaintance with which is assumed by many of the selections. Most of this necessarily concise introductory work is found in the introductions to parts 1 and 2.

It may be useful to repeat that the organization of this volume is only one possible ordering of its selections. Instead, for example, they could be presented chronologically, which could reveal how much more complex were the affiliations, cross-references, and debates than any simple organizational schema can indicate. Alternative groupings of articles to highlight other connections are conceivable. For example, there could be a section which deals with narrative and excess (not just the contributions of Thompson and Linderman in part 1, but also the reading of *Young Mr. Lincoln* by the editors of *Cahiers du cinéma* and Heath's synthetic essay "Narrative Space" in part 4, as well as others). Or, it is possible to collect all the explicitly feminist essays into one group. It was decided here to spread feminist arguments throughout the volume in order to suggest their wide-ranging, fundamental importance in film theory; however, in some circumstances it might be more useful to read them all at once or successively. These examples show that many organizational possibilities exist. Obviously, if this book is used in a classroom, an instructor may well wish to arrange the readings in different ways, for his or her own pedogogical purposes.

One final point has to do with the selections made. Readers familiar with the film-theoretical milieu which is the concern of this book will surely note the absence of at least some names which have played important roles in that milieu. This can only be acknowledged, with the statement that inescapable limitations of space made difficult decisions necessary.

Notes

1. See J. Dudley Andrew, *The Major Film Theories* (New York: Oxford University Press, 1976) for a standard but intentionally ahistorical account of arguments within the tradition of classical film theory. It should be noted that Andrew's perspective is somewhat different from those of most of the writers included in this anthology.

2. For example, see "Film Form: New Problems," in Sergei Eisenstein, *Film Form*, trans. Jay Leyda (New York: Harcourt, Brace, 1949); and "The Evolution of the Language of Cinema," in André Bazin, *What Is Cinema?*, vol. 1, trans. Hugh Gray (Berkeley: University of California Press, 1967).

Work of film theorists referred to but not cited in full in this preface can be found in their contributions to this anthology.

Acknowledgments

The idea for this anthology was originally conceived in a series of discussions with Michael Silverman of Brown University regarding the state of film theory during and after the 1970s, and from classroom experiences of teaching that theory. The selection of items to be included and their final ordering owes much to these conversations. I gratefully acknowledge his contribution.

Certain individuals have my gratitude for significant contributions made on short notice. I received crucial linguistic assistance from my colleague in Foreign Languages and Screen Studies at Clark University, Marcia Butzel. Stephen Dirado took time off from his own remarkable photographic art to perform the relatively workaday task of reproducing stills. Claire Bloom helped with a rearrangement of text at an important point in the project.

This project received support from the Clark University Faculty Development Fund.

All my students of the past few years at Clark University, Columbia University, and New York University have had no choice but to put up with my insistence on the value of recent theory. They have greatly contributed to my understanding of that theory and to the selection process here, often in complicated ways of which they may be unaware. I thank them all.

And I also wish to thank my editor at Columbia University Press, Bill Germano. His general belief in the significance of theory and film studies, and his enthusiasm for this project in particular, are responsible for the existence of this book.

Finally, and as always, Mary Ann Doane provided me with intellectual assistance and emotional support—both necessary conditions for the completion of this project.

Part One

Structures of Filmic Narrative

Introduction: The Saussurian Impulse and Cinema Semiotics

At the high point of the so-called structuralist movement (centered in France in the mid-1960s), there was intensive interest in analyzing diverse phenomena investigated in a number of distinct fields (e.g., anthropology, sociology, philosophy, literature, film) by "reading" their objects of analysis through a concept of structure derived from certain aspects of classical structural linguistics. The "linguistic approach" was employed widely, on artifacts ranging from cultural phenomena with obvious bases in verbal language (such as, myth which is verbally transmitted and literary narrative) to those whose linguistic bases are not so obvious. It had a decisive impact in the study of cinema.

One way of explaining the conceptual impact of structuralism is by beginning from a major issue of film theory on which structuralism has had an important effect: the extent to which cinematic signification can be comprehended in terms of a systematics. The elegant and fertile framework for investigating linguistic signifying systems provided by structural linguistics led film theorists to give this question new kinds of attention. In particular, the definitions of linguistic structure of most importance for structuralism generally and film theory in particular stemmed directly from the proposals advanced by Ferdinand de Saussure in his *Course in General Linguistics,* first compiled in 1915.[1] There Saussure sought to provide the foundations for a modern linguistics, but he also proposed that the conceptual framework he developed might be applied to a general science of signs—"semiology." Saussure was not the only thinker to envision such a science, but his distinctions and terminology had a great effect on the attempt to devise first a structuralist and then a post-structuralist cinema semiotics in the 1960s and 1970s. It will therefore be useful to review some of his conceptualizations before outlining some basic issues in cinema semiotics.

Saussure proposed to investigate any language as an abstract, closed system of elements and rules which subtends actual usages of a language and which could generate any number of concrete utterances. The distinction between *langue* (the underlying system) and *parole* (the particular utterances) was a fundamental principle of his linguistics because he argued that the first object of linguistics should be *langue*. The question then becomes what are the units and relations composing *langue*.

Saussure calls the basic elements of a language *signs*. Western thought has generally considered any instance of representation by dividing it into three components: (1) the perceivable material which appears to stand for something else (graphic marks in writing, sonic disturbances of air in speech, etc.); (2) the mental state called up by or associated with that perceivable material ("meaning"); and (3) real-world objects, processes, etc. to which the first two components supposedly correspond or refer. Saussure calls the first (perceivable material) the *signifier* and the second ("meaning") the *signified*. For him these are the two inescapable faces of that basic unit of signification, the sign, inseparably joined like the two sides of a piece of paper.

Crucially, Saussure argues that in verbal language the connection between signifier and signified is virtually always arbitrary; that is, while a sign is a unity of signifier and signified, there is no natural connection between the two. In a given usage of verbal language, meaning occurs on the basis of an unconscious but collectively legislated convention of a given tongue, such as French or Chinese. It is only through such conventionalization that signifier and signified can be associated to produce the kinds of suppleness and subtlety of meaning which can be found in verbal expressions. Note that this makes the conception of the signifier more complex than at first appears: a signifier is not just perceivable material which stands for something in the world (a referent) on a one-to-one basis; even if it did this, a signifier *also* and *simultaneously* exists as an entity of the group, a collective phenomenon. The sign is therefore a mental entity. (But its basis is not necessarily in consciousness, since language users certainly do not have to be explicitly and consciously aware of the structures of language.)

The premise of the arbitrariness of the sign permits Saussure to conceive of language as requiring a relatively abstract underlying system *(langue)*, for in this account the system organizing signs is what permits meaning to be produced— not any inherent characteristics of a given signifier or signified. But a further result of this approach is the conception of such systems as radically closed: Saussure moves to banish concern with the referent from the work of the linguist. The linguist is concerned with reconstructing *langue*, the unconscious but finite system which is the condition for the possibility of speech *(parole)*. The study of *parole* cannot in itself be the linguist's goal: there are an infinite number of concrete utterances possible in any tongue; each is caught up in and inflected by concrete speech situations; and any given instance of *parole* is by itself not systematizable. However, *parole* can be studied to build inferentially a less concrete entity that logically must subtend it, namely *langue*.

Saussure's conception of the linguist's objective is thus the construction of an abstract, closed system. This necessitates a number of additional arguments and methodological propositions, which have to do both with the general charac-teristics of such systems and with prescriptions for studying them. Among the latter, for example, is the recommendation that language should be studied less in its *diachronic* (changing over time) aspects than as a *synchronic* cross-section of a mass of signs and rules for producing understandable utterances. But perhaps the most far-reaching definition Saussure provides is for that of the key relation in the linguistic system, the one which gives definition to the various components of *langue:* what he names as *difference.*

Having argued that signs are not determined by their concrete, positive qualities such as a specific relation to a referent but by their position in the system as a whole, Saussure traces out implications. A signifier has linguistic value only in relation to other signifiers, that is, to what in the linguistic system it is *not;* a sign is defined negatively. On this relational account, signification is determined not just by what is present in an instance of *parole,* but what is not said, is absent. These negative relations, absences, dominate language.[2]

On a generalized level, Saussure sums up these negative relations with the term *difference:* language is to be conceived fundamentally as a system of differ-ences among signifiers. The linguist studies differential relations. There are two fundamental axes of such relations, the *syntagmatic* and the *paradigmatic* (which Saussure calls the "associative"). The syntagmatic is comprised of the rule-governed relationships among signs present in an actual, concrete signifying "chain" such as a sentence; it is the realm of combination. The paradigmatic is constituted by the relationships among all the possible (therefore implicit, absent) alternatives to each element of a signifying chain; it is the realm of substitution. For example, in the sentence "The big pig ate Nate," at the level of the moneme, the paradigmatic set of adjectives which could fit into the position occupied by *big* might include *small* and *white,* but not *from,* and still be syntagmatically correct and reasonable ("understandable"), given the relationships permitted by the *langue* underlying English. Note that both syntagmatics and paradigmatics study the regulation of difference. Individual items of any paradigm or syntagm are distinguished from one another only as clusters of features which can be recognized as pertinent differences, and these vary among different tongues.

Of course, *langue* is a complex, multileveled system, so such relations would presumably be sought at several levels. Phonology based on these principles, for example, highlights the fact that from the range of possible sounds the human voice can produce, only a limited number signify in a given tongue, and that the relevance of a specific sound is mandated by the collective structure of differences which are pertinent in a given tongue. For example, if the first sound of the English word *big* is unvoiced rather than voiced, it registers a pertinent phonological difference in the *langue* of English and becomes *pig,* another sign with another signified. It is the joining, or *articulation* of pertinent sounds which form meaningful units—suffixes, prefixes, words, etc. These meaningful units achieve their place in language because they can be read through a collective structure of differential relations: *big* and *pig* are components of a large system of differences which enables meaning to emerge from such arbitrary signifiers.

There is in addition another linguistic articulation, whereby such meaningful units are in turn joined together into sentences, groups of differentiated words which are ordered according to certain rules and which, according to common sense, express a "complete thought." This "thought" may aspire to the status of anything from an emotional expression of the speaker to a referential description of physical processes. If the "communication" is "successful," then meaning will shine through the network of differences which formed it. This leads to an apparent peculiarity: if, as common sense would have it, language should be used to manifest intended meanings, this occurs by obscuring the basis of language—the relation of difference. In anticipation of kinds of arguments which will be presented below, we can here point out that one possible conclusion of this account of signification is the contention that meaning is a unifying impulse which obscures the basic heterogeneity of signifying materials and processes which produce it.

In the history of linguistics, Saussure's formulations represent a seminal moment. Their implications can be charted through a number of now classic works, ranging from Roman Jakobson on phonology to Noam Chomsky on syntax. Yet, despite Saussure's own call for a more general semiology based on identical or similar principles, it is not immediately evident that his distinctions are applicable to all kinds of sign processes. Can it be said that *all* sign systems have as their basic perceivable units arbitrary signifiers? What of visual images, one of our chief concerns here, which so often seem to be based on resemblance to a real-world object? Certainly cinema—which, because of its utilization of photography and recorded sound, appears at first glance to produce not just representations *of* reality but presentations *from* reality—might seem to be poor ground for a Saussurian semiology. How can one argue that cinematic signification is founded on a relational structure of differences? Indeed, in the history of thinking about film, one forceful argument has traditionally been that cinema, by its very nature, depends on a *positive* relationship to something in the real world, a relationship which is outside any artificial or arbitrary system of image-signs; for if cinema is primarily used as a photographic medium, there must be objects which can be filmed.

Furthermore, suppose there were good counterarguments for the arbitrariness of cinematic signifiers. In itself, this still would not necessarily justify the appeal to *linguistic* structures as aiding in the understanding of *cinematic* systematicity. Of course, it may well be possible to argue for the universal validity of categories of verbal *langue* for understanding signification in general, in part because every normal human being seems to be born with the capacity for language use. This is supported by the fact that language is a central aspect of every human culture of which we know. But such an argument can work in another direction. On the surface, at least, not all sign systems have such universality; indeed, if cinema is a sign system, it is one which has existed in a very small number of cultures in human history. Conceivably, this could lead to a case that the culturally widespread characteristics of linguistic structure are not comparable to cinematic systems.

Nevertheless, it was precisely Saussure who provided a starting point for the semiological inquiry into cinema which was so important by the late 1960s. Distinctions between cinema and verbal language were taken into account either by new emphases in the conceptualization of cinema or by modifications in Saussurian methodological premises. For example, it proved possible to emphasize a number of "arbitrary" aspects of film images taken as signifiers. If the cinema image is derived through photography from the graphic procedures of Renaissance painters, it can be argued that the basis of the image is a number of *conventions* of visual representation. Those conventions turn out to have exemplary importance for the theoretical status of such images. One effect of the argument for the basic conventionality of cinematic image was to open the way for a utilization of the idea of difference in cinematic signification. This Saussurian concept underwent a number of developments and modifications whose discussion is best postponed until we come to consider psychoanalytic theory in part 2. However, we should note here certain aspects of the influence of conceptions of an underlying *langue*—or a widespread, fundamental signifying system—for the semiological investigation of cinema.

On this question of systematicity, structuralist-influenced analysis made by its breakthrough by developing the already existing notion of "classical cinema." This is a concept whose most important use had previously been in the writings of André Bazin. It denotes a set of formal and stylistic boundaries defined by a certain fundamental stability of editing and camerawork practices and by certain generic conventions. Taken together these were, according to Bazin, the epitome of Hollywood filmmaking before *Citizen Kane*. Bazin argued that *Citizen Kane* and certain other films marked a rupture in film history, after which different constructions of narrative space and time would lead to a more realist approach to the world by means of cinema, which embodied a progressive realization of the latter's ontological nature.[3]

In the two and one-half decades since his death, other theorists, critics, and historians—as often as not unsympathetic to Bazin's phenomenological realist aesthetic—have expanded the concept of classical cinema. For some, it does not merely indicate the parameters of form and style in Hollywood cinema of the 1930s, but extends roughly from World War I to the breakup of the Hollywood studio system in the 1950s and 1960s, or even to the present, insofar as this system persists through the formal organization of international commercial film and perhaps television in an era when the industry's financial structure is somewhat different. Furthermore, where Bazin might stress the moral significance of film style as an approach to and/or attitude toward reality, other kinds of thinkers instead stressed the ideological components of these parameters of filmmaking, so intimately linked to the film industry of the most powerful capitalist nation.

Behind this enormous expansion of the concept of classical cinema lies the idea that Hollywood filmmaking has dominated our conception of what a "normal" movie is since the formation of the film studio apparatus between roughly 1910 and the early 1920s. Thus the U.S. film industry can be treated not only as the most powerful economic force among national cinemas, but relatedly as the most influential model of filmmaking practice in history. The claim is that there are certain identifiable parameters of form and style which have for most of film history served as norms and limitations throughout the world, and these norms are associated most closely with the kinds of films produced most successfully and extensively in the American narrative film industry. (While this kind of filmmaking is now often connoted by the appellation "classical cinema," the phrase "mainstream cinema" is sometimes employed with a gain in clarity.)

To anyone who has studied film history, the impact, both economic and aesthetic, of the American film industry will probably seem undeniable. but here we are concerned with another question, namely the search for a systematizable object which will permit the semiotician to formulate something in cinema comparable to *langue* in verbal language. The investigation of classical narrative cinema, in the extended sense of that term, has provided such an object. Even if we leave aside the question of whether cinema as such has anything strictly comparable to the linguistic system, it is still possible to argue that cinema *in its historical actuality* has norms so dominant and long-lasting (for a medium less than one hundred years old) that such norms can be treated as the parameters of a system which can hold the methodological place occupied by *langue* in Saussurian linguistics. This classical system is the basis for what we ordinarily take as understandable, and pleasurable, movies.

Thus, Bazin might argue that ultimately every film image is unique in that it records an absolutely unrepeatable segment of real space and time. But such writers as Raymond Bellour built on certain aspects of the early work of Christian Metz to discover a system of repetitions and regulated differences established both within individual films of the classical cinema and over a large body of films. Further, it was argued by such writers that the paradigmatic orderings of images (and sounds during the greater part of the medium's history) are based on certain identifiable types of narrative organization, with each image and sound answerable first of all to its place in the presentation of a story; that is, every image and sound of classical film responds to certain pervasive narrational principles which regulate the flow of sensations and meanings to the spectator. The norms of signification in cinema would therefore always require some minimum of *diegesis*—a fictional space, time, and world—and diegetic constructions are narrational. The attractiveness of this kind of analysis of filmic narrative and the concept of a dominant or "classical" narrative was further reinforced by the flowering of "narratology" in the study of myth and literature.[4]

A classical text thus becomes identifiable to investigators on the basis of a number of overlapping qualities, not all of which are necessarily present in each instance but which do permit of a certain regulated range of variations. Exemplary headings under which some chief examples of such characteristics cluster include: a restricted economy of narrative form; enough stylistic transparency to insure that elements are deployed primarily at the service of plot and character; and a certain recirculation of figures of mise-en-scène, camerawork, editing, and/or genre, both within individual films and through the classical system as a whole. It could even be argued that in superficially non-narrative kinds of films such as documentaries images and sounds are, in many respects, usually organized according to formal and stylistic parameters drawn from classical narrative cinema or at least are most often organized in response to those parameters. There are two emphases of general importance, then, that came from this investigation: first, that signification in cinema is indeed systematizable as a network of structural repetitions and differences; and, second, that a number of conceptualizations from theories of narrative rooted in Saussure can be centrally useful in the semiotics of cinema.

All this might seem of evident utility for the concerns of an academic or esoteric criticism. We now have large-scale generalizations which provide professors with the rationale for microscopic analyses of the patterns of constructing images and sounds in a tremendous number of films—and hence the basis for a large number of articles in academic journals. However, it is by no means a historical accident that this approach to cinema became so attractive at a time when the institution of the university was a center of directly political concerns. For if there is a system of norms, then we can inquire about the foundations and determinants of such systems, and about the implications of deviation or (from a different perspective) oppositional practices and systems. Further, if the systematic norms of image/sound construction are conceived of as sociohistoric and cultural entities, then so can deviations be conceived of as cultural politics. It is true that this is yet another departure from a strictly Saussurian semiology of cinema, for which a postulated cinematic signifying system would be describable in the same form which Saussure attributes to *langue*. Not only are the dominant structures underpinning signification seen in historical terms, but now opposition to such structures is contemplated. In Saussurian linguistics such opposition is, strictly speaking, impossible on this side of meaning, for to oppose the structure of *langue* is to produce non-sense. At most, one may play at the edges of the parameters of the linguistic system, as in certain kinds of poetry and literature.[5]

On the other hand, when attempts were made to develop new conceptualizations of cultural politics in cinema from the earlier tendencies of structuralism and post-structuralism, the Saussurian heritage remained evident. In Saussure the privileged formal figure is the binary opposition: every term in a signifying system is fundamentally definable only in a relation of difference to that which it is not; that is, in relation to at least one other term. The application of this principle to social and cultural analysis had already been shown as feasible in the analyses of myth, seminal for structuralist narrative theory, performed by the anthropologist Claude Levi-Strauss.[6] By the early 1970s, instead of—or in addition to—employing the figure of the binary opposition as a means of decoding the semantic structure of a text, some of the more politicized cinema semioticians often used it on another level. They differentiated among two classes of films: those which fit clearly into the paradigms of the classical filmmaking system, now seen as integral components of cultural and/or representational systems characteristic of advanced capitalism; and those which opposed classical paradigms of filmmaking. Such formulations of a cultural politics ranged from promotion of certain kinds of avant-garde film making to polemical calls for alternative views of film history which would denaturalize dominant modes of cinematic signification by giving proper importance to other actual or possible practices.[7]

But if the intellectual climate made such a cultural politics attractive, those same impulses could lead to doubts about the ultimate implications of the systemics which was being constructed in film theory. The structuralist-Saussurian tendency in cinema semiotics had put forward a powerful analysis of classical cinema by investigating it as a system; therefore, this tendency included a strong proclivity to reveal a certain fundamental repetition in all films made within this cinema. The years during which these approaches were most aggressively formulated in film theory—the late 1960s to mid-1970s—saw the development and working-out of kinds of political-cultural impulses that not only crystallized in France in 1968, but were felt in varying degrees and through various manifestations in a number of Western nations. In particular, early in this period there was indeed a strong film-theoretical temptation to conceptualize absolutely opposed textual traits as markers of oppositional cinema, for this permitted a political evaluation which supported stylistically radical artistic practices. It is clear that this could and sometimes did lead to the polemical overvaluation of formally defined textual characteristics as being oppositional in themselves. It should be noted, however, that this was part of a more general tendency which opened the way for important explorations. Not only in theory and criticism but also in filmmaking there were important interrogations of the cinematic and cultural potential of textual traits which might be defined as against the classical system of signification (e.g., uneconomical use of elements of narrative form, stylistic and formal opacity, a stoppage of the recirculation of normally repeated figures or a hyperbolization and laying-bare of such recirculation).

This temptation, which we might label binary cultural politics, nevertheless led to difficulties for those who came to structuralist theorization seeking radically alternative conceptualizations of cinema at the service of an oppositional cultural politics. To treat oppositional filmmaking simply as a radical otherness to dominant practices conceived on a Saussurian model of *langue* is to attribute to the latter a totalized determining power. That is, from a theoretical standpoint, such a binary sociocultural analysis makes "the" signifying system into a structurally unified totality underlying and penetrating all individual instances of signification within that dominant system. Every mainstream film will ultimately have to be analyzed as being a particular instance of a general totality. The result is a model of signification where analysis is complete when all has been placed structurally within the dominant system—which is ultimately only to reproduce that dominance in theory. Analysis of a film or films can cease when its textual complicity is demonstrated.

For those seeking new definitions of a cultural politics, such a totalized, closed system could soon become a critically and politically suffocating premise. Where is transformation, where is history, where is politics in all this? The effects of such totalizing power are located by analysis at the level of practice (the dominant practices are the measure of what shall and shall not be comprehended as disruptive). But as theoretical presumptions, they can mandate a conception that may only be able to demonstrate the impossibility of disruption *within* the system and consign opposition to a structural place of *exterior* importance. It becomes difficult to understand where is the political, historical, and/or theoretical common ground on which the two poles struggle and engage with one another.

The desire to conceptualize a cultural politics was only one distinctive strand in the intellectual history of the period. It serves here as an example, one which remained especially important in film culture, of a general set of complex theoretical debates around structuralist conceptions. These discussions were already in progress by the late 1960s, and if we define of structuralism in a very strict way (limiting it to the application of Saussurian principles only), the structuralist moment in film theory was relatively brief. Even as that tendency was being forcefully explored in the study of cinema, a number of arguments converged in a general move which did not embody simple abandonment of all interest in systematicity, but did inflect conceptions of signifying systems in crucial ways. Certain aspects of the resulting "post-structuralism" became central to developments in film theory. (In fact, any linear presentation of the development of these arguments can only be heuristic; critiques were most often simultaneous, at least in film theory, with the kind of mobilizations of structuralism discussed above, and the former had effects on the latter.) In particular, conceptions having to do with a "theory of the subject" on the basis of not only semiotic theory but also psychoanalytic and ideological theory, rapidly became central to film-theoretical argumentation. We can postpone discussion of this until the next part of this anthology.

Here, it is enough to resume our gloss on the concept of signifying system by pointing out that one central concern of critiques of structuralism involved reconsideration of the structuralist predisposition to treat signifying systems and/or individual instances of texts produced in a given system as relatively coherent totalities. For some critics and theorists, the oppositional utility of structuralist conceptions consisted in part in a challenge to traditional aesthetics, a central aspect of which was said to be the notion of an artwork as a self-contained, organically unified entity. It was thought that the self-sufficiency of the work was put in question by seeing it as a regulated play of differences, understandable not in itself but only in relation to the larger system. However, the extraordinary generalizing power which methodology rooted in Saussure confers on analysis of the signifying system (conceptualized on the model of *langue*) tended to reinstate that unity, redefined and on other levels. Contradiction and heterogeneity could still be shut out in textual analysis, though by placement of the work through the concept of the signifying system rather than at the level of its own uniqueness.

As opposed to this, there developed a predisposition toward suspicion of appearances of unity and totality, whether produced by individual texts being studied or by analysts seeking systematicity. From various perspectives, including psychoanalytic theories of signification and social theory, it was argued that contradiction as well as unity, heterogeneity as well as homogeneity, might be a goal of analysis—even the analysis of a relatively well-developed signifying system. In fact, this claim could actually be presented from the perspective of semiotic theory as deriving from certain of Saussure's conceptions, and hence as an internal critique of Saussurian structuralism. It may be true that the "experience" of many instances of signification is that of a finalization, a completion of meaning and hence a unity; and if so, one might argue that "experience" is rooted in a greater totality which can be called "signifying system." But if we follow Saussure in conceiving of all signs as defined by a structure of differences, then signification is the action of difference. Stopping analysis when one has unified that action under the rubric of meaning would thus be to participate in the finalization, and actually to contribute to the obfuscation of fundamental signifying mechanisms.[8]

This leads to the possibility that words such as structure and system, if they are to be retained, should not be theorized as completely closed and totalized entities. Let us accept for now the validity of describing a film text as "classical," and let us suppose that such a text is read, in the first instance, as an individual polished unity or with an implicit awareness of a general signifying system. Nevertheless—or even because of this—it may be that theory and critical analysis should read such texts more deeply and aggressively, seeking the processes of difference and disjuncture which produce that sense of unity. This would be to ask how surface homogeneity occurs on the basis of heterogeneous components rather than, as it were, accepting the text and/or signifying system at their own word.

Thus, it becomes conceivable that over and above the analyzable totalities and unities imposed by a signifying system, a certain "excess" can be found even in the most classical film. Then it becomes possible that critical analysis may be able to discover cases of films produced within the classical system but which nevertheless take some of its mechanisms to such an extreme that the film exceeds certain of the aspects which seem to unify it. This kind of argument can be made on a number of levels ranging from that of perception (as Kristin Thompson points out in her contribution below, aspects of perceivable material can be said to escape determination by the signifying structure) to ideology (as in a famous collective reading of *Young Mr. Lincoln* performed in 1970 by the editors of *Cahiers du cinéma,* who found a number of crucial moments where the logic of the film's ideological project breaks down into contradiction and incoherence; this analysis is included in part 4 of the present volume).

This type of argument necessitates a fundamental complexity in the conceptual framework of any postulated cinema semiotics. Most simply, we can note here one major consequence. The goal of abstracting a closed system of signification that directly comprehends all individual film texts by describing their processes as being either inside or outside that system must be transformed. Elements which appear excessive, heterogeneous, incoherent from the perspective of a purportedly totalized signifying system and/or apparently "unified" text must be accounted for. And the means of suppressing—or repressing—them must be included in the description of a purported totality. This is not simply to reject systemic investigation of signification, but it is minimally to begin from a more complex view of the regularities of filmic signification. For many important film theorists, lines of argument such as this necessitated appeals to other kinds of explanatory and investigative frameworks. Some of the major approaches taken in this regard will be covered in later parts of this book.

The items included in part 1 exemplify some of the major approaches in the conceptualization of a cinematic signifying system and, more particularly, classical cinema; the Saussurian impulse in such work; some ideological–political implications of this project; and the concept of excess.

The first selection is the most recently written. David Bordwell's essay is a theoretical overview of one of the privileged objects of investigation in film theory in the 1960s and 1970s, namely classical cinema. He provides an important summary of the concept from a Neoformalist perspective, drawing on his researches into the history of Hollywood cinema and narrative theory.

The investigations conducted by Christian Metz throughout the 1960s and early 1970s on questions of cinema in relation to linguistics and semiology were, for film theory, probably the most influential contributions made by any single individual. "Problems of Denotation in the Fiction Film" summarizes many of the chief problems with which he was concerned in the 1960s as he addressed the question of whether a Saussurian semiology of cinema is possible. It includes a presentation of the *grande syntagmatique* (the large syntagmatic category of the image track), his often noted working proposal of a typology of categories of syntagmatic organization in mainstream cinema.

Included in this part are two articles by Raymond Bellour which are important investigations into the formulation and processes of difference in classical films. In "Segmenting/Analyzing" Bellour explores the functioning of segmentation in an entire classical film, *Gigi*. Not only an analysis of the film, this article is just as much a methodological meditation on the possibilites of cinema semiology, as exemplified by Metz's *grande syntagmatique*. The second article by Bellour, "The Obvious and the Code," deals with the operations of difference on a more microscopic level, by analyzing patterns of repetition and variation in a segment from *The Big Sleep*.

It is noteworthy that even though the above articles are intended to present and/or exemplify the semiotic conceptualization of the classical cinematic system of signification, each of them to a greater or lesser degree grapples with questions and difficulties raised by that conceptualization. Thus, for example, in his analysis of *Gigi*, Bellour does not just "apply" the categories of the *grande syntagmatique*, but interrogates them even as he interrogates the construction of the classical film; and he ends by demonstrating the possibility that the analysis of repetition and difference must be extended to the level of character structure, summarizing the variations at play with allusions to psychoanalytic terminology.

In "The-Spectator-in-the-Text: The Rhetoric of *Stagecoach*," Nick Browne explicitly centers his investigation of a sequence from a famous classical film on an issue normally considered to be outside the bounds of a strictly Saussurian semiology: how do the patterns of classical filmmaking appeal to a spectator? Browne provides not only a model of close textual analysis, but also an exploration of explanatory claims that can be made on the basis of textual analysis. In its concern with the appeal to the spectator as a rhetorical act, this article should be compared to several selections appearing later in this anthology, some of which are critiqued by Browne.

Jean-Luc Godard was one of the most important film makers for the period during which semiological investigations of classical cinema were sometimes allied with radical calls for a new cultural politics of cinema. In "Godard and Counter-Cinema: *Vent d'Est*," Peter Wollen uses a Godard film as an occasion for outlining what he sees as Godard's binary cultural politics. Even in this clear, deliberately schematic article, which summarizes a number of the classical and non-classical textual characteristics of concern to a cultural politics, Wollen includes cautionary notes regarding the problems of an oppositional project defined purely in binary terms.

In "The Concept of Cinematic Excess," Kristin Thompson confronts aspects of film texts which surpass mechanisms describable by a functional account of narrative structures. Using examples from *Ivan the Terrible*, she demonstrates how the concept of excess challenges theories and readings of films which stop when unifying structures have been located.

In "Uncoded Images in the Heterogeneous Text," Deborah Linderman is also concerned with excess. Her reading of Dreyer's *The Passion of Joan of Arc* illustrates how concentration on excess can lead to an interest in the penetration of textual mechanisms by ideology and vice-versa. Indeed, this article anticipates the introduction of other kinds of questions and additional terminologies in the following parts of this anthology.

Notes

1. Ferdinand de Saussure, *Course in General Linguistics,* trans. Wade Baskin (New York: McGraw-Hill, 1966).

2. This is why the signifier is, for Saussure, not simply perceivable material but (in the paradigmatic case of spoken language) a "sound-image." The term emphasizes not only that a singifier is inseparable from a signified but also that the signifier as "material" is not a determinate signifier because it is perceived as such, but is perceived as such because it is already a unit in a system of differential relations. See, for example, *Course in General Linguistics,* pp. 66–67.

3. See "The Evolution of the Language of Cinema" in André Bazin, *What is Cinema?,* vol. 1, trans. Hugh Gray (Berkeley: University of California Press, 1967).

4. The work of Roland Barthes provides summaries of shifting attitudes in "narratology" and toward "the classical text" in literature which had some influence in film theory. For example, see Barthes' overview "Introduction to the Structural Analysis of Narrative" (1966) in *Image-Music-Text,* ed. and trans. Stephen Heath (New York: Hill and Wang, 1977); Barthes, "The Realistic Effect" (1968), trans. Gerald Mead in *Film Reader* (1978), no. 3; and Barthes, *S/Z,* trans. Richard Miller (New York: Hill and Wang, 1974).

The distinction between *diegesis* and *mimesis* is found in Plato and Aristotle, and appears in twentieth-century literary theory as an opposition in modes of narration between "telling" and "showing" the story events. Christian Metz credits Etienne Souriau with importing the term into film theory to denote "the film's *repesented* instance." The use of the term emphasizes how narrative cinema "tells" stories by "showing," so that Plato's original distinction is untenable in any absolute sense. Genette makes a similar point about litertature in his summary of this opposition. See Gérard Genette, *Narrative Discourse: An Essay in Method,* trans. Jane E. Lewin (Ithaca: Cornell University Press, 1980), pp. 162–69, and Christian Metz, *Film Language: A Semiotics of the Cinema,* trans. Michael Taylor (New York: Oxford University Press, 1974), pp. 97–98.

5. One classic example of the Saussurian heritage extended to poetics is in the work of Roman Jakobson. See his "Closing Statement: Linguistics and Poetics," in *Style in Language,* ed. Thomas A. Sebeok (Cambridge, MA: MIT Press, 1960); for example, the discussion of the relation between the poetic function and the referential function of an utterance on pp. 367–74.

6. For considerations of method and the generalizability of linguisitic procedures to sociocultural phenomena, see Claude Lévi-Strauss, *Structural Anthropology,* trans. Claire Jacobson and Brooke Grundfest Schoepf (New York: Basic Books, 1963).

7. Compare, for example, the analytic use to which Peter Wollen put the figure of the binary opposition in his discussion of Hawks and Ford in *Signs and Meanings in the Cinema* (Bloomington and London: Indiana University Press, 1969, rev. 1972), pp. 74–105, to the more polemical development of systemic, political oppositions among types of film making in Noël Burch and

Jorge Dana, "Propositions," *Afterimage* (1974), no. 5, pp. 40–66, or Jean-Louis Comolli and Jean Narboni, "Cinema/Ideology/Criticism (1)," in *Screen Reader 1* (London: Society for Education in Film and Television, 1977), which originally appeared in *Cahiers du cinéma* in 1969 and which was published in English in *Screen* in 1971. While the latter two delimit intermediate cases between the extremes of systemic-political complicity and radical opposition, even these intermediate positions are defined in the context of a binary opposition between two radically different categories of textuality.

8. For one of the most influential examples of this kind of critique of Saussurianism, see Jacques Derrida, *Of Grammatology*, trans. Gayatri Chakravorty Spivak (Baltimore: Johns Hopkins University Press, 1976; original French publication 1967), esp. part 1, ch. 2, "Linguistics and Grammatology."

David Bordwell
Classical Hollywood Cinema: Narrational Principles and Procedures

Three aspects of narrative can, at least provisionally, be kept distinct. A narrative can be studied as *representation,* how it refers to or signifies a world or body of ideas. This we might call the "semantics" of narrative, and it is exemplified in most studies of characterization or realism. A narrative can also be studied as a *structure,* the way its components combine to create a distinctive whole. An example of this "syntactic" approach would be Vladimir Propp's morphology of the magical fairy tale.[1] Finally, we can study a narrative as an *act,* a dynamic process of presenting a story to a perceiver. This would embrace considerations of source, function, and effect; the temporal progress of information or action; and concepts like the "narrator." This is the study of *narration,* the "pragmatics" of narrative phenomena. What follows concerns itself with narration in classical Hollywood cinema between 1917 and 1960, but it does not singlemindedly stick to this aspect. It is common for any one narrative analysis to focus on one aspect but to bring in others as needed. Lévi-Strauss, for instance, uses a concept of narrative structure to disclose deeper levels of meaning, what the myth represents: syntax is a tool for revealing semantics. In this essay, I introduce issues of representation (especially denotative representation) and structure (especially dramaturgical structure) in order to highlight how classical Hollywood narration constitutes a particular configuration of normalized options for representing the story and manipulating composition and style. Since this is a précis of an

Adapted from David Bordwell, *Narration in the Fiction Film* (Madison: University of Wisconsin Press, 1985), reprinted by permission of the University of Wisconsin Press.

extensive body of research, it will have an unfortunately programmatic, *ad hoc* air about it, but the readers can refer to the end of the article for the evidence upon which these claims are based.[2] Unusual nomenclature is glossed below.*

The Straight Corridor

The classical Hollywood film presents psychologically defined individuals who struggle to solve a clear-cut problem or to attain specific goals. In the course of this struggle, the characters enter into conflict with others or with external circumstances. The story ends with a decisive victory or defeat, a resolution of the problem and a clear achievement or nonachievement of the goals. The principal causal agency is thus the character, a distinctive individual endowed with an evident, consistent batch of traits, qualities, and behaviors. Although the cinema inherits many conventions of portrayal from theater and literature, the character types of melodrama and popular fiction get fleshed out by the addition of unique motifs, habits, or behavioral tics. In parallel fashion, the star system has as one of its functions the creation of a rough character prototype which is then adjusted to the particular needs of the role. The most "specified" character is usually the protagonist, who becomes the principal causal agent, the target of any narrational restriction, and the chief object of audience identi-fication. These features of the syuzhet come as no surprise, though already there are important differences from other narrational modes (e.g., the comparative absence of consistent and goal-oriented characters in art-cinema narration).

Of all such modes, the classical one conforms most closely to the "canonic story" which story-comprehension researchers posit as normal for our culture.

Fabula: Russian formalist term for the narrative events in causal chronological sequence. (Sometimes translated as "story.") A construct of the spectator.

Syuzhet: Russian formalist term for the systematic presentation of fabula events in the text we have before us. (Sometimes translated as "plot.")

Narration: the process of cueing a perceiver to construct a fabula by use of syuzhet patterning and film style.

Knowledgeability: the extent to which the narration lays claim to a range and depth of knowledge of fabula information.

Self-consciousness: the degree to which the narration acknowledges its address to the spectator.

Communicativeness: the extent to which the narration withholds or communicates fabula information.

Compositional motivation: justifying the presence of an element by its function in advancing the syuzhet.

Realistic motivation: justifying the presence of an element by virtue of its conformity with some extratextual reality.

Artistic motivation: justifying the presence of an element by its calling attention to itself as a distinct device.

Transtextual motivation: justifying the presence of an element by reference to the category of texts to which this one belongs (e.g., by appealing to genre conventions).

In fabula terms, the reliance upon character cause and effect and the definition of the action as the attempt to achieve a goal are salient features of the canonic format.[3] At the level of the syuzhet, the classical film respects the canonic pattern of establishing an initial state of affairs which gets violated and which must then be set right. Indeed, Hollywood screenplay-writing manuals have long insisted on a formula which has been revived in recent structural analysis: the plot consists of an undisturbed stage, the disturbance, the struggle, and the elimination of the disturbance.[4] Such a syuzhet pattern is the inheritance not of some monolithic construct called the "novelistic" but of specific historical forms: the well-made play, the popular romance, and, crucially, the late nineteenth-century short story.[5] The characters' causal interactions are thus to a great extent functions of such overarching syuzhet/fabula patterns.

In classical fabula construction, causality is the prime unifying principle. Analogies between characters, settings, and situations are certainly present, but at the denotative level any parallelism is subordinated to the movement of cause and effect.[6] Spatial configurations are motivated by realism (a newspaper office must contain desks, typewriters, phones) and, chiefly, by compositional necessity (the desk and typewriter will be used to write causally significant news stories, the phones form crucial links among characters). Causality also motivates temporal principles of organization: the syuzhet represents the order, frequency, and duration of fabula events in ways which bring out the salient causal relations. This process is especially evident in a device highly characteristic of classical narration—the deadline. A deadline can be measured by calendars *(Around the World in Eighty Days)*, by clocks *(High Noon)*, by stipulation ("You've got a week but not a minute longer"), or simply by cues that time is running out (the last-minute rescue). That the climax of a classical film is often a deadline shows the structural power of defining dramatic duration as the time it takes to achieve or fail to achieve a goal.

Usually the classical syuzhet presents a double causal structure, two plot lines: one involving heterosexual romance (boy/girl, husband/wife), the other line involving another sphere—work, war, a mission or quest, other personal relationships. Each line will possess a goal, obstacles, and a climax. In *Wild and Wooly* (1917), the hero Jeff has two goals—to live a wild western life and to court Nell, the woman of his dreams. The plot can be complicated by several lines, such as countervailing goals (the people of Bitter Creek want Jeff to get them a railroad spur, a crooked Indian agent wants to pull a robbery) or multiple romances (as in *Footlight Parade* and *Meet Me in St. Louis*). In most cases, the romance sphere and the other sphere of action are distinct but interdependent. The plot may close off one line before the other, but often the two lines coincide at the climax: resolving one triggers the resolution of the other. In *His Girl Friday,* the reprieve of Earl Williams precedes the reconciliation of Walter and Hildy, but it is also the condition of the couple's reunion.

The syuzhet is always broken up into segments. In the silent era, the typical

Hollywood film would contain between 9 and 18 sequences; in the sound era, between 14 and 35 (with postwar films tending to have more sequences). Speaking roughly, there are only two types of Hollywood segments: "summaries" (compromising Metz's third, fourth, and eighth syntagmatic types) and "scenes" (Metz's fifth, sixth, seventh, and eighth types.)[7] Hollywood narration clearly demarcates its scenes by neoclassical criteria—unity of time (continuous or consistently intermittent duration), space (a definable locale), and action (a distinct cause-effect phase). The bounds of the sequence will be marked by some standardized punctuations (dissolve, fade, wipe, sound bridge).[8] Raymond Bellour points out that the classical segment tends also to define itself microcosmically (through internal repetitions of style or story material) and macrocosmically (by parallels with other segments of the same magnitude).[9] We must also remember that each film establishes its own scale of segmentation. A syuzhet which concentrates on a single locale over a limited dramatic duration (e.g., the one-night-in-a-haunted-house film) may create segments by character entrances or exits, a theatrical *liaison des scènes*. In a film which spans decades and many locales, a series of dissolves from one small action to another will not necessarily create distinct sequences.

The classical segment is not a sealed entity. Spatially and temporally it is closed, but causally it is open. It works to advance the causal progression and open up new developments.[10] The pattern of this forward momentum is quite codified. The montage sequence tends to function as a transitional summary, compressing a single causal development, but the scene of character action—the building block of classical Hollywood dramaturgy—is more intricately constructed. Each scene displays distinct phases. First comes the exposition, which specifies the time, place, and relevant characters—their spatial positions and their current states of mind (usually as a result of previous scenes). In the middle of the scene, characters act toward their goals: they struggle, make choices, make appointments, set deadlines, and plan future events. In the course of this, the classical scene continues or closes off cause-effect developments left dangling in prior scenes while also opening up new causal lines for future development. At least one line of action must be left suspended, in order to motivate the shifts to the next scene, which picks up the suspended line (often via a "dialogue hook"). Hence the famous "linearity" of classical construction—a trait not characteristic of Soviet montage films (which often refuse to demarcate scenes clearly) or of art-cinema narration (with its ambiguous interplay of subjectivity and objectivity).

Here is a simple example. In *The Killers* (1946), the insurance investigator Riordan has been hearing Lieutenant Lubinsky's account of Ole Anderson's early life. At the end of the scene, Lubinsky tells Riordan that they're burying Ole today. This dangling cause leads to the next scene, set in the cemetery. An establishing shot provides spatial exposition. While the clergyman intones the funeral oration, Riordan asks Lubinsky the identity of various mourners. The last, a solitary old man, is identified as "an old-time hoodlum named Charleston." Dissolve to a pool hall, with Charleston and Riordan at a table drinking and talking about Ole. During the burial scene, the Lubinsky line of inquiry is closed off and the Charleston line is initiated. When the scene halts, Charleston is left suspended, but he is picked up immediately in the exposition of the next scene. Instead of a complex braiding of causal lines (as in Rivette) or an abrupt breaking of them (as in Antonioni, Godard, or Bresson), the classical Hollywood film spins them out in smooth, careful linearity.

The linkage of localized causal lines must eventually terminate. How to conclude the syuzhet? There are two ways of regarding the classical ending. We can see it as the crowning of the structure, the logical conclusion of the string of events, the final effect of the initial cause. This view has some validity, not only in the light of the tight construction that we frequently encounter in Hollywood films but also given the precepts of Hollywood screenwriting. Rule books tirelessly bemoan the pressures for a happy ending and emphasize the need for a logical wrap-up. Still, there are enough instances of unmotivated or inadequate plot resolutions to suggest a second hypothesis: that the classical ending is not all that structurally decisive, being a more or less arbitrary readjustment of that world knocked awry in the previous eighty minutes. Parker Tyler suggests that Hollywood regards all endings as "purely conventional, formal, and often, like the charade, of an infantile logic."[11] Here again we see the importance of the plot line involving heterosexual romance. It is significant that of 100 randomly sampled Hollywood films, over 60 ended with a display of the united romantic couple—the cliché happy ending, often with a "clinch"—and many more could be said to end happily. Thus an extrinsic norm, the need to resolve the plot in a way that provides "poetic justice," becomes a structural constant, inserted with more or less motivation into its proper slot, the epilogue. In any narrative, as Meir Sternberg points out, when the syuzhet's end is strongly precast by convention, the compositional attention falls on the retardation of outcome accomplished by the middle portions; the text will then "account for the necessary retardation in quasi-mimetic terms by placing the causes for delay within the fictive world itself and turning the middle into the bulk of the represented action."[12] At times, however, the motivation is constructed to be inadequate, and a discordance between preceding causality and happy denouement becomes noticeable as an ideological difficulty; such is the case with films like *You Only Live Once, Suspicion, The Woman in the Window,* and *The Wrong Man.*[13] We ought, then, to be prepared for either a skillful tying up of all loose ends or a more or less miraculous appearance of what Brecht called bourgeois literature's mounted messenger. "The mounted messenger guarantees you a truly undisturbed appreciation of even the most intolerable conditions, so it is a sine qua non for a literature whose sine qua non is that it leads nowhere."[14]

The classical ending may be a sore spot in another respect. Even if the ending resolves the two principal causal lines, some comparatively minor issues may still be left dangling. For example, the fates of secondary characters may go unsettled. In *His Girl Friday,* Earl Williams is reprieved, the corrupt administration will be thrown out of office, and Walter and Hildy are reunited, but we never learn what happens to Molly Malloy, who jumped out a window to distract the reporters. (We know only that she was alive after the fall.) One could argue that in the resolution of the main problem we forget minor matters, but this is only a partial explanation. Our forgetting is promoted by the device of closing the film with an *epilogue,* a brief celebration of the stable state achieved by the main characters. Not only does the epilogue reinforce the tendency toward a happy ending; it also repeats connotative motifs that have run throughout the film. *His Girl Friday* closes on a brief epilogue of Walter and Hildy calling the newspaper office to announce their remarriage. They learn that a strike has started in Albany, and Walter proposes stopping off to cover it on their honeymoon. This plot twist announces a repetition of what happened on their first honeymoon and recalls that Hildy was going to marry Bruce and live in Albany. As the couple leave, Hildy carrying her suitcase, Walter suggests that Bruce might put them up. The neat recurrence of these motifs gives the narration a strong unity; when such details are so tightly bound together, Molly Malloy's fate is more likely to be overlooked. Perhaps instead of "closure" it would be better to speak of a "closure effect," or even, if the strain of resolved and unresolved issues seems strong, of "pseudo-closure." At the level of extrinsic norms, though, the most coherent possible epilogue remains the standard to be aimed at.

Commonplaces like "transparency" and "invisibility" are on the whole unhelpful in specifying the narrational properties of the classical film. Very generally, we can say that classical narration tends to be omniscient, highly communicative, and only moderately self-conscious. That is, the narration knows more than any or all characters, it conceals relatively little (chiefly "what will happen next"), and it seldom acknowledges its own address to the audience. But we must qualify this characterization in two respects. First, generic factors often create variations upon these precepts. A detective film will be quite restricted in its range of knowledge and highly suppressive in concealing causal information. A melodrama like *In This Our Life* can be slightly more self-conscious than *The Big Sleep,* especially in its use of acting and music. A musical will contain codified moments of self-consciousness (e.g., when characters sing directly out at the viewer). Second, the temporal progression of the syuzhet makes narrational properties fluctuate across the film, and these too are codified. Typically, the opening and closing of the film are the most self-conscious, omniscient, and communicative passages. The credit sequence and the first few shots usually bear traces of an overt narration. Once the action has started, however, the narration becomes more covert, letting the characters and their interaction take over the transmission of information. Overt narrational activity returns at certain conventional moments: the beginnings and endings of scenes (e.g., establishing shots, shots of signs, camera movements out from or in to significant objects, symbolic dissolves), and that summary passage known as the "montage sequence." At the very close of the syuzhet, the narration may again acknowledge its awareness of the audience (musical motifs reappear, characters look to the camera or close a door in our face), its omniscience (e.g., the camera retreats to a long-shot), and its communicativeness (now we know all). Classical narration is thus not equally "invisible" in every type of film nor throughout any one film; the "marks of enunciation" are sometimes flaunted.

The communicativeness of classical narration is evident in the way that the syuzhet handles gaps. If time is skipped over, a montage sequence or a bit of character dialogue informs us; if a cause is missing, we will typically be informed that something isn't there. And gaps will seldom be permanent. "In the beginning of the motion picture," writes one scenarist, "we don't know anything. During the course of the story, information is accumulated, until at the end we know everything."[15] Again, these principles can be mitigated by generic motivation. A mystery might suppress a gap (e.g., the opening of *Mildred Pierce*), a fantasy might leave a cause still questionable at the end (e.g., *The Enchanted Cottage*). In this respect, *Citizen Kane* remains somewhat "unclassical": the narration supplies the annswer to the "Rosebud" mystery, but the central traits of Kane's character remain partly undetermined, and no generic motivation justifies this.

The syuzhet's construction of time powerfully shapes the fluctuating overtness of narration. When the syuzhet adheres to chronological order and omits the causally unimportant periods of time, the narration becomes highly communicative and unselfconscious. On the other hand, a montage sequence compresses a political campaign, a murder trial, or the effects of Prohibition into moments, and the narration becomes overtly omniscient. A flashback can quickly and covertly fill a causal gap. Redundancy can be achieved without violating the fabula world if the narration represents each story event several times in the syuzhet, through one enactment and several recountings in character dialogue. Deadlines neatly let the syuzhet unselfconsciously respect the durational limits that the fabula world sets for its action. When it is necessary to suggest repeated or habitual actions, the montage sequence will again do nicely, as Sartre noted when he praised *Citizen Kane's* montages for achieving the equivalent of the "frequentative" tense: "He made his wife sing in every theater in America."[16] When the syuzhet uses a newspaper headline to cover gaps of time, we recognize both the narration's omniscience and its relatively low profile. (The public record is less self-conscious than an intertitle "coming straight from" the narration.) More generally, classical narration reveals its discretion by posing as an *editorial* intelligence that selects certain stretches of time for full-scale treatment (the scenes), pares down others a little, presents others in highly compressed fashion (the montage sequences), and simply scissors out events that are inconsequential. When fabula duration is expanded, it is done through crosscutting.

Overall narrational qualities are also manifested in the film's manipulation of space. Figures are adjusted for moderate self-consciousness by angling the bodies more or less frontally but avoiding to-camera gazes (except, of course, in optical point-of-view passages). That no causally significant cues in a scene are left unknown testifies to the communicativeness of narration. Most important is the tendency of the classical film to render narrational omniscience through spatial *omnipresence*.[17] If the narration plays down its knowledge of effects and upcoming temporal developments, it does not hesitate to reveal its ability to change views at will. Cutting within a scene and crosscutting between various locales testify to the narration's omnipresence. Writing in 1935, a critic claims that the camera is omniscient in that it "stimulates, through correct choice of subject matter and set-up, the sense within the percipient of 'being at the most vital part of the experience—at the most advantageous point of perception' throughout the picture."[18] Whereas Miklos Jancso's long takes create spatial patterns that refuse omnipresence and thus drastically restrict the spectator's knowledge of story information, classical omnipresence makes the cognitive schema we call "the camera" into an *ideal* invisible observer, freed from the contingencies of space and time but then discreetly confining itself to codified patterns for the sake of story intelligibility.

By virtue of its handling of space and time, classical narration makes the fabula world an internally consistent construct into which narration seems to step from the outside. Manipulation of mise-en-scène (figure behavior, lighting, setting, costume) creates an apparently independent profilmic event, which becomes the tangible story world framed and recorded from without. This framing and recording tends to be taken as the narration itself, which can in turn be more or less overt, more or less "intrusive" on the posited homogeneity of the story world. Classical narration thus depends upon the notion of the "invisible observer."[19] Bazin, for instance, portrays the classical scene as existing independently of narration, as if on a stage.[20] The same quality is named by the notion of "concealment of production": the fabula seems not to have been constructed but appears to have preexisted its narrational representation. (In production, in some sense, it often did: for major films of the 1930s and thereafter, Hollywood set designers created three-dimensional tabletop mock-ups of sets within which models of cameras, actors, and lighting units could be placed to predetermine filming procedures.)[21]

This invisible-observer narration is itself often fairly effaced. The stylistic causes of this I shall examine shortly, but we can already see that classical narration quickly cues us to construct story logic (causality, parallelisms), time, and space in ways that make the events "before the camera" our principal source of information. For example, it is obvious that Hollywood narratives are highly redundant, but this effect is achieved principally by patterns attributable to the story world. Following Susan Suleiman's taxonomy,[22] we can see that the narration assigns the same traits and functions to each character on her or his appearance; different characters present the same interpretive commentary on the same character or situation; similar events befall different characters; and so on. Information is for the most part repeated by characters' dialogue or demeanor. There is, admittedly, some redundancy between narrational commentary and depicted fabula action, as when silent film expository intertitles convey crucial information or when nondiegetic music is pleonastic with the action (e.g., "Here Comes the Bride" in *In This Our Life*). Nevertheless, in general, the narration is so constructed that characters and their behavior produce and reiterate the necessary story data. The Soviet montage cinema makes much stronger use of redundancies between narrational commentary and fabula action. Retardation operates in analogous fashion: the construction of the total fabula is delayed principally by inserted lines of action (e.g., causally relevant subplots, interpolated comedy bits, musical numbers) rather than by narrational digressions of the sort found in the "God and Country" sequence of *October*. Similarly, causal gaps in the fabula are usually signaled by character actions (e.g., the discovery of clues in detective films). The viewer concentrates on constructing the fabula, not on asking why the narration is representing the fabula in this particular way—a question more typical of art-cinema narration.

The priority of fabula causality and an integral fabula world commits classical narration to unambiguous presentation. Whereas art–cinema narration can blur the lines separating objective diegetic reality, characters' mental states, and inserted narrational commentary, the classical film asks us to assume clear distinctions among these states. When the classical film restricts knowledge to a character, as in most of *The Big Sleep* and *Murder My Sweet,* there is nonetheless a firm borderline between subjective and objective depiction. Of course, the narration can set traps for us, as in *Possessed* (1947), when a murder that appears to be objective is revealed to have been subjective (a generically motivated switch, incidentally); but the hoax is revealed immediately and unequivocally. The classical flashback is revealing in this connection. Its *presence* is almost invariably motivated subjectively, since a character's recollection triggers the enacted representation of a prior event. But the *range of knowledge* in the flashback portion is often not identical with that of the character doing the remembering. It is common for the flashback to show us more than the character can know (e.g., scenes in which s/he is not present). An amusing example occurs in *Ten North Frederick*. The bulk of the film is presented as the daughter's flashback, but at the end of the syuzhet, back in the present, she learns for the first time information we had encountered in "her" flashback! Classical flashbacks are typically "objective": character memory is a pretext for a nonchronological syuzhet arrangement. Similarly, optically subjective shots become anchored in an objective context. One writer notes that a point-of-view shot "must be motivated by, and definitely linked to, the objective scenes [shots] that precede and follow it."[23] This is one source of the power of the invisible–observer effect: the camera seems always to include character subjectivity within a broader and definite objectivity.

Classical Style

Even if the naive spectator takes the style of the classical Hollywood film to be invisible or seamless, this is not much critical help. What makes the style so self-effacing? The question cannot be answered completely until we consider the spectator's activity, but we may start with Yuri Tynyanov's suggestion: "Pointing to the 'restraint' or 'naturalism' of the style in the case of some film or some director is not the same as sweeping away the role of style. Quite simply, there are a variety of styles and they have various roles, according to their relationship to the development of the syuzhet."[24] Three general propositions, then.

(1) On the whole, classical narration treats film technique as a vehicle for the syuzhet's transmission of fabula information.

Of all modes of narration, the classical is most concerned to motivate style compositionally, as a function of syuzhet patterning. Consider the very notion of what we now call a shot. For decades, Hollywood practice called a shot a "scene," thus conflating a material stylistic unit with a dramaturgical one. In filmmaking practice, the overriding principle was to make every instantiation of technique obedient to the character's transmission of fabula information, which would invariably make bodies and faces the focal points of attention. Given the recurrent causal structure of the classical scene (exposition, closing off of an old causal factor, introduction of new causal factors, suspension of a new factor), the filmmaker can deploy film techniques isomorphically with respect to this structure. The introduction phase typically includes a shot which establishes the characters in space and time. As the characters interact, the scene is broken up into closer views of action and reaction, while setting, lighting, music, composition, and camera movement enhance the process of goal formulation, struggle, and decision. The scene usually closes on a portion of the space—a facial reaction, a significant object—that provides a transition to the next scene.

While it is true that sometimes a classical film's style becomes "excessive," decoratively supplementing denotative syuzhet demands, the use of technique must be minimally motivated by the characters' interactions. "Excess," such as we find in Minnelli or Sirk, is often initially justified by generic convention. The same holds true for even the most eccentric stylists in Hollywood, Busby Berkeley and Josef von Sternberg, each of whom required a core of generic motivation (musical fantasy and exotic romance, respectively) for his experiments.

(2) In classical narration, style typically encourages the spectator to construct a coherent, consistent time and space of the fabula action.

Many other narrational norms value disorienting the spectator (albeit for different purposes). Only classical narration favors a style which strives for utmost denotative clarity from moment to moment. Each scene's temporal relation to its predecessor will be signaled early and unequivocally (by intertitles, conventional cues, a line of dialogue). Lighting must pick out figure from ground; color must define planes; in each shot, the center of story interest will tend to be centered in relation to the sides of the frame. Sound recording is perfected so as to allow for maximum clarity of dialogue. Camera movements aim at creating an unambiguous, voluminous space. "In dollying," remarks Alan Dwan, "as a rule we find it's a good idea to *pass* things. . . . We always noticed that if we dollied past a tree, it became solid and round, instead of flat."[25] Hollywood makes much use of the *anticipatory* composition or camera movement, leaving space in the frame for the action or tracking so as to prepare for another character's entrance. Compare Godard's tendency to make framing wholly subservient to the actor's immediate movement with this comment of Raoul Walsh's: "There is only one way in which to shoot a scene, and that's the way which shows the audience what's happening next."[26] Classical editing aims at making each shot the logical outcome of its predecessor and at reorienting the spectator through repeated setups. Momentary disorientation is permissible only if motivated realistically. Discontinuous editing, as in Slavko Vorkapich's sequence of the earthquake in *San Francisco,* is motivated by the chaos of the action depicted. Stylistic disorientation, in short, is permissible when it conveys disorienting story situations.

(3) Classical style consists of a strictly limited number of particular technical devices organized into a stable paradigm and ranked probabilistically according to syuzhet demands.

The stylistic conventions of Hollywood narration, ranging from shot composition to sound mixing, are intuitively recognizable to most viewers. This is because the style deploys a limited number of devices, and these devices are regulated as alternative depictive options. Lighting offers a simple example. A scene may be lit "high-key" or "low-key." There is three-point lighting (key, fill, and backlighting on figure, plus background lighting) versus single-source lighting. The cinematographer also has several degrees of diffusion available. Now in the abstract all choices are equiprobable, but in a given context, one alternative is more likely than its mates. In a comedy, high-key lighting is more probable; a dark street will realistically motivate single-source lighting; the closeup of a woman will be more heavily diffused than that of a man. The "invisibility" of the classical style in Hollywood relies not only on highly codified stylistic devices but also upon their codified functions in context.

Or recall the ways of framing the human figure. Most often, a character will be framed between *plan-american* (the knees-up framing) and medium closeup (the chest-up framing); the angle will be straight-on, at shoulder or chin level. The framing is less likely to be an extreme long-shot or an extreme closeup, a high or low angle. And a bird's eye view or a view from straight below are very improbable and would require compositional or generic motivation (e.g., as an optical point of view or as a view of a dance ensemble in a musical).

Most explicitly codified into rules is the system of classical continuity editing.

The reliance upon an axis of action orients the spectator to the space, and the subsequent cutting presents clear paradigmatic choices among different kinds of "matches." That these are weighted probabilistically is shown by the fact that most Hollywood scenes begin with establishing shots, break the space into closer views linked by eyeline-matches and/or shot/reverse shots, and return to more distant views only when character movement or the entry of a new character requires the viewer to be reoriented. Playing an entire scene without an establishing shot is unlikely but permissible (especially if stock or location footage or special effects are employed); mismatched screen direction and inconsistently angled eyelines are less likely; perceptible jump cuts and unmotivated cutaways are flatly forbidden. This paradigmatic aspect makes the classical style, for all its "rules," not a formula or a recipe but a historically constrained set of more or less likely options. [27]

These three factors go some way toward explaining why the classical Hollywood style passes relatively unnoticed. Each film will recombine familiar devices within fairly predictable patterns and according to the demands of the syuzhet. The spectator will almost never be at a loss to grasp a stylistic feature because s/he is oriented in time and space and because stylistic figures will be interpretable in the light of a paradigm.

When we consider the relation of syuzhet and style, we can say that the individual film is characterized by its obedience to a set of extrinsic norms which govern both syuzhet construction and stylistic patterning. The classical cinema does not encourage the film to cultivate idiosyncratic intrinsic norms; style and syuzhet seldom enjoy prominence. A film's principal innovations occur at the level of the fabula—i.e., "new stories." Of course, syuzhet devices and stylistic features have changed over time. But the fundamental principles of syuzhet construction (preeminence of causality, goal-oriented protagonist, deadlines, etc.) have remained in force since 1917. The stability and uniformity of Hollywood narration is indeed one reason to call it classical, at least insofar as classicism in any art is traditionally characterized by obedience to extrinsic norms. [28]

The Logic of Classical Spectatorship

The stability of syuzhet processes and stylistic configurations should not make us treat the classical spectator as passive material for a totalizing machine. The spectator performs particular cognitive operations which are no less active for being habitual and familiar. The Hollywood fabula is the product of a series of particular schemata, hypotheses, and inferences.

The spectator comes to a classical film very well prepared. The rough shape of syuzhet and fabula is likely to conform to the canonic story of an individual's goal-oriented, causally determined activity. The spectator knows the most likely stylistic figures and functions. The spectator has internalized the scenic norms of exposition, development of old causal line, and so forth. The viewer also knows the pertinent ways to motivate what is presented. "Realistic" motivation, in this mode, consists of making connections recognized as plausible by common opinion. ("A man like this would naturally . . .") Compositional motivation consists of picking out the important links of cause to effect. The most important forms of transtextual motivation are recognizing the recurrence of a star's persona from film to film and recognizing generic conventions. Generic motivation, as we have seen, has a particularly strong effect on narrational procedures. Finally, artistic motivation—taking an element as being present for its own sake—is not unknown in the classical film. A moment of spectacle or technical virtuosity, a thrown-in musical number or comic interlude: the Hollywood cinema intermittently welcomes the possibility of sheer self-absorption. Such moments may be highly reflexive, "baring the device" of the narration's own work, as when in *Angels Over Broadway* a destitute playwright reflects, "Our present plot problem is money."

On the basis of such schemata the viewer projects hypotheses. Hypotheses tend to be probable (validated at several points), sharply exclusive (rendered as either/or alternatives), and aimed at suspense (positing a future outcome). In Phil Rosen's *Roaring Timber* (1937), a landowner enters a saloon in which our hero is sitting. The owner is looking for a tough foreman. Hypothesis: he will ask the hero to take the job. This hypothesis is probable, future-oriented, and exclusive (either the man will ask our hero or he won't). The viewer is helped in framing such hypotheses by several processes. Repetition reaffirms the data on which hypotheses should be grounded. "State every important fact three times," suggests scenarist Frances Marion, "for the play is lost if the audience fails to understand the premises on which it is based."[29] The exposition of past fabula action will characteristically be placed within the early scenes of the syuzhet, thus supplying a firm basis for our hypothesis-forming. Except in a mystery film, the exposition neither sounds warning signals nor actively misleads us; the primacy effect is given full sway. Characters will be introduced in typical behavior, while the star system reaffirms first impressions. ("The moment you see Walter Pidgeon in a film you know he could not do a mean or petty thing.")[30] The device of the deadline asks the viewer to construct forward-aiming, all-or-nothing causal hypotheses: either the protagonist will achieve the goal in time or s/he will not. And if information is unobtrusively "planted" early on, later hypotheses will become more probable by taking "insignificant" foreshadowing material for granted.

This process holds at the stylistic level as well. The spectator constructs fabula time and space according to schemata, cues, and hypothesis-framing. Hollywood's extrinsic norms, with their fixed devices and paradigmatic organization, supply the viewer with firm expectations that can be measured against the concrete cues emitted by the film. In making sense of a scene's space, the spectator need not mentally replicate every detail of the space but need only construct a rough relational map of the principal dramatic factors. Thus a "cheat cut" is easily ignored because the spectator's cognitive processes rank cues by their pertinence to constructing the ongoing causal chain of the fabula, and on this scale, the changes in speaker, camera position, and facial expression are more noteworthy than say, a slight shift in hand positions.[31] The same goes for temporal mismatches.

What is rare in the classical film, then, is Henry James's "crooked corridor," the use of narration to make us jump to invalid conclusions.[32] The avoidance of disorientation we saw at work in classical style holds good more broadly as well. Future-oriented "suspense" hypotheses are more important than past-oriented "curiosity" ones, and surprise is less important than either. In *Roaring Timber*, imagine if the landowner had entered the bar seeking a tough foreman, offered the job to our hero, and he had replied in a fashion that showed he was not tough. Indeed, one purpose of foreshadowing and repetition is exactly to avoid surprises later on. Of course, if all hypotheses were steadily and immediately confirmed, the viewer would quickly lose interest. Several factors intervene to complicate the process. Most generally, schemata are by definition abstract prototypes, structures, and procedures, and these never specify all the properties of the text. Many long-range hypotheses must await confirmation. Retardation devices, being unpredictable to a great degree, can introduce objects of immediate attention as well as delay satisfaction of overall expectation. The primacy effect can be countered by what psychologists call a "recency effect" which qualifies and perhaps even appears to negate our first impression of a character or situation. Furthermore, the structure of the Hollywood scene, which almost invariably ends with an unresolved issue, insures that an event-centered hypothesis carries interest over to the next sequence. Finally, we should not underestimate the role of rapid rhythm in the classical film; more than one practitioner has stressed the need to move the construction of story action along so quickly that the audience has no time to reflect—or get bored. It is the task of classical narration to solicit strongly probable and exclusive hypotheses and then confirm them while still maintaining variety in the concrete working out of the action.

The classical system is not simpleminded. Recall that under normal exhibition circumstances the film viewer's rate of comprehension is absolutely controlled. The cueing of probable, exclusive, and suspense-oriented hypotheses is a way of adjusting dramaturgy to the demands of the viewing situation. The spectator need not rummage very far back into the film, since his or her expectations are aimed at the future. Preliminary exposition locks schemata into place quickly, and the all-or-nothing nature of most hypotheses allows rapid assimilation of information. Redundancy keeps attention on the issue of immediate moment, while judicious lacks of redundancy allow for minor surprises later. In all, classical narration manages the controlled pace of film viewing by asking the spectator to construe the syuzhet and the stylistic system in a single way: construct a denotative, univocal, integral fabula.

Implications and Avenues

By virtue of its centrality within international film commerce, Hollywood cinema has crucially influenced most other national cinemas. After 1917, the dominant forms of filmmaking abroad were deeply affected by the models of storytelling presented by the American studios. Yet the Hollywood cinema cannot be identified with classicism *tout court*. The "classicism" of 1930s Italy or 1950s Poland may mobilize quite different narrational devices. (For instance, the happy ending seems more characteristic of Hollywood than of other classicisms.) But in most such cinemas classical narration's *principles* and *functions* can be considered congruent with those outlined here. A group of Parisian researchers has come to comparable, if preliminary, conclusions about French films of the 1930s.[33] Noël Burch has shown that in the German cinema, a mastery of classical style is displayed as early as 1922, in Lang's *Dr. Mabuse Der Spieler*.[34] As a narrational mode, classicism clearly corresponds to the idea of an "ordinary film" in most cinema-consuming countries of the world.

The many variants of classicism make any overall periodization of the mode very difficult. Even the history of Hollywood norms is notoriously hard to delineate with any precision. This is partly because significant periods in the history of studios or technology will not necessarily coincide with changes in stylistic or syuzhet processes. Broadly speaking, we could periodize classical Hollywood narration on three levels. With respect to *devices,* we could trace changes within classical narrational paradigms, according to what options come into favor at certain periods. Here we should look not only for innovations but for normalization, patterns of majority or customary practice. Connecting scenes by dissolves is possible but rare in the silent cinema, yet it is the favored transition between 1929 and the late 1950s. On the dimension of narrational *systems,* we could study the principles that constitute narrative causality, time, and space. Spatial continuity within a scene can be achieved by selecting from several functionally equivalent techniques, but such continuity rests on broader principles, such as the positing of the 180°-line, or axis of action; and changes in this postulate can be traced across the history of cinema. We could also study the fluctuations of the more abstract narrational *properties* over time. For instance, narration in the 1920–1923 American silent cinema tends to be somewhat more self-conscious than in the later 1920s, chiefly because of a greater use of expository intertitles in the earlier period. Similarly, an insistently overt suppressiveness emerges in many films associated with the grouping known as *film noir.* I can here only hint at the manifold possibilities; we await a thorough history of classical storytelling and style.

Where, we might finally ask, does all this leave two important critical issues: authorship and ideology? In this space, only sketchy answers can be suggested. It seems evident that an auteur's work can be identified by its characteristic narrational principles and patterns. Hitchcock and Fuller's films are more self-conscious than, say, those of Hawks and Preminger. Moreover, we can associate consistent stylistic choices with directorial signatures: Ophuls' preference for tracking shots over cut-ins, Lubitsch's use of closeups. Most important is the fact that any distinct authorial approach to narration typically remains within classical bounds, creating extrinsic norms that conform to or amplify intrinsic ones. Authorial difference in Hollywood thus dramatizes the range and limits of the classical paradigm. As for the ideological significance of classical narration, all the principles and procedures I have considered could be analyzed in this regard. The goal-oriented hero, the appeal to principles of unity and realism, the functions of temporal and spatial coherence, the centrality of the invisible observer, the arbitrariness of closure—each bears the traces of social-historical processes of production and reception. The predominance of three-point lighting appeals to canonized conceptions of glamor and beauty; the treatment of heterosexual romance links Hollywood classicism to dominant conceptions of sexual relations. The 180-degree system not only bears the traces of a mode of production seeking speedy and economical filmmaking; it also continues a tradition of spatial representation at work since the Greek theater. Each film works with, or with and against, ideological and economic protocols.

What is important, however, is that even in this most ordinary cinema, the spectator constructs form and meaning according to a process of knowledge, memory, and inference. No matter how routine and "transparent" classical film viewing has become, it remains an activity. Any alternative or oppositional cinema will mobilize narration to call forth activities of a different sort.

Notes

1. V. Propp, *Morphology of the Folktale* (Austin: University of Texas Press, 1968).

2. This essay refers to material discussed at length in chapters 1 to 7 of David Bordwell, Janet Staiger, and Kristin Thompson, *The Classical Hollywood Cinema: Film Style and Mode of Production to 1960* (New York: Columbia University Press, 1985). A general background for the discussion is David Bordwell and Kristin Thompson, *Film Art: An Introduction* (Reading MA: Addison-Wesley, 1979).

3. Perry W. Thorndyke, "Cognitive Structures in Comprehension and Memory of Narrative Discourse," *Cognitive Psychology* (1977), 9:84–96. For an example of an approach to a different narrative cinematic mode, see my article "The Art Cinema as a Mode of Film Practice," *Film Criticism* (Fall 1979), 4(1):56–64.

4. Eugene Vale, *The Technique of Screenplay Writing* (New York: Grosset and Dunlap, 1972), pp. 135–60; Stephen Heath, "Film and System: Terms of Analysis," *Screen* (Spring 1975), 16(1):48–50.

5. See Bordwell, Staiger, and Thompson, *The Classical Hollywood Cinema*, chapters 14–18.

6. Rick Altman stresses the need to consider the importance of character parallels as "paradigmatic" relations in the classical text. It is true that analogies and contrasts of situation or character occur in classical films, but these relations are typically dependent upon logically prior causal relations. Rick Altman, "The American Film Musical: Paradigmatic Structure and Mediatory Function," in Altman, ed., *Genre: The Musical* (London: Routledge and Kegan Paul, 1981), pp. 197–207.

7. Christian Metz, "Problems of Denotation in the Fiction Film," in *Film Language*, tr. Michael

Taylor (New York: Oxford University Press, 1974), pp. 108–46 [included in this anthology—ED.].

8. Raymond Bellour, "The Obvious and the Code," *Screen* (Winter 1974–75), 15(4):7–8 [included in this anthology—ED.]. See also Alan Williams, "Narrative Patterns in 'Only Angels Have Wings,' " *Quarterly Review of Film Studies* (November 1976), 1(4):357–72.

9. Raymond Bellour, "To Analyze, to Segment," in Altman, ed., *Genre* pp. 107–16 [included in this anthology—ED.]

10. Thierry Kuntzel, "The Film-Work II," *Camera Obscura* (1980), 5:25.

11. Parker Tyler, *The Hollywood Hallucination* (New York: Simon and Schuster, 1970), p. 177.

12. Meir Sternberg, *Expositional Modes and Temporal Ordering in Fiction* (Baltimore: Johns Hopkins University Press, 1978), p. 178.

13. See Richard Dyer, *Stars* (London: British Film Institute, 1979), p. 65, and David Bordwell, "Happily Ever After, Part II," in *The Velvet Light Trap* (1982), no. 19, pp. 2–7.

14. Bertolt Brecht, *Collected Plays,* ed. Ralph Manheim and John Willett (New York: Vintage, 1977), 2:331.

15. Vale, *Technique of Screenplay Writing,* p. 81.

16. Jean-Paul Sartre, "Quand Hollywood veut faire penser," *L'Écran français* (3 August 1945), no. 5, p. 3.

17. I borrow the term from Seymour Chatman, *Story and Discourse: Narrative Structure in Fiction and Film* (Ithaca: Cornell University Press, 1978), p. 103.

18. A. Lindsley Lane, "The Camera's Omniscient Eye," *American Cinematographer* (March 1935), 16(3):95.

19. The clearest statement of the "invisible observer" notion is to be found in V. I. Pudovkin, *Film Technique* (New York: Grove, 1960), pp. 67–71.

20. André Bazin, *What Is Cinema?* trans. Hugh Gray (Berkeley: University of California Press, 1966), p. 32.

21. See Hal Herman, "Motion Picture Art Director," *American Cinematographer* (November 1947), 28(11):396–97, 416–17; Herman Blumenthal, "Cardboard Counterpart of the Motion Picture Setting," *Production Design* (January 1952), 2(1):16–21.

22. Susan Rubin Suleiman, *Authoritarian Fictions: The Ideological Novel as a Literary Genre* (New York: Columbia University Press, 1983), pp. 159–71.

23. Herb Lightman, "The Subjective Camera," *American Cinematographer* (February 1946), 27(2):46, 66–67.

24. Yury Tynyanov, "Fundamentals of the Cinema," in Christopher Williams, ed., *Realism in the Cinema* (London: Routledge and Kegan Paul, 1980), p. 149. I have modified the translation slightly.

25. Peter Bogdanovich, *Alan Dwan* (Berkeley: University of California Press, 1970), p. 86.

26. Quoted in Thomas Elsaesser, "Why Hollywood," *Monogram* (April 1971), no. 1, p. 8.

27. Because norms are guidelines that rank options probabilistically, we ought not to be too quick to disclose "transgressions" of classical style. For instance, Peter Lehman claims that subjective framings of a character's to-camera stare in *Dr. Jekyll and Mr. Hyde* (1932) are "quite at odds with the usual Hollywood paradigm." Yet optical point-of-view shots are not forbidden by classical protocols; they are just less likely than other alternatives. Similarly, Lehman points out a discontinuity when Jekyll leaves an establishing shot and supposedly turns his back; cut to Ivy looking at the camera and tossing a garter at it. I would suggest three things here. First, the cues seem ambiguous as to whether Jekyll in fact turns his back; he could still be watching offscreen. A later shot, of his feet turned toward Ivy as the garter lands before him, reinforces some such spatial hypothesis. Second, the playfulness of the point-of-view pattern is not unlike the whimsical play with space in Lubitsch and other innovative classical directors. Finally, we should recall that *Dr. Jekyll and Mr. Hyde* begins with a lengthy traveling shot from Jekyll's optical point of view, before we have been introduced to the character. Optical subjectivity thus constitutes an important part of the film's intrinsic norm. One could argue that Ivy's glance into

an ambivalent offscreen eye simply amplifies the film's narrational norm. See Peter Lehman, "Looking at Ivy Looking at Us Looking at Her: The Camera and the Garter," *Wide Angle* (1983), 5(3):59–63.

28. "There are, of course, periods tending toward maximally attainable harmony and stability; they are usually called periods of classicism." Jan Mukařovský, "The Aesthetic Norm," in *Structure, Sign, and Function: Selected Essays by Jan Mukařovský*, trans. and ed. by John Burbank and Peter Steiner (New Haven: Yale University Press, 1978), p. 54.

29. Frances Marion, *How to Write and Sell Film Stories* (New York: Covici-Friede, 1937), p. 144.

30. Richard Mealand, "Hollywoodunit," in Howard Haycraft, ed., *The Art of the Mystery Story* (New York: Grosset and Dunlap, 1946), p. 300.

31. It is thus somewhat misleading for Vance Kepley to assert that the restaurant scene in *His Girl Friday* creates "a shifting cinematic space not unlike what Burch finds in *Ivan the Terrible* and what other theorists find in such non-classical directors as Ozu." Eisenstein and Ozu make mismatches more prominent than does Hawks. The point is not that Hawks's scene has no spatial incompatibilities, but the classical spectator is simply cued to overlook them. See Vance Kepley, Jr., "Spatial Articulation in the Classical Cinema: A Scene From *His Girl Friday*," *Wide Angle* (1983), 5(3):50–58.

32. Sternberg, *Expositional Modes*, p. 71.

33. Michèle Lagny, Marie-Claire Ropars, and Pierre Sorlin, "Analyse d'un ensemble filmique extensible: Les Films français des années 30," in *Théorie du film*, ed. J. Aumont and J. L. Leutrat (Paris: Albatros, 1980), pp. 132–64.

34. Noël Burch, "Fritz Lang: German Period," in Richard Roud, *Cinema: A Critical Dictionary*, ed. (New York: Viking, 1980), 2:583–88.

[2]

Christian Metz
Problems of Denotation
in the Fiction Film

The film semiologist tends, naturally, to approach his subject with methods derived from linguistics. Consequently, wherever the language of cinematography differs from language itself, film semiology encounters its greatest obstacles. Let us begin immediately with the points of *maximum difference*. There are two of them: there is the problem of the *motivation* of signs (see part 1) and that of the *continuity* of meanings (see part 3). Or, if one prefers, the question of the arbitrariness of signs (in the Saussurian sense) and the question of discrete units.

1. Cinematographic Signification Is Always More or Less Motivated, Never Arbitrary

Motivation occurs on two levels: on that of the relationship between the denotative signifiers and signifieds, and that of the relations between the connotative signifiers and signifieds.

Denotation: The motivation is furnished by analogy—that is to say, by the

This is a combination and modification by the author of three articles written in 1966–1967. It was published in this form as a chapter in Christian Metz, *Essais sur la signification au cinéma* (Paris: Klincksieck, 1968). The 1971 edition of this book was translated as *Film Language: A Semiotics of the Cinema*, trans. Michael Taylor (New York: Oxford University Press, 1974). The following selection is reprinted here by permission of Oxford University Press. Occasional changes have been made in the translation for reasons of terminological consistency, and the footnotes of the translation have been revised and extended to accord with the 1971 French edition.

perceptual similiarity between the signifier and the signified. This is equally true for the sound track (the sound of a cannon on film resembles a real cannon sound) as for the image track (the image of a dog is like the dog).

We therefore have visual analogy and auditory analogy; for the cinema is derived from photography and from the phonograph, which are both modern technologies of *mechanical duplication*. Of course, the duplication is never perfect; between the object and its image there are many perceptible differences, which film psychologists have studied. But, from the point of view of semiotics, it is not necessary that the signifier and the signified be *identical*. Simple analogy provides sufficient motivation.

For, even when it partially distorts its model, mechanical duplication does not *analyze* into specific units. There is no actual transformation of the object, but a simple partial *distortion,* which is purely perceptual.

Connotation: Connotative meanings are motivated, too, in the cinema. But in this case the motivation is not necessarily based on a relationship of perceptual analogy. We should remember that, in his distinction between intrinsic and extrinsic semes, Eric Buyssens had already observed that analogy is only one of the forms of motivation.

We will not insist upon the problems of cinematographic connotation here, for this is a study of denotation. Suffice it to say that cinematographic connotation is always symbolic in nature: The signified motivates the signifier but goes beyond it. The notion of *motivated overtaking (depassement motivé)* may be used to define almost all filmic connotations. Similarly, one says that the cross is the symbol of Christianity because, although Christ dies on a cross (the motivation), there are many more things in Christianity than there are in a cross (the "overtaking").

The *partial motivation* of filmic connotations does not prevent them from giving rise quite often to codifications or to conventions, which are more or less extended according to the case. Here is a simple example: In a talking film in which the hero has, among other diegetic peculiarities, the habit of whistling the first bars of a certain tune—and provided that this fact has been clearly impressed upon the spectator from the beginning of the film—the mere appearance of the tune of the sound track (in the visual absence of the hero himself) will be sufficient to suggest the totality of the character later in the film after the hero has gone on a long journey or even vanished. It is not without powerful connotations that the character may have been thus designated. In this simplified example we see that the hero has not been "symbolized" by some arbitrary characteristic, but by a feature entirely his own (thus, lack of *total* arbitrariness). Yet in the whole character there was more than just the familiar tune; other features, which belong to him also, could have been chosen to "symbolize" him (and would have involved other connotations). There is, then, some arbitrariness in the relationship between the connotative signifier (the melody) and the connotative signified (the character).[1]

Even the subtlest and most ingenious cinematographic connotations are based then on this simple principle, which we might state as follows: A visual or an auditory theme—or an arrangement of visual and auditory themes—once it has been placed in its correct syntagmatic position within the discourse that constitutes the whole film, takes on a value greater than its own and is increased by the additional meaning it receives. But this addition itself is never entirely "arbitrary," for what the theme symbolizes in this manner is an integral situation or whole process, *a part of which in fact it is,* within the story told by the film (or which the spectator knows to be an actual part of life). in short, the connotative meaning *extends over* the denotative meaning, but without *contradicting* or *ignoring* it. Thus the partial arbitrariness; thus the absence of total arbitrariness.

2. Range and Limits of the Concept of Analogy

The concept of analogy must nevertheless be handled with caution. It is true that, for an actual semiotics of the cinema, analogy serves as a kind of stopping block: Wherever analogy takes over filmic signification (that is, notably the meaning of each visual element taken separately), there is a lack of specifically cinematographic codification. That is why I believe filmic codes must be sought on other levels: the codes peculiar to connotation (including partially "motivated" codes for the pure "arbitrary" does not exhaust the codifiable field) or the codes of denotation-connotation related to the discursive organization of image groups (see also, for example, the "large syntagmatic category of the image track" [*"la grande syntagmatique de la bande images"* is sometimes referred to simply as "the *grande syntagmatique*" in other translations and in English-language articles.—ED.] parts 5 and 6 below). But, for a general semiotics, the analogous portions of filmic signification would not constitute a point of stopping off; for many things that are assumed to be "acquired" by the film analyst and therefore are a kind of absolute beginning *after which* the cinematographic experience unfolds, are in turn the complex, terminal products of *other* cultural experiences and various organizations whose field of action, being more general, includes a great deal more than the cinema alone. Among the codes that are extracinematographic by nature, but that nevertheless intervene on the screen under cover of analogy, one must point out as a minimum—without prejudice to more complex and sensitive enumerations—the *iconology* specific to each sociocultural group producing or viewing the films (the more or less institutionalized modalities of object representation, the processes of recognition and *identification* of objects in their visual or auditive "reproduction," and, more generally, the collective notions of what an image is), and, on the other hand, up to a certain point, *perception* itself (visual habits of identification and construction of forms and figures, the spatial representations peculiar to each culture, various auditory structures, and so on). Characteristically, codes of this type function, so to speak, at the heart of analogy and are experienced by the viewers as a part of the most ordinary and natural visual or auditory decipherment.

Contrary to what I believed four years ago (notably in "The Cinema: Language or Language System?"),[2] it does not seem at all impossible to me, today, to assume that *analogy is itself coded without, however, ceasing to function authentically as analogy in relation to the codes of the superior level*—which are brought into play only on the basis of this first assumption. Many of the misunderstandings and arguments about these subjects derive from the fact that no one has yet attempted to draw up a halfway complete list of the different heterogeneous and superimposed codes copresent in any cultural activity of some importance, and no one has yet tried to clarify the precise organization of their interactions.[3]

In any event, it seems to me that one can distinguish at least two main types of signifying organization: *cultural* codes and *specialized* codes. The first define the culture of each social group; they are so ubiquitous and well "assimilated" that the viewers generally consider them to be "natural"—basic constituents of mankind itself (although they are clearly *products*, since they vary in space and time). The handling of these codes requires no *special* training—that is to say, no training other than that of living, and having been raised, in a society. On the other hand the codes I have called "specialized" concern more specific and restricted social activities. They appear more explicitly as codes, and they require a special training—to a large or small extent depending on the case (relatively "small" in the cinema)—that is to say, a training even the "native" person, possessing the culture of his group, cannot dipense with.

This bipartition is fairly useful in the study of gesticulatory codes, which I take here simply as examples. The so-called expressive, affective, spontaneous, natural, or speech-accompanying gestures *already* constitute a first level of codification, since it is known that the same gesture has different meanings from culture to culture, while the same meaning is expressed by different gestures. Gestures like those that make up the "sign language" of the deaf and dumb (and in general all gestures said to be "artificial," "conventional," "codified," or "ruled," and so on) represent *another* level of codification, which is used in particular social situations and the training for which constitutes a separate activity. A Frenchman, born and raised in France, does not need to be specially taught the gestures expressing anger, refusal, resigned acceptance, or the gesture that stands for "Come here!"—but, though he is French, he will need to be specially taught the sign language of the deaf and dumb (in his own language); otherwise he will never know it.

The purely cinematographic signifying figures studied here (montage, camera movements, optical effects, "rhetoric of the screen," interaction of visual and auditory elements, and so on) constitute specialized codes—although relatively "easy" ones, as we will see later—that function above and beyond photographic and phonographic analogy. The iconological, perceptual, and other codes are cultural codes, and they function in good part *within* photographic and phonographic analogy, as Umberto Eco,[4] to whom the hypothesis advanced in these pages owes much, has rightly pointed out.

So far, I have been speaking about denotation (the literal sense of the film). But among the large body of connoted significations in the cinema (the "symbolic sense" of all varieties), there are a certain number that, outside of the specifically cinematographic codifications, intrude to the film by means of perceptual analogy each time an object or an ordering of objects (visual or auditory) "symbolizes" within the film what it would have symbolized outside of the film—that is to say, within culture (with the chance that it will carry *in addition,* and only in the film, symbolic significations that will then derive from its location within the cinematographic discourse proper). "Objects" (and characters must also be included)—that is to say, the different basic elements of filmic discourse—do not enter the film in a virgin state; they carry with them, before even "cinematographic language" can intervene, a great deal more than their simple literal identity—which does not prevent the spectator belonging to a given culture from deciphering this "increment" at the same time that he identifies that object. This is the concept of the *im-segno* as formulated by Pier Paolo Pasolini, who does not, however, sufficiently insist on the fact that the *im-segno,* in the cinema, is located at the very center of the perceptual analogy between the object and its image.[5]

This new specific level of organization, which is constituted by the cultural connotations peculiar to objects, has an extremely complex relationship to *iconology* (about which I spoke a little earlier); complex in itself, even more complex when it occurs in the framework of a film. Between these two levels of intelligibility there is all the difference that separates denotation from connotation—but also the similarity implied by their common root in the actual perception of the spectators. This is why, provisionally, I use the term *iconography* to designate the prefilmic connotations of objects, in order to distinguish them from—and at the same time draw them closer to—the *iconology* (likewise prefilmic) that organizes the denotation of those same objects.

3. The Cinema as Such Has Nothing Corresponding to the Double Articulation of Verbal Languages

Let us note first that the cinema has no *distinctive* units (I mean distinctive units of its own).[6] It does not have anything corresponding to the phoneme or to the relevant phonic feature on the level of expression, nor, on the level of content, does it have anything equivalent to the seme in Algirdas Julien Greimas's sense, or in Bernard Pottier's sense.[7]

Even with respect to the signifying units, the cinema is initially deprived of discrete elements. It proceeds by whole "blocks of reality," which are actualized with their total meaning in the discourse. These blocks are the "shots." The discrete units identifiable in the filmic discourse on another level—for, as we shall see, there is another level—are not equivalent to the first articulation of spoken languages.

Certainly, it is true that montage is in a sense an analysis, a sort of articulation of the reality shown on the screen. Instead of showing us an entire landscape, a filmmaker will show us successively a number of partial views, which are broken down and ordered according to a very precise intention. It is well known that the nature of the cinema is to transform the world into discourse.

But this kind of articulation is not a true articulation in the linguistic sense.[8] Even the most partial and fragmentary "shot" (what film people call the closeup) still presents a complete segment of reality. The closeup is only a shot taken closer than other shots.

It is true that the film *sequence* is a real unit—that is to say, a sort of coherent *syntagma* within which the "shots" react (semantically) to each other. This phenomenon recalls up to a certain point the manner in which words react to each other within a sentence, and that is why the first theoreticians of the cinema often spoke of the shot as a word, and the sequence as a sentence. But these were highly erroneous identifications, and one can easily list five radical differences between the filmic "shot" and the linguistic word:[9]

(1) Shots are infinite in number, contrary to words, but like statements, which can be formulated in a verbal language.

(2) Shots are the creations of the filmmaker, unlike words (which pre-exist in lexicons), but similar to statements (which are in principal the invention of the speaker).

(3) The shot presents the receiver with a quantity of undefined information, contrary to the word. From this point of view, the shot is not even equivalent to the sentence. Rather, it is like the complex statement of undefined length (how is one to describe a film shot completely by means of natural language?).

(4) The shot is an actualized unit, a unit of discourse, an assertion, unlike the word (which is a purely virtual lexical unit), but like the statement, which always refers to reality or a reality (even when it is interrogative or jussive). The image of a house does not signify "house," but "Here is a house"; the image contains a sort of index of actualization,[10] by the mere fact that it occurs in a film.

(5) Only to a small extent does a shot assume its meaning in paradigmatic contrast to the other shots that might have occurred at the same point along the filmic chain (since the other possible shots are infinite in number), whereas a word is always a part of at least one more or less organized semantic field. The important linguistic phenomenon of the clarification of present units by absent units hardly comes into play in the cinema. Semiologically, this confirms what the aestheticians of the cinema have frequently observed; namely, that the cinema is an "art of presence" (the dominance of the image, which "shuts out" everything external to itself).

The filmic "shot" therefore resembles the statement rather than the word. Nevertheless, it would be wrong to say that it is equivalent to the statement. For there are still great differences between the shot and the linguistic statement. Even the most complex statement is reducible, in the final analysis, to discrete elements (words, morphemes, phonemes, relevent features), which are fixed in number and in nature.

To be sure, the filmic shot is also the result of an ordering of several elements (for example, the different visual elements in the image—what is sometimes called the *interior montage*), but these elements are indefinite in number and undefined in nature, like the shot itself. The analysis of a shot consists in progressing from a nondiscrete whole to smaller nondiscrete wholes: One can decompose a shot, but one cannot reduce it.

All that can be affirmed, therefore, is that a shot is less unlike a statement than a word, but it does not necessarily resemble a statement.

4. The "Grammar" of Cinema: A Rhetoric or a Grammar?

After the preceding paragraphs one might suppose that the "grammar" of cinema is a rhetoric rather than a true grammar, since the *minimum unit* (the shot) is not determined, and consequently codification can affect only the *large units.*

Thus, the *dispositio* (or large syntagmatic category), which is one of the principal parts of classical rhetorics, consists in prescribing determined orderings of undetermined elements: Judiciary discourse, for example, must contain five parts (*exordium,* recital of facts, and so on), but each one of these parts remains free in length and internal composition. Practically all the figures of "cinematographic grammar"—that is to say, the corpus of units that (1) signify (as opposed to being "distinctive"), (2) are discrete, (3) are of large magnitude, and (4) are proper to the cinema and common to all films—obey this same principle. Thus "alternate montage" (alternating images equals simultaneity of the referents) is an ordering that is both *codified* (i.e., the fact of alternating itself) and *significant* (since the alternating signifies simultaneity). But the length and the internal composition of the ordered elements (i.e., the alternating images) remains entirely free.

Nevertheless, it is at this point that one of the main difficulties in the semiotics of the cinemā arises. *For this rhetoric I have just mentioned is also, in other aspects, a grammar*—and, as Pier Paolo Pasolini rightly points out,[11] the nature of the semiotics of film is that grammar and rhetoric are not separate in it.

Why do filmic orderings that are codified and significant constitute a grammar? Because they organize not only filmic connotation but also, and *primarily,* denotation. The specific signified of alternate montage involves, as we have seen, the literal temporality of the plot—the first message of the film—even if the alternating order automatically entails various denotations.

It is impossible to maintain that the "grammar" of film concerns primarily denotation unless one immediately defines what is meant by *primarily.* It is, so to speak, a synchronic *primarily:* The thing that characterizes the *functioning* of filmic orderings is that it is primarily thanks to them that the spectator understands the literal sense of the film. From the *diachronic* perspective, on the contrary, filmic orderings are codified primarily for purposes of connotation rather than denotation. One can always "tell a story" merely by means of iconic analogy, and indeed that is what the earliest filmmakers did (when, for example, they photographed a music-hall sketch) in the period when a specific cinematographic language did not yet exist (1895–1900 and even, in part, the period of 1900–15). The principal figures of cinematographic language were originally elaborated with the aim of making the story more "alive" or more "moving"— that is to say, for connotative purposes. The empirical history of the cinema leaves us in no doubt on this matter. Nevertheless, there immediately occurred a kind of vast semiological cross-fertilization: The concern with connotation resulted in increasing, organizing, and codifying denotation, thus putting an end to the *exclusive* rule of iconic analogy as a means of denotation. Here again is the example of alternate montage: It was invented in order to premit certain "effects of style" and composition, but it became a pattern of denotative intelligibility, since movie spectators henceforth knew that the alternating of images on the screen was always liable to signify that, in the most literal temporality of the fiction, the events presented were simultaneous.

It is therefore quite true, as the film aesthetician Jean Mitry has remarked, that, in the cinema, even more than elsewhere, connotation is nothing other than a form of denotation.[12] Consider our example again: a filmmaker wants to show two events that are simultaneous in the fiction (signified of denotation equals, among other things, simultaneity). He has the choice, for a corresponding denotative signifier, between alternate montage and a more ordinary form of montage in which the two events are presented one after the other without alternating (the second event being then antedated by some device, such as a title saying "Meanwhile," or some indication in the dialogue, or in some detail of the image, etc.) The impression that the spectator will finally derive (i.e., signified of connotation) will not at all be the same in the two instances, and the concrete feeling of a close simultaneity between the two facts will be stronger with the use of alternate montage. Yet the signified of denotation (i.e., approximate simultaneity) will have been correctly understood in both cases, while the form of denotation will not have been the same in the two instances, and consequently the connotation will have been modified.

In short, films are able to connote without generally requiring *special* (i.e., separate) connotors because they have the most essential signifiers of connotation at their permanent disposal: the choice between several ways of structuring denotation. On the other hand, it is because *denotation itself is structured,*[13] because today it is no longer the mere automatic functioning of iconic analogy, and because the cinema is a great deal more than just photography, that films can connote without the permanent assistance of discontinuous connotors. Thus, by way of semiotics, we arrive at an observation that film aestheticians frequently make: Namely, that *preexisting* symbols (whether social, psychoanalytic, etc.) that are artificially tacked on to filmic continuity represent a poor and simplistic approach, and that the essential part of cinematographic symbolism lies elsewhere (the symbol must be "born out of the film").

5. The Large Syntagmatic Category of the Image Track [La Grande syntagmatique de la bande-images]

So far, I have examined only the status of "cinematographic grammar," and I have said nothing about its *content*. I have not given the table of the codified orderings of various kinds used in film.

It is not possible here to give this table in its complete form, with all the explanations required by each one of the indicated orderings, and with the *principles of commutation* between them (and consequently to enumerate them.)[14]

Let us content ourselves, then, with the almost unpolished "result" —the table itself in a summarized form—and only that part of it that outlines the large syntagmatic category of the image track (i.e., the codified and signifying orderings on the level of the *large* units of the film,[15] and ignoring the elements of sound and speech). Naturally this problem constitutes only one of the chapters of "cinematographic syntax."

In order to determine the number and the nature of the main syntagmatic *types* used in current films, one must start from common observation (existence of the "scene," the "sequence," "alternate montage," etc.) as well as on certain "presemiotic" analyses by critics, historians, and theoreticians of the cinema ("tables of montage," various classifications, etc.)[16] This preliminary work must account for several points of importance—that is why it in no way precludes the viewing of numerous films—and it must then be organized into a coherent body—that is to say, into a list of all the main types of image orderings occurring in films under the various headings into which they are naturally classified.

One thus arrives at a first "tabulation" of the syntagmatic components of films—a chart remaining fairly close to the concrete filmic material, but which, from the point of view of semiological theory, is as yet insufficiently developed. I will not trace here this first stage, which is indispensable but which one must go beyond, for it has already been outlined in *Communications* (no. 8, 1966),[17] and orally, at the Second Film Festival of Pesaro (Italy, May 1966).[18] I will remind the reader simply that I had distinguished six main types: the autonomous shot, the scene, the sequence, the descriptive syntagma, the alternating syntagma (including three subcategories: alternate, alternating, and parallel), and the frequentative syntagma (also with three subtypes: full frequentative, "bracket" frequentative, and semifrequentative).

Since then, I have sought to establish a second general table of syntagmatic categories in film. This was described in the review *Image et son* (no. 201, 1967);[19] it was also presented at the Conference of Semiotics at Kazimierz, Poland, in September 1966;[20] it is the table reproduced on the adjacent page, and it will be the basis for my analysis of Jacques Rozier's film *Adieu Philippine,* which appears later in this book.[21]

This second table differs from the first on two specific points and on a question of general method. The specific points: First, it appeared that the "frequentative"—which is by the way relatively rare—is not a type of image-ordering to be placed on the same level as the others; rather it is a specific modality liable to affect in certain precise cases some of the remaining types.[22] Second, the unitary status I had given to the "alternating syntagma" (which included, notably, the alternate and parallel syntagmas, relegating them to the position of subtypes) strikes me as being a little artificial today, for the appearance on the screen of images alternating in series is a fairly common phenomenon, and can give rise to very different significations.[23] The alternating syntagma and the frequentative syntagma therefore are no longer indicated as such in the new chart.

As for the difference of method: It appears that the different types and subtypes that composed the first table, where they were presented in the purely enumerative form of a list, can be redistributed into a system of successive dichotomies, according to a procedure commonly used in linguistics. This scheme gives us a better outline of the *deep structure* of the choices that confront the filmmaker for each one of the "sequences" of his film. In this way, an empirical and purely inductive classification could later be converted into a deductive system; in other words, a factual situation, initially ascertained and clarified, later showed itself to be more logical than one might have predicted (see table).

At present, then, I distinguish eight main types of autonomous segments, that is, "sequences" (but henceforth I will reserve the term "sequence" for only two of these eight types, numbers 7 and 8).

The autonomous segment is a subdivision of the first order in film; it is therefore a part of a film, and not a part of a part of a film. (If an autonomous section is composed of five successive shots, each one of these shots is a part of a part of the whole film—that is to say, a nonautonomous segment). It is clear nevertheless that the "autonomy"of the autonomous segments themselves is not an *independence*, since each autonomous segment derives its final meaning in relation to the film as a whole, the latter being the *maximum syntagma* of the cinema.

In distinguishing between the "shot" and the "sequence," everyday language clearly indicates that there are two things in the cinema (without prejudice to eventual intermediate levels): On the one hand there is the minimum segment, which is the shot (see *Film Language: A Semiotics of the Cinema,* pages 106–7),

General Table of the Large Syntagmatic Category of the Image-track ["Grande syntagmatique de la bande-images"]

In italics: the syntagmatic types that are initially identifiable in films (inductive method), but which are arrived at last in the system (deductive method)—that is to say, the eight main syntagmatic types. Each of these types is given the number it had in the text.

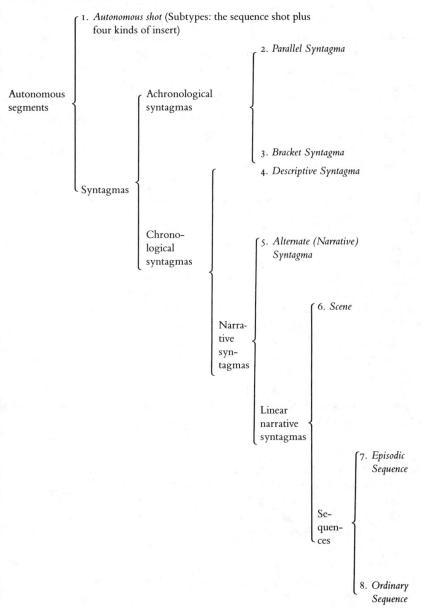

1. *Autonomous shot* (Subtypes: the sequence shot plus four kinds of insert)

Autonomous segments

Syntagmas

Achronological syntagmas

2. *Parallel Syntagma*

3. *Bracket Syntagma*

Chronological syntagmas

4. *Descriptive Syntagma*

Narrative syntagmas

5. *Alternate (Narrative) Syntagma*

6. *Scene*

Linear narrative syntagmas

Sequences

7. *Episodic Sequence*

8. *Ordinary Sequence*

and on the other hand the autonomous segment. This, as we will see shortly, does not prevent a minimum segment from being occasionally autonomous.

Let us now examine our eight syntagmatic types.

(1) A first pertinence allows us to distinguish autonomous segments constituted by a single shot—that is to say, *autonomous shots*—from the seven other varieties of autonomous segment, which all contain several shots. The latter are therefore all *syntagmas* (autonomous segments having more than one minimum segment). In the case of the autonomous shot, on the contrary, a single shot presents an "episode" of the plot. The autonomous shot is therefore the only instance where a single shot constitutes a primary, and not a secondary, subdivision of the film. Similarly, in literature the sentence is a unit smaller than the paragraph, but some paragraphs contain only one sentence (in linguistics the same could be said of the relation between the phoneme and the moneme, or between the moneme and the statement; in other words, we are dealing with a phenomenon that is common in semiotics). In short, some of the autonomous segments of a film are syntagmas,[24] and others are not; conversely, some of the shots in a film are autonomous and others are not.

The autonomous shot includes several subtypes: There is, on the one hand, the famous "sequence shot" of the modern cinema (an entire scene treated in a single shot; the shot derives its autonomy from the unity of "action"); on the other hand, there are the various kinds of shot that owe their autonomy to their status as syntagmatic *interpolations* and could be collectively termed *inserts*. If one selects the *cause* of their interpolative nature as a principle of classification, one will notice that up to now there have been only four types of insert in the cinema: the *nondiegetic* insert (i.e., image having a purely comparative function; showing an object which is external to the action of the film); the *subjective* insert (i.e., image conveying not the present instance, but an absent moment experienced by the hero of the film.[25] Examples: images of memory, dream, fear, premonition, etc.); the *displaced diegetic* insert (an image that, while remaining entirely "real," is displaced from its normal filmic position and is purposely intruded into a foreign syntagma. Example: Within a sequence showing the pursuers, a single shot of the pursued is inserted); and, finally, the *explanatory* insert (the enlarged detail, in a magnifying-glass effect. The detail is removed from its empirical space and is presented in the abstract space of a mental operation. Example: closeup of a visiting card or letter).

(2 and 3) Among the syntagmas (autonomous segments composed of several shots), a second criterion allows us to distiguish between *nonchronological* and chronological syntagmas. In the first variety, the temporal relationship between the facts presented in the different images is not defined by the film (i.e., temporary withdrawal of the signified of temporal denotation); in the second kind it is.

I have so far identified two main types of nonchronological syntagma. One of them is well known by film aestheticians and is called "parallel montage sequence" (I prefer to say *parallel syntagma,* to save the word "sequence" for other uses). Definition: montage brings together and interweaves two or more alter-ating "motifs," but no precise relationship (whether temporal or spatial) is assigned to them—at least on the level of denotation. This kind of montage has a direct symbolic value (scenes of the life of the rich interwoven with scenes of the life of the poor, images of tranquility alternating with images of disturbance, shots of the city and of the country, of the sea and of wheat fields, and so on).

The second type of nonchronological syntagma has not (to my knowledge) been identified before, but it is easily isolated in films. Definition: a series of very brief scenes representing occurrences that the film gives as typical samples of a same order of reality, without in any way chronologically locating them in relation to each other, in order to emphasize their presumed kinship within a category of facts that the filmmaker wants to describe in visual terms.[26] None of these little scenes is treated with the full syntagmatic breadth it might have commanded; it is taken as an element in a system of allusions, and therefore it is the series, rather than the individual, that the film takes into account. Thus the series is equivalent to a more ordinary sequence, and so it constitutes an autonomous segment (this is a kind of filmic equivalent to conceptualization). Example: the first erotic images of *Une Femme mariée* (Jean-Luc Godard, 1964) sketch a global picture of "modern love" through variations and partial repeti-tions; or again, the succeeding shots of destruction, bombings, and grief at the beginning of *Quelque part en Europe* (Geza Radvanyi, 1947) are an exemplary illustration of the idea of the "Disasters of War."

Let us call this construction of images the *bracket syntagma,* since it suggests that, among the occurrences that it groups together, there is the same kind of relationship as that between the words in a typographical bracket. In the bracket syntagma it is frequently the case that different successive evocations are strung together through optical effects (dissolves, wipes, pan shots, and, less commonly, fades). This use, which has a redundant function, provides the sequence with a common thread and confirms the viewer's impression that the sequence must be taken as a whole, and that he must not attempt to link the short partial scenes directly to the rest of the narrative. Example: in *The Scarlet Empress* (Joseph von Sternberg, 1935), the sequence that constructs the terrifying yet fascinating image of Tzarist Russia that the future empress imagines as a little girl (prisoners tied to giant bell clappers, the executioner with his axe, and so on).[27]

Thus, among the nonchronological syntagmas, it is the presence or absence of a systematic alternating of images in interwoven series that allows us to distinguish between the parallel syntagma and the bracket syntagma (presence equals parallel syntagma; absence equals bracket syntagma). The bracket syn-tagma directly groups all the images together; the parallel syntagma contains two or more series, each one having several images, and these series alternate on the screen (A B A B, etc.).

(4) In the *chronological* syntagmas, the temporal relationships between the facts that successive images show us are defined on the level of denotation (i.e., literal temporality of the plot, and not just some symbolic, "profound" time). But these precise relationships are not necessarily those of consecutiveness; they may also be relations of *simultaneity.*

There is one syntagmatic type in which the relationship between *all* the motifs successively presented on the screen is one of simultaneity: the *descriptive syntagma* (i.e., various filmic descriptions).[28] It is the only case of consecutiveness on the screen that does not correspond to any diegetic consecutiveness. (Remember that the screen is the location of the signifier, and the diegesis is the location of the signified). Example: the description of a landscape (a tree, followed by a shot of a stream running next to the tree, followed by a view of a hill in the distance, etc.). In the descriptive syntagma, the only intelligible relation of coexistence between the objects successively shown by the images is a relation of *spatial* coexistence.

This in no way implies that the descriptive syntagma can only be applied to *motionless* objects or persons. A descriptive syntagma may very well cover an action, provided that it is an action whose only intelligible internal relationship is one of spatial parallelism at any given moment in time—that is to say, an action the viewer cannot mentally string together in time. Example: a flock of sheep being herded (views of the sheep, the shepherd, the sheepdog, etc.). In the cinema as elsewhere, description is a modality of discourse, and not a substantial characteristic of the object of discourse; the same object can either be *described* or *told*, depending on the logic of what is said about it.[29]

(5) All chronological syntagmas other than the descriptive syntagma are *narrative syntagmas*—that is to say, syntagmas in which the temporal relationship between the objects seen in the images contains elements of consecutiveness and not only of simultaneity.[30] But within the narrative syntagmas there are two divisions: The syntagma may interweave several distinct temporal progressions, or, on the contrary, it may consist of a single succession encompassing all the images. Thus, the alternate narrative syntagma (or *alternate syntagma*) is distinguished from the various sorts of linear narrative syntagma.

The alternate syntagma is well known by theoreticians of the cinema under the names "alternate montage," "parallel montage," "synchronism," etc., depending on the case. Typical example: shot of the pursuers, followed by a shot of the pursued, and back to a shot of the pursuers. Definition: The montage presents alternately two or more series of events in such a way that within each series the temporal relationships are consecutive, but that, between the series taken as wholes, the temporal relationship is one of simultaneity (which can be expressed by the formula "Alternating of images equals simultaneity of occurrences").[31]

(6) Within the *linear narrative syntagmas* (i.e., a single succession linking together all the acts seen in the images), a new criterion lets us make yet another

distinction: Succession may be *continuous* (without break or ellipsis) or discontinuous (jumps). Naturally one must not count as true ellipses—that is to say, as *diegetic breaks*—what might be called simple camera breaks (i.e., temporal continuity is interrupted by a displacing of the camera, or by a cutaway, and is then taken up again at the exact chronological point it had meanwhile reached).

When succession is continuous (i.e., with no diegetic breaks), we have the only kind of syntagma in the cinema that resembles a "scene" in the theater—or a scene in everyday life—that is to say, it represents a spatiotemporal integrality experienced as being without "flaws" (by "flaw" I mean those brusque effects of appearance or disappearance that are the frequent corollaries of the very multiplicity of shots, which film psychologists have studied and which constitute one of the major differences between filmic perception and real perception).[32] This is the *scene properly speaking* (or simply scene). It was the only construction known to the early filmmakers; it still exists today, but merely as one type among other types (it is therefore commutable). Example: conversation scenes (the presence on the soundtrack of a coherent succession of linguistic statements has the effect of rendering a unitary, "flawless" visual construction more probable—though not obligatory).

Thus, through means that are *already* filmic (separate shots that are later combined), the scene reconstructs a unit *still* experienced as being "concrete": a place, a moment in time, an action, compact and specific. The signifier is fragmentary in the scene—a number of shots, all of them only partial "profiles" *(Abschattungen)*—but the signified is unified and continuous. The profiles are interpreted as being taken from a common mass—for what one calls "viewing a film" is in fact a very complex phenomenon, constantly involving three distinct activities (perception, restructuring of the visual field, and immediate memory), which propel each other on, and, as fast as it comes in, never cease working on the information they furnish to themselves.

(7 and 8) Distinct from, and opposed to, the scene are the various kinds of linear narrative syntagma in which the temporal order of the facts presented is *discontinuous.* They are the *sequences proper.* (In cinematographic circles, the term "sequence" used to indicate a purely filmic construction—in contrast to "scene" in the theater—but, in time, the word has come to designate any sequence of shots having a unity—that is to say, any autonomous segment except the autonomous shot. Therefore, in current usage, "sequence" is equivalent to what I would call the *autonomous syntagma,* of which my table lists seven varieties. That is why I specify "sequences proper" for the two kinds of sequence I will now define.)

Within the sequence proper (i.e., single, discontinuous temporal order), one finds two species. The temporal discontinuity may be unorganized and, so to speak, scattered—and the viewer skips the moments that have, to his mind, no direct bearing on the plot: This is the *ordinary sequence,* a syntagmatic type very common in the cinema. On the other hand, the discontinuity may be *organized* and may therefore be the principle of structure and intelligibility in the sequence, in which case we have what I would call the *episodic sequence*. Definition: The sequence strings together a number of very brief scenes, which are usually separated from each other by optical devices (dissolves, etc.) and which succeed each other in chronological order.[33] None of these allusive little scenes is treated with the syntagmatic thoroughness it might have commanded, for the scenes are taken not as separate instances but only in their totality, which has the status of an ordinary sequence and which therefore constitutes an autonomous segment. In its extreme form (that is, when the successive episodes are separated by a long diegetic duration), this construction is used to condense gradual progressions. In Orson Welles's *Citizen Kane* (1941), the sequence portraying the gradual deterioration of the relationship between the hero and his first wife shows a chronological series of quick allusions to dinners shared by the couple in an atmosphere that is decreasingly affectionate; the scenes, treated in a succession of pan shots, are connected over intervening periods of months. In a less spectacular but structurally identical form, the episodic sequence is used to represent, through a series of regularly distributed (and less "striking") abridgments, various kinds of minor diegetic progression of less extended total duration by systematically isolating some of their succeeding "moments."

The ordinary sequence and the episodic sequence are both sequences in the proper—including the extracinematographic—sense of the word: the concept of a single concatenation plus the concept of discontinuity. However, in the episodic sequence, each one of the images constituting the series appears distinctly as the symbolic summary of one stage in the fairly long evolution condensed by the total sequence. In the ordinary sequence, each one of the units in the narrative simply presents one of the unskipped moments of the action. Consequently, in the first case each image stands for more than itself[34] and is perceived as being taken from a group of other possible images representing a single phase of a progression[35] (which, in relation to the integrality of the syntagma, does not prevent each of the allusions from having its own location along the axis of time). But in the ordinary sequence each image represents only what it shows.

For all that, the ordinary sequence itself already constitutes a more specifically filmic narrative unit, and one that is more removed from the conditions of real perception, than the film scene (and *a fortiori* the theater scene); unlike the scene, the sequence is not the locus of the coincidence—even in principle—of screen time and diegetic time (time of the signifier and time of the signified). The sequence is based on the unity of a more complex action (although it is still single, contrary to what occurs, for example, in the parallel syntagma or in the bracket syntagma), an action that "skips" those portions of itself it intends to leave out and that is therefore apt to unfold in several different locations (unlike the scene). A typical example is the sequence of escape (in which there is an approximate unity of place, but one that is essential rather than literal: that is, the "escape location," that paradoxical unit, the mobile locus). Thus, one encounters diegetic breaks within the sequence (and not just camera interruptions, as in the scene), but these hiatuses are considered insignificant—at least on the level of denotation[36]—and are to be distinguished from those indicated by the fades or by any other optical device between two autonomous segments.[37] Indeed, the latter are reputed to be oversignificant, even in denotation: We are told nothing, yet we are informed that a great deal could be told us (the fade is a segment that shows nothing but is very visible), and the "skipped moments" emphasized in this way are presumed to have influenced the events narrated by the film (unlike diegetic breaks within the sequence) and to be therefore necessary in some way, despite their absence, to the literal intellection of whatever follows.

This second version of my table of the large syntagmatic category is not necessarily the last one,[38] for it is the nature of intellectual investigation to be progressive and, of semiotics, to be a work of patience. Furthermore, the requirements known in linguistics under the name *formalization* usually lead one to proceed in gradual stages, particularly in an area that is, semiologically, still unexplored. After all, the more important point is perhaps not that a certain structure of images, subsumed here under a single type, may one day be more exactly analyzed (whether by me or by someone else) as corresponding, according to the specific case, to two different types—or other adjustments of this variety. The semiotics of the cinema is still taking its first steps. But it is precisely for that reason that my intention in this essay was to give the reader an idea of the problems confronting the student of film when he begins to use methods derived from linguistics and applies them in ways that are altogether new.

6. Relations Between the Large Syntagmatic Category and the Concept of Cinematographic "Montage"

Each of the eight main syntagmatic types—with the exception of the autonomous shot, where the problem does not occur—may be effected in one of two ways: either by recourse to *montage proper* (as was usually the case in the cinema of the past) or by means of *subtler forms of syntagmatic ordering* (as is often the case in the modern cinema). Combinations that avoid *collage*-juxtaposition (i.e., continuity shooting, long shots, sequence shots, using the resources of the "wide screen," and so on) are nonetheless *syntagmatic* constructions, examples of montage in the broad sense, as Jean Mitry has clearly shown.[39] It is true that the concept of montage as irresponsible, magical, and all-powerful manipulation has become obsolete. However, montage as the *structuring of intelligible coherence by means of various "conjunctures"* is by no means "outmoded," since film is always *discourse,* and therefore the locus of many different actualized elements.[40]

Example: A filmic description can be made in a single "shot," apart from any kind of montage, simply through camera movements. The intelligible structure ordering the different visual elements is the same as that linking the different *shots* within a classical descriptive syntagma. Montage proper is an *elementary* form of the large syntagmatic category of film, for each "shot" theoretically isolates a single visual element. Thus the *relation between visual elements* coincides with the relation between shots, rendering analysis easier than in the complex (and culturally "modern") forms of the cinematographic syntagmatic category.

Consequence: A deeper analysis of the syntagmatic category in modern films would require revising the status of the autonomous shot—at the very least in its form of "sequence shot"—because, up to a certain point, it may contain image structures that, in the seven other syntagmatic types, continue to exist in a free "undetermined" state. (This is the phenomenon expressed very approximately, in a simple juxtaposition of words, by the term "sequence shot.")

7. Remark on the Diachronic Evolution of Cinematographic Codes

The large syntagmatic category of the cinema is not immutable; it has a diachronic aspect. It evolves distinctly *faster* than languages do, a circumstance derived from the fact that art and language are more closely interrelated in film than in the verbal field. The creative filmmaker exerts more influence on the diachronic evolution of cinematographic language than the imaginative writer on the evolution of his idiom, for idiom may exist in the absence of art, whereas the cinema must be an art to become a language[41] with a partial denotative code. Remember, also, that filmmakers constitute a limited social group (creative group), whereas the users of language are coextensive as a group with society itself (user group).[42]

Nevertheless, the large syntagmatic category of the cinema ensures a codification that is coherent for every diachronic "state." Too great a deviation from this codification at any given moment results in the nonintelligence—for the mass of the spectators—of the film's literal meaning (example: certain "avant-garde" films).

8. "Natural Logic" and Conventional Codification in Filmic Ordering

Cinematographic "grammar" is codified, but it is not arbitrary. The distinction between the arbitrary and the motivated does not at all coincide, in this case, with that between the "free" and the codified.

The syntagmatic types in which denotation is not *analogous* retain a certain amount of *naturalness*[43] in their relationship of the signified to the signifier. Thus, in the alternate syntagma, denotation is not analogous—since the images alternate while the facts are presumably simultaneous and not alternating—yet, it has been shown that the intelligibility of this kind of montage is based on a spontaneous form of interpolation that the spectator practices quite naturally[44] (i.e., as soon as the rhythm of the alternating becomes sufficiently rapid, the spectator is able to guess that a series of events, A, is continuing to unfold in the diegesis, while only a fragment of the series of events, B, is being shown on the screen).

But this "natural" characteristic is not total, and therefore we can speak only of partial codification. Among the possible image structures (a fairly large number of which should exist), only a few are conventionalized; among the more or less natural (or *logical*) patterns of intelligibility on which the cinema *could* build its syntagmatic orderings, only a very few are retained—and they become *effective* patterns of intellection and are almost always grasped by the normal, adult spectator belonging to a society acquainted with the cinema. It is striking that, compared to all the conceivable image orderings, only a very small number is actually used. Just as in semantics there is the arbitrariness of lexicalization, in the cinema one has the arbitrariness of grammaticalization.

This alliance between natural logic and conventioanl codification has a consequence that has been singled out, with varying degrees of clarity, by psycho-sociologists, educators, filmologists, and the specialists of "popular animation": The practice of the cinema, both in its creating and in its viewing, requires a certain *apprenticeship*, but this apprenticeship is very *slight* compared to the one language demands. On the phylogenetic level, the evolution of cinematographic language took approximately twenty years (from 1895 to 1915 roughly: from Lumière to Griffith)—this is both a long time and a very short time. On the ontogenetic level, it is known that, before approximately the age of twelve years, a child is not able to grasp the literal meaning of an ordinary modern feature film in its whole continuity, but after that age he is gradually able to do so without having to undergo massive schooling such as the learning of a foreign language (or even a thorough knowledge of the mother tongue) requires. This is also true of adults in societies without cinema (black Africa, etc.): At first contact, they do not immediately understand the complex films of our societies, but later they are able to grasp them quite rapidly. All investigations agree on these points.[45]

9. Syntagmatic and Paradigmatic Categories in the "Grammar of Film"

The large syntagmatic category outlined above also constitutes a *paradigmatic category*—since, at any given moment in the making of his film, the filmmaker must choose from a limited series of types of syntagmatic ordering. Thus we have *paradigms* of *syntagmas*, and, to a certain extent, this situation resembles that which exists in the syntaxes of many languages (example: the choice among several types of clause: final clause, consecutive clause, and so on).

"Paradigmatic" and "syntagmatic" must not, as Louis Hjelmslev pointed out,[46] be assimilated, respectively, to "smallest units" and "largest units." The distinction between *ordering* and *choice* is one thing; the distinction between *large segments* and *small segments* is something else. There are syntagmatic phenomena on the level of the small segments (i.e., the syllable in verbal languages), and, conversely, paradigmatic phenomena on the level of the large segments (such as, precisely, the aspects mentioned here of the grammar of the cinema).[47]

10. The Respective Positions of the "Large" and the "Small" Elements In Relation to the Definition of a Properly Cinematographic Signifying System

It is even possible—although it is still too early to affirm this positively—that the *paradigmatic category of the large units* constitutes by itself—in a certain way that will be explained—the major part of the total paradigmatic category of "cinematographic language." In this respect there are already four remarks that can be made.

(1) Various filmic paradigms, which remain to be studied and have not been examined here (camera movements, internal structures of the "shot," "dissolves" and other optical devices, main types of relationship between sound and sight, etc.), share with the paradigms I have just analyzed the common characteristic of being concerned with syntagmatic elements that are already quite "large": This is true of entire *shot sequences,* of the entire *shot* itself, of the *relationship* of visual elements (that is, the relationship between two or more visual or sound elements that are isolated from the totality of the shot but that are themselves taken as totalities with their various perceptive aspects), and of the *relationship between the aspects* of the visual elements (each one of these "aspects," even when isolated from the other aspects of the same object, still possesses a complex and global quality). In linguistic terms, one might say that the *frame of reference*—or the *domain,* as Zellig Harris uses the word—of the different properly cinematographic figures remains remarkably "large," even when it is at its "smallest."

(2) Although, since the advent of the talking movie, *speech* has become an important element in films (occasionally the most important) and although its very presence introduces units that are really small—since they are the units of language—into the total cinematographic message, only a portion of the study of this verbal element—precisely a portion that considers large segments—pertains to a specifically filmic semiotics: that is, the analysis of the principal types of relationship between speech and image, or between speech and the rest of the sound track (music, "real noises," etc.). For the investigation of the filmic aspects of speech must not make us forget that the reason speech has become so important in the cinema is because, precisely, it is speech—that is to say, because it enriches film with the faculties of language; to this extent, its study

(and therefore, of course, the study of the smallest units) falls largely outside of the theory of the cinema itself.

(3) Among the other *facts* of the paradigmatic category of films that should be studied, the greater number pertain to *differential analyses*—that is, analyses that, taking the "filmic fact" as more or less acquired,[48] direct their attention to its specific manifestations, whether they are films as unique "works," the different parts of films as unique parts, or even the different kinds of film groups (always unique) corresponding, depending on the case, to the total *"oeuvre"* of a film-maker, the cinematographic "genre" (western, etc.), the "style" of a "period," of a country, of a "school," etc. (See, for example, the concept of "film stylistics" that Raymond Bellour outlines in great detail.)[49] These are all investigations quite separate from the study of actual cinematographic language—for the latter is an independent signifying system, and each film (or part of a film or group of films) is in turn another independent signifying system. Moreover—and although these differential analyses may, as a whole, ultimately consider elements that are smaller than those examined in the study of cinematographic language— these smaller elements risk remaining fairly "large," at least in the sense outlined in paragraph 1.

(4) Finally, if one day (whether through the study of films in general or through the study of a particular film) elements are isolated that, in comparing their syntagmatic magnitude to the total "scope" of the film track, deserve, in one way or another, to be qualified as "small," one may well discover that they have no discrete units (and consequently no paradigms) other than those that might be derived from a general semantics, or a semiotics of cultures or objects, etc. That is to say, one would find no discrete units specific to cinematographic language; for what defines the latter, indeed, is a certain mode of reproducing and ordering "fragments of reality" that are not specifically filmic in themselves (this is what is called "making a film"). The mechanical character of the basic filmic operation (photographic and phonographic duplication) has the conse-quence of integrating into the final product chunks of signification whose internal structure remains afilmic, and which are governed mainly by cultural paradigms. When some of these "fragments of reality" have been specially produced for the film (i.e., *mise-en-scène*), this production itself—other than the fact that it is never a radical reconstruction, for objects cannot be made over (or only in language can they be recast)—is never entirely obedient to systems that are unique to the art of film, but rather in large part to those same cultural significations that intrude into the filming of an object or of a more or less preexisting occurrence.

What I am saying is this: In the current state of the semiotics of film (and of the general theory of semiotics, for that matter), it is impossible to locate precisely the threshold separating elements we call "large" from those we term "small." Is its place in the *filmed object*—that is to say, in the visual or sound element (i.e., "automobile" in a certain image, the "train sound" accompaying another image)? If this is the case, how is one to *break down* and *categorize* such "objects"? Does the threshold extend to the *aspect* of the filmed object (the "color" and "size" of the automobile; the "violent roar" of the train sound)? And if this is the case, how, again, is one to isolate these aspects? Perhaps, even, it is located in the *parts* of the filmed objects (the "hood" of the car, the "beginning" of the train sound)? How are these parts to be handled?

For the time being, these problems all seem insoluble. *Languages* indeed break down into precise units the same experiences that the cinema presents in another way; and that is why one considers as acquired to the cinema units that in fact derive directly from the maternal language of the film analyst. That, however, is also why filmic analysis requires a metalanguage that, although it is better suited to the realities of the film thanks to its signifieds, is nevertheless obliged to borrow those signifieds from one or another natural language. Simply, this metalanguage is at present still at the stage of stammering.

And yet, however uncertain its location, the existence of the threshold between the "small" and the "large" elements is beyond doubt. There are two reasons for this—and perhaps they are really one and the same reason.

(1) Even in the cases where the filming manipulates the filmed object to a maximum—whether it is by previous *mise-en-scène,* in the actual *shooting* (angle and axial distance, choice of film, choice of lens, etc.), or by *breakdown* of the shots and *montage* (i.e., discursive ordering of the various shots)—it is unable, *beyond a certain degree,* to analyze and to reconstruct the very thing it is manipulating: This derives from that incoercible minimum, photographic fidelity— that is to say (despite everything else), from the mechanical nature of the basic filmic operation. Even in trick or stunt sequences, the constituent fragments themselves are not "faked" except for those trick sequences based not on decomposition but on a total alteration (accelerated sequence)—even then, however, certain aspects cannot be faked (the form and the direction of motion are retained in the accelerated sequence). Consequently, no matter how far one displaces the threshold between the "large" and the "small" toward the "small," one will always encounter elements beyond that threshold that should, with precision, be termed "small," if one agrees to designate thus the level of magnitude below which and beyond which the filmic vehicle as such is no longer able to effect commutations among the elements it integrates and can then only reproduce them—and, by the same token, it is no longer able to reproduce, by means of the elements themselves, all the significations (whether literal or variously symbolic, entirely or only partially systematized) that cluster around them, *beyond the film*—that is to say, in culture.

(2) *From the semantic point of view,* these elements, however "small" they may be, are always larger than the smallest units of verbal language (Greimas's semes, for example) and even some linguistic units that are already quite large (the

word). In the case of the visual elements or aspects of visual elements I have just discussed, the smallest of the filmic elements still contained a *quantity of information* that could not be conveyed by anything less than a sentence in language. As a result, we may state that, *for a semantic body of the same magnitude,* languages *already* provide a highly complex analysis (for the sentence comprises several monemes, a syntax, etc., and, in fact, carries the integrality of idiom)—whereas cinematographic language has not *even begun* to speak. In this same respect it is also a very refined language: It allows others to speak before intervening, and when it does intervene, its discourse is enriched by all that it previously refrained from delivering.

Thus, when it reaches the level of the "small" elements, the semiotics of the cinema encounters its limits, and its competence is no longer certain. Whether one has desired it or not, one suddenly finds oneself referred to the myriad winds of culture, the confused murmurings of a thousand other utterances: the symbolism of the human body, the language of objects, the system of colors (for color films) or the voices of chiaroscuro (for black and white films), the sense of clothing and dress, the eloquence of landscape. In each of these cases—and in each of the cases not mentioned here—the study (indispensable, by the way) of the properly filmic creations of the appropriate significations will provide us with no essential paradigm: for those great creative tropes of meaning and of humanity will remain imbedded in culture where only a very general semantics can illuminate them—even if their deep scattered appearance in films contributes, in return, to their partial reformulation.[50]

Verbal language can display specific units already on the level of its smallest elements (relevant phonic and semantic features, phonemes, monemes, etc.) because it analyzes and reconstructs human experience *from end to end,* providing the different aspects of this experience with phonic substitutes that, in themselves, have nothing in common with what they are meant to indicate. Conversely, "cinematographic language" can begin displaying specific units only after it has reached the level of fairly large elements, because its analysis and reconstruction of human experience are only *partial.* In a way peculiar to it, it orders and states the different aspects of this experience, which it begins by taking in the form of "blocks" that are largely pre-existent to its enterprise. Thus we are brought around to some of the favorite observations—though formulated differently—of film aestheticians: That the cinema is a language of reality—and that its specific nature is to transform the world into discourse, but so that its "worldness" is retained. Note, also, that it is to a great extent thanks to this characteristic of total reconstruction that verbal language is, in fact, language proper, human language *par excellence*—and that the absence of a similar virtue contributes greatly to the fact that cinematographic language (resembling in this respect many other systems of signification) cannot presume to have an anthropological importance as central, permanent, ancient, and universal as language itself, even in recent industrial societies where "audiovisual" semiotics plays a capital role.

11. Film and Diegesis: The Semiotics of the Cinema and the Semiotics of the Narrative

The reader will perhaps have observed in the course of this article (and especially in the definition of the different types of autonomous segment) that it is no easy matter to decide whether the large syntagmatic category in film involves the *cinema* or the cinematographic *narrative*. For all the units I have isolated are located *in* the film but in *relation* to the plot. This perpetual seesaw between the screen instance (which signifies) and the diegetic instance (which is signified) must be accepted and even erected into a methodological principle, for it, and only it, renders commutation possible, and thus identification of the units (in this case, the autonomous segments).

One will never be able to analyze film by speaking *directly* about the diegesis (as in some of the film societies, *ciné clubs*, in France and elsewhere, where the discussion is centered around the plot and the human problems it implies), because that is equivalent to examining the signifieds without taking the signifiers into consideration. On the other hand, isolating the units without considering the diegesis *as a whole* (as in the "montage tables" of some of the theoreticians of the silent cinema) is to study the signifiers without the signifieds—since the nature of narrative film is to narrate.

The autonomous segments of film correspond to as many diegetic *elements*, but not to the "diegesis" itself. The latter is the *distant signified* of the film taken as a whole: Thus a certain film will be described as "the story of an unhappy love affair set against the background of provincial bourgeois French society toward the end of the nineteenth century," etc. The partial elements of the diegesis constitute, on the contrary, the *immediate signifieds* of each filmic segment. The immediate signified is linked to the segment itself by insoluble ties of semiological reciprocity, which form the basis of the principle of commutation.

The necessity of this seesawing I have just described is nothing other than the consequence of an underlying cultural and social fact: The cinema, which could have served a variety of uses, in fact is most often used to *tell stories*—to the extent that even supposedly nonnarrative films (short documentary films, educational films, etc.) are governed essentially by the same semiological mechanisms that govern the "feature films."[51]

Had the cinema not become thoroughly narrative, its grammar would undoubtedly be entirely different (and would perhaps not even exist). The reverse of this coin, however, is that a given narrative receives a very different semiological treatment in the cinema than it would in a novel, in classical ballet, in a cartoon, and so on.

There are therefore two distinct enterprises, neither of which can replace the other: On the one hand, there is the semiotics of the narrative film, such as the one I am attempting to develop; on the other hand, there is the structural analysis of actual narrativity—that is to say, of the narrative taken *independently from the vehicles carrying it* (the film, the book, etc.)[52] The study of the narrative, we know, is currently enjoying a great deal of interest. A scholar like Claude Brémond, for example, is directing his investigations toward that very precise "layer of signification" *(couche signifiante)* that a narrative constitutes before the intervention of the narrative "props." I agree entirely with this author as to the autonomy of the narrative layer itself:[53] The *narrated event,* which is a signified in the semiotics of narrative vehicles (and notably of the cinema), becomes a signifier in the semiotics of narrativity.

Conclusion

The concept of a "cinematographic grammar" is very much out of favor today; one has the impression, indeed, that such a thing cannot exist. But that is only because it has not been looked for in the right place. Students have always implicitly referred themselves to the *normative grammar of particular languages* (namely, their maternal languages), but the linguistic and grammatical phenomenon is much vaster than any single language and is concerned with the *great and fundamental figures of the transmission of all information.* Only a general linguistics and a general semiotics (both nonnormative and simply analytical disciplines) can provide the study of cinematographic language with the appropriate methodological "models." It does not suffice merely to observe that there is nothing in the cinema corresponding to the consecutive clause in French, or to the Latin adverb, which are extremely particular linguistic phenomena, are not necessary, and are not universal. The dialogue between the film theoretician and the semiologist can commence only beyond the level of such idiomatic specifications or such restrictive prescriptions. *The fact that must be understood is that films are understood.* Iconic analogy alone cannot account for the intelligibility of the co-occurrences in filmic discourse. That is the function of the large syntagmatic category.

Notes

1. This amounts to saying that *ellipsis* and *symbol,* regarded in their deepest principle, are no longer two different things in the cinema. Rather they constitute the present face (symbol) and the absent face (ellipsis) of a single representation, through which the film, *by the mere fact that*

it must always select what it shows and what it does not show, transforms the world into articulated discourse.

2. See "The Cinema: Language or Language System?" in Christian Metz, *Film Language: A Semiotics of the Cinema* (New York: Oxford University Press, 1974), pp. 39–41. Hereinafter cited as *as Film Language*). [EDITOR'S NOTE: This is the same collection in which "Problems of Denotation in the Fiction Film" appears. "The Cinema: Language or Language System?" was originally published in 1964.]

3. The discussions that have taken place in recent years about the semiotics of the cinema have made it appear more and more clearly that *the cinema as a whole* is a locus where many signifying systems are superimposed and interwoven—and that *cinematographic language* is only one of these systems. As for me, I would willingly classify the totality of the "codes" that intervene in the total cinematographic message into five main levels of organization that would be superimposed in a hierarchy (see "The Cinema: Language or Language System?", pp. 61–63, note p. 61, in Metz, *Film Language*). But this is only a hypothesis.

4. U Eco, notably in his contribution to the round-table discussion on the theme of *Ideology and Language in the Cinema,* held in the framework of the Third Festival of the New Cinema (*Pesaro III,* Italy, June 1967). The substance of his discussion was reprinted in *Appunti per una semiologia delle communicazioni visivi* (Florence: Universita di Firenze, Bompiani Editore, 1967), pp. 139–52.

In his contribution to the discussion at Pesaro, Umberto Eco raised a number of objections to the concept of analogy presented here; in the paragraphs above I have taken into account my conversations with him at Pesaro, reminders of which one will also find in his *Appunti,* p. 141.

5. For references concerning Pasolini's theory of the *"im-segno,"* and for a résumé and discussion of his theory, see "The Modern Cinema and Narrativity" in *Film Language,* esp. pp. 211–16. The concept of the im-segno, despite my objections to it, is a stimulating one and has helped me greatly to clarify my own thoughts about superposition of several distinct levels of organization at the heart of the "cinema" as a totality.

6. I mean to say that cinematographic language as such lacks distinctive units. For, as a totality, the cinema contains various other signifying systems, each one of which behaves differently in relation to the problem of articulations. On this point, see Metz, "The Cinema: Language or Language System?" note, pp. 61–63.

The most obvious example—there are others less apparent—of the superposition of codes within the total cinematographic institution (superpositions that complicate the problem of the articulations in the cinema) is provided by the occurrence of the *verbal element* in talking films: The effect of its intervention is to integrate the doubly articulated significations into the global message of the film but not into the specific language of the "cinema."

7. A. J. Greimas, *Sémantique structurale* (Paris: Larousse, 1966). B. Pottier, *Systematique des éléments de relation* (doctoral thesis, 1955; Paris: Klincksieck, 1962). The concept of the seme, in the sense we are interested in here, is defined in Pottier's thesis, although the actual term occurs later, in *Recherches du l'analyse sémantique en linguistique et en traduction mécanique* (Publications de la faculté des lettres de Nancy, 1963).

8. See "Some Points in the Semiotics of the Cinema" in *Film Language,* pp. 98–99.

9. The following passage is a repetition of the passage in *Film Language,* p. 26.

10. In André Martinet's sense. See André Martinet, *Elements of General Linguistics,* trans. Elizabeth Palmer (London: Faber and Faber, 1960), p. 116.

11. P. Pasolini, "Le Cinéma de poésie," contribution to the First Festival of the New Cinema (*Pesaro I,* Italy, June 1965). Published in *Cahiers du cinéma* (October 1965), no. 171, pp. 55–64. The passage referred to: pp. 55–56.

12. Jean Mitry, *Esthétique et psychologie du cinéma* (Paris: Ed Universitaires, 1965); vol. 2.

13. On this point, see "Some Points in the Semiotics of the Cinema" in *Film Language.*

14. See *Cinéma et langage* (doctoral thesis), in progress. [EDITOR'S NOTE: This work was subsequently completed and published as *Langage et cinéma* (Paris: Larousse, 1971), and it has

been translated as Christian Metz, *Language and Cinema*, trans. Donna-Jean Umiker-Sebeok (The Hague: Mouton, 1974).]

15. That is to say, on a level roughly corresponding to that of the "sequence" in the usual sense of that word. The term "large syntagmatic category" is therefore meant to indicate the difference between this approach and, for example, a shot-by-shot analysis, or an analysis within the shot itself. But one must not forget that an even broader syntagmatic level also exists: groups of sequences, "main parts" of the film, return or repetition of extended motifs, etc.

In fact, as we will see further on (part 10 of this chapter) it may well be that all the units making up cinematographic language are "large." But they are more or less so, since they do not belong all to the same type.

My "large syntagmatic category" consists in breaking the film down into segments of a certain magnitude. But this is not the only magnitude possible. For example, one must point out that, in the Italian review *Cinema e film* ([Spring 1967], no. 2, pp. 198–207, "Premesse sintagmatiche ad un' analisi di 'Viaggio in Italia'"), Adriano Apra and Luigi Martelli analyzed a passage from Rossellini's *Viaggio in Italia* on several simultaneous levels: They isolated "autonomous segments," using my chart, but they also identified (and rightly so) units that were larger and smaller than my "autonomous segments." Similarly, when a linguist refers to a given verbal statement, he may give a complete account of it—*represent* it integrally, as Noam Chomsky would say—in terms of phonemes or in terms of morphemes.

What we call a film is a set of sequences; it is also a series of shots, and a succession of "episodes" as well, etc. Each of these levels alone may account for the total material of the film; but, in order to know the film's total structure, one must, at least theoretically, have analyzed the film successively on all its levels.

16. The word "type" is used here in the sense that one speaks, for example, of the ablative absolute as a type peculiar to Latin. A type in grammar is a productive analogical matrix.

Among the authors who have devised tables of montage, or classifications of various kinds— or who have studied separately a specific type of montage—I am indebted notably to Eisenstein, Pudovkin, Kuleshov, Timochenko, Béla Balázs, Rudolf Arnheim, André Bazin, Edgar Morin, Gilbert Cohen-Séat, Jean Mitry, Marcel Martin, Henri Agel, François Chevassu, Anne Souriau . . . and one or two others perhaps whom I have unintentionally overlooked.

Because there is not enough room here, I will not (at least in this text) indicate how the various classifications of these authors are distributed in relation to each specific point of my chart. But it must not be forgotten that, among the various "image constructions" identifiable in films, some were defined and analyzed (very ingeniously at times) before the appearance of an actual semiological method. There were also larger attempts at classification, which are extremely instructive even in their failings. Semiotics as we now understand it must always rest on a double support: on the one hand, upon linguistics, and, on the other hand, upon the theory peculiar to the field under consideration.

17. In "La Grande syntagmatique du film narratif," one of the three articles that were fused together to form this text.

18. "Considerations sur les éléments sémiologiques du film," a paper presented at the round-table discussion, *Per una nuova coscienza critica del linguaggio cinematografico (Pesaro II*, Italy, 1966). Minutes published in *Nuovi Argomenti* (Italy) n.s., no. 2 (April–June 1966), See pp. 46–66 for my contribution "Considerationi sugli elementi semiologici del film." (This text is not reproduced here; the first part presented an early version of my table of the large syntagmatic category.)

19. In "Un Problème de sémiologie du cinéma," one of the three articles this text is based on.

20. "Problèmes de denotation dans le film de fiction: Contribution à une sémiologie du cinéma" (the third of the inital articles).

21. This study constitutes section 3 (chapters 6 and 7) of *Film Language*.

22. What I used to call the "full frequentative" *(fréquentatif plein"*—see *Communications*, [1966], no. 8, p. 122) is in fact, with its images alternating in series, simply a frequentative variant of the parallel syntagma or the alternate syntagma, depending on the case. Indeed it became

apparent that the "close succession of repetitive images" *(ibid.,* p. 121) could not be distinguished from the alternating of images in series (which characterizes parallel and alternate syntagmas) by any strict *initial* commutation—that is to say, by a commutation made before the analyst is supposed to have isolated the *signified* of the alternating. It is precisely the fact that the viewer who is well acquainted with the cinema always already knows the signifieds which had led me to believe mistakenly that, on a purely formal level (i.e., the distributional level), an alternating /ABAB. . ./ is always an alternating /A-B-A-B . . ./, so that the relevant difference between "ordinary" alternating (parallel or alternate syntagmas) and "frequentative" alternatings (i.e., frequentative variations of the same syntagmas) must be sought on another level—and this brings us to the level of subtypes. (It is, known well, enough, in linguistics to what degree too great a familiarity with the signifieds obscures or distorts, one or another characteristic of the signifier, which is theoretically very apparent; as when one analyzes a foreign language one speaks fluently, with grammatical categories unconsciously borrowed from one's own language).

What I used to call the "semifrequentative" *(Communications* [1966] no. 8, p. 122) is also a frequentative variant—but of the episodic sequence in this instance. Similarly, and for the same reasons, what I used to call the bracket frequentative is simply a frequentative variant of the bracket syntagma.

The unitary classification into a large syntagmatic type on the same level as other syntagmatic types of several frequentative variants affecting different image structures in different ways presented an additional drawback, because it resulted in artificial unifications that partially distorted the reality of the facts of filmic ordering. Test analyses directed at passages of various films have shown specifically that, although the frequentative modality was accompanied by an alternating of images in series, in the instance of my earlier "full frequentative," the same modality of the *signified* was able to establish itself perfectly well without any alternating effect, in the instances of my earlier "bracket frequentative" or "semifrequentative" categories. Consequently, the relative unity, which will doubtless have to be retained for the totality of the frequentative variants of different segments, will probably have to be sought elsewhere than in the mere fact of alternation.

23. On this question, see *Film Language,* note, p. 103. The fact that, in my new table, there is no longer a *single* large syntagmatic type that is defined *only* by the fact of alternating does not imply that the *criterion of alternating* has no reality (the problem is to determine on what level it occurs); for it is quite evident that there are passages in films where images alternate in series, and others where they do not. But it has not appeared productive to state this pertinence *right from the beginning* of the classification, for other criteria, in the same place, allow us to establish general conclusions more rapidly (see the problems of "convenience" and "simplicity" in linguistic formalization).

24. My table therefore contains eight syntagmatic types, but only seven syntagmas. The autonomous shot is by definition not a syntagma; it is nevertheless a syntagmatic type, since it is one of the types that occur in the global syntagmatic structure of the film. More generally speaking, syntagmatic analysis is a part of semiotics in which one is *initially* confronted with "discourses" that are always syntagmas of different magnitudes, but in which the units one *isolates as one proceeds* are not necessarily all syntagmas—for some of them may not be divisible in every case.

It was the existence of autonomous shots that led me to use the term "autonomous segments" (rather than "autonomous syntagmas") for the different syntagmatic types, in order to have a term corresponding to all the types ("autonomous segment" had the further advantage of being contrasted to "minimum segment").

25. On this point see "Le Cinéma, monde et récit," in *Critique* (May 1965) no. 216. (article not included here [i.e. in *Film Language*—ED.]

26. It was this circumstance (brief interruption of the vectoral temporality that constitutes the usual order of films) that, in my first version of the table of the large syntagmatic categories (see *Communication* [1966], no. 8, p. 122), led me to subsume this type of montage under the

"frequentative" category. But in fact it appears more and more clearly that, in the cinema, the order of temporal consecutiveness may be interrupted more than one way (see, for example, the parallel syntagma, or the descriptive syntagma), and that the bracket construction per se is not necessarily iterative (it links together *several facts* of the same order, but without especially suggesting that each one of these facts ocurred *several times;* similarly, although "thematic repetitions" are not excluded from this construction, they are not the rule, either). The fact remains that the bracket syntagma, by its very nature, may often appear with a frequentative modality as well (whence my initial error).

27. In this example the optical device employed was the dissolve. Moreover the same sequence is also a good example of the bracket syntagma with a frequentative modality.

28. I have already spoken about description and its relationship to narration and to the image in another context, in "Notes Toward a Phenomenology of the Narrative" in *Film Language.*

29. A good example of this can be seen in autonomous segment no. 45 of *Adieu Philippine* (see *Film Language,* pp. 167–68).

30. For one will *also* find simultaneities in filmic narratives: Even when the film narrates, it does so with the image, and it is the nature of the latter frequently to show several things at the same time. It is therefore not the *presence of simultaneity* but the *absence of consecutiveness* that allows us to distinguish between "description' and "narration" in the cinema.

31. Next to the alternating syntagma, there is one (and perhaps several) specific ordering(s) of images whose precise place in the "film's logic" is not yet clear to me. A good example of this can be seen in autonomous segment no. 32 of *Adieu Philippine,* and the question is discussed in relation to that segment in my analysis of the film; see *Film Language,* pp. 163–64. I have temporarily placed this type, with a question mark, under the alternating syntagma, from which it is less removed than from any other type of syntagma.

32. Particularly A. Michotte van den Berck, "Le Caractére de 'réalité' des projections ciné-matographiques," *Revue internationale de filmologie* (October 1948), pp. 249–61, esp. pp. 252–54 ("l'effêt-écran").

33. That is the major difference between the episodic sequence and the bracket syntagma. Otherwise, as one can readily see, the two types have many characteristics in common.

34. This is true even on the denotative level (literal meaning of the film). It is, so to speak, the basic rule for this type of syntagma. The fact that on the connotative level (affective repercussions, symbolic extensions, etc.) every image indicates more than it shows is another problem and is not germane to this analysis.

35. This circumstance explains why, in the first version of my syntagmatic table (see *Com-munications* [1966], no. 8, p. 122), I had associated this variety of montage with the "frequentative" category (though with the reservation implied in calling it "semifrequentative"). In fact, however, since this structure somehow consists in delegating an image to exemplify a virtual body of other images, it is based on a technique of *condensation* more than on a form of *iteration* (and there is no iteration either on the level of the syntagma taken as a whole, since the images, like the corresponding phases of the evolution the film condenses, succeed each other in chronological order). Therefore the syntagmatic type considered here has nothing *inherently* frequentative about it. It nonetheless is liable—as are certain other of the eight main types of montage (see note 22). —to appear at times under a variant form with the addition of a frequentative modality—whence my initial error.

36. Since, for the understanding of the connotative signifieds (and notably the style of the different films and filmmakers), the number and the nature of these interruptions are obviously of great importance.

37. This, of course, does not imply that optical effects always occur between two contiguous autonomous segments.

38. It is possible, in particular, that the autonomous shot (type 1 of my table) is a class rather than a single, terminal type, for it includes fairly numerous and varied image structures; it is the only one of my types having so many subtypes—and this sort of "bulge" may indicate insufficient

formalization of the corresponding point. Also, as we shall see in part 6 below, the autonomous shot is somehow apt to "contain" all the other varieties of shot. Finally, it can be said that the first dichotomy—which separates the autonomous shot from the seven other types, i.e., from all the syntagmas—is based on a characteristic of the *signifier* (i.e., "a single shot, or several shots?"), whereas the distinctions between the syntagmas are derived from the signified (despite various identifiable traits in the corresponding signifiers). These three reasons might eventually compel us to revise the status of the autonomous shot, which would entail bringing some changes to the general disposition of the chart. Perhaps there are even *two* tables of the syntagmatic category in the image track (ultimately very similar to each other, or at least *homologous* on many points)—a table of the syntagmas and one of the combinations internal to the autonomous shot ("free" and "determnined" syntagmatic categories, as with morphemes in American linguistics)? The situation would then resemble—in methodology if not in substance—that of many languages, whose phonological systems are more easily understood if one conceives of them as comprising two subsystems, one of "vowels" and one of "consonants."

I remind the reader also that the problems raised by the category of "alternating syntagmas" (see *Film Language*, pp. 105-7, and note, 22 above) have not been entirely resolved as is shown by my discussion of autonomous segment no. 32 of *Adieu Philippine* (see *Film Language*, pp. 163–64, with note p. 164).

39. Mitry, *Esthétique* 9–61.

40. See my article "'Montage' et le discours dans le film. Un problème de sémiologie diachronique du cinéma," *Word* (April–December, 1967), 23 (1–3):388–95. This issue constituted the first volume ("General Linguistics") of *Linguistic Studies Presented to Anbré Martiet*.

41. See "The Cinema: Language or Language System?" Also my article "Une Etape dans la réflexion sur le cinéma," *Critique* (March 1965), no 214, pp. 227–48, esp. pp. 228–30.

42. See "Some Points in the Semiotics of the Cinema."

43. For the precise meaning of this term, see "The Cinema: Language or Language System?" second note, p. 78.

[EDITOR'S NOTE: The point is important enough to quote the note to which Metz here refers. In the earlier essay, Metz has recourse to the concept of naturalness when he follows the philosopher Mikel Dufrenne in calling "expressive" that signification wherein "'meaning' is somehow immanent to a thing, is directly released from it, and merges with its very form." But later Metz added a footnote at this point. It modifies his earlier unproblematized acceptance of the category of naturalness as follows:

Today, I would say rather that expressiveness is a meaning established without recourse to a *special* and explicit code. But not without recourse to vast and complex sociocultural *organizations*, which are represented by other forms of codification...In general, if the sum of the effects of meaning we call *expressive*, or *motivated*, or *symbolic*, etc., appears to be "natural"—and is indeed so in a certain way, for example to a phenomenology or a psychology of meaning—it is mainly because the effects are very deeply rooted in cultures, and because they are rooted at a level that, in these cultures, lies far beyond the various explicit, specialized, and properly informative codes. One can of course argue whether these deep significatory organizations existing at these distant levels can be rightly considered as proper codes. But, whatever the case, they are more or less organized systems, which can convey meaning and vary from one human group to another. If as a general rule the system-user experiences them not as codes but as effects of natural meaning, that is because he has sufficiently "assimilated" them to the extent that he does not possess them *in a separate state*. Thus, as a paradoxical consequence, the deepest cultural codifications are experienced as the most natural. Other codifications—which are cultural too, but are more superficial ore more specialized—are, on the contrary, much more easily identified by the user as conventional and separate systems.

In the text above, I gave, among other examples of *expressiveness*, what we quite rightly call "facial expression." Certainly, it is not through the effect of "cinematographic language" (nor of any other explicitly informative code) that the film spectator is able to decipher the expressions he reads on the hero's face. However, it is not through the effect of nature itself either, for the expressions of the face have meanings that vary considerably from one civilization to another (think of the difficulty one experiences in trying to understand the facial expressions in a Japanese film). Nevertheless, it remains true that in films of our own culture we understand them quite naturally—that is to say, through the effect of a knowledge that is very old and very deep in us, that functions by itself, and that—for us—is henceforth merged with perception itself.]

44. By Souriau, in his study discussed in "Some Points in the Semiotics of the Cinema."

45. On this problem of filmic intellection, see "The Cinema: Language or Language System?"

46. "La Structure morphologique," a paper written for the Fifth International Congress on Linguistics, 1939 (the congress was interrupted by the declaration of war, but the paper had been printed before the congress convened). Reprinted in *Essais linguistiques* (Copenhagen: Nordisk Sprog-og Kulturforlag, 1959), pp. 113–38. See esp. pp. 123–28.

47. This distinction between two distinctions is fairly simple in principle. But it is much less simple to discern clearly its application in a new and concrete area: This is, indeed, where I failed in earlier investigations. On this point, see *Film Language* second note, p. 74.

48. Gilbert Cohen-Séat's term *(Essai sur les principes d'une philosophie du cinéma,* P.U.F., 1946).

49. Raymond Bellour, "Pour une stylistique du film," *Revue d'esthetique* (April–June 1966), 19(2):161–78. To exclude from the field of the "semiotics of the cinema" studies like Bellour's, when they are rigorously conducted, would only result in a quibbling over terms and definitions, which, in the present state of cinematographic studies, would be altogether useless and unresolvable. It is nevertheless true that, relative to the body of work remaining to be done, such studies can only be a *phase,* or an immediate *task* distinct from the study of cinematographic language in general. It is therefore important whether one considers the stylistics of film as a part of film semiotics or as a separate area of investigation. Even in the verbal domain the relationship between stylistics and pure linguistics is far from being clear. One way or another, the term "stylistics" seems to me well suited to the kind of investigation described by Raymond Bellour.

50. Further on in *Film Language,* I return to this problem in a somewhat different perspective, in the context of an analysis of Pasolini's theory of the "im-segno." Cf. chapter 8, "Modern Cinema and Narrativity," pp. 211–16. See also my analysis of *L'Avventura,* chapter 3, p. 74.

51. On this question of the "encounter of cinema and narrativity," and on its importance, see "The Cinema: Language or Language System?" and "Some Points in the Semiotics of the Cinema" in *Film Language.*

52. I took this point of view in "Notes Toward a Phenomenology of Narrative."

53. See particularly C. Brémond, "Le Message narratif" *(Communications* [1964], no. 4, special issue: "Recherches sémiologiques," pp. 4–32, esp. pp. 31–32.) Also, "La Logique des possibles narratifs" *(Communications* [1966], no. 8, special issue: "L'Analyse structurale du récit," pp. 60–76).

[3]

Raymond Bellour
Segmenting/Analyzing

1. 1/47

The film opens. Paris, the Bois de Boulogne, the Avenue des Acacias. The choryphaeus (commentator) of the musical comedy (Honoré) introduces himself and in a voice that is part song, part speech states the theme: "Little Girls": a theme immediately focused by the appearance of its instigator: "This story is about a little girl in particular. . . . Her name is Gigi." Gigi passes by and slips away, opening up the theme to the narrative which borrows her name.

The film ends. The theme is taken up again: same setup, same place, same shot. But now, behind the commentator a couple comes into view, moving in a different, mythical, time, a time apparently outside the narrative since it constitutes the solution of the narrative's enigma: Gigi, accompanied by her husband, Gaston.

Classical cinema (especially American classical cinema) depends heavily on such "rhyming" effects. They carry narrative difference through the ordered network of resemblances; by unfolding symmetries (with varying degrees of refinement) they bring out the dissymmetry without which there would be no narrative. The classical film from beginning to end is constantly repeating itself because it is resolving itself. This is why its beginning often reflects its end in a final emphasis; in this, the film acknowledges that it is a result, inscribing the systematic condition of the course it follows by signing with a final paragraph the operation which constructs it throughout.

First published in *Quarterly Review of Film Studies* (August 1976), 1:331–53 and reprinted by permission of the author. The translation here used is from *Genre: The Musical*, ed. Rick Altman (London: Routledge and Kegan Paul and the British Film Institute, 1981) and is reprinted by permission of the British Film Institute.

In this instance the repetition-resolution effect has a specific, but very common, character and this is its whole strength; it operates on a broad scale and very precisely, *from segment to segment,* that is, from one major narrative unit to another, from one major syntagmatic unit to another.

But what actually is a segment for the purposes of analysis? This comes down to asking first: with what kind of truth and applicability does the *grande syntagmatique* endow the definition of the segment and the reality of analysis?

2. On the *Grande Syntagmatique*

Much has been written about the *grande syntagmatique:* for it, against it, based on it. The work for has perhaps been excessively subservient. That against has recently lacked intellectual generosity and imagination. I shall not recapitulate. But at the same time I shall assume familiarity. However, I shall need to retrace the line which carries it in the thinking of Christian Metz, in order to set my own procedure in context.

The constitution of the *grande syntagmatique* combines two complementary lines of thought, determined by the logic of discovery. This is in 1966, just two years after the impetus provided by *"Cinéma: langue ou langage?"*[1] On the one hand it is necessary to demonstrate by means of a code, i.e. *this* code that *some* code is involved; in other words that codicity is no less effective in cinema than in other fields, and that it is possible to try to master it and activate it there. Something no classification, taxonomy, "montage table", etc... had been able to demonstrate, either because they were too formal, or not formal enough. In this sense, the *grande syntagmatique* is a theoretical operator: it actualizes the concrete possibility of a semiology of the cinema because it brings its virtualness onto a material level. Moreover, this specific code seems, from both logical and historical viewpoints, to be preeminently suited to illuminating the cultural makeup of film as the basis of fiction, using a closed series of commutable syntagmatic types.

The interacting pressure of these two lines of thought explains, how Metz was able to yield, though only in part, to the immediately punctured illusion of having "found" THE code of cinema. Very soon, indeed almost at once, the *grande syntagmatique* ceases to be THE code, to become quite simply a (specific) code among others (an assertion *Language and Cinema*[2] goes over again and again to the point of dizziness on the level of codes). But the shadow of ambiguity is valuable. For while the *grande syntagmatique* may be one code among other codes which juxtapose and cross it, it envelops them and is superior to them in the proper sense of the word: that is, manifestly, as the consequence and condition of the fiction.

On the other hand, from its origins, or almost so, the *grande syntagmatique* was the object of a patient and rigorous self-criticism on Metz's part. It is therefore constantly deepened by contradictions turned on itself, in step with a logic of still improbable effects, which in a sense undermines the direct positivity of the code but augments its potential pressure. From the first *Essais*, Metz confronted three basic objections. First, the gap between the autonomous shot and the seven other syntagmatic types; the sequence-shot (as the name indicates) through a kind of spatiotemporal expansion proves to contain the possibilities of seven other types; it thus imposes the need for a genuine bipartition of the initial chart.[3] Then in the seven other types, the discrepancy between the "hard" and "soft" types (which emerges in a concrete form in the syntagmatic analysis of *Adieu Philippine*). For example, between the bracketed syntagma and the non-diegetic insert on the one hand, said to be "clear configurations, 'recognised' with certainty and no possibility of error"; and on the other hand, the ordinary sequence and the scene, said to "have fairly fluid contours so that it is sometimes difficult to draw them out of the mass and isolate them from the general filmic flux."[4] (I would add to these a vacillation, first between the scene and the sequence, then between successions of scenes and/or sequences and weak instances of the episodic sequence, which sometimes raises questions.) Finally, the third and in my view most important point: "The set of problems posed by the fact of alternation" which the two complementary forms (one achronological, the other chronological) of parallel and alternate syntagma are powerless to resolve.

The solution would seem to assume that a rigorous semiological theory be established in order to account for *two facts* that are both pronounced in films though neither of them has yet been satisfactorily explained: (1) the phenomenon of what one might call the *transformation of the insert* (an autonomous segment with a single insert can easily be "transformed" into an autonomous segment comprising multiple inserts and thus into an alternate type... (2) the distinction between *true alternation* (which establishes a narrative "doubling" in the film) and *pseudo-alternation* (which may be reduced to a mere visual alternation within a unitary space or else derives simply from the fact that the *filmed subject* itself assumes a vaguely "alternating" aspect within a certain relationship).[5]

Finally a third line of thought deriving logically from the other two: through the methodological investigation carried out by *Language and Cinema,* the code becomes genuinely a code; in other words, radically detached from the filmic text for which it is simply an abstract exponent, actualized there in the concrete form of the autonomous segment.[6] In an article written soon after, this concern prompted Metz to establish the triple criterion of demarcation for the autonomous segment in the "diegetic film" (actually put into operation by Metz with his syntagmatic analysis of *Adieu Philippine*): "The analyst of the classical film is justified in considering as a single autonomous segment any passage in the film which is not interrupted by a major change in the course of the plot, by punctuation, or by the abandonment of one syntagmatic type for another."[7] The autonomous segment is thus consciously set off to the side of the text, in the direction of its obligatory intercodicity and of textual analysis.

All this has meant that today, Metz thinks (as I know from talking to him at length) that a new version of the *grande syntagmatique* is possible. (If so, why not do it, you may ask. Quite simply because science exists only as borne by a desire, and desires are displaced—as Freud discovered. Only the imaginary realm of science believes that one always insists on finishing—in a limited period—what one has begun.) The new version of the *grande syntagmatique* would need to break down the positivist illusions frequently linked to the beginnings of any formalization. It would thus more surely guard against the new positivism which the evolution of linguistics might tend to project onto film theory, by seeking simply to replace the structural model by the generative and transformational model. In safeguarding itself against both, the new version could combine the advances they have made. It would be wary of the plurality of levels which prohibits a strictly Chomskian model from ever rejoining its object, film, in the singularity of its textual system. Cinema will never be a language, nor film a grammar. It is not by chance that Nicolas Ruwet's poetic and musicological analyses owe as much if not more to the structural model as to the generative and transformational. But on the other hand, the new version of the *grande syntagmatique* would need to reinforce the level of abstraction in order to stamp out definitively any flattening structural effect, or any descriptive application between code and text, thus correcting earlier inadequacies. It would thus need to constitute a body of spatiotemporal matrices, where the present syntagmatic types, together with their complements and necessary modifications, would be arranged into an ordered series. Then the surface level, that is, the level of textual actualization, would alone merit the name autonomous segment, presenting analysis with the constantly renewed singularity of a precise decomposition of the filmic chain.

This very special situation of the *grande syntagmatique* as a problematical, incomplete code, on the one hand prime and primary, on the other, a code among others, seems to have had two opposing results in the field of specific film analyses. Numerous works have developed in the direct line of the *grande syntagmatique*, either applying it literally, or occasionally seeking to perfect it by trying to diversify, enrich, and lend flexibility to one or other of its types (but still necessarily remaining within the bouunds of Metz's self-critique, which implies its transformation). These works thus reasserted the determining stability of this code, its capacity for historical and stylistic induction, and its specific, practical (descriptive) and analytical instrumentality in the textual study of the large narrative units.[8]

On the other hand, a number of textual analyses developed within the movement to establish a semiology of cinema and with a more or less explicit reference to Metz's thinking found themselves not ignoring but skirting the test of the *grande syntagmatique*. For some this was doubtless because they only placed themselves on the level of the segment (or fragment) in order to concentrate on the work of its smaller units. Or because they started from a segment or a number of segments (or fragments) in order to evaluate their function in the productivity of the textual whole.[9] But this detour extends even to analyses bearing on a film as a whole and thus more or less consciously situated within the perspective defined by Metz as that of the global textual system. I have in mind consciously bringing together works of very varied nature and intention, *Foetus astral*, by Jean Monod and Jean-Paul Dumont,[10] the collective work of *Cahiers du Cinéma* on *Young Mr. Lincoln*,[11] the book by Claude Bailblé, Michel Marie, and Marie-Claire Ropars on *Muriel*,[12] Stephen Heath's long study on *Touch of Evil*,[13] and my own analysis of *North by Northwest*.[14] The detour is all the more notable in the last two examples in that the analyses (in other ways very different) depend on a segmentation: a primitive or semiprimitive segmentation which justified Stephen Heath's note following his découpage: "The segmentation here operates at the level of the narrative signified according to the simple criteria of unity of action, unity of characters, unity of place: it has no analytic status other than that of allowing reference to the film as narrative." I ought to have added that note to the découpage tables in my own study, were it not obvious that, like Stephen Heath's they constantly brushed up against the *grande syntagmatique*, without seeking to constrain it and above all without risking being constrained by it.

This is the risk I should like to take here, because of what it seems to me that it can teach us. Starting from the *grande syntagmatique* and going well beyond it, I will concentrate on the systematic modeling of the narrative units of the classic American film. Perhaps as a *genre* film, which is profoundly coded, *Gigi* shows this modeling better than others. But I remain convinced that, within the irreducible arrangement of each of its textual instances, such a modeling process governs the majority of the films of American high "classicism."

This beginning of an analysis of *Gigi* does not aim to fill any gap between the present state of the *grande syntagmatique* and a second, as yet, virtual state. Analysis could no doubt situate that gap and consider it in terms of its own logic. But no more. Here therefore, the *grande syntagmatique* is fully applied (that is, with all its "lacks") as the operator of the analysis: given first, the descriptive logicalization it effects on its own level; then, the syntagmatic reference it opens up in the analysis by its capacity to instigate a generalized syntagmatic segmentation. As we shall see, segmentation is a *mise-en-abîme*, a "plumbing of depth", a process which has no end theoretically–which does not mean that it has no meaning, in fact that is its whole meaning. Through the differential play it sets up between various levels, segmentation allows us to experience the increased plurality of textual effects.

But the present analysis is only a beginning, and within such limited bounds it is by definition far more the setting in place of an analytical framework, a setting in perspective, than analysis itself. I have limited myself to a major extent (but on the level of the smaller units, minimally) to the recording of the differential rhyming and repetition effects which structure the development of the narrative. Their fundamental determining role in the constitution of the classical film at the level of the fragment, the segment, or the film as a whole has been shown by earlier analyses.[15] To me it seemed striking to make them stand out within the crossing of levels at work here. I could obviously not do much more than categorize and list these rhyming effects; what I could not do was produce them in the logic of their textual progression, the material work of their traversal: analysis is not reducible to its framework. Imagination, mine and yours, has to give back to the elements I have broken down the space that constitutes and is constituted by them; in other words, their textual volume.

3. Segmental

The syntagmatic breakdown of *Gigi* which reveals 47 autonomous segments in the image track of the film (1 to 47 in the summary table at the end of this article) calls for a number of observations.

(a) The extreme redundancy between the three demarcatory criteria demonstrates a high degree of classicalness.

(b) In this sound and musical film, the image is sovereign on the level of syntagmatic demarcation. The instrumental or vocal numbers are lower or equal to the segmental limits, with one exception—Gigi's song ("I Don't Understand the Parisians") straddles segments 9 and 10, so creating a kind of autonomous sound segment. The voice and dialogue are strictly subject to the phenomenality of the image, its temporal outline. As far as the music is concerned, while its fades occasionally do not coincide with the fades of the segmental demarcation, overall and in relation with the song, it simply reinforces the stability of the autonomous segments of the image. The *grande syntagmatique* of the image track in the classical film, because of the power specific to the diegesis, is clearly something like THE code—the one which permits the rest.

(c) This strict application of the *grande syntagmatique* ran up against two difficulties:

(i) On the fringes of the scene/sequence vacillation (not generally very strong here) two hesitations in the breakdown: between segments 10 and 11, and within the very long segment 30. A (relatively) slight impression of continuity led me to mark a segment in the first instance. In the second I hesitated over a sequence/scene/sequence tripartition (found as a/b/c in the subsegmentation).

(ii) The impossibility, in a film which includes no alternating syntagma on the significative level, of giving an account of the alternations (where does the true begin or the pseudo end?) which more or less structure numerous segments: 1, 8, 13, 15, 17, 21 (an episodic sequence which is at the same time an alternate syntagma, but lacks simultaneity between the two temporal series, like the alternate syntagma of *Adieu Philippine*, which Metz used as a basis for raising the question of alternation), 24, 25, 26 (in which the segmental level loses a true scene between Honoré and Mamita), 30, 35 (a bastardized episodic sequence whose first two episodes are a kind of summary of an alternate syntagma) and 47.

The autonomous shot, despite its frequency (9 segments), brings few complications—here again the classic model is in full play.

This breakdown demonstrates two conditions essential to the development of the textual logic.

(a) First the high number of repetitions and rhymes which, within the mirror effect of segments 1–47, operate *from segment to segment*. Not through their syntagmatic forms, of course. At this level, the syntagmatic type is simply one pertinence among others, although profoundly different: as a specific exponent of the textual surface it affects, it is the form in which pertinences of varying stability (places, characters, actions, musical or sung motifs) are inscribed in the cinematic signifier, their disposal within each segment being what conveys the narration from segment to segment.[16] In this sense, what I am here calling segmental (i.e.; the textual surface delimited by different forms of autonomous segments) corresponds to the level Metz calls "suprasegmental" in terms of codic units.

One has only to refer to the summary table to recognize the operations taking place, the repetitions, scored by differences, between segments

$$4 \text{ and } 37 \quad 15 \text{ and } 41\text{–}42$$
$$6, 16, \text{ and } 20 \quad 19, 27, \text{ and } 32$$
$$7 \text{ and } 31 \quad 23 \text{ and } 46$$
$$8, 28, \text{ and } 29 \quad 24, 25, \text{ and } 26$$
$$14 \text{ and } 40 \quad 36 \text{ and } 39.$$

(b) From segment 36, certain of these operations touch a large number of the final segments of the film (37, 39, 40, 41–42, 46, 47). Such concentration is worth noting: it shows how, through its segmental outlines, the film resolves itself by repetition, through a kind of generalized condensation of the narrative which, on the formal level, conveys it to its ending.

But these chains of repetition-resolution effects are inscribed within the bounds of autonomous segments only to break them down in multiple ways. For if the classical film tends, as Metz saw clearly, toward the sequence (the autonomous segment)[17] far more than toward the shot, it does so at the cost of an equally profound tendency to inscribe the segment within a system of narrative commutation with units which are both superior and, above all, inferior to the segment, with a bearing well beyond the divisions of the filmic chain.[18] These two major movements simultaneously attract and repel, contradict and complement each other. This is what makes it both necessary and difficult to distinguish them: their (decomposable) merging, which turns the film into the space of a generalized segmentality, is the condition which transforms the filmic surface into a textual volume.

4. Suprasegmental/Infrasegmental

On the one hand the classical film thus tends toward units which can be superior to the segment (suprasegment or macrosegment), even though they very often coincide with it. Both ordinary and specialized language refers to these as "sequences"; they often correspond to "units of scenario."[19] They are generally determined by a kind of global unity of space, place, and action. In *Gigi* this is the case with segments 24, 25, and 26, all situated at Trouville in the course of the same day and involving the same characters (thus constituting a kind of episodic suprasequence). It is also the case, in a very different way, with segments 12 and 13, the one denoting, by means of an extremely rapid autonomous shot, the front of the Palais de Glace (neither Gaston nor Gigi are visible, but we know that they are walking towards the building and that they are going to go in); the other, the scene which unfolds inside the rink. But unity of place is not an imperative, if the narrative movements prove too dissimilar in spite of the transitions which bind them; it thus seems more correct not to combine segment 27 (XVI), where Alicia persuades Mamita to accelerate Gigi's education, and segments 28 and 29 (XVII), which are devoted to the educational sessions. The suprasegment is a kind of unified minor dramatic mold, which is what justifies its also being able to cover several different locations in succession. Hence segments 3, 4, 5, and 6 (III), which preside over the meeting of Gaston and Honoré, or segments 30 and 31 (XVIII) and 43, 44, 45, and 46 (XXVI), which present in one block Gaston's contradictory reactions to Gigi's transformation.

The determination of the suprasegment is obviously less rigorous than that of the autonomous segments because it is not determined by any cinematic specificity but derives solely from the pressure of the textual system. It is therefore to a profound degree subject to the singularity of each film; and it depends on analysis which gives it an intermediary function between the segments and the large film sections (A, B, C, D, E here) which distribute the dramaturgy of the narrative. Its interest, like that of any découpage operation, is primarily descriptive and involves circumscribing the rhyming effects which unite or superimpose themselves on those of the autonomous segments. Through a kind of internal tautology, the segments grouped into a suprasegment rhyme among themselves all the more strongly within this new unit. An operation which in one sense adds little but is nevertheless striking since it concentrates the rhyming effect in the narrative succession. This is so in the case of segments 24, 25, and 26 at Trouville mentioned earlier, which group three "sequences" supported by the same characters; likewise segments 28 and 29 which bring together into one "education" syntagma the two episodic sequences in Alicia's apartment. But the most eloquent are clearly those large-scale rhymes which are established across the film from suprasegment to suprasegment: the one clear example relates to the two "Maxim's" sets, which unite segments 14 and 15 and segments 40, 41, and 42, in VIII and XXV, respectively. There are other effects at work between sets, but their nature is more partial and is determined by the complementary test of subsegmentation.

For in this film, as in the classical film generally, it is clearly on the level of the units lower than the segment that the multiple echo-play, which structures and constrains the progressive resolution of the textual system throughout, is systematized in a much broader way. At this lower level, let us consider what I shall call *elementary* subsegmentation; i.e., the subsegmentation which defines two or more successive times within the continuity of the same segment, each circumscribing a small scene. I mean this in the dramatic, not syntagmatic sense, obviously.

It will be recalled that Metz invoked a third criterion to determine the demarcation between two autonomous segments: "a major change in the course of the plot." The criterion is clearly imprecise: what is a major change? But this is to pose the question badly. For demarcation in terms of the "plot itself"[20] is nearly always obvious: the absence of the two other criteria almost automatically entails the transparency of the third. This stems from the fact that the classical film defines its segmental units by a series of breaks in the signified of temporal denotation: only a major change in the course of the plot can manifest the break when it is not done by punctuation or variation in treatment. The imprecise criterion is therefore the sure one. Through a kind of tautological proof, a narrative change which entails no segmental mark can only be a 'minor' change; but in return, the minor change will often be far less minor than others which are nevertheless sanctioned by segmental demarcation, precisely because the change introduced into the course of the plot by the other two criteria would not exist without them (except in cases of redundancy of course, and these are always numerous). Consider for example the mutation introduced into the narrative by the appearance of a character (major or minor as the case may be) and inversely, the slightness of the change denoted by the demarcation through punctuation bettween the autonomous shot of the façade of the Palais de Glace and the scene inside which follows. In other words, segmental découpage determined by the multiple inscription of the signified of temporal denotation in the filmic signifier only half coincides (occasionally more, occasionally less) with the unfolding of the plot and the succession of narrative actions. Hence a series of dissociations which open the way to an operation of subsegmentation.

The episodic sequence (and the same would be true of the bracket syntagma) has a particular privilege in this context, arising out of the precise demarcation of each episode. This demarcation is effected again (but at a lower level, as a subsegmentation) by the diegesis itself, in most cases by internal punctuation (for the sake of consistency, let us call it a subpunctuation). On the one hand episodes are thus almost always linked together (as are the segments in certain suprasegments) by a succession of rhyming effects, as in the case of the various episodes of segments 14, 21, 28, and 29.[21] On the other, a certain episode may establish rhyming effects over a distance with some segment or subsegment.

This is how the overall rhyme linking segments 14 and 20 takes its precise shape: the fourth episode of segment 14 (14d), in which Liane and Gaston enter Maxim's, is repeated by segment 40, where Gigi and Gaston enter in their turn.

Inversely, the criteria of subsegmentation in the other segments are determined outside any specific inscription in the cinematic signifier. Their indisputable indeterminate character should not be taken as a cause for hesitation. True scenes are constituted nevertheless. They rest on disjunctions provoked by characters' entries and exits, particularly emphatic in this *genre* film and strongly marked by the dynamic of theatrical representation. The locations, actions, instrumental and vocal motifs clearly all give powerful support to the stage scene effects organized between characters. But they do not have the same degree of pertinence: the instrumental or vocal motifs, because their limits are almost always inferior or equal to the segment, only partly coinciding with that of the subsegment; the actions, because they are not truly divisible into segments in the same way and tend to be diluted in the overall mass of narrative signifieds; the locations, because the temporal form which distributes them is already the precise object of the *grande syntagmatique*.

Scenes thus appear, opening up multiple networks of rhymes. Right from segment 1, the fifteen shots which succeed each other before Gigi appears show Honoré in the position of commentator (1a), as he will be again in the first episode of segment 14 (14a); then again in subsegment 34b, after the disappearance of Gaston. In the same way in segment 32, the disappearance of Gigi in shot 154 opens a brief scene between Mamita and Gaston which responds to the one which preceded it in segment 7 and the one which succeeds it by the same means in subsegment 30b, before being renewed in segment 31.[22]

On the other hand, the subsegmental division allow the establishment of new commutations on the basis of intermediary sets between the subsegment and the segment, the segment and the suprasegment. Thus the first "education set" which overlaid segment 8 and subsegment 9a following it finds it full echo in suprasegment XVII (28 and 29). In the same way the very long subsegment 30c, subsegment 43b, and the short segments 44 and 45 mark with a very sharp repetition effect Gaston's two departures and returns, which prelude his decision first to keep Gigi, then to marry her. In this way an overall rhyme is established between subsegment 30c and segment 31 on the one hand, and segments 43, 44, 45, and 46 on the other; suprasegment XXVI in other words. This last rhyme serves to increase in a major way the condensation which brings together in the final section (E) a series of earlier elements from the four other sections. Space does not allow for a demonstration of the subtle way in which condensation, in this last example, only touches segment XXVI from the starting point of the earlier effect which condenses (precondenses) suprasegments XIV and XXVI in suprasegment XVIII. But to make the text's productive return on itself fully readable, it would be necessary to go much further into the decomposition of its elements; i.e., it would be necessary to subsegment the subsegmentation.

5. (Sub–Supra) Segmental/Textual

For subsegmentation goes much further than this. Up till now I have channeled it into scene effects, corresponding to one or more shots; and in the first case, always either to very long shots (like 34b) or to the more specifically determined units in the episodic sequence.[23] I have, moreover, simply brought out successive dissociations in terms of a linearity which sometimes corresponds exactly to the truth of the text, but more often only in part, mimicking its truth with a representative approximation which is neither altogether false nor altogether true.[24] This is the reason for my qualification of that first subsegmentation as *elementary*.

Complex subsegmentation goes much beyond this. It might be called *micro-segmentation*—indicating a movement, which is the progressive work of textual and analytical pressure. For here there is no longer anything which corresponds to the precise distinction between segmentation and subsegmentation. Before segmental demarcation there are only degrees of narrative expansion. This is why complex segmentation does not have anything to do with the limits of the shot, even though the play that is set up with the demarcatory boundary of the shot in turn constitutes a textual pertinence and a stylistic index.

Here I can only give two very summary examples of this movement.[25]

(a) *Segment 33*. Shot 302 shows Gigi in her room (this décor appears here for the first time); she is alone, stretched out on the bed, stroking her cat, and she gets up to open the door to Gaston within the continuity of the same shot. This beginning of a scene is soon matched by a true scene, the long autonomous shot of segment 38, in which Gigi is singing in her room, holding her cat in her arms. The simplicity of this arrangement shows clearly the way in which the film proceeds through the varied duplication of its successive elements. More-over it completes the condensation effect operating between the fifth section of the film and the four others: from segment 37 to segment 47 there is none which does not repeat a moment, a segment, or a subsegment, from the four others, scored by the variation which carries the film to its end.

The three quite unequal subsegments which follow (b/c/d) are inscribed along three axes which, because the subsegmentation is not developed, only emerge incompletely: the first, which covers almost the whole of the segment (302–7), is inscribed in the series of scenes between Gigi and Gaston; the second, deter-mined by Mamita's appearance in shot 308, is inscribed in the series of multiple scenes or scene fragments between Gigi, Mamita, and Gaston (in particular, it ushers in the dramatic and equally very brief 43a); the third, after Gigi has rushed to her room, is inscribed by means of a second internal split in shot 308, in the series of scenes, peaceful and dramatic by turns, which bring together Mamita and Gaston.

(b) *Segment 47.* Here again, internal splitting of the shot brings out three minuscule subsegments in the last two shots of the film: (a) in shot 348, Honoré is singing, leaning on a tree in close medium shot; (b) in shot 349, Gigi and Gaston advance at a slant across the lawn and go toward a cab which they climb into, followed by the camera which then loses them to rejoin (c), within the continuity of the same shot, Honoré in the same fixed frame of the preceding shot.

This final example gives a clear indication of how the progressive decomposition of the dramatic instances of the filmic chain, opened up by the decomposition of the *grande syntagmatique,* leads of itself and more or less inevitably toward internal analysis of the segments on the one hand, and on the other toward a comparative analysis of the segments which echo each other. It can be seen that the final segment, which displays a clearcut classicism, is constructed on an a/b/a alternation which reproduces that of the initial segment of which it is the resolution: in both places, it is clearly between Honoré and "the rest" that a narrative alternation is established. But at the start it is done in 21 shots which would need to be broken down; for example, it would be seen that neither the first nor the last shot shows Honoré, and that the last shows Gigi alone, because the narrative is beginning; in the final segment it is accomplished in two shots which both show Honoré, and in between the two, Gigi, but with her husband Gaston.

At this microsystematic level, analysis encounters the increased dispersion and constraint of the specific codes (codes of camera movement, looks, scale of shots, etc. . . . .) deployed within and throughout the macrosystematic code of the *grande syntagmatique.* Analysis meets anew with the voluminous pressure of the textual system, the full organic play of its differential repetitions. For example, the segmental analysis thus increased, operating from segment to segment as from suprasegment to subsegment, would end by constructing, on the basis of the multiple scenes "at Gigi's," the immense paradigm of entries and exits (there are others, but this is the most obvious) sustaining the microsystematic structuration of the narrative units of the film (the large, the medium, and the less large, which, as Metz clearly saw, are still remarkably large precisely because they are the smallest).[26]

6. Segmental/Familial/Conjugal

To conclude, let me note a final, fundamental effect, proper to many American classical films, whereby the textual volume multiplies and closes off doubly the field of its own expansion. The systematic accumulation of symmetries and dissymmetries throughout the filmic chain, decomposed by the work of a generalized segmentation, constantly mimics and reproduces (because the one produces the other) the schema of family relations which founds the narrative space.

Gigi on the one hand, Gaston on the other, are two children brought up, in accordance with their sex, by a substitute mother (Mamita) and a substitute father (Honoré). A triple dissymmetry is incribed in this symmetry, which pledges Gigi and Gaston to each other from the outset.

(a) One man, Honoré, corresponds to two women, Mamita and Alicia, in the role of adoptive substitute parent.

(b) A genealogical gap makes Gaston Honoré's nephew and Gigi the grandchild of Mamita and grand-niece of Alicia.

(c) A clear difference in age between Gigi and Gaston reproduces this genealogical gap, making one already a man, the other still a child.

The mutual feeling between Gigi and Gaston is crystalized in the suprasegment (XV) at Trouville. These three segments (the analysis lacked the opportunity to go into this point) are partly constructed on a narrative alternation which juxtaposes Gigi and Gaston on the one hand, and on the other, Honoré and Mamita, who meet in the film for the first and last time. They seem to be bound by an old love and go so far as to evoke the marriage which might have united them. This retrospective marriage clearly simply serves to reflect the as yet potential marriage of Gigi and Gaston. But it suggests much more than that. At this precise moment, the bar of dissymmetry jumps from one generation to another, with the help of a single reply. When Mamita tells Honoré with an insistence of no use to the plot, but necessary to the symbolic level: "Gigi is my granddaughter," Honoré's gallantry, which is structural in the proper sense, prompts him to reply: "Granddaughter, no. Daughter." What clearer way of indicating that the children they have not had are obviously those they have both adopted, whom the film is to unite in marriage. In this way, an incest fiction, so favored by the classic-romantic imagination, is established. The dissymmetry obviously reappears, like Alicia, who is absent from this four-term structure. But the dissymmetry of the structures serves what it hides and allows to be resolved: thanks to a discrepancy in age, Gigi is to recover in Gaston the substitute for a father even more strangely absent than the mother who is heard singing as a voice-off, and Gaston recovers in Mamita the obvious substitute for a mother of whom not a word is spoken.

This then is the story the film tells us, within a narrative which makes of the segmental the textual condition for a happy slide from the familial into the conjugal, and so assigns itself as an object the resolution of Oedipus. This is the effect of textual production which I tried to grasp in terms that were both different and rigorously complementary, in an analysis of Alfred Hitchcock's *North by Northwest,* as an effect I called "symbolic blockage."

Section	Supra-segment	Segment	Place	Sub-segment	Characters	Shots	Syntagma	Music	Action
	0	0	Titles over engravings			x		Champagne Gigi	
A	I	1	The Bois	a	Honoré	1–15	sequence	"Bois" theme	Honoré introduces the Bois de Boulogne and himself: the bachelor stockholder and a lover of women.
				b	Honoré Gigi	16–21		"Little Girls" theme by Honoré	He praises little girls and introduces Gigi, playing with some friends. She passes behind him and goes off through the Bois.
	II	2	At Gigi's (ext./int.)		Gigi Mamita	22–24	sequence	Mother's singing voice-off	Gigi arrives at her grandmother Mamita's and is reminded that it is the day of her visit to Aunt Alicia.
	III	3	Paris At Gaston's (ext.)		/Honoré/	25	autonomous shot	"Little Girls" variation	A cab crosses a square and stops in front of a luxurious building.
		4	At Gaston's (int.)		Gaston tradesman valet	26	autonomous shot		His uncle's visit is announced to Gaston Lachaille. He finishes dealing with a few matters and goes out.
		5	At Gaston's (ext.)		Honoré Gaston	27–28	sequence		The meeting between the uncle and the nephew who go off in a cab across Paris

Section	Supra-segment	Seg-ment	Place	Sub-segment	Characters	Shots	Syntagma	Music	Action
		6	Paris		Honoré Gaston	29–40	scene	"It's a bore" theme, then sung by Honoré/Gaston	Honoré praises the charms of life (Paris, wine, women, high society). Gaston responds that everything bores him and stops the cab.
IV		7	At Gigi's (ext./int.)		Gaston Mamita	41–48	scene		Gaston arrives at Mamita's. They talk about Gigi. Gaston is astonished by the "lessons" Alicia is giving her.
V		8	At Alicia's (ext./int.)		Alicia Gigi	49–64	sequence		Gigi arrives at Alicia's running. The lesson is on how to eat ortolans. Conversation on marriage.
		9	At Alicia's (int.)	a	Alicia Gigi	65–67	scene		Lesson (continuation): jewels, cigars. Conversation on love and art. Alicia leaves.
				b	Gigi	68–71	scene	"The . . .	Gigi inveighs against the Parisians and love and goes off.
VI		10	Le Jardin des Tuileries		Gigi	72–75	sequence	. . . Parisians" by Gigi	Gigi continues singing as she crosses the Tuileries and ends up sitting on a bench.
		11	Le Jardin des Tuileries		Gigi Gaston	76–82	scene		Gaston arrives in a cab, recognizes Gigi ("Gaston, do you make love all the time?") and teases her as he takes her along to the Palais de Glace where he is meeting Liane d'Exelmans.

									The façade of the Palais de Glace
VII		12	The skating rink (ext.)		/Gigi Gaston/	83	autonomous shot	waltz	
		13	the skating rink (int.)		Gigi Gaston Liane skating teacher	84–90	sequence	waltz	They enter and sit down. On the rink are Liane and her skating teacher. Gigi finds her common and vulgar and leaves suddenly. Liane joins Gaston and reminds him that they are to meet Honoré at Maxim's. They leave.
B	VIII	14	At Maxim's (entrance)	a	Honoré (+x)	91	episodic sequence	Maxim's theme	Honoré introduces Maxim's and praises it.
				b	Baron de la Cour. Girl.	91–92		Maxim's theme chorus in speech/song	The Baron de la Cour enters with a "belle."
				c	Honoré. Girl	92–93		" "	Honoré enters with a "belle."
				d	Gaston Liane	93–94		" "	Gaston enters with Liane.
		15	At Maxim's (room)		Gaston Liane Honoré	95–105	sequence	"She is so gay tonight", by Gaston	At the table, Liane is in high spirits, Gaston gloomy. "She is not thinking of me." Honoré asks Liane to dance. Liane grows more and more exuberant. Gaston increasingly bad-tempered.

Section	Supra-segment	Seg-ment	Sub-segment	Place	Characters	Shots	Syntagma	Music	Action
IX		16		At Honoré's (int.)	Gaston Honoré Manuel	106–121	scene	"It's a bore" by Honoré/Gaston, then Manuel	Gaston arrives at his uncle's to announce that Liane is being unfaithful with the skating master. Honoré takes him to Honfleur where the couple are hiding, to settle the affair in a gentlemanly way.
X		17		At Honfleur (ext./int.)	Honoré Gaston Liane skating teacher	122–134	sequence		Honoré and Gaston arrive at an inn and surprise the couple. Gaston offers the man a thousand francs to disappear and says goodbye to Liane, who faints.
		18		Newspaper	(Gaston Liane)	135	autonomous shot		A front page with a photo of Liane. "Sugar Prince breaks with Liane d'Exelmans."
XI		19		At Alicia's	Alicia Mamita	136	autonomous shot		Alicia and Mamita comment on Liane's "suicide."
XII		20		At Honoré's	Gaston Honoré Manuel	137	autonomous shot		Gaston arrives at Honoré's and is congratulated by Honoré on his first suicide; he dissuades him from shutting himself away and advises him rather to live it up.

C	XIII	21	At Gigi's (int.)	A	a	/Gigi/ (Gaston)	138	sequence	Gigi's hands hold an illustrated program: "Gaston Lachaille opens Pré Catelan for a gigantic party."
			Pré Catelan/B	B	b	Gaston Honoré	139–141		Honoré enjoying himself at a table with several girls while Gaston yawns.
			At Gigi's (int.)	A	a	/Gigi/ (Gaston)	142		Gigi's hands hold an illustrated program: "Who will be Gaston Lachaille's Queen at the battle of flowers?"
			The Bois	C	c	Gaston	143–144		In a flower-covered float, Gaston, looking bored beside a girl.
			At Gigi's (int.)	A	a	/Gigi/ (Gaston)	145		Gigi's hands hold an illustrated program: "Two thousand guests invited to Gaston Lachaille's masked ball."
			At Gaston's	D	d	Gaston Honoré	146–148		Honoré looks for Gaston in the costumed crowd and finds him slumped in a corner on a couch.
			At Gigi's (int.)	A	a	/Gigi/ (Gaston)	149		Gigi's hands hold an illustrated program: "Gaston Lachaille invites the opera company home."

Section	Supra-segment	Seg-ment	Place	Sub-segment	Characters	Shots	Syntagma	Music	Action
	XIV	22	At Gigi's (int.)	a	Gigi Mamita Gaston	149–154	scene	"Little Girls" whistled by Gigi	The bell rings. Gigi gets up and opens the door to Gaston. Mamita is preparing a cassoulet in the kitchen. Gaston decides to put off his party and sends Gigi with an apology.
				b	Mamita Gaston	155–156		Mother's voice off	Mamita and Gaston talk about Honoré.
		23	At Gigi's (int.)		Gigi Gaston Mamita	157–175	scene	"Champagne" by Gigi, Gaston, Mamita	Gaston and Gigi play cards. Gigi makes him promise that if she wins he will take her with him to Trouville. She cheats and wins. Gaston is furious but gives in, agrees to take them. They sing and dance with Mamita as they empty a bottle of champagne.
	XV	24	At Trouville The beach The sea		Gigi Gaston Girl Man Honoré Mamita	176–183	sequence	"Champagne"	While Gaston and Gigi frolic in the water, Honoré is about to pass a note to a girl when he catches sight of Mamita on the beach, greeting him. He puts away the note and a man goes into the girl's cabin.

			Location	Characters	Frame	Type	Music	Description
		25	At Trouville Tennis	Gigi Gaston Girl Man Honoré Mamita	184–194	sequence	"Champagne"	Honoré arrives on the tennis court. The girl, dressed to kill, is solemnly playing with her admirer on one side. On the other, Gaston is playing with Gigi, who is running about like a mad thing under the amused eye of Mamita.
		26	At Trouville The terrace The beach	Gigi Gaston Girl Honoré Mamita	195–223	sequence	"I remember it well" by Honoré/Mamita	Gigi and Gaston on the beach with a pair of donkeys. Mamita watches from the terrace, laughing. Honoré is about to follow the girl as she comes into the hotel when he catches sight of Mamita and goes to sit beside her. They evoke past love at length. Night falls. Gigi and gaston return, dragging the donkeys.
D	XVI	27	At Alicia's (int.)	Mamita Alicia	224–225	scene		Alicia warns an amazed Mamita about Gaston's likely passion for Gigi and persuades her to speed up Gigi's education before the return of Gaston, who has left for Monte-Carlo.

Section	Supra-segment	Seg-ment	Place	Sub-segment	Characters	Shots	Syntagma	Music	Action
XVII		28	At Alicia's (int.)	a	Alicia Gigi	236	episodic sequence	"Little Girls"	The lesson in manners: how to serve coffee, which Gigi spills.
				b	" "	237			Lesson in manners: how to walk, how to sit down. Not very successful.
				c	" "	238			Lesson in manners: tasting wine, on which Gigi gets tipsy.
				d	" "	239			Lesson in manners: choosing a cigar, which Gigi snaps in two.
		29	At Alicia's (int.)	a	Alicia Mamita Gigi mannequin couturier	240–246	episodic sequence	"Little Girls"	Presentation of a dress, which Mamita and Gigi like, Alicia doesn't like.
				b	Alicia Mamita Gigi etc...	247–250			
				c	Alicia Mamita Gigi etc...	251–254			A second dress, which Mamita and Gigi like, Alicia doesn't like.
				d	Alicia Mamita Gigi etc...	255–256			A third dress, which Mamita and Gigi don't like and Alicia chooses.

XVIII	30	At Gigi's (int.)	A	a	Gigi Mamita Gaston	257–268	sequence	"Little Girls"	Gigi tries on the dress and is aghast. Gaston arrives at Gigi's. She rushes straight into her room and returns in a white dress. Gaston, who doesn't accept the metamorphosis, loses his temper and leaves, then returns to invite Gigi to tea at the "Reservoirs." Mamita is against it and Gigi goes back to her room.
		From Gigi's/B back to Gigi (ext.)		b	Mamita Gaston	269–275		"She is a babe," by Gaston	Mamita explains to gaston that she cannot let Gigi go out with him alone. Gaston loses his temper, insults Mamita and leaves.
				c	Gaston	276–289		"Gigi" by Gaston	He walks across Paris as far as the Tuileries, where he met Gigi earlier, and returns. When he left, Gigi was only a charmless child; on his return, a girl with whom he is in love.
XIX	31	At Gigi's (ext.)			Gaston Mamita	290–291	scene		he rings and asks mamita to receive him.
	32	At Alicia's (int.)			Alicia Mamita	292–301	scene		Mamita reports to Alicia Gaston's proposal on keeping Gigi: a private apartment, a car, etc.

Section	Supra-segment	Segment	Place	Sub-segment	Characters	Shots	Syntagma	Music	Action
XX	33		At Gigi's A (bedroom)	a	Gigi	302	sequence	"I remember it well"	Gigi comes out of her room to open the door to Gaston.
			At Gigi's B (living room)	b	Gaston Gigi	302–308			Gigi refuses Gaston's proposals, bursts into tears when she learns that he loves her.
			At Gigi's (living room)	c	Gaston Gigi Mamita	308			Mamita rushes in, Gigi runs to her room.
			At Gigi's (living room)	d	Mamita Gaston	308			Gaston says goodbye to Mamita and leaves.
XXI	34		At the restaurant	a	Honoré Gaston	309–311	scene		Gaston arrives in a restaurant where Honoré is having lunch and explains his disappointment to him. Honoré consoles him and invites him to join him that evening with "Michèle" at Maxim's.
				b	Honoré	312		"Poor boy," by Honoré	Honoré congratulates himself on having reached an age where conflicts like this don't matter.
XXII	35		On the telephone A	a	Mamita	313	episodic sequence		Mamita telephones in tears.
			At Alicia's B	b	Alicia	314			Alicia puts down the telephone and has a cab called.
			In Paris C	c	(Alicia)	315			A cab crosses a square in Paris.

			Characters	Shots	Type	Music	Description
		36	Alicia Mamita Gigi Gaston	316–325	scene		At Gigi's	Alicia arrives at Gigi's and reproaches Mamita for her clumsiness. Gaston rings, he has received Gigi's letter. She comes out from her room for a moment to tell him that she would rather be unhappy with him than without him and returns to her room. Gaston goes out. The two sisters look at each other.
E	XXIII	37	Gaston jeweler	326	autonomous shot		At Gaston's	Gaston chooses a jewel for Gigi.
	XXIV	38	Gigi	327	autonomous shot	"Say a prayer for me tonight" by Gigi	At Gigi's (bedroom)	Gigi mentally prepares herself for the evening she is to experience.
		39	Gigi Alicia Mamita Gaston	328–329	scene		At Gigi's (int./ext.)	Gigi emerges from her room in an evening dress. She kisses Alicia and Mamita, opens the door to Gaston's ring and they go out.
	XXV	40	Gigi Gaston	330–331	sequence	Maxim's theme	At Maxim's (entrance)	Gaston and Gigi enter Maxim's and move to a table.
		41	Gigi Gaston Honoré	332–335	sequence	"She is so gay tonight"	At Maxim's (inside)	At the table. Gigi applies Alicia's lesson to perfection: the coffee, the cigar, and the jewelry. They get up to dance, as they pass greeting a surprised Honoré who recognizes Gigi.

Section	Supra-segment	Segment	Sub-segment	Place	Characters	Shots	Syntagma	Music	Action
		42		At Maxim's (entrance hall)	Gigi Gaston Honoré	336–337	sequence		Gaston offers Gigi his gift. Gigi exclaims like a real woman of the world over the beauty of the diamonds which she offers to the room to admire. Gaston is angered and leaves, dragging her to the exit.
XXVI		43	a	From Gigi's/A (ext.)	Gigi Gaston Mamita	338	sequence		He drags Gigi by the hand up the steps. Gigi throws herself tearfully into Mamita's arms. Gaston goes back down the steps and walks across Paris.
	B		b		Gaston	339–340			
		44		Les Tuileries	Gaston	341	autonomous shot	"She is a babe" / "Gigi"	He passes in front of the Tuileries fountain, stops, and turns back.
		45		Toward's Gigi's (ext.)	Gaston	342–344	sequence		He retraces his steps and goes slowly up Gigi's stairway.
		46		At Gigi's (int.)	Gaston Gigi Mamita	345–347	scene		Mamita and Gigi are sitting up. Mamita goes to open the door to Gaston and begs him to avoid a scandal. Gaston asks Mamita for Gigi's hand. She rushes into his arms tenderly.
XXVII		47		The Bois	Honoré Gigi Gaston	348–349	sequence	"Little Girls" by Honoré	Honoré sings. Gigi and Gaston appear and leave in a cab. Honoré goes on singing.
	Repeat			Ending on painting		a shot			

Notes

1. TRANSLATOR'S NOTE: This celebrated work by Christian Metz first appeared in *Communications* in 1964, as one of his *Essais sur la signification au cinéma (ESC)*, initially published in a variety of journals. *ESC*, vol. 1 appeared in book form in 1968 (Paris: Klincksieck). The English translation by Michael Taylor appeared as *Film Language: A Semiotics of the Cinema* (New York: Oxford University Press, 1974). *ESC* vol. 2 was published by Klincksieck in 1972.

2. TRANSLATOR'S NOTE: *Langage et cinéma* (Paris: Larousse, 1971). English translation by Donna Jean Umiker-Sebek, *Language and Cinema* (The Hague: Mouton, 1974).

3. *Film Language*, p. 134. *ESC*, 2:203–4. [See Metz, "Problems of Denotation in the Fiction Film" in this volume—ED.]

4. *ESC*, 2:206.

5. *Film Language*, p. 164, note.

6. "A purely logical entity which, by itself, does not take place in the film;. . . in this code of the large syntagmatic category, the distinctive units do not consist of filmic segments, but of sorts of abstract exponents each of which is attached to a filmic segment" (*Language and Cinema*, pp. 201–2). "The autonomous segment is not a unit of the 'film,' but a unit of the systems of the film" (*Ibid.*, p. 190, note 8).

7. *ESC*, 2:129.

8. I have in mind here the works of Adriano Aprà and Luigi Martelli on *Viaggio in Italia* ("Premesse sintagmatiche ad un 'analise di *Viaggio in Italia*" *Cinema e Film* [Spring 1967], 1–2); Jean-Claude Bernardet on the Brazilian film *Sao Paulo, sociedade anonima* (Metz, *A significacào uo cinema* [Sao Paulo, 1972]); Jan Toft on *Battleship Potemkin* (Christian Metz og Eisenstein, *Exil* [October 1973] vol. 7, no. 1); Genevieve Jacquino on the didactic film (forthcoming); Francis Ramirez and Christian Rolot on the films of the modern French comedy school (forthcoming); and the more partial utilizations of the *grande syntagmatique* by Roger Odin on a part of Grémillon's *Gardiens de phare* ("Semiologie et analyse de film-lecture de codes," *Travaux de linguistque*, [Saint-Etienne: Ed. l'Université de Saint-Etienne, 1972]), vol. 2; and by John Ellis on *Passport to Pimlico* ("Made in Ealing," *Screen* [1975], vol. 16, no. 1) and Stephen Heath on *Touch of Evil* ("*Touch of Evil*" in the same issue).

9. For example, Kari Hanet, "The Narrative Text of *Shock Corridor*," *Screen* (1974–75), vol. 15, no. 4, and Thierry Kuntzel, "Le travail du film 2" *Communications*, (1975) no. 23.

10. Jean Monod and Jean-Paul Dumont, *Foetus Astral* (Paris: Christian Bourgeois, 1970).

11. Editors of *Cahiers du cinéma*, "Young Mr. Lincoln de John Ford, texte collectif" *Cahiers du cinéma* (August–September 1970), no. 223 [translation included in this anthology—ED.]

12. Claude Bailblé, Michel Marie, and Marie-Claire Ropars, *Muriel* (Paris: Galilee, 1975).

13. Already cited.

14. Raymond Bellour, "Le blocage symbolique," *Communications* (1975), no. 23.

15. Raymond Bellour, "*Les Oiseaux:* Analyse d'une séquence," *Cahiers du Cinéma* (October 1968), no. 216; "L'Evidence et le code," *Cinema: théorie, lectures* (Paris: Klincksieck, 1973) ["The Obvious and the Code," included in this volume—ED.]; "Le Blocage symbolique."

16. Only the punctuation mark, when it is demarcatory, constitutes a pertinence of the same order as the syntagmatic type, because it participates in a specific code (the straight cut is obviously part of that code when it is substitutable for the punctuation mark). See *ESC*, 2:122–24.

17. "It seeks not the shot, but the sequence, which is a permanent concern and problem: actions, epochs, landscapes, must be distributed and organized over the totality of the film: regroupings both superior to the shot (= unit of shooting) and inferior to the *work* (the maximal unit) must be established." *ESC*, 2:120–21.

18. In their syntagmatic analysis of *Viaggio in Italia*, Adriano Aprà and Luigi Martelli have

very carefully noted the need for complementary segmentations: one at the superior or "structural" level, constituting units which they call *cineperiodo* (after the cine-phrase adopted by the Russian formalists), the other at the inferior level, called "grammatical" (through an odd abuse of words current for a few years in Italy). But in spite of everything they remian essentially with Metz's autonomous segments and compromise their work of decomposition and pre-analysis largely by the distinction they make between the grammatical and the structural, which avoids the fundamental problem of the single and plural (i.e., textual) articulation of the different levels of description possible.

19. *Film Language*, p. 181.

20. *ESC*, 2:127.

21. And all the episodic sequences except segment 35, whose bastardized character I have underlined.

22. At this level, the specific pertinence established between the segments by the differences between the syntagmatic types is displaced in the form of an opposition between segment and subsegment (with, as we have just seen, the intermediary case of subsegments constituted by the episodes of episodic sequences).

23. With one exception, 43a. This clearly underlines the way that from the moment the breakdown becomes textual, it is constantly opening up depths. To avoid being inaccurate I did not wish to credit Gaston alone with segment 43, where he brings Gigi and Mamita into one shot; on the other hand, in order to be exact, I ought to have divided subsegment 43a again into two subsegments, Gigi-Gaston and Gigi-Gaston-Mamita, which would be perfectly practicable for numerous other scenes.

24. This is quite striking for the set of segments which rest totally or in part on alternations of a more or less structuring kind at various levels. By definition, they impel more strongly than the rest toward an approximation which can only be broken down by a deeper subsegmentation.

25. The first figures in the summary table along with the other operations, to show that what is involved is always only the same operation displaced. I have not included the second, more complex example, which can be described by analysis alone.

26. *ESC*, 2: 138–40.

—translated by Diana Matias

Raymond Bellour
The Obvious and the Code

Take as the example twelve shots from *The Big Sleep*. They are inscribed between two major "scenes." The first, in Eddy Mars' garage—where Vivian enters the action on Marlowe's side for the first time—culminates in the death of Canino; the second, in Geiger's house, is the end of the film—Eddy Mars' death brings the open series of enigma and peripeteia to a close and sets the seal on the emergence of a couple. In between the two there are twelve shots showing Vivian and Marlowe in the car on the way from the garage to the house.

As a specific unit of code, they correspond exactly to what Christian Metz in his *grande syntagmatique* calls a *scene;* that is, an autonomous segment, characterized by a chronological coincidence between "the unique consecutiveness of" the signifier (deployment on the screen) and the unique consecutiveness of the signified (= the time of the fiction)."[1] On the other hand, as a specifically textual unit, they also constitute what, in work toward a description of the classic narrative film, I have chosen to call a segment;[2] that is, a moment in the filmic chain which is delimited both by an elusive but powerful sense of dramatic or fictional unity and by the more rigorous notion of identity of setting and characters of the narrative. (When, as is most often the case, the two pertinences do not overlap completely, i.e. when a significant variation in location or character appears within one and the same segment, the segment divides into subsegments). In this case the dramatic unity is obvious—a pause between two strong times marked by the deaths of Canino and Eddy Mars, respectively, and a resumption of verbal relations between Vivian and Marlowe. Identity of characters and location is absolute—throughout the segment we have a car, and

Published as "L'Évidence et le code," in *Cinéma: théorie, lectures,* ed. Dominique Noguez (Paris: Ed. Klincksieck, 1973) and translated in *Screen* (Winter 1974–75, 15:7–17. Reprinted by permission of the author, and translation used by permission of the Society for Education in Film and Television.

the two main characters in intimate conversation. Finally, the segmental nature of the shots is reinforced by an element which, for all that is not inherent in its definition, is often consubstantial with it in the classic narrative; the twelve shots open and close on lap dissolves—a punctuation which here functions as a (redundant) sign of demarcation.[3]

The interest of this segment lies in its relative poverty. Even an attentive viewer will not be sure to retain anything but the impression of a certain amount of vague unity. Questioned, he will very likely hazard the view that the segment consists of a long take supported by dialogue, or at best, of two or three shots. But Hawks needed twelve shots to secure the economy of this segment. Undoubtedly, that economy was designed in order not to be perceived, which is in fact one of the determining features of the American cinema. But it exists, and from it the classic mode of narration draws a part of its power. It is true, as Metz has observed, that that mode "is geared towards the sequence and it is the sequence (and not the shot) which is its preoccupation, its constant problem."[4] But the organic material of this preoccupation is the prior set of formal, hierarchically ordered relations between the shots. What I want to show here is how the simplest narrative fact imaginable—two characters talking in a car—can come to set into play a series of elementary but subtle operations which ensure its integration into the development of a narration. It is on this level that the—relative—poverty of this segment is exemplary.

According to Rivette's famous formula, "obviousness is the mark of Howard Hawks' genius,"[5] No doubt—provided we recognize the extent to which that obviousness only comes to the fore insofar as it is coded.

The text of the segment is constituted by the concerted action of six codes, listed from (a) to (f) in the accompanying recapitulatory diagram. The first three concern variations in scale between the shots, whether they are static or moving, and camera angle (symbolized by the arrow). These are three specific codes which manifest the potentialities of one of the five purports of expression proper to all sound film, i.e. the image-band.[6] The three others are nonspecific codes; the presence or absence of this or that character or characters from the units considered (and note the lack of extension of this code here—there is no shot without a character), whether they express themselves in dialogue or not, and finally whether these units are of greater or lesser duration, does not depend on cinema. In the case of the last code, a relative imprecision will be noted—the times of each shot are brought into clear opposition, and this is just one of the multiple abstractions to which the codes subject the text. As for those elements consigned to the seventh column, they do of course come within a code, but its extension differs radically from that of the remaining six. It differs in two senses: as a code of narrative actions it is of itself broader than the rest, pluricodic from the outset through the different levels on which its elements are located; in addition, it only takes on its specific value as code in the light of the

	Framing	S/M	Angle	Characters	Speech	Time	Elements of Narration
1	MS → MCS	M	↗	VM	–	+	
2	CS	S	↗	VM	+VM	+	
3	CU	S	↗	M	+M	–	
4	CU	S	↑	V	+VM	–	
5	CU	S	↗	M	+M	–	
6	CU	S	↑	V	+MV	–	V: ' I guess I am in love with you '
7	CS	S	↗	VM	+VM	++	Marlowe's movement as he takes a corner
8	CU	S	↑	V	+M	–	
9	CU	S	↗	M	+M	–	
10	CS	S	↗	VM	+VM	+	M : ' I guess I am in love with you '
11	CU	S	↑	V	–	–	
12	CS	S	↗	VM	–	+	Vivian puts her hand on Marlowe's arm
	a	b	c	d	e	f	

body of the text (for example the film) for which it determines one of the principal semantic axes. It is a reflection of this extension that it figures here in only a restricted number of elements capable of entering into combination with the action of the other six codes in the circumscribed space of twelve shots.

The most direct oppositions of the segment emerge between shots 1 and 2. Shot 1 is the only moving shot; it tracks in to frame the front right window of the car, and (from medium shot to medium-close shot) delimits two frames which are to have no equivalent in the remainder of the segment. I should stress (something which does not seem to have constituted a distinct code but might have done so) that it is the only shot taken outside the car. A fourth—correlative—opposition is marked in the transition between presence and absence of dialogue. But from shot 1 to 2 the narration is at pains to soften any excessive difference, ensuring continuity on three levels: through the relative identity of duration of the shots, the combined presence of the two main characters in both shots, and above all, by maintaining the initial camera angle (from left to right) which is the simplest way of ensuring a sense that one is watching one and the same shot (see plates).

Shot 3 starts from an unevenly graduated transition (it is static like shot 2, and preserves the same camera angle as shots 1 and 2) to introduce another series of differences. The two characters/one character (Marlowe) change has its three correlates: passage from medium-close shot to closeup, from long take to short take, and the centering of the dialogue on one character.

Shot 4 refines this beginning of a system. We pass naturally from one character to the other, from Marlowe to Vivian, as if shot 2 had been divided to show us in turn the hero and the heroine, giving each of them the same reduction in framing and duration. But only at the cost of a double difference: Vivian does not speak alone in shot 4 as Marlowe did in shot 3. Instead they both talk. And above all, the angle changes completely to show Vivian full face, enclosed by

1

5

2

6

3

7

4

8

the space of the car interior—the reverse of Marlowe, beside whose face the night landscape continues to flow, discernible through the left front window of the car.

Thereafter the segment organizes itself on this twofold opposition alternating between two characters and one character, and between each of the two characters. But while the static nature of the shot, the distribution of the scale of framing and the camera angle remain invariable, the other pertinences undergo notable changes.

(a) First, the distribution of the characters. The shots which show the characters alone follow a very precisely graded pattern which complicates the initial 2/1–1 alternation. This pattern may be broken down as follows: four alternating shots (3–6), then two (8–9), then one (11). Inevitably, within the gradual contraction that marks the curve of the segment and ensures its internal acceleration (what might be called its "suspense"), a privileged status is assigned to Vivian, who figures in shot 11. Note that this privilege is secured by a delicate transition which inverts the initial data of the alternation—M/V/M/V order which succeeds shot 2, becomes V/M after shot 7, as if to pave the away for the absence of Marlowe in the last occurrence.

(b) But the privilege conceded within one code (presence in the image) is overthrown in another (presence in the dialogue belonging to each shot). We have already noted that while Marlowe alone speaks in shot 3 where he is alone in the image, Marlowe and Vivian both talk in shot 4 which shows Vivian alone, an opposition which is continued in shots 5 and 6. The shots which follow accentuate this imbalance in accordance with a progression which is at the same time inverse, similar, and different to that of the image-presence progression. For Marlowe alone speaks in shots 8 and 9, which show the two characters alternately, and while he does not speak in shot 11, where Vivian marks her privilege in the image, she—far from speaking—is quite silent.[7]

This silence, which opposes this shot of Vivian to the whole anterior series of shots showing one character, is followed by another silence. Shot 12, which shows both Vivian and Marlowe again, is silent, thereby giving the other end of the segment a symmetry with shot 1, whose singularity in relation to those that follow has been noted. A folding effect which clearly demonstrates the way in which the narration, even down to its details, proceeds through a differential integration of its constituent elements.

(c) Third, time. While the two characters–long take/one character–short take equivalence is respected throughout the segment, the first term of the opposition undergoes profound internal variation. Shot 7 is in fact much longer than its corresponding shots 1, 2, 10, and 12, to the point where it is almost as long as the whole set of remaining eleven shots. The strategic placement of this shot will be noted—it occurs in the middle of the segment, thus delimiting a beginning which makes it possible, and an end which it motivates and which echoes the beginning through a multiple process, a process simultaneously of equivalence through symmetry, of resolution through repetition and variation, and of acceleration in balancing.

The arrangement shown by the work of the codes is the same one that shapes the meaning of the fiction. From the mass of narrative elements ebbing and flowing throughout the segment (conversations, turning on a deepening of the relations of the enigma, and the more or less continuous-discontinuous field of the characters' actions and reactions) I have isolated only two phrases and two gestures. ". . . I guess I am in love with you." This phrase, which occurs twice, uttered first by Vivian and then by Marlowe, clearly shows the extent to which the reduplication effect—in this instance a simple mirror effect linked to the admission of love—is constitutive of the narrative. But this is so at the cost of an inversion which underscores the fact that repetition is constitutive only inasmuch as it takes its starting point from the difference circumscribing it, within a movement of bi-motivation which is in fact the specific necessity of this type of narrative. It is in shot 6, in which she appears alone, that Vivian makes the first admission of love whose effect carries over into shot 7, thereby justifying among other things its exceptional length. Inversely, it is in shot 10, in which Vivian and Marlowe appear together, that he reiterates the admission whose effect focuses on shot 11, which shows Vivian alone and silent.

The two gestures, on the contrary, are relatively heterogeneous. But they are of interest, the first—Marlowe gripping the steering wheel on a difficult swerve—by specifying him, as he has been throughout the film, as belonging on the side of action; the second, Vivian's tender gesture, coming as an explicit and conclusive response to the admission of love, in that it lets us place her clearly within a feeling only recognized and expressed by her once she has committed herself in the action on Marlowe's side.

This double narrative inflection moreover has its effect on at least two of the codic implications of the narrative, whose articulation appears that much more strongly motivated as a result. On the one hand the divergence between presence in the dialogue and presence in the image which privilege Marlowe and Vivian respectively; on the other, the difference in camera angle, concentrated on Vivian and abstracting her face on the surface of the screen. Easiliy recognizable here is a double sign of the mythologization of the woman. Hawks, we might note, is one of the Hollywood directors who has most profoundly reorientated the Hollywood tradition of the woman-object. The well-known independence and initiative of his heroines brings to certain of his couples—and to none more than that of *The Big Sleep*—the slightly legendary character of a relationship of adult reciprocity. But this is only achieved through the codified marks, which, in this instance, make it the woman whose magnified face simultaneously, and wholly expresses and receives the admission of love.

Nevertheless, it would be overly simple to move to a neat conclusion and find something like the "secret" of the text in this correspondence, to see it as the rationale of the text, discovered in its meaning, or even in a meaning. On the other hand, if there is nothing but meaning, and if it has a meaning, in the sense that one might say it has a direction, this must, I think, be expressed in quite a different way. In these films, let's say in the classic American cinema, meaning is constituted by a correspondence in the balances achieved—as a law of the text in development—throughout its numerous codic and pluri-codic levels, in other words, its systems. Multiple in both nature and extension, these cannot be reduced to any truly unitary structure or semantic relationship.

But, to confine ourselves to what has been produced by this analytical description of twelve shots isolated from a film which can justifiably figure as one of the models of American high classicism, we note:

(a) The number of shots, which is relatively high given the exigencies of the action. This allows for a discontinuity capable of ensuring a certain degree of variation of the filmic space within the given time.

(b) This variation, which the narrative adopts as one of its basic options is, on the other hand, limited by a profound tendency toward repetition. Repetition essentially takes the upper hand through a number of strictly similar shots: on the one hand shots 3, 5, and 9 of Marlowe, and on the other, shots 4 and 6 of Vivian. (The similarity in question is, of course, on the level of the codes, which constrain the constitutive variation of dialogues, actors' comportment, etc.)

(c) This tendency toward repetition, which as we saw also expresses itself clearly through numerous relationships of partial similarity between shots (and beyond that between codes), carries with it a natural aftereffect. It underscores the codic differences which give effectiveness to the basic variation constituted by the successive plurality of the shots. These differences are powerful and discrete in their distribution and transitions, having as their primary object to ensure the natural continuity of the narrative—that is, to sustain its artifice, but without ever making it too obvious. A balance which in its own specific mode echoes that inscribed in the playing of the actors and the style of the photography.[8]

(d) This balance thus reveals a constant relationship from shot to shot between symmetry and dissymmetry, which is moreover reinforced by a general arrangement in the segment as a whole. In this respect, we might recall the unequal deployment of the shots alternating between Vivian and Marlowe around the central axis represented by shot 7, which is itself inscribed into the alternation on another level. It is not surprising, therefore, that it should be the regulated opposition between the closing off of symmetries and the opening up of dissymmetries which gives rise to the narrative, to the very fact that there is a narrative.

A particular arrangement will, however, be noted which seems to me not specific to but profoundly characteristic of the American cinema. The progressive relationship (in the literal sense) outlined above seems more or less to resolve itself within each unit of narration—in this case within a short segment of twelve shots which might be taken for a secondary transition—by means of a suspension and folding effect, as if to allow the segment to close back on itself more effectively and leave the new fold the problem of unrolling its new elements. Take the final shot, for example. It is conclusive and synthetic undoubtedly, by virtue of Vivian's tender gesture which closes off the dialogue marked by their double avowal. But it is also so in another way: by the silence between the characters which only has its equivalent in shot 1, it ensures a kind of overall symmetry, but it is tipped over into dissymmetry, so to speak, because it is opposed to the shot it recalls through the identity it sustains with shots 2, 7, and 10, the final silence being the distinguishing mark.

Notes

1. Raymond Bellour and Christian Metz, "Entretien sur la sémiologie du cinéma," *Semiotica* 4(1):10. For more detailed discussion, see Christian Metz, *Essais sur la signification au cinéma* (Paris: Klincksieck, 1968), pp. 130–31.

2. Particularly in a work in progress on Vincente Minnelli's *Gigi*. [See "Segmenting/Analyzing" in this anthology—ED.].

3. See on this point the valuable distinctions established by Christian Metz, "Ponctuations et démarcations dans le film de diègèse," *Essais sur la signification au cinéma*, 2:126–29).

4. *Ibid*, pp. 120–21.

5. "Génie de Howard Hawks," *Cahiers du Cinéma* (May 1953), no. 23, p. 16.

6. On this opposition between specific and nonspecific codes and the correlative ideas cinema/film, see the whole of Christian Metz's book *Langage et Cinéma* (Paris: Larousse, 1971) *(Language and Cinema* [The Hague: Mouton, 1974]). Following on Metz (see esp. pp. 169–80) one might bring in here the notion of degree of specificity to establish a gradation between the specific codes; only the static/moving code is specific in an absolute way here. The pictorial arts have variations in scale and in angle, although within a radically different extension of the notion of a work or of textual closure. Film contains them within itself (except a film made up of a single shot filmed from a fixed camera position and without internal variation among the subjects filmed, in other words, almost a nonfilm), whereas it requires several paintings, etchings, or photographs to constitute an equivalent variability. It is in this sense that the frame, while it is the smallest unit into which the filmic chain can be broken down, cannot be retained as a pertinent unit for the theory of cinema and film analysis except at the cost of prior loss of the notion of specificity.

7. Note here the difficulty sometimes encountered by clear distinctions. At a viewing, even a viewing slowed down by a projector which allows for reduction in speed, shot 11 appears to be silent, following a cut on Marlowe's admission "I guess I am in love with you." On the viewing table, on the other hand, the "you" seems fairly clearly to straddle the two shots. This effect is certainly not negligible, since it was intended in the editing and it accentuates the motivational relation in the succession of the two shots. It suggests once again the need to question the theoretical status of all that is only clearly apparent on the level of the frame.

8. A distinction needs to be made here between these two methods of balance, which correspond to each other and support each other, both equally aimed at giving the illusion of naturalness by the regulated control of artifice. While both are *codified,* to the degrree demanded by the need to produce the illusion, only the first is *coded,* i.e., capable of formulation into relatively strict systematic relationships. That is why the playing of the actors or the arrangements of tones in the image, which express themselves in the first case in terms of gestural dynamics and in the second in terms of intensity of light, resist analysis which inversely finds its chosen ground in the coded or codable elements (to stress clearly its character as a construction). It should be added that what falls to a greater extent into the codified in one instance may in another instance fall to a greater extent into the coded: for example, the arrangement of lighting and certain features of the actors' playing in certain German expressionist films.

—*translated by Diana Matias*

[5]

Nick Browne
The Spectator-in-the-Text:
The Rhetoric of *Stagecoach*

The sequence from John Ford's *Stagecoach* shown in the accompanying stills
raises the problem of accounting for the organization of images in an instance
of the "classical" fiction film and of proposing the critical terms appropriate for
that account. The formal features of these images—the framing of shots and
their sequencing, the repetition of setups, the position of characters, the direction
of their glances—can be taken together as a complex structure and understood
as a characteristic answer to the rhetorical problem of telling a story, of showing
an action to a spectator. Because the significant relations have to do with seeing—
both in the ways the characters "see" each other and the way those relations are
shown to the spectator—and because their complexity and coherence can be
considered as a matter of "point of view," I call the object of this study the
"specular text."

Explanations of the imagery of the classical narrative film are offered by
technical manuals and various theories of editing. Here, though, I wish to
examine the connection between the act of narration and the imagery, specifically
in the matter of the framing and the angle of view determined by setups, by
characterizing the narrating agency or authority which can be taken to rationalize
the presentation of shots. An explanation of this kind necessarily involves clarifying in some detail the notion of the "position of the spectator." Thus we must
characterize the spectator's implied position with respect to the action, the way
it is structured, and the specific features of the process of "reading" (though not

in the sense of interpretation). Doing so entails a description (within the terms of the narrative) of the relation of literal and fictional space that comprehends what seems, ambiguously, like the double origin of filmic images.

An inquiry into the forms of authority for the imagery and the corresponding strategies which implicate the viewer in the action has few precedents, yet it raises general but basic questions about filmic narration that begin to clarify existing accounts of the relation of narrative to image. The sequence from *Stagecoach* is interesting as a structure precisely because, in spite of its simplicity (it has no narrative or formal eccentricity) it challenges the traditional premises of critical efforts to account for the operation and effects of "classical" film style.

The traditional rationale for the presentation of imagery is often stated by the camera's relation to the spectator. For instance, a basically dramatic account has it that the shots should show essentially what a spectator would see if the action were played on a stage, and if at each moment he had the best view of the action (thus the changing angles only supply "accents"). Editing would follow the spectator's natural course of attention as it is implied by the action of the *mise-en-scène*. In such a mode the question of agency—that is, who is "staging" and making these events appear in this way—is referred not to the author or narrator but to the action itself, fully embodied in the characters. Everything that happens must be exhibited clearly for the eye of the spectator. On this theory, all the structures of the presentation are directed to a place external to the scene of the action—to the final authority, the ideal spectator. Oudart's recent account (*Film Quarterly*, Fall 1974) proposes that imagery is paradigmatically referred to the authority of the glance of the "absent one," the offscreen character within the story who in the countershot is depicted within the frame; the spectator "identifies" with the visual field of the "owner" of the glance. The "system of the suture" is an explanation that establishes the origin of the imagery by reference to the agency of character, but, surprisingly, it does not consider (indeed it seems to deny) the final agency, the authority of the narrator. The traces of the action of the narrator may seem to be effaced by this system, but such an effect can only be the result of a certain more general rhetoric. Thus I am proposing an account in which the structure of the imagery, whatever its apparent forms of presentation, refers jointly to the action of an implied narrator (who defines his position with respect to the tale by his judgments) and to the imaginative action occasioned by his placing and being placed by the spectator. Neither the traditional nor the more recent theories seem fully adequate to this problematic.

Thus the problem that arises from *Stagecoach* is to explain the functioning of the narrator and the nature and effects of spectator placement; specifically, describing and accounting for in detail a filmic rhetoric in which the agency of the narrator in his relation to the spectator is enacted jointly by the characters and the particular sequence of shots that show them. To describe this rhetoric in a rigorous and illuminating way means clarifying in filmic terms the notions of "narrative authority," "point of view," and "reading," and showing that these concepts are of use precisely because they arise naturally from the effort to account for the concrete structures of the text.

The moment in the story that the sequence depicts is the taking of a meal at the Dry Fork station on the stage's way to Lordsburg. Earlier in the film, the prostitute Dallas (the woman in the dark hat) has been run out of town by the Ladies' Law and Order League and has been put aboard the stagecoach. There she joined, among others, a cavalry officer's wife named Lucy (in the white hat) and Hatfield, her chivalrous but distant escort. Just before the present scene, the Ringo Kid (John Wayne), who has broken out of jail to avenge his brother's murder, has been ordered aboard by the sheriff when discovered by the side of the road. The sequence begins immediately after a vote among the members of the group to decide whether to go on to Lordsburg and ends shortly before the end of the scene when the group exits the station. For purposes of convenience I have called shots 4, 8, and 10, which are from the same setup, series A, and shots 3, 7, 9, and 11, series B.

One of the rationales that might be proposed to account for the setups, the spatial fields they show, the sequence of shots, is their relation to the "psychology" of the characters. How, if at all, are the setups linked to the visual attention, as with the glance, or say the interests of a character in the story? In the shot/reverse shot pattern which is sometimes, wrongly I think, taken as an exclusive paradigm of the "classical" style, the presence of the shot on the screen is "explained" or read as the depiction of the glance of the offscreen character, who, a moment later, is shown in the reverse shot. But because only a few shots of this sequence (or of most films) follow this pattern, we shall be pressed to a different formulation. The general question is how the two setups of the two major series of shots—series A from the head of the table and series B from the left side—are to be explained.

Series A is related to the visual attention of the woman at the head of the table, Lucy. The connection between the shots and her view, especially in the modulation of the force and meaning of that view, must, however, be established. These shots from A are readable as the depiction of Lucy's glance only retrospectively, after series B has shown her at the head of the table and after the animation conveyed in the dolly forward has implied its significance. The point remains, however, that the shots of series A are finally clearly authorized by a certain disposition of attention of one of the characters.

In contrast to series A, the series B shots from the left of the table are like the opening and closing shots (1, 12) in not being associated with or justified spatially as the depiction of anyone's glance. Can the placement of these shots be justified either as the "best angle" for the spectator or as the depiction of some other more complex conception of "psychology" of character than an act of attention in a glance? Persons to whom these shots might be attributed as

1

4a DALLAS: Thank you.

2 RINGO: Set down here, ma'am.

4b

3a

4c

3b

5

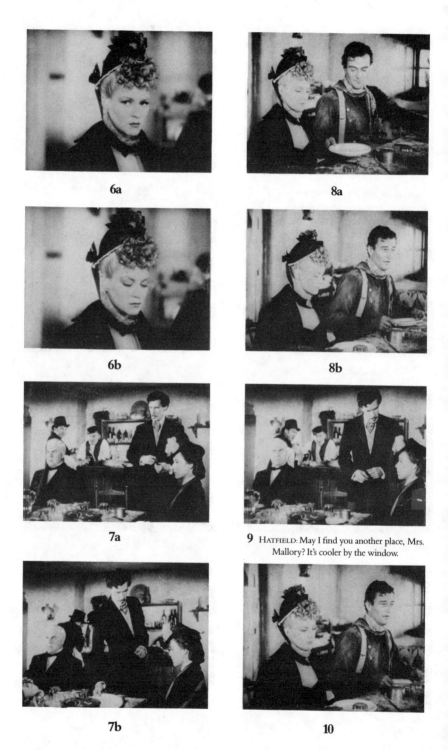

6a

8a

6b

8b

7a

9 HATFIELD: May I find you another place, Mrs. Mallory? It's cooler by the window.

7b

10

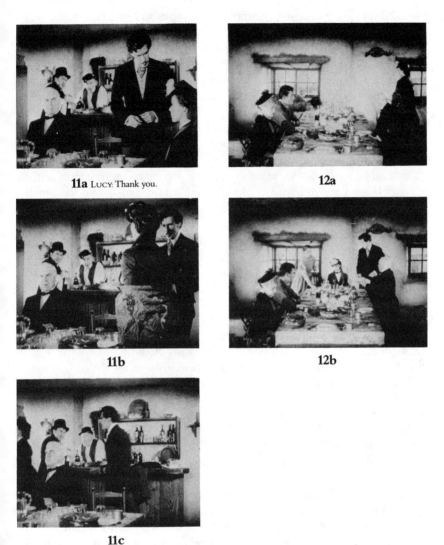

11a LUCY: Thank you.

12a

11b

12b

11c

views would be Dallas or the outlaw Ringo, for they satisfy one condition: they are out of the A-series frame. As series A shows, in this style the association of a shot with a glance is effected by a coincidence of geographical places, eye and camera. But here, quite plainly, neither Dallas nor Ringo is in a position to view from this angle. And in each shot, Lucy is in the frame.

To attribute the shots of series B—to justify their placement spatially—to some conception of character psychology requires some other justification than the mere representation of somebody's glance. What kind of psychological account could explain the alternation of these precise framings? What kind of

mental disposition, ensemble of attitude, judgment, and intention, is this framing significant of? Whose disposition? On what basis would such an attribution
be effected? If establishing the interpretation of the framing depended on or was
referred to a character's "state of mind," which in fact changes significantly over
the course of the sequence for each of the major characters (Dallas, Ringo, and
Lucy), how would it be possible to accommodate those changing feelings to
the fixity of setup? The fact of the fixity of setup denies that the explanation for
camera placement can as a principle be referred to a psychology of character(s)
based on the kind of emotional changes—surprise, repudiation, naiveté, humiliation—that eventuate in the sequence.

As another hypothesis we could say that the particular compositional features
of series B are a presentation not of the "mind" of any single character but of a
state of affairs within the group, a relationship among the parties. What is the
state of affairs within this society that the framing depicts? There are two
significant features of the composition from setup B: the relation of Lucy in the
immediate foreground to the group behind her, a group whose responsiveness
to events repeats the direction of her own attention, and her relation, spatially,
to Dallas and Ringo, who, excluded by the left edge of the frame, are outside.
The permanent and underlying fact about the mise-en-scène which justifies the
fixity of camera placement is its status as a social drama of alliance and antag-
onism between two social roles—Lucy, an insider, a married woman and defender of custom; and Dallas, outsider and prostitute who violates the code of
the table. The camera setups and the spatial fields they reveal, the compositional
exclusion of the outlaw couple and their isolation in a separate space, with the
implied assertion of Lucy's custodial relation to the body of legitimate society,
respond to and depict in formal terms the social "positions" of the characters.
In the kind of dramatic presentation they effect, the features of the framing are
not justified as the depiction of personal psychology considered as changes of
feeling; instead, by their emphasis on social positions, or types, they declare a
psychology of intractable situations.

The framing of series B from the left of the table does not represent literally
or figuratively any single person's view; rather, it might be said, it depicts, by
what it excludes and includes, the interplay of social positions within a group.
This asymmetry of social position of Lucy over Dallas extends as well to formal
and compositional features of the sequence. Though setup B represents both
positions, Dallas's negatively, it makes Lucy's position privileged in the formal
mechanism of narrative exposition. The fundamental narrative feature of the
sequence is a modification and inflection of the logic of shot/countershot. Here
it is an alternation of series A and B around, not two characters, but either
Lucy's eye or body. That is, in series A Lucy is present as an eye, as the formal
beholder of the scene. Alternately, in B, Lucy is shown bodily dominating the
foreground, and as the eye to which the views of series A are referred. Formally
the narration proceeds by alternatingly shifting Lucy's presence from the level

of the depicted action, as body (B), to the level of representation, as the invisible eye (A), making Lucy's presence the central point of spatial orientation and legibility. In shots 5 and 6, the closeup of the exchange of looks between the two women, the formal asymmetry is the difference of their frontality, and the shot of Lucy is from a place that Dallas could not literally occupy. Lucy's frontality (5) marks a dispossession, a displacement, that corresponds to Dallas's social "absence" in the entire sequence—to her exclusion from the frame in B, to her isolation as the object of Lucy's scornful glance in A. By contrast to Lucy's presence everywhere, as body and eye, Dallas's eye is never taken as the source of authority for a shot. Her eye is averted. She is always, in both A and B, the object of another's gaze—a condition that corresponds to the inferiority of her social position, and to her formal invisibility—she cannot authorize a view.

The shots of setup B, which might be called "objective," or perhaps "nobody's" shots, in fact refer to or are a representation of Lucy's social dominance and formal privilege. B shows a field of vision that closely matches Lucy's *conception* of her own place in that social world: its framing corresponds to her alliance with the group and to her intention to exclude the outsiders, to deny their claim to recognition. It is, in other words, not exactly a description of Lucy's subjectivity but an objectification of her social self-conception. Though Lucy is visible in the frame, series B might be said, metaphorically, to embody her point of view.

This explanation seems cogent as far as it goes. But there are some further issues that arise from the passage, in the way it is experienced, that suggests that the foregoing analysis of the justification of these formal features is incomplete as an account of the grounds for the effects the passage produces and theoretically limited in terms of explaining the strategies of framing and other premises of the narration.

Simply put, the experience of the passage is a feeling of empathy for Dallas's exclusion and humiliation, and a repudiation of Lucy's prejudice as unjust, two feelings brought together by a sense of inevabililty of the conflict. There is, in other words, a curious opposition between the empathetic response of a spectator toward Dallas and the underlying premises of the mechanism of the narrative which are so closely related, formally, to Lucy's presence, point of view, and interests. It is this sense of incongruity between feeling and formal structure that occasions the following effort to consider the sequence in terms of the ways it produces its effects, that is, rhetorically.

One question about a formal matter which draws attention to the limitations of a structural account based on a conception of the social order is why the outsiders are seen from a position that is associated with Lucy's place at the table, her gaze. This fact, and the action of the audience within the film, casts doubt on two theories of agency. Our attention as spectators, in the shots of series B, does not follow the visual attention of any depicted characters. These shots might perhaps be read as statements of the "interests" of characters, the nature of their social positions, but that is already a kind of commentary or interpretation that needs explanation. The actions of the men at the bar, the audience within the film, disprove the traditional rationale for editing stated by reference to an ideal spectator: as "placed" spectators we anticipate, not follow, the movements of their attention (2,3); the object of their attention is sometimes out of the frame we see (3b) and what they see is shown only from a view significantly different from any simply "accented" or "best view," indeed from a place they could not occupy; and sometimes (7b, 8) they have turned away, uninterested, but the screen doesn't go black. In general, an adequate account of the formal choices of the passage must be quite different from an account of the event as if it were staged for the natural attention of a spectator, depicted or real. To ask why the spectator sees in the way he does refers to a set of premises distinguishable from an account based on the attention of either a character or an ideal spectator. It refers to the concrete logic of the placement of the implied spectator and to the theory of presentation that accounts for the shaping of his reponse. Such an account makes the "position" of the spectator, the way in which he is implicated in the scene, the manner and location of his presence, his point of view, problematical.

It is this notion of the "position of the spectator" that I wish to clarify insofar as that notion illuminates the rhetorical strategies, particularly choice of setup (implying scale and framing) that depicts the action. In contemporary French film theory, particularly in the work of Comolli and Baudry, the notion of the "place" of the spectator is derived from the central position of the eye in perspective and photographic representation. By literally substituting the epistemological subject, the spectator, for the eye, in an argument about filmic representation, the filmic spectator is said to be "theological," and "centered" with respect to filmic images. Thus the theory of the filmic spectator is treated as if subject to the Derridean critique of center, presence, etc. French theory is wrong to enforce this analogy based on the position of the eye in photographic perspective, because what is optical and literal in that case corresponds only to the literal place of the spectator in the projection hall, and not at all to his figurative place in the film, nor to his place as subject to the rhetoric of the film, or reader or producer of the sense of the discourse. Outside a French ideological project which fails to discriminate literal and figurative space, the notion of "place" of the spectator, and of "center," is an altogether problematic notion whose significance and function in critical discussion has yet to be explicated.

The sequence from *Stagecoach* provides the terms in which the notion of the position of the spectator might be clarified, provided we distinguish, without yet expecting full clarification, the different senses of "position." A spectator is (a) seated physically in the space of the projection hall and (b) placed by the camera in a certain fictional position with respect to the depicted action; moreover (c), insofar as we see from what we might take to be the eye of a character, we are invited to occupy the place allied to the place he holds, in, for example, the social system; and finally (d), in another figurative sense of place, it is the only way that our response can be accounted for, that we can identify with a character's position in a certain situation.

In terms of the passage at hand, the question is then: how can I describe my "position" as spectator in identifying with the humiliated position of one of the depicted characters, Dallas, when my views of her belong to those of another, fictional character, Lucy, who is in the act of rejecting her? What is the spectator's "position" in identifying with Dallas in the role of the passive character? Dallas in averting her eyes from Lucy's in shot 6 accepts a view of herself in this encounter as "prostitute" and is shamed. However, in identifying with Dallas in the role of outcast, presumably the basis for the evocation of our sympathy and pity, our response as spectator is not one of shame, or anything even analogous. We do not suffer or repeat the humiliation. I understand Dallas's feeling but I am not so identified with her that I reenact it. One of the reasons for this restraint is that though I identify with Dallas's abject position of being seen as an unworthy object by someone whose judgment she accepts, I identify with her as the object of another's action. Indeed, in a remarkable strategy, I am asked to see Dallas through Lucy's eyes. That as spectator I am sharing Lucy's view and, just as important, her manner of viewing, is insisted on most emphatically by the dolly forward (4) and by disclosures effected by shot/countershot, thus placing me in a lively and implicated way in a position fully associated with Lucy's place at the head of the table.

Insofar as I identify with Dallas, it is not by repeating her shame, but by imagining myself in her position (situation). The early scenes of the film have carefully prepared us to believe that this exclusion is an unjust act. When the climactic moment arrives, our identification with Dallas as an object of view is simultaneously established as the ground for repudiating the one whose view we share and are implicated in. Though I share Lucy's literal geographical position of viewing at this moment in the film, I am not committed to her figurative point of view. I can, in other words, repudiate Lucy's view of or judgment on Dallas, without negating it as a view, in a way that Dallas herself, captive of the other's image, cannot. Because our feelings as spectators are not "analogous" to the interests and feelings of the characters, we are not bound to accept their views either of themselves or of others. Our "position" as spectator then is very different from the previous senses of "position"; it is defined neither in terms of orientation within the constructed geography of the fiction nor in terms of social position of the viewing character. On the contrary, our point of view on the sequence is tied more closely to our attitude of approval or disapproval and is very different from any literal viewing angle or character's point of view.

Identification asks us as spectators to be two places at once, where the camera is and "with" the depicted person—thus its double structure of viewer/viewed.

As a powerful emotional process it thus throws into question any account of the position of the spectator as centered at a single point or at the center of any simply optical system. Identification, this passage shows, necessarily has a double structure in the way it implicates the spectator in the position of both the one seeing and the one seen. This sequence, however, does establish a certain kind of "center" in the person of Lucy. Each of the shots is referred alternatingly to the scene before her eye or the scene of her body, but it is a "center" that functions as a principle of spatial legibility, and is associated with a literal point within the constructed space of the fiction. This center stands, though, as I have suggested, in a very complicated relation to our "position" as spectator. That is, the experience of the passage shows that our identification, in the Freudian sense of an emotional investment, is not with the center, either Lucy or the camera. Rather, if, cautiously, we can describe our figurative relation to a film in geographical terms, of "in," "there," "here," "distance" (and this sequence, as part of its strategy as a fiction, explicitly asks us to by presenting action to us from the literal view of a character), then as spectators, we might be said to formally occupy someone else's place, to be "in" the film, all the while being "outside" it in our seats. We can identify with a character and share her "point of view" even if the logic of the framing and selection of shots of the sequence deny that she has a view or a place within the society that the mise-en-scène depicts. There are significant differences between structures of shots, views, and identification: indeed, this sequence has shown, as a principle, that we do not "identify" with the camera but with the characters, and hence do not feel dispossessed by a change in shots. For a spectator, as distinct perhaps from a character, point of view is not definitively or summarily stated by any single shot or even set of shots from a given spatial location.

The way in which we as spectators are implicated in the action is as much a matter of our position with respect to the unfolding of those events in time as in their representation from a point in space. The effect of the mode of sequencing, the regular opposition of insiders and outsiders, is modulated in ways that shape the attitudes of the spectator/reader toward the action. This durational aspect emphasizes the process of inhabiting a text with its rhythms of involvement and disengagement in the action, and suggests that the spectator's position, his being in time, might appropriately be designated the "reader-in-the-text." His doubly structured position of identification with the features and force of the act of viewing and with the object in the field of vision are the visual terms of the dialectic of spectator placement. The rhetorical effort of shots 2–6 is directed to establishing the connection between shots and a "view," to endowing the position at the head of the table with a particular sense of a personalized glance. Shot 2, like 4, cannot at the moment it appears on the screen be associated with Lucy's glance. The shot/countershot sequencing discloses Lucy's location, and the turn of the head (3b) establishes a spatial relation between A and B; the animation, or gesture, implied by the dolly forward, combined with the emotional intensity implied by the choice of scale (5, 6) is read in terms of a personalized agency and clarified by what is shown in the visible field, Lucy's stern face (5). It is a rhetoric that unites the unfolding shots and gives meaning to this depicted glance—affront. It creates with the discrete shots (2, 3, 4) the impresseion of a coherent act of viewing, a mental unity whose meaning must make itself felt by the viewer at the moment of confrontation (5, 6) to effect the sense of repudiation of Lucy's view and the abjectness of Dallas. It takes time— a sequence of shots, in other words—to convey and specify the meaning of an act of viewing.

Reading, as this instance shows, is in part a process of retrospection, situating what could not be "placed" at the moment of its origin and bringing it forward to an interpretation of the meaning of the present moment. As such it has a complex relation to the action and to the spatial location of viewing. But the process of reading also depends on forgetting. After the climactic moment (5, 6) signaling Dallas's averting her eyes, a different temporal strategy is in effect. Lucy has looked away in 7b, and in subsequent shots from the head of the table, our attention is directed not so much to the act of showing, and what it means— unawareness (2), recognition (4), rejection (6)—but rather in 8 and 10 is directed at the action within the frame. The spectator's forgetting of what the dramatic impact depended on just a few moments before (here the personalized force that accompanied the act of showing the shot as a glance) is an effect of placement that depends on an experience of duration which occludes a previous significance and replaces it with another, a process we might call fading.

The modulation of the effects of fading is what, to take another example, is at issue in the interpretation of the shots of both series A and B. I have argued above that the setup and field of B correspond to Lucy's understanding of her place in the social system—to her point of view in the metaphorical sense. This interpretation corresponds to the general impression of the first six shots, taken together, as representing Lucy's manner of seeing. Shot 7 initiates a new line of dramatic action that poses the question of what Lucy will do now, and also begins a process not exactly of rereading, but a search for a new reading of the meaning of the setups. At this moment (7b), Lucy has turned her attention away from Dallas and is now turned toward Hatfield; and Ringo, previously occupied with his table etiquette (2, 4) is looking (8b, 10) intently out of frame right. The initial sense of the setup B is partially replaced by but coexists with another: that the depicted action in the frame is now being viewed by someone looking from outside the frame, namely Ringo, who is waiting expectantly for something to happen. The view from the left of the table is readable, not exactly as Lucy's self-conceptions as before, and not as a depiction of Ringo's glance, but as a representation of his interest in the scene, his point of view (again, in the metaphorical sense). Similarly, shots 8 and 10, showing Dallas and Ringo, no longer seem to characterize Lucy as the one doing the seeing, as in 4 and 6; they have become impersonal. The rigidity and opposition of setups A and B correspond to the rigidity of social position, but our reading of the changing secondary significances of the framing is an effect of fading that is responsive to acts of attention and seeing depicted within the frame.

Our anticipation, our waiting to see what will happen, is provoked and represented on the level of the action by the turning around of the audience-in-the-film (Billy and Doc Boone in 3b, 9). Our own feeling, because of our visual place to the left of the table, is closer to Ringo's than to theirs. Certainly the distention and delay of the climactic moment by a virtual repetition (9, 11a) of those shots of a hesitating Lucy (unnecessary for simple exposition) produce a sense of our temporal identification with Ringo (8b, 10), necessary for the success of the moment as drama—its uncertainty and resolution. The drama depends for the lesson it demonstrates not on Lucy's self-regard before a general public as previously, but on being watched by the parties to be affected. It is Ringo's increasingly involved presence as an authority for a view, even though he mistakenly thinks he is being ostracized, that makes the absent place left by Lucy's departure so evidently intended as a lesson in manners, so accusingly empty. By these strategies and effects of duration—retrospection, fading, delay, and anticipation—the reading of emphasis on the act of showing or what is shown, the significance of angle and framing, can be modulated. Together these means define features of a rhetoric which, though different from the placement effected by visual structures, also locate and implicate the reader/spectator in the text.

The spectator's place, the locus around which the spatiotemporal structures of presentation are organized, is a construction of the text which is ultimately the product of the narrator's disposition toward the tale. Such structures, which in shaping and presenting the action prompt a manner and indeed a path of reading, convey and are closely allied to the guiding moral commentary of the film. In this sequence the author has effaced himself, as in other instances of indirect discourse, for the sake of the characters and the action. Certainly he is nowhere visible in the same manner as the characters. Rather he is visible only through the materialization of the scene and in certain masked traces of his action. The indirect presence to his audience that the narrator enacts, the particular form of self-effacement, could be described as the masked displacement of his narrative authority as the producer of imagery from himself to the agency of his characters. That is, the film makes it appear as though it were the depicted characters to whom the authority for the presentation of shots can be referred—most evidently in the case of a depiction of a glance, but also, in more complex fashion, in the reading of shots as depictions of a "state of mind." The explanation of the presence of the imagery is referred by the film not to the originating authority who stands invisible, behind the action, but to his masks within the depicted space.

In accord with the narrator's efforts to direct attention away from his own activity, to mask and displace it, the narrator of *Stagecoach* has a visible persona,

Lucy, perform a significant formal function in the narration: to constitute and to make legible and continuous the depicted space, by referring shots on the screen alternately to the authority of her eye or the place of her body. The literal place of the spectator in the projection hall, where in a sense all the shots are directed, is a "center" that has a figurative correspondence on the level of the discourse in the "place" that Lucy occupies in the depicted space. But because Lucy performs her integrative function not exactly by her being at a place, the head of the table, but by enacting a kind of central consciousness that corresponds to a social and formal role, a role which for narrative purposes can be exploited by shifting the views representing the manner of her presence, the notion of "center" might be thought of not as a geographical place but as a structure or function. As such, this locus makes it possible for the reader himself to occupy that role and himself to make the depicted space coherent and readable. For the spectator, the "center" is not just a point either in the projection hall or in the depicted geography, but is the result of the impression produced by the functioning of the narrative and of his being able to fictionally occupy the absent place.

Locating this function, "inscribing" the spectator's place on the level of the depicted action, has the effect of making the story seem to tell itself by reference not to an outside author but to a continuously visible, internal narrative authority. This governing strategy, of seeming to internalize the source of the exposition in characters, and thus of directing the spectator's attention to the depicted action, is supported by other features of the style: shot/countershot, matching of glances, continuity.

Consequently, the place of the spectator in his relation to the narrator is established by, though not limited to, identifications with characters and the views they have of each other. More specifically his "place" is defined through the variable force of identification with the one viewing and the one viewed— as illustrated in the encounter between Lucy and Dallas. Though the spectator may be placed in the "center" by the formal function Lucy performs, he is not committed to her view of things. On the contrary, in the context of the film, that view is instantly regarded as insupportable. Our response to Dallas supports the sense that the spectator's figurative position is not stated by a description of where the camera is in the geography of the scene. On the contrary, though the spectator's position is closely tied to the fortunes and views of characters, our analysis suggests that identification, in the original sense of an emotional bond, need not be with the character whose view he shares, even less with the disembodied camera. Evidently, a spectator is several places at once—with the fictional viewer, with the viewed, and at the same time in a position to evaluate and respond to the claims of each. This fact suggests that like the dreamer, the filmic spectator is a plural subject: in his reading he is and is not himself.

In a film, imagining ourselves in a character's place by identification, in respect to the actual situation, is a different process, indeed a different order of fiction than taking a shot as originating from a certain point within the fictional geography. The relation though between the literal space of the projection hall and the depicted space of the film image is continuously problematic for a definition of the "thatness" of the screen and for an account of the place of the spectator. If a discourse carries a certain impression of reality, it is an effect not exactly of the image but rather of the way the image is placed by the narrative or argument. My relation to an image on the screen is literal because it can be taken as being directed to a physical point, my seat (changing that seat doesn't alter my viewing angle on the action), as though I were the fixed origin of the view. On the other hand, the image can also be taken as originating from a point in a different kind of space, recognizably different in terms of habitability from that of the projection hall: it is from a fictional and changeable place implied by an origin contained in the image. The filmic image thus implies the ambiguity of a double origin—both from my literal place as spectator and from the place where the camera is within the imaginative space.

One structural result of the ambiguous relation of literal and depicted space and of the seemingly contradictory efforts of the text to both place and displace the spectator is the prohibition against the "meeting," though no such act is literally possible, of actor's and spectator's glances, a prohibition that is an integral feature of the sequence as a "specular text." In its effect on the spectator, the prohibition defines the different spaces he simultaneously inhabits before the screen. By denying his presence in one sense, the prohibition establishes a boundary at the screen that underscores the fact that the spectator can have no actual physical exchange with the depicted world, that he can do nothing relevant to change the course of the action. It places him irretrievably outside the action.

At the same time, the prohibition is the initial premise of a narrative system for the representation of fictional space and the means of introducing the spectator imaginatively into it. The prohibition effects this construction and engagement by creating an obliquity between our angle of viewing and that of the characters which works to make differences of angle and scale readable as representations of different points of view. As such it plays a central part in our process of identification or nonidentification with the camera and depicted characters. It provides the author an ensemble of narrative forms—an imaginary currency consisting of temporary exchange, substitution, and identification—that enables us, fictionally, to take the place of another, to inhabit the text as a reader.

Establishing agency by either the authority of character or of spectator corresponds in its alternative rhetorical forms to the articulation of the ambiguity of the double origin of the image. In a particular text it is the narration that establishes and arbitrates the spectator's placement between these two spaces. *Stagecoach* makes definite efforts to imply that not only is the spectator not there, not present in his seat, but that the film-object originates from an authority within the fictional space. The narration seems to insist that the film is a free-standing entity which a spectator, irrelevant finally to its construction, could only look on from the outside. On the other hand, in the ways that I have described, the film is directed in all its structures of presentation toward the narrator's construction of a commentary on the story and toward placing the spectator at a certain "angle" to it. The film has tried not just to direct the attention but to place the eye of the spectator inside the fictional space, to make his presence integral and constitutive of the structure of views. The explanation the film seems to give of the action of narrative authority is a denial of the existence of a narrator different from character and an affirmation of the dominating role of fictional space. It is a spatial mode not determined by the ontology of the image as such but is in the last instance an effect of the narration.

Masking and displacement of narrative authority are thus integral to establishing the sense of the spectator "in" the text, and the prohibition to establishing the film as an independent fiction, different from dream in being the product of another, that can nevertheless be in-habited. Fascination by identification with character is a way the integrity of fictional space is validated, and because the spectator occupies a fictional role, is a way too that the film can efface the spectator's consciousness of his position. As a production of the spectator's reading, the sense of reality that the film enacts, the "impression of the real," protects the account the text seems to give of the absent narrator.

The cumulative effect of the narrator's strategy of placement of the spectator from moment to moment is his introduction into what might be called the moral order of the text. That is, the presentational structures which shape the action both convey a point of view and define the course of the reading, and are fundamental to the exposition of moral ideas—specifically a discussion about the relation of insiders to outsiders. The effect of the distinction between pure and impure is the point of the sequence, though as a theme it is just a part of the total exposition. The sequence thus assists in the construction of attitudes toward law and custom and to those who live outside their strictures. It introduces the question of the exercise of social and customary (as distinguished from legal) authority. To the extent we identify with Ringo and Dallas—and the film continuously invites us to by providing multiple grounds: the couple's bravery, competence, and sincerity—the conventional order and the morality it enforces is put in doubt. Without offering a full interpretation of the theme of *Stagecoach,* which would I think be connected with the unorthodox nature of their love and the issue of Ringo's revenge and final exemption from the law by the sheriff, I can still characterize the spectator's position at this particular moment in the film.

It amounts to this: that though we see the action from Lucy's eyes and are invited by a set of structures and strategies to experience the force and character of that view, we are put in the position finally of having to reject it as a view that is right or that we could be committed to. The sequence engages us on this point through effecting an identification with a situation in which the outsider is wronged and thus that challenges Lucy's position as the agent of an intolerant authority. We are asked, by the manner in which we must read, by the posture we must adopt, to repudiate Lucy's view, to see behind the moral convention that supports intolerance, to break out of a role that may be confining us. As such, the importance of the sequence in the entire film is the way it allies us emotionally with the interests and fortunes of the outsiders as against social custom, an identification and theme that, modulated in subsequent events, continues to the end of the film. The passage, lifted out of its context, but drawing on dispositions established in previous sequences, is an illustration of the process of constructing a spectator's attitudes in the film as a whole through the control of point of view. Whether or not the western genre can in general be characterized by a certain mode of identification, as, for example, in the disposition or wish to see the right done, and whether *Stagecoach* has a particularly significant place in the history of the genre by virtue of its treatment of outsiders, is an open question. In any case the reader's position is constituted by a set of views, identifications, and judgments that establish his place in the moral order of the text.

Like the absent narrator who discloses himself and makes his judgments from a position inseparable from the sequence of depicted events that constitute the narrative, the spectator, in following the story, in being subject of and to the spatial and temporal placement and effects of exposition, is in the process of realizing an identity we have called his position. Following the trajectory of identifications that establishes the structure of values of a text, "reading" as a temporal process could be said to continuously reconstruct the place of the narrator and his implied commentary on the scene. In this light, reading, as distinct from interpretation, might be characterized as a guided and prompted performance that (to the extent a text allows it, and I believe *Stagecoach* does) recreates the point of view enacted in a scene. As a correlative of narration, reading could be said to be the process of reenactment by fictionally occupying the place of the narrator.

Certain formal features of the imagery—framing, sequencing, the prohibition, the "invisibility" of the narrator—I have suggested, can be explained as the ensemble of ways authority implicitly positions the spectator/reader. As a method, this analysis of *Stagecoach* points to a largely unexplored body of critical problems associated with describing and accounting for narrative and rhetorical signifying structures. The "specular text" and the allied critical concepts of "authority," "reading," "point of view," and "position of the spectator," however provisional, might be taken then as a methological initiative for a semiotic study of filmic texts.

Selected Bibliography

Baudry, Jean-Louis. "Ideological Effects of the Basic Cinematographic Apparatus." *Film Quarterly* (Winter 1974–75). [Included in this anthology—ED.]

Cavell, Stanley. *The World Viewed* (New York: Viking Press, 1971).

Comolli, Jean-Louis. "Technique et Idéologie: Camera, Perspective, Profondeur de Champ." *Cahiers du Cinéma* (May–June 1971). [Other installments from this series are included in this anthology—ED.]

Dayan, Daniel. "The Tutor Code of Classical Cinema." *Film Quarterly* (Fall 1974). [Cf. Kaja Silverman, "Suture," in this anthology–ED.]

Guzzetti, Alfred. "Narrative and the Film Image." *New Literary History* (Winter 1975).

Lubbock, Percy. *The Craft of Fiction*. (New York: Viking Press, 1957).

[6]

Peter Wollen

Godard and Counter-Cinema:
Vent d'Est

More and more radically Godard has developed a counter-cinema whose values are counterposed to those of orthodox cinema. I want simply to write some notes about the main features of this counter-cinema. My approach is to take seven of the values of the old cinema, Hollywood-Mosfilm as Godard would put it, and contrast these with their (revolutionary, materialist) counterparts and contraries. In a sense, the seven deadly sins of the cinema against the seven cardinal virtues. They can be set out schematically as follows:

Narrative transitivity	Narrative intransitivity
Identification	Estrangement
Transparency	Foregrounding
Single diegesis	Multiple diegesis
Closure	Aperture
Pleasure	Un-pleasure
Fiction	Reality

Obviously, these somewhat cryptic headings need further commentary. First, however, I should say that my overall argument is that Godard was right to break with Hollywood cinema and to set up his counter-cinema and, for this alone, he is the most important director working today. Nevertheless, I think there are various confusions in his strategy, which blunt its edges and even, at times, tend to nullify it—mainly, these concern his confusion over the series of terms: fiction/mystification/ideology/lies/deception/illusion/representation. At the end of these notes, I shall touch on some of my disagreements. First, some remarks on the main topics.

Published in *Afterimage* (1972), no. 4; and reprinted here by permission of the author.

1. Narrative Transitivity v. Narrative Intransitivity. (One thing following another v. gaps and interruptions, episodic construction, undigested digression.)

By narrative transitivity, I mean a sequence of events in which each unit (each function that changes the course of the narrative) follows the one preceding it according to a chain of causation. In the Hollywood cinema, this chain is usually psychological and is made up, roughly speaking, of a series of coherent motivations. The beginning of the film starts with establishment, which sets up the basic dramatic situation—usually an equilibrium, which is then disturbed. A kind of chain reaction then follows, until at the end a new equilibrium is restored.

Godard began to break with this tradition very early. He did this, at first, in two ways, both drawn from literature. He borrowed the idea of separate chapters, which enabled him to introduce interruptions into the narrative, and he borrowed from the picaresque novel. The picaresque is pseudo-autobiographical form which for tight plot construction substitutes a random and unconnected series of incidents, supposed to represent the variety and ups-and-downs of real life. (The hero is typically marginal to society, a rogue-errant, often an orphan, in any case without family ties, thrown hither and thither by the twists and turns of fortune.)

By the time he arrives at *Vent d'Est,* Godard has practically destroyed all narrative transitivity. Digressions which, in earlier films, represented interruptions to the narrative have hypertrophied until they dominate the film entirely. The basic story, as much of it as remains, does not have any recognizable sequence but is more like a series of intermittent flashes. Sometimes it seems to be following a definite order in time, but sometimes not. The constructive principle of the film is rhetorical, rather than narrative, in the sense that it sets out the disposition of an argument, point by point, in a sequence of 1–7, which is then repeated, with a subsidiary sequence of theory A and B. There are also various figures of amplification and digression within this structure.

There are a number of reasons why Godard has broken with narrative transitivity. Perhaps the most important is that he can disrupt the emotional spell of the narrative and thus force the spectator, by interrupting the narrative flow, to reconcentrate and refocus his attention. (Of course, his attention may get lost altogether.) Godard's cinema, broadly speaking, is within the modern tradition established by Brecht and Artaud, in their different ways, suspicious of the power of the arts—and the cinema, above all—to "capture" its audience without apparently making it think, or changing it.

2. Identification v. Estrangement. (Empathy, emotional involvement with a character v. direct address, multiple and divided characters, commentary.)

Identification is a well-known mechanism though, of course, in the cinema there are various special features which mark cinematic identification off as a

distinct phenomenon. In the first place, there is the possibility of double identification with the star and/or with the character. Second, the identification can
only take place in a situation of suspended belief. Third, there are spatial and
temporal limits either to the identification or, at any rate, to the presence of the
imago. (In some respects, cinematic identification is similar to transference in
analysis, though this analogy should not be taken too far.)

Again, the breakdown of identification begins early in Godard's films and
then develops unevenly after that, until it reaches a new level with *Le Gai Savoir.*
Early devices include nonmatching of voice to character, introduction of "real
people" into the fiction, characters addressing the audience directly. All these
devices are also used in *Vent d'Est,* which takes especially far the device of
allowing voices to float off from characters into a discourse of their own on the
soundtrack, using the same voice for different characters, different voices for
the same character. It also introduces the "real life" company into the film itself
and, in a rather complicated figure, introduces Gian-Maria Volonte, not simply
as an actor (Godard shows the actors being made up) but also as intervening in
the process of "image-building." As well as this, there is a long and extremely
effective direct address sequence in which the audience is described—somewhat
pejoratively—from the screen and invited into the world of representation.

It is hardly necessary, after the work of Brecht, to comment on the purpose
of estrangement effects of this kind. Clearly, too, they are closely related to the
breakup of narrative transitivity. It is impossible to maintain "motivational"
coherence when characters themselves are incoherent, fissured, interrupted,
multiple, and self-critical. Similarly, the ruse of direct address breaks not only
the fantasy identification but also the narrative surface. It raises directly the
question "What is this film for?" superimposed on the orthodox narrative
questions "Why did that happen?" and "What is going to happen next?" Any
form of cinema which aims to establish a dynamic relationship between filmmaker and spectator naturally has to consider the problem of what is technically
the register of discourse, the content of the enunciation, as well as its designation,
the content of the enunciate.

3. Transparency v. Foregrounding. ("Language wants to be overlooked"—
Siertsema v. making the mechanics of the film/text visible and explicit.)

Traditional cinema is in the direct line of descent from the Renaissance discovery
of perspective and reformulation of the art of painting, expressed most clearly
by Alberti, as providing a window on the world. The camera, of course, is
simply the technological means toward achieving a perfect perspective construction. After the Renaissance the painting ceased to be a text which could be"read,"
as the iconographic imagery and ideographic space of pre-Renaissance painting
were gradually rejected and replaced by the concept of pure representation. The
"language" of painting became simply the instrument by which representation

of the world was achieved. A similar tendency can be seen at work with attitudes to verbal language. From the seventeenth century onward, language was increasingly seen as an instrument which should efface itself in the performance of its task—the conveyance of meaning. Meaning, in its turn, was regarded as representation of the world.

In his early films Godard introduced the cinema as a topic in his narrative—the "Lumière" sequence in *Les Carabiniers,* the film within a film in *Le Mépris.* But it was not until his contribution to *Loin du Vietnam* that the decisive step was taken, when he simply showed the camera on screen. In the post-1968 films the process of production is systematically highlighted. In *Vent d'Est* this shows itself not simply in taking the camera behind the scenes, as it were, but also in altering the actual film itself: thus the whole worker's control sequence is shown with the film marked and scratched, the first time that this has happened in Godard's work. In previous films, he had not gone further that using special film stock (*Les Carabiniers*) or printing sequences in negative (*Les Carabiniers, Alphaville*).

At first sight, it looks as if the decision to scratch the surface of the film brings Godard into line with other avant-garde filmmakers, in the American "underground" especially. However, this is not really the case. In the case of the American filmmakers marking the film is best seen alongside developments in painting that have dominated, particularly in the U.S.A., in recent years. Broadly speaking, this involves a reduction of film to its "optical" substrate. Noise is amplified until, instead of being marginal to the film, it becomes its principal content. It may then be structured according to some calculus or algorithm, or submitted to random coding. Just as, in painting, the canvas is foregrounded, so in cinema, the film is foregrounded.

Godard, however, is not interested in this kind of "designification" of the image by foregrounding "noise" and then introducing a new constructive principle appropriate to this. What he seems to be doing is looking for a way of expressing negation. It is well known that negation is the founding principle of verbal language, which marks it off both from animal signal systems and from other kinds of human discourse, such as images. However, once the decision is made to consider a film as a process of writing in images, rather than a representation of the world, then it becomes possible to conceive of scratching the film as an erasure, a virtual negation. Evidently the use of marks as erasures, crossing out an image, is quite different from using them as deliberate noise or to foreground the optical substrate. It presupposes a different concept of "film writing" and "film reading."

Some years ago, Astruc, in a famous article, wrote about *le caméra-stylo.* His concept of writing—*écriture*—was closer to the idea of style. Godard, like Eisenstein before him, is more concerned with "image-building" as a kind of picto-graphy, in which images are liberated from their role as elements of representation and given a semantic function within a genuine iconic code, something like the baroque code of emblems. The sequences in which the image of Stalin is discussed are not simply—or even principally—about Stalin's politics as much as they are about the problem of finding an image to signify "repression." In fact, the whole project of writing in images must involve a high degree of foregrounding, because the construction of an adequate code can only take place if it is glossed and commented upon in the process of construction. Otherwise, it would remain a purely private language.

4. Single Diegesis v. Multiple Diegesis. (A unitary homogeneous world v. heterogeneous worlds. Rupture between different codes and different channels.)

In Hollywood films, everything shown belongs to the same world, and complex articulations within that world—such as flashbacks—are carefully signaled and located. The dominant aesthetic is a kind of liberalized classicism. The rigid constraints of the dramatic unities have been relaxed, but mainly because they were over-strict and limiting, whereas the basic principle remains unshaken. The world represented on the cinema must be coherent and integrated, though it need not observe compulsory, statutory constraints. Time and space must follow a consistent order. Traditionally, only one form of multiple diegesis is allowed— the play within a play—whereby the second, discontinuous diegetic space is embedded or bracketed within the first. It should be added that there are some exemplary cases of transgression of single diegesis within literature, such as Hoffmann's *Life of Tomcat Murr,* which consists of Tomcat Murr's life—the primary diegesis—interleaved at random with pages from another text—the life of Kreisler—supposedly bound into the book by mistake by the bookbinder. The pages from the secondary diegesis begin and end in the middle of sentences and are in the wrong order, with some missing. A novel like Sterne's *Tristram Shandy,* however, simply embeds a number of different diegesis on the play-within-a-play model. (Of course, by recursion this principle can be taken to the breaking point, as Borges has often pointed out.)

Godard uses film-within-a-film devices in a number of his early works. At the same time the primary diegesis begins to develop acute fissures and stresses. In *Le Mépris,* for example, there is not only a film-within-a-film, but many of the principal characters speak different languages and can only communicate with each other through an interpreter (an effect entirely lost in some dubbed versions, which have to give the interpreter meaningless remarks to speak). The first radical break with single diegesis, however, comes with *Weekend,* when characters from different epochs and from fiction are interpolated into the main narrative: Saint-Just, Balsamo, Emily Brontë. Instead of a single narrative world, there is an interlocking and interweaving of a plurality of worlds.

At the same time that Godard breaks down the structure of the single diegesis, he also attacks the structure of the single, unitary code that expressed it. Not only do different characters speak different languages, but different parts of the film do too. Most strikingly, there is a rupture between sound track and images: indeed, the elaboration of this rupture dominates both *Le Gai Savoir* and *Pravda*. The text becomes a composite structure, like that of a medieval macaronic poem, using different codes and semantic systems. Moreover, these are not simply different but also often contradictory. *Vent d'Est,* for instance, presents alternative ways of making a film (the Glauber Rocha sequence) only to reject them. It is one of the assumptions of contemporary linguistics that a language has a single, unitary semantic component, just as it has a single syntax. In fact, this is surely not the case. The semantic component of a language is composite and contradictory, permitting understanding on one level, misunderstanding on another. Godard systematically explores the areas of misunderstanding.

5. Closure v. Aperture. (A self-contained object, harmonized within its own bounds v. open-endedness, overspill, intertextuality—allusion, quotation, and parody).

It has often been pointed out that in recent years, the cinema has become "self-conscious" in contrast to the "innocent" days of Hollywood. In itself, however, self-consciousness is quite compatible with closure. There is a use of quotation and allusion that simply operates to provide a kind of "surplus" of meaning, as the scholastics used to say, a bonus for those who catch the allusion. The notorious "Tell me lies" sequence in *Le Petit Soldat,* borrowed from *Johnny Guitar,* is of this kind: it does not make much difference whether you recognize it or not and, even if you do, it has no effect on the meaning of the sequence. Or else quotation can be simply a sign of eclecticism, primarily a stylistic rather than semantic feature. Or, as with Makavejev's use of quotation, the objective may be to impose a new meaning on material by inserting it into a new context: a form of irony.

Godard, however, uses quotation in a much more radical manner. Indeed, his fondness for quotation has always been one of the distinguishing characteristics of his films. At the beginning of his career, Godard used to give instructions to the cameraman almost entirely in terms of shots from previous films, and at a more explicit level, there are endless direct quotes, both from films and from painting and literature. Whole films contain obvious elements of pastiche and parody: *Une Femme est une Femme* is obviously derivative from the Hollywood musical, *Les Carabiniers* from Rosselini, *Le Mépris* is "Hawks and Hitchcock shot in the manner of Antonioni". . . it would be possible to go on endlessly.

However, as Godard's work developed, these quotations and allusions, instead of being a mark of eclecticism, began to take on an autonomy of their own, as structural and significant features within the films. It becomes more and more impossible to understand whole sequences and even whole films without a degree of familiarity with the quotations and allusions which structure them. What seemed at first to be a kind of jackdaw mentality, a personality trait of

Godard himself, begins to harden into a genuine polyphony, in which Godard's own voice is drowned out and obliterated behind that of the authors quoted. The film can no longer be seen as a discourse with a single subject, the film-maker/auteur. Just as there are a multiplicity of narrative worlds, so too there are a multiplicity of speaking voices.

Again, this takes us back to the period before the rise of the novel, the representational painting, to the epoch of the battle of the books, the logomachia. Perhaps the author who comes most to mind is Rabelais, with his endless counterposition of quotations, his parodies, his citation of authorities. The text/film can only be understood as an arena, a meeting place in which different discourses encounter each other and struggle for supremacy. Moreover, these discourses take on an independent life of their own. Instead of each being corked up in its bottle with its author's name on it as a label, the discourses escape, like genies, are let out to intermingle and quarrel.

In this sense, Godard is like Ezra Pound or James Joyce, who, in the same way, no longer insist on speaking to us in their own words but can be seen more as ventriloquist's dummies, through whom are speaking—or rather being writ-ten—palimpsests, multiple *Niederschriften* (Freud's word) in which meaning can no longer be said to express the intention of the author or to be a representation of the world, but must like the discourse of the unconscious be understood by a different kind of decipherment. In orthodox logic and linguistics, context is only important as an arbiter between alternative meanings (amphibologies, as they are called in logic). In Godard's films, the opposite process is at work: the juxtaposition and recontextualization of discourses leads not to a separating-out of meanings but to a confrontation.

6. Pleasure v. Unpleasure. (Entertainment, aiming to satisfy the spectator, v. provocation, aiming to dissatisfy and hence change the spectator.)

The attack on "entertainment" cinema is part of a broader attack on the whole of "consumer society." Cinema is conceived of as a drug that lulls and mollifies the militancy of the masses, by bribing them with pleasurable dreams, thus distracting them from the stern tasks which are their true destiny. It is hardly necessary to insist on the asceticism and Puritanism—repressiveness—of this conception that unflinchingly seeks to put the reality principle in command over the pleasure principle. It is true that the short-term (cinematic) dream is some-times denounced in the name of a long-term (millenarian) dream and short-term (false, illusory, deceptive) satisfactions contrasted with long-term (real, genuine, authentic) satisfactions, but this is exactly the kind of argument which is used to explain the accumulation of capital in a capitalist society by the saving principle and postponement of consumption.

Brecht was careful never to turn his back on entertainment and, indeed, he even quotes Horace in favor of pleasure as the purpose of the arts, combined, of course, with instruction. This is not to say that a revolutionary cinema should distract its spectators from realities, but that unless a revolution is desired (which means nothing less than coinciding with and embodying collective fantasies) it will never take place. The reality principle only works together with the pleasure principle when survival itself is at stake, and though this may evidently be the case in a revolutionary situation, it is not so in the advanced capitalist countries today. In a situation in which survival is—at least relatively—nonproblematic, the pleasure principle and the reality principle are antagonistic, and since the reality principle is fundamentally adaptive, it is from the pleasure principle that change must stem. This means that desire and its representation in fantasy, far from being necessary enemies of revolutionary politics—and its cinematic auxiliary—are necessary conditions.

The problem, of course, concerns the nature of the fantasies on the one hand, and the way in which they are presented in the text/film on the other hand, the way in which fantasy scenarios are related to ideologies and beliefs and to scientific analysis. A revolutionary cinema has to operate at different levels— fantasy, ideology, science—and the articulation of these levels, which involve different modes of discourse and different positions of the subject, is a complicated matter.

In *Vent d'Est* the "struggle against the bourgeois notion of representation" certainly does not rule out the presence of fantasy: fantasy of shooting the union delegate, fantasies of killing shoppers in a supermarket. Indeed, as long as there are images at all, it is impossible to eliminate fantasy. But the fantasies are almost entirely sadomasochistic in content, and this same fantasy content also seems to govern the relationship between filmmaker and spectator, rather on the lines of the relationship between the flute player in the film and his audience. A great many of the devices Godard uses are designed to produce a collective working relationship between filmmaker and audience, in which the spectator can collaborate in the production/consumption of meaning. But Godard's view of collective work is conceived of in very imprecise terms. "Criticism" consists of insults and interrogation. The fantasy content of the film is not articulated correctly with the ideology or political theory. This, in turn, seems to spring from a suspicion of the need for fantasy at all, except perhaps in the sadomasochistic form of prevocation.

7. Fiction v. Reality. (Actors wearing make-up, acting a story v. real life, the breakdown of representation, truth.)

Godard's dissatisfaction with fiction cinema begins very early. Already in *Vivre sa Vie* nonfiction is introduced—the chapter on the economics and sociology of prostitution. There is almost no costume drama in Godard's career, until— ironically enough—*Vent d'Est*. Even within the framework of fiction, he has stuck to contemporary life. His science fiction films *(Alphaville, Anticipation)* have all been set in a kind of future-in-the-present, without any paraphernalia of special effects or sets.

As with all the features I have described, the retreat from (and eventually attack on) fiction has proceeded unevenly through Godard's career, coming forward strongly in, for instance, *Deux ou Trois Choses,* then receding again. Especially since May 1968, the attack on fiction has been given a political rationale (fiction = mystification = bourgeois ideology), but at the beginning, it is much more closely connected with Godard's fascination (Cartesian, rather than Marxist) with the misleading and dissembling nature of appearances, the impossibility of reading an essence from a phenomenal surface, of seeing a soul through and within a body or telling a lie from a truth. At times Godard seems almost to adopt a kind of radical Romanticism, which sees silence (lovers' silence, killers' silence) as the only true communication, when reality and representation, essence and appearance, irreducibly concide: the moment of truth.

Obviously, too, Godard's attitude to fiction is linked with his attitude to acting. This comes out most clearly in *Une Femme Mariée,* when the actor is interrogated about his true self, his relationship to his roles. Godard is obsessed with the problem of true speech, lying speech, and theatrical speech. (In a sense, these three kinds of speech, seen first in purely personal terms, are eventually policitized and given a class content. The bourgeoisie lie, the revisionists lie, though they should speak the truth, the revolutionaries speak the truth, or, rather stammer an approach to the truth.) Godard has long shown a horror of acting, based originally on a "logocentric" antipathy to anybody who speaks someone else's words, ironic in the circumstances. Eventually, Godard seems to have reformulated his attitude so that actors are distrusted for speaking other people's words as if they were their own. This accompanies his growing recognition that nobody ever speaks in his own words, hence the impossibility of genuine dialogue and the reduction of dialogue to reciprocal—or often unilateral—interviewing. In *Vent d'Est* there is almost no dialogue at all (only a number of variants of monologue) and this must relate to the caricature of collective work Godard puts forward.

Interviewing is, of course, the purest form of linguistic demand, and the demand Godard makes is for the truth. Yet it never seems to be forthcoming, not surprisingly, since it cannot be produced on demand. It is as if Godard has a lingering hope that if people could find their own words, they might produce it miraculously in our presence, but if not, then it has to be looked for in books, which are the residues of real words. This kind of problematic has been tormenting Godard throughout his cinematic career. In *A Bout de Souffle,* for instance, there is the central contrast between Michel Poiccard/Laszlo Kovacs— an honest impostor—and Patricia, whose mania for honesty reveals her in the end as a deceiver.

The early films tend to explore this kind of problem as one between different levels, but in the post-1968 films, there seems to have been a kind of flattening out, so that fiction = acting = lying = deception = representation = illusion = mystification = ideology. In fact, as anybody reflecting on Godard's earlier films must surely know, these are all very different categories. Ideology, for instance, does not depend primarily on lies. It depends on the acceptance of common values and interests. Similarly mystification is different from deception: a priest does not deceive his congregation about the miracle of the mass, in the same way that a conjurer deceives his audience, by hiding something from them. Again, the cinema is a form of representation, but this is not the same as illusion or *trompe l'oeil*. It is only possible to obliterate these distinctions by defining each of them simply in terms of their departure from truth.

The cinema cannot show the truth, or reveal it, because the truth is not out there in the real world, waiting to be photographed. What the cinema can do is produce meanings, and meanings can only be plotted not in relation to some abstract yardstick or criterion of truth but in relation to other meanings. This is why Godard's objective of producing a countercinema is the right objective. But he is mistaken if he thinks that such a countercinema can have an absolute existence. It can only exist in relation to the rest of the cinema. Its function is to struggle against the fantasies, ideologies, and aesthetic devices of one cinema with its own antagonistic fantasies, ideologies, and aesthetic devices. In some respects this may bring it closer—or seem to bring it closer—to the cinema it opposes than *Vent d'Est* would suggest. *Vent d'Est* is a pioneering film, an avant-garde film, an extremely important film. It is the starting point for work on a revolutionary cinema. But it is not that revolutionary cinema itself.

Kristin Thompson
The Concept of Cinematic Excess

"No, no, I'll take no less, than all in full excess." —*Handel's Semele*

"Analytically there is something ridiculous about it." —*Roland Barthes*[1]

Recently certain writers have moved away from the traditional concept of criticism as an activity designed purely to explain the narratively functional aspects of the work. Following essentially, I believe, in the direction opened by the Russian Formalists, these critics have suggested that films can be seen as a struggle of opposing forces. Some of these forces strive to unify the work, to hold it together sufficiently that we may perceive and follow its structures. Outside any such structures lie those aspects of the work which are not contained by its unifying forces—the "excess." The term is used by Stephen Heath in his essay "Film and System: Terms of Analysis"; there he asserts:

Just as narrative never exhausts the image, homogeneity is always an *effect* of the film and not the filmic system, which is precisely the production of that homogeneity. Homogeneity is haunted by the material practice it represses and the tropes of that repression, the forms of continuity, provoke within the texture of the film the figures—the edging, the margin—of the loss by which it moves; permanent battle for the resolution of that loss on which, however, it structurally depends, mediation between image and discourse, narrative can never contain the whole film which permanently exceeds its

This article was published as chapter 9 from Kristin Thompson, *Eisenstein's "Ivan the Terrible": A Neoformalist Analysis,* copyright © 1981 by Princeton University Press. The chapter was revised from an earlier article in *Ciné-Tracts* (Summer 1977), no. 2 and is reprinted by permission of Princeton University Press. The earlier article is here reprinted.

fictions. "Filmic system," therefore, always means at least this: the "system" of the film in so far as the film is the organization of a homogeneity *and* the material outside inscribed in the operation of that oganization as its contradiction.[2]

"Homogeneity" is here the unifying effect I have mentioned. Heath suggest that the material of the image in film creates a play which goes beyond this unity. A film depends on materiality for its existence; out of image and sound it creates its structures, but it can never make all the physical elements of the film part of its set of smooth perceptual cues. The critic concentrates neither wholly upon the coherent elements nor wholly upon the excess; he/she deals with the tensions between them. I am using the Russian Formalist definition of narrative as an interplay between plot and story; plot is the actual presentation of events in the film, while story is the mental reconstruction by the spectator of these events in their "real," chronological order (partly on the basis of codes of cause and effect). Heath is talking about the classical Hollywood film, which typically strives to minimize excess by a thoroughgoing motivation. Other films outside this tradition do not always try to provide an apparent motivation for everything in the film, and thus they leave their potentially excessive elements more noticeable.

Roland Barthes' essay "The Third Meaning" ("Le Troisième sens") lays out a similar idea that the materiality of the image goes beyond the narrative structures of unity in a film. The choice of the term "meaning" is a misleading one, since these elements of the work are precisely those which do not participate in the creation of narrative or symbolic meaning; Barthes himself calls it "the obtuse meaning," and says: "it does not even indicate an *elsewhere* of meaning . . . it rather frustrates meaning–subverting not the content but the entire practice of meaning."[3] For this reason I prefer to use Heath's term, "excess," rather than Barthes'.

But Barthes is ultimately clearer as to what he considers part of this filmic excess. Heath's analysis of *Touch of Evil* provides examples that tend to confuse his term rather than clarify it. He calls the scenes in Tanya's place in that film excess because they "have no narrative function,"[4] even though this is clearly not the case. These scenes provide *relatively* little causal material to forward the proairetic, in comparison with the other scenes of the film. They do, however, contain a considerable amount of semic material about Hank Quinlan and hence provide motivation for his behavior in the rest of the film; Tanya's place provides the connection between Quinlan and Menzies that allows the latter to engage Quinlan in the final incriminating conversation. These are not the only narrative functions these scenes play, but they will serve to indicate that Heath has chosen a rather easy way out of the problem by dismissing whole scenes as excess when they are simply different from more causally dense portions of the narrative. Heath also resorts to a psychoanalytic explanation for excess, indicating that it is the material which must be repressed by the film; see, for example, his discussion of the character of the "night man" as a figure of excess.[5] But none of this comes to terms with Heath's own claim (possibly derived from Barthes) that the excess arises from the conflict between the *materiality* of a film and the unifying structures within it. Heath, in fact, never analyzes a scene into its material and structural components to find examples of excess.

Barthes' entire essay, on the other hand, is based specifically on the material aspects of film as the source of its excess. He in fact analyzes only still photographs, but his conclusions are applicable to film (and also to the material qualities of the film's sound, which Barthes ignores). At one point, Barthes claims that excess does not weaken the meaning of the structures it accompanies: "if the signification is exceeded by the obtuse meaning, it is not thereby denied or blurred."[6] This seems doubtful, however. Presumably the only way excess can fail to affect meaning is if the viewer does not notice it; this is a matter of training and background. Certainly a steady and exclusive diet of classical narrative cinema seems to accustom people to ignoring the material aspects of the artwork, since these are usually so thoroughly motivated as to be unobtrusive. But the minute a viewer begins to notice style for its own sake or watch works which do not provide such thorough motivation, excess comes forward and must affect narrative meaning. Style is the use of repeated techniques which become *characteristic* of the work; these techniques are foregrounded so that the spectator will notice them and create connections between their individual uses. Excess does not equal style, but the two are closely linked because they both involve the material aspects of the film. Excess forms no specific patterns which we could say are characteristic of the work. But the formal organization provided by style does not exhaust the material of the filmic techniques, and a spectator's attention to style might well lead to a noticing of excess as well. Elsewhere Barthes acknowledges that his "obtuse meaning" does indeed affect our perception of meaning in a distractive way; speaking of certain qualities of photographic image, he asks, "are they not a kind of blunting of a too-obvious meaning, a too-violent meaning?. . . do they not cause my reading to skid?"[7] This image of a skidding perception is interesting, because it is not far from the kinds of metaphors the Russian Formalists chose to describe the effects of delaying devices in a narrative, such as "staircase construction." In each case, there is an attempt to describe a movement away from a direct progression through an "economical" structure. Barthes also speaks of the obtuse meaning as separate from the diegesis of the film; referring to a frame enlargement from *Ivan the Terrible,* he says:

The obtuse meaning is clearly counternarrative itself. Diffused, reversible, caught up in its own time, it can, if one follows it, establish only another script that is distinct from the shots, sequences, and syntagmas. . . . Imagine "following" not Euphrosinia's machinations, nor even the character (as a diegetic entity or as a symbolic figure), nor even, further, the countenance of the Wicked Mother, but only, in this countenance, that grimace, that black veil, the heavy, ugly dullness of that skin. You will have another temporality, neither diegetic nor oneiric, you will have another film.[8]

Probably no one ever watches *only* these nondiegetic aspects of the image through an entire film. Nevertheless, they are constantly present, a whole "film" existing in some sense alongside the narrative film we tend to think of ourselves as watching.

The idea that the critic's job might include the pointing-out of this excess may startle some. But we have been looking at the neat aspects of artworks so long that we may forget their disturbing, rough parts. As Barthes says, "The *present* problem is not to destroy the narrative, but to subvert it."[9] For the critic, this means the realization that he/she needs to talk about those aspects of the work that are usually ignored because they don't fit into a tight analysis.

The concept of excess need not be used only in semiotic, structuralist, or post-structuralist analyses. It fits into a critical approach based on Russian Formalism as well. For, while the Formalists did not come up with the idea of excess as such, they did move in a direction that implied it. When Viktor Shklovski says, "the language of poetry is not a comprehensive language, but a semi-comprehensible one,"[10] we must assume that the incomprehensible elements are so because they do not fit neatly into the unified relationships in the work; they must be explained as tending toward excess. Shklovski also makes a distinction between "material" and "form"; in speaking of music he says, "We have found, not form and content, but rather material and form, i.e., sounds and the disposition of sounds."[11] The process of "disposition" of materials into structures does not eliminate their original materiality. Thus the Formalists seem to have at least approached the realization that excessive elements provide a large range of possibilities for the roughening of form; the material provides a perceptual play by inviting the spectator to linger over devices longer than their structured function would seem to warrant.

Of course, no element in a work is strictly excessive to the degree that it has no connections to the other elements (except perhaps simple technical errors—the airplane in the sky of a biblical epic scene). As the Soviet filmmakers of the postrevolutionary period realized, simply to place two things together is to create a perception of them as related. This is one reason why excess is so difficult to talk about: most viewers are determined to find a necessary function for any element the critic singles out. For some reason, the claim that a device has *no* function beyond offering itself for perceptual play is disturbing to many people. Perhaps this tendency is cultural, stemming from the fact that art is so often spoken of as unified and as creating perfect order, beyond that possible in nature.

But if part of the difficulty of talking about excess stems from its novelty as a concept, the critic is also faced with the fact that excess tends to elude analysis. For example, take Barthes' description of Efrosinia given in the above quotation. That one *can* look at the visual figure in the images quite apart from her narrative function seems reasonably certain; we may go further and say with some confidence that one can perceive the visual figure even while following the narrative function it fills. But a discussion of the *qualities* of the visual figure at which we look seems doomed to a certain subjectivity. We may not agree that the texture of Efrosinia's skin has a "heavy, ugly dullness." The fact, however, that we can agree it has *some* texture opens the possibility of analysis. The critic and his/her reader must resist the learned tendency to try and find a narrative significance in every detail, or at least they must realize that a narrative function does not exhaust the material presence of that detail. Our conclusion must be that, just as every film contains a struggle of unifying and disunifying structures, so every stylistic element may serve at once to contribute to the narrative and to distract our perception from it.

Excess is not only counternarrative; it is also counterunity. To discuss it may be to invite the partial disintegration of a coherent reading. But on the other hand, pretending that a work is exhausted by its functioning structures robs it of much that is strange, unfamiliar, and striking about it. If the critic's task is at least in part to renew and expand the work's power to defamiliarize, one way to do this would be precisely to break up old perceptions of the work and to point up its more difficult aspects.

I shall follow Barthes' essay in drawing my examples from *Ivan the Terrible*. The act of "pointing" must be my principal tool here, since other means of analysis are designed for nonexcessive structures. (Barthes says in his essay, "I am not describing, I cannot manage that, I am merely designating a site.")[12] Analysis implies finding relationships between devices. Excessive elements do not form relationships, beyond those of coexistence. The Russian Formalists, however, give us a tool which may at least make the process of pointing somewhat systematic: motivation.[13] Strong realistic or compositional motivation will tend to make excessive elements less noticeable; the perception of the narratively and stylistically significant will dominate. But at other times, a lack of these kinds of motivations may direct our attention to excess.

More precisely, excess implies a gap or lag in motivation. Even though the presence of a device may not be arbitrary, its motivation can never completely control our perception of the film as material object. To a large extent, the spectator's ability to notice excess is dependent upon his/her training in viewing films. The spectator who takes films to be simple copies of reality will probably tend to subsume the physicality of the image under a general category of verisimilitude; that shape on the screen looks as it does because "those things really look like that." Another spectator, trained to look at films as romantic expressions of the artist, might attempt to see every aspect of every shot as conveying "meaning," "personal vision," and the like; the image looks the way it does because that is how the artist saw the world. At the other extreme, the "art for art's sake" viewer—the "empty" formalist—will tend to ignore motivation in favor of a totally free play of the "aesthetic" elements. All these approaches tend to vitiate the tension in the work between unified and excessive elements. The current study attempts to suggest an alternative.

A film displays a struggle by the unifying structures to "contain" the diverse elements that make up its whole system. Motivation is the primary tool by which the work makes its own devices seem reasonable. At that point where motivation fails, excess begins. To see it, we need to stop assuming that artistic motivation creates complete unity (or that its failure to do so somehow constitutes a fault). There are at least four ways in which the material of the film exceeds motivation.

First, narrative function may justify the presence of a device, but it doesn't always motivate *the specific form that individual element will take.* Quite often, the device could vary considerably in form and still serve its function adequately. Perhaps its color is vital, but its shape could be different. With an infinite number of points in space, we must assume that there is some range of camera placements which would frame the scene adequately to its function. In *Ivan the Terrible,* Ivan must be an impressive character, but his impressiveness could be created in many ways. The actual choices are relatively arbitrary: a pointed head, a musical theme, closeups with a crowd in deep focus, and so on.

Second, the medium of cinema is such that its devices exist through time. Motivation is insufficient to determine *how long* a device needs to be on the screen in order to serve its purpose. (Indeed, for different spectators, the requisite time is probably different.) We may notice a device immediately and understand its function, but it may then continue to be visible or audible for some time past this recognition. In this case, we may be inclined to study or contemplate it apart from its narrative or compositional function; such contemplation necessarily distracts from narrative progression. (In Russian Formalist terms, the perception of narrative progression involves the spectator's mental construction of a chronological set of story events "behind" the concrete presentation of plot action in the film.) On the other hand, the device may be more obscure and require a longer process of interpretation to make sense; how can motivation determine the length of time necessary for this perceptual activity? Noel Burch's concept of "legibility"[14] provides a rough guide. A large number of items within a single space will require a greater duration for complete scanning than a smaller number of items. But this determination can only be relative; the specific length must always be arbitrary to a certain degree. Repeated viewings of a film are likely to increase the excessive potentials of a scene's components; as we become familiar with the narrative (or other principle of progression), the innate interest of the composition, the visual aspects of the decor, or the structure of the musical accompaniment, may begin to come forward and capture more of our attention. The legibility has shifted for us; we now can simply *recognize* the unifying narrative elements, rather than having to perceive them for the first time. As a result, we now have time to contemplate the excessive aspects. The function of the material elements of the film is accomplished, but their perceptual interest is by no means exhausted in the process.

Third, a single bit of narrative motivation seems to be capable of functioning almost indefinitely. It may justify many devices which have virtually the same connotation, even though they may vary greatly in form. Thus Ivan's basic function in *Ivan the Terrible* is to formulate and embody the goal of unifying Russia. This symbolic position motivates the extremely redundant expression of Ivan's scenes in every cinematic channel; the film must confirm and reconfirm Ivan's adequacy to the goal he represents. This redundancy does not advance the narrative in every case; rather it tends to expand the narrative "vertically." After a point, the repeated use of multiple devices to serve similar functions tends to minimize the importance of their narrative implications; instead, they become foregrounded primarily through their own innate interest.

Fouth and last, a single motivation may serve to justify a device which is then repeated and varied many times. By this repetition, the device may far outweigh its original motivation and take on an importance greater than its narrative or compositional function would seem to warrant. This kind of excess is extremely common in *Ivan*. The introduction of the bird motif, for example, is realistically motivated; a couple of the objects in the coronation ceremony have historically authentic bird emblems on them (the scepter, the little rug on the dais). But later the birds become less integral to the action at hand. They have associations, but these associations are relatively arbitrary; the birds on the wall behind Ivan's throne during his argument with Philip, for example, have minimal narrative connotations. We cannot say that the various instances of birds in the film are unmotivated, for they all relate to each other and hence form a unified structure. But they do draw attention to themselves far beyond their importance in the functioning of the narrative.

With these characteristics of excess in mind, let us look at some examples from *Ivan*. Some of these may seem trivial; they will certainly not always be the kind of thing the critic ordinarily points out. But taken together, they should suggest the wealth of excessive details which make the film a rich perceptual field.

Ivan's excess becomes readily apparent if we compare it with a more stand-ardized usage like that of the classical Hollywood cinema. One critic whose approach is largely tied to the classical Hollywood narrative style, Pauline Kael, finds *Ivan* difficult to enjoy; while she admits its grandeur, she says, "we may stare at it in a kind of outrage. True, every frame looks great—it's a brilliant collection of stills—but as a movie, it's static, grandiose, and frequently ludicrous . . ."[15] In our terms, this "outrage" is in part the rejection of excess, the reluctance to consider the uneconomical or unjustified. *Ivan,* with its broken rhythms of acting, its systematic mismatches of mise-en-scène at cuts, and its constant heightening of stylistic devices, stands in contrast to the Hollywood cinema. Here style becomes foregrounded to an unusual degree, necessarily calling attention to the material of the film.

The composition of visual elements within the frame may become a rich source of excess. Striking arrangements abound in *Ivan;* they become particularly prominent because Eisenstein uses so many static or nearly static shots to explore space and further the narrative. The long shots of Ivan's tent on the hill at Kazan would be an example of this; the arrangement of curved lines of soldiers and a group of banners provide a striking composition in which little movement occurs (part 1, 281–82).[16] The series of shots of Boyars and ambassadors in the courtyard at the beginning of the illness sequence in part 1 invites our attention to small shifts of space, to faces and textures of fur and brocade, to the changing visual overtone of the cathedral icon, and to the rhythmic chiming of the various bells. In the opening coronation scene, three bald European ambassadors speak and shake their heads, but of at least equal interest is the pattern formed by their heads in the center of three large white ruffs (1, 9).

The deep focus shots in the Alexandrov sequence of part 1 place Ivan in closeup with the crowd on the snow-covered plain beyond. In each shot, Ivan moves his head—up in the first, down in the second (796, 800). These head movements are unmotivated; they seem to exist only to play on shifting graphic relationships between Ivan's profile and the curved shape of the crowd beyond, the amazing juxtapositions of space and volume, the texture of Ivan's hair and skin against the whiteness, and the vertical montage relations of sound and image.

The four shots of Ivan's return to Moscow in part 2 also play on formal values. Since all four shots show the same basic action—the galloping of the procession of Oprichniki and coach—we must conclude that one shot would convey as much narrative information as four (or six or eight). Formal interest rests in the rhythm of the fast music in conjunction with the swift movement and in the small shifts of the church spire in the background at the cuts. Shot 99 (the second of the segment) has almost the same setup as shot 98. Shot 100 shifts to a longer view of the whole scene, but shot 101 again has almost the same framing. These small changes (a violation of Hollywood's "30° rule" that every shot should be distinctly different from its neighbors in order to clearly motivate the cut) create variations that add nothing except as perceptual material.

The textures, colors, and shapes of the costumes are frequent sites for excess in *Ivan*. For example, the glitter of light on the costumes of Vladimir and Efrosinia in the beaver lullaby scene becomes very prominent. The contrast of Philip's plain black cloth cassock with Ivan's heavy fur cloak provides the basis for considerable play in the scene of their argument early in part 2. In shot 213, Philip turns suddenly and moves to the throne to lean over and speak directly to Ivan; the shifting train swirls behind him and stretches into a series of diagonal folds as he moves. Later, as Philip stalks away, shouting his curse back to Ivan, the long shot frames the entire empty throneroom (216). First Philip moves away, turns briefly to shout back, then continues out; during this, Ivan moves right and then across left to follow Philip. The indirect, hesitating movements of the two men in black against the light flagstones on the floor set up swirling patterns of visual interest and excess. In the Livonian scene, Sigismund leans forward in closeup until his head seems to be suspended in the center of a set of radiating black and white lines (his ruff; shot 84, part 2). In the same scene, one knight wears armor decorated with huge, curling feathers, elaborately backlit (68).

Excess is present in the way things happen. The tassel of Pimen's rosary drags lightly over the carvings on the gold Bible in a closeup during the illness sequence (1, 455). Ivan's sweeping turn as he carries the poisoned cup to Anastasia is unnecessary in relation to the action. Efrosinia's behavior as she sings the lullaby is strange in a way which goes beyond the narrative connotations. Ivan's kiss on Malyuta's brow before the execution in part 2 slips away from the straightforward causal motivation of the scene.

The style of many devices is highly exaggerated in *Ivan,* compared to that in the classical narrative film. Elements of the acting like the sweeping gestures and the staring eyes stand out as strange; we may recognize their function in the filmic system, but this will not obliterate their peculiarity. ("Peculiar" and "strange" here have only positive connotations; these qualities are a large part of *Ivan's* appeal.) The Hollywood norm has accustomed us to clear, seamless space; now we are confronted with frequent, pointless shifts and gaps. Ivan's device of cubistic editing constitutes a perceptual game.[17] If the spectator consciously notices the cubistic cuts, he/she may indeed be drawn aside from the smoother structures to notice more and more subtle instances of this spatial instability. Indeed, any stylistic disjunction may lead the spectator into an awareness of excess—unless he/she strives too hard to recuperate them.

Problematic or unclear elements are likely to become excess. Many of the icons in the cathedral, for example, are never seen in their entirety. They are realistically motivated as portions of a reasonably authentic historical setting; but because they are only partially visible, they invite inspection in an attempt (necessarily fruitless) at identification. Half-glimpsed hallways, partially darkened corners of rooms, slightly out-of-focus backgrounds, and other similar visual presences may all tend to draw the eye, particularly on repeated viewings. What are we to make of the black-clad body that lies in the background of one shot of the execution scene of part 2 (285)? The body is not there in any other shot, nor is there the faintest narrative motivation for its presence; it is not one of the Boyars, nor is there any suggestion that an Oprichnik dies or faints in this scene. Beyond the frequent use of confused spatial cues in the cutting, there is also one point where the geography is flagrantly inconsistent. When Efrosinia leaves the wedding banquet to check on the progress of the riot, she goes out by a little door and emerges outside at the head of the stairway. Later, she receives Demyan's report in a little archway at the foot of this same stairway; yet when the pair go through the door in this archway, they (at least Efrosinia—Demyan has disappeared during the cut of the interior of the hall) are coming in the same little doorway by which Efrosinia has previously exited.

Certain props carry interest beyond their function in the narrative. The repeated closeups of the emblems of Riga, Reval, and Narva at the beginning of the poisoning sequence are only tangential to the narrative; we would undoubtedly be able to understand Ivan's speech without these "visual aids." But their carvings attract attention. Similarly, the coffin and its trappings in the scene of Ivan's mourning are striking and elaborate: Anastasia lies in a hollowed-out log, surrounded by a fan of shining decorations like a peacock's tail.

We may find some of the most extreme examples of excess in the Fiery Furnace play scene. The play's function in the narrative is clear, but its manner of execution tends toward excess. Barthes speaks briefly of this scene in discussing excess, pointing to the three boys and, "the schoolboy absurdity of their mufflers diligently wrapped around their necks."[18] The mufflers work in with the general principles of the playlet's style, with a heightening of signification accomplished in the various channels by adding a symbolic device to the literal one: the boys stand over fire, but also light candles to imply that they are in the fire; they are tied together, but also wear mufflers to heighten the concept of "bound-ness"; they step into the furnace, but the Chaldeans also turn cartwheels to mark the moment (to suggest a sense of falling or confusion?). But beyond this function, Barthes' description seems to me right; there *is* something about those mufflers that goes beyond their symbolic participation in the playlet. Their individual decorative pattern and strangeness in this context convey a quality which is perhaps, as Barthes says "absurd," perhaps amusing, touching, or all three. The same is true for other aspects of the scene: the Chaldeans' painted grimaces, the cymbal crashes, the boys' haloes, and the rest, all have qualities beyond their immediate functions.

I have said almost nothing about sound, but clearly it can have its excessive features as well. The strange, jangling bell toward which Vladimir glances in the courtyard scene of the illness sequence of part 1 would be one example. Birds are heard chirping in only one shot of the scene of the herald toward the end of part 1. Malyuta's repetitions of the word "pes" (pronounced "pyos," meaning "dog") in his conversation with Ivan before the executions in part 2 seem to me rather comic, mainly because of the sound of the word itself and the injured tones in which he delivers the lines. In general, music has a great potential to call attention to its own formal qualities apart from its immediate function in relation to the image track. The tendency of the actors to speak their lines in separate bits with long pauses between also tends, I suspect, to call attention to the sounds and rhythms of the dialogue.

A couple of obvious devices in the film that seem strongly excessive: the shifts between color and black-and-white stock, which inevitably must cause a perceptual shock dependent entirely upon the material of the images; and the use of two identical shots from the coronation sequence (1, 58–59) of two young women spectators in the Fiery Furnace scene of part 2 (334–35). In the latter case, we can recuperate the repetition logically by positing that the device helps create a narrative parallel between the two scenes; nevertheless the two shots stand out as disturbing elements because we know they are physically the *same* shots—they violate our expectations about the temporal distinctness of the two scenes.

These few indications from *Ivan* must suffice to help define the excess concretely. I can do no more than indicate; a systematic analysis is impossible. Why then bother with excess at all? What is its value? Beyond renewing the perceptual freshness of the work, it suggests a different way of watching and listening to a film. It offers a potential for avoiding the traditional, conventionalized views of what film structure and narrative should be—views which fit in perfectly with the methods of filmmaking employed in the classical commercial narrative cinema. The spectator need not assume that the entire film consists only of the unified system of structures we call form and style; he/she need not assume that film is a means of communication between artist and audience. Hence the spectator will not go to a film expecting to discern what it is "trying to say," or to try and reassemble its parts into some assumed, preordained whole.

An awareness of excess may help change the status of narrative in general for the viewer. One of the great limitations for the viewer in our culture has been the attitude that film equals narrative, and that entertainment consists wholly of an "escapism" inherent in the plot. Such a belief limits the spectator's participation to understanding only the chain of cause and effect. The fact that we call this understanding the ability to "follow" the narrative is not accidental. The viewer goes along a preordained path, trying to come to the "correct" conclusions; skillful viewing may consist of being able to anticipate plot events before they occur (as with the detective story, which becomes a game in guessing the identity of the criminal before the final revelation). This total absorption in narrative has some unpleasant consequences for the act of viewing. The viewer may be capable of understanding the narrative, but has no context in which to place that understanding; the underlying arbitrariness of the narrative is hidden by structures of motivation and naturalization. A narrative is a chain of causes and effects, but, unlike the real world, the narrative world requires one initial cause which itself has no cause. The choice of this initial cause is one source of the arbitrariness of narrative. Also, once the hermeneutic and proairetic codes are opened in a narrative, there is nothing which logically determines how long the narrative will continue; more and more delays could prolong the chain of cause and effect indefinitely. Thus the initiation, progression, and closure of fictional narratives is largely arbitrary. Narratives are not logical in themselves; they only make use of logic. An understanding of the plot, then, is only a limited understanding of one (arbitrary) portion of the film. But if one looks beyond narrative, at both the unified and the excessive elements at work on other levels, the underlying principles of the film (such as the hermeneutic code and the patterns of motivation) may become apparent. The viewer is no longer caught in the bind of mistaking the causal structure of the narrative for some sort of inevitable, true, or natural set of events which is beyond questioning or criticism (except for superficial evaluation on the grounds of culturally defined conventions and canons of verisimilitude).

One example of the result of a willingness to view films for excess as well as for unified structures is the genre of experimental films which examines already-existing films. These often consist of optical printer alterations of the original film, emphasizing the material of the image. Ken Jacobs' *Tom, Tom, the Piper's Son* (1969) is one such film, which takes a short silent film of the primitive period and blows up and repeats portions of the various shots to create a feature-length film. Narrative begins to break down and tiny gestures, grain, and individual frames become foregrounded. Joseph Cornell made *Rose Hobart* (late 1930s) by taking an obscure American adventure picture *(East of Borneo,* 1932) and turning it into a play on the concept of narrative by isolating individual shots, cutting them together out of order, and repeating shots. He substituted a musical track for the original sound and specified that the film be shown through a purple filter. The result hints obliquely at the original narrative, but generally concentrates on the gestures and appearance of Rose Hobart, a minor Hollywood actress, and on the absurdly exotic studio jungle settings. These, as well as some of Stan Lauder's loop films, suggest the structural possibilities an awareness of excess can create. I don't mean to imply that the spectator and critic will be led to aesthetic creations of their own as a result of watching for excess. But Jacobs' and Cornell's films demonstrate the kinds of perceptual shifts which might take place once one becomes aware of excess.

Once the narrative is recognized as arbitrary rather than logical, the viewer is free to ask why individual events within its structures are as they are. The viewer is no longer constrained by conventions of reading to find a meaning or theme within the work as the solution to a sort of puzzle which has a right answer. Instead, the work becomes a perceptual field of structures which the viewer is free to study at length, going beyond the strictly functional aspects. Each film dictates the way it wants to be viewed by drawing upon certain conventions and ignoring or flouting others. But if the viewer recognizes these conventions and refuses to be bound by them, he/she may strive to avoid having limitations imposed upon his/her viewing without an awareness of that imposition. Obviously there is no completely free viewing situation; we are always guided by our knowledge and cultural tradition. But a perception of a film which includes its excess implies an awareness of the structures (including conventions) at work in the film, since excess is precisely those elements which escape unifying impulses. Such an approach to viewing films can allow us to look further into a film, renewing its ability to intrigue us by its strangeness; it also can help us to be aware of how the whole film—not just its narrative—works upon our perception.

142 *Kristin Thompson*

Notes

1. Roland Barthes, "The Third Meaning," trans. Richard Howard, *Artforum* (January 1973), 11(5):47.

2. Stephen Heath, "Film and System: Terms of Analysis, Pt. I," *Screen* (Spring 1975), 16(1):100.

3. Barthes, "The Third Meaning," p. 49.

4. Heath, "Film and System," p. 67.

5. *Ibid.*, pp. 73–74.

6. Barthes, "The Third Meaning," p. 47.

7. *Ibid.*

8. *Ibid.*, p. 49.

9. *Ibid.*, p. 50. Italics in original.

10. Viktor Shklovski, "The Resurrection of the World," trans. Richard Sherwood, *20th Century Studies* (December 1972), nos. 7–8, p. 46.

11. Viktor Shklovski, "Form and Material in Art," trans. Charles A. Moser and Patricia Blake, in *Dissonant Voices in Soviet Literature,* ed. Patricia Blake and Max Hayward (New York: Harper and Row, 1964), p. 21.

12. Barthes, "The Third Meaning," p. 48.

13. Boris Tomashevski, "Thematics," in *Russian Formalist Criticism; Four Essays,* trans. and ed. Lee T. Lemon and Marion J. Reis (Lincoln: University of Nebraska Press, 1965), pp. 78–87.

14. Noel Burch, *Theory of Film Practice,* trans. Helen R. Lane (New York: Praeger, 1973), p. 52.

15. Pauline Kael, *Kiss Kiss Bang Bang* (Boston: Little Brown, 1968), p. 288.

16. Shot numbers are as given in Sergei Eisenstein, *Ivan the Terrible* (New York: Simon and Schuster, 1970).

17. See Burch's comparison of *Ivan's* cutting to the painting style of Gris in *Theory of Film Practice,* pp. 37–39.

18. Barthes, "The Third Meaning," p. 48.

[8]

Deborah Linderman
Uncoded Images in the Heterogeneous Text

1. The Heterogeneous Text

Following long-standing imperatives, we are accustomed to think of the classical text as an holistic and unitary system, self-contained by the singularity of its determinations and bound by conditions of intelligibility. But as Barthes, at the very least, has been telling us, the classical text is "really" a set of segments separately articulated, and its modality is piecemeal.[1] It is comprised of a "braid" of codes from other texts and other voices, but also from scraps and fragments of unaestheticized discourse, cultural formulas that have been retranscribed by being made to pass through the controlling codes of a given textual system. The effect of this braiding or burnishing of the text is to disguise its segmentary modality and make it appear natural, endowed with mimetic truth and narrative fluency; whereas narrative in fact is the integration of atomistic units—words, images—into a higher-level story formation by their conduction to a single end or terminus.

In other words, the integrity (organicity) of the text is assured by its tendentious unfolding, for the laws of narrative motion entail that all signifiers of difference are introduced into the text only to be resolved symmetrically into a sameness; the narrative folds over itself even as it seems to unfold. Thus part of a code will appear at one site of the text to disappear, then reappear "later"

Published in *Wide Angle* (1979), 3(3):54–63, and reprinted by permission of the Johns Hopkins University Press and the author.

(since unfolding is held to a linear temporality); its erasure entailing both its succeeding "different" signifier and the future mode of its recontextualization, its resolution into sameness, or homogeneity. The "textness"—i.e. overdetermination—of the text, then, is constituted by a system of perpetual and perpetuating deferrals of meaning, whereby heterogeneous signifiers are mobilized in linear chains along the syntagm, one chain tending to borrow surplus meanings from another until all meanings are appropriated by the totalizing claims of the textual system. Textual overdetermination has ideological value, since it assures the appearance of continuity to discontinuous segments and thus blocks, or seems to, the infiltration of extratextual, alien, nonappropriatable meanings that would reveal because of their very "inappropriateness" (a) the seams of the textualizing process and (b) risky, dangerous, or repressed ideation not aesthetically bindable.

But the burnished surface of the aesthetic text can be deidealized and rescored into zones. To take the text apart at the seams is to look for the presence in it of countertextual, interruptive locutions that may be embedded in the heterogeneous quotations, phrases, formulas, already-written discourse which each text, as it were, rewrites. Psychoanalysis readily offers as models for a theory of the text as a transcursive discourse the dream, the joke and the paralogism, all of which have in common the disruption of biunivocality by signifiers of difference—contraband, extra or nontendentious meanings not wholly appropriatable to an end. These sites of alterity are the sites of multiple articulations unfolding all at once; the nodal points at which the heterogeneous means of production of the text are bared. Its heterogeneity recovered, the text has no final term: it is precisely interminable. There is no total context which *de*termines everything in the text; instead, signifiers of alterity force one to acknowledge in it irresolute coding and nonresolvable fields of meaning. Such alterity may take the form of traces, incomplete and alien simulacra from *other* contexts, undelimited and not integratable by the narrative into the dominant textual matrix. But not fully excludable from it either, inasmuch as conflictual processes gain articulation through traces, which perhaps ought to be considered the markers of an ambivalent formation, a substitution or compromise and a sign that the text is not to be taken at face value. Alterity is ulterior, comprising a threat to the stability of the textual system by announcing that the representations of the narrative have "failed" to contain and appropriate—make appropriate—all textual ideation. For to deidealize a text is ultimately to unbind it. Foreign simulacra, multiple filaments of meaning, multiple embeddings, all hint at preemptive ideological content which, given full force or voice, would unbind the burnished text and underdetermine it.

We could provisionally call such traces *undercoded,* but the problem with this, Eco's term,[2] is that it presupposes an organic context. For Eco contends that once the labor of decoding for such a sign has been done and the dominant textual codes been cracked, an undercoded sign can become *overcoded* by being integrated through polysemantic linkages with the macrostructure. Eco's premise is to disallow as semiotic material whatever cannot be accommodated by a coding system, from which it follows that the meanings of an undercoded sign become accessible if the position of that sign is contextually resolved. Yet such a premise makes impossible the structuration of a heterogeneous text, which may be ennervated with nonrecuperable content, unnameable meanings that have escaped social coding altogether. If a sign context cannot be totalized, it ought not to be considered an actualization or fulfillment of consciousness.[3] And the inscription of inadvertent meanings into a text is an inscription of meanings which interfere with the totalization of context and reveal ambivalent intentionality. One need not talk here of the unconscious of a given person or of the "fallacies" of intention at all: one need only propose a discourse, an author, a text, as a forcefield that mediates the inscription of cultural imperatives, any discourse thus bearing the sanctions and proscriptions of the socius and of the historical moment of its production. Ambivalent intentionality, then, may reveal how the pressures of censorship in the symbolic order are mediated by a transcribing agent and may testify only to the blockages imposed by social coding. Ultimately an undercoded sign is not synonymous with an uncoded sign, for if there is *stuff* in the text which has eluded social coding, then there is also an untextualized conflictual field not bindable by signifying processes.

In Dreyer's silent film *The Passion of Joan of Arc* (1928), which will exemplify a heterogeneous text, uncoded material tells us what kind of stuff it is that the text represses, i.e., cannot transform to its own final terms. This material is deposited in the text in a series of surplus, "extra," shots that are indeed unbound: they could be completely excised from both the narrative track and the image track without damage to the textual system. They are primarily cutaways and inserts which have not been fully appropriated by the dominant diegesis and which countermand the metalanguage of the text. The purport of this alien material is to signify the impossible position of the feminine in the symbolic order of the patriarchy. It is obviously logical that there should be a strong connection between uncoded, unbound signs and a heterogeneous narrative structure; a homogeneous narrative structure, if there really is such a thing, could not support the presence of inarticulatable meanings among a set of full-fledged representations. But like the dream censor, the film censor cannot stop censorious ideation from sneaking past all checks and balances. Hence it is doubtful that a homogeneous text, even the most so-called classical text, is anything but a postulate in search of closure.

2. Controlled Inscription

The metalanguage of a text is not a separate code abstracted from it and existing outside, beyond, and above a target language; rather it is implanted within the so-called object language and is constituted by the narrative itself as a set of directives for how to read the object text. The force of this set of directives is ideological in that precisely because the metalanguage of a text is not separate from but hidden in its fictions, its directive coercions are suppressed. The metalanguage of Dreyer's film comports with the dominant ideology of the heroism of the Christian martyr, and the chief directive of the metalanguage is to read the text according to a familiar discourse based on the Christian formulation of life beyond life and salvation through suffering and various types of humiliation. The following excerpts from the English language subtitles of the film will make the point. They conform to Quicherat's transcripts (1838) of the historical trial of the real Joan of Arc and define her as the saint not perceived as such "in time" because of the wordly blinders and inferior vision of her prosecutors. There is, of course, no metalingual directive to read for preemptive ideological content within the discourse.

EXAMPLE A

Priest:	*Why do you wear man's dress? Do you want a woman's gown?*
Joan:	*When I have done what God sent me to do, I shall resume woman's dress.*
Priest:	*Then it is by God's command that you dress like a man? . . . What reward do you hope to obtain from our Lord?*
Joan:	*The salvation of my soul.*
Priest:	*Rank blasphemy!*

EXAMPLE B

Joan:	*Get the judges. I repent. I have lied to save my life. Hasten. I have done a great wrong.*
Priest:	*You still believe that you are God's emissary?*
Massieu:	*That answer signs her death warrant!*
Joan:	*What I did, I did through fear of being burned alive.*
Massieu:	*We have come to prepare you for death.*
Joan:	*Already? What manner of death?*
Massieu:	*At the stake! . . . And the great victory?*
Joan:	*My martyrdom.*
Massieu:	*And your deliverance?*
Joan:	*My death!*

EXAMPLE C

Priest:	*This is not a trial. It is persecution. To me she seems a saint.*

As Example A indicates—and one could adduce many more such quotations from the subtitles—the issue of her heresy is conflated with the issue of the feminine status of Joan of Arc, and Dreyer's legacy of historical material is rich in problematics in this respect. For the historical Joan of Arc was tried not only for heresy and treason but also for sorcery, the last because she was a female who wore the disguise of the male symbolic order and who heard voices. She is represented by Dreyer as having no access to the codes of the symbolic order—

a male hand guides hers to fashion some sort of signature and she barely speaks at all—a representation consistent with the known fact of her actual illiteracy; but the historical case was stronger still. Not only was she a warrior superman, her voice virtually stilled to silence, her body cloaked in an armature; but she also obeyed an unreal speech, dislocated and prophetic, a substitution perhaps for that marginal speech of the female within the patriarchy. Thanks to which margin, she can find a symbolic space to hide herself. Joan of Arc was condemned as a heretic (not a traitor), but sorcery was plainly part of the verdict ("This witch is cunning . . . She will slip through our fingers. We must use craft to catch her.") because she refused the mediation of the church hierarchy, listening to her own mandates instead, whatever displacements these might in fact represent. Hence her political significance is specifically feminist. Dreyer notably shows us nothing of her military career and very little indeed of any political background at all. His flat spare sets and stark closeups that wring narratives out of the faces of Joan of Arc's male interrogators act in the text to repress political articulation. The mob, a sign precisely of political force, acquires textual space and becomes materially visible in shots of weeping women and of hand-to-hand combat only as the sacrificial immolation finally commences. This sacrifice, the gradual erasure of Joan of Arc from the text and its mobilization toward closure, lifts the ban against intradiegetic commentary on her sociopolitical status, the figure of the martyr being "refigured" and recontextualized by the eruption of a combative populace.

Until this eruption the enunciatory structure of the film consists mainly of chains of Dreyer's famous closeups, that of Falconetti alternating with those of her various interrogators. The narrative integrates this material alternation of shots into a series of unremitting interrogations, an effort by a powerful amalgam of priests and soldiers to penetrate—whether by questions or by offers of literal torture—her disguises and her womanhood. Yet although the enunciations of the classical film would logically objectify this effort by a set of shot/reverse shots based on penetration by the gaze, a model of matched glances and a relay of looks, in this film Falconetti is isolated both affectively and spatially in such a way as to create a curious deflection of the look. Partly the deflection is accomplished by her prevailingly dolorous affect: her eyes are cast upward in a stare at nothing the spectator can see, her brow is knit into an expression of the agony that is piteous, the pity that is piety, and Joan of Arc's virtual muteness is compensated by a painful ecstasy of constantly overflowing tears. The dolorous affect assures that with one exception to be noted, Joan of Arc meets no gaze; it thus seals off the space around her representation and imparts to it the aura of an icon presented by the camera to the spectator tropically for reverence instead of viewing. Moreover, although the camera tends to traverse the course of the glance of the interrogators and to align the spectator with that look and its particular signification, it is always interrupted in this motion before suturing the respective fields of the judges and their victim. Joan of Arc is repeatedly presented on the cut, and so her actual as well as affective space remains atomized. Whereas despite the fact that they are in many shots similarly atomized, the males do exchange the look and the word via a short lateral pan. The result is the sublim(iz)ation of the figure of Joan of Arc, who is in the first place derealized by her face and in the second situated in a delocalized, idealized space. In short, while the narrative appropriates the icon of the face into a representation of transcendence, the unmatched alternating closeups produce an inherent instability in the material enunciations of the film. The logic of that instability loosens the narrative and disperses the text to heterogeneity, as we shall see, the material codes of the film thus directly supporting its modes of production of meaning.

Three of the first twelve shots of the initial sequence of the film—(1) the Bible encircled from top to bottom in chains; (2) her feet in boots, bound at the ankles with the same chains; (3) her hand placed in oath on the same bound book, the zoned Word of the repressive patriarchy—picture for us by a movement of metonymy both her exclusion from and her imprisonment within the regime of the symbolic, the chains binding her within, the oath enforcing her ascription to this regime. An uneasy, indeed impossible relation to the patriarchy makes any choice, any resolution of choices, only a misrepresentation, mistaken. But the film is stabilized nonetheless by Joan of Arc's long silences and equally durable tears and by the mandate of its own metalanguage, as we have seen.

Further evidence of the violence suppressed by the textuality of the text appears in two other sequences, each of which is susceptible of a reading that will absorb it into the metalanguage but which still appears to articulate *another* discourse. The interrogators ask Joan of Arc who taught her her Paternoster. The already slow tempo of the film is further retarded between every question and answer. She cries in answering "my mother" and refuses to repeat the prayer. The Word of the father taught by the mother could hardly bear reciting. A conflictual relation to the maternal legacy within the patristic, monotheistic order forecloses articulation and manifests itself in refusal. But there is no scream, no hysterical enactment, no lasting resistance, no radical rupture in a system of controls that force the female into disfigurement and sublimation. The sequence is paradigmatically completed later in the film when a false priest again tries to bribe out of her the Paternoster, token of her cultural inscription, by presenting a forged letter with a false signature of King Charles ostensibly enlisting her military support: "I am preparing to march on Rouen with a great army. I send you this priest that you may place your confidence in him. . . . " Under these, the terms of a masculine mandate, the recitation is elicited, a symbolic acquiescence that perversely links her faith to the possibility of power within a masculine regime—an androgynous submission to the figure of the father (god, king, priest, professor). Ironically at this point the matching of glances between Joan of Arc and the false priest bind her to her chief betrayor. The metalanguage coerces this submission into an act of heroism rendering her earlier refusal parenthetical, aside of the point.

Godard has introduced into *Letter to Jane* a well-known still of Falconetti wearing a mock-up of a crown of thorns. Godard and Gorin in their lengthy narration of that film propose that Jane Fonda is paradigmatically linked with Joan of Arc, among others, for the "inward look of existential crisis," the look without a reverse shot. And while it is in fact the case, born out in the film's enunciations as well as its representation, that Joan of Arc has renounced the possibility of a reverse shot by renouncing her otherness and going in drag, her martydom thus being an extreme and radical act of autism, the mock crown could operate as a sign in the film of otherness, a site of satire to contravene all social valorizations. Kristeva has referred to the female as "this eternal satire of the community,"[4] meaning that the feminine is a positionality of repression that absorbs, reflects, and embodies the disavowals of culture; that the pleasure of the feminine therefore is chiefly in a capacity to imagine the *return* of the feminine, as repressions return, indigenously through the cracks of culture. But under the terms of the metalanguage, Joan of Arc appears to take the mock crown without this imagination and without mockery, for it achieves a simple equation of her passion with the passion of Christ. The pertinent sequence which leads ultimately to her recantation quoted in example B above begins with some court fools twirling this crown on the tips of their lances, spinning it off and tossing it about: they finally impose it on her head, and her face immediately assumes the expression of sorrow. All possibility of jest and satire therefore resides only with the fools. Her hair is then shaven from her head in the conventional procedure of exacting penitence; as it is swept up for trash, she looks merely piteous, but a reaction shot at the crown being likewise swept up has her abruptly recoiling in shock. Her recantation follows, and it is clear that between the equally inauthenticating options of permanent silence and imprisonment, on the one hand, and a resonantly manipulative suicide on the other, she will as potent woman prefer to be empowered. The mock crown thus becomes doubly and ironically valorized—a crown of wordly power, or of power at least. Imprisonment and silence, of course, are truer options in the sense of expressing more clearly her position within the patriarchy. It is clear that at its manifest level, the text can find no unitary, textual, way to propose that Joan of Arc is deformed by the impossibility of her options within the paternal order. Hiding in it, inscribing herself into power through its symbolic mediations, she must also be sacrificed by it, for culture has found ways to purge itself of whomever collapses the strict bipolar positions of its coding systems and thus obstructs the courses of its political and commercial exchange.

3. Woman as Waste

Embracing both of the double parameters of martyrdom, the one ecstatic and submissive to the patriarchy, the other melancholic and autodestructive,[5] Dreyer's Joan of Arc describes the inviable, doublebinding logic of the feminine. Situated on "this side of the threshold of repression,"[6] which is to say on the side of culture—as virgin, martyr, saint, nurse, mother, mistress—she obligingly accedes to the despotism of the paternal Word and Law so as to maintain the economy of "civilization and its discontents." For under the terms of the primal, Oedipal repression, the accession of the polymorphous body to the localizing, univocalizing tyranny of the signifier is also an accession to bodily zoning—the learning of forbidden zones that means the stabilization of the Oedipal crisis and the entry into culture. Hereafter, the body accedes to the Word. It renounces pre-Oedipal modalities of the tie to the mother, laughter, babble, hysteria, rhythm, desire, that seize the body in a rush across zones, that ultimately press against the Word and erupt through it, by disguise and displacement willy-nilly. The heterogeneous drives of the body, genitally localized by the Oedipal acquiescence to the demands of the socius, exist on *that side* of the boundary of repression, the other side, the site of otherness. That side of the boundary of repression is the feminine, on the side of delocalized pleasure and hysterical rushes, jouissant, fitfully visible only through the cracks of culture, therefore dangerous, imaginary, bacchic. Culture calls her when it sees her "intuitive," a seer, a sorceress, a witch, "instinctual," pregnant. Bearing the name of the father and of the child's father, she cannot find a name to call her own. Godard says in *Weekend,* "Christianity is the refusal to know oneself and the death of language." The feminine is what the masculine refuses to know about itself; it is the symbolic expiation by the two sexes of the possibilities of the body— especially the constant discourse of the body with death—through forms of masochism or indeed through martyrdom. This expiation protects social commerce; it keeps the channels of exchange pure of contaminating imprint from a maternal legacy and the maternal trace thus exists in culture only in disguise, in a conflictual format. Safeguarded by this twisting of the maternal sign, purity of exchange is the assignation of determinate values: X is worth exactly Y, a salvation for a martyrdom. This perverse frugality has longstanding endorsement. Augustine, for example, as quoted by Kristeva, writes in praise of virginity in *On the Holy Virginity,* but nevertheless maintains that "As far as I think, however, no one would dare prefer virginity to martyrdom."[7] Which is to say that extremities of masochism are to be preferred even over *undying* sublimation, a deformed heroism to be embraced in the name of every effort of the socius to inscribe onto the surface of the body its own idealizations.

4. Surplus Inscription

The flat sets and idealizing closeups of Dreyer's film and the excision of background or depth of field comport with a privative narrative that abstracts and transcendentalizes the story of Joan of Arc. But although the narrative itself, with its focalization on the trial and passion specifically, is a tightly framed construct, the tendency of the enunciations toward atomization and dispersal seems to admit into the text several apparently superfluous, extra if not "wasted" shots, not bound by the diegesis and indeed virtually parenthetical. Each of these shots could plainly be removed from the film with no loss of meaning to the metalanguage. Each is intercut with the long sequence of Joan of Arc's immolation and thus represents, if only for very brief duration, other action "taking place" simultaneously, though it is unclear in spatial terms where exactly this action is and what its relevance is to the central action. The shots are not point-of-view shots, nor do they appear in the text anchored by any pertinent consciousness other than the spectator's. In a way they seem to be mere flourishes of style, shots there only to be ultimately denied. Yet perhaps these images are precisely impertinent, i.e., threatening to "take the place of" the martyrdom. Because while each shot can be read according to the demands of the diegesis, none at the same time really counts for it. The subjects of the shots are either grotesques or freakish angles of the camera. Are they fanciful embellishments at the surface of the narrative, there to "say something" about the grotesque sacrifice, or are they uncoded signs that mark the sites of deeper alterity in the text? Both?

(1) A sword swallower, wheel balancer, and other circus figures;
(2) A contortionist twisted over himself; both one and two could be read as signs for "the carnival of this world";
(3) A dwarf in a cart wheeling somewhere at great speed: this stunted world;
(4) A baby suckling; this image is edited into two closeups, separated by a cut back to Joan of Arc at the stake. Should she have done this if she were normal?
(5) An overhead shot of a phalanx of soldiers, but the camera angle changes although the camera itself does not move as they charge past it; the image registers their radical foreshortening in relation to the camera.
(6) An exceedingly low-angle shot, the camera appearing to be positioned directly below a transparent drawbridge across which move figures of the mob; the motion within the frame distorts the angle of these figures: the position of the camera and the movement of its subject collaborate to derange perspective within the image in both five and six.

Prior to these shots, we have seen only a church courtroom, some priests, and a militia, nothing of the wider social context of Joan of Arc's operation. Thus these shots do have a rationale, i.e., they are motivated, since they bring into visibility the mob on the sidelines and generate its eruption into combat. Significantly, however, the shots of actual combat are obscured in a chiaroscuro haze of smoke from the very pyre of the martyr: as is well known, the death of the sacrificial hero is a ritual purgation which, by a combination of idealization (my god, you have burned a saint) and effigy magic, assures the stabilization of the social order. A ritual suicide appropriates to itself the accumulated evils, ills, and pressures of the tribe, but in such a way instead of sharpening political focus operates precisely to obfuscate it. While it is not completely outrageous to force these shots which rupture the surface of the narrative back into the terms of the narrative, to do so is to deny their interruptive structure. Let us materialize the represented sidelines of the action into the margin of the discourse resituating these shots now scattered in the narrative in that margin. The shots are then marginal glosses, and as we know the margin is infinite. Therefore these shots infinitize the narrative. Rather than fulfilling a univocal field of intentionality, they record an undelimited tension that has usurped the boundaries of the narrative and exposed its polyvocality. Joan's mistaken choice of martyrdom is glossed by contortion and deformity; the limits of her range of options by the explicit antonymity martyrdom/motherhood; the violence of her story by the extremities of perspective within the image, caused by both camera movement and movement in the frame; this sudden, localized, derangement of the image track expressing the impossibility of finding a stable vantage from which to bind, frame, and authenticate her victimization. Image surplus, narrative surplus; the uncoded images propose a testing of limits, subvert the ostensible limits of the text, and press for a way to articulate its central but radically decentered problematic, which is a question of social positioning. How to situate the feminine among authenticating options?

Still counting, among the final shots of the film, a penultimate (the stake at which Joan of Arc has been burned is juxtaposed with a cross) diagrams the mispositioning to which we have been witness. The metalanguage forces a valorizing synonymity between the two implements of masochistic heroism. Yet the disfigured logic of such closure is underlined by the brutal literalism of the juxtaposition—a dissolve or a superimposition would better serve the purposes of sublimity. The stake remains stubbornly literal and material. And further, an irony—in case we want to read an irony—has no point unless it cuts both ways. The enunciations of his camera may have suggested to Dreyer a doubt of which he himself was hardly conscious. At least the representation which he has, we might say, hit upon is of a martyrdom taken in good conscience but bad faith. The heterogeneous text, like the heterogeneous body, would appear to embarrass perversity.

Notes

1. Roland Barthes, *S/Z*, trans. Richard Miller, (New York: Hill and Wang, 1974), *passim*.
2. Umberto Eco, *A Theory of Semiotics* (Bloomington: Indiana University Press, 1976), pp. 129–39.
3. See Samuel Weber, "It," *Glyph* (1978), no. 4, p. 11.
4. Julia Kristeva, *About Chinese Women*, trans. Anita Barrows (New York: Urizen Books, 1977), p. 15.
5. *Ibid.*, pp. 27–28.
6. *Ibid.*, p. 14.
7. *Ibid.*, p. 27.

Part Two

Subject, Narrative, Cinema

Introduction:
Text and Subject

Part 1 of this anthology presented influential arguments concerning certain means for analyzing cinematic signification for systematic regularities and some consequent implications. Emphasis was on the fact that in the study of film this question has often been inflected by Saussurian linguistics and on consideration of the feasibility of a binary cultural politics. Part 1 also introduced issues circulating around concepts such as excess, which, while not necessarily negating the investigation of systemic conceptualizations of cinema, at least necessitate their being elaborated and supplemented. In fact, the necessity for such a supplement was indicated by virtually all the contributors to part 1.

Given such considerations, concepts such as structure and system could be retained for a semiotics of cinema, but only if they were deployed in a more complex way. These concepts depend on a project which ultimately lumps a large amount of signification together; but when mobilized in a radical fashion, they can be connected to arguments which interrogate and modify the very ideas of unity and totality. This would then also affect conceptions of individual texts.

Once the unity of a text is seen as problematic and complex, characterizing a film as a discursive entity whose processes are defined solely by its inclusion within (or exclusion from) a closed signifying system becomes difficult. To position films through critical and theoretical analysis would now require a different kind of framework, one which provides for a more nuanced awareness of the play of textual impulses. If the hypothesis that signification is systematic— regularized and thus somehow regulated—is to be maintained, an account of cinematic signification must comprehend excess, incoherence, contradiction, heterogeneity. These must now be included in descriptions and explanations even of purportedly totalizing signifying systems. The question may seem somewhat paradoxical or oxymoronic, but it can be put a little more concretely. How and why are such potentially disrupting impulses (from the viewpoint of systematicity) mobilized, suppressed, utilized, and/or repressed? One focal basis for answering such questions in film theory was the argument that, if the concept of signifying system is to be retained, it would have to be described dynamically. Terms which emphasize a constant *activity*, a *process*, would have be used in conceptualizing textuality and signifying systematicity.

Some film theorists prominent in the earlier discussions of the potential of a semiotics approach have indeed argued that changes in emphasis along these lines occurred.[1] These changes are summarized by a number of interacting terms, for example, from a focus on *structure* to a focus on *operations*, or from an interest in the *énoncé* (the "enunciated," the "statement" itself—the patterns of organizing signifying elements in an instance of signification) to an interest in the *énonciation* (the "enunciation"—the relation of those patterns to the concrete signifying situation and the positions of "speaker" and "listener" they presuppose). Now of course such shifts in emphases did not simply occur in a chronologically smooth progression; some of these concerns are clearly present in work which dates from the late 1960s and early 1970s, while efforts to define the parameters of cinematic signifying structures were produced later, and the two conceptual tendencies interpenetrated each other.

But it seems evident that in the history of cinema semiotics, there has often existed a self-conscious distinction between the two tendencies with the structuralist tendency being logically prior. More pertinent here than temporal precedence is the fact that insofar as changes in emphases did occur, film theory was in many ways partaking of more general trends in what came to be called "post-structuralism." These larger theoretical tendencies affected debate in such diverse areas as the general theory of the sign, philosophy, social theory, and psychoanalysis. What especially links film theory to the post-structuralism of the 1970s is the great impact of that sector of post-structuralism which claimed to be producing new elaborations of theories of human subjectivity. Therefore, before proceeding with the remainder of this anthology, it will be useful to introduce some of the relevant aspects of what has been called the theory of the subject.

The term *subject* denotes a fundamental human mental activity of interacting with things in the world by opposing them to one's own consciousness, as in the philosophical (epistemological) distinction between subject and object. However, by the 1970s French post-structuralists, including such divergent thinkers as Louis Althusser, Roland Barthes, Jacques Derrida, Michel Foucault, Julia Kristeva, and Jacques Lacan, had from varying but intertwining perspectives all proposed that the traditional philosophical conception of the subject is misleading in important respects. Against the strong Cartesian tradition in French intellectual history, they argued in different ways that the self-awareness of human subjectivity is founded on a central misrecognition by the subject—or self, or ego—that *it* is somehow central to the processes of knowing the world. In general, these post-structuralists at that time argued that the subject's knowledge of world and self is shaped by discourse. Ultimately this could be to say that human subjectivity finds itself through a discursive universe which produces and reproduces that subjectivity and, often enough, its constitutive illusions.

In what follows, we will consider two interrelated areas of human existence to explore two significant examples of contexts for theorizing and analyzing such misrecognition. One of these areas is described in social theory and one in psychoanalytic theory. In particular, some of the work of Louis Althusser and Jacques Lacan, two thinkers whose work was important to film-theoretical discussion in the 1970s, will be stressed.

To be aware of oneself as a distinct mental entity, a consciousness, is to have identity. Phenomenologically, of course, this is a constant, everyday experience which enables one to confront existence and undertake activities as a "continuous" human being; that is, I remain conscious that I am the "same" person today I was yesterday, which is a guarantee of my identity. Such self-awareness, however, can also be described with reference to processes not reducible to the unique experience by an individual of his or her own consciousness. It is possible to argue that such consciousness is a product, or construct, rather than an irreducible *a priori*. Such an argument would rest on an account of how this mode of subjectivity is produced and how it functions.

If one attempts this kind of argument from the perspective of social theory, the claim would be that to take the position of a self-aware subject is to participate in a process valuable to social institutions and/or to a society. In that case one's identity is produced as a result of ongoing social processes. Such a perspective was advanced influentially during the 1960s and early 1970s in Louis Althusser's reformulations of Marxist theories of ideology.[2]

For Althusser ideology is a requisite component of any society. It consists in a vast network of representational systems that provide the means with which individuals may think of their existence. But since it operates by delimiting as well as providing possible significations of existence, that massive representational network Althusser calls ideology is restrictive of thought and experience. He argues that such restrictions are crucial components of social organization and order: To maintain themselves over time, societies require that their multitude of agents have a minimal commonality of "consciousness," which means that those possibilities and limitations on thought and experience must to a significant degree be produced *as an integral part of* any lasting societal organization. This perspective leads Althusser to suggest that the category of the subject is a necessary (if not sufficient) support for the workings of ideology.

Such a conception, if accepted, has clear theoretical and methodological consequences for any semiotics, since it envisions representational systems as intricately knotted with broad processes of social organization. But here we will concentrate on the category of the subject in such a framework. For Althusser, ideology exists in an uncountable number of signifying entities. From the viewpoint of "consciousness," it can be said that we are "surrounded" from birth by signifying discourses which necessarily provide the paths by which we understand and experience. But from another perspective it is these discourses which construct individual social agents as human subjects. Insofar as any instance of signification presumes an addressee or "listener," it aims at something which is presumed to be able to understand—a *someone*. An individual is addressed in such discursive processes as a coherent consciousness, a subject.

The mechanisms by which discourses assume and thus appeal to a purportedly pre-existing subject—and thereby are in fact prior connditions for its production—Althusser sums up with the term *interpellation*. This term can name the act whereby a member of parliament questions a minister who is obligated to respond and assume responsibility for the actions of his or her government. Althusser metaphorically theorizes that all human individuals as social agents are constantly being interpellated. The discourses which interpellate them are not simply autonomous, but are amalgamated with social institutions, ranging from religion (one is called to account by an overarching authority) to legal practices (one is called to take responsibility as a legal subject for one's thoughts and actions) to everyday activities throughout a social formation.

If it still seems puzzling that Althusser would place such emphasis on ideology as *representational* processes and then focus on what can be called a "subject effect" as a *social* function, then we might elaborate a bit on the centrality of this effect to discursive practices. Every time an individual "uses" a signifying system, such as verbal language, the very form of that system includes "places" that attest to the existence of subjects of signification. In the fundamental, therefore privileged system of verbal language, examples include personal pronouns and verb tense—which always is relative to the present time of the speaker and thus assumes a subject of language in time. This subject is ultimately posited in discourse as the sender and/or comprehender of significations. In this context, it can be said that Althusser focuses attention on a conflation of levels: the sender and/or comprehender of significations, able to speak and understand, is conflated with a social subject mandated by social institutions, able to "choose," "responsible" for his or her acts, ultimately culpable for antisocial behavior. Since it is ideology, a kind of discursive environment, that provides the mediations for understanding actual existence, an individual's placement as a social subject is a placement as subject "in" discourse.[3]

On this view, then, the human subject is a function of a social formation which assumes and thereby continually constructs it in practices, in institutions, and therefore through discourse, without which there cannot be social practices and institutions, as a universal category of "lived experience." By constructing subjects in ideology—which is, ultimately, a framework for understanding existence beneficial to a given social order—the social formation works to maintain its own relative stability through time (both in the lifetime of an individual's experience and across the time of successive generations). The experience of subjectivity is intricately interlocked with the reproduction by a social formation of itself as a "natural" state of things. In classical accounts, of course, the production of what exists as "natural" is the operation of ideology.

Such a perspective has direct implications for film theory. If ideology consists in a universe of discursive representationality, then insofar as cinema works as representation and/or as a component of discursive systems of representation, filmic signifying systems can and should be investigated as ideology. If discursive effects are inseparable from interpellating individuals as subjects, then even film theory conceptualizing cinema as ideology should inquire about the mechanisms through which an individual film spectator "recognizes" himself or herself as subject in the film viewing process. In fact, this became a question consistently raised in film analysis during the 1970s, though not always from the explicit premise of social interpellation. Given the importance of the politicized wing of semiotic investigators of cinema, one would expect the fundamental repetitions identified in investigations stemming from the structuralist tendency to be related to questions of cinema as ideology: what concepts, myths, ideas, etc. are being thus recirculated? But such researches were further tied to a strong interest in what came to be called the study of "the position of the subject" or "subject-positioning" in cinema: how do dominant cinematic strategies strive to position the spectators as subjects, and what are the possibilities for contesting this positioning? This line of inquiry proved to be one of the strongest and most fertile in recent film theory.

However, if one examines a film for the mechanisms by which it offers a position or positions for the spectator to recognize himself or herself as subject, one will encounter a certain lack in the theory of ideology. A theory of ideology is not a specific account of human subjectivity as such, but an account of the production, circulation, and constraints of what is taken as knowledge and/or positions proper to knowledge in a given social formation. Thus, if one agrees with Althusser that the category of the subject is of special importance for ideological formations, there is a theoretical need for exploring the attraction of "subjecthood." What profit is there for an individual human being in assuming the positionality defined by that category? The very notions of interpellation and spectator-positioning seem to assume individuals who already desire to recognize themselves as subjects. Hence, an understanding of that desire is necessary even to pose those issues in the analysis of films.

Given the linkage of ideology and this desire with discursivity, the attraction, the *appeal,* of signifying processes requires a more specific theorization. This amounts to asking for an elaborate and rigorous account of relationships among text, meaning, pleasure, and spectatorial position. What are the processes by which specific discursive patterns appeal to an individual as subject? Social theory alone could not answer this question. But the ways one responds to this question will determine how one analyzes film texts and theorizes cinema.

In cinema semiotics of the 1970s, this issue was most often met by treating signification in terms provided by particular kinds of psychoanalytic theory. Now, if one attributes any validity to the psychoanalytic enterprise, this move will not seem too surprising. It is possible to view even classical psychoanalysis precisely as an account of the individual's desire for identity, for secure subjective positionality, against forces which constantly threaten it. Freud's "discovery" of the unconscious is inseparable from his account of human identity as being founded on a repression which is a necessary condition for forming a sense of self.

For Freudians, primary experiences of identity are constructed against a radical anxiety, summarized as castration anxiety. Processes of desire, sexuality, and fantasy are intertwined with consciousness of self, which is produced to counter against that founding anxiety and is always in dialectic with it. As a result, the normal experience of identity occurs only on condition that its basic processes are hidden from the "I" thus constructed. This is an essential Freudian point: there is always a fundamental *mis*recognition involved in the individual's desire to find—or recognize—his or her self as stable and secure.

The thesis that the unconscious is the basis for the existence of self-consciousness ("ego") can therefore serve as an explanation of the generalized desire of individual humans to seek secure subjective positions. Classical psychoanalytical conceptions could therefore be of great importance to the theorization of how films appeal to human subjects. In addition, however, the psychoanalytic theory utilized in recent cinema semiotics has often been inflected by the work of Jacques Lacan. Much of the conceptual apparatus for the most influential work on subject-positioning in cinema has been provided by his formulations. It will therefore be useful to outline briefly a few aspects of those formulations which have been especially evident in film-theoretical argument.[4]

We may begin with Lacan's heavy emphasis on the "entry" of a human infant "into" language. This occurs around the period of the child's discovery of sexual difference and the Oedipal conflicts traditionally highlighted in psychoanalytic thought. There are two general points of interest for semiotics in this. The first is simply that it leads Lacan to stress the importance of signification (especially in verbal language) for psychoanalytic investigations, and hence his work has often been used to develop connections between semiotics and psychoanalysis. The second is that Lacan explicitly follows Saussure in conceiving of language as a system of differences, which channels those connections in very specific ways.

For a Saussurian semiologist, the relation of difference is fundamental to signification, an *a priori* of language which becomes the premise of the analyst's work. Lacan goes beyond the givenness of difference, building on the terms of *linguistic* investigation to emphasize the role assigned to difference in *psychoanalytic* thought. Linguistics, strictly speaking, does not answer the question of how an individual human comes to recognize aspects of its universe in their differences. Psychoanalysis can answer that this recognition is not only a precondition for the individual to become a signifying being, but is also tied to the human's development as a sexed subject. In the classical psychoanalytic account of the genesis of the subject, the discovery of the possibility of difference coalesces around the relation of the individual to the difference between male and female bodies. At the time the child begins recognizing sexual difference, it has already begun to acquire a sense of identity, but that sense of selfhood is "pre-Oedipal:" narcissistic, all-encompassing, and essentially asocial. The Oedipal phase, revolving around the discovery of sexual difference by the child, completes the transformation of the infant into a social subject.

Lacan's far-reaching supplement to this classical psychoanalytic account is to argue that the existence of signifying processes is central to the transition and far-reaching consequences associated with Oedipal experiences. It is a major tenet of classical psychoanalysis that during the Oedipal crisis there normally occurs the more or less permanent "splitting" of the psyche between what is available to consciousness and the unconscious. The individual assumes the identity of a sexed subject, as the unconscious and repression become a constant fact of that subject. Lacan adds that fundamental to the Oedipal knotting of identity and sexuality is symbolization. That is, as an individual comes to awareness of self as a separate subject who is sexed, he or she "enters" what Lacan calls the *symbolic order,* and becomes a subject in language as well.

The importance of symbolization and language for Freud has always been evident, for example in his concern with dream symbolization and slips of the tongue. But the implications of Lacan's theoretical emphasis on this perspective are nevertheless enormous. He ultimately means that the relations of the subject posited as central by psychoanalysis—for example, between conscious and unconscious, and of the individual to other bodies and to objects—cannot be understood without taking the framework of signifying systematicity into account. Among other things this approach can provide the basis for an account of the appeal of representational processes.

Some of the articles included in the following part of this anthology summarize important aspects of Lacanian thought, and in this introduction the aim is only to highlight some Lacanian emphases of more specific pertinence to cinema. Nevertheless, it will first be useful to outline four general hypotheses common in Lacanian approaches to signification:

1. *Difference as a linguistic (or semiotic) concept is associated with difference as a psychoanalytic category.*

Lacan's linguistics is a Saussurian linguistics, for which signification takes place as a play of pertinent systemic differences among signifiers. For Lacan, this ties signification to the psychoanalytic account of the infant which stresses that in order to acquire identity individual humans must learn to recognize differences in the world. Primary awareness of difference in the child's universe focuses on an experience of the body, coalescing through the castration complex around sexual differentiation. That is, for psychoanalysis the discovery of difference is inextricably associated with a phantasmatic attack upon one's own body.

On the one hand, the formation of identity requires a founding awareness of one's own body precisely as *one's* own. But in that case, an attack upon it is an extreme psychic threat. Hence, the harshness of the child's dilemma: in order to become a self-aware human individual—a subject—the child must experience that founding anxiety. Now, this is roughly the same time that the child "acquires" language, and for Lacan this means the onset of awareness of bodily difference in the experience of castration is not separable from the practical comprehension of the principle of difference in signification. But in that case—if a central strand of the Oedipal "knot" is the establishing of the individual's identity in language and signification—the symbolic order is entered on the basis of dread.

2. *The impression of coherent meaning is produced in signifying practi· ·s against heterogeneity and difference; this coherence therefore works for the constant reassurance and production of the subject's full identity.*

Let us suppose, with Lacan, that the developing self-consciousness of the child comes terrified into signifying systematicity. What would such a developing self-consciousness seek there? What could a signifying system offer it? Presumably, there would have to be some reassurance against the central anxiety which psychoanalysis labels as castration. Therefore, at least from the subject's perspective, signifying systems would have to include something at the service of coherent identity, of a security of self. This occurs on the level of meaning. The impression of a reassuringly adequate relation between signifier and signified and/or sign and referent is achieved in practice for the subject, despite the fact of the arbitrariness of the sign and the basis of language in what threatens the subject—difference. (However, we will shortly indicate how that achievement is only a qualified one.) Thus, Lacanian psychoanalysis is (among other things) an account of how, in and through signification, the individual is "sutured" into "secure" meaning at the service of "stable" identity.

To understand why secure meaning should confirm the subject in its identity, briefly consider the purported attributes of an utterance which seems "adequate." Such an utterance is said to "communicate a thought" originating in the speaking subject to a listening subject who then understands that thought. Very simply, any such instance of language use will offer both subjects a secure position insofar as an impression of delimitable meaning is achieved: *I* speak and *you* understand.

Now, such adequation is often described as a relation of substitutibility between sign and referent or between signifier and signified. But that is not the lesson here; rather, it is precisely to the extent that the sign or signifier can be thus comprehended as adequate that the subject is safely positioned as such. This is because that adequation is an experience of guaranteed understanding and/or knowledge by the subject: it is *I* who comprehend, it is *my* capacities which are demonstrated in "sending" and "receiving" "communications." (And this approach can be extended to the framework of understanding or being entertained by a film).

But note that this effect occurs as one of unificaton and homogeneity. The principle of difference, at work in and defining the very material employed as the basis of signification, is to be overlooked or overcome in search of meaning as *coherent,* and this coherence is then attributed to the very being of the subject(s) of the speech situation. Thus, while a position for the subject is therefore achieved as the apparent effect of a determination of signifier by signified, actually the crucial effect lies in the homogenizing aspect. Since Lacan accepts the Saussurian account, however, this appearance can only be a constitutive illusion of the subject. In actuality, the signifiers are the locus of the play of difference subtending signification and meaning, so the determinations of the speech situation are the reverse of its appearance: it is the signifier which determines the subject as a certain position in meaning—not the subject which determines the signified by the act of communicating his or her thoughts.

Thus, it is not the subject who uses the signifying system, but the signifying system which defines the subject. It is not the subject who "speaks" the signified, but the signifier which "speaks" the subject. But this is precisely what the subject cannot consistently recognize while maintaining its own existence, for processes of difference cannot be separated from the experience of the castration complex. This is why the subject, though it exists "through" the play of differences, has a stake in overvaluing a homogenizing signified as against the system of differences which determines signification.

From a logical viewpoint based on the principle of noncontradiction, there is something of the illogical, the paradoxical, the impossible about the functioning of the subject in and through the symbolic order. The child must be able to comprehend difference in the world in order to exist in signification and therefore culture, but the function of difference is tied to the terror of castration anxiety and therefore demands repression. Yet the linguistic system, the most determinant signifying system for Lacan, is founded precisely on a system of differences, so that any instance of language use is potential evidence of that which threatens the subject. Thus, if the consciousness of the child is formed in language to seek security in the face of difference, and if it enters the symbolic order in such a quest, there would seem to be no permanent solution available in signification to the subject. It could only seek temporary, recurrent solutions to its dilemmas of identity.

3. *Subjective life can be described as the constant interrelations between processes of the imaginary order and the symbolic order.*

To put it simply, the law of noncontradiction is not determinant in the unconscious. There must be psychic processes which can repetitively find this logically dubious homogeneity against the symbolic order *for the subject* as a stable identity. For a subject to recognize itself as secure and stable in language, it must read "through" the materiality of language as a structuring of differences and in spite of the latter find evidence of self-coherence.

Most generally, this unifying, coherence-seeking impulse is what Lacan calls the *imaginary order.* On the one hand, the imaginary names those psychic forces which are fundamentally contrary to the symbolic: the imaginary, rooted in pre-Oedipal formations of the nascent sense of self, seeks coherence for the ego and therfore an end to difference against castration. The symbolic, on the other hand, is built on difference and therefore inseparable from the experience of castration. Thus, the imaginary order strives toward the assumption of full identity *against* the symbolic.

On the other hand, these two orders of subjectivity are intricately and inevitably interdependent. If the quest of the imaginary is for an absolute and permanent confirmation of identity, it cannot put aside the signifying system whose constitution threatens such stability, but must work *through* it. Once castration and repression have occurred, the individual is irreversibly "in" the symbolic, so it is only "through" the symbolic that the imaginary can seek reassurance—by means of "positions" in signifying processes which (temporarily but repetitively) provide for the reconfirmation of the subject's identity.

But furthermore, the symbolic requires the imaginary. How could signification exist without "beings" who "wish" to assume positions of subjects of language and in language? This is the fundammental Lacanian dialectic: there is the necessity of the imaginary to find a sense of coherence and wholeness, which impels the subject to seek confirmation of coherent identity "outside" itself, in its relation to "the other". But the subject can only experience this "outside" as "the Other," that is, with the mediation of the symbolic, which was entered by means of the Oedipal experience and all that implies in psychoanalytic thought. The subject, then, is always seeking to overcome the alienation and threats to the sense of self which follows from the period of castration and entry into the symbolic order. The goal of the imaginary is an impossible one, so it can at most be achieved temporarily in substitutions, whether of objects or in signification. Or rather, it is signifying structures which define what can count as such a satisfaction, no matter what the "material" of that satisfaction is. But since in the last instance only substitutions are attainable (the sign can never be the thing), identity must always deal with its own ultimate lacks.

4. Signification occurs in the face of lack with the phallus as a privileged signifier of desire.

We have seen that in Lacanian psychoanalysis, the constant, definitional threat to the coherence of the subject classically attributed to castration overlaps with the relation of the subject to signification in general and language in particular. As indicated by Freud, the search for subjective security is unending (this is what is established in the psychoanalytic concept of castration). Insofar as the subject achieves security by finding homogeneous meaning, the conception of signification as the play of differences combined with the thesis of the arbitrariness of the sign deprive confirmations of identity of any absolute success.

Since the subject's relation to the world—to otherness—is through signification, *the real* (another special Lacanian term) is ultimately unreachable in any direct way, but is only constructed in the symbolic, as "reality."[5] Underlying the discursive constructions through which the subject is constantly in search of itself, there is always a basic inadequacy to signification, a lack. From the perspective of the imaginary, then, there is always something tenuous for the subject. On the level of signification, no matter how much a given discourse is shaped to apply pressure toward unification, adequacy, clear meaning, reference to the real, and so forth, it will also manifest more or less strongly its own heterogeneous processes, that is, the discursive production of that pressure. As Saussure banishes the referent from the processes of signification that produce meaning, Lacan banishes any direct contact with the real outside signification from the experience of the subject. Thus, if the imaginary pushes for an absolute assurance in representation, representation is never what it seems, so the problem is insoluble.

The fundamental lack in signification translates into an underlying lack in being and identity. This is why the connection of signification to castration is more than analogy. As a way of emphasizing this, we can here note that the drastic consequences which the necessary inadequacies of signification have for subjective life by outlining Lacan's conception of the phallus as the fundamentally important signifier (rather than a bodily part).

The child enters the symbolic order looking for ways to defend its sense of self, which is, on the basis of the Oedipal crisis, now felt to be lacking. It is the terms of that lack and their special relation to signification which the concept of the phallus as signifier apprehends. The triangular structure of mother, child, and father is treated by Lacan not as a sociological reality, but *as a structure;* the three terms are defined by their relations to one another, as structural functions. That is, it does not matter whether there is a "real" father or mother; rather what matters is a set of relations which introduces lack into the universe of the infant.

Now, it is precisely difference, lack, which finds its signifier in the phallus. Lacan emphasizes this in relation to certain other psychoanalytic concepts, such as that of desire. A subject's desire for total love is inevitably included in any demand or request signified to an Other for a particular object of need. (Structurally, the model here is an infant's demand to the mother.) But that desire finds its unconscious token in this privileged signifier of lack, the phallus. We must return once more to the concept of castration to explicate this.

In the Oedipal scenario a dyadic relation of mother to child is broken and made into a triangular relation when the child must confront the intervention of a third term, the father. In this scenario, the child processes the consequent shocks and traumas in such a way to result in the advent of the subject as split (between conscious and a repressed unconscious), as signifying, as sexual (male or female), and as a desiring being. These consequences occur by the fantastic representation of lack: the penis which is an attribute of the father but not of the mother is converted into a signifier, and through that conversion that the child enters the symbolic order.

Without going into detail on all the theoretical twists and turns, some Lacanian emphases on this matter include the following: first, from now on in subjective life, the penis is no longer a bodily part, but a signifier—the phallus. (Indeed, how could the "missing" phallic attribute of the mother even be anything but a fantastic signifier?) Second, the phallus as signifier is a signifier of difference (this links the castration complex and the symbolic order) and therefore at some level must be understood as such by the subject in order to become a sexed being and in order to enter signification. That is, the child must comprehend the principle of difference in order to be a signifying being, which means that difference must be signified; that function is occupied by the phallus. Thus, even though the phallus might be conceived as that which is the subject's ultimate desire, it nevertheless continues to be the signifier of lack itself.

Third, Lacan places great stress on the psychoanalytic concept of desire, and the phallus is the ultimate token or signifier for desire. In the Oedipal structure, the recognition of difference occurs when the child discovers the mother as lacking and therefore imputes to her a consequent desire for that which she lacks: the phallus of the father. Thus, for the child the phallus is that which the mother desires. It is in the desire of the mother that desire is initiated in the child. To maintain the full, dyadic relation to the mother, the child would like to assume the function which the phallus occupies in the desire of the mother, that is, would like to *be* the phallus which the mother lacks. But this is of course impossible, for the phallus is a fantastic signifier; so the child will have to be satisfied with an unending series of substitutes for what it is not, namely the phallus for the mother.

This initiation of the subject into desire helps explain why desire can never be permanently satisfied: it is unending because a perfect object which would terminate it can never be found. Thus, the processes of desire can only be specified on the level of inadequate substitutions—of signs. And the phallus both provides the signifier around which the fixations of meaning (imaginary stoppages of desire) coalesce, while it simultaneously signifies the principle of difference which determines that any object will always be lacking. The concept of the phallus as signifier once again highlights paradoxical situation of a subject seeking stasis (identity), but which always must do this in dynamic processes.[6]

The Lacanian triad of the imaginary order, the symbolic order, and the real models a fundamental view of subjective processes. Having outlined that triad, we can now begin returning to a more direct consideration of film theory. Lacan's intricate account can be seen as explicating the category of the unified, coherent subject as a reality of experience, but as a *produced* reality, a construct. From one perspective, as Lacan would claim, this is only an elaboration of the classical psychoanalytic insight that a sense of self is inseparable from repressive mechanisms, and that what is repressed is precisely what necessitates the remarkable defenses of identity. But the conception of the human psyche resulting from this elaboration, with its emphasis on and theorization of operations of signification, might be extremely attractive for a semiotics seeking a level of explanation which supercedes the definition and implementation of structural categories, as well as for filling out the concept of interpellation as a generalized social mechanism. For example, the centrality thus posited of the phallus as signifier is one of the elements of Lacanian theory which has made it useful for feminist film theorists (it provides an account of phallocentric desire in relation to representation) and simultaneously has made it problematic for them (it becomes difficult to conceive of desire in a nonphallocentric way).

Just as pertinent here, we can note that, despite its stress on verbal language, Lacan's theorization of the processes of desire which move an individual to assume a position of a supposedly self-conscious subject in language and representation has its special attractions for a semiotics of *visual* representation. One general tendency in psychoanalytic thought is to seek cases or events which are especially revealing of widespread structures and processes underlying conscious experience. This has led to a common practice of privileging certain scenarios in order to explore such underlying processes. Lacanian psychoanalysis stresses mechanisms by which an infant acquires identity in relation to the universe of signification. In so doing, this psychoanalysis often privileges scenarios in which visual perception has a central function. This emphasis has been exploited by a number of film theorists drawn to psychoanalytic accounts of the spectator as subject.

Take, for example, the pre-Oedipal, narcissistic phase of the development of the ego—what some psychoanalytic theorists might call the primary identification against which all subsequent assumptions of identity (secondary identifications) will be measured and at some level found failing by the psyche. To mark the acquisition of that narcissistic sense of self, Lacan privileges the phenomenon of a six-to eighteen-month-old infant's delight at *seeing* its own image in a mirror and thereby recognizing its body as a coherent whole. However, Lacan stresses a simultaneous *misrecognition* of the image by the child, who sees it as visual evidence of his or her own "presence" in entities outside its body. During this "mirror phase," there is a triumphant, joyous experience of full, unthreatened, coherent identity wherein the infant finds its self reflected in its relation to everything in the world. At this stage, the individual exists more or less purely in the imaginary order (which is thus named in part because a certain relation to imagery is central to the description of its effects).

Similarly, the discovery of difference—which for Lacan threatens the imaginary, narcissistic identity of the mirror phase and initiates the individual into the symbolic order—has privileged scenarios that rely on visual perception even in classical psychoanalysis. Important scenarios of encounters with sexual difference in the primal scene (when the child discovers the parents having intercourse) and the "moment" originating fetishism (when the child "sees" that the mother has no penis and takes this as evidence of the possibility of castration) are founded on the child's misunderstanding of a visual experience of human bodies.

Again, these are only privileged scenarios and cases to be explored for underlying psychical structures. One thing they do register, however, is the early overdevelopment of the visual sense (for psychoanalysis, the scopic drive) on the part of the infant, manifested as a precocious visual curiosity. Vision can therefore be treated as crucial in primary assumptions of identity and in threats against that identity. In that case, defenses against such threats and in the service of secure and stable subjectivity would likely take place in part, at least, in the register of the visual. Thus, visual representation in this account has its own special functions in the ongoing processes of subjectivity, and these could be of central interest to a semiotic investigaion of the visual aspects of cinema.

In a more general sense, however, this theoretical framework indicates that all representational processes share certain aspects in their appeals to individuals as subjects. Any representational entity regardless of its material characteristics (whether image, writing, speech, or something else) must include some kind of compensation to the benefit of the continual production of coherent identity as a counter to the constant fact of difference. Of course, there must be distinctions among various modes of signification and hence a specificity in the psychic economy of a given medium's participation in this general process; these are of central importance to any film theory. But it is also of importance to note the general perspective provided by a Lacanian semiotics.

The appeal of representational entities to subjects is explained by the thesis of the mutual imbrication of imaginary and symbolic orders. The imaginary is the realm of an impossible, ideal security of being underlying the pursuit of identity. Identity is continually being constructed against a lack of wholeness, a lack which, measured against the plentitude of identity of primary narcissism, can never be recovered. The symbolic is the regime which perpetually reactivates the threat (always embodying the fact of difference) and provides a means of temporarily overcoming that threat by providing reconfirming but never finalized positionalities in meaning.

Despite Lacan's own stress on the symbolic order as a *linguistically* organized fact, psychoanalytic conceptions and Lacan's emphasis on the relations between subjective positionality, representational systems and processes, and desire have often been treated by film theorists as a complement to a general semiotics. They have also sometimes been treated as filling in certain gaps in an interpellation theory of ideology. It is certainly true that contradictions between the two latter theories could also be adduced. But we have tried to highlight concerns which both share: an insistence on the importance of representational processes, an emphasis on the category of the subject, a focus on mechanisms of misrecognition seen as inseparable from signification.

Over the past several years, textual operations have often been approached by film theorists in relation to such issues. Those operations are thus often conceived of as addressing or appealing to a subject (or, more precisely, a psychic entity which works to maintain the status of a self-aware subject over and against the forces which threaten that status). The analysis of how images and sounds construct spectatorial positions has become one of the most significant kinds of investigations in contemporary film theory and criticism. Cinema, groups of films, and individual films are interrogated as sign processes for the ways in which they are implicated in the general, constant processes of constructing social and psychical identity.

The items selected for part 2 all consider filmic narrative from the perspective of subject-positioning. Furthermore, almost all of them include explicit explanations of and/or meditations on psychoanalytic approaches to that issue. Thus, this part functions to bring together several articles that present the theorization of how films address subjects and psychoanalytic theory in relation to cinematic narrative.

One of the most significant critics of his era, Roland Barthes, provides an elegant gloss on the concept of the spectating subject in "Diderot, Brecht, Eisenstein." Finding commonalities between theater, painting, and cinema, Barthes outlines a connection between spectating and fetishism. In addition, he considers some of the consequences of this view of textuality for a cultural politics, and calls into question the notion of a binary cultural politics by introducing a third kind of textuality which he calls "music" and "the Text."

Colin MacCabe argues that the classical text shares fundamental characteristics and goals of realism, and that this commonality can be understood by theorizing the position of the spectating subject. His view of the relation of signification to the subject is grounded in a useful presentation of Lacanian conceptions. He further argues for the pertinence of this view of signification for making sociopolitical distinctions among different kinds of filmic textuality.

Laura Mulvey's "Visual Pleasure and Narrative Cinema" includes another presentation of psychoanalytic theory in relation to cinema. Though there is some reference to Lacan, Mulvey tends to mobilize Freud more directly than MacCabe. This article's significance lies in part in its landmark appropriation of psychoanalytic theory for feminist approaches to cinema. Both Barthes and MacCabe, in different ways, call attention to the need to theorize looking and vision in cinema in relation to spectatorial position. But Mulvey's concentration on the male look at the woman and her mobilization of the psychoanalytic conceptions of voyeurism and fetishism in their explicitly sexual configurations to understand classical cinema makes feminist argument central to any psychoanalytic understanding of classical cinema.

In one of the earliest responses to Mulvey, Paul Willemen sums up aspects of her argument, offers some sympathetic critiques on certain points, and suggests that scopophiliac elements exist in the avant-garde cinema as well as the classical cinema. He illustrates his argument by considering the mobilization of such impulses in the work of Stephen Dwoskin.

The term "suture" comes into film theory from Lacanian thought. It is a metaphor for the relation of a subject to a signifying chain—an interaction of the impulse to coherent identity which, figuratively speaking, must maintain itself through the gaps of difference, heterogeneity, and contradiction embodied in the construction of any signifying chain. As Kaja Silverman presents the notion, it "can be understood as the process whereby the inadequacy of the subject's position is exposed in order to facilitate (i.e., create the desire for) new insertions into a cultural discourse which promises to make good that lack." Silverman provides an overview of the different ways this notion of suture has been employed in film theory; develops it through analyses of films *(Psycho, Lola Montez, Gilda);* and establishes relations between lack as conceived in the notion of suture and a feminist account of spectatorship found in the work of Laura Mulvey.

Julia Kristeva's "Ellipsis on Dread and the Specular Seduction" meditates on the relation of the threat of subjective dispersal as it is impinged upon by "the fascinating specular" of cinema. It thus addresses issues raised by Silverman in more general terms: the relation of subjective threat to subjective reassurance—of the possibility of lack to desire—and the function of cinema in that relation.

Christian Metz's "The Imaginary Signifier" is a synthetic inquiry into the utility of psychoanalytic conceptions in film theory, and possibly the single most important and most often cited article on that question. Metz's shift in theoretical frameworks (from Saussurian linguistics in "Problems of Denotation in the Fiction Film" to Freud, Lacan, et al). is explained in this article not as a rejection of the semiotic enterprise but as a development of it. Metz asks, "What contribution can Freudian psychoanalysis make to the study of the cinematic signifier" and outlines the kinds of links he sees between psychoanalysis and semiotics.

In the portions of "The Imaginary Signifier" not included in this volume, Metz explains that he is concerned with the kind of film which gives pleasure (is a "good object"), precisely indicates the type of psychoanalysis he is concerned with, and meditates on the possibilities of psychoanalytic study of what he calls the film script. The bulk of the portions here republished run through the applicability and limitations of psychoanalytic concepts central to the theorization of cinema: identification, the mirror phase, the scopic drives, disavowal and fetishism, and so forth. These are considered in light of some of the traditional issues of film theory (e.g., what are the differences and similarities between film and theater) and some less traditional issues (e.g., the extent to which the pleasure of the cinematic experience has something of the illegitimate about it.) "The Imaginary Signifier" can thus serve here both as an influential overview of the intervention of psychoanalysis in recent film theory and as a transition to part 3, which is concerned in part with the ways such conceptions have been mobilized to understand the construction and specific dispositions of filmic technology.

Notes

1. For example, Christian Metz, *The Imaginary Signifier: Psychoanalysis and the Cinema* (London: Macmillan, and Bloomington: Indiana University Press, 1982), p. 3.

2. See esp. "Marxism and Humanism," in Louis Althusser, *For Marx,* trans. Ben Brewster (New York: Pantheon Books, 1969); and, on the subject and the thesis of interpellation (discussed below), "Ideology and Ideological State Apparatuses (Notes Towards an Investigation)," in Louis Althusser, *Lenin and Philosophy and Other Essays,* trans. Ben Brewster (New York: Monthly Review Press, 1971).

3. This link between signifying form and social institutions via the concept of the subject is not made as explicitly by Althusser himself. However, insofar as the category of the subject has been of interest in film theory from a sociocultural perspective, a jump such as this seems necessary.

On the provisions made in structures of verbal language for subject effects, one constant reference has been the work of Emile Benveniste. See his articles such as "Relationships of Person in the Verb," "The Correlations of Tense in the French Verb," "The Nature of Pronouns," and "Subjectivity in Language" all included in his collection *Problems in General Linguistics,* trans. Mary Elizabeth Meek (Coral Gables, FL: University of Miami Press, 1971). For example, see p. 224: "It is in and through language that man *[sic]* constitutes himself as a *subject*. . ."

4. There is now a good deal of Lacan's work available in English translation. For film theory, a useful place to begin remains "The mirror stage as formative of the function of the I. . ." in Jacques Lacan, *Ecrits: A Selection,* trans. Alan Sheridan (New York: Norton, 1977). Other selections in *Ecrits: A Selection* of special interest for the discussion below include "The Agency of the Letter in the Unconscious or Reason Since Freud" and "The Signification of the Phallus."

5. For an explication of the Lacanian distinction between "the real" and "reality" in the context of a discussion of cinema and film theory, see Stephen Heath, *"Anata mo,"* *Screen* (Winter 1976–1977), 17(4):49–66.

6. See Jacqueline Rose, "Introduction—II" in *Feminine Sexuality: Jacques Lacan and the école freudienne,* ed. Juliet Mitchell and Jacqueline Rose, trans. Jacqueline Rose (New York: Norton, 1983), for a careful explication of and commentary on Lacan's conception of the phallus and its relation to desire, e.g. pp. 37–43.

[9]

Roland Barthes
Diderot, Brecht, Eisenstein

For André Techiné

Let us imagine that an affinity of status and history has linked mathematics and acoustics since the ancient Greeks. Let us also imagine that for two or three millennia this effectively Pythagorean space has been somewhat repressed (Pythagoras is indeed the eponymous hero of Secrecy). Finally, let us imagine that from the time of these same Greeks another relationship has been established over against the first and has got the better of it, continually taking the lead in the history of the arts—the relationship between geometry and theater. The theater is precisely that practice which calculates the place of things *as they are observed*: if I set the spectacle here, the spectator will see this; if I put it elsewhere, he will not, and I can avail myself of this masking effect and play on the illusion it provides. The stage is the line which stands across the path of the optic pencil, tracing at once the point at which it is brought to a stop and, as it were, the threshold of its ramification. Thus is founded—against music (against the text)—*representation*.

Representation is not defined directly by imitation: even if one gets rid of notions of the "real," of the "vraisemblable," of the "copy," there will still be representation for so long as a subject (author, reader, spectator, or voyeur) casts his *gaze* toward a horizon on which he cuts out the base of a triangle, his eye (or his mind) forming the apex. The "Organon of Representation" (which today it is becoming possible to write because there are intimations of *something else)* will have as its dual foundation the sovereignty of the act of cutting out *[découpage]* and the unity of the subject of that action. The substance of the various arts will therefore be of little importance; certainly, theater and cinema are direct expressions of geometry (unless, as rarely, they carry out some research on the voice, on stereophony), but classic (readable) literary discourse, which has for such a long time now abandoned prosody, music, is also a representational, geometrical discourse in that is cuts out segments in order to depict them: to discourse (the classics would have said) is simply "to depict the tableau one has in one's mind." The scene, the picture, the shot, the cut-out rectangle, here we have the very *condition* that allows us to conceive theater, painting, cinema, literature, all those arts, that is, other than music and which could be called *dioptric arts.* (Counterproof: nothing permits us to locate the slightest tableau in the musical text, except by reducing it to a subservience to drama; nothing permits us to cut out in it the slightest fetish, except by debasing it through the use of trite melodies.)

As is well known, the whole of Diderot's aesthetics rests on the identification of theatrical scene and pictorial tableau: the perfect play is a succession of tableaux, that is, a gallery, an exhibition; the stage offers the spectator "as many real tableaux as there are in the action moments favorable to the painter." The tableau (pictorial, theatrical, literary) is a pure cut-out segment with clearly defined edges, irreversible and incorruptible; everything that surrounds it is banished into nothingness, remains unnamed, while everything that it admits within its field is promoted into essence, into light, into view. Such demiurgic discrimination implies high quality of thought: the tableau is intellectual, it has something to say (something moral, social), but it also says that it knows how this must be done; it is simultaneously significant and propaedeutic, impressive and reflexive, moving and conscious of the channels of emotion. The epic scene in Brecht, the shot in Eisenstein are so many tableaux; they are scenes which are *laid out* (in the sense in which one says *the table is laid),* which answer perfectly to that dramatic unity theorized by Diderot: firmly cut out (remember the tolerance shown by Brecht with regard to the Italian curtain-stage, his contempt for indefinite theaters—open air, theater in the round), erecting a meaning but manifesting the production of that meaning, they accomplish the coincidence of the visual and the ideal *découpages.* Nothing separates the shot in Eisenstein from the picture by Greuze (except, of course, their respective projects: in the latter moral, in the former social); nothing separates the scene in epic theater from the Eisenstein shot (except that in Brecht the tableau is offered to the spectator for criticism, not for adherence).

Is the tableau then (since it arises from a process of cutting out) a fetish object? Yes, at the level of the ideal meaning (Good, Progress, the Cause, the triumph of just History); no, at that of its composition. Or rather, more exactly, it is the very *composition* that allows the displacement of the point at which the fetish comes to a halt and thus the setting further back of the loving effect of the *découpage*. Once again, Diderot is for us the theorist of this dialectic of desire; in the article on "Composition," he writes: "A well-composed picture *[tableau]* is a whole contained under a single point of view, in which the parts work together to one end and form by their mutual correspondence a unity as real as that of the members of the body of an animal; so that a piece of painting made up of a large number of figures thrown at random onto the canvas, with neither proportion, intelligence, nor unity, no more deserves to be called a *true composition* than scattered studies of legs, nose, and eyes on the same cartoon deserve to be called a *portrait* or even a *human figure*." Thus is the body expressly introduced into the idea of the tableau, but it is the whole body that is so introduced—the organs, grouped together and as though held in cohesion by the magnetic power of the segmentation, function in the name of a transcendence, that of the *figure,* which receives the full fetishistic load and becomes the sublime substitute of meaning: it is this meaning that is fetishized. (Doubtless there would be no difficulty in finding in post-Brechtian theater and post-Eisensteinian cinema mises-en-scène marked by the dispersion of the tableau, the pulling to pieces of the "composition," the setting in movement of the "partial organs" of the human figure, in short the holding in check of the metaphysical meaning of the work—but then also of its political meaning; or, at least, the carrying over of this meaning toward *another* politics).

Brecht indicated clearly that in epic theater (which proceeds by successive tableaux) all the burden of meaning and pleasure bears on each scene, not on the whole. At the level of the play itself, there is no development, no maturation; there is indeed an ideal meaning (given straight in every tableau), but there is no final meaning, nothing but a series of segmentations each of which possesses a sufficient demonstrative power. The same is true in Eisenstein: the film is a contiguity of episodes, each one absolutely meaningful, aesthetically perfect, and the result is a cinema by vocation anthological, itself holding out to the fetishist, with dotted lines, the piece for him to cut out and take away to enjoy (isn't it said that in some *cinémathèque* or other a piece of film is missing from the copy of *Battleship Potemkin*—the scene with the baby's pram, of course—it having been cut off and stolen lovingly like a lock of hair, a glove or an item of women's underwear?). The primary force of Eisenstein is due to the fact that *no image is boring,* you are not obliged to wait for the next in order to understand and be delighted; it is a question not of a dialectic (that time of the patience required for certain pleasures) but of a continuous jubilation made up of a summation of perfect instants.

Naturally, Diderot had conceived of this perfect instant (and had given it thought). In order to tell a story, the painter has only an instant at his disposal, the instant he is going to immobilize on the canvas, and he must thus choose it well, assuring it in advance of the greatest possible yield of meaning and pleasure. Necessarily total, this instant will be artificial (unreal; this is not a realist art), a hieroglyph in which can be read at a single glance (at one grasp, if we think in terms of theater and cinema) the present, the past, and the future; that is, the historical meaning of the represented action. This crucial instant, totally concrete and totally abstract, is what Lessing subsequently calls (in the *Laocoön)* the *pregnant moment.* Brecht's theater, Eisenstein's cinema are series of pregnant moments: when Mother Courage bites on the coin offered by the recruiting sergeant and, as a result of this brief interval of distrust, loses her son, she demonstrates at once her past as tradeswoman and the future that awaits her— all her children dead in consequence of her money-making blindness. When (in *The General Line)* the peasant woman lets her skirt be ripped up for material to help in repairing the tractor, the gesture bears the weight of a history: its pregnancy brings together the past victory (the tractor bitterly won from bureaucratic incompetence), the present struggle, and the effectiveness of solidarity. The pregnant moment is just this presence of all the absences (memories, lessons, promises) to whose rhythm History becomes both intelligible and desirable.

In Brecht, it is the *social gest* which takes up the idea of the pregnant moment. What then is a social gest (how much irony has reactionary criticism poured on this Brechtian concept, one of the clearest and most intelligent that dramatic theory has ever produced!)? It is a gesture or set of gestures (but never a gesticulation) in which a whole social situation can be read. Not every gest is social: there is nothing social in the movements a man makes in order to brush off a fly; but if this same man, poorly dressed, is struggling against guard-dogs, the gest becomes social. The action by which the canteen-woman tests the genuineness of the money offered is a social gest; as again is the excessive flourish with which the bureaucrat of *The General Line* signs his official papers. This kind of social gest can be traced even in language itself. A language can be gestual, says Brecht, when it indicates certain attitudes that the speaker adopts toward others: "If thine eye offend thee, pluck it out" is more gestual than "Pluck out the eye that offends thee" because the order of the sentence and the asyndeton that carries it along refer to a prophetic and vengeful situation. Thus rhetorical forms may be gestual, which is why it is pointless to criticize Eisenstein's art (as also that of Brecht) for being "formalizing" or "aesthetic": form, aesthetic, rhetoric can be socially responsible if they are handled with deliberation. Representation (since that is what we are concerned with) has inescapably to reckon with the social gest; as soon as one "represents" (cuts out, marks off the tableau and so discontinues the overall totality), it must be decided whether the gesture is social or not (when it refers not to a particular society but to Man).

What does the actor do in the tableau (the scene, the shot)? Since the tableau is the presentation of an ideal meaning, the actor must present the very knowledge of the meaning, for the latter would not be ideal if it did not bring with it its own machination. This knowledge which the actor must demonstrate—by an unwonted supplement—is, however, neither his human knowledge (his tears must not refer simply to the state of feeling of the Downcast) nor his knowledge as actor (he must not show that he knows how to act well). The actor must prove that he is not enslaved to the spectator (bogged down in "reality", in "humanity"), that he guides meaning toward its ideality—a sovereignty of the actor, master of meaning, which is evident in Brecht, since he theorized it under the term "distanciation." It is no less evident in Eisenstein (at least in the author of *The General Line,* which is my example here), and this not as a result of a ceremonial, ritual art—the kind of art called for by Brecht—but through the insistence of the social gest which never ceases to stamp the actors' gestures (fists clenching, hands gripping tools, peasants reporting at the bureaucrat's reception desk). Nevertheless, it is true that in Eisenstein, as in Greuze (for Diderot an exemplary painter), the actor does sometimes adopt expressions of the most pathetic quality, a pathos which can appear to be very little "distanced"; but distanciation is a properly Brechtian method, vital to Brecht because he represents a tableau for the spectator to criticize; in the other two, the actor does not necessarily have to distance: what he has to present is an ideal meaning, and it is sufficient therefore that he "bring out" the production of this value, that he render it tangible, intellectually visible, by the very excess of the versions he gives it; his expression then signifies an idea—which is why it is excessive—not some natural quality. All this is a far cry from the facial affectations of the Actors' Studio, the much praised 'restraint' of which has no other meaning than its contribution to the personal glory of the actor (witness in this respect Brando's grimacings in *The Last Tango in Paris).*

Does the tableau have a subject (a topic)? Nowise; it has a meaning, not a subject. The meaning begins with the social gest (with the pregnant moment); outside of the gest, there is only vagueness, insignificance. "In a way," writes Brecht, "subjects always have a certain naivety, they are somewhat lacking in qualities. Empty, they are in some sort sufficient to themselves. Only the social *gest* (criticism, strategy, irony, propaganda, etc.) introduces the human element." To which Diderot adds (if one may put it like that): the creation of the painter or the dramatist lies not in the choice of a subject but in the choice of the pregnant moment, in the choice of the tableau. It matters little, after all, that Eisenstein took his "subjects" from the past history of Russia and the Revolution and not— "as he should have done" (so say his censors today)—from the present of the construction of socialism (except in the case of *The General Line);* battleship or czar are of minor importance, are merely vague and empty "subjects," what alone counts is the gest, the critical demonstration of the gesture, its inscription— to whatever period it may belong—in a text the social machination of which is cleary visible: the subject neither adds nor subtracts anything. How many films are there now "about" drugs, in which drugs are the "subjects"? But this is a subject that is hollow; without any social gest, drugs are insignificant, or rather, their significance is simply that of an essential nature—vague, empty, eternal: "drugs lead to impotence" (*Trash*), "drugs lead to sucide" (*Absences répétées*). The subject is a false articulation: why this subject in preference to another? The work only begins with the tableau, when the meaning is set into the gesture and the coordination of gestures. Take *Mother Courage*: you may be certain of a misunderstanding if you think that its "subject" is the Thirty Years War, or even the denunciation of war in general; its *gest* is not there, but in the blindness of the tradeswoman who believes herself to live off war only, in fact, to die of it; even more, the gest lies in the *view* that I, spectator, have of this blindness.

In the theater, in the cinema, in traditional literature, things are always seen *from somewhere*. Here we have the geometrical foundation of representation: a fetishist subject is required to cut out the tableau. This point of meaning is always the Law: law of society, law of struggle, law of meaning. Thus all militant art cannot but be representational, legal. In order for representation to be really bereft of origin and exceed its geometrical nature without ceasing to be representation, the price that must be paid is enormous—no less than death. In Dreyer's *Vampyr*, as a friend points out, the camera moves from house to cemetery recording *what the dead man sees*: such is the extreme limit at which representation is outplayed; the spectator can no longer take up any position, for he cannot identify his eye with the closed eyes of the dead man; the tableau has no point of departure, no support, it gapes open. Everything that goes on before this limit is reached (and this is the case of the work of Brecht and Eisenstein) can only be legal: in the long run, it is the Law of the Party which cuts out the epic scene, the filmic shot; it is this Law which looks, frames, focuses, enunciates. Once again Eisenstein and Brecht rejoin Diderot (promoter of bourgeois domestic tragedy, as his two successors were the promoters of a socialist art). Diderot distinguished in painting major practices, those whose force is cathartic, aiming at the ideality of meaning, from minor practices, those which are purely imitative, anecodotal—the difference between Greuze and Chardin. In other words, in a period of ascendency every physics of art (Chardin) must be crowned with a metaphysics (Greuze). In Brecht, in Eisenstein, Chardin and Greuze coexist (more complex, Brecht leaves it to his public to be the Greuze of the Chardin he sets before their eyes). How could art, in a society that has not yet found peace, cease to be metaphysical? that is, significant, readable, representational? fetishist? When are we to have music, the Text?

It seems that Brecht knew hardly anything of Diderot (barely, perhaps, the *Paradoxe sur le comédien*). He it is, however, who authorizes, in a quite contingent way, the tripartite conjuncture that has just been proposed. Round about 1937, Brecht had the idea of founding a *Diderot Society*, a place for pooling theatrical experiments and studies—doubtless because he saw in Diderot, in addition to the figure of a great materialist philosopher, a man of the theater whose theory aimed at dispensing equally pleasure and instruction. Brecht drew up the program for this society and produced a tract which he contemplated sending out. To whom? To Piscator, to Jean Renoir, to Eisenstein.

—translated by Stephen Heath

Colin MacCabe
Theory and Film:
Principles of Realism and Pleasure

Film theory has undergone an extraordinary expansion and mutation in the last few years. Without wishing to specify either their relative importance or their interdependence, one could indicate three factors which have contributed to this growth: increasingly heterogenous developments within filmic practice: an enlarged educational investment; and a growing concern with the general theoretical problems of signification. The result of these complex determinants is that, while developing its own specific area of analysis, film theory has come in recent years to have more and more to contribute to many of the most important and central cultural debates. *Screen* has participated actively in this process and it is through a consideration of one crucial area of discussion, namely realism, that we can attempt to understand the impetus and direction of *Screen's* work in the recent past. Brecht remarked that realism was not simply a matter for aesthetic debate but was one of the crucial questions of our age.[1] The problems of realism occur in an acute and critical form in the cinema, and perhaps no single topic concentrates so many of the developments that have taken place in film theory.

If we say that realism is, and has been, the dominant aesthetic in film, it is important to realize that this dominance does not date from film's inception. At the moment of its invention, various possibilities remained upon to film; possibilities which were closed down by a set of ideological choices, and the manner of this closure is of great interest to the study of ideology.[2] But if we recognize the extent to which realism became dominant in film only after the development

Published in *Screen* (Autumn 1976), vol. 17, no. 3, and reprinted by permission of the Society for Education in Film and Television.

of sound, and after film production throughout the world had been hegemonized in Hollywood, it is still the case that realism has been the dominant aesthetic since the Second World War. Whether we look to Hollywood, where realism is purchased at almost any price, or to the Italian neorealist cinema, we find that the struggle is to represent reality as effectively as possible; in both cinemas the possibility as such of the representational relation is taken for granted. If cinéma-vérité opposed Hollywood, this opposition was in terms of the effacement of style, where a pristine representation, an authentic relation between film and fact, was contaminated by arrangement and conscious intervention. Only in the early 1960s do we begin to find filmic practices which question the very validity of the representational relation. Within the Continental tradition, and owing an explicit debt to neorealism and particularly to Rossellini, the films of Godard began an investigation of film which took as its object the very processes of representation as well as the problem of what was represented. At the same time, in America, the development of cheaper filmmaking technology allowed many of the theoretical concerns of modern American painting to find a practical application in film. The name of Warhol can serve as an index of this development. But if these practices can best be articulated outside any representational problematic, the theoretical debates around them have constantly lagged behind those practices, and very often, the most important factor contributing to this backwardness has been difficulties with the problem of realism. At the same time a traditional realism remains the dominant force within the commercial cinema, where, if many of the tricks and effects of other cinemas area constantly borrowed, films like *Nashville* or *American Graffiti* reproduce the major strategies and procedures of films like *Giant* or *The Chase*. Finally, realism poses a constant problem within the Marxist theoretical and political tradition as a legacy of the primacy attached to it in the Soviet Union in the 1930s. It is thus difficult in any field of cinema to avoid the term, and indeed it is vitally necessary to examine it and its consequences in some detail.

Realism and Empiricism

As a starting point one could take the objection that realism cannot be dominant in the cinema because Hollywood cinema is not realistic. By the criteria of one of the great realist critics, André Bazin, for a film to be realistic, it must locate its characters and action in a determinate social and historical setting. Most Hollywood films, it could be argued, fail to do this and are, therefore, unrealistic. But Bazin's characterization of realism is much more centrally concerned with a transparency of form which is reduplicated within Hollywood filmic practice. Bazin's criteria for distinguishing between films can only be based on nonfilmic concerns. (It should be said in advance that although these considerations will tend to collapse Hollywood and neorealist cinema together, there is a different reading of Bazin which could disengage from his text a set of incoherences which can be articulated so as to produce distinctions between neorealism and much Hollywood cinema such that the value judgments Bazin wished to confer on the postwar Italian cinema could be retained without a commitment to Bazin's theory of representation.)[3]

For Bazin, as for almost all realist theorists, what is in question is not just a rendering of reality but the rendering of a reality made more real by the use of aesthetic device. Talking of the use of convention within the cinema, Bazin writes that such a use may be made "at the service or at the disservice of realism, it may increase or neutralize the efficacy of the elements of reality captured by the camera. . . One can class, if not hierarchize, the cinematographic styles as a function of the gain of reality that they represent. We shall thus call *realist* any system of expression, any narrative procedure which tends to make more reality appear on the screen."[4] This "more" is not quantative but qualitative: it measures the extent to which the essence of the object represented is grasped. For Bazin the essence is attained through globality and totality; it is understood as coherence. Rossellini's vision is assessed in terms of the globality of the real that it represents: this globality

does not signify, completely the contrary, that neorealism can be reduced to same objective documentaryism. Rossellini likes to say that the basis of his conception of mise-en-scène lies in a love not only of his characters but also of reality just as it is, and it is exactly this love which forbids him to dissociate that which reality has united; the character and the decor. Neorealism is defined neither by a refusal to take up a position with regard to the world nor by a refusal to judge it but it supposes in fact a mental attitude; it is always reality seen through an artist, refracted by his consciousness, but by all his consciousness, and not by his reason or his passion or his belief and reconstituted from dissociated elements.[5]

The central nature of the artistic activity becomes the presentation of a reality more real than that which could be achieved by a simple recording. The play on the notions of "real" and "reality" which is involved in Bazin's conception (the artist produces a reality more real than reality) is also the central feature of empiricism. In *Reading Capital,* Louis Althusser locates the specific feature of empiricism not in the confrontation between subject and object which is postulated as anterior to any knowledge (though to be sure empiricism relies on this), but rather in its characterization of the knowledge to be obtained as defined by the object of which it is knowledge. Althusser writes: "The whole empiricist process of knowledge lies in that operation of the subject named abstraction. To know is to abstract from the real object its essence, the possession of which by the subject is then called knowledge."[6] The whole empiricist conception thus depends on two notions of real and ultimately two notions of object, and this play suppresses the process at work in the production of knowledge. Bazin too starts out with the reality of everyday life and ends up with the greater reality of the filmmaker's representation of it. What must be hidden by the "author" is the process by which this "greater reality" is arrived at, for, of course, on this account the "greater reality" is there all along just waiting to be seen. Thus, for Bazin, any concept of process which would call both subject and object into play instead of positing them as constitutive moments is eliminated. This finds clear expression in his discussion of de Sica's *Bicycle Thieves:*

As the disappearance of the actor is the result if an overcoming of the style of acting, the disappearance of the mise-en-scène is equally the fruit of a dialectical process of the style of narration. If the event is sufficient unto itself without the director having need to illuminate it by angles or the special position of the camera, it is true that it has come to that perfect luminosity which permits art to unmask a nature which finally resembles it.[7]

All interference by the subject must be reduced to a minimum because such interference involves subject and object in a process which destroys their full and punctual autonomy. The triumph of *Bicycle Thieves* is that it completely does away with the cinematic process. Bazin writes: *"Bicycle Thieves* is one of the first examples of pure cinema. There are no more actors, no more story, no more mise-en-scène, that is to say finally in the aesthetic illusion of reality—no more cinema."[8] The revelation of reality is the prime task of the cinema, and all aesthetic devices are simply there to unmake themselves so that we too can experience, as the artist experienced before us, that moment at which reality presents itself as whole.

Contradiction and the Real

Against this traditional analysis, I argue that film does not reveal the real in a moment of transparency, but rather that film is constituted by a set of discourses which (in the positions allowed to subject and object) produce a certain reality. The emphasis on production must be accompanied by one on another crucial Marxist term, that of contradiction. There is no one discourse that produces a certain reality—to believe so is to fall into the idealism complementary to the empiricism already discussed. A film analysis is dealing with a set of contradictory discourses transformed by specific practices. Within a film text these may be different "views" of reality which are articulated together in different ways. Most documentaries (including the anthropological films Mick Eaton and Ivan Ward discuss in their article "Anthropology and Film" in this number of *Screen*) bind the images together by the verbal interpretation of the voiceover commentary. Classical fictional cinema, on the other hand, has the crucial opposition between spoken discourses which may be mistaken and a visual discourse which guarantees truth—which reveals all. For this opposition to be set up, the spectator must be placed in a position from which the image is regarded as primary. The movement of this placing can be grasped by considering a third group of films which find their constitutive principle in the refusal so to place the spectator. In a film such as the Dziga-Vertov Group's *Wind from the East* a set of political discourses and images are juxtaposed so that, although what the Second Female Voice says is what the filmmakers regard as politically correct, it neither subdues the images, as in the documentary, nor is judged by them. None of the discourses can be read off one against the other. There is no possibility of verification, no correspondence between sound and image enabling the spectator to enter the realm of truth. This dislocation between sound and image focuses attention on the position of the spectator—both in the cinema and politically. These juxta-positions make the spectator constantly aware of the discourses that confront him as discourses—as, that is, the production of sets of positions—rather than allowing him to ignore the process of articulation by entering a world of correspondence in which the only activity required is to match one discourse against the realm of truth.

It might here be objected that "filmic discourse" has not been defined with sufficient precision. Rather than giving an exact definition, one must indicate the range of application of the term. Within language studies, from at least the Renaissance onward, "discourse" is the term used to indicate a shifting of attention from the formal oppositions which the linguist attempts to define and articulate to the way in which these formal oppositions relate to the speaking subject. When we talk of "discourse" we move away from a conception of language as a set of significant oppositions independent of the speaking subject (Saussure's *langue*) to focus on the position of the speaking subject within the utterance. With discourse we become interested in the dialectical relation be-tween speaker and language in which language always already offers a position to the speaker, and yet, at the same time, the act of speaking may itself displace that position. In filmic terms this means the kinds of combinations of words and images which can be differentiated in terms of different positions allocated to the viewer. I hope to make clear the kinds of elements involved in this combination later in my examination of *American Graffiti*. For the moment it can be stated that it is neither a question of the filmmaker using a transparent discourse to render the real nor of her or him inventing a discourse which produces a real. Instead the production of a film must be understood as involving a work, a practice, a transformation on and of the discourses available. One such practice, which I have called classical realism,[9] and shall analyze in *American Graffiti,* involves the homogenization of different discourses by their relation to one dominant discourse—assured of its domination by the security and trans-parency of the image. The fact that one such practice involves this homogeni-zation is a matter of ideological and political but not normative interest. My aim in this article is to demonstrate how the practices which articulate the different elements in the discourses which constitute a filmic text have certain political effects. For the moment, and against a traditional realist emphasis, one could say that, at any given time, it is the contradictory positions available discursively to the subject, together with the positions made available by non-linguistic practices, that constitute the reality of the social situation.

It is contradiction that Bazin wishes at all costs to conceal and coherence that furnishes him with his crucial emphasis. The coherence and the totality of the artist's vision provide the final criterion of reality—subject and object confront one another in full luminosity. This luminosity draws attention to the fact that the relation is visual—that all we have to do in the cinema is look. It is here that we begin to analyze the practices of classical realist cinema, for the distinguishing feature of these practices is the production of a perfect point of view for the audience—a point of vision.

The Point of View and the Look

Jacques Lacan has offered an analysis of vision which is of great relevance to any attempt to understand the reality of film. For Lacan, vision offers a peculiarly privileged basis to an *imaginary* relation of the individual to the world.[10] This imaginary relationship is characterized by the plenitude it confers on both subject and object, caught as they are outside any definition in terms of difference—given in a full substantial unity. The imaginary is central to the operations of the human psyche and is constituted as such in early infancy. Somewhere between the sixth and eighteenth month, the small human infant discovers its reflection in the mirror; an apprehension of unity all the more surprising in that it normally occurs before motor control has ensured that unity in practice. The specular relation thus established in this, the mirror phase, provides the basis for primary narcissism, and is then transferred onto the rest of the human world where the other is simply seen as another version of the same—of the "I" which is the center of the world. It is only with the apprehension of genital difference that the child leaves the comfortable world of the imaginary to enter into the world of the symbolic. The symbolic is understood by Lacan (after Lévi–Strauss) not as a set of one-to-one relationships but as a tissue of differences which articulate the crucial elements within the child's world. It is the acceptance of a potential lack (castration) which marks the child's access to the symbolic and to language. Language in the realm of the imaginary is understood in terms of some full relation between word and thing: a mysterious unity of sign and referent. In the symbolic, language is understood in terms of lack and absence—the sign finds its definition diacritically through the absent syntagmatic and paradigmatic chains it enters into. As speaking subjects we constantly oscillate between the symbolic and the imaginary—constantly imagining ourselves granting some full meaning to the words we speak, and constantly being surprised to find them determined by relations outside our control. But if it is the phallus which is the determining factor for the entry into difference, difference has already troubled the full world of the infant. The imaginary unity has already been disrupted by the cruel separation from those objects originally understood as part of the subject—the breast and the feces. The phallus becomes the dominating metaphor for all these previous lacks. Lacan defines the centrality of the phallus for the entry into the symbolic and language when he describes the phallus as "the signifier destined to designate the effects, taken as a set, of signified, insofar as the signifier conditions these effects by its presence as signifier."[11] The signified here is exactly the imaginary full meaning constantly contaminated by the signifier's organization along constitutive and absent chains.

In *Le Séminaire XI,* Lacan attempts to demonstrate the relation between the symbolic and the imaginary at the level of vision and to demonstrate the existence of lack within the scopic field (this lack being the condition of the existence of desire within the visual field—a desire which can find satisfaction in a variety of forms). Taking the Holbein picture *The Ambassadors* (the National Gallery, London), Lacan comments on the death's-head hidden in the picture by a trick of perspective and only visible from one particular angle. The rest of the picture is caught in the world of the imaginary—the spectator is the all-seeing subject and, as if to emphasize the narcissistic nature of the relation, Holbein fills the picture with Renaissance emblems of vanity. However, the death's-head, perceived when we leave the field of the picture, reintroduces the symbolic. For the death's-head draws attention to the fact that we see the picture at a distance and from a particular angle (if we think back to Bazin's quotation about *Bicycle Thieves,* it is clear that for him cinema must obliterate distance and angles). With the introduction of the spectator's position the objects simply and substantially there are transformed into a set of differential relationships; a set of traces left by a paint brush; an organized area of space which, from one particular point, can be read as an object. That the object thus seen is a skull is in no way surprising when we consider that the entry into the symbolic can be most simply described as the recognition of the world independently of my consciousness— as the recognition, that is, of the possibility of my own death. Holbein's picture demonstrates a congruence between the organization of language and the or- ganization of the visual field. Just as the constitutive elements of language must be absent in the moment of speaking, so the constitutive nature of the distance and position of the viewing subject must be absent from the all-embracing world of vision. *The Ambassadors* reintroduces the look into vision. As such it bears witness to the separation (castration) on which vision is based, but which it endlessly attempts to ignore.

The intervention of the symbolic in the imaginary is already in evidence at the very opening of the mirror phase. For the infant verifies its reflection by looking to the mother who holds it in front of the mirror. It is the mother's look that confirms the validity of the infant's image, and with this look we find that at the very foundation of the dual imaginary relationship there is a third term already unsettling it. The mother verifies the relationship for the child, but at the cost of introducing a look, a difference where there should be only similitude. The fact that this look which both sets up and potentially destroys the full visual field is felt as castration explains why, traditionally, the eye is always evil. We are now in a position to grasp Lacan's claim that the visual is organized in terms of the look *(le regard)*—defined by the others' look that it is not—and of the blot *(la tache)*, the fact that any visual field is already structured so that certain effects will be seen, Lacan writes:

The function of the blot and the look is, at one and the same time, that which commands the most secretly, and that which always escapes the grip of, that form of vision which finds its contentment in imagining itself as consciousness. [12]

Bazin wishes to do away with the camera because it constantly threatens the world of imaginary plenitude and must therefore be repressed at all costs. In its place a visual world is instituted from which the look, any trace of castration, has been expelled. The distinction between the symbolic and the imaginary can be understood in cinematic terms by contrasting the look and the point of view. The point of view is always related to an object. [13] But insofar as the object is a given unity there is always the possibility of seeing it together with all the possible points of view—there is always the possibility of a point of overview. The point of view preserves the primacy of vision, for what is left out of one point-of-view shot can always be supplied by another. The look, however, is radically defective. Where the point of view is related to an object, the look is related to other looks. The look's field is not defined by a science of optics in which the eye features as a geometrical point but by the fact that the object we are looking at offers a position from which we can be looked at—and this look is not punctual but shifts over the surface. It is important that it is a head that looks back at us from Holbein's painting.

From this account of the pleasure involved in vision it might seem that the ideal film would show us a static perspective. But this is to ignore the dialectic of pleasure and desire revealed to us by Freud. [14] If, on the one hand, there is a tendency toward stasis, toward a normalization of excitation within the psyche, there is also a compulsion to repeat those moments at which the stasis is set in motion, at which the level of excitation rises to unbearable heights. The small boy in *Beyond the Pleasure Principle* in his endless game of *fort-da* ceaselessly throws away the object at the end of the string only to draw it back and start again. This action, which Freud tells us reproduces the experience of separation from the mother, shows that it is exactly the moment of anxiety, of heightened tension, the moment of coming which is relived in a constant cycle, which threatens itself. What lies beyond the pleasure principle is not a threatening and exterior reality but a reality whose virulence knows no cessation, the reality of those constitutive moments at which we experience ourselves in the very moment of separation; which moments we are compelled to repeat in that endless movement which can find satisfaction only in death. Desire is set up only by absence, by the possibility of return to a former state—the field of vision becomes invested libidinally only after it has been robbed of its unity by the gaze of the other. The charm of classical realism is that it introduces the gaze of the other but this introduction is always accompanied by the guarantee of the supremacy of the point of view; the threat appears so that it can be smoothed over, and it is in that smoothing that we can locate pleasure—in a plenitude which is fractured but only on condition that it will be reset. Here the stock terms demonstrate what is at stake: the motion pictures, the movies, the flicks; it is the threat of motion, of displacement that is in question, but this threat is overcome from the start.

The logic of this contradictory movement can be understood on the basis of the set of interchanges that take place between screen and viewer—that complicated circulation which ensures that I am not only a spectator in the cinema but also, by a process of identification, a character on the screen. The cinema constantly poses me as the constant point of a fixed triangle and it constantly obscures and effaces the complicated progress of the shots, the impossible movements of that point by the logic of events on the screen. To analyze this process we need the concepts elaborated by Benveniste to distinguish between the *sujet de l'énonciation* and the *sujet de l'énoncé*.[15] Benveniste suggests that to arrive at a logical understanding of tenses and to understand fully the importance of language for subjectivity, the speaker as the producer of the discursive chain, *le sujet de l'énonciation,* must be distinguished from the speaker as the grammatical subject, *le sujet de l'énoncé.* The distance between these two subjects gives us a formal linguistic account of the distance between the philosophical subject, *le sujet de l'énoncé,* the "I," judge of the correspondence between world and language, and the psychoanalytic subject, the *sujet de l'énonciation,* the "it," unable to distinguish between word and world and constantly threatening and unmasking the stability of the "I." Applied to film this is the distinction between the spectator as viewer, the comforting "I," the fixed point, and the spectator as he or she is caught up in the play of events on the screen, as he or she "utters," "enounces" the film. Hollywood cinema is largely concerned to make these two coincide so that we can ignore what is at risk. But this coincidence can never be perfect because it is exactly in the divorce between the two that the film's existence is possible. This bringing into play of the process of the text's production takes us out of the classical field of semiotics, the field of the *énoncé* in which the text is treated as the assertion of a set of disjunctions permuted to produce actions, and into the question of the production of these very disjunctions. The subject is neither the full presence of traditional "auteur" criticism nor the effect of the structure of traditional structuralism; it is divided in the movement between the two. The contradiction betweeen *énonciation* and *énoncé* is also the contradiction between narrative and discourse. Narrative is always propelled by both a heterogeneity and a surplus—a heterogeneity which must be *both* overcome *and* prolonged. The narrative begins with an incoherence but already promises the resolution of that incoherence. The story is the passage from ignorance to knowledge, but this passage is denied as process—the knowledge is always already there as the comforting resolution of the broken coherence (every narration is always a suspense story). Narrative must deny the time of its own telling—it must refuse its status as discourse (as articulation), in favor of its self-presentation as simple identity, complete knowledge.

American Graffiti: **An Example**

To understand a film like *American Graffiti,* its reality and its pleasure—the reality of its pleasure—it is necessary to consider the logic of that contradiction which produces a position for the viewer but denies that production. To admit that production would be to admit of position, and the position that has been produced is the position of the point of view, promising, as Bazin wished, that the event is sufficient to itself and needs no illumination from angles or the special position of the camera—promising, in short, a suprapositional omniscience, the full imaginary relation. In *American Graffiti* this contradiction of a process of production and the denial of that process take form around the fact that we know, from the beginning of the narrative, that Curt Henderson will leave the town and yet that we hover, in suspense, over a decision which, once resolved, is obvious. The question, as always in classical realism, is one of identity. This identity may be questioned and suspended, but it is, in a deferred moment, asserted and read back over the text. Nor is this reading back an optional extra. Without it the very concept of identity and truth, the very concept of character, on which classical realism rests would disintegrate. If the hero were not really good (or bad or whatever) all along then there would be no point to the story—the narrative would become merely the retailing of successive states of affairs. The resolution of the identity of Curt Henderson is also the production for the viewer of that point of view from which he can watch the film, but the pleasure of this production is provided by two looks which threaten to disturb that point of view, to displace an identity. These looks are each of a different order and I want to consider them separately, for one remains within the order of pleasure guaranteed by the point of view while the other threatens a disruption of a very different order.

The first look that introduces the moment of heterogeneity and surplus which is the impetus of the narrative comes from the girl in the white T-bird.[16] Securely placed within a point-of-view shot (Curt Henderson's) it nevertheless troubles a full imaginary identity—throwing open an uncertainty about Curt and his future on the night he has to decide whether to leave town. It is explicitly a gaze of sexuality and introduces the unsettling evidence of woman's desire as the girl mouths "I love you." *American Graffiti* thus traverses the classical path of narrative in that it is a desperate attempt to deny sexuality, the knowledge of which provides its first impetus. The girl's glance introduces a look into our point of view and calls attention to our position as we become separated from our full being in the world (as Curt becomes an other for someone he does not know, so he becomes aware of his position, loses the full security of the imaginary). In order to replace ourselves fully in the world it is necessary to refind an origin which can function as a guarantee of identity. In order to overcome the unsettling gaze of the mother we must find a father, someone who will figure as that moment of originating identity and power which will deny the possibility of the interplay of looks. It is this search that Curt Henderson undertakes. His progress from the schoolteacher to the Pharaohs to Wolfman Jack is the search for a father who will confirm him in his identity and expunge the possibility of difference; who will reassert the point of view over the look. In the scene in the radio studio we have another very heavily marked point-of-view sequence (three shots of Curt watching, two of Wolfman Jack performing, in exactly the same sequence as we had earlier seen the blonde at the traffic lights) which provides the knowledge to overcome the earlier threat.

It might be objected that this approach ignores the complicated intercrossing of the stories of the four boys. But not only can one find the same logic at play in two of the other three (Milner constitutes a special case), it would also be a mistake to think they are on the same level. *Nashville* and *American Graffiti* are two of a set of films which, although they have borrowed tricks and devices from other cinemas, remain within a traditional Hollywood practice. The two most obvious tricks are the refusal to weight the sound track in the traditional manner, a development drawing on such different sources as Welles, Godard, and cinéma-vérité, and, on the other hand, a proliferation of characters such that the dominance of narrative has been replaced by the freedom of the "slice of life". Both these novelties function as noise rather than structure. A close analysis of the sound shows that a traditional weighting is given to those elements necessary for the development of the narrative. Equally, the proliferation of characters does not affect the traditional movement of narrative. Rivette's *Out One: Spectre* is an example of a film which does break down narrative by proliferation of character, but at the cost of an enormous extension of the duration of the film and a genuine inability to find it an *end*.

It is Curt Henderson's point of view which offers within the narrative that knowledge and security we enjoy as we sit in the cinema, and it is this visual primacy which indicates his traditional centrality to the narrative. For Curt accomplishes the final imaginary task—he discovers the father. For everyone else Wolfman Jack is a name which finds its reality only in the differential world of sound, but Curt is able to reunite name and bearer so that a full presence can provide the certainty of what he is and what he must do—he is a *seer* and must leave town in order to see the world. The girl's gaze troubled this identity, but in the final shots of the film Curt is in a position where that gaze cannot trouble him. Before she knew who and where he was—now the positions are reversed.

And it is from the point of view of the plane that the film accomplishes the progress toward the knowledge implicit in it from the beginning. The primacy of Curt's progress for an understanding of the film is underlined when the final titles tell us that he is now a writer living in Canada. The implication is that it is he who has written the story, he has conferred on us his point of view.

The other look within the film is of a different order and radically displaces the point of view, introducing a far more threatening moment of separation for the spectator. This look does not occur within the diegetic space between characters but in the space between screen and audience. John Milner and Carol attack a car whose occupants have been so foolish as to throw something at them, racing around it letting out its tires and covering it in foam. As this happens, changes of camera position are no longer motivated either by point-of-view shots or by diegetic considerations—for a moment we have lost our position and point of view as the camera breaks the 180-degree rule, though this losing of position has a certain diegetic motivation in the actions of John and Carol. Most significantly, we see the film lights appear beside the car. The diegetic space is broken up as the film looks back at us. This encounter with the real, this movement into the symbolic is the moment of ecstasy in which Carol squirts foam all over the car and Milner lets out all the tires (a sexual symbolism obvious enough), showing us that the pleasure involved here is of a more radical nature—a pleasure of tension and its release. If Curt provides the pleasure of security and position, John Milner functions as that threatening repetition which can only end in death and which offers no position but rather ceaseless motion. This is not to suggest that Milner offers any real alternative in the film; if he did it would contaminate the pleasure provided by Curt more significantly. But as the representative of an element which finds its definition outside the synchronic space of the other characters, he introduces time in a potentially threatening way. The political nature of the film, as will be argued later, depends on a repression of time outside a process of natural growth. Milner introduces, admittedly in a minimal way, a time which is not reducible to this natural cycle—his attitude to the culture is different from that of the other boys, because he is older than they.

The Question of the Audience

What has been said so far may seem to have removed all questions of realism and film from any consideration of their social conditions of production and reception. Concentration on the organization of the text has proposed a viewer caught only within an atemporal movement between the symbolic and the imaginary and confronted only by the reality of difference. It might seem from this that film and, by implication, art in general are caught in an eternal battle between the imaginary fullness of ideology and the real emptiness of the symbolic. Nothing could be further from my intentions in this article. My aim is to introduce certain general concepts which can be used to analyze film in a determinate social moment. That the breaking of the imaginary relation between text and viewer is that first prerequisite of political questions in art has, I would hold, been evident since Brecht. That the breaking of the imaginary relationship can constitute a political goal in itself is the ultraleftist fantasy of the surrealists and of much of the avant-garde work now being undertaken in the cinema. In certain of their formulations this position is given a theoretical backing by the writers of the *Tel Quel* group.

I hope that my analysis of *American Graffiti* has sketched in outline how the process of the production of a point of view for the spectator is effaced by mechanisms of identification. What is politically important about this textual organization is that it removes the spectator from the realm of contradiction. But it is not just contradiction in general that is avoided but a specific set of contradictions—those raised by the impact of the Vietnam War on American society. Portrait of a pre-Vietnam America, the film presents to us the children of the Kennedy Generation in the age of innocence—an innocence that we can regard from our position of knowledge. But this knowledge presupposes us outside politics now, outside contradiction. Indeed, Curt Henderson is a writer living in Canada, reflecting on an earlier reality of America that could not be sustained. (The fact that the writer is living in Canada is a further index of the repression of Vietnam—he has presumably dodged the draft, but this remains unspoken: to interrogate that decision would introduce contradiction.) The passing of innocence is reduced in the film to the process of growing up—there is no way in which external forces could be introduced into the homogeneous society of small-town California. Toad grows up and goes off to die at An Loc, but this is simply part of a human cycle. The position of the viewer after the Vietnam War is simply held to be the same but different—the position of the imaginary. The Vietnam War is repressed and smoothed over.

However, if this is our criticism of the film it is clear that what we object to is not the fact that bits of reality have somehow got left out, but rather the whole relation of the film to its audience. The audience and their representations are the terms of the "realism" of any film or work of art—not some preexistent reality which it merely conveys. Nor should this be thought novel within the socialist tradition, for I would argue that Engels' and Lenin's comments on realism are prompted by these considerations, and if they used what tools they had to hand and are thus given to talking in representational terms, then we, seventy years later, should not be worried about discarding these terms.

In his letter to Minna Kautsky of November 26, 1885 on her novel *The Old and the New,* Engels wrote that he had nothing against politically didactic writing, but then went on to say:

But I believe the tendency must spring forth from the situation and the action itself, without explicit attention called to it; the writer is not obliged to offer to the readers the future historical solution of the social conflicts he depicts. Especially in our conditions, the novel primarily finds its readers in bourgeois circles, circles not directly related to our own, and there the socialist tendentious novel can fully achieve its purpose, in my view, if, by conscientiously describing the real mutual relations, it breaks down the conventional illusions dominating them, shatters the optimism of the bourgeois world, causes doubts about the validity of the existing order, and this without directly offering a solution or even, under some circumstances, taking an ostensibly partisan stand.[17]

Within this passage Engels is using more than one criteron of realism. He calls not simply for a description of the real mutual relations but for one such that they will be directly related to their audience. The text is determined not only by the situation to be represented but by its audience as well. These considerations also dominate Lenin's writing on literature. In the articles on Tolstoy which contain his most lengthy consideration of literary matters, the present political conjuncture is always dominant. Before all else it is essential to grasp the political situation to which they are addressed. They are written to combat two prevailing views of Tolstoy—opposed but complementary. On the one hand, Lenin wishes to wrest Tolstoy from those reactionary critics who want to clasp the religious Tolstoy to their bosom and thus present him as fundamentally in favor of the status quo. On the other hand, Lenin is concerned to correct those on the left like Plekhanov who see no more in Tolstoy than a religious mystic and thus reject his work as of no value. Left and right within this circle can agree on the identity of Tolstoy. Lenin, however, protests that there is no such identity, but rather a set of contradictions which must be grasped and understood as an urgent political task. Lenin never ceases to emphasize that the reality of Tolstoy is contradictory—that it is composed both of a bitter and undying enmity for the social system which has brought about the social conditions in Russia but that this enmity goes together with the most reactionary mystical and religious ideology with the result that Tolstoy*ism* is a profound obstacle to revolutionary change in Russia. In addition to this emphasis on change and contradiction Lenin is emphatic that Tolstoy is typical, that he "represents" the period 1861–1905, the period, that is, between the freeing of the serfs and the unsuccessful revolution of 1905. Understanding the contradiction that is Tolstoy is important because it "represents" on the literary level the political problem of the peasantry in Russia—the peasantry is a force of great revolutionary potential and yet it is held back by a very reactionary ideology. Only by understanding these two contradictory facets can one correctly analyze the situation in Russia.

It is important to have these facts clear before considering the problem of the vocabulary Lenin uses in these articles, a vocabulary of expression and representation which finds its most characteristic form in the metaphor of the mirror.

Indeed the first article on Tolstoy is entitled "Leo Tolstoy as the Mirror of the Russian Revolution" and it begins with the following paragraph:

To identify the great artist with the revolution (of 1905) which he has obviously failed to understand, and from which he obviously stands aloof, may at first sight seem strange and artificial. A mirror which does not reflect things correctly could hardly be called a mirror. Our revolution, however, is an extremely complicated thing. Among the mass of those who are directly making and participating in it there are many social elements which have obviously not understood what is taking place and which also stand aloof from the real historical tasks with which the course of events has confronted them. And if we have before us a really great artist, he must have reflected in his work at least some of the aspects of the revolution. [18]

Thus this mirror that is Tolstoy and his work are so described that the metaphor cannot function coherently. Not only is it a mirror that does not reflect, it is also a mirror that participates in a process without understanding it and, as a participant, must presumably be affected by and affect that process. It is a mirror that acts. A mirror that alters the very scene it is reflecting. To complete the paragraph Lenin adds an assertion which has nothing to do with what has gone before. In any case, he argues, Tolstoy is a great artist, and if this is so then his work *must* reflect his time. Thus within Lenin's text we can discern two claims. First that to understand Tolstoy is to understand the period 1861–1905 (here Tolstoy is a mirror but a mirror which acts) and second that the relation between Tolstoy and his time is the necessary relation that holds between a great artist and the society in which he lives and works.

These opening remarks provide Lenin with the space to go on to say that Tolstoy is of such supreme importance not because he represents a reactionary peasant ideology which already exists, but rather because he produces an ideology which the peasant is likely to espouse. And this production of ideology is not a separate activity from Tolstoy's writing. Ideology is produced within the work of literature; insofar as the artist is able to grasp and articulate the social changes taking place within the world of individuals and feelings, within the world of identification, he will offer an explanation of them: he will proffer an ideology. Insofar as the reader is offered both a description and an explanation of his or her own life (and the description and explanation are one and the same process), he or she may adopt the ideological viewpoint of the text. It is here that ideology accomplishes its real effects, as the representation of the real conditions of existence affects those conditions themselves. Tolstoy's skill as a writer is part and contradictory parcel of his importance as a reactionary ideologue, and both must be understood to understand the peasantry. For Lenin, as for Engels, [19] what is at issue is not simply the reality external to the text but the reality of the text itself. We must understand the text's effectivity within the social process, which is to say we have to consider the relation between reader and text in its historical specificity.

Conclusions and Consequences

In an earlier article,[20] I argued for a typology of texts classified according to the organization of discourses within them. What was crucial was not the content of the text but the relations inscribed for the reader. The real was not an external object represented in the text but the relation between text and reader which reduplicated or cut across the subject's relation to his or her experience. Classically, realism depended on obscuring the relation between text and reader in favor of a dominance accorded to a supposedly given reality; but this dominance, far from sustaining a "natural" relation, was the product of a definite organization which, of necessity, effaced its own workings. In so far as the "reality" thus granted dominance was in contradiction with the ideologically dominant determinations of reality, then a text could be deemed progressive, but nevertheless such an organization was fundamentally reactionary; for it posed a reality which existed independently of both the text's and the reader's activity, a reality which was essentially noncontradictory and unchangeable. Alternatively, one could have an organization of discourses which broke with any dominance and which, as such, remained essentially subversive of any ideological order. At the end of the article I raised the question as to whether there could be a revolutionary film which would subvert the traditional position of the spectator in a more positive fashion than the simple deconstruction of the subversive film or whether any such positivity inevitably replaced one in a position of imaginary dominance.

Although I think that the earlier article can be read in a more favorable light, there is no doubt that it is contaminated by formalism; by a structuralism that it claimed to have left behind. Traditional criticism holds text and author/reader separate, with the author able to inject meaning which is then passed on to the reader. The position outlined in my article made the subject the effect of the structure (the subject is simply the sum of positions allocated to it) but it preserved the inviolability and separateness of the text—no longer given as an immutable content fixed in its determinations by reality through the author, but rather as immutable structure determining reality and author/reader in their positions. But the text has no such separate existence. If we dissolve the reader into the text in the system of identification which I have outlined in this article, it is impossible to hold text and reader (or author as first reader) separate. Rather it is a question of analyzing a film within a determinate social moment so that it is possible to determine what identifications will be made and by whom, the way Lenin analyses Tolstoy.[21] The text has no separate existence, and for this reason it is impossible to demand a typology of texts such as I proposed in my earlier article. Rather each reading must be a specific analysis which may use certain general concepts but these concepts will find their articulation within the specific analyses and not within an already defined combinatory.

Realism is no longer a question of an exterior reality nor of the relation of reader to text, but one of the ways in which these two interact. The filmmaker must draw the viewer's attention to his or her relation to the screen in order to make him or her "realize" the social relations that are being portrayed. Inversely one could say that it is the "strangeness" of the social relations displayed which draws the viewer's attention to the fact of watching a film. It is at the moment that an identification is broken, becomes difficult to hold, that we grasp in one and the same moment both the relations that determine that identity and our relation to its representation.[22] Oshima's *Death by Hanging* offers an excellent example of a film in which the indissociability of "the real" from reality is demonstrated, in which the learning of our position in the cinema is also the learning of the social reality of Japan. (It would be in terms of the way that the artist analyzes our moments of constitutive separation in terms of social reality that one might formulate a justification for Lenin's unsubstantiated claim that any great artist must "reflect" the great social changes of his time.) In *Death by Hanging*, R, having failed to die, must learn who he is so that he can be hanged again fully conscious of his crime. As he learns to take up his position sexually and socially so that he can understand why he, a Korean subproletarian, raped and murdered a Japanese girl, so we too are learning what it is to sit in the cinema. The documentary style of the opening of the film merges into fiction and then fantasy without any of the conventional markers. We have constantly to refind our place, both in the execution hut and in the story. Subjective shots are eschewed, as are the normal rules for the organization of cinematic space. One of the results of the lack of subjective shots is that they can be used to great effect at certain moments, as when R confronts the girl he will attack. At the narrative level we are constantly unsure both of the status of events (fact, fiction, or fantasy within fiction) but also of how to understand the "ridiculous" prison officers. As we watch the Education Officer there is a kind of irony at work which completely undercuts any position of knowledge. In a film like *American Graffiti* we can find a very classical irony whereby we are constantly aware that everything is too perfect to be true, but this irony simply confirms us in our dominance, for the perfection guarantees the imaginary truth of the story. In *Death by Hanging*, the comic antics of the Education Officer deprive us of any fixed position from which we could gather his activities into a coherent "character." Unable to "place" him, we are forced to pay attention to him, to listen to his ridiculous logic, outside any certain realm of truth. The irony of *Death by Hanging* dissolves any area of truth which could be established by judging its correspondence to reality. Story of an identity (R must learn who he is), *Death by Hanging* dissolves the identity into a set of relationships which once grasped can be transformed. It is because he has understood them as a set of relationships that R can transform them at the end of the film. The introduction of his sister introduces a reality into his fantasies which means that he can no longer act them out in the real world. As this introduction of a radical otherness destroys R's fantasies, so the film destroys our fantasies by the introduction of its own reality. At the end of the film we no longer have our fantasies of Koreans, of executions, but only on the condition that we no longer have our fantasy of the cinema.

The cost of ignoring these considerations can be seen in the TV play *The Lump,* produced by Tony Garnett, written by Jim Allen, and directed by Jack Gold in 1969. Posed once again as a problem of identity—will the young student who has taken part in the strike on the building site be won to the truth of the revolutionary cause, or will he prefer to opt out and reveal his weakness?—*The Lump* contains all its material within the most conventional diegetic and cinematic space. As a result of this imprisonment it is impossible for the filmmakers to introduce any historical component—the relations of the present struggle to the Russian Revolution or to the experience of Thomas Hardy—without such forced diegetic motivation—a poster of Lenin, the example of the slogan "Peace, Land, Bread," a bedside copy of *Jude the Obscure*—that the purpose of the reference is lost except on those who know it already. At the same time it is impossible to introduce any element of criticism or information which would not fracture the transparent space and make us aware that we are watching a "political" film. Thus there can be no criticism of the attitude to women within the text (women are expunged completely from this world of identity except for Yorky's comment that he wants "to get a leg over"), nor can there be any real information about the conditions of the Irish workers that cannot be "realistically" conveyed in a short speech by a character. The introduction of any of these elements might be held to destroy the popular appeal of the film and deprive the makers of the possibility of arousing the support of a mass audience for the scandals of the building industry, and more generally for the support of left-wing views. But the content of the left-wing commitment is so vague, as a necessary consequence of the refusal to introduce the spectator to his or her own constitutive contradictions, that it is doubtful whether anybody is won by the film to anything. The mechanisms at work in *The Lump* are the same as those used in *The Sweeney* to elicit sympathy for a copper who bends the rules. One can lend this sympathy for an hour without having to change one's attitudes or beliefs because of the occultation of the relation between viewer and text which allows the spectator to remain both on and off screen in that interchange I have already sketched. It is by the interruption of that channel that one begins engagement with the real—until then there is simply the endless repetition of the imaginary.

Notes

This article originated in a paper written for a SEFT Weekend on Realism and the Cinema. The films planned for screening at that school were *American Graffiti,* as an example of a Hollywood-made film in the modern, more "realistic" style, *The Lump,* as an example of the use of fictionalized documentary for political ends within the mass media, and *Death by Hanging,* as an example of a film which while superficially "nonrealist" can lay claim to inclusion within

Brecht's definitions of realism. These three films accordingly constitute the main sources of examples in this article.

1. "Realism is an issue not only for literature: it is a major political, philosophical and practical issue and must be handled and explained as such." Bertolt Brecht, "Against George Lukacs," *New Left Review* (March–April 1974), no. 84, p. 45.

2. This should not be taken to imply that the cinematic apparatus is ideologically neutral, but that its ideological effects are only one of the determinants of what became the dominant cinema and its ideological effects. Stephen Heath has begun the investigation of this inscription in "On Screen, in Frame," *Quarterly Review of Film Studies* (Autumn 1976), vol. 1, no. 3.

3. A good survey of Bazin's comments on realism can be found in Christopher Williams, "Bazin on Neo-Realism," *Screen* (Winter 1973–74), 14(4):61–68.

4. André Bazin, *Qu' est-ce que le cinéma?* (Paris: Ed. du Cerf, 1962), 4:22.

5. *Ibid.,* p. 154.

6. Louis Althusser, *Reading Capital,* trans. Ben Brewster (London: New Left Books, 1970), pp. 35–36.

7. Bazin, *Qu'est-ce que le cinéma?* p. 57.

8. *Ibid.,* p. 59.

9. In Colin MacCabe, "Realism and the Cinema: Notes on Some Brechtian Theses," *Screen* (Summer 1974), 15(2):7–27. For a criticism of the positions put forward in that article, see below.

10. The analysis of a Holbein painting which is discussed in this section can be found in "Du regard comme objet petit a" in Jacques Lacan, *Le Séminaire XI* (Paris: Ed. du Seuil, 1973), pp. 65–109. My understanding of the issues has benefited from Christian Metz's "The Imaginary Signfier," *Screen* (Summer 1975), pp. 16(2):14–76. [excerpts from that article are included in the present anthology—ED.], and Jacqueline Rose's British Film Institute Educational Advisory Service seminar paper "The Imaginary, the Insufficient Signifier," mimeographed.

11. Jacques Lacan, *Ecrits* (Paris: Ed. du Seuil, 1966), p. 690.

12. Lacan, *Le Séminaire XI,* p. 71.

13. See Edward Branigan, "Formal Permutations of the Point-of-View Shot," *Screen* (Autumn 1975), 16(3):54–64.

14. For a summary of Freud's argument in its Lacanian reformulation, see Colin MacCabe, "Presentation of 'The Imaginary Signifier'," *Screen* (Summer 1975), 16(2):7–13.

15. See Emile Benveniste, *Problems of General Linguistics* (Coral Gables, FL: University of Miami Press: 1971), part 5.

16. The analysis of the interplay of identification and vision leans heavily on two earlier articles in *Screen*—Stepehn Heath's "Film and System, Terms of Analysis" (Spring 1975), 16(1):7–77 and (Summer 1975), 16(2):91–113; and Laura Mulvey, "Visual Pleasure and Narrative Cinema," (Autumn 1975), 16(3):6–18 [included in this anthology—ED.].

17. *Marx and Engels on Literature and Art: A Selection of Writings,* ed. Lee Baxandall and Stefan Morawski (St. Louis: Telos Press, 1973), pp. 112–13.

18. In V.I. Lenin, *On Literature and Art* (Moscow: Progress Publishers, 1967). For a detailed consideration of Lenin's use of the metaphor of the mirror, see Pierre Macherey, *Pour une théorie de la production litteraire* (Paris: Librairie Francis Maspero, 1967), pp. 125–58. The translation of Macherey, *A Theory of Literary Production* (London: Routledge, 1978) includes also an appendix of Lenin's articles on Tolstoy, including that quoted here.

19. And also, I would argue, for Marx—see his letter to Ferdinand Lassalle of April 19, 1859. See *Marx and Engels on Literature Art,* pp. 105–8.

20. MacCabe, "Realism and the Cinema."

21. Such an analysis, it must be emphasized, has nothing to do with a counting of heads but is a class analysis. Its validity will be determined in its relations to practice, both political and cinematic.

22. This is the burden of the argument in Colin MacCabe, "The Politics of Separation," *Screen* (Winter 1975–76), 16(4):46–61.

[11]

Laura Mulvey
Visual Pleasure and
Narrative Cinema

I. Introduction

A. A Political Use of Psychoanalysis. This paper intends to use psycho-analysis to discover where and how the fascination of film is reinforced by preexisting patterns of fascination already at work within the individual subject and the social formations that have molded him. It takes as starting point the way film reflects, reveals, and even plays on the straight, socially established interpretation of sexual difference which controls images, erotic ways of looking, and spectacle. It is helpful to understand what the cinema has been, how its magic has worked in the past, while attempting a theory and a practice which will challenge this cinema of the past. Psychoanalytic theory is thus appropriated here as a political weapon, demonstrating the way the unconscious of patriarchal society has structured film form.

The paradox of phallocentrism in all its manifestations is that it depends on the image of the castrated woman to give order and meaning to its world. An idea of woman stands as linchpin to the system: it is her lack that produces the phallus as a symbolic presence, it is her desire to make good the lack that the phallus signifies. Recent writing in *Screen* about psychoanalysis and the cinema has not sufficiently brought out the importance of the representation of the female form in a symbolic order in which, in the last resort, it speaks castration and nothing else. To summarize briefly: the function of woman in forming the

Published in *Screen* (Autumn 1975), vol. 16, no. 3, and reprinted by permission of the Society for Education in Film and Television.

patriarchal unconscious is twofold: she first symbolizes the castration threat by her real absence of a penis and, second, thereby raises her child into the symbolic. Once this has been achieved, her meaning in the process is at an end; it does not last into the world of law and language except as a memory which oscillates between memory of maternal plenitude and memory of lack. Both are posited on nature (or on anatomy in Freud's famous phrase). Woman's desire is subjected to her image as bearer of the bleeding wound, she can exist only in relation to castration and cannot transcend it. She turns her child into the signifier of her own desire to possess a penis (the condition, she imagines, of entry into the symbolic). Either she must gracefully give way to the word, the Name of the Father and the Law, or else struggle to keep her child down with her in the half-light of the imaginary. Woman then stands in patriarchal culture as signifier for the male other, bound by a symbolic order in which man can live out his fantasies and obsessions through linguistic command by imposing them on the silent image of woman still tied to her place as bearer of meaning, not maker of meaning.

There is an obvious interest in this analysis for feminists, a beauty in its exact rendering of the frustration experienced under the phallocentric order. It gets us nearer to the roots of our oppression, it brings an articulation of the problem closer, it faces us with the ultimate challenge: how to fight the unconscious structured like a language (formed critically at the moment of arrival of language) while still caught within the language of the patriarchy. There is no way in which we can produce an alternative out of the blue, but we can begin to make a break by examining patriarchy with the tools it provides, of which psycho-analysis is not the only but an important one. We are still separated by a great gap from important issues for the female unconscious which are scarcely relevant to phallocentric theory: the sexing of the female infant and her relationship to the symbolic, the sexually mature woman as nonmother, maternity outside the signification of the phallus, the vagina . . . But, at this point, psychoanalytic theory as it now stands can at least advance our understanding of the status quo, of the patriarchal order in which we are caught.

B. Destruction of Pleasure as a Radical Weapon. As an advanced represen-tation system, the cinema poses questions of the ways the unconscious (formed by the dominant order) structures ways of seeing and pleasure in looking. Cinema has changed over the last few decades. It is no longer the monolithic system based on large capital investment exemplified at its best by Hollywood in the 1930s, 1940s and 1950s. Technological advances (16mm, etc.) have changed the economic conditions of cinematic production, which can now be artisanal as well as capitalist. Thus it has been possible for an alternative cinema to develop. However self-conscious and ironic Hollywood managed to be, it always restricted itself to a formal mise-en-scène reflecting the dominant ideolog-ical concept of the cinema. The alternative cinema provides a space for a cinema to be born which is radical in both a political and an aesthetic sense and challenges the basic assumptions of the mainstream film. This is not to reject the latter moralistically, but to highlight the ways in which its formal preoccupations reflect the psychical obsessions of the society which produced it, and, further, to stress that the alternative cinema must start specifically by reacting against these obsessions and assumptions. A politically and aesthetically avant-garde cinema is now possible, but it can still only exist as a counterpoint.

The magic of the Hollywood style at its best (and of all the cinema which fell within its sphere of influence) arose, not exclusively, but in one important aspect, from its skilled and satisfying manipulation of visual pleasure. Unchallenged, mainstream film coded the erotic into the language of the dominant patriarchal order. In the highly developed Hollywood cinema it was only through these codes that the alienated subject, torn in his imaginary memory by a sense of loss, by the terror of potential lack in fantasy, came near to finding a glimpse of satisfaction: through its formal beauty and its play on his own formative obsessions. This article will discuss the interweaving of that erotic pleasure in film, its meaning, and in particular the central place of the image of woman. It is said that analyzing pleasure, or beauty, destroys it. That is the intention of this article. The satisfaction and reinforcement of the ego that represent the high point of film history hitherto must be attacked. Not in favor of a reconstructed new pleasure, which cannot exist in the abstract, nor of intellectualized unpleasure, but to make way for a total negation of the ease and plenitude of the narrative fiction film. The alternative is the thrill that comes from leaving the past behind without rejecting it, transcending outworn or oppressive forms, or daring to break with normal pleasurable expectations in order to conceive a new language of desire.

II. Pleasure in Looking/Fascination with the Human Form

A. The cinema offers a number of possible pleasures. One is scopophilia. There are circumstances in which looking itself is a source of pleasure, just as, in the reverse formation, there is pleasure in being looked at. Originally, in his *Three Essays on Sexuality*, Freud isolated scopophilia as one of the component instincts of sexuality which exist as drives quite independently of the erotogenic zones. At this point he associated scopophilia with taking other people as objects, subjecting them to a controlling and curious gaze. His particular examples center around the voyeuristic activities of children, their desire to see and make sure of the private and the forbidden (curiosity about other people's genital and bodily functions, about the presence or absence of the penis and, retrospectively, about the primal scene). In this analysis scopophilia is essentially active. (Later, in *Instincts and their Vicissitudes*, Freud developed his theory of scopophilia further, attaching it initially to pregenital autoeroticism, after which the pleasure of the look is transferred to others by analogy. There is a close working here of the relationship between the active instinct and its further development in a narcissistic form). Although the instinct is modified by other factors, in particular the constitution of the ego, it continues to exist as the erotic basis for pleasure in looking at another person as object. At the extreme, it can become fixated into a perversion, producing obsessive voyeurs and Peeping Toms, whose only sexual satisfaction can come from watching, in an active controlling sense, an objectified other.

At first glance, the cinema would seem to be remote from the undercover world of the surreptitious observation of an unknowing and unwilling victim. What is seen of the screen is so manifestly shown. But the mass of mainstream film, and the conventions within which it has consciously evolved, portray a hermetically sealed world which unwinds magically, indifferent to the presence of the audience, producing for them a sense of separation and playing on their voyeuristic fantasy. Moreover, the extreme contrast between the darkness in the auditorium (which also isolates the spectators from one another) and the brilliance of the shifting patterns of light and shade on the screen helps to promote the illusion of voyeuristic separation. Although the film is really being shown, is there to be seen, conditions of screening and narrative conventions give the spectator an illusion of looking in on a private world. Among other things, the position of the spectators in the cinema is blatantly one of repression of their exhibitionism and projection of the repressed desire onto the performer.

B. The cinema satisfies a primordial wish for pleasurable looking, but it also goes further, developing scopophilia in its narcissistic aspect. The conventions of mainstream film focus attention on the human form. Scale, space, stories are all anthropomorphic. Here, curiosity and the wish to look intermingle with a fascination with likeness and recognition: the human face, the human body, the relationship between the human form and its surroundings, the visible presence of the person in the world. Jacques Lacan has described how the moment when a child recognizes its own image in the mirror is crucial for the constitution of the ego. Several aspects of this analysis are relevant here. The mirror phase occurs at a time when the child's physical ambitions outstrip his motor capacity, with the result that his recognition of himself is joyous in that he imagines his mirror image to be more complete, more perfect than he experiences his own body. Recognition is thus overlaid with misrecognition: the image recognized is conceived as the reflected body of the self, but its misrecognition as superior projects this body outside itself as an ideal ego, the alienated subject, which, reintrojected as an ego ideal, gives rise to the future generation of identification with others. This mirror-moment predates language for the child.

Important for this article is the fact that it is an image that constitutes the matrix of the imaginary, of recognition/misrecognition and identification, and hence of the first articulation of the "I," of subjectivity. This is a moment when an older fascination with looking (at the mother's face, for an obvious example) collides with the initial inklings of self-awareness. Hence it is the birth of the long love affair/despair between image and self-image which has found such intensity of expression in film and such joyous recognition in the cinema audience. Quite apart from the extraneous similarities between screen and mirror (the framing of the human form in its surroundings, for instance), the cinema has structures of fascination strong enough to allow temporary loss of ego while simultaneously reinforcing the ego. The sense of forgetting the world as the ego has subsequently come to perceive it (I forgot who I am and where I was) is nostalgically reminiscent of that presubjective moment of image recognition. At the same time the cinema has distinguished itself in the production of ego ideals as expressed in particular in the star system, the stars centering both screen presence and screen story as they act out a complex process of likeness and difference (the glamorous impersonates the ordinary.)

C. Sections II.A and B have set out two contradictory aspects of the pleasurable structures of looking in the conventional cinematic situation. The first, scopophilic, arises from pleasure in using another person as an object of sexual stimulation through sight. The second, developed through narcissism and the constitution of the ego, comes from identification with the image seen. Thus, in film terms, one implies a separation of the erotic identity of the subject from the object on the screen (active scopophilia), the other demands identification of the ego with the object on the screen through the spectator's fascination with and recognition of his like. The first is a function of the sexual instincts, the second of ego libido. This dichotomy was crucial for Freud. Although he saw the two as interacting and overlaying each other, the tension between instinctual drives and self-preservation continues to be a dramatic polarization in terms of pleasure. Both are formative structures, mechanisms not meaning. In themselves they have no signification, they have to be attached to an idealization. Both pursue aims in indifference to perceptual reality, creating the imagized, eroticized concept of the world that forms the perception of the subject and makes a mockery of empirical objectivity.

During its history, the cinema seems to have evolved a particular illusion of reality in which this contradiction between libido and ego has found a beautifully complementary fantasy world. In *reality* the fantasy world of the screen is subject to the law which produces it. Sexual instincts and identification processes have a meaning within the symbolic order which articulates desire. Desire, born with language, allows the possibility of transcending the instinctual and the imaginary, but its point of reference continually returns to the traumatic moment of its birth: the castration complex. Hence the look, pleasurable in form, can be threatening in content, and it is woman as representation/image that crystallizes this paradox.

III. Woman as Image, Man as Bearer of the Look

A. In a world ordered by sexual imbalance, pleasure in looking has been split between active/male and passive/female. The determining male gaze projects its fantasy onto the female figure, which is styled accordingly. In their traditional exhibitionist role women are simultaneously looked at and displayed, with their appearance coded for strong visual and erotic impact so that they can be said to connote *to-be-looked-at-ness*. Woman displayed as sexual object is the leitmotif of erotic spectacle: from pinups to striptease, from Ziegfeld to Busby Berkeley, she holds the look, plays to and signifies male desire. Mainstream film neatly combined spectacle and narrative. (Note, however, how in the musical song-and-dance numbers break the flow of the diegesis.) The presence of woman is an indispensable element of spectacle in normal narrative film, yet her visual presence tends to work against the development of a story line, to freeze the flow of action in moments of erotic contemplation. This alien presence then has to be integrated into cohesion with the narrative. As Budd Boetticher has put it:

> What counts is what the heroine provokes, or rather what she represents. She is the one, or rather the love or fear she inspires in the hero, or else the concern he feels for her, who makes him act the way he does. In herself the woman has not the slightest importance.

(A recent tendency in narrative film has been to dispense with this problem altogether; hence the development of what Molly Haskell has called the "buddy movie," in which the active homosexual eroticism of the central male figures can carry the story without distraction.) Traditionally, the woman displayed has functioned on two levels: as erotic object for the characters within the screen story, and as erotic object for the spectator within the auditorium, with a shifting tension between the looks on either side of the screen. For instance, the device of the showgirl allows the two looks to be unified technically without any apparent break in the diegesis. A woman performs within the narrative, the gaze of the spectator and that of the male characters in the film are neatly combined without breaking narrative verisimilitude. For a moment the sexual impact of the performing woman takes the film into a no-man's-land outside its own time and space. Thus Marilyn Monroe's first appearance in *The River of No Return* and Lauren Bacall's songs in *To Have or Have Not*. Similarly, conventional closeups of legs (Dietrich, for instance) or a face (Garbo) integrate into the narrative a different mode of eroticism. One part of a fragmented body destroys the Renaissance space, the illusion of depth demanded by the narrative; it gives flatness, the quality of a cut-out or icon rather than verisimilitude to the screen.

B. An active/passive heterosexual division of labor has similarly controlled narrative structure. According to the principles of the ruling ideology and the physical structures that back it up, the male figure cannot bear the burden of sexual objectification. Man is reluctant to gaze at his exhibitionist like. Hence the split between spectacle and narrative supports the man's role as the active one of forwarding the story, making things happen. The man controls the film fantasy and also emerges as the representative of power in a further sense: as the bearer of the look of the spectator, transferring it behind the screen to neutralize the extradiegetic tendencies represented by woman as spectacle. This is made possible through the processes set in motion by structuring the film around a main controlling figure with whom the spectator can identify. As the spectator identifies with the main male protagonist,[1] he projects his look on to that of his like, his screen surrogate, so that the power of the male protagonist as he controls events coincides with the active power of the erotic look, both giving a satisfying sense of omnipotence. A male movie star's glamorous characteristics are thus not those of the erotic object of the gaze, but those of the more perfect, more complete, more powerful ideal ego conceived in the original moment of recognition in front of the mirror. The character in the story can make things happen and control events better than the subject/spectator, just as the image in the mirror was more in control of motor coordination. In contrast to woman as icon, the active male figure (the ego ideal of the identification process) demands a three-dimensional space corresponding to that of the mirror recognition in which the alienated subject internalized his own representation of this imaginary existence. He is a figure in a landscape. Here the function of film is to reproduce as accurately as possible the so-called natural conditions of human perception. Camera technology (as exemplified by deep focus in particular) and camera movements (determined by the action of the protagonist), combined with invisible editing (demanded by realism) all tend to blur the limits of screen space. The male protagonist is free to command the stage, a stage of spatial illusion in which he articulates the look and creates the action.

C.1. Sections III. A and B have set out a tension between a mode of representation of woman in film and conventions surrounding the diegesis. Each is associated with a look: that of the spectator in direct scopophilic contact with the female form displayed for his enjoyment (connoting male fantasy) and that of the spectator fascinated with the image of his like set in an illusion of natural space, and through him gaining control and possession of the woman within the diegesis. (This tension and the shift from one pole to the other can structure a single text. Thus both in *Only Angels Have Wings* and in *To Have and Have Not*, the film opens with the woman as object of the combined gaze of spectator and all the male protagonists in the film. She is isolated, glamorous, on display, sexualized. But as the narrative progresses she falls in love with the main male protagonist and becomes his property, losing her outward glamorous characteristics, her generalized sexuality, her showgirl connotations; her eroticism is subjected to the male star alone. By means of identification with him, through participation in his power, the spectator can indirectly possess her too.)

But in psychoanalytic terms, the female figure poses a deeper problem. She also connotes something that the look continually circles around but disavows: her lack of a penis, implying a threat of castration and hence unpleasure. Ultimately, the meaning of woman is sexual difference, the absence of the penis as visually ascertainable, the material evidence on which is based the castration complex essential for the organization of entrance to the symbolic order and the law of the father. Thus the woman as icon, displayed for the gaze and enjoyment of men, the active controllers of the look, always threatens to evoke the anxiety it originally signified. The male unconscious has two avenues of escape from this castration anxiety: preoccupation with the reenactment of the original trauma (investigating the woman, demystifying her mystery), counterbalanced by the devaluation, punishment, or saving of the guilty object (an avenue typified by the concerns of the *film noir*); or else complete disavowal of castration by the substitution of a fetish object or turning the represented figure itself into a fetish so that it becomes reassuring rather than dangerous (hence overvaluation, the cult of the female star). This second avenue, fetishistic scopophilia, builds up the physical beauty of the object, transforming it into something satisfying in itself. The first avenue, voyeurism, on the contrary, has associations with sadism: pleasure lies in ascertaining guilt (immediately associated with castration), asserting control, and subjecting the guilty person through punishment or forgiveness. This sadistic side fits in well with narrative. Sadism demands a story, depends on making something happen, forcing a change in another person, a battle of will and strength, victory/defeat, all occurring in a linear time with a beginning and an end. Fetishistic scopophilia, on the other hand, can exist outside linear time as the erotic instinct is focused on the look alone. These contradictions and ambiguities can be illustrated more simply by using works by Hitchcock and Sternberg, both of whom take the look almost as the content or subject matter of many of their films. Hitchcock is the more complex, as he uses both mechanisms. Sternberg's work, on the other hand, provides many more example of fetishistic scopophilia.

C.2. It is well known that Sternberg once said he would welcome his films being projected upside down so that story and character involvement would not interfere with the spectator's undiluted appreciation of the screen image. This statement is revealing but ingenuous. Ingenuous in that his films do demand that the figure of the woman (Dietrich, in the cycle of films with her, as the ultimate example) should be identifiable. But revealing in that it emphasizes the fact that for him the pictorial space enclosed by the frame is paramount rather than narrative or identification processes. While Hitchcock goes into the investigative side of voyeurism, Sternberg produces the ultimate fetish, taking it to the point where the powerful look of the male protagonist (characteristic of traditional narrative film) is broken in favor of the image in direct erotic rapport with the spectator. The beauty of the woman as object and the screen space coalesce; she is no longer the bearer of guilt but a perfect product, whose body, stylized and fragmented by closeups, is the content of the film and the direct recipient of the spectator's look. Sternberg plays down the illusion of screen depth; his screen tends to be one-dimensional, as light and shade, lace, steam, foliage, net, streamers, etc. reduce the visual field. There is little or no mediation of the look through the eyes of the main male protagonist. On the contrary, shadowy presences like La Bessière in *Morocco* act as surrogates for the director, detached as they are from audience identification. Despite Sternberg's insistence that his stories are irrelevant, it is significant that they are concerned with situation, not suspense, and cyclical rather than linear time, while plot complications revolve around misunderstanding rather than conflict. The most importance absence is that of the controlling male gaze within the screen scene. The high point of emotional drama in the most typical Dietrich films, her supreme moments of erotic meaning, take place in the absence of the man she loves in the fiction. There are other witnesses, other spectators watching her on the screen; their gaze is one with, not standing in for, that of the audience. At the end of *Morocco*, Tom Brown has already disappeared into the desert when Amy Jolly kicks off her gold sandals and walks after him. At the end of *Dishonored*, Kranau is indifferent to the fate of Magda. In both cases, the erotic impact, sanctified by death, is displayed as a spectacle for the audience. The male hero misunderstands and, above all, does not see.

In Hitchcock, by contrast, the male hero does see precisely what the audience sees. However, in the films I shall discuss here, he takes fascination with an image through scopophilic eroticism as the subject of the film. Moreover, in these cases the hero portrays the contradictions and tensions experienced by the spectator. In *Vertigo* in particular, but also in *Marnie* and *Rear Window*, the look is central to the plot, oscillating between voyeurism and fetishistic fascination. As a twist, a further manipulation of the normal viewing process which in some sense reveals it, Hitchcock uses the process of identification normally associated with ideological correctness and the recognition of established morality and shows up its perverted side. Hitchcock has never concealed his interest in voyeurism, cinematic and noncinematic. His heroes are exemplary of the symbolic order and the law—a policeman *(Vertigo)*, a dominant male possessing money and power *(Marnie)*—but their erotic drives lead them into compromised situations. The power to subject another person to the will sadistically or to the gaze voyeuristically is turned onto the woman as the object of both. Power is backed by a certainty of legal right and the established guilt of the woman (evoking castration, psychoanalytically speaking). True perversion is barely concealed under a shallow mask of ideological correctness—the man is on the right side of the law, the woman on the wrong. Hitchcock's skillful use of identification processes and liberal use of subjective camera from the point of view of the male protagonist draw the spectators deeply into his position, making them share his uneasy gaze. The audience is absorbed into a voyeuristic situation within the screen scene and diegesis which parodies his own in the cinema. In his analysis of *Rear Window,* Douchet takes the film as a metaphor for the cinema. Jeffries is the audience; the events in the apartment block opposite correspond to the screen. As he watches, an erotic dimension is added to his look, a central image to the drama. His girlfriend Lisa had been of little sexual interest to him, more or less a drag, so long as she remained on the spectator side. When she crosses the barrier between his room and the block opposite, their relationship is reborn erotically. He does not merely watch her through his lens, as a distant meaningful image, he also sees her as a guilty intruder exposed by a dangerous man threatening her with punishment, and thus finally saves her. Lisa's exhibitionism has already been established by her obsessive interest in dress and style, in being a passive image of visual perfection; Jeffries' voyeurism and activity have also been established through his work as a photojournalist, a maker of stories and captor of images. However, his enforced inactivity, binding him to his seat as a spectator, puts him squarely in the fantasy position of the cinema audience.

In *Vertigo,* subjective camera predominates. Apart from one flashback from Judy's point of view, the narrative is woven around what Scottie sees or fails to see. The audience follows the growth of his erotic obsession and subsequent despair precisely from his point of view. Scottie's voyeurism is blatant: he falls in love with a woman he follows and spies on without speaking to. Its sadistic side is equally blatant: he has chosen (and freely chosen, for he had been a successful lawyer) to be a policeman, with all the attendant possibilities of pursuit and investigation. As a result, he follows, watches, and falls in love with a perfect image of female beauty and mystery. Once he actually confronts her, his erotic drive is to break her down and force her to tell by persistent cross-questioning. Then, in the second part of the film, he reenacts his obsessive involvement with the image he loved to watch secretly. He reconstructs Judy as Madeleine, forces her to conform in every detail to the actual physical appearance of his fetish. Her exhibitionism, her masochism, make her an ideal passive counterpart to Scottie's active sadistic voyeurism. She knows her part is to perform, and only by playing it through and then replaying it can she keep Scottie's erotic interest. But in the repetition he does break her down and succeeds in exposing her guilt. His curiosity wins through and she is punished. In *Vertigo,* erotic involvement with the look is disorientating: the spectator's fascination is turned against him as the narrative carries him through and entwines him with the processes that he is himself exercising. The Hitchcock hero here is firmly placed within the symbolic order, in narrative terms. He has all the attributes of the patriarchal superego. Hence the spectator, lulled into a false sense of security by the apparent legality of his surrogate, sees through his look and finds himself exposed as complicit, caught in the moral ambiguity of looking. Far from being simply an aside on the perversion of the police, *Vertigo* focuses on the implications of the active/looking, passive/looked-at split in terms of sexual difference and the power of the male symbolic encapsulated in the hero. Marnie too performs for Mark Rutland's gaze and masquerades as the perfect to-be-looked-at image. He too is on the side of the law until, drawn in by obsession with her guilt, her secret, he longs to see her in the act of committing a crime, make her confess, and thus save her. So he too becomes complicit as he acts out the implications of his power. He controls money and words, he can have his cake and eat it.

IV. Summary

The psychoanalytic background that has been discussed in this article is relevant to the pleasure and unpleasure offered by traditional narrative film. The scopophilic instinct (pleasure in looking at another person as an erotic object), and, in contradistinction, ego libido (forming identification processes) act as formations, mechanisms, which this cinema has played on. The image of woman as (passive) raw material for the (active) gaze of man takes the argument a step further into the structure of representation, adding a further layer demanded by the ideology of the patriarchal order as it is worked out in its favorite cinematic form—illusionistic narrative film. The argument returns again to the psychoanalytic background in that woman as representation signifies castration, inducing voyeuristic or fetishistic mechanisms to circumvent her threat. None of these interacting layers is intrinsic to film, but it is only in the film form that they can reach a perfect and beautiful contradiction, thanks to the possibility in the cinema of shifting the emphasis of the look. It is the place of the look that defines cinema, the possibility of varying it and exposing it. This is what makes cinema quite different in its voyeuristic potential from, say, striptease, theater, shows, etc. Going far beyond highlighting a woman's to-be-looked-at-ness, cinema builds the way she is to be looked at into the spectacle itself. Playing on the tension between film as controlling the dimension of time (editing, narrative) and film as controlling the dimension of space (changes in distance, editing), cinematic codes create a gaze, a world, and an object, thereby producing an illusion cut to the measure of desire. It is these cinematic codes and their relationship to formative external structures that must be broken down before mainstream film and the pleasure it provides can be challenged.

To begin with (as an ending), the voyeuristic-scopophilic look that is a crucial part of traditional filmic pleasure can itself be broken down. There are three different looks associated with cinema: that of the camera as it records the profilmic event, that of the audience as it watches the final product, and that of the characters at each other within the screen illusion. The conventions of narrative film deny the first two and subordinate them to the third, the conscious aim being always to eliminate intrusive camera presence and prevent a distancing awareness in the audience. Without these two absences (the material existence of the recording process, the critical reading of the spectator), fictional drama cannot achieve reality, obviousness, and truth. Nevertheless, as this article has argued, the structure of looking in narrative fiction film contains a contradiction in its own premises: the female image as a castration threat constantly endangers the unity of the diegesis and bursts through the world of illusion as an intrusive, static, one-dimensional fetish. Thus the two looks materially present in time and space are obsessively subordinated to the neurotic needs of the male ego. The camera becomes the mechanism for producing an illusion of Renaissance space, flowing movements compatible with the human eye, an ideology of representation that revolves around the perception of the subject; the camera's look is disavowed in order to create a convincing world in which the spectator's surrogate can perform with verisimilitude. Simultaneously, the look of the audience is denied an intrinsic force: as soon as fetishistic representation of the female image threatens to break the spell of illusion, and the erotic image on the screen appears directly (without mediation) to the spectator, the fact of fetishization, concealing as it does castration fear, freezes the look, fixates the spectator, and prevents him from achieving any distance from the image in front of him.

This complex interaction of looks is specific to film. The first blow against the monolithic accumulation of traditional film conventions (already undertaken by radical filmmakers) is to free the look of the camera into its materiality in time and space and the look of the audience into dialectics, passionate detachment. There is no doubt that this destroys the satisfaction, pleasure, and privilege of the "invisible guest," and highlights how film has depended on voyeuristic active/passive mechanisms. Women, whose image has continually been stolen and used for this end, cannot view the decline of the traditional film form with anything much more than sentimental regret.[2]

Notes

1. There are films with a woman as main protagonist, of course. To analyze this phenomenon seriously here would take me too far afield. Pam Cook and Claire Johnston's study of *The Revolt of Mamie Stover* in Phil Hardy, ed., *Raoul Walsh* (Edinburgh; Edinburgh Film Festival and Vineyard Press, 1974), shows in a striking case how the strength of this female protagonist is more apparent than real.

2. This article is a reworked version of a paper given in the French Department of the University of Wisconsin, Madison, the spring of 1973.

[12]

Paul Willemen
Voyeurism, The Look, and Dwoskin

1

Most definitions of cinematic specificity exclude from their considerations the complex interaction of looks at play in the filmic process. On the contrary, the objectness of the film text is emphasized in its autonomous, self-enclosed separation from the viewer—thus relegating the problem of the look to the realm of individual subjectivity. Looking itself thus becomes an unproblematic activity irrevocably tied to subjective intentionality. Christian Metz emphasized this particular approach by insisting that, although film functions in many ways like a mirror, it differs from the mirror in one crucial aspect: it doesn't reflect an image of the spectator's own body: "film is not exhibitionist. I look at it but it doesn't look at me looking at it. . . . the visible is entirely on the side of the screen."[1] The spectator is cast in the role of "invisible subject" identifying itself to the camera as the punctual source of the look which constitutes the image along the lines of a monocular perspective. Having split the cinematic operation into two distinct realms, film studies can be separated into on the one hand semiological study of the text as an autonomous object and on the other the psychology of the spectator. Such a separation opens wide the door to the two main idealist traditions dominating film criticism (and filmmaking): the film text becomes either a Kantian "object for itself" (Ding an sich), as in mechanical structuralism in the more primitive forms of semiology; or the text exists solely by the grace

Published in *Afterimage* (1976), no. 6, pp. 40–50, and reprinted by permission of the author.

of the individual consciousness of the viewer whose subjective intentionality determines the way he/she sees the text. The latter form of idealism leads to statements decreeing that there are as many ways of appreciating a film as there are individual spectators.

In a short article in the *Times Higher Education Supplement* (March 26, 1976), Stephen Heath writes that since "the encounter of Marxism and psychoanalysis on the terrain of semiotics," film can now be studied as a specific signifying practice:

signifying indicates the recognition of film as a system or series of systems of meaning, film as articulation. *Practice* stresses the process of this articulation, which it thus refuses to hold under the assumption of notions such as 'representation' and 'expression'; it takes film as a work of production of meanings and in doing so brings into the analysis the question of the positioning of the subject within that work, its relations of the subject, what kind of 'reader' and 'author' it constructs. *Specificity* is both [the] codes particular to cinema *and* the heterogeneity of its particular effect, its particular inscriptions of subject and meaning in ideology. Directed in this way the study of film is neither 'contents' nor 'forms' but, breaking the deadlock of that opposition, of operations, of the process of film and the relations of subjectivity in that process.

It is in this context of the study of the relations of subjectivity in the filmic process that the problem of the look and the modes of its inscription acquire their full significance.

The remarkably few studies of this problem of the look in the cinema have tended to concentrate either on the organization of intradiegetic looks within the Hollywood narrative cinema (30-degree and 180-degree rules, eyeline matches, etc.) and their implications of involvement (via identification) or separation (via suturing effects) for the spectator; or on more formalist studies of points-of-view structures without taking into account that the point of view of the camera is not identical with that of the spectator. If indeed the spectator can be said to have a point of view. In fact, the viewing subject is itself caught in a complex interaction of different looks from different places. In Hollywood cinema, as Metz correctly points out, the spectator is inscribed as 'invisible' but that does not mean that he/she is not also subjected to a look, merely that the look at the viewing subject is effaced through a series of aesthetic strategies. The viewer of Hollywood cinema is allowed to imagine himself/herself as "invisible": "conventional films tend to suppress all marks of the subject, of the [filmic] uttering (enunciation), so that the spectator may have the *impression* [my emphasis] of being that subject but as an empty and absent subject, reduced to the mere faculty of vision . . . all the seen is rejected towards the side of the pure object." Metz continues to describe this as "a drastically split situation in which the double denial without which there would be no story *(histoire)* is maintained at all costs; the scene ignores that it is seen . . . and that ignorance allows the viewer to ignore himself/herself as voyeur."[2] In another essay, I attempted to show that a film text is always traversed by two sets of marks relating to the looks of two different subjects, one assigned to the place of the author, the other to the place of the viewer, with the viewing subject in fact, as an instance incorporating that irrevocable split and vacillating between the two terms.[3] As J. Lacan put it: "Certainly, the tableau is in my eye. But I, I am in the tableau . . . in the scopic relation, the subject hangs in an essential vacillation on a fantasy which hinges on a specific object: the look."[4]

What needs to be studied is the variety of the modalities of the inscription of the look in the filmic process. A good starting point can be found in a remarkable essay by Laura Mulvey, "Visual Pleasure and Narrative Cinema" [included in this anthology—ED.], where she outlines an initial approach to the problem.

Mulvey distinguishes three different looks: (1) the camera's look as it records the profilmic event, (2) the audience's look at the image and (3) the look the characters exchange within the diegesis. What Metz referred to as the inscription of the reader as an invisible, empty and absent subject, Mulvey explains in the following terms: "The conventions of narrative film deny the first two [looks] and subordinate them to the third, the conscious aim being always to eliminate intrusive camera presence and prevent a distancing awareness in the audience." Such a distancing awareness occurs precisely when the viewer is confronted with marks of the subject, which directly interpellates the viewer-addressee of a constructed message, forcing him/her to abandon the cloak of invisibility which allowed the viewer to fantasize himself/herself as a subject of the discourse.[5]

As regards the look cast by the spectator Mulvey divides it into two types: (1) the spectator can be in direct scopophilic contact with an object of desire or (2) he/she can be fascinated with the image of his/her like, identifying with this ideal ego and thus, in a roundabout way, gain control and possession of the desired object within the diegesis. In this way, the spectator's look at the spectacle and the intradiegetic looks can be articulated to each other via the spectator's narcissistic identification with his/her representative in the diegesis.

This distinction between the two types of looks cast by the viewer is in some ways open to question. It is true that the traditional forms of cinema are dedicated to the legitimization and perpetuation of a patriarchal order, and that in such a context, the object of the look is traditionally the female form displayed for the gaze and enjoyment of men as the active controllers of the look. However, the real basis for the distinction between direct scopophilic contact with the object of desire and mediated contact/possession of that object must be sought in the origins of the scopophilic drive itself. In *Instincts and Their Vicissitudes* Freud wrote that "At the beginning of its activity, the scopophilic instinct is autoerotic: it has indeed an object, but that object is the subject's own body." The identification of the woman as the privileged object of the scopophilic drive is therefore already the product of a displacement. Mulvey doesn't allow sufficient room for the fact that in patriarchy the direct object of scopophilic desire can also be male. If scopophilic pleasure relates primarily to the observation of one's sexual like (as Freud suggests), then the two looks distinguished by Mulvey are in fact varieties of one single mechanism: the repression of homosexuality. The narcissistic identification with an ideal ego in the diegesis would therefore not be a mere mediation in order to get at a desired woman, but the contemplation of the male hero would in itself be a substantial source of gratification for a male viewer—as is demonstrated time and again in the contemporary American cinema's celebration of male couples. In such films, the suggested homosexual gratification appears to be in direct proportion to the degree women are humiliated in/eliminated from the diegesis. Gratification of the scopophilic drive necessarily reactivates traces of primary narcissim, a fact not sufficiently stressed in Mulvey's account, undermining the rigor of the distinction between the two types of viewer's looks she describes.

However, it remains true that in patriarchy the female form is a privileged object of scopophilic desire. Mulvey continues her argument by pointing out that the contemplation of the female form itself trails problems in its wake, as it cannot fail to evoke, in return, the anxiety it originally signified, i.e., castration. She explains that the male unconscious has two avenues of escape from this evocation of castration anxiety: (1) a preoccupation with the reenactment of the original trauma, i.e., investigating the woman, the perpetual recommencing of attempts to see her guilty secret, counterbalanced by the devaluation/punishment/saving of the object culpable of provoking the anxiety; (2) a complete disavowal of castration by substituting a fetish object, even to the point of turning the represented figure itself into a fetish, as happened with the star cult. Finally, Mulvey underlines that the first escape route has close links with sadism, a drive which also is aimed at repressing castration anxieties provoked in the subject. She links this sadistic component of voyeurism to the need for a narrative, as sadism depends on making something happen to something/someone else, while fetishistic scopophilia can exist outside linear time, happily contemplating a frozen image. Here again, the distinction between the two ways of coping with castration fears appears a bit hasty. The former route i.e., the recurrent investigation of the female form, is itself a form of fetishism: "I know she is castrated, and yet. . . let's look again." This attitude reproduces the traditional fetishistic split between belief and knowledge. So, both escapes are equally implicated in fetishism but offer different strategies of coping.

In her desire to pinpoint the various scopophilic mechanisms at play in the narrative films Mulvey overlooks the fact that in so-called nonnarrative films exactly the same mechanisms are at play: scopophilia, fetishism, and sadism. The sadistic aggression of the woman, evident in narrative films, is easily paralleled by the aggression of the fetish frame or the emulsion, as in some avant-garde films. Mulvey's article ends with what appears to be an error prompted by her concern to relate a feminist politics to an avant-garde orthodoxy. Undoubtedly, the kind of voyeuristic pleasure which involves sadistic/fetishistic pleasure at the expense of an objectification of the image of women must be attacked and destroyed. But this does not mean that it is possible, or indeed, desirable, to expel these drives from the filmic process altogether, as such a move would simply abolish cinema itself. It is essential if cinema is to continue to exist that the scopophilic drive be granted some satisfaction. What matters is not whether this pleasure is present or absent, but the positioning of the subject in relation to it. To put it in Stephen Heath's terms, what kind of "reader" or "author" it constructs.

2

Having described the three looks at play in the filmic process, the two different looks of the viewer and the two escapes from castration anxiety, Mulvey finishes her essay with the statement: "This complex interaction of looks is specific to film." However, few films proposed the inscription of the look in its different modalities as their central paradigm. Most of Stephen Dwoskin's work stands as an isolated example of an attempt to work through this particular problematic. The reasons why this should have gone largely unnoticed (or at least uncommented) are to be found in the nature of the debates at present shaping the landscape of avant-garde filmmaking. Battle lines appear to have been drawn around the issue of cinematic specificity, in Metzian terms: specifically cinematic signifiers vs. filmic signifiers. Such a division neatly sidesteps the issue that signifieds cannot be expelled, just as it is impossible to present a sheet of paper with only one side. What is a signifier or a signified depends entirely on the level on which the analysis operates: a signified on one level can become a signifier on another level. But even the more sophisticated participants in the debate ignore the central cinematic fact of the inscription of the look, as this object cannot be unambiguously located on either side of the division between signified and signifier. Moreover, such a division borders on and is often invaded by the old and familiar form/content opposition. Dwoskin's films, by focusing on the look itself, break the deadlock of that opposition, and simultaneously see themselves relegated to marginality, or even rejected outright by anyone holding to the old binary opposition: proponents of classic narrative films object to Dwoskin's formal concerns (see the reactions at the Cannes festival to the showing of *Dyn Amo*) while "structural" filmmakers object to Dwoskin's use of a narrative and the presence of diegetic signifiers. Dwoskin is not even mentioned in P. Adams Sitney's book, *Visionary Film*, nor in *Structural Film Anthology*, edited by P. Gidal—in spite of Dwoskin's insistent foregrounding of specifically cinematic codes relating to processing, developing, and printing techniques, e.g., *Dirty* and *Me Myself & I*. Dave Curtis, in his *Experimental Cinema*, simply dismisses Dwoskin as a maker of conventional documentaries, a view that would certainly not be shared by the producer of Panorama.

A detailed analysis of Dwoskin's films would require a period of study much longer than the one available for the production of this article. I will therefore attempt to back up my thesis that Dwoskin's films engage with the crucial and specifically cinematic problem of the place and functioning of the look only by referring to a few fairly randomly chosen examples. Incidentally, this also means that a whole series of other important aspects of Dwoskin's films will not be dealt with in this essay (e.g., the importance and the function of music, verbal language, the play on the "structural" elements in his films, etc.)

For there to be a look, there has to be a subject and an object demarcating it, in the same way that for there to be a message there has to be a sender and a receiver. As in the structure of fantasy, the object and subject may change places, the term of their articulation remains. In this instance: the look. However, as Laura Mulvey points out, there are—as a rule—three looks in the cinema: intradiegetic, camera/profilmic event, viewer/film. In nonfigurative cinema, the intradiegetic look is absent while the camera/profilmic event look is still present, but erased in that no identifiable, recognizable object is being looked at. The third look is still present. In conventional narrative cinema, attempts are made to make the viewer/film look coincide with the camera/profilmic event look, and a considerable panoply of strategies is deployed to erase the marks of the presence of the camera's look as distinct from the viewer's. This is not to say that the camera sees something different, just that the camera sees differently. *Me Myself & I* focuses precisely on this difference. By varying the processing of the exposed film, the different modalities of the camera's look at the profilmic event are foregrounded, while the viewer's look at the image necessarily remains constant. Entry into the diegesis by means of narcissistic identification—an ever present danger when using a profilmic event involving human figures—is prevented largely by camera movements and the proximity of the camera to its profilmic scene. So, although there is a recognizable profilmic event, entry to it is barred and what remains are the two looks: the camera's and the viewer's. Another film exploring the material independence of the camera's look is *Take Me*. In *Experimental Cinema*, Dave Curtis describes the film in these terms: "A girl directly tries to seduce the camera, giving a come-on to the audience and the camera responds." Already, it appears that Curtis confuses the look of the camera with that of the audience and fails to make the distinction demanded by the text: the relation between the girl and the camera is not the same as that between the girl and the audience, as becomes evident in the rest of Curtis's own description: "but the relationship is peculiar, the girl retires from a kiss with her mouth smeared with paint. She persists, slowly becoming covered with paint . . . It is as though both the audience and the girl are being punished for their (mutual) complicity in a vicarious sexual relationship." Indeed, the mutual vicarious sexual relationship between girl and audience is one of voyeurism, with the camera inscribed as "other" agency, source of a different look with different effects on both girl and viewer. The role of the camera in this film is even more significant than Curtis' description suggests: in the voyeuristic relationship between viewer and girl the camera also functions as signifier of desire—the desire which supports the voyeuristic relationship in the first place. The paint which gradually covers the body of the girl, then, acquires the status of traces imprinted on the object of voyeurism, traces which are imprinted by the signifier of desire and betraying the tactile elements present in the desire for physical possession implied/denied by the voyeuristic relation. A critical account of the film would have to denounce the fact that the sadistic components redoubling the voyeurism are not themselves redirected toward the viewer, thus leaving the viewer's sadism as an unquestioned—and therefore uncriticized—given. In a later film, *Girl*, Dwoskin explores the implications of the scopophilic drive more fully. The film consists of one long static take of a naked girl standing on a bath mat. As the take continues, we become aware that the girl is uncomfortable: she fidgets about, tries to cover herself with her hands and arms, etc. However, the take continues, in silence, until the film runs out.

In his essay, *Instincts and Their Vicissitudes,* Freud observed that an instinct (drive) may undergo a reversal into its opposite or may turn round upon the subject. This is precisely what happens during the viewing of *Girl:* the act of sadistic viewing rebounds on the subject as the viewer becomes aware that the look upon the girl is having disagreeable effects on her, and instead of the "innocent" pleasure of watching a naked girl, the viewer now has to confront the considerable sadistic components present in his/her act of looking and by implication, confront the castration fears provoked by the investigation of the naked female form in the diegesis. The film also demonstrates that in the filmic process, there are not just three looks, as described in Mulvey's article, but four: the look at the viewer must be added. J. Lacan described his fourth look as being not "a look that can be seen, but a look imagined by men in the field of the other." It is this look which "surprises me in the act of voyeurism and occasions a feeling of shame." It is this look which, in Sartre's *Being and Nothingness,* constitutes me in relation to the Other. In the filmic process, this look can be represented as the look which constitutes the viewer as visible subject. A tangible signifier of the look (not to be confused with the look itself, which is "imagined") could be found in the reflection of the light of the screen/projection beam back onto the faces of the viewers. This look begins to play an ever more important role in *Girl* as the film progresses: as the viewer has to confront his/her sadistic voyeurism, the presence of the imagined look in the field of the other makes itself increasingly felt, producing a sense of shame at being caught in the act of voyeurism. By this time, the viewing subject has become the exhibitionist. The scopic drive has been turned back onto the subject and the active aim has become a passive one, delegating the role of actively viewing sadist, in a displacing gesture, onto the camera—sometimes, wrongly, identified with the filmmaker. The scopic drive has thus been turned back upon the subject (girl/viewer) and has been reversed into its opposite (looking at/being looked at). This can, quite understandably, be accompanied by a change from voyeuristic pleasure to unpleasure combined with a refusal to acknowledge one's unstable position in the viewing process. It must be stressed that the fourth look is not of the same order as the other three, precisely because the subject of the look is an imaginary other, but this doesn't make the presence of the look any the less real. But although it is ever present in all filmic experiences, the overwhelming majority of films as well as the other aspects of the cinematic institution, such as theaters, projection conditions, etc., conspire to minimize its effects, the aim being to try and erase it altogether. It is perhaps this fourth look which prompted theater managers to decide that the most expensive seats in a theater should be at the back: there one has the impression of being better protected against the danger of being overlooked in one's voyeuristic pleasure, a protection people appear to be willing to pay for. In fact, the presence of the fourth look has considerable implications regarding the social experience of film going and may offer an insight into the differences between the subject/object/spectacle relations in cinema and theater.

The same complex dialectic of looks—all four of them—occurs in *Dyn Amo,* this time involving a decentering of the camera's look by the main actress' "direct" appeal, across the barrier of the screen, to the viewer, summoning him/ her to come to her assistance in the diegesis. In fact, the whole film could be regarded as a textbook demonstration of the entire complex of drives mentioned in Mulvey's essay: the film plays expertly upon the distinctions and gradual transitions between a spectacle especially designed for an audience (both within the diegesis and in the actual film theater), involving conscious sexual provocation, and the voyeuristic spectacle where the object is supposed to be unaware of the look directed at it, followed by a reinscription of the look, but this time directed at the viewer. There are also many aspects of the film problematizing the sadistic and fetishistic components implicated in the act of pleasurable viewing, but these too are redirected at the viewer by means of the fourth look. In this sense, *Dyn Amo* is an advance on an earlier orchestration of looks engineered by Dwoskin, *Chinese Checkers,* where the fourth look is not explicitly inscribed in the text, which makes the text more unproblematically pleasurable and therefore more politically suspect, as the implicit sexism is not foregrounded as a specific problem. In *Chinese Checkers,* the camera's look is distinguished by its mobility and its ability to vary the distance between lens and profilmic object, while the intradiegetic look is exchanged between two women who gradually appear to merge into one almost abstract entity: female eroticism, but still subjected to a controlling gaze which is itself not interpellated. As happens in almost all Dwoskin's films, the libidinal energy involved in the act of watching a film is displaced and crystallized in the diegesis and placed before us *(Vorgestellt)* in the form of erotic activities. In a sense, it is the very vagueness of the generalized eroticism of the diegetic activities which allows the exploration of the implications of the act of looking itself. It is the inscription of the look in relation to these activities which teases out the questions raised by the fact that the subject hangs on to a fantasy which hinges on the look.

It would be possible to quote many more examples of Dwoskin's skilled mise-en-scène of the look. At one time, he even plays on the distinction (i.e., the possible confusion) between the look of the camera and that of the filmmaker, together with a putting into question of the narcissistic relation which both viewer and filmmaker (who is also a viewer, but in another place) entertain with a character in the diegesis: *Behindert*. However, the present series of examples may suffice to back up the original thesis that Dwoskin's films focus on an aspect of the filmic process which, in spite of its specificity to the cinema, has been consistently overlooked. Simultaneously, and perhaps inevitably, Dwoskin's films explore the ramifications that this complex interaction of looks has regarding "the process of films and the relations of subjectivity in that process." Moreover, it is no accident that the more limited the scope of the films' exploration of the problem of the look, the more suspect the films become politically. Only Dwoskin's more complex films encourage the viewer to become aware of the kind of structure of subjectivity in which he/she is implicated when indulging his/her scopophilic drive in relation to projected images.

Note: Peter Gidal pointed out to me that up to circa 1972 Dwoskin was in no sense marginal or neglected. He argued that among avant-garde filmmakers working in Britain, Dwoskin had been the main (almost the sole) beneficiary of critical attention. Although I would still argue that Dwoskin has always been "marginal," the alleged neglect only covers the period from *Times For* onward, i.e., from the time the inscription of the fourth look became dominant in his films.

Notes

1. C. Metz, *Histoire/discours*, in *Langue, discours, société* (Paris 1975). [Now published as part of Metz, *The Imaginary Signifier: Psychoanalysis and the Cinema*, trans. Celia Britton et al. (London: Macmillan; Bloomington: Indiana University Press, 1982)—ED.]

2. *Ibid.*

3. P. Willemen, "Pursued: The Fugitive Subject" in *Raoul Walsh*, Edinburgh Film Festival, 1974.

4. J. Lacan, *Le Séminaire* (Paris: Ed. du Seuil, 1973.)

5. Moreover, Mulvey appears to overstate the case against traditional Hollywood narrative. Camera movements have always, even in Hollywood films, been fairly obtrusive and have always drawn attention to themselves, e.g., Anthony Mann's crane shots, Corman's dolly shots and zooms, etc. But it is true that even the look of the camera has consistently been subordinated to the logic of intradiegetic looks.

[13]

Kaja Silverman
Suture [Excerpts]

. . . The concept of suture attempts to account for the means by which subjects emerge within discourse. As I have already indicated, although that concept has been most intensely theorized in relation to cinematic texts, its initial formulation comes from Jacques-Alain Miller, one of Lacan's disciples. We will look briefly at that formulation before turning to the cinematic one.

Miller defines suture as that moment when the subject inserts itself into the symbolic register in the guise of a signifier, and in so doing gains meaning at the expense of being. In "Suture (elements of the logic of the signifier)," he writes:

Suture names the relation of the subject to the chain of its discourse. . . it figures there as the element which is lacking, in the form of a stand-in. For, while there lacking, it is not purely and simply absent. Suture, by extension—the general relation of lack to the structure of which it is an element, inasmuch as it implies the position of a taking-the-place-of.[1]

Miller's account of suture locates the emphasis in orthodox Lacanian places; the key terms in his definition of it are "lack" and "absence." Indeed, as Miller describes it, suture closely resembles the subject's inauguration into language, illustrated by Lacan with the *"fort"/"da"* game. A given signifier (a pronoun, a personal name) grants the subject access to the symbolic order, but alienates it not only from its own needs but from its drives. That signifier stands in for the absent subject (i.e. absent in being) whose lack it can never stop signifying.

The French theoretician Jean-Pierre Oudart subsequently transported the concept of suture into film studies, where it has been used to probe the precise nature of cinematic signification—to answer the frequently pondered questions "What is the cinematic equivalent for language in the literary text?" and "What is cinematic syntax?" These formal speculations have not preempted those about subjectivity but have been integrated into them. The theory of suture has been rendered more complex with each new statement about it, so that it now embraces a set of assumptions not only about cinematic signification, but about the viewing subject and the operations of ideology. Rather than retracing each argument in turn, we will here attempt to provide a synthesis of the contributions made by Jean-Pierre Oudart, Daniel Dayan, Stephen Heath, [and] Laura Mulvey. . . .

Suture: The Cinematic Model

Theoreticians of cinematic suture agree that films are articulated and the viewing subject spoken by means of interlocking shots. They are thus in fundamental accord with Noel Burch's remark that "Although camera movements, entrances into and exits from frame, composition and so on can all function as devices aiding in the organization of the film object . . . the shot transition [remains] the basic element [of that organization]."[2] Shot relationships are seen as the equivalent of syntactic ones in linguistic discourse, as the agency whereby meaning emerges and a subject-position is constructed for the viewer.

However, some theoreticians conceptualize those relationships differently from others. Whereas Oudart and Dayan find the shot/reverse shot formation to be virtually synonymous with the operations of suture, Heath suggests that it is only one element in a much larger system, and emphasizes features of the editing process which are common to all shot transitions. We will begin by discussing the shot/reverse shot formation. . . .

. . . [T]he shot/reverse shot formation derives its real importance and interest for many of the theoreticians of suture because it demonstrates so lucidly the way in which cinema operates to reduplicate the history of the subject. The viewer of the cinematic spectacle experiences shot 1 as an imaginary plenitude, unbounded by any gaze, and unmarked by difference. Shot 1 is thus the site of a *jouissance* akin to that of the mirror stage prior to the child's discovery of its separation from the ideal image which it has discovered in the reflecting glass.

However, almost immediately the viewing subject becomes aware of the limitations on what it sees—aware, that is, of an absent field. At this point shot 1 becomes a signifier of that absent field, and *jouissance* gives way to unpleasure. Daniel Dayan offers a very clear summary of this transition in "The Tutor Code of Classical Cinema":

When the viewer discovers the frame—the first step in reading the film—the triumph of his former *possession* of the image fades out. The viewer discovers that the camera is hiding things, and therefore distrusts it and the frame itself which he now understands to be arbitrary. He wonders why the frame is what it is. This radically transforms his mode of participation—the unreal space between characters and/or objects is no longer perceived as pleasurable. It is now the space which separates the camera from the characters. The latter have lost their quality of presence. The spectator discovers that his possession of space was only partial, illusory. He feels dispossessed of what he is prevented from seeing. He discovers that he is only authorized to see what happens to be in the axis of the gaze of another spectator, who is ghostly or absent.[3]

Jean-Pierre Oudart refers to the spectator who occupies the missing field as the "Absent One." The Absent One, also known as the Other, has all the attributes of the mythically potent symbolic father: potency, knowledge, transcendental vision, self-sufficiency, and discursive power. It is, of course, the speaking subject of the cinematic text, a subject which, as we have already indicated, finds its locus in a cluster of technological apparatuses (the camera, the tape recorder, etc.). We shall see that this speaking subject often finds its fictional correlative in an ideal paternal representation.

The speaking subject has everything which the viewing subject, suddenly cognizant of the limitations on its vision, understands itself to be lacking. This sense of lack inspires in that subject the desire for "something else," a desire to see more.

However, it is equally important that the presence of the speaking subject be hidden from the viewer. Oudart insists that the classic film text must at all costs conceal from the viewing subject the passivity of that subject's position, and this necessitates denying the fact that there is any reality outside the fiction.

The shot/reverse shot formation is ideally suited for this dual purpose, since it alerts the spectator to that other field whose absence is experienced as unpleasurable while at the same time linking it to the gaze of a fictional character. Thus a gaze within the fiction serves to conceal the controlling gaze outside the fiction; a benign other steps in and obscures the presence of the coercive and castrating Other. In other words, the subject of the speech passes itself off as the speaking subject.

For Oudart, cinematic signification depends entirely upon the moment of unpleasure in which the viewing subject perceives that it is lacking something, i.e., that there is an absent field. Only then, with the disruption of imaginary plenitude, does the shot become a signifier, speaking first and foremost of that thing about which the Lacanian signifier never stops speaking: castration. A complex signifying chain is introduced in place of the lack which can never be made good, suturing over the wound of castration with narrative. However, it is only by inflicting the wound to begin with that the viewing subject can be made to want the restorative of meaning and narrative.

Stephen Heath emphasizes the process of negation which occurs concurrently with a film's positive assertions—its structuring absences and losses. In "Narrative Space," he writes:

Film is the production not just of a negation but equally, simultaneously, of a negativity, the excessive foundation of the process itself, of the very movement of the spectator as subject in the film; which movement is stopped in the negation and its centering positions, the constant phasing in of subject vision ("this but not that" as the sense of the image in flow). [4]

The unseen apparatuses of enunciation represent one of these structuring loses, but there are others which are equally important. The classic cinematic organization depends upon the subject's willingness to become absent to itself by permitting a fictional character to "stand in" for it, or by allowing a particular point of view to define what it sees. The operation of suture is successful at the moment that the viewing subject says, "Yes, that's me," or "That's what I see."

Equally important to the cinematic organization are the operations of cutting and excluding. It is not merely that the camera is incapable of showing us everything at once, but that it does not wish to do so. We must be shown only enough to know that there is more, and to want that "more" to be disclosed. A prime agency of disclosure is the cut, which divides one shot from the next. The cut guarantees that both the preceding and the subsequent shots will function as structuring absences to the present shot. These absences make possible a signifying ensemble, convert one shot into a signifier of the next one, and the signified of the preceding one.

Thus cinematic coherence and plentitude emerge through multiple cuts and negations. Each image is defined through its differences from those that surround it syntagmatically and those it paradigmatically implies ("this but not that"), as well as through its denial of any discourse but its own. Each positive cinematic assertion represents an imaginary conversion of a whole series of negative ones. This castrating coherence, this definition of a discursive position for the viewing subject which necessitates not only its loss of being but the repudiation of alternative discourses, is one of the chief aims of the system of suture.

Most classic cinematic texts go to great lengths to cover over these "cuts." Hitchcock's *Psycho*, on the other hand, deliberately exposes the negations upon which filmic plentitude is predicated. It unabashedly foregrounds the voyeuristic dimensions of the cinematic experience, making constant references to the speaking subject, and forcing the viewer into oblique and uncomfortable positions *vis-à-vis* both the cinematic apparatuses and the spectacle which they produce.

Psycho not only ruptures the Oedipal formation which provides the basis of the present symbolic order but declines to put it back together at the end. The final shot of Norman/mother, which conspicuously lacks a reverse shot, makes clear that the coherence of that order proceeds from the institution of sexual difference, and the denial of bisexuality.

Finally, *Psycho* obliges the viewing subject to make abrupt shifts in identification. These identifications are often in binary opposition to each other; thus the viewing subject finds itself inscribed into the cinematic discourse at one juncture as victim, and at the next juncture as victimizer. These abrupt shifts would seem to thwart the process of identification, as would all the other strategies just enumerated. However, quite the reverse holds true. The more intense the threat of castration and loss, the more intense the viewing subject's desire for narrative closure.

Psycho's opening few shots take in the exterior of a group of city buildings, without a single reverse shot to anchor that spectacle to a fictional gaze. The transition from urban skyline to the interior of a hotel room is achieved by means of a trick shot: the camera appears to penetrate the space left at the bottom of a window whose venetian blind is three-quarters closed. The viewing subject is made acutely aware of the impossibility of this shot—not just the technical but the "moral" impossibility, since the shot in question effects a startling breach of privacy.

Our sense of intruding is accentuated by the first shot inside the hotel room, which shows us a woman (Marion), still in bed, and her lover (Sam) standing beside the bed, half-undressed, with a towel in his hands. His face is cropped by the frame, so that he preserves a certain anonymity denied to Marion, who will be the object of numerous coercive gazes during the film. From the very outset, the viewer is not permitted to forget that he or she participates in that visual coercion.

Marion and Sam exchange a series of embraces before leaving the hotel room. Their lovemaking is interrupted by a discussion about Sam's marital status, and the strain imposed by their clandestine meetings. Marion expresses an intense desire to have their relationship "normalized"—to be inserted through marriage into an acceptable discursive position. Sam comments bitterly on the economic obstacles in the way of such a union. Later in the same day when Marion is entrusted with $40,000 which is intended to buy someone else's marital bliss, and when the man who gives it to her announces that he never carries more money than he can afford to lose, Marion decides to achieve her culturally induced ambitions through culturally taboo means.

The sequence which follows is an extremely interesting one in terms of suture. In the first shot of that scene Marion stands in the doorway of her bedroom closet, her right side toward the camera, wearing a black brassiere and half-slip. A bed separates the camera from her, and in the left far corner there is a vanity-table and mirror. Suddenly the camera moves backward to reveal a corner of the bed not previously exposed, on which lies the envelope of stolen money. It zooms in on the money, then pans to the left and provides a closeup of an open suitcase, full of clothing. During all of this time, Marion is facing the closet, unable to see what we see.

There is a cut to Marion, who turns and looks toward the bed. Once again the camera pulls back to reveal the packet of money. In the next shot, Marion adjusts her hair and clothes in front of the vanity table and mirror. She turns to look at the bed, and we are given a reverse shot of the stolen envelope. This particular shot/reverse shot formation is repeated. Finally, Marion sits down on the bed, puts the money in her purse, picks up the suitcase, and leaves.

This sequence achieves a number of things: It establishes the fascination of the money, not only for Marion but for us (we can't help looking at it, even when Marion's back is turned). It delimits a claustral transactional area, an area from which all mediating objects (i.e., the bed) are eventually removed, from which Marion can no longer emerge. The film resorts more and more obsessively to shot/reverse shots in the following episodes, suggesting Marion's absolute entrapment within the position of a thief. Finally, it associates the money with a transcendental gaze, a gaze which exceeds Marion's, and that can see her without ever being seen—one which knows her better than she knows herself.

The privileged object in the shot/reverse shot formations which punctuate the second half of this episode is the packet of money, not Marion. Indeed, the entire spatial field is defined in relation to that spot on the bed where the $40,000 lies; positioned in front of it, we look for a long time at the contents of the room before its human inhabitant ever casts a significant glance at anything. By privileging the point of view of an inanimate object, Hitchcock makes us acutely aware of what Oudart would call the "Absent One"—i.e., of the speaking subject. Our relationship with the camera remains unmediated, "unsoftened" by the intervention of a human gaze.

Far from attempting to erase our perception of the cinematic apparatus, the film exploits it, playing on the viewing subject's own paranoia and guilt. We enjoy our visual superiority to Marion, but at the same time we understand that the gaze of the camera—that gaze in which we participate—exceeds us, threatening not only Marion but anyone exposed to the film's spectacle.

It would appear that the system of suture cannot be too closely identified with that shot/reverse shot formation in which the function of looking is firmly associated with a fictional character, since by violating that convention Hitchcock throws a much wider net over his audience. He thereby forces the viewing subject to take up residence not only within one of the film's discursive positions (that of victim), but a second (that of sadistic and legalistic voyeur). The whole operation of suture can be made *more* rather than less irresistible when the field of the speaking subject is continually implied. Two other episodes in *Psycho* demonstrate the same point.

The earlier of these inscribes the law into the fictional level of the film through the figure of a highway patrolman. An opening long-shot shows Marion's car pulled over to the side of a deserted road. A police car pulls into frame and parks behind it. In the next shot the patrolman climbs out of his car, walks over to the driver's side of Marion's automobile, and looks through the window. A third shot shows us what he sees—a sleeping Marion. A succession of almost identical shot/reverse shot formations follow, by means of which the superiority of the legal point of view is dramatized. The patrolman knocks on Marion's window and at last she wakes up. We are now provided with a shot/reverse shot exchange between the two characters, but although Marion does in fact look back at the person who has intruded upon her, his eyes are concealed by a pair of dark glasses.

The policeman interrogates Marion about her reasons for sleeping in her car, and she explains that she pulled over because of fatigue. She asks: "Have I broken a law?" The conversation is as oblique as the exchange of looks—rather than answering her question, the patrolman asks: "Is there anything wrong?" His question is neither casual nor solicitous; it is a threat, backed up by a series of quick shot/reverse shots which expose Marion yet further to the scrutiny of a law which it seems impossible to evade, and impossible to decipher.

The police officer asks to see Marion's license. Again the question is far from innocent; "license" has as broadly existential a meaning as the word "wrong" in the earlier question. After she gives him her driver's license, the patrolman walks around to the front of the car to write down the license plate number. We see him through the windshield, still protected by his dark glasses from any personal recognition. The reverse shot discloses not Marion, but the license plate which seems to speak for her with greater authority, and to do so through a legal discourse which renders her even more passive.

The policeman permits Marion to resume her journey, but he tails her for several miles. Her paranoia during this period is conveyed through a group of alternating frontal shots of her driving, and reverse shots of her rearview mirror. The patrol car is clearly visible in both—Marion is now doubly inscribed.

Several sequences later, as Marion continues on her journey in the rain and darkness, the voices of her boss, of the man whose money she has stolen, and of a female friend are superimposed on the sound track, speaking about Marion and defining her even more fully. This device is the acoustic equivalent of all those shots which we have seen, but which Marion has been unable to see because her back was turned, because she was looking in another direction, or because she was asleep. It serves, like those shots, to reinforce the viewing subject's consciousness of an Other whose transcendent and castrating gaze can never be returned, and which always sees one thing: guilt.

The famous shower sequence not only further disassociates the film's spectacle from any of its characters but suggests how much larger the system of suture is than any shot formation. The scene begins with Marion undressing in a motel bedroom, watched through a peephole by Norman, her eventual killer. She goes into the bathroom and flushes down the torn pieces of paper on which she has just taken stock of her financial situation (she has decided to return the stolen money, and wants to calculate how much of it she has spent). Marion then closes the bathroom door, effectively eliminating the possibility of Norman or anyone else within the fiction watching her while she showers. Once again the camera insists on the primacy of its own point of view.

Marion steps inside the bath, and we see her outline through the half-transparent curtain. Then, in a shot which parallels the earlier one in which we seem to slip through the bottom of the hotel window, we penetrate the curtain and find ourselves inside the shower with Marion. The film flaunts these trick shots, as if to suggest the futility of resisting the gaze of the speaking subject.

There are nine shots inside the shower before Marion's killer attacks. They are remarkable for their brevity, and for their violation of the 30-degree rule (the rule that at least 30 degrees of space must separate the position of the camera in one shot from that which follows it in order to justify the intervening cut). Some of the theoreticians of suture argue that the narrative text attempts to conceal its discontinuities and ruptures, but the shower sequence repeatedly draws our attention to the fact of the cinematic cut. This episode also includes a number of obtrusive and disorienting shots—shots taken from the point of view of the shower head at which Marion looks. When the stabbing begins, there is a cinematic cut with almost every thrust of the knife. The implied equation is too striking to ignore: the cinematiac machine is lethal; it too murders and dissects. The shower sequence would seem to validate Heath's point that the coherence and plenitude of narrative film are created through negation and loss.

We have no choice but to identify with Marion in the shower, to insert ourselves into the position of the wayward subject who has strayed from the highway of cultural acceptability, but who now wants to make amends. The vulnerability of her naked and surprisingly small body leaves us without anything to deflect that transaction. Marion's encounter with the warm water inside the shower not only suggests a ritual purification, but a contact so basic and primitive as to break down even such dividing lines as class or sexual difference. Finally, the whole process of identification is formally insisted upon by the brevity of the shots; the point of view shifts constantly within the extremely confined space of the shower, making Marion the only stable object, that thing to which we necessarily cling.

That identification is not even disrupted when the cutting activity is mirrored at the level of the fiction, and a bleeding, stumbling Marion struggles to avoid the next knife wound. It is sustained up until the moment when Marion is definitively dead, an inanimate eye now closed to all visual exchanges. At this point we find ourselves in the equally appalling position of the gaze which has negotiated Marion's murder, and the shading of the corners of the frame so as to simulate the perspective of a peephole insists that we acknowledge our own voyeuristic implication.

Relief comes with the resumption of narrative, a resumption which is effected through a tracking shot from the bathroom into the bedroom. That tracking shot comes to rest first upon the packet of money, then upon an open window through which Norman's house can be seen, and finally upon the figure of Norman himself, running toward the motel. When Norman emerges from his house, adjacent to the motel, the full extent of our complicity becomes evident, since we then realize that for the past five or ten minutes we have shared not his point of view, but that of a more potent and castrating Other. But the envelope of money rescues us from too prolonged a consideration of that fact.

The $40,000 assures us that there is more to follow, and that even though we have just lost our heroine, and our own discursive postion, we can afford to finance others. What sutures us at this juncture is the fear of being cut off from narrative. Our investment in the fiction is made manifest through the packet of money which provides an imaginary bridge from Marion to the next protagonist.

Psycho is relentless in its treatment of the viewing subject, forcing upon it next an identification with Norman, who with sober face and professional skill disposes of the now affect-less body of Marion, cleans the motel room, and sinks the incriminating car in quicksand. Marion is subsequently replaced in the narrative by her look-alike sister, and Norman's schizophrenia dramatizes the same vacillation from the position of victim to that of victimizer which the viewing subject is obliged to make in the shower sequence and elsewhere. *Psycho* runs through a whole series of culturally overdetermined narratives, showing the same cool willingness to substitute one for another that it adopts with its characters. Moreover, the manifest context of these narratives yields all too quickly to the latent, undergoing in the process a disquieting vulgarization. We understand perfectly the bourgeois inspiration of Marion's marital dreams, and the spuriousness of the redemptive scenario she hopes to enact by returning the money. Similarly, Norman's Oedipal crisis is played more as farce than melodrama, replete with stuffed birds and hackneyed quarrels in which he plays both parts.

The film terrorizes the viewing subject, refusing ever to let it off the hook. That hook is the system of suture, which is held up to our scrutiny even as we find ourselves thoroughly ensnared by it. What *Psycho* obliges us to understand is that we want suture so badly that we'll take it at any price, even with the fullest knowledge of what it entails—passive insertions into preexisting discursive positions (both mythically potent and mythically impotent); threatened losses and false recoveries; and subordination to the castrating gaze of a symbolic Other.

In fact, the more the operations of enunciation are revealed to the viewing subject, the more tenacious is its desire for the comfort and closure of narrative—the more anxious it will be to seek refuge within the film's fiction. In so doing, the viewing subject submits to cinematic signification, permits itself to be spoken by the film's discourse. For the theoreticians of suture, the viewing subject thereby reenacts its entry into the symbolic order. . . .

We have seen that the match of subject and cinematic discourse occurs not just at the level of the shot but at that of the story—that films reinterpellate the viewer into preestablished discursive positions not only by effacing the signs of their own production but through the lure of narrative. The standard format of the classic cinematic text duplicates within the fiction as a whole the paradigm of the shot/reverse shot, disrupting the existing symbolic order, dislocating the subject-positions within it, and challenging its ideals of coherence and fullness only in order subsequently to reaffirm that order, those positions and those ideals.

Sometimes it is recognizably the same order which is restored at the end of the film. Thus *It's a Wonderful Life* calls into question the potency of George Bailey and the authenticity of the structures of the family and capitalism only so that it can revalidate them. In other cases a new order seems to replace one which has been fractured. For instance, in *Marnie* a "false" coherence (the coherence of a matriarchy) gives way to a "true" coherence (the coherence of a patriarchy). However, the new order always turns out to have been the original order, temporarily interrupted. The system of suture functions not only constantly to reinterpellate the viewing subject into the same discursive positions, thereby giving that subject the illusion of a stable and continuous identity, but to rearticulate the existing symbolic order in ideologically orthodox ways.

We observed earlier, in relation to *Psycho,* that the insertion of the viewer into the cinematic discourse is facilitated through the cuts by means of which films are articulated. That insertion also involves another cutting operation, that implied by sexual difference. It is imperative to note that the identifications and erotic investments of classic cinema—like those established during the Oedipus complex—produce a sexually differentiated subject. Not only are classic cinema's subject positions organized along sexual lines, but so is the desire it inaugurates. Indeed, the entire system of suture is inconceivable apart from sexual difference. As Claire Johnston points out in "Towards a Feminist Film Practice: Some Theses":

As a process, a practice of signification, suture is an ideological operation with a particular function in relation to paternal ideology in that out of a system of differences it establishes a position in relation to the phallus. In so doing it places the spectator in relation to that position. . . . It is this imaginary unity, the sutured coherence, the imaginary sense of identity set up by the classic film which must be challenged by a feminist film practice to achieve a different constitution of the subject in relation to ideology.[5]

One of the chief mechanisms by which the system of suture conceals the apparatuses of enunciation is by setting up a relay of glances between the male characters within the fiction and the male viewers in the theater audience, a relay which has the female body as its object. Similarly, one of the most effective strategies at its disposal for deflecting attention away from the passivity and lack of the viewing subject's own position is by displacing those values onto a female character within the fiction. (Needless to say, this displacement assuages the anxieties only of the male viewer; it heightens those of the female viewer.) Often the entire narrative is organized around a demonstration and an interrogation of the female character's castrated condition, a demonstration and an interrogation which have as their ultimate aim the recovery of a sense of potency and wholeness for both the male character and the male viewer. This narrative organization reflects the paradigm which suture establishes at the level of the shot; in both cases an absence is first revealed, and then covered over through a skillful displacement from the level of enunciation onto that of the fiction. We will discuss the relationship between suture and sexual difference in greater detail in the following section.

Suture and Sexual Difference

. . . [Laura] Mulvey's argument [in "Visual Pleasure and Narrative Cinema"[6]] bears a striking resemblance to the suture theory. Both posit a cinematic adventure in which plentitude is fractured by difference and lack, only to be sealed over once again. For the theoreticians of suture, the salvage activity is carried out by means of the movement from one shot to the next. For Mulvey, as for the many feminist film theoreticians who have worked along similar lines,[7] the lack which must be both dramatized and contained finds its locus in the female body. The various absences upon which classic cinema turns, from the excluded real to the hidden camera and tape recorder, are in effect signified *through* woman. As Jacqueline Rose observes in "The Cinematic Apparatus: Problems in Current Theory," the female subject

> is structured as image around this reference [to the excluded real] and. . . thereby *comes* to represent the potential loss and difference which underpins the whole system. . . . What classical cinema performs or "puts on stage" is this image of woman as other, dark continent, and from there what escapes or is lost to the system; at the same time as sexuality is frozen into her body as spectacle, the object of phallic desire and/or identification.[8]

"Visual Pleasure and Narrative Cinema" suggests a kind of "thematics" which complements and enriches that part of the suture argument which is more strictly concerned with the level of enunciation. It also demonstrates the impossibility of thinking about any part of the classic cinematic organization—including editing—apart from sexual difference. Indeed, the two theoretical models achieve a particulary tight join at precisely that point most stressed by

Oudart and Dayan, i.e., the shot/reverse shot formation. Not only can a metaphoric connection be established between the two halves of that formation on the one hand, and the alignment of female spectacle with male vision on the other, but the former provides the ideal vehicle for the latter. Classic cinema abounds in shot/reverse shot formations in which men look at women. We will examine below some of the other ways in which cinematic articulation relies upon the female figure.

However, before doing so I would like to return to the two representational strategies isolated by Mulvey for neutralizing the anxiety aroused by female lack. The first of these, we recall, involves an interrogation calculated to establish either the female subject's guilt or her illness, while the second negotiates her erotic overinvestment. Mulvey associates the former alternative with narrative progression, and the latter with narrative interruption. In other words, whereas investigation of the guilty or sick woman always entails a diegetic coercion, fetishism of the female form sometimes serves to rupture the diegesis and so to "dis-place" the viewer. These two very different resolutions to the problem of castration anxiety warrant a careful analysis, since the second contains the potential to subvert the first. As we will see, the model described by Mulvey can give rise to at least two transgressive representations. One of these representations, brilliantly exploited by *Lola Montes,* transfers to woman qualities which are normally the exclusive property of the phallus, most notably the capacity to transcend narrative.

Max Ophuls' highly self-conscious film can almost be read as a disquisition about the status of the female image in classic cinema. Its elaborately orchestrated narrative unfolds through the interrogation of Lola, an interrogation which establishes that she is both "fallen" and unwell. In addition the film quite literally circles around Lola-as-spectacle, and although that spectacle is nothing if not fetishized, it is nonetheless fully contained within the narrative. It thus not only dramatizes both of the solutions cited by Mulvey for neutralizing the male viewer's anxiety but shows how they can be combined.

At the same time, *Lola Montes* gives us another series of female images which remain much more fragmented, and which threaten the coherence not only of the diegesis but of the dominant symbolic order. Ultimately those images are consolidated within the main narrative, but the strain which they exert upon it suggests that they represent an important area of resistance to traditional power relations.

Ophuls' film moves back and forth between two temporal planes, one of which situates the viewer in a continuous present tense, and the other of which locates the viewer in a discontinuous past. The sequences from the film's present tense all take place in a circus whose one and only theme is the rise and descent of a *femme fatale.* Lola's climb to fame and fall to ignominy are dramatized in a variety of ways, ranging from pantomime to trapeze acts. The show is written, directed, and produced by the ringmaster, who is in the business of selling scandals. However, it is billed as "the whole truth and nothing but the truth," the real-life story of Lola Montes told in "her own inimitable words."

Parts of that story are narrated by the ringmaster. Other parts are extracted in the form of set speeches from Lola, who particularly toward the end of the film requires frequent prompting. However, portions of her past are also conveyed to us through flashbacks, and they are connected with her much more intimately than the lines she speaks. Not only do the usual conventions governing flashbacks serve to link them with Lola's consciousness, but they are invariably signaled by a lap dissolve of her face over a remote object or landscape.

The flashbacks differ from the circus performance in other important respects as well. Whereas Lola's movements are rigorously supervised in the latter, in the former they are characterized by an unusual freedom and spontaneity. Our first glimpse of her in the circus proves paradigmatic in this respect: she sits on a fixed base while the camera circles vertiginously around her. Later, dressed in a white wedding dress and bridal crown, Lola remains immobile in the middle of an even more dazzling display of movement; she is stationed on a rotating platform, surrounded by a second platform which rotates in the opposite direction. These two sequences underscore the fact that in the circus Lola does not so much move as submit to movement. They thus anticipate the film's final shot, in which a caged and altogether tamed Lola extends her hand through the bars to be kissed by a long line of male spectators.

The last enclosure contrasts strikingly with the carriage in which Lola travels in all but two of the flashbacks. That vehicle permits her not only to leave one country and enter another at will, but to break off one relationship and begin another whenever she chooses to do so; even when she travels in someone else's carriage her own follows closely behind. It is while seated in the latter that she makes her most revealing statement: "For me, life is movement."

That remark is borne out again and again in the flashback scenes. Lola repeatedly breaks away from or interrupts rituals within which she has been assigned a relatively passive place—a prearranged marriage, a marital union in which she is called upon to act the part of a martyr, a Spanish dance, a military procession, a royal audience. Indeed, she effects her dramatic ascent entirely through actions which defy the norm.

In each of these situations Lola makes a spectacle of herself. In other words, she invites the male gaze, draws visual attention to herself. However, it is important to note that the alignment of male look with female image does not here work in the usual way, since far from locating power on the male side that visual transaction confers it on the female side. Thus whereas in the circus episodes the scopic exchange functions to subordinate Lola, in the flashback scenes it provides the agency whereby she assumes power.

The very different status of the male gaze in the film's two temporal registers can be explained by the fact that in one instance Lola's exhibitionism is passive but in the other active. In the circus scenes she is constrained by the ringmaster's look to conform to a preestablished representation, and obliged night after night to repeat the same part. In the flashback scenes, however, Lola exercises fascination and control over numerous male gazes through an elaborate masquerade, an ongoing performance in which she both scripts and constantly changes the parts she plays. Her recourse to the principle of unpredictability is as vital as the artistic control she wields, and may indeed be synonymous with it, since, as we suggested above, it permits her to disrupt the many narratives which would otherwise contain her.

Lola's capacity to transgress the diegetic flow is inscribed into the film's formal operations as well as its fiction. The fluctuation between the sustained storytelling efforts of the ringmaster and the fragmented and nonlinear memories which proceed from Lola's consciousness introduce into the film's structure a tension which is not neutralized until her literal and metaphoric fall. Like her scandals, those memories have the quality of a "cut-out or icon" which Mulvey associates with the fetishist solution, situating the film in a "no-man's-land outside its own time and space." In short, they run counter to the flow of the circus narrative. However, after her jump Lola entirely succumbs to the tyranny of the ring-master's gaze, and her memories cease to function as a point of resistance to the passivity and masochism of her present plight. The flashbacks abruptly terminate, and she takes her place inside the gilded cage.

The one flashback which the ringmaster shares with Lola proves critical in determining the ultimate assimilation of past to present. That flashback also clarifies the very different terms under which Lola will be obliged to play to the male gaze once she joins the circus. In it the ringmaster pays Lola a private visit and offers to sell her as "the most scandalous woman in the world." Although she declines his offer, we know from certain other signs of acquiescence that she will eventually capitulate. For instance, he tells her to stop pacing and she does so—she submits, that is, to the restrictions which he verbally places on her movements, permits herself to be positioned by him. Similarly, when he informs her that she smokes too much, she throws away her cigar.

Even more significant is Lola's response to the ringmaster's assertion that men come to watch her dance only because of her beauty: she sits down in front of a mirror and regards her reflection, as if for the first time. In effect, she subordinates herself to this view of her. For the first time Lola submits to the look of another, is contituted through and dominated by the male gaze.

Lola Montès uses its governing circus metaphor as a means of foregrounding the centrality of a passive and compliant female representation to the operations of classic cinema. Not only does the ringmaster write his narrative across the surface of Lola's body, but the film shows itself to be dependent upon that same surface for its own articulation. Composition, *mise-en-scène*, lighting, camera movement, and shot matches all function to display Lola, and that display in turn provides them with their formal coherence.

At the same time that Ophuls' film dramatizes the "ideal" relationship between the fetishized female image and narrative progression, it also suggests ways in which that image can be used to subvert or disrupt the diegesis. Like Sternberg's *Blonde Venus* or *Morocco*, *Lola Montès* indicates that the power relations which are inscribed into classic cinema through its scopic regime are by no means as stable as is the regime itself. In other words, the identification of the female subject with specularity and the male subject with vision does not necessarily assure the latter a dominant position. The construction of woman-as-fetish carries with it certain dangers for male subjectivity. Not only does that construction facilitate the detachment of the female image from narrative control, but it can challenge the very assumption upon which the existing symbolic order depends—the assumption, that is, that woman is castrated or lacking. In short, the fetish can become indistinguishable from the phallus. This is, of course, precisely what happens in some of the flashback sequences in *Lola Montès*.

Yet another "perverse" resolution of the castration anxiety discussed by Mulvey involves the privileging of lack and passivity over potency and aggressivity. This resolution, like the one in which the woman aspires to the position of the phallus, leaves intact the scopic regime of classic cinema. Indeed, both are only made possible by the preservation of that regime.

The famous strip sequence from Charles Vidor's 1946 film, *Gilda*, provides a particularly vivid dramatization of the second way in which the construction of woman-as-fetish can challenge the system of which it is a part. The episode in question represents the climactic moment in a plot which is notable for its masochistic excess: the title character has earlier made a toast to her own destruction, referred to herself as the "dirty laundry," married someone who frightens her, and encouraged Johnny Farrell, the man she loves, to imagine her a whore.

The strip sequence is in fact an extension of the last of these projects. It takes place after the assumed death of Gilda's first husband, and her remarriage to Johnny—a marriage which, due to Johnny's sexual jealousy, has never been consummated. Gilda goes to the casino, where he works, to assure him once again that her seeming promiscuity has only been a masquerade. When he casts renewed aspersions on her fidelity, she decides to play her assigned part to the hilt.

Like most of the other episodes of ritual self-humiliation engineered by Gilda, this one relies on the equation of female subjectivity with spectacle, and male subjectivity with the look. Here she does not play just to Johnny's gaze but to those of the casino staff, a large group of predominantly male customers, and a detective. Initially she contents herself with singing and swaying to an erotically self-lacerating song, but when she is encouraged by the onlookers to remove her clothes she promptly complies, only stopping when she is dragged from the floor by one of Johnny's henchmen.

This song-and-dance number provides a classic example of what Mulvey calls the "fetishist" solution to the problem of female lack. However, it deviates from Mulvey's model in that the erotic overvaluation of Gilda's body (her arms, her face, her hair, the black sheath she wears, the necklace and gloves she tosses to the crowd) does not serve to conceal her castration, but to flaunt it. It also involves a rather noisy demonstration of female guilt, in that it is intended by Gilda to provide the final, irrefutable evidence of her promiscuity. Finally, that demonstration is not orchestrated by the male subject, but is "voluntarily" supplied by the female subject; Gilda not only engages in a self-incriminating striptease, but sings a song about the age-old evil of woman ("Put the Blame on Mame").

The film thus superimposes the two rather contradictory strategies isolated by Mulvey as calculated to neutralize the male subject's castration anxieties. The insufficient figure loudly proclaims her guilt, and through her song, dance, and striptease simultaneously fosters the overvaluation of her physical attributes. Confession and fetishism do not here work to deflect attention away from female lack to male potency, but to inspire in the viewer (fictional and actual) the desire to have it fully revealed—to have it revealed, moreover, not as a repellent but as a pleasurable sight.

Perhaps most remarkably, the conjunction of castration and overvaluation results in a kind of masochistic eroticism in which Johnny participates not only as viewer but as spectacle. When Gilda is pulled away at the end of her act she says to Johnny: "You wanted that. Now you should be happy. You wanted everyone to know that Johnny Farrell's wife is a tramp." She thereby suggests that Johnny wants not only her exposure, but his own; that his position, like hers, is a passive and masochistic one. The viewing subject is no more exempt from this passivity and masochism than is Johnny; whether that subject identifies with Gilda or Johnny, the result is at least in this respect the same.

Suture can be understood as the process whereby the inadequacy of the subject's position is exposed in order to facilitate (i.e., create the desire for) new insertions into a cultural discourse which promises to make good that lack. Since the promised compensation involves an ever greater subordination to already existing scenarios, the viewing subject's position is a supremely passive one, a fact which is carefully concealed through cinematic sleight-of-hand. This sleight-of-hand involves attributing to a character within the fiction qualities which in fact belong to the machinery of enunciation: the ability to generate narrative, the omnipotent and coercive gaze, the castrating authority of the law.

The shot/reverse shot formation merely constitutes one device for achieving this transfer. As Mulvey suggests, others include spying on the woman, diagnosing her illness, forcing her to confess, or better yet (as in *Lola Montes*) writing a narrative by means of which she is defined. It is no accident that in the films described by Mulvey the woman is *made* to confess by a male character.

Gilda threatens to reveal this cinematic sleight-of-hand when she freely "confesses" to the crimes and natural disasters caused by women throughout history. Perhaps even more disruptive is the fact that she renders so transparent the degree to which her guilt is culturally inherited and written. However, most remarkable is the way in which the film acknowledges and dwells upon the lures of castration. Gilda exercises fascination precisely by virtue of those things she lacks—money, legal authority, power, the omnipotent and coercive gaze. She insists upon her inadequacy, repeats words ("decent?") which might be used to put her beyond the pale, drinks to her own downfall, invites men to undress her, and sings lyrics which underscore female guilt.

Vidor's film thus poses a temptation which suture is intended to overcome; the temptation to refuse cultural reintegration, to skid off course, out of control, to prefer castration to false plenitude. That danger, like the one suggested by *Lola Montes*, is implicit in classic cinema's scopic regime. It represents a point of female resistance within the very system which defines woman as powerless and lacking. . . .

Notes

1. Jacques-Alain Miller, "Suture (elements of the logic of the signifier)," *Screen* (1977–78), vol. 18, no. 4 [The original French publication of this article was in 1966. In the present context, a chronological listing of original publications on cinema and suture considered central by the author may be of interest: Jean-Pierre Oudart, "Cinema and Suture," *Screen* (1977–78), vol. 18, no. 4, originally published in *Cahiers du cinéma* (April and May 1969), nos. 211 and 212; Daniel Dayan, "The Tutor-Code of Classical Cinema," *Film Quarterly* (Fall 1974), vol. 23, no. 1; and Stephen Heath, "Notes on Suture," *Screen*, (1977–78), vol. 23, no. 4—ED.]
2. Noel Burch, *Theory of Film Practice,* trans. Helen R. Lane (New York: Praeger, 1973), p. 12.
3. Daniel Dayan, "The Tutor-Code of Classical Cinema," in *Movies and Methods,* ed. Bill Nichols (Berkeley: University of California Press, 1976), p. 448.
4. Stephen Heath, "Narrative Space," *Screen* (1976), vol. 17, no. 3 [included in this anthology—ED.].
5. Claire Johnston, "Towards a Feminist Film Practice: Some Theses," *Edinburgh Magazine,* (1976), no. 1, p. 56.
6. Laura Mulvey, "Visual Pleasure and Narrative Cinema," *Screen* (1975), vol. 16, no. 3 [included in this anthology—ED.].
7. See Mary Ann Doane, "Misrecognition and Identity," *Ciné-Tracts* (1980), vol. 3, no. 3, and "Woman's Stake: Filming the Female Body," *October* (1981), no. 17, pp. 23–31; Teresa de Lauretis, "Through the Looking-Glass," in *The Cinematic Apparatus,* ed. Teresa de Lauretis and Stephen Heath (London: Macmillan, and New York: St. Martin's, 1980), pp. 187–202 [included in this anthology—ED.], and "Woman, Cinema, and Language," *Yale Italian Studies* (1980), 1(2):5–21; Sandy Flitterman, "Woman, Desire, and the Look: Feminism and the Enunciative Apparatus in Cinema," *Ciné-Tracts* (1978), vol. 2, no. 1; Leslie Stern, "Point of View: The Blind Spot," *Film Reader* (Evanston, Ill.: Northwestern University Film Division/School of Speech, 1977), no. 5, pp. 214–36; and Linda Williams, "Film Body: An Implantation of Perversions," *Ciné-Tracts* (1981), vol. 3, no. 4 [included in this anthology—ED.], and "When the Woman Looks" [published in Mary Ann Doane, Patricia Mellencamp and Linda Williams, eds., *Re-Vision: Essays in Feminist Film Criticism,* American Film Institute Monograph no. 3 (Frederick, MD: University Publications of America, 1984)—ED.].
8. Jacqueline Rose, "The Cinematic Apparatus: Problems in Current Theory," in *The Cinematic Apparatus,* p. 182.

Julia Kristeva
Ellipsis on Dread and the Specular Seduction

"Even though man be disquieted in vain, surely he walketh in the image."
—St. Augustine

What I see has nothing to do with the specular which fascinates me. The glance by which I identify an object, a face, my own, another's, delivers my identity which reassures me: for it delivers me from *frayages,*[1] nameless dread, noises preceding the name, the image—pulsations, somatic waves, color frequencies, rhythms, tones. Intellectual speculation derives from this identifying, labeling glance: the hysteric knows something of the process when, endlessly unable to find a sufficiently satisfying mirror, she finds herself at last in the theory itself— target of all sensible and senseless intentions, shelter where one can *know without seeing oneself,*[2] for one has relegated to another (philosophical contemplation) the problem of representing an (my) identity as reassuring as *trompe-l'oeil* because it covers over and darkens the dread, the *frayages.* For speculation socializes me and reassures others as to my good intentions in both meanings and morals; but, in regard to my dreamed body, sets forth to them only that which the physician's speculum reveals: a de-eroticized surface which I concede to him in the wink of an eye by which I make him believe he is not an *other,* but has only to look at me as I myself would do if I were he—complicity of the barrier operating on the hither side of the retina, snare which captures him rather than me.

Published as "Ellipse sur la frayeur et la séduction spéculaire" in *Communications* (1975) no. 23, and translated in *Wide Angle* (1979), 3(3):42–47. Reprinted by permission of the author, and translation used by permission of the Johns Hopkins University Press.

However, once *frayage/frayeur*[3] erupts into the *seen*, that *seen* stops being simply reassuring, *trompe-l'oeil*, or invitation to speculation, and becomes the *fascinating specular*. Cinema seizes us precisely in this place. Doubtless it does more than that. All images, and those of the other visual arts as well, are assuredly and variously on the same path. In this note, however, I am not treating any particular element of film history but rather that peculiar impact of the image projected on the screen, which one looks at, seeing it completely differently from the way one sees objects intervening in or surrounding an action. At the intersection between the vision of a real object and hallucination, the cinematographic object brings into the *identifiable* (and surely nothing is more identifiable than the visible/seeable) that which remains beyond identification: the drive unsymbolized, unfixed in the object—the sign—language, or, in more brutal terms, it brings in aggressivity. And calls on the fantasm to recognize itself therein: to perpetuate or empty itself, according to the capacity of the image to distance itself from itself.

Everything specular is fascinating because it bears the trace, in the visible, of this aggressivity, this unsymbolized drive: unverbalized and hence unrepresented. Thus let us name *specular* that visible sign which calls on the fantasm because it includes an excess of visual traces, useless for the sheer identification of objects, being chronologically and logically anterior to the famous "mirror phase." This information has little to do with "referent" (or with object) but rather with the attitude of the subject to the object; thus we are already dealing with that contract of desire which is the *expressible* (the *lekton* of the Stoics), whose existence makes of the sign (that is, the image) a symptom (that is, the specular). Let us call these supplemental informations "lektonic traces": it will be a matter of a well-regulated distribution of variants of what Freud calls "primary" processes, or preverbal, "semiotic" processes, in the complete "symbolic" functioning of a speaking subject, made up of language as well as representation: displacements, condensations, tones, rhythms, colors, patterns—always in excess as compared with the represented, the signified.

Matisse, Klee, Rothko, Schoenberg, and Webern remind us that modern art—painting, sculpture, music—found its privileged domain in the arrangement of these lektonic traces, to the detriment of the image-sign of a referent. The fact that the products of these artists let themselves be thought—or rather, let themselves be specularized—by a formalism borrowed from Euclidean geometry or from topology, could only leave an impression of a tendency in modern art toward "mathematical abstraction" among those who suppress the "lektonic" value of a signifying practice: those who suppress that dimension in which the subject chooses to trace, for others and hence in the expressible (image or word) his aggressivity and/or his dread. Or else we might posit these latter entities as underlying mathematical writing as well: "Writing comes out of terror."[4]

From its very beginnings, cinema seems to follow this tendency of modern art in general, when it pursues, notably in Eisenstein, an obstinate project of incorporating what I have called a network of "lektonic traces" into the referential image-sign. Meticulous organization of space, rigorous positioning of each object, calculated intervention of every sound and every bit of dialogue—all were meant to add a "rhythmic," "plastic" dimension to the *too visible:* an enigma not to be made too immediately obvious, and into which is figured the film-maker's anguish which must arouse the spectator's anguish more profoundly than the referential image-sign could do. Thus Eisenstein's course for filmmakers in which he sets out the exemplary situation as regards the specular, since it calls on the fantasm of that fundamental "invisible"—the primal scene: "The return of the soldier who finds his wife pregnant." For this he deploys—in the arrange-ment of objects, actors, and dialogue—an artistry worthy of the most learned topologist, and destined either to provoke or to quench the conflicted desire of knowing whose child it is. "All the elements of the scene must express in a spatial and temporal manner the internal content of the drama. Our solution (for the episode in question) consists of the clear confrontation between two tendencies represented by two spatial complexes differently characterized—one straight and frontal, the other oblique, diagonal." Eisenstein designs it thus:

His course, as we know, abounds in such diagrams. Always the same search for "lektonic traces," elements left unaccounted for in the too-visible, too-signifying sign, in terms of filmic *discourse*: "It is only when one can understand the signifier *(oboznacenije)* not as a set of congealed signs for phenomena, but rather when one apprehends it dynamically, in the numberless multiplicities of its eternally variable particular manifestations, that the signifier loses its indirect character of heavy pun or deadened symbol."[5] These positions are also found in Eisenstein's considerations of cinematographic image and of rhythm: "organic" for him, "metric" for Pudovkin, "melodic" for Walt Disney—rhythm is always an indis-pensable internal necessity for what representation in the cinema means to him.[6]

Presymbolic *frayage,* which is the mark of the aggressivity and/or the anguish aroused by the contract of desire with someone else, is laid down in the most archaic, hence the most pregnant manner, in this figuring which is, for the visible, the "rhythm" of space and color, serving, from this level, to incite and consume the aggressivity and/or the anguish of the viewer. No doubt this effect is obtained to the maximum when the image itself signifies aggressivity. Rep-resented horror is the specular par excellence: might not Hitchcock be the filmmaker par excellence, uniting Eisensteinian rhythm with the vision of terror? The modern public registers the fact clearly: from the most "sophisticated" to the most "vulgar," we cannot resist vampires or the massacres of the Western. Catharsis, that regulatory function necessary to every society, comes to us no longer by way of Oedipus, Electra, or Orestes, but through the gunshots of any

Western or the alternation between horror and prettification found in porno films. The sillier the better, moreover, for what really counts is that the specular present—through its direct signified (object or represented situation)—and that it figure through its plastic rhythm (that network of lektonic elements, sound, tone, color, space, pattern) the drive—the aggression—which has come back to us from the other without reply, and which has consequently remained uncaptured, unsymbolized, unconsumed.

F. is a year old and speaks in nothing but echolalia: rhythm, intonation, variable intensities; and it seems he sees objects only as encumbering and accidental extensions of his own still dispersed body. The microphone can record his voice without any protest from him: recordings of the drama between broadcast and breathing, choking sounds, painful regulations between intensities and frequencies, but already in the process of being organized by the primal computer: rhythm. A few months later, objects begin to exist: F. sees them, hides them, loses them. He also sees the tape recorder, and whatever strategy we may devise to keep the recorder from interfering with his movements, the mere sight of it elicits tears. As if the earlier vocal dramas had now been projected upon the visible object; the intolerable nature of vocal apprenticeship demanded by the adult, hence the waste product of the adult, has left its stain on a visible object which is now charged with representing the drive underlying the verbal function.

At the very moment when simple echolalia is becoming a symbolic function— for it is beginning to designate separate objects seen as such—the drive, which used to be consumed in echolalia, is seen as represented by an object, in metonymic relation to it, which becomes "the bad object." But it is also because this seen object has become possible, because the object is *there* from now on, support and captation of aggressivity and anguish, that the apprenticeship of language as a system of communicative signs is assured.

In the current of friendships and loves, dreams do not wait for the analyst's couch: they circulate like gifts. A. has a recurrent nightmare: he is four years old, he is on his "pot" in the bathroom. When the excrement overflows the bowl and is transformed into a "big animal," something between a frog and a crocodile, but with transparent skin, like the membrane of an eye, suddenly. A.'s father enters, sees the animal, and threatens punishment. Exemplary montage between anal drive, the subordination to the father for anal coitus (fantasy of the anal penis and of cloacal birth), and a grafting, on the same desiring vector, of the glance which is always the eye of the other, menacing and seductive, the paternal eye. Let us note the lack of dissociation between the object as offal, itself not yet separated from the body, and the paternal eye, which figures the first instance of visual and/or symbolic representation. The lack of distinction between object-offal/eye–symbolic instance is invariably accompanied by another: the hesitation in regard to sexual difference: active or passive, seeing or seen, my eye or his[7] eye, "man" or erotic-object-used-sadistically-by-the-father ("woman"). If the clear separation of these two orders, at the two levels, assures repression and the subject's mastery over his body, over the signifier and over others, nothing guarantees that this separation will remain forever clear and definitive. Dream, that private cinema of the public, is there to remind us how dramatic and endlessly uncompleted is the apprenticeship of symbolism (image or speech), as well as the acceptance of sexual difference. The economy of dream recalls it (primary processes plus representation and secondary processes) even when it is not so spectacularly explicit as the dream of A. Nightmare or dream of delights, but always seductive: the specular will be the prize for a pleasure refused, graft of a *jouissance*[8] which has not been able to take place, will never take place enough, in the waking life.)

All semiotic material (color, malleable mass, sound, etc.) lends itself to this rhythmization, this cathartic representation. The specular remains no less the absolute master. Why? Because it is through the glance, first and foremost, that the body—fragmented by the rhythms and intonations of echolalia, multiplied, cut in pieces, neither male nor female—constitutes itself as one and identifiable: the image, before the word whose path it prepares, creates an identity for us which will be imaginary from that point on. The consequences: not only does the specular absorb primitive pulsional *frayages*, unsymbolized aggressivities, but it provides for them, and for that very reason is seductive. The specular: final and most efficient repository for aggressions and anxieties, and magisterial provider/seducer. Seductive: that is, flowing from *frayages* (rhythms, somatic waves, color frequencies) toward that impossible target where the eternally unfinished series of images is supposed to converge, a convergence which would finally constitute an "I" identical to itself, freed at last from that period, prior to the mirror phase, when the "I" depended on the mother, was more or less indistinguishable from her. From that point on, the "I" would be able to attract others by addressing the (aggressive) drive toward them in the form of a (desiring) call. It is in the specular, then, that the drive's derivation ends its course, and it is from the specular that the identificatory lure begins, with its narcissistic dance.

Chronologically in the child's development, and logically in the functioning of the adult, the specular remains the most advanced support for the inscription of the drive in relation to sound or tactile material, for example. Thus the specular is also the earliest point of origin for signs, for narcissistic identifications, and for the phantasmatic terror one speaking identity holds for another. Terror and seduction. That the one has to do with dependency on the mother, and the other an appeal addressed to the father, the male and female must both be equally aware. In that which the specular proposes to man and woman as a node connecting terror and seduction (the drive's traces *and* the signifying derivation—imaged, contractual, desiring, socializing), man and woman find themselves *differently*. But if they enter the game, they will both be led to cross both zones and attempt both identifications—maternal, paternal. Test of sexual difference—

of homosexuality, that brush with psychosis—they never stop letting it be intimated, even they don't let it be seen: Eisenstein, Hitchcock.

This terror/seduction node, which could have had (and doubtless *has*) analytic effects (cf. psychological crises, or else the capitalization circuits which unleash all pictural innovation) becomes, through cinematographic commerce, a kind of cut-rate seduction. One quickly pulls the veil over the terror, and only the cathartic relief remains; in mediocre pot-boilers, for example, in order to remain within the range of petty bourgeois taste, film plays up to narcissistic identification, and the viewer is satisfied with the "three-buck" seduction.[9]

But the greatest specular seduction has nothing to do with that. One dreams it with or without image: the body blasted open, borne up on tonal litters, an eye that X-rays the viscera, movie camera following the twisted tunnels of the cavities, or the blue-red-green that rides on wings, on horseback. . . One listens to it: Mozart, Schoenberg. One gives it shape: Don Juan, the ideal specular hero, seductive because he is the master who defies fathers and the connoisseur of women never satisfied with one alone, transforming in a series of mistresses the silenced passion for a mother, and his love for the father—in a reciprocal murder;[10] always ambivalent, law and transgression, terror and fascination. If one needed an emblem for the specular, it would be Don Juan. No visual art can measure up to it: untenable rivalry.

I dream of an impossible film: *Don Juan* by Eisenstein and Hitchcock with music by Schoenberg. Invisible.[11] Empty hall. But what a rite of terror and seduction! Moreover, Schoenberg would have been able to find the solution to the debate he himself called a false one, between his Moses and his Aaron: between (divine) menace which strikes with imageless thunder and the gaiety of the idolaters seduced by the golden calf.

St. Augustine once again states and consolidates the truth of the phanatasmic and symbolic order for two thousand years of Christianity, when he specifies the *image* as constitutive of the *mens;* as *"immascible."*[12] The symbolic order is assured as soon as there are images, in which one unfailingly believes, for belief itself is an image: the two sorts of image are constituted by the same processes and start with the same terms: memory, sight, and love or will. We shall not discuss the theological implications of this concept for the Christian faith. Let us only note that, for St. Augustine, however deformed or vitiated an image may be, from the moment that it *is*, it supports the transcendental quest, even and perhaps all the more so if it is not the image of an identifiable object. Knowing this permits him that marvelous gesture of inverting Scripture: "Surely every man walketh in a *vain show [= image]*: surely they are disquieted in vain: he heapeth up riches, and knoweth not who shall gather them,"[13] *(Psalms,* 39, 6). For these lines St. Augustine substitutes the following: "Even though man be disquieted in vain, surely he walketh in the image."[14]

Specular fascination captures terror and restores it to the symbolic order. Christian art—in the penumbra of churches more than anywhere else—understands, multiplies, and exploits this fascination. Calm reigns before the sight of hell captured in the image.

With cinema, the semiotic efficacy of monotheism attains its peak: nothing better than film to accomplish the Augustinian insight: "Even though man be disquieted in vain, surely he walketh in the image." For in the filmic fascination, the spectator "heapeth up riches" more than is possible anywhere else, multiple signs (disgorgers of anguish), and "he knoweth not who shall gather them" (believes himself sheltered from the power that projects those identificatory supports for him).

No antifilm possible, then? Must all spectacle be paid for in advance, and chalked up to Order's account? There remains, here as elsewhere, the laugh: but, when it is the image laughing, identity crumbles and the "Great Dictator" is sawed in half. *Chaplin, or Specular Mortification:* the worm in the successful order of psychosis incarnate, eating away at it and laughing with full knowledge of what it is doing. *The Great Dictator,* a new era in occidental imagery: "Even though man walketh in the image, he walketh no more." The film actor in Chaplin, but also the discrepancy or conflict between sound and image, discourse and representation, or the "impious fracturing of projection" possible in camera movement itself (Godard, Bresson), hold the spectator, still inside a phantasm, but at a distance from his own fascination.

It was probably necessary that specular fascination arrive at its peak of perfection in the cinema, so that both its dread and its seduction might break out in laughter and in distantiation. Without this demystification, the cinema would be nothing but another Church.

Translator's Notes and Author's Citations

Substantive notes are the translator's; citations are the author's.

1. In *Edinburgh Magazine* (1976) no. 1, p. 62, Geoffrey Nowell-Smith translates Kristeva's *frayage* (Freud's *Bahnung*) as "pathway" or "facilitation." I have chosen to leave the term in French, since I am unable to find an English equivalent which satisfies me. The word, coming from physiology, describes "a phenomenon consisting in the fact that the passage of a neural flow [flux nerveux] in the conductors becomes easier through repetition." This dictionary definition makes the term feel close to but not identical with either of the two psychological entities we call conditioning or imprinting.

2. *Savior sans se voir:* I feel compelled to point out a typical sample of the poetic wordplay found throughout the original, which cannot possibly be realized in translation. (Italics mine.)

3. Deriving from the verb *frayer* (to trace out, open out, make way, beat a track, etc.), the noun *frayage* is often used in this essay in juxtaposition with *frayeur* (terror, dread), with which it has no etymological connection. Kristeva is clearly availing herself of the poetic resonances generated by this juxtaposition.

4. Sollers, *Paradise.*

5. S. Eisenstein, *Selected Works* (in Russian) (Moscow: Iskusstvo, 1966), 4:58, 60.

6. See S.M. Eisenstein, *Au-delà des étoiles* (Paris: Union Generale d'Editions, 1974), pp. 276 ff.

7. *Son oeil:* his eye? her eye? his/her eye? I have chosen *his,* assuming from the context that the reference is to the eye of the father.

8. Jouissance is left in French in order that it maintain its double meaning: enjoyment, orgasm. Certainly both implications are operating here.

9. In the original: *la séduction a cinq ou dix francs.*

10. [The complex play of this sentence invites some elaboration. One example is the linguistic association between master *(maître)* and mistresses *(maîtresses).* More complicated is an ambiguity around the adjective "silenced," which is a straightforward English rendering of *tue,* past participle of the verb *taire* (to silence someone). But the French term also resembles forms of the verb *tuer* (to kill) and can (as the author has pointed out in correspondence) be read in ambiguity with the latter's past participle *tuée.* Hence, there is a wordplay established which associates the silencing of a passion and killing. As the sentence is composed, this leads to the introduction of the term "murder."

In addition, we might note in this sentence an inversion of the Oedipal scenario of love for the mother and murder of the father. Instead, there is love for the father, while (silencing) killing is on the side of the relationship to a mother, indicating (as the author has pointed out in correspondence) Don Juan's identification with the mother.—ED.]

11. *(In)visible:* the word(s) can be construed as (in)visible *or* (un)seeable. I have resorted to both in this translation; the words *visible* and *invisible* occur very often in the text.

12. *Immascible:* assuming this to be a neologism, I leave it in the French. [There are at least three words which might be associated with this neologism: first, *image* (image), which appears in this paragraph; second, *immiscible,* from the verb *immiscer* (to mix up, to involve, to introduce or twist someone into an affair; or in its reflexive form, to interfere, to meddle); and *cible* (target, aim, purpose, object).—ED.]

13. Here Kristeva quotes the Vulgate version of *Psalms* 39:6, and then its French equivalent. I have chosen to give the King James version.

14. Using the biblical quotation above as a model, I am proposing here my own version of the author's rendering of St. Augustine's "inversion."

—Translated by Dolores Burdick
(with revision based on comments of the author)

[15]

Christian Metz
The Imaginary Signifier
[Excerpts]

The Investigator's Imaginary

I ask myself: what in fact is the object of this text? What is the *driving uncertainty* without which I should not have the desire to write it, and thus would not be writing it? What is my imaginary at this moment? What is it that I am trying, even without illusions, to bring to a conclusion?

It seems to me that it is a *question,* in the material sense of the word—a sentence terminating in a question mark—and that, as in dreams, it is inscribed right there in front of me, armed from head to toe. I shall unfold it here, with, of course, that slightly obsessional coefficient which is party to any aspiration to rigor.

So let me spell it out: "What contribution can Freudian psychoanalysis make to the study of the cinematic signifier?"

This is, in other words, the manifest content of my dream, and its interpretation will (I hope) constitute my text. I can already see three vital points, three nodal points in it. Let me examine them separately (*The Interpretation of Dreams*

Excerpted from the article published as "Le Signifiant imaginaire" in *Communications* (1975), no. 23, and translated in *Screen* (Summer 1975), 16(2):46–76. It is included in Christian Metz, *The Imaginary Signifier: Psychoanalysis and the Cinema* (London and Basingstoke: Macmillan, 1982; and Bloomington: Indiana University Press, 1982); excerpts from chapter 2 and chapters 3–5 inclusive reprinted by permission of Macmillan Publishers, Ltd. and Indiana University Press. Translation used by permission of the Society for Education in Film and Television.

invites us to do so, as does the minimal necessity of having a "plan"), and associate freely from each of them. They are the words "contribution," Freudian psychoanalysis," and above all "cinematic signifier."

Psychoanalysis, Linguistics, History

"Contribution," then, first of all: this term tells me that psychoanalysis cannot be the only discipline concerned in the study of the cinematic signifier, and that its offering has to be articulated with others. To begin with, and fairly directly, with that of classical semiology—based on linguistics—a guiding principle in my earliest filmic investigations and today in those of several others. Why "directly"? Because linguistics and psychoanalysis are both sciences of the symbolic and are even, come to think of it, the only two sciences whose immediate and sole object is the fact of signification as such (obviously all sciences are concerned with it, but never so frontally or exclusively). To be slightly cavalier, linguistics—together with its close relations, notably modern symbolic logic—can be regarded as taking for its share the exploration of the secondary process, and psychoanalysis that of the primary process:[1] that is to say, between them they cover the whole field of the *signification-fact* taken in itself. Linguistics and psychoanalysis are the two main "sources" of semiology, the only disciplines that are semiotic through and through.

That is why both in turn have to be set within the horizon of a *third perspective,* which is, as it were, their common and permanent background: the direct study of societies, historical criticism, the examination of infrastructures. This time the junction is much less easy (if the other one can be described as easy), for the signifier has its own laws (primary and secondary), and so does political economy. Even technically, if one thinks of the daily work of the investigator, of his reading, his documentation, etc., the "dual competence" which was not impossible a moment ago now becomes a bit of a gamble: thus in the case of the cinema, where is the semiotician who could seriously claim, given his education and his specialized conceptual tools, to be able to explain the role of capitalist monopolies in the film industry in as pertinent and rigorous a way as economists like Henri Mercillon and his disciples have? In cinematic studies as in others, semiology (or semiologies) cannot replace the various disciplines that discuss the social fact itself (the source of all symbolism), with its laws that determine those of the symbolic without being identical with them: sociology, anthropology, history, political economy, demography, etc. It cannot replace them, nor must it repeat them (danger of ritual repetition or "reductionism"). It must take them into account, move forward on its own front (it too is materialist in its own way), and mark the anchorage points in all the cases in which the state of research already makes this possible (for example, the spectator's psychism as a factor of historical adjustment and a link in the chain of the money circuit). In other words, it must be inscribed in advance, by a kind of epistemological anticipation (but one which must not become the pretext for a voluntary paralysis), in the perspective of a true knowledge of man—a perspective still only present as a dotted line in most of its circuit, and a knowledge in the singular, very different from today's "human sciences," so often gnawed by scientism and yet necessary, for today is not tomorrow—of a state of knowing in which the way the development of technologies and balances of social forces (society in its physical state, as it were) finally comes to influence inflections peculiar to the work of the symbolic such as the order of "shots" or the role of "sound off" in some cinematic subcode, in some genre of films, for example, would be *known* in all the reality of the intermediate mechanisms without which only a global inkling and postulation of causality is possible.

Here I am touching on the famous problem of "relative autonomies" but not necessarily (although the two things are often confused) on a simple distinction between infrastructures and superstructures. For if it is clear that the cinema as an industry, its modes of financing, the technological development of film stock, the average income of the spectators (enabling them to go more or less often to the cinema), the price of seats, and many other things belong fully to infrastructural studies, it does not follow that, by some mechanical symmetry, the symbolic (primary or secondary) is exclusively superstructural in its order. It is partly so, of course, and even largely so in its most apparent strata, in its manifest content, in those of its features that are directly related to precise social facts and change when the latter change: e.g., in linguistics broad sectors of the lexicon (but already much less of phonology or syntax), in psychoanalysis the various historical variants of the Oedipus complex—or perhaps the Oedipus complex itself, which is far from being the whole of psychoanalysis—which are clearly linked to the development of the institution of the family. But signification also has more buried and permanent springs (ones by definition less visible, less striking to the mind) whose validity extends, in our present state of knowledge, to the whole of humanity, i.e., to man as a biological "species." Not that the symbolic is something "natural," nonsocial; on the contrary, in its deepest foundations (which are always structures and not "facts"), signification is no longer just a consequence of social development; it becomes, along with the infrastructures, a party to the constitution of sociality itself, which in its turn defines the human race. The partial "uncoupling" of the laws of signification from short-term historical developments does not mean a naturalization of the semiotic (its *psychologization),* but on the contrary reemphasizes its radical, as it were, definitional sociality. There is always a moment after the obvious observation that it is man who makes the symbol when it is also clear that the symbol makes man: this is one of the great lessons of psychoanalysis,[2] anthropology,[3] and linguistics.[4]

Abstracting from the immense sector in which it is specifically *cultural* (varying in a time scale which is of the same order as that of history), the symbolic is thus not precisely a superstructure.[5] This does not make it an infrastructure, unless one departs from the strict (Marxist) sense of the term, and there is nothing to be gained from such a mélange. Rather, in its deeper strata it represents a kind of *juxtastructure,* to use a term which has already been put forward[6] for other phenomena of the same kind, a juxtastructure in which are expressed, in the last analysis, certain characteristics of man as an animal (and as an animal different from all other animals, i.e., as a nonanimal too). I shall only recall two well-known examples of these "laws" (of these aspects of "The Law" as Lacan would say) that help underpin all significatory work: in linguistics, in all known idioms, double articulation, the paradigm/syntagm opposition, the necessary duplication of the logical generation of sentences into a categorial component and a transformational component; in psychoanalysis, in all known societies, the prohibition of incest (and yet sexual procreation, as in all the higher animals) along with the inevitable corollary of these two as it were contradictory facts, the very remarkable relationship (whether or no it consists of an Oedipus complex of the classical type) which each human offspring must definitely enter into with respect to its father and mother (or to a more diffuse world of kin) and thus a variety of major consequences such as repression, the division of the psychical apparatus into several systems which are relatively ignorant of one another, hence the permanent coexistence in human productions (such as films) of two irreducible "logics," one of which is "illogical" and opens permanently on to a multiplicity of overdeterminations, etc.

To sum up, the influence of linguistics and of psychoanalysis may lead gradually, in combination, to a relatively autonomous science of the cinema (= "semiology of the cinema"), but the latter will deal *simultaneously* with facts which are superstructural and others which are not, without for all that being specifically infrastructural. In both these aspects its relation to truly infrastructural studies (cinematic and general) will continue to hold. It is on these three levels that the symbolic is social (hence it is entirely social). But, like the society which creates it and which it creates, it too has a materiality, a kind of *body*: it is in this almost physical state that it concerns semiology and that the semiologist desires it. . . .

Identification, Mirror

"What contribution can Freudian psychoanalysis make to the knowledge of the cinematic signifier?" That was the question/dream I posed (the scientific imaginary wishing to be symbolized), and it seems to me that I have now more or less *unwound* it; unwound but no more; I have not given it an answer. I have simply paid attention to what it was I wished to say (one never knows this until one has written it down), I have only questioned my question: this unanswered character is one that has to be deliberately accepted, it is constitutive of any epistemological procedure.

Since I have wished to mark the places (as empty boxes some of which are beginning to fill without waiting for me, and so much the better), the places of different directions of work, and particularly of the last, the psychoanalytic exploration of the signifier, which concerns me especially, I must now begin to inscribe something in this last box; must take further, and more plainly in the direction of the unconscious, the analysis of the investigator's desire that makes me write. And to start with, of course, this means asking a new question: among the specific features of the cinematic signifier that distinguish the cinema from literature, painting, etc. which ones by nature call most directly on the type of knowledge that psychoanalysis alone can provide?

Perception, Imaginary

The cinema's signifier is *perceptual* (visual and auditory). So is that of literature, since the written chain has to be *read,* but it involves a more restricted perceptual register: only graphemes, writing. So too are those of painting, sculpture, architecture, photography, but still within limits, and different ones: absence of auditory perception, absence in the visual itself of certain important dimensions such as time and movement (obviously there is the time of the look, but the object looked at is not inscribed in a precise and ordered time sequence forced on the spectator from outside). Music's signifier is perceptual as well, but, like the others, less "extensive" than that of the cinema: here it is vision which is absent, and even in the auditory, extended speech (except in song). What first strikes one then is that the cinema is *more perceptual,* if the phrase is allowable, than many other means of expression; it mobilizes a larger number of the axes of perception. (That is why the cinema has sometimes been presented as a "synthesis of all the arts"; which does not mean very much, but if we restrict ourselves to the quantitative tally of the registers of perception, it is true that the cinema contains within itself the signifiers of other arts: it can present pictures to us, make us hear music, it is made of photographs, etc.)

Nevertheless, this as it were numerical "superiority" disappears if the cinema is compared with the theater, the opera, and other spectacles of the same type. The latter too involve sight and hearing simultaneously, linguistic audition and nonlinguistic audition, movement, real temporal progression. Their difference from the cinema lies elsewhere: they do not consist of *images,* the perceptions they offer to the eye and the ear are inscribed in a true space (not a photographed one), the same one as that occupied by the public during the performance;

everything the audience hears and sees is actively produced in its presence, by human beings or props which are themselves present. This is not the problem of fiction but that of the definitional characteristics of the signifier: whether or no the theatrical play mimes a fable, its *action,* if need be mimetic, is still managed by real persons evolving in real time and space, *on the same stage or "scene" as the public.* The "other scene," which is precisely not so called, is the cinematic screen (closer to fantasy from the outset): what unfolds there may, as before, be more or less fictional, but the unfolding itself is fictive: the actor, the "décor," the words one hears are all absent, everything is *recorded* (as a memory trace which is immediately so, without having been something else before), and this is still true if what is recorded is not a "story" and does not aim for the fictional illusion proper. For it is the signifier itself, and as a whole, that is recorded, that is absence: a little rolled-up perforated strip which "contains" vast landscapes, fixed battles, the melting of the ice on the River Neva, and whole lifetimes, and yet can be enclosed in the familiar round metal tin, of modest dimensions, clear proof that it does not "really" contain all that.

At the theater, Sarah Bernhardt may tell me she is Phèdre or, if the play were from another period and rejected the figurative regime, she might say, as in a type of modern theater, that she is Sarah Bernhardt. But at any rate, I should see Sarah Bernhardt. At the cinema, she could make the same two kinds of speeches too, but it would be her shadow that would be offering them to me (or she would be offering them in her own absence). Every film is a fiction film.

What is at issue is not just the actor. Today there are a theater and a cinema without actors, or in which they have at least ceased to take on the full and exclusive function which characterizes them in classical spectacles. But what is true of Sarah Bernhardt is just as true of an object, a prop, a chair for example. On the theater stage, this chair may, as in Chekhov, pretend to be the chair in which the melancholy Russian nobleman sits every evening; on the contrary (in Ionesco), it can explain to me that it is a theater chair. But when all is said and done it is a chair. In the cinema, it will similarly have to choose between two attitudes (and many other intermediate or more tricky ones), but it will not be there when the spectators see it, when they have to recognize the choice; it will have delegated its reflection to them.

What is characteristic of the cinema is not the imaginary that it may happen to represent, but the imaginary that it *is* from the start, the imaginary that constitutes it as a signifier (the two are not unrelated; it is so well able to represent it because it is it; however, it is it even when it no longer represents it). The (possible) reduplication inaugurating the intention of fiction is preceded in the cinema by a first reduplication, always already achieved, which inaugurates the signifier. The imaginary, by definition, combines within it a certain presence and a certain absence. In the cinema it is not just the fictional signified, if there is one, that is thus made present in the mode of absence; it is from the outset the signifier.

Thus the cinema, "more perceptual" than certain arts according to the list of its sensory registers, is also "less perceptual" than others once the status of these perceptions is envisaged rather than their number or diversity; for its perceptions are all in a sense "false." Or rather, the activity of perception which it involves is real (the cinema is not a fantasy), but the perceived is not really the object, it is its shade, its phantom, its double, its *replica* in a new kind of mirror. It will be said that literature, after all, is itself only made of replicas (written words, presenting absent objects). But at least it does not present them to us with all the really perceived detail that the screen does (giving more and taking as much, i.e., taking more). The unique position of the cinema lies in this dual character of its signifier: unaccustomed perceptual wealth, but at the same time stamped with unreality to an unusual degree and from the very outset. More than the other arts, or in a more unique way, the cinema involves us in the imaginary: it drums up all perception, but to switch it immediately over into its own absence, which is nonetheless the only signifier present.

The All-Perceiving Subject

Thus film is like the mirror. But it differs from the primordial mirror in one essential point: although, as in the latter, everything may come to be projected, there is one thing and one thing only that is never reflected in it: the spectator's own body. In a certain emplacement, the mirror suddenly becomes clear glass.

In the mirror the child perceives the familiar household objects, and also its object par excellence, its mother, who holds it up in her arms to the glass. But above all it perceives its own image. This is where primary identification (the formation of the ego) gets certain of its main characteristics: the child sees itself as an other, and beside an other. This other other is its guarantee that the first is really it: by her authority, her sanction, in the register of the symbolic, subsequently by the resemblance between her mirror image and the child's (both have a human form). Thus the child's ego is formed by identification with its like, and this in two senses simultaneously, metonymically and metaphorically: the other human being who is in the glass, the own reflection which is and is not the body, which is like it. The child identifies with itself as an object.

In the cinema, the object remains: fiction or no, there is always something on the screen. But the reflection of the own body has disappeared. The cinema spectator is not a child and the child really at the mirror stage (from around six to around eighteen months) would certainly be incapable of "following" the simplest of films. Thus, what *makes possible* the spectator's absence from the screen—or rather the intelligible unfolding of the film despite that absence—is the fact that the spectator has already known the experience of the mirror (of the true mirror), and is thus able to constitute a world of objects without having first to recognize himself within it. In this respect, the cinema is already on the side of the symbolic (which is only to be expected): the spectator knows that objects exist, that he himself exists as a subject, that he becomes an object for others: he knows himself and he knows his like: it is no longer necessary that this similarity be literally *depicted* for him on the screen, as it was in the mirror of his childhood. Like every other broadly "secondary" activity, the practice of the cinema presupposes that the primitive undifferentiation of the ego and the nonego has been overcome.

But *with what*, then, does the spectator identify during the projection of the film? For he certainly has to identify: identification in its primal form has ceased to be a current necessity for him, but he continues, in the cinema—if he did not the film would become incomprehensible, considerably more incomprehensible than the most incomprehensible films—to depend on that permanent play of identification without which there would be no social life (thus, the simplest conversation presupposes the alternation of the *I* and the *you;* hence the aptitude of the two interlocutors for a mutual and reversible identification). What form does this *continued* identification, whose essential role Lacan has demonstrated even in the most abstract reasoning[7] and which constituted the "social sentiment" for Freud[8] (= the sublimation of a homosexual libido, itself a reaction to the aggressive rivalry of the members of a single generation after the murder of the father), take in the special case of one social practice among others, cinematic projection?

Obviously the spectator has the opportunity to identify with the *character* of the fiction. But there still has to be one. This is thus valid only for the narrative-representational film and not for the psychoanalytic constitution of the signifier of the cinema as such. The spectator can also identify with the actor, in more or less "afictional" films in which the latter is represented as an actor, not a character, but is still offered thereby as a human being (as a perceived human being) and thus allows identification. However, this factor (even added to the previous one and thus covering a very large number of films) cannot suffice. It only designates secondary identification in certain of its forms (secondary in the cinematic process itself, since in any other sense all identification except that of the mirror can be regarded as secondary).

An insufficient explanation, and for two reasons, the first of which is only the intermittent, anecdotal, and superficial consequence of the second (but for that reason more visible, and that is why I call it the first). The cinema deviates from the theater on an important point that has often been emphasized: it often presents us with long sequences that can (literally) be called "inhuman"—the familiar theme of cinematic "cosmomorphism" developed by many film theorists—sequences in which only inanimate objects, landscapes, etc. appear and which for minutes at a time offer no human form for spectator identification:

yet the latter must be supposed to remain intact in its deep structure, since at such moments the film *works* just as well as it does at others, and whole films (geographical documentaries, for example) unfold intelligibly in such conditions. The second, more radical reason is that identification with the human form appearing on the screen, even when it occurs, still tells us nothing about the *place of the spectator's ego* in the inauguration of the signifier. As I have just pointed out, this ego is already formed. But since it exists, the question arises precisely of *where it is* during the projection of the film (the true primary identification, that of the mirror, forms the ego, but all other identifications presuppose, on the contrary, that it has been formed and can be "exchanged" for the object or the fellow subject). Thus when I "recognize" my like on the screen, and even more when I do not recognize it, where am I? Where is that someone who is capable of self-recognition when need be?

It is not enough to answer that the cinema, like every social practice, demands that the psychical apparatus of its participants be fully constituted, and that the question is thus the concern of general psychoanalytic theory and not that of the cinema proper. For my *where is it?* does not claim to go so far, or more precisely tries to go slightly further: it is a question of the *point* occupied by this already constituted ego, occupied during the cinema showing and not in social life in general.

The spectator is absent from the screen: unlike the child in the mirror, he cannot identify with himself as an object, but only with objects which are there without him. In this sense the screen is not a mirror. The perceived, this time, is entirely on the side of the object, and there is no longer any equivalent of the own image, of that unique mix of perceived and subject (of other and I) which was precisely the figure necessary to disengage the one from the other. At the cinema, it is always the other who is on the screen; as for me, I am there to look at him. I take no part in the perceived; on the contrary, I am *all-perceiving*. All-perceiving as one says all-powerful (this is the famous gift of "ubiquity" the film makes its spectator); all-perceiving, too, because I am entirely on the side of the perceiving instance: absent from the screen, but certainly present in the auditorium, a great eye and ear without which the perceived would have no one to perceive it, the instance, in other words, which *constitutes* the cinema signifier (it is I who make the film). If the most extravagant spectacles and sounds or the most unlikely combination of them, the combination furthest removed from any real experience, do not prevent the constitution of meaning (and to begin with do not *astonish* the spectator, do not really astonish him, not intellectually: he simply judges the film as strange), that is because he knows he is at the cinema.

In the cinema the *subject's knowledge* takes a very precise form without which no film would be possible. This knowledge is dual (but unique). I know I am perceiving something imaginary (and that is why its absurdities, even if they are extreme, do not seriously disturb me), and I know that it is I who am perceiving it. This second knowledge divides in turn: I know that I am really perceiving, that my sense organs are physically affected, that I am not fantasizing, that the fourth wall of the auditorium (the screen) is really different from the other three, that there is a projector facing it (and thus it is not I who am projecting, or at least not all alone), and I also know that it is I who am perceiving all this, that this perceived-imaginary material is deposited in me as if on a second screen, that it is in me that it forms up into an organized sequence, that therefore I am myself the place where this really perceived imaginary accedes to the symbolic by its inauguration as the signifier of a certain type of institutionalized social activity called the "cinema."

In other words, the spectator *identifies with himself,* with himself as a pure act of perception (as wakefulness, alertness): as the condition of possibility of the perceived and hence as a kind of transcendental subject, which comes before every *there is.*

A strange mirror, then, very like that of childhood, and very different. Very like, as Jean-Louis Baudry has emphasized,[9] because during the showing we are, like the child, in a submotor and hyperperceptive state; because, like the child again, we are prey to the imaginary, the double, and are so paradoxically through a real perception. Very different, because this mirror returns us everything but ourselves, because we are wholly outside it, whereas the child is both in it and in front of it. As an *arrangement* (and in a very topographical sense of the word), the cinema is more involved on the flank of the symbolic, and hence of secondariness, than is the mirror of childhood. This is not surprising, since it comes long after it, but what is more important to me is the fact that it is inscribed in its wake with an incidence at once so direct and so oblique, which has no precise equivalent in other apparatuses of signification.

Identification with the Camera

The preceding analysis coincides in places with others which have already been proposed and which I shall not repeat: analyses of *quattrocento* painting or of the cinema itself which insist on the role of monocular perspective (hence of the *camera*) and the "vanishing point" that inscribes an empty emplacement for the spectator-subject, an all-powerful position which is that of God himself, or more broadly ̄of some ultimate signified. And it is true that as he identifies with himself as look, the spectator can do no other than identify with the camera, too, which has looked before him at what he is now looking at and whose stationing (= framing) determines the vanishing point. During the projection this camera is absent, but it has a representative consisting of another apparatus, called precisely a "projector." An apparatus the spectator has behind him, *at the back of his head,*[10] that is, precisely where fantasy locates the "focus" of all vision.

All of us have experienced our own look, even outside the so-called *salles obscures* [= cinemas], as a kind of searchlight turning on the axis of our own necks (like a pan) and shifting when we shift (a tracking shot now): as a cone of light (without the microscopic dust scattered through it and streaking it in the cinema) whose vicariousness draws successive and variable slices of obscurity from nothingness wherever and whenever it comes to rest. (And in a sense that is what perception and consciousness are, a *light*, as Freud put it,[11] in the double sense of an illumination and an opening, as in the arrangement of the cinema, which contains both, a limited and wandering light that only attains a small part of the real, but on the other hand possesses the gift of casting light on it). Without this identification with the camera certain facts could not be understood, though they are constant ones: the fact, for example, that the spectator is not amazed when the image "rotates" (= a pan) and yet he knows he has not turned his head. The explanation is that he has no need to turn it really, he has turned it in his all-seeing capacity, his identification with the movement of the camera being that of a transcendental, not an empirical subject.

All vision consists of a double movement: projective (the "sweeping" search-light) and introjective: consciousness as a sensitive recording surface (as a screen). I have the impression at once that, to use a common expression, I am "casting" my eyes on things, and that the latter, thus illuminated, come to be deposited within me (we then declare that it is these things that have been "projected," on to my retina, say). A sort of stream called the look, and explaining all the myths of magnetism, must be sent out over the world, so that objects can come back up this stream in the opposite direction (but using it to find their way), arriving at last at our perception, whch is now soft wax and no longer an emitting source.

The technology of photography carefully conforms to this (banal) fantasy accompanying perception. The camera is "trained" on the object like a firearm (= projection) and the object arrives to make an imprint, a trace, on the receptive surface of the filmstrip (= introjection). The spectator himself does not escape these pincers, for he is part of the apparatus, and also because pincers, on the imaginary plane (Melanie Klein), mark our relation to the world as a whole and are rooted in the primary figures of orality. During the performance the spectator is the searchlight I have described, duplicating the projector, which itself dupli-cates the camera, and he is also the sensitive surface duplicating the screen, which itself duplicates the filmstrip. There are two cones in the auditorium: one ending on the screen and starting both in the projection box and in the spectator's vision insofar as it is projective, and one starting from the screen and "deposited" in the spectator's perception insofar as it is introjective (on the retina, a second screen). When I say that "I see" the film, I mean thereby a unique mixture of two contrary currents: the film is what I receive, and it is also what I release, since it does not preexist my entering the auditorium and I only need close my eyes to suppress it. Releasing it, I am the projector, receiving it, I am the screen;

in both these figures together, I am the camera, which points and yet which records.

Thus the constitution of the signifier in the cinema depends on a series of mirror effects organized in a chain, and not on a single reduplication. In this the cinema as a topography resembles that other "space," the technical equipment (camera, projector, filmstrip, screen, etc.), the objective precondition of the whole institution: as we know, the apparatuses too contain a series of mirrors, lenses, apertures, and shutters, ground glasses, through which the cone of light passes: a further reduplication in which the equipment becomes a metaphor (as well as the real source) for the mental process instituted. Further on we shall see that it is also its fetish.

In the cinema, as elsewhere, the constitution of the symbolic is only achieved through and above the play of the imaginary: projection-introjection, presence-absence, fantasies accompanying perception, etc. Even when acquired, the ego still depends in its underside on the fabulous figures thanks to which it has been acquired and which have marked it lastingly with the stamp of the lure. The secondary process does no more than "cover" (and not always hermetically) the primary process which is still constantly present and conditions the very possibility of what covers it.

Chain of many mirrors, the cinema is at once a weak and a robust mechanism: like the human body, like a precision tool, like a social institution. And the fact is that it is really all these at the same time.

And I, at this moment, what am I doing if not adding to all these reduplications one more whereby theory is attempting to set itself up? Am I not looking at myself looking at the film? This *passion for seeing* (and also hearing), the foundation of the whole edifice, am I not turning it, too, on (against) that edifice? Am I not still the voyeur I was in front of the screen, now that it is this voyeur who is being seen, thus postulating a second voyeur, the one writing at present, myself again?

On the Idealist Theory of the Cinema

The place of the ego in the institution of the signifier, as transcendental yet radically deluded subject, since it is the institution (and even the equipment) that gives it this place, surely provides us with an appreciable opportunity the better to understand and judge the precise epistemological import of the idealist theory of the cinema which culminates in the remarkable works of André Bazin. Before thinking directly about their validity, but simply reading texts of this kind, one cannot but be struck by the great precision, the acute and immediately sensitive intelligence that they often demonstrate; at the same time they give the diffuse impression of a permanent ill-foundedness (which affects nothing and yet affects everything); they suggest that somewhere they contain something like a weak point at which the whole might be overturned.

It is certainly no accident that the main form of idealism in cinematic theory has been phenomenology. Bazin and other writers of the same period explicitly acknowledged their debt to it, and more implicitly (but in a more generalized fashion) all conceptions of the cinema as a mystical revelation, as "truth" or "reality" unfolding by right, as the apparition of what is [*l'étant*], as an epiphany, derive from it. We all know that the cinema has the gift of sending some of its lovers into prophetic trances. However, these cosmophanic conceptions (which are not always expressed in an extreme form) register rather well the "feeling" of the *deluded ego* of the spectator; they often give us excellent descriptions of this feeling, and to this extent there is something scientific about them and they have advanced our knowledge of the cinema. But the *lure of the ego* is their blind spot. These theories are still of great interest, but they have, so to speak, to be put the other way round, like the optical image of the film.

For it is true that the topographical apparatus of the cinema resembles the conceptual apparatus of phenomenology, with the result that the latter can cast light on the former. (Besides, in any domain, a phenomenology of the object to be understood, a "receptive" description of its appearances, must be the starting point; only afterward can *criticism* begin; psychoanalysts, it should be remembered, have their own phenomenology.) The *there is* of phenomenology proper (philosophical phenomenology) as an ontic revelation referring to a perceiving subject (= "perceptual *cogito*"), to a subject for which alone there can be anything, has close and precise affinities with the installation of the cinema signifier in the ego as I have tried to define it, with the spectator withdrawing into himself as a pure instance of perception, the whole of the perceived being "out there." To this extent the cinema really is the "phenomenological art" it has often been called, by Merleau-Ponty himself, for example.[12] But it can only be so because its objective determinations make it so. The ego's position in the cinema does not derive from a miraculous resemblance between the cinema and the natural characteristics of all perception; on the contrary, it is foreseen and marked in advance by the institution (the equipment, the disposition of the auditorium, the mental system that internalizes the two), and also by more general characteristics of the physical apparatus (such as projection, the mirror structure, etc.), which although they are less strictly dependent on a period of social history and a technology, do not therefore express the sovereignty of a "human vocation," but inversely are themselves shaped by certain specific features of man as an animal (as the only animal that is not an animal): his primitive *Hilflosigkeit*, his dependence on another's care (the lasting source of the imaginary, of object relations, of the great oral figures of feeding), the motor prematurity of the child which condemns it to an initial self-recognition by sight (hence outside itself) anticipating a muscular unity it does not yet possess.

In other words, phenomenology can contribute to knowledge of the cinema (and it has done so) insofar as it happens to be like it, and yet it is on the cinema *and* phenomenology in their common illusion of *perceptual mastery* that light must be cast by the real conditions of society and man.

On Some Subcodes of Identification

The play of identification defines the cinematic situation in its generality, i.e., *the* code. But it also allows more specific and less permanent configurations, "variations" on it, as it were; they intervene in certain coded figures which occupy precise segments of precise films.

What I have said about identification so far amounts to the statement that the spectator is absent from the screen *as perceived*, but also (the two things inevitably go together) present there and even "all-present" as *perceiver*. At every moment I am in the film by my look's caress. This presence often remains diffuse, geographically undifferentiated, evenly distributed over the whole surface of the screen; or more precisely *hovering*, like the psychoanalyst's listening, ready to catch on preferentially to some motif in the film, according to the force of that motif and according to my own fantasies as a spectator, without the cinematic code itself intervening to govern this anchorage and impose it on the whole audience. But in other cases, certain articles of the cinematic codes or subcodes (which I shall not try to survey completely here) are made responsible for suggesting to the spectator the vector along which his permanent identification with his own look should be extended temporarily inside the film (the perceived) itself. Here we meet various classic problems of cinematic theory, or at least certain aspects of them: subjective images, out-of-frame space, looks (looks and no longer the look, but the former are articulated to the latter).

There are various sorts of subjective image, and I have tried elsewhere (following Jean Mitry) to distinguish between them.[13] Only one of them will detain me for the moment, the one which "expresses the viewpoint of the filmmaker" in the standard formula (and not the viewpoint of a character, another traditional subcase of the subjective image): unusual framings, uncommon shot angles, etc., as for example in one of the sketches which make up Julien Duvivier's film *Carnet de bal* (the sketch with Pierre Blanchar, shot continuously in tilted framings). In the standard definitions one thing strikes me: I do not see why these uncommon angles should express the viewpoint of the filmmaker any more than perfectly ordinary angles, closer to the horizontal. However, the definition is comprehensible even in its inaccuracy: precisely because it is uncommon, the uncommon angle makes us more aware of what we had merely forgotten to some extent in its absence: an identification with the camera (with "the author's viewpoint"). The ordinary framings are finally felt to be nonframings: I espouse the filmmaker's look (without which no cinema would be possible), but my consciousness is not too aware of it. The uncommon angle reawakens me and (like the cure) teaches me what I already knew. And then, it obliges my look to stop wandering freely over the screen for the moment and to scan it along more precise lines of force which are imposed on me. Thus for a moment I become directly aware of the *emplacement* of my own presence-absence in the film simply because it has changed.

Now for looks. In a fiction film, the characters look at one another. It can happen (and this is already another "notch" in the chain of identifications) that a character looks at another who is momentarily out-of-frame, or else is looked at by him. If we have gone one notch further, this is because everything out-of-frame *brings us closer to the spectator,* since it is the peculiarity of the latter to be out-of-frame (the out-of-frame character thus has a point in common with him: he is looking at the screen). In certain cases the out-of-frame character's look is "reinforced" by recourse to another variant of the subjective image, generally christened the "character's point of view.": the framing of the scene corresponds precisely to the angle from which the out-of-frame character looks at the screen. (The two figures are dissociable, moreover: we often know that the scene is being looked at by someone other than ourselves, by a character, but it is the logic of the plot, or an element of the dialogue, or a previous image that tells us so, not the position of the camera, which may be far from the presumed emplacement of the out-of-frame onlooker.)

In all sequences of this kind, the identification that founds the signifier is *twice relayed,* doubly duplicated in a circuit that leads it to the heart of the film along a line which is no longer hovering, which follows the inclination of the looks and is therefore governed by the film itself: the spectator's look (= the basic identification), before dispersing all over the surface of the screen in a variety of intersecting lines (= looks of the characters in the frame = second duplication), must first "go through"—as one goes through a town on a journey, or a mountain pass—the look of the character out-of-frame (= first duplication), himself a spectator and hence the first delegate of the true spectator, but not to be confused with the latter since he is inside if not the frame then at least the fiction. This invisible character, supposed (like the spectator) to be seeing, will collide obliquely with the latter's look and play the part of an obligatory inter-mediary. By offering himself as a crossing for the spectator, he inflects the circuit followed by the sequence of identifications, and it is only in this sense that he is himself seen: as we see through him, we see ourselves not seeing him.

Examples of this kind are much more numerous and each of them is much more complex than I have suggested here. At this point textual analysis of precise film sequences is an indispensable instrument of knowledge. I just wished to show that in the end there is no break in continuity between the child's game with the mirror and, at the other extreme, certain localized figures of the cinematic codes.

The mirror is the site of primary identification. Identification with one's own look is secondary with respect to the mirror, i.e., for a general theory of adult activities, but it is the foundation of the cinema and hence primary when the latter is under discussion: it is *primary cinematic identification* proper ("primary identification" would be inaccurate from the psychoanalytic point of view; "secondary identification," more accurate in this respect, would be ambiguous for a cinematic psychoanalysis). As for identifications with characters, with their own different levels (out-of-frame character, etc.), they are secondary, tertiary cinematic identifications, etc.; taken as a whole in opposition to the identification of the spectator with his own look, they constitute secondary cinematic identification in the singular.[14]

"Seeing a Film"

Freud noted, vis-à-vis the sexual act,[15] that the most ordinary practices depend on a large number of psychical functions which are distinct but work consecutively, so that all of them must be intact if what is regarded as a normal performance is to be possible (it is because neurosis and psychosis dissociate them and put some of them out of court that a kind of commutation is made possible whereby they can be listed retrospectively by the analyst). The apparently very simple act of *seeing a film* is no exception to this rule. As soon as it is subjected to analysis it reveals to us a complex, multiply interconnected imbrication of the functions of the imaginary, the real, and the symbolic, which is also required in one form or another for every procedure of social life, but whose cinematic manifestation is especially impressive, since it is played out on a small surface. (To this extent the theory of the cinema may some day contribute something to psychoanalysis, even if, through force of circumstances, this "reciprocation" remains very limited at the moment, the two disciplines being very unevenly developed.)

In order to understand the fiction film, I must both "take myself" for the character (= an imaginary procedure) so that he benefits, by analogical projection, from all the schemata of intelligibility that I have within me, and not take myself for him (= the return to the real) so that the fiction can be established as such (= as symbolic): this is *seeing-real*. Similarly, in order to understand the film (at all), I must perceive the photographed object as absent, its photograph as present, and the presence of this absence as signifying. The imaginary of the cinema presupposes the symbolic, for the spectator must first of all have known the primordial mirror. But as the latter instituted the ego very largely in the imaginary, the second mirror of the screen, a symbolic apparatus, itself in turn depends on reflection and lack. However, it is not fantasy, a "purely" symbolic-imaginary site, for the absence of the object and the codes of that absence are really produced in it by the *physis* of an equipment: the cinema is a body (a *corpus* for the semiologist), a fetish that can be loved.

The Passion for Perceiving

The practice of the cinema is only possible through the perceptual passions: the desire to see (= scopic drive, scopophilia, voyeurism), which was alone engaged in the art of the silent film, the desire to hear which has been added to it in the sound cinema (this is the *pulsion invocante,* the invocatory drive, one of the four main sexual drives for Lacan;[16] it is well known that Freud isolated it less clearly and hardly deals with it as such).

These two sexual drives are distinguished from the others in that they are more dependent on a lack, or at least dependent on it in a more precise, more unique manner, which marks them from the outset, even more than the others as being on the side of the imaginary.

However, this characteristic is to a greater or lesser degree proper to all the sexual drives insofar as they differ from purely organic instincts or needs (Lacan), or in Freud from the self-preservation drives (the "ego drives" which he tended subsequently to annex to narcissism, a tendency he could never quite bring himself to pursue to its conclusion). The sexual drive does not have so stable and strong a relationship with its 'object' as do for example hunger and thirst. Hunger can only be satisfied by food, but food is quite certain to satisfy it; thus instincts are simultaneously more and less difficult to satisfy than drives; they depend on a perfectly real object for which there is no substitute, but they depend on nothing else. Drives, on the contrary, can be satisfied up to a point outside their objects (this is sublimation, or else, in another way, masturbation) and are initially capable of doing without them without putting the organism into immediate danger (hence repression). The needs of self-preservation can neither be repressed nor sublimated; the sexual drives are more labile and more accommodating, as Freud insisted[17] (more radically perverse, says Lacan.)[18] Inversely, they always remain more or less unsatisfied, even when their object has been attained; desire is very quickly reborn after the brief vertigo of its apparent extinction, it is largely sustained by itself as desire, it has its own rhythms, often quite independent of those of the pleasure obtained (which seemed nonetheless its specific aim); the lack is what it wishes to fill, and at the same time what it is always careful to leave gaping, in order to survive as desire. In the end it has no object, at any rate no real object; through real objects which are all substitutes (and all the more numerous and interchangeable for that), it pursues an imaginary object (a "lost object") which is its truest object, an object that has always been lost and is always desired as such.

How, then, can one say that the visual and auditory drives have a stronger or more special relationship with the absence of their object, with the infinite pursuit of the imaginary? Because, as opposed to other sexual drives, the "perceiving drive"—combining into one the scopic drive and the invocatory drive—*concretely represents the absence of its object* in the distance at which it maintains it and which is part of its very definition: distance of the look, distance of listening. Psychophysiology makes a classic distinction between the "senses at a distance" (sight and hearing) and the others all of which involve immediate proximity and which it calls the "senses of contact" (Pradines): touch, taste, smell, coenesthetic sense, etc. Freud notes that voyeurism, like sadism in this respect, always keeps apart the *object* (here the object looked at) and the *source* of the drive, i.e., the generating organ (the eye); the voyeur does not look at his eye.[19] With orality and anality, on the contrary, the exercise of the drive inaugurates a certain degree of partial fusion, a coincidence (= contact, tendential abolition of distance) of source and aim, for the aim is to obtain pleasure at the level of the source organ (= "organ pleasure")[20] e.g., what is called "pleasure of the mouth."[21]

It is no accident that the main socially acceptable arts are based on the senses at a distance, and that those which depend on the senses of contact are often regarded as "minor" arts (e.g., the culinary arts, the art of perfumes, etc.) Nor is it an accident that the visual or auditory imaginaries have played a much more important part in the histories of societies than the tactile or olfactory imaginaries.

The voyeur is very careful to maintain a gulf, an empty space, between the object and the eye, the object and his own body: his look fastens the object at the right distance, as with those cinema spectators who take care to avoid being too close to or too far from the screen. The voyeur represents in space the fracture which forever separates him from the object; he represents his very dissatisfaction (which is precisely what he needs as a voyeur), and thus also his "satisfaction" insofar as it is of a specifically voyeuristic type. To fill in this distance would threaten to overwhelm the subject, to lead him to consume the object (the object which is now too close so that he cannot see it anymore), to bring him to orgasm and the pleasure of his own body, hence to the exercise of other drives, mobilizing the senses of contact and putting an end to the scopic arrangement. *Retention* is fully part of perceptual pleasure, which is thereby often colored with anality. Orgasm is the object rediscovered in a state of momentary illusion; it is the fantasy suppression of the gap between object and subject (hence the amorous myths of "fusion"). The looking drive, except when it is exceptionally well developed, is less directly related to orgasm than are the other component drives; it favors it by its excitatory action, but it is not generally sufficient to produce it by its figures alone, which thus belong to the realm of "preparatives." In it we do not find that illusion, however brief, of a lack filled, of a nonimaginary, of a full relation to the object, better established in other drives. If it is true of all desire that it depends on the infinite pursuit of its absent object, voyeuristic desire, along with certain forms of sadism, is the only desire whose principle of distance symbolically and spatially evokes this fundamental rent.

The same could be said, making the necessary modifications of course, about the invocatory (auditory) drive, less closely studied by psychoanalysis hitherto, with the exception of writers like Lacan and Guy Rosolato. I shall merely recall that of all hallucinations—and what reveals the dissociation of desire and real object better than the hallucination?—the main ones by far are visual and auditory hallucinations, those of the senses at a distance (this is also true of the dream, another form of hallucination).

The Scopic Regime of the Cinema

However, although this set of features seems to me to be important, it does not yet characterize the signifier of the cinema proper, but rather that of all means of expression based on sight or hearing, and hence, among other "languages," that of practically all the arts (painting, sculpture, architecture, music, opera, theater, etc.) What distinguishes the cinema is an extra reduplication, a supplementary and specific turn of the screw bolting desire to the lack. First because the spectacles and sounds the cinema "offers" us (offers us at a distance, hence as much *steals* from us) are especially rich and varied: a mere difference of degree, but already one that counts: the screen presents to our apprehension, but absents from our grasp, more "things." (The mechanism of the perceiving drive is identical for the moment, but its object is more endowed with matter; this is one of the reasons why the cinema is very suited to handling "erotic scenes" which depend on direct, nonsublimated voyeurism.) In the second place (and more decisively), the specific affinity between the cinematic signifier and the imaginary persists when film is compared with arts such as the theater in which the audiovisual given is as rich as it is on the screen in the number of perceptual axes involved. Indeed, the theater really does "give" this given, or at least slightly more really: it is physically present, in the same space as the spectator. The cinema only gives it in effigy, inaccessible from the outset, in a primordial *elsewhere*, infinitely desirable (= never possessible), on another scene which is that of absence and which nonetheless represents the absent in detail, thus making it very present, but by a different itinerary. Not only am I at a distance from the object, as in the theater, but what remains in that distance is now no longer the object itself, it is a delegate it has sent me while itself withdrawing. A double withdrawal.

What defines the specifically cinematic *scopic regime* is not so much the distance kept, the "keeping" itself (first figure of the lack, common to all voyeurism), as the absence of the object seen. Here the cinema is profoundly different from the theater as also from more intimate voyeuristic activities with a specifically erotic aim (there are intermediate genres, moreover: certain cabaret acts, striptease, etc.): cases where voyeurism remains linked to exhibitionism, where the two faces, active and passive, of the component drive are by no means so dissociated; where the object seen is present and hence presumably complicit; where the perverse activity—aided if need be by a certain dose of bad faith and happy illusion, varying from case to case, moreover, and sometimes reducible to very little, as in true perverse couples—is rehabilitated and reconciled with itself by being, as it were, undividedly taken in charge by two actors assuming its constitutive poles (the corresponding fantasies, in the absence of the actions, thus becoming interchangeable and shared by the play of reciprocal identification). In the theater, as in domestic voyeurism, the passive actor (the one seen), simply because he is bodily present, because he does not go away, is presumed to consent, to cooperate deliberately. It may be that he really does, as exhibitionists in the clinical sense do, or as, in a sublimated fashion, does that oft-noted triumphant exhibitionism characteristic of theatrical acting, counterposed even by Bazin to cinematic representation. It may also be that the object seen has only accepted this condition (thus becoming an "object" in the ordinary sense of the word, and no longer only in the Freudian sense) under the pressure of more or less powerful external constraints, economic ones, for example, with certain poor strippers. (However, they must have consented at some point; rarely is the degree of acceptance zero, except in the case of *victimization,* e.g., when a fascist militia strips its prisoners: the specific characteristics of the scopic arrangement are then distorted by the overpowerful intervention of another element, sadism.) Voyeurism which is not too sadistic (there is none which is not so at all) rests on a kind of *fiction,* more or less justified in the order of the real, sometimes institutionalized as in the theater or striptease, a fiction that stipulates that the object "agrees," that it is therefore exhibitionist. Or more precisely, what is necessary in this fiction for the establishment of potency and desire is presumed to be sufficiently guaranteed by the physical presence of the object: "Since it is there, it must like it," such, hypocritical or no, deluded or no, is the retrenchment needed by the voyeur so long as sadistic infiltrations are insufficient to make the object's refusal and constraint necessary to him. Thus, despite the distance instituted by the look—which transforms the object into a *picture* (a *tableau vivant*[22]) and thus tips it over into the imaginary, even in its real presence—that presence, which persists, and the active consent which is its real or mythical correlate (but always real as myth) reestablish in the scopic space, momentarily at least, the illusion of a fullness of the object relation, of a state of desire which is not just imaginary.

It is this last recess that is attacked by the cinema signifier, it is in its precise emplacement (*in its place,* in both senses of the word) that it installs a new figure of the lack, the physical absence of the object seen. In the theater, actors and spectators are present at the same time and in the same location, hence present one to another, as the two protagonists of an authentic perverse couple. But in the cinema, the actor was present when the spectator was not (= shooting), and the spectator is present when the actor is no longer (= projection): a failure to meet of the voyeur and the exhibitionist whose approaches no longer coincide (they have "missed" one another). The cinema's voyeurism must (of necessity) do without any very clear mark of consent on the part of the object. There is no equivalent here of the theater actors' final "bow." And then the latter could see their voyeurs, the game was less unilateral, slightly better distributed. In the darkened hall, the voyeur is really left alone (or with other voyeurs, which is worse), deprived of his other half in the mythical hermaphrodite (a hermaphrodite not necessarily constituted by the distribution of the sexes but rather by that of the active and passive poles in the exercise of the drive). Yet still a voyeur, since there is something to see, called the film, but something in whose definition there is a great deal of "flight": not precisely something that hides, rather something that *lets* itself be seen without *presenting* itself to be seen, which has gone out of the room before leaving only its trace visible there. This is the origin in particular of that "recipe" of the classical cinema which said that the actor should never look directly at the audience (= the camera).

Thus deprived of rehabilitatory agreement, of a real or supposed consensus with the other (which was also the Other, for it had the status of a sanction on the plane of the symbolic), cinematic voyeurism, *unauthorized* scopophilia, is from the outset more strongly established than that of the theater in direct line from the primal scene. Certain precise features of the institution contribute to this affinity: the obscurity surrounding the onlooker, the aperture of the screen with its inevitable keyhole effect. But the affinity is more profound. It lies first in the spectator's solitude in the cinema: those attending a cinematic projection do not, as in the theater, constitute a true "audience," a temporary collectivity; they are an accumulation of individuals who, despite appearances, more closely resemble the fragmented group of readers of a novel. It lies on the other hand in the fact that the filmic spectacle, the object seen, is more radically ignorant of its spectator, since he is not there, than the theatrical spectacle can ever be. A third factor, closely linked to the other two, also plays a part: the *segregation of spaces* that characterizes a cinema performance and not a theatrical one. The "stage" and the auditorium are no longer two areas set up in opposition to each other within a single space; the space of the film, represented by the screen, is utterly heterogeneous, it no longer communicates with that of the auditorium: one is real, the other perspective: a stronger break than any line of footlights. For its spectator the film unfolds in that simultaneously very close and definitively inaccessible "elsewhere" in which the child *sees* the amorous play of the parental couple, who are similarly ignorant of it and leave it alone, a pure onlooker whose participation is inconceivable. In this respect the cinematic signifier is not only "psychoanalytic"; it is more precisely Oedipal in type.

In this set of differences between the cinema and the theater, it is difficult to be precise about the relative importance of two types of conditioning, and yet they are definitely distinct: on the one hand the characteristics of the signifier (alone envisaged here), i.e., the supplementary degree of absence that I have tried to analyze, and on the other the socio–ideological circumstances that marked the historical birth of the two arts in a divergent manner. I have broached the latter topic elsewhere in my contribution to the *Hommage à Emile Benveniste* [part 2 of my book *The Imaginary Signifier*] and I shall only recall that the cinema was born in the midst of the capitalist epoch in a largely antagonistic and fragmented society, based on individualism and the restricted family (= father—mother—children), in an especially superegotistic bourgeois society, especially concerned with "elevation" (or façade), especially opaque to itself. The theater is a very ancient art, one which saw the light in more authentically ceremonial societies, in more integrated human groups (even if sometimes, as in Ancient Greece, the cost of this integration was the rejection into a nonhuman exterior of a whole social category, that of the slaves), in cultures which were in some sense closer to their desire (= paganism): the theater retains something of this deliberate civic tendency toward ludico–liturgical "communion," even in the degraded state of a fashionable rendezvous around those plays known as *pièces de boulevard.*

It is for reasons of this kind too that theatrical voyeurism, less cut off from its exhibitionist correlate, tends more toward a reconciled and community-orientated practice of the scopic perversion (of the component drive). Cinematic voyeurism is less accepted, more "shamefaced."

But it is not just a question of global determinations (by the signifier or by history); there are also the personal efforts of the writers, producers, and actors. Like all general tendencies, the ones I have signaled are unevenly manifest from work to work. There is no need to be surprised that certain films accept their voyeurism more plainly than do certain plays. It is at this point that the problems of political cinema and political theater would come in, and also those of a politics of the cinema and the theater. The militant use of the two signifiers is by no means identical. In this respect the theater is clearly at a great advantage, thanks to its "lesser degree of imaginariness," thanks to the direct contact it allows with the audience. The film which aims to be a film of intervention must take this into account in its self-definition. As we know, this is by no means easy.

The difficulty also lies in the fact that cinematic scopophilia, which is "nonauthorized" in the sense I have just pointed out, is at the same time authorized by the mere fact of its institutionalization. The cinema retains something of the prohibited character peculiar to the vision of the primal scene (the latter is always surprised, never contemplated at leisure, and the permanent cinemas of big cities, with their highly anonymous clientele entering or leaving furtively, in the dark, in the middle of the action, represent this transgression factor rather well)—but also, in a kind of inverse movement which is simply the "reprise" of the imaginary by the symbolic, the cinema is based on the legalization and generalization of the prohibited practice. Thus it shares in miniature in the special regime of certain activities (such as the frequentation of *maisons de tolérance*, very well named in this respect) that are both official and clandestine, and in which neither of these two characteristics ever quite succeeds in obliterating the other. For the vast majority of the audience, the cinema (rather like the dream in this) represents a kind of enclosure or "reserve" which escapes the fully social aspect of life although it is accepted and prescribed by it: going to the cinema is one lawful activity among others with its place in the admissible pastimes of the day or the week, and yet that place is a "hole" in the social cloth, a *loophole* opening on to something slightly more crazy, slightly less approved than what one does the rest of the time.

Theater Fiction, Cinema Fiction

Cinema and theater do not have the same relation to fiction. There is a fictional cinema, just as there is a fictional theater, a "nonfiction" cinema just as there is a nonfiction theater, because fiction is a great historical and social figure (particularly active in our Western tradition and perhaps in others), endowed with a force of its own which leads it to invest various signifiers (and inversely, to be more or less expelled from them on occasion). It does not follow that these signifiers have an even and uniform affinity with it (that of music, after all, finds it particularly uncongenial, and yet there is such a thing as program music). The cinematic signifier lends itself the better to fiction in that it is itself fictive and "absent." Attempts to "defictionalize" the spectacle, notably since Brecht, have gone further in the theater than in the cinema, and not by chance.

But what interests me here is rather the fact that this unevenness is still apparent if one compares only the fictional theater with the fictional cinema. They are not "fictional" in quite the same way, and it was this that I had been struck by in 1965 when I compared the "impression of reality" produced by these two forms of spectacle.[23] At that time my approach was a purely phenomenological one, and it owed very little to psychoanalysis. However, the latter confirms me in my earlier opinion. Underlying all fiction there is a dialectical relationship between a real instance and an imaginary instance, the former's job being to *mimic* the latter: there is the representation, involving real materials and actions, and the represented, the fictional properly speaking. But the balance established between these two poles and hence the precise nuance of the *regime of belief* that the spectator will adopt varies tolerably from one fictional technique to the other. In the cinema as in the theater, the represented is by definition imaginary; that is what characterizes fiction as such, independently of the signifiers in charge of it. But the representation is fully real in the theater, whereas in the cinema it too is imaginary, the material being already a reflection. Thus the theatrical fiction is experienced more—it is only a matter of a different "dosage," of a difference of economy, rather, but that is precisely why it is important—as a set of real pieces of behavior actively directed at the evocation of something unreal, whereas cinematic fiction is experienced rather as the quasi-real presence of that unreal itself; the signifier, already imaginary in its own way, is less palpably so, it plays more into the hands of the diegesis, it tends more to be swallowed up by it, to be credited to its side of the balance sheet by the spectator. The balance is established slightly closer to the represented, slightly further from the representation.

For the same reason, fictional theater tends to depend more on the actor (representer), fictional cinema more on the character (represented). This difference has often been emphasized by the theory of the cinema, where it constitutes an already classical theme. In the psychoanalytic field it has also been noted, by Octave Mannoni in particular.[24] Even when the cinema spectator does identify with the actor rather than with the part (somewhat as he does in the theater), it is with *the actor as "star"*, i.e., still as a character, and a fabulous one, itself fictional: with the best of his parts.

It may be said that there are much simpler reasons for this difference, that in the theater the same part can be interpreted by various actors from one production to another, that the actor thus becomes "detached" from the character, whereas in the cinema there are never several productions (several "casts") for one film, so the part and its unique interpreter are definitively associated with one another. This is quite true, and it does affect the very different balance of forces between actor and character in theater and cinema. But it is not a "simple" fact, nor is it independent of the distance between the respective signifiers; on the contrary, it is but one aspect of that distance (merely a very striking one). If the theatrical part can have a variety of interpreters, that is because its representation is real and mobilizes people who are really present each evening (and who are not therefore necessarily always the same). If the cinematic part is fastened once and for all to its interpreter, it is because its representation involves the reflection of the actor and not the actor himself, and because the reflection (the signifier) is *recorded* and is hence no longer capable of change.

Disavowal, Fetishism

As can be seen, the cinema has a number of roots in the unconscious and in the great movements illuminated by psychoanalysis, but they can all be traced back to the specific characteristics of the institutionalized signifier. I have gone a little way in tracing some of these roots, that of mirror identification, that of voyeurism and exhibitionism. There is also a third, that of fetishism.

Since the famous article by Freud that inaugurated the problem,[25] psychoanalysis has linked fetish and fetishism closely with castration and the fear it inspires. Castration, for Freud, and even more clearly for Lacan, is first of all the mother's castration, and that is why the main figures it inspires are to a certain degree common to children of both sexes. The child who sees its mother's body is constrained by way of perception, by the "evidence of the senses," to accept that there are human beings deprived of a penis. But for a long time—and somewhere in it forever—it will not interpret this inevitable observation in terms of an anatomical difference between the sexes (= penis/vagina). It believes that all human beings originally have a penis and it therefore understands what it has seen as the effect of a mutilation which redoubles its fear that it will be subjected to a similar fate (or else, in the case of the little girl after a certain age, the fear that she has already been subjected to it). Inversely, it is this very terror that is projected on to the spectacle of the mother's body, and invites the reading of an absence where anatomy sees a different conformation. The scenario of castration, in its broad lines, does not differ whether one understands it, like Lacan, as an essentially symbolic drama in which castration takes over in a decisive metaphor all the losses, both real and imaginary, that the child has already suffered (birth trauma, maternal breast, excrement, etc.), or whether on the contrary one tends, like Freud, to take that scenario slightly more literally. Before this *unveiling of a lack* (we are already close to the cinema signifier), the child, in order to avoid too strong an anxiety, will have to double up its belief (another cinematic characteristic) and from then on forever hold two contradictory opinions (proof that in spite of everything the real perception has not been without effect): "All human beings are endowed with a penis" (primal belief) and "Some human beings do not have a penis" (evidence of the senses). In other words, it will, perhaps definitively, retain its former belief *beneath* the new one, but it will also hold to its new perceptual observation while *disavowing* it on another level (= denial of perception, disavowal, Freud's *Verleugnung*). Thus is established the lasting matrix, the affective prototype of all the splittings of belief which man will henceforth be capable of in the most varied domains, of all the infinitely complex unconscious and occasionally conscious interactions which he will allow himself between "believing" and "not believing" and which will on more than one occasion be of great assistance to him in resolving (or denying) delicate problems. (If we were all a little honest with ourselves, we would realize that a truly integral belief, without any "underside" in which the opposite is believed, would make even the most ordinary everyday life almost impossible.)

At the same time, the child, terrified by what it has seen or glimpsed, will have tried more or less successfully in different cases, to *arrest* its look, for all its life, at what will subsequently become the fetish: at a piece of clothing, for example, which masks the frightening discovery, or else precedes it (underwear, stockings, boots, etc.). The fixation on this "just before" is thus another form of disavowal, of retreat from the perceived, although its very existence is dia- lectical evidence of the fact that the perceived has been perceived. The fetishistic prop will become a precondition for the establishment of potency and access to orgasm *[jouissance]*, sometimes an indispensable precondition (true fetishism); in other developments it will only be a favorable condition, and one whose weight will vary with respect to the other features of the erotogenic situation as a whole. (It can be observed once again that the defense against desire itself becomes erotic, as the defense against anxiety itself becomes anxiogenic; for an analogous reason: what arises "against" an affect also arises "in" it and is not easily separated from it, even if that is its aim.) Fetishism is generally regarded as the "perversion" par excellence, for it intervenes itself in the "tabulation" of the others, and above all because they, like it (and this is what makes it their model), are based on the avoidance of castration. The fetish always represents the penis, it is always a substitute for it, whether metaphorically (= it masks its absence) or metonymically (= it is contiguous with its empty place). To sum up, the fetish signifies the penis as absent, it is its negative signifier; supple- menting it, it puts a "fullness" in place of a lack, but in doing so it also affirms that lack. It resumes within itself the structure of disavowal and multiple belief.

These few reminders are intended above all to emphasize the fact that the dossier of fetishism, before any examination of its cinematic extensions, contains two broad aspects which coincide in their depths (in childhood and by virtue of structure) but are relatively distinct in their concrete manifestations, i.e., the problems of belief (= disavowal) and that of the fetish itself, the latter more immediately linked to erotogenicity, whether direct or sublimated.

Structures of Belief

I shall say very little about the problems of belief in the cinema. First because they are at the center of my article "The Fiction Film and Its Spectator" included in the book *The Imaginary Signifier.* Second because I have already discussed them in this part apropos of identification and the mirror: I have tried to describe, outside the special case of fiction, a few of the many and successive twists, the "reversals" (reduplications) that occur in the cinema to articulate together the imaginary, the symbolic, and the real; each of these twists presupposes a division of belief; in order to work, the film does not only require a splitting, but a whole series of stages of belief, imbricated together into a chain by a remarkable machinery. In the third place, because the subject has already been largely dealt with by Octave Mannoni in his remarkable studies of the theatrical illusion,[26] with reference to the fictional theater. Of course, I have said above that theatrical fiction and cinematic fiction are not fictional in the same way; but this deviation concerned the representation, the signifying material and not the represented, i.e., the fiction-fact as such, in which the deviation is much smaller (at any rate so long as one is dealing with *spectacles* such as theater and cinema—written fiction obviously presents somewhat different problems). Mannoni's analyses are just as valid for the fiction film, with the single reservation that the divergences in representation that I have already discussed are borne in mind (at the end of the chapter on the passion for perceiving).

I shall rest content to adapt these analyses to a cinematic perspective, and not feel obliged to repeat them (not so well) in detail. It is understood that the audience is not duped by the diegetic illusion, it "knows" that the screen presents no more than a fiction. And yet, it is of vital importance for the correct unfolding of the spectacle that this make-believe be scrupulously respected (or else the fiction film is declared "poorly made"), that everything is set to work to make the deception effective and to give it an air of truth (this is the problem of *verisimilitude*). Any spectator will tell you that he "doesn't believe it," but everything happens as if there were nonetheless someone to be deceived, someone who really would "believe in it." (I shall say that behind any fiction there is a second fiction: the diegetic events are fictional, that is the first; but everyone pretends to believe that they are true, and that is the second; there is even a third: the general refusal to admit that somewhere in oneself one believes they are genuinely true.) In other words, asks Mannoni, since it is "accepted" that the audience is incredulous, *who is it who is credulous* and must be maintained in his credulousness by the perfect organization of the machinery (of the machination)? This credulous person is, of course, another part of ourselves, he is still seated *beneath* the incredulous one, or in his heart, it is he who continues to believe, who disavows what he knows (he for whom all human beings are still endowed with a penis). But by a symmetrical and simultaneous movement, the incredulous person disavows the credulous one; no one will admit that he is duped by the "plot." That is why the instance of credulousness is often projected into the outer world and constituted as a separate person, a person completely abused by the diegesis: thus in Corneille's *L'Illusion comique,* a play with a significant title, the character Pridamant, the *naïf,* who does not know what theater is, and *for whom,* by a reversal foreseen in Corneille's plot itself, the representation of the play is given. By a partial identification with this character, the spectators can sustain their credulousness in all incredulousness.

This instance which believes and also its personified projection have fairly precise equivalents in the cinema: for example, the credulous spectators at the *"Grand Café"* in 1895, frequently and complacently evoked by the incredulous spectators who have come *later* (and are no longer children), those spectators of 1895 who fled their seats in terror when the train entered La Ciotat station (in Lumière's famous film), because they were afraid it would run them down. Or else, in so many films, the character of the "dreamer"—the sleeping dreamer—who during the film believed (as we did!) that it was true, whereas it was he who saw it all in a dream and who wakes up at the end of the film (as we do again). Octave Mannoni compares these switches of belief with those the ethnologist observes in certain populations in which his informers regularly declare that "long ago we used to believe in the masks" (these masks are used to deceive children, like our Father Christmas, and adolescents learn at their initiation ceremonies that the "masks" were in fact adults in disguise); in other words, these societies have always "believed" in the masks, but have always relegated this belief to a "long ago": they still believe in them, but always in the aorist tense (like everyone). This "long ago" is childhood, when one really was duped by masks; among adults, the beliefs of "long ago" irrigate the unbelief of today, but irrigate it by denegation (one could also say: by *delegation,* by attributing credulity to the child and to former times).

Certain cinematic subcodes inscribe disavowal into the film in the form of less permanent and more localized figures. They should be studied separately in this perspective. I am not thinking only of films which have been "dreamt" in their entirety by one of their characters, but also of all the sequences accompanied by a "voice-off" commentary, spoken sometimes by a character, sometimes by a kind of anonymous "speaker." This voice, precisely a voice "off," beyond jurisdiction, represents the rampart of unbelief (hence it is the opposite of the Pridamant character, yet has the same effect in the last analysis). The distance it establishes between the action and ourselves comforts our feeling that we are not duped by that action: thus reassured (behind the rampart), we can allow ourselves to be duped by it a big longer (it is the speciality of naive distanciations to resolve themselves into alibis). There are also those "films within a film" which downgear the mechanism of our belief-unbelief and anchor it in several stages, hence more strongly: the included film was an illusion, so the including film (the film as such) was not, or was somewhat less so.[27]

The Cinema as Technique

As for the fetish itself, in its cinematic manifestations, who could fail to see that it consists fundamentally of the equipment of the cinema (= its "technique"), or of the cinema as a whole as equipment and as technique, for fiction films and others? It is no accident that in the cinema some cameramen, some directors, some critics, some spectators demonstrate a real "fetishism of technique," often noted or denounced as such ("fetishism" is taken here in its ordinary sense, which is rather loose but does contain within it the analytical sense that I shall attempt to disengage). As strictly defined, the fetish, like the apparatus of the cinema, is a *prop,* the prop that disavows a lack and in doing so affirms it without wishing to. A prop, too, which is, as it were, placed on the body of the object; a prop which is the penis, since it negates its absence, and hence a partial object that makes the whole object lovable and desirable. The fetish is also the point of departure for specialized practices, and as is well known, desire in its modalities is all the more "technical" the more perverse it is.

Thus, with respect to the desired body—to the body of desire rather—the fetish is in the same position as the technical equipment of the cinema with respect to the cinema as a whole. A fetish, the cinema as a technical performance, as prowess, as an *exploit,* an exploit that underlines and denounces the lack on which the whole arrangement is based (the absence of the object, replaced by its reflection), an exploit which consists at the same time of making this absence forgotten. The cinema fetishist is the person who is enchanted at what the machine is capable of, at the *theater of shadows* as such. For the establishment of his full potency for cinematic enjoyment *[jouisssance]* he must think at every moment (and above all *simultaneously*) of the force of presence the film has and of the absence on which this force is constructed.[28] He must constantly compare the result with the means deployed (and hence pay attention to the technique), for his pleasure lodges in the gap between the two. Of course, this attitude appears most clearly in the "connoisseur," the cinephile, but it also occurs, as a partial component of cinematic pleasure, in those who just go to the cinema: if they do go it is partly in order to be carried away by the film (or the fiction, if there is one), but also in order to *appreciate* as such the machinery that is carrying them away: they will say, precisely when they have been carried away, that the film was a "good" one, that it was "well made" (the same thing is said in French of a harmonious body).

It is clear that fetishism, in the cinema as elsewhere, is closely linked to the good object. The function of the fetish is to restore the latter, threatened in its "goodness" (in Melanie Klein's sense) by the terrifying discovery of the lack. Thanks to the fetish, which covers the wound and itself becomes erotogenic, the object as a whole can become desirable again without excessive fear. In a similar way, the whole cinematic institution is, as it were, *covered* by a thin and omnipresent garment, a stimulating prop through which it is consumed: the ensemble of its equipment and its tricks—and not just the celluloid strip, the *pellicule* or "little skin" which has been rightly mentioned in this connection[29]—of the equipment which *needs* the lack in order to stand out in it by contrast, but which only affirms it insofar as it ensures that it is forgotten, and which lastly (its third twist) needs it also not to be forgotten, for fear that at the same stroke the fact that *it* caused it to be forgotten will be forgotten.

The fetish is the cinema in its *physical* state. A fetish is always material: insofar as one can make up for it by the power of the symbolic alone one is precisely no longer a fetishist. At this point it is important to recall that of all the arts the cinema is the one that involves the most extensive and complex equipment; the "technical" dimension is more obtrusive here than elsewhere. Along with television, it is the only art that is also an industry, or at least is so from the outset (the others become industries subsequently: music through the gramophone record or the cassette, books by mass printings and publishing trusts, etc.) In this respect only architecture is a little like it; there are "languages" that are *heavier* than others, more dependent on "hardware."

At the same time as it localizes the penis, the fetish represents by synecdoche the whole body of the object as desirable. Similarly, interest in the equipment and technique is the privileged representative of *love for the cinema*.

The Law is what permits desire: the cinematic equipment is the instance thanks to which the imaginary turns into the symbolic, thanks to which the lost object (the absence of what is filmed) becomes the law and the principle of a specific and instituted signifier, which it is legitimate to desire.

For in the structure of the fetish there is another point on which Mannoni quite rightly insists and which directly concerns my present undertaking. Because it attempts to disavow the evidence of the senses, the fetish is evidence that this evidence has indeed been *recorded* (like a tape stored in the memory). The fetish is not inaugurated because the child still believes its mother has a penis (= order of the imaginary), for if it still believed it completely, as "before," it would no longer need the fetish. It is inaugurated because the child now "knows very well" that its mother has no penis. In other words, the fetish not only has disavowal value, but also *knowledge value*.

That is why, as I said a moment ago, the fetishism of cinematic technique is especially well developed among the "connoisseurs" of the cinema. That is also why the theoretician of the cinema necessarily retains within him—at the cost of a new backward turn that leads him to interrogate technique, to symbolize the fetish, and hence to maintain it as he dissolves it—an interest in the equipment without which he would not be motivated to study it.

Indeed, the equipment is not just physical (= the fetish proper); it also has its discursive imprints, its extensions in the very text of the film. Here is revealed the specific movement of theory: when it shifts from a fascination with technique to the critical study of the different *codes* that this equipment authorizes. *Concern for the signifier* in the cinema derives from a fetishism that has taken up a position as far as possible along its cognitive flank. To adapt the formula by which Octave Mannoni defines disavowal (= "I know very well, but all the same . . ."), the study of the signifier is a libidinal position which consists in weakening the "but all the same" and profiting by this saving of energy to dig deeper into the "I know very well," which thus becomes "I know nothing at all, but I desire to know."

Fetish and Frame

Just like the other psychical structures that constitute the foundation of the cinema, fetishism does not intervene only in the constitution of the signifier but also in certain of its more particular configurations. Here we have *framings* and also certain *camera movements* (the latter can anyway be defined as progressive changes in framing).

Cinema with directly erotic subject matter deliberately plays on the edges of the frame and the progressive if need be incomplete revelations allowed by the camera as it moves, and this is no accident. Censorship is involved here: censorship of films and censorship in Freud's sense. Whether the form is static (framing) or dynamic (camera movements), the principle is the same; the point is to gamble simultaneously on the excitation of desire and its nonfulfilment (which is its opposite and yet favors it), by the infinite variations made possible precisely by the studios' technique on the exact emplacement of the *boundary* that bars the look, that puts an end to the "seen," that inaugurates the downward (or upward) tilt into the dark, toward the unseen, the guessed-at. The framing and its displacements (that determine the *emplacement*) are in themselves forms of "suspense" and are extensively used in suspense films, though they retain this function in other cases. They have an inner affinity with the mechanisms of desire, its postponements, its new impetus, and they retain this affinity in other places than erotic sequences (the only difference lies in the *quantum* which is sublimated and the *quantum* which is not). The way the cinema, with its wandering framings (wandering like the look, like the caress), finds the means to reveal space has something to do with a kind of permanent undressing, a generalized striptease, a less direct but more perfected striptease, since it also makes it possible to dress space again, to remove from view what it has previously shown, to *take back* as well as to retain (like the child at the moment of the birth of the fetish, the child who has already seen, but whose look beats a rapid retreat): a striptease pierced with "flashbacks," inverted sequences that then give new impetus to the forward movement. These veiling-unveiling procedures can also be compared with certain cinematic "punctuations," especially slow ones strongly marked by a concern for control and expectation (slow fade-ins and fade-outs, irises, "drawn out" lap-dissolves like those of Sternberg.)[30]

"Theorize," he says . . . (Provisional Conclusion)

The psychoanalytic constitution of the cinema signifier is a very wide problem, one containing, so to speak, a number of "panels." I cannot examine them all here, and there will surely be some that I have not even mentioned.

However, something tells me that (for the present) I can stop here. I wanted to give a first idea of the field I perceive and, to begin with, to assure myself that I was indeed perceiving it (I was not certain of it all at once).

Now I shall turn back on this study itself as an unfolding of my initial dream. Psychoanalysis does not illuminate only the film, but also the conditions of desire of whoever makes himself its theoretician. Interwoven into every analytical undertaking is the thread of a self-analysis.

I have loved the cinema, I no longer love it, I still love it. What I have wished to do in these pages is to keep at a distance, as in the scopic practice I have discussed, that which in me (= in everyone) *can* love it: to retain it as *questioned*. As questioning, too, for in wishing to construct the film into an object of knowledge one extends, by a supplementary degree of sublimation, the passion for seeing that made the cinephile and the institution themselves. Initially an undivided passion, entirely occupied in preserving the cinema as a good object (imaginary passion, passion for the imaginary), it subsequently splits into two diverging and reconverging desires, one of which "looks" at the other; this is the theoretical break, and like all breaks it is also a link: that of theory with its object.

I have used words like "love of the cinema." I hope I will have been understood. The point is not to restrict them to their usual meaning, the meaning suggested by "archive rats" or fanatical "Macmahonites" (who provide no more than exaggerated examples). Nor is the point to relapse into the absurd opposition between the affective and the intellectual. The point is to ask why many people go to the cinema when they are not obliged to, how they manage to "assimilate" the rules of this game which is exceedingly complex and historically fairly new, how they themselves become cogs of the instutition. For anyone who asks this question, "loving the cinema" and "understanding film" are no more than two closely mingled aspects of one vast sociopsychical machinery.

As for the person who looks at this machine itself (the theoretician who desires to know it), I have said that he was necessarily sadistic. There is no sublimation, as Freud himself insisted, without "defusion of the drives." The good object has moved to the side of knowledge and the cinema becomes a bad object (a dual displacement which makes it easy for "science" to stand back). The cinema is "persecuted," but this persistence is also a reparation (the knowing posture is both aggressive and depressive), a reparation of the specific kind, peculiar to the semiologist; the *restoration* to the theoretical body of what has been taken from the *institution,* from the code which is being "studied."

To study the cinema: what an odd formula! How can it be done without "breaking" its beneficial image, all that idealism about film as an "art" full and simple, the seventh of the name? By breaking the toy one loses it, and that is the position of the semiotic discourse; it feeds on this loss, it puts in its place the hoped for advance of knowledge: it is an inconsolable discourse that consoles itself, that takes itself by the hand and goes to work. Lost objects are the only ones one is afraid to lose, and the semiologist is he who rediscovers them *from the other side: "Il n'y a de cause que de ce qui cloche"*—"there is a cause only in something that doesn't work."[31]

Notes

Translator's notes in brackets.

1. If I see this division as a deliberate simplification (but perhaps that is precisely why it is useful), this is for various reasons, two of which are more important than the rest: (1) psychoanalysis has not introduced only the idea of the primary process, but also the very distinction between the primary and the secondary (hence it has "refounded" the secondary); (2) inversely, certain linguists, such as Emile Benveniste, for example, in his studies of personal pronouns, go beyond the study of the pure "statement" and through their reflections on the enunciation enter on a road which leads closer to the "primary," to the constitution of the subject, etc.

2. Lacan: "The order of the symbol can no longer be conceived as constituted by man, but rather as constituting him," translated from "Le Séminaire sur 'La Lettre volée,' " *Ecrits* (Paris: Editions du Seuil, 1966), p. 46.

3. E.g. Lévi-Strauss: myths think themselves out among themselves.

4. See Benveniste's notion that, in a sense, it is *langue* that "contains" society rather than the reverse; "Sémiologie de la langue," *Problémes de linguistique générale* (Paris: Gallimard, 1974), 2:62.

5. It will be remembered that this is what Stalin said of language. Lacan recalls it maliciously; "The Agency of the Letter in the Unconscious," *Ecrits: A Selection*, trans. A. Sheridan (London: Tavistock, 1977), p. 176, note 7.

6. L. Séve, *Marxisme et théorie de la personnalité*, Editions Sociales, 1969, p. 200. A juxtastructural phenomenon differs from a superstructural phenomenon in two respects: (1) it is not exactly a *consequence* of the "base" since it forms part of it, in addition to the strictly infrastructural determinations; and (2) it represents the biological element in man: as such it is distinct from the "social base" and "as it were *laterally engaged* with it."

7. Lacan, "Le Temps logique et l'assertion de certitude anticipée," *Ecrits*, pp. 197–213.

8. Freud, "The Ego and the Id," 19:26, 30 (on "desexualized social sentiment"); see also (on the subject of paranoia) "On Narcissism: An Introduction," 14:95–96, 101–2. [All references to Freud's work in this essay are references to J. Strachey, ed., *Standard Edition of the Complete Psychological Works of Sigmund Freud* (London: Hogarth, 1953–66.)]

9. Jean-Louis Baudry, "Cinéma: effets idéologique produit par l'appareil de base," *Cinéthique* (1970), nos. 7–8, pp. 1–8, translated as "Ideological Effects of the Basic Cinematographic Apparatus," *Film Quarterly* (1974–75) 28(2):39–47; "Le Dispositif: Approches métapsychologiques de l'impression de réalité," *Communications* (1975) 23:56–72, translated as "The Apparatus," *Camera Obscura* (1976), no. 1, pp. 104–26. [These articles are included in this anthology— ED.]

10. [*Derrière la tête* means "at the back of one's mind" as well as "behind one's head."] See André Green, "L'Ecran bi-face, un oeil derrière la tête," *Psychoanalyse et cinéma*, January 1, 1970 (no further issues appeared), pp. 15–22. It will be clear that in the passage that follows my analysis coincides in places with that of André Green.

11. Freud, "The Ego and the Id," 19:18; *The Interpretation of Dreams*, 5:615 (= consciousness as a sense organ) and 574 (= consciousness as a dual recording surface, internal and external);

"The Unconscious," 14:171 (psychical processes are in themselves unconscious, consciousness is a function that *perceives* a small proportion of them), etc.

12. Merleau–Ponty, "The Film and the New Psychology," lecture to the Institut des Hautes Etudes Cinématographiques (March 13, 1945), translated in *Sense and Nonsense* (Evanston, Ill.: Northwestern University Press, 1964), pp. 48–59.

13. See section 2 of Christian Metz, "Current Problems of Film Theory," *Screen* (1973), 14(1–2): 45–49.

14. On these problems see Michel Colin, "Le Film: Transformation du texte du roman," unpublished thesis (Mémoire de troisième cycle), 1974.

15. Freud, *Inhibitions, Symptoms, and Anxiety*, 20:87–88.

16. See especially Lacan, *The Four Fundamental Concepts of Psycho-Analysis*, trans A. Sheridan (London: Hogarth Press, 1977), pp. 180 and 195–96.

17. Freud, "Repression," 14:146–47; "Instincts and Their Vicissitudes," 14:122 and 134 note; "The Ego and the Id," 19:30; "On Narcissism: An Introduction," 14:94, etc.

18. More precisely: lending themselves through their peculiar characteristics to a perversion which is not the drive itself but the subject's position with respect to it (Lacan, *The Four Fundamental Concepts*, pp. 181–83). Remember that for Freud as well as for Lacan, the drive is always "componential" (the child is polymorphously perverse, etc.).

19. Freud, "Instincts and their Vicissitudes," 14:129–30.

20. *Ibid.*, 14:138.

21. Lacan, *The Four Fundamental Concepts*, pp. 167–168.

22. See the paragraph with this title in Jean François Lyotard's article "L'Acinéma," *Revue d'Esthétique* (1973) nos. 2–4, pp. 357–69 [included in this anthology—ED.]

23. C. Metz, "On the Impression of Reality in the Cinema," in *Essais sur la signification au cinéma*, vol. I (Paris: Klincksieck, 1968), translated as *Film Language: A Semiotics of the Cinema*, trans. M. Taylor (New York: Oxford University Press, 1974).

24. See O. Mannoni, "L'Illusion comique ou le théâtre du point de vue de l'imaginaire," in *Clefs pour l'imaginaire ou l'autre scène* (Paris: Seuil, 1969), p. 180.

25. Freud, "Fetishism," 21:152–57. See also Octave Mannoni's important study, "Je sais bien, mais quand même. . ." [I know very well, but all the same. . .], in *Clefs pour l'imaginaire ou l'autre scène.*

26. Mannoni, "L'Illusion comique ou le théâtre du point de vue de l'imaginaire."

27. A startling (though only partial) resemblance to the case of "dreams within a dream"; see Freud, *The Interpretation of Dreams*, 4:338.

28. I have studied this phenomenon at slightly greater length in "Trucage et cinéma" in *Essais sur la signification au cinéma* (Paris: Klincksieck, 1972), 2:173–92.

29. Roger Dadoun, " 'King Kong'; du monstre comme démonstration," *Littérature* (1972), 8:109; Octave Mannoni, *Clefs pour l'imaginaire ou l'autre scène*, p. 180.

30. Reading this article in manuscript, Thierry Kuntzel has pointed out to me that in this paragraph I perhaps lean slightly too far toward fetishism and fetishism alone in discussing filmic figures that depend just as much on *cinematic perversion* in general: the hypertrophy of the perceptual component drive with its mises-en-scène, its progressions/retentions, its calculated postponements, etc. This objection seems to me (after the event) to be correct. I shall have to come back to it. Fetishism, as is well known, is closely linked to perversion, although it does not exhaust it. Hence the difficulty. For the cinematic effects I am evoking here (playing on the framing and its displacements), the properly fetishistic element seems to me to be the *bar*, the edge of the screen, the separation between the seen and the unseen, the "arrestation" of the look.

Once the seen or the unseen are envisaged rather than their intersection (their edge), we are dealing with scopic perversion itself, which goes beyond the strict province of the fetish.

31. Lacan, *The Four Fundamental Concepts,* p. 22. [Lacan contrasts a *cause,* as an occult property, with a law, in which "causes" are smoothly absorbed as variables in a function; the unconscious, however, will remain a cause in the occult sense, because its order exceeds any particular function; it is the Law rather than a law, *enunciation* rather than *statement,* *"lalangue"* rather than a *langue*—hence its privileged manifestation in the lapse, the mistake, the point at which discourse "limps".]

—translated by Ben Brewster

Part Three

Apparatus

Introduction

In part 2 theorization of the position of the spectating subject was presented mainly in relation to films organized as narratives. This was in part because narrative structure and processes continue to be of central interest to many film theorists working on subject-positioning. It might also be noted that clearly, the development of the opposition between classical (or at least mainstream) fictional film and nonclassical cinema is not necessarily suppressed by this focus. However, there is another emphasis concerning the positioning of the subject which makes the question of oppositional textual forms even more difficult: what has been called the question of "the cinematic apparatus."

Are there subject effects specific to cinema, to the kind of machine it is, to the kind of viewing situation it generally involves? In "Ellipsis on Dread and the Specular Seduction," in part 2, Kristeva suggested that cinema might have a special relation to "specular fascination." In "The Imaginary Signifier" Metz outlined a number of specifics of the film viewing situation—the theater is dark, the projector is behind the spectator, the image is framed (cf. Barthes' "Diderot, Brecht, Eisenstein"), etc.; and these were said in themselves to have implications for the positionality of the spectator. To what extent, then, is spectatorial position already determined by the machinery of cinema? Are there ideological and psychic determinants and/or implications in that machinery? Such questions were raised throughout the time that the articles in the last part were produced; indeed, Metz himself was openly influenced by investigations into such issues when he wrote "The Imaginary Signifier."

The conceptual framework used to discuss these questions has generally been similar to that introduced in the previous parts of this collection; hence, the metalanguage tends to be from semiotics, psychoanalysis, and the theory of ideology. What we might briefly highlight here is a central issue which such studies raise, and we shall put that issue as harshly as possible: are there genuine, radical variational or oppositional possibilities? If the cinematic machinery in itself is treated as a *necessary* manifestation of certain kinds of subjective positioning, or as *necessarily* imbued with a certain ideology of vision and visual representation, then to that extent it becomes more difficult to conceive of oppositional practices in a film.

The difficulty is that the apparatus itself in any of its uses will carry the baggage of complicity along with it; it might even be argued that at such levels questions of textuality become moot. This will happen if the investigation of subject-positioning and the specular are too strongly localized in the machinery which subtends any use of cinema. The implications can be debilitating for both film theory and film practice. Suppose, for example, that specularity is thought to be a necessary aspect of the cinematic apparatus, and that such specularity is then described from a feminist perspective which adduces a necessary link between visual pleasure and male scopic perversions, which are therefore said to shape the organization of visual representation in patriarchal sociocultural formations. Does this mean that *any* filming of a female body is ideologically suspect?[1]

What emerges in such a harsh formulation are two separate regimes of subject construction: that of the apparatus itself, and that of signifying processes (often especially those of narrative) which to a large degree operate beyond cinema (e.g., storytelling existed long before film and endures in many other media). If the first is in effective operation, and the second as it is manifested in films must always be supported by the first, does the second ultimately matter? In fact, there are many ways of arguing that it does. For example, one can propose that certain kinds of deployment of narrative can be set in contradiction to the tendencies of apparatus, as Kristeva does at the end of "Ellipsis on Dread and the Specular Seduction." The critique of the apparatus from the viewpoint of subject construction need not lead to a reduction wherein the filmic apparatus is considered *only* in terms of its fundamental machinery. Rather, what would be necessary is an investigation of the joining, the "articulation" of that fundamental machinery with various regimes of signification (see Stephen Heath's "Narrative Space" in part 4, for example.)

For what has to be kept in mind is the impulse which leads to the study of "the" apparatus. The purpose is not to instantiate some kind of simplistic technological determinism. Most of the prominent theorists who have written in this area have been concerned precisely with the *junctures* of film and culture. That is, they have been concerned with the cultural determinations which produce the cinematic apparatus, and, inversely, how and why certain realms of representation serve as components of sociocultural formations. In that case, to see the apparatus as determinant in itself misses the point of the entire project. That point is precisely the apparatus as a conjuncture of determinants and effectivities, one nodal point of a social construction of knowledge, desire, pleasure, signifying adequacies, etc. Thus, as often as not, when the apparatus is theorized, the writer will have in mind not simply "the cinema machine" in a literal sense (e.g., the basic camera-projector mechanism), but this literal machine in the context of a larger social and/or cultural and/or institutional "machine," for which the former is only a point of convergence of several lines of force of the latter. (It is also possible that some distinctions may have been blurred by translations from French which have rendered both *appareil* [apparatus in the sense of machine, mechanisms] and *dispositif* [apparatus in the more general sense of device, arrangement, disposition] into English as "apparatus.")

Perhaps this is only to insist that a critique of totality, discussed elsewhere in these introductions, would apply also to the conceptualization of the cinematic apparatus. If one investigates the apparatus by outlining the spectatorial ideals of a certain technology of representation—its aspirations, as it were, for the subject—this is not the same as finding an automatically and universally efficacious implementation of those ideals. To theorize the apparatus is not necessarily to depict the continuous territory of an ontology of cinema in all its totalizing effectivity. Instead, it can be to map an element of the often rocky and disjunctive terrain on which we find and construct both the history of signification in general and the history of filmic signification in particular.

Finally, this might be the place to note that theoretical approaches concerned with subject, narrative, apparatus, signification, etc. do not necessarily ignore classical film theory. Older debates can often be taken up but with new premises and often in radical disagreement with some of the previous ways the issues were posed. For example, issues of cinematic specificity are not treated as problems of essence or aesthetic purity, but rather as questions of the particularity of film's participation in generalized semiotic, social, and/or psychoanalytic processes. If all representational entities appeal in some way to the spectator's self-recognition, then what is it, Metz asked in "The Imaginary Signifier," that cinema does in this respect which no other signifying practice does in quite the same way? To take another example, André Bazin's treatment of the historical development of cinema as based on a natural, unavoidable spectatorial desire to invest faith in the reality (i.e., the referential validity) of the image receives a kind of answer from writers such as Jean-Louis Baudry (in this part) and Jean-Louis Comolli (see part 4). They also find a desire to believe in the image, but they explain the development and utilization of the cinematic apparatus on the basis of an "ideology of the visible." Instead of describing cinema as a response to a natural human desire, they describe a cinematic apparatus which participates in the psychic and social construction of spectators whose subjectivity is then reconfirmed by belief in the image.

The articles grouped together in part 3 include influential presentations of the conception of "the apparatus" in relation to the theory of the subject. This group of articles also includes considerations of questions of opposition, and the relation of text and textual strategies to cinema as apparatus.

If there is a single most influential writer on cinema as apparatus, it is undoubtedly Jean-Louis Baudry. Two of his articles are republished here. The first, "Ideological Effects of the Basic Cinematographic Apparatus," is one which influenced Metz's conception of primary cinematic identification. Baudry considers the image-making methods and capacities of the cinematic machine *(l'appareil)* not only in the context of a psychoanalytic framework but also in light of some objectives of idealist philosophy epitomized in Husserl. It is this connection which allows him to analyze the apparatus ideologically.

In "The Apparatus: Metapsychological Approaches to the Impression of Reality in the Cinema," Baudry approaches the referential effect of cinema as an aspect of the viewing situation, elaborating a comparison of it with the scene of representation as presented by Plato, taken as exemplary of idealist philosophy. He reads Plato's scene through Freud and into the cinematic apparatus *(le dispositif)*. Baudry proposes that the cinematic "reality effect," which has elicited so much commentary, can be considered as a subject effect rooted in regression, in the psychoanalytic sense of that term.

The sound track has undoubtedly received less attention in studies of the apparatus and theoretical tendencies affected by such studies. Reasons for this neglect include the fact that film theory has traditionally evinced more interest in image than in sound (there are undoubtedly symptomatic, historical reasons for this); and that psychoanalytic conceptions of the subject tend to appeal to scenarios of vision and investigate, precisely, the *specular*. There has nevertheless been increasing attention to the sound track. Some of the major issues raised by the sound track in this context are indicated by two articles included here.

In "The Silences of the Voice," Pascal Bonitzer begins from a consideration of the voice in documentaries and news reporting, focusing especially on voice-over commentary; as he does this, he also sketches out some implications of his argument in relation to narrative and the apparatus. His central concern is the heterogeneity which sound potentially embodies in relation to the fascinating specularity of the image. How is that heterogeneity contained, when the existence of voice-off is evidence of an appeal of knowledge that can be radically separate from the reality-effect of the image? What are the consequences for the conceptualization of subject-positioning and a politically militant use of documentary and cinema in general? Bonitzer argues that the cinematic apparatus is deployed not simply as image and sound, but in such a way that it is dominated by the look and the voice.

In "The Voice in the Cinema: The Articulation of Body and Space," Mary Ann Doane considers sound with special attention to a psychoanalytic conception of the attraction of unity—as a phantasmatic image of bodily perfection. Her aim is a theoretical understanding of relations of sound and image, and their relation to the pleasure of the spectator in dominant cinema. After a discussion whose major focus is also the voice, she concludes by marking out difficulties and opportunities for oppositional practices from a feminist perspective.

In "Acinema," Jean-François Lyotard begins from a more or less traditional definition of cinema as "the inscription of movement." He then proceeds to a theorization of the pleasure of representational and narrative art forms, focusing attention on the Freudian conception of the dialectic between the drives (potentially dispersive) and identity (unifying). He then conceptualizes an "acinema," an oppositional formation which situates itself at the two extremes (extreme mobility and extreme immobility). As does Doane, Lyotard starkly poses a crucial question for any oppositional cinema—its relation to totality and pleasure.

Teresa de Lauretis's "Through the Looking-Glass" was a response to an international conference on the cinematic apparatus which took place in 1978. She takes a critical perspective toward two central pressure points in the juncture of semiotics and the study of cinema: the Saussurian tendency in semiotics and the place allotted to women and female subjectivity in psychoanalytic and ideological/cultural theories. De Lauretis highlights the danger that theories mobilized to deal with dominant cinema as norm ultimately may capitulate to it; given, for example, the phallocentric emphases of Freudian and Lacanian psychoanalyses, to what extent could they ever provide the basis for an account of nonphallocentric representation? To what extent can transformation be imagined on the basis of a semiotics which sees the signifier as determinant and the signifying system as always already in place? She is not necessarily arguing for the abandonment of the issues as they are posed by this kind of theory, but for the development of these questions in new ways. She thus provides a properly distanced summary of many of the issues raised around questions of the subject and the apparatus.

Note

1. This extreme example is drawn from discussion at an international conference on the cinematic apparatus held in 1978. It is recorded in Teresa de Lauretis and Stephen Heath, eds., *The Cinematic Apparatus* (London: Macmillan, 1980). See the remarks by the filmmaker and theoretician Peter Gidal on p. 169.

16

Jean-Louis Baudry
Ideological Effects of the Basic
Cinematographic Apparatus

At the end of *The Interpretation of Dreams,* when he seeks to integrate dream
elaboration and its particular "economy" with the psyche as a whole, Freud
assigns to the latter an optical model: "Let us simply imagine the instrument
which serves in psychic productions as a sort of complicated microscope or
camera." But Freud does not seem to hold strongly to this optical model, which,
as Derrida has pointed out,[1] brings out the shortcomings of graphic representation in the area earlier covered by his work on dreams. Moreover, he will later
abandon the optical model in favor of a writing instrument, the "mystic writing
pad." Nonetheless, this optical choice seems to prolong the tradition of Western
science, whose birth coincides exactly with the development of the optical
apparatus which will have as a consequence the decentering of the human
universe, the end of geocentrism (Galileo).

But also, and paradoxically, the optical apparatus camera obscura will serve
in the same period to elaborate in pictorial work a new mode of representation,
perspectiva artificialis. This system, recentering or at least displacing the center
(which settles itself in the eye), will ensure the setting up of the "subject"[2] as the
active center and origin of meaning. One could doubtless question the privileged
position which optical instruments seem to occupy on the line of intersection
of science and ideological productions. Does the technical nature of optical
instruments, directly attached to scientific practice, serve to conceal not only
their use in ideological products but also the ideological effects which they may

Published in *Cinéthique,* (1970), nos. 7–8 and used here by permission of the author. Translation
© 1974 by the Regents of the University of California; reprinted from *Film Quarterly* (Winter
1974–75), 28(2):39–47, by permission of the Regents.

themselves provoke? Their scientific base would ensure them a sort of neutrality and help to avoid their being questioned.

But already a question: if we are to take account of the imperfections of these instruments, their limitations, by what criteria may these be defined? If, for example, one can speak of a restricted depth of field as a limitation, doesn't this term itself depend on a particular conception of reality for which such a limitation would not exist? Contemporary media are particularly in question here, to the extent that instrumentation plays a more and more important role in them and that their distribution is more and more extensive. It is strange (but is it so strange?) that emphasis has been placed almost exclusively on their influence, on the effects that they have as finished products, their content, the field of the signified if you like; the technical bases on which these effects depend and the specific characteristics of these bases have, however, been ignored. They have been protected by the inviolability that science is supposed to provide. We would like to establish for the cinema a few guidelines which will need to be completed, verified, improved.

We must first establish the place of the instrumental base in the set of operations which combine in the production of a film (we omit consideration of economic implications). Between "objective reality" and the camera, site of inscription, and between the inscription and the projection are situated certain operations, a *work* which has as its result a finished product. To the extent that it is cut off from the raw material ("objective reality") this product does not allow us to see the transformation which has taken place.

Equally distant from "objective reality" and the finished product, the camera occupies an intermediate position in the work process which leads from raw material to finished product. Though mutually dependent from other points of view, *découpage* [shot breakdown before shooting] and *montage* [editing, done afterward] must be distinguished because of the essential difference in the signifying raw material on which each operates: language (scenario) or image. Between the two complementary stages of production a mutation of signifying material takes place (neither translation nor transcription, obviously, for the image is not reducible to language) precisely in the place occupied by the camera. Finally, between the finished product (possessing exchange value, a commodity) and its consumption (use value) is introduced another operation effected by a set of instruments. Projector and screen restore the light lost in the shooting process, and transform a succession of separate images into an unrolling which also restores, but according to another scansion, the movement seized from "objective reality" (see the diagram).

Cinematographic specificity thus refers to a *work*, that is, to a process of transformation. The question becomes: is the work made evident, does consumption of the product bring about a "knowledge effect" [Althusser], or is the work concealed? If the latter, consumption of the product will obviously be accompanied by ideological surplus value. On the practical level, this poses the

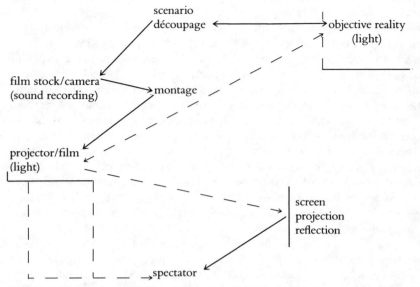

The disposition of elements and the broken lines indicating the ideological process are clarified in the text.

question of by what procedures the work can in fact be made "readable" in its inscription. These procedures must of necessity call cinematographic technique into play. But, on the other hand, going back to the first question, one may ask, do the instruments (the technical base) produce specific ideological effects, and are these effects themselves determined by the dominant ideology? In which case, concealment of the technical base will also bring about an inevitable ideological effect. Its inscription, its manifestation as such, on the other hand, would produce a knowledge effect, as actualization of the work process, as denunciation of ideology, and as critique of idealism.

The Eye of the Subject

Central in the process of production[3] of the film, the camera—an assembly of optical and mechanical instrumentation—carries out a certain mode of inscription characterized by marking, by the recording of differences of light intensity (and wavelength for color) and of differences between the frames. Fabricated on the model of the camera obscura, it permits the construction of an image analogous to the perspective projections developed during the Italian Renaissance. Of course, the use of lenses of different focal lengths can alter the perspective of an image. But this much, at least, is clear in the history of cinema:

it is the perspective construction of the Renaissance which originally served as model. The use of different lenses, when not dictated by technical considerations aimed at restoring habitual perspective (such as shooting in limited or extended spaces which one wishes to expand or contract) does not destroy [traditional] perspective but rather makes it play the role of norm. Departure from the norm, by means of a wide-angle or telephoto lens, is clearly marked in comparison with so-called "normal" perspective. We will see in any case that the resulting ideological effect is still defined in relation to the ideology inherent in perspective. The dimensions of the image itself, the ratio between height and width, seem clearly taken from an average drawn from Western easel painting.

The conception of space which conditions the construction of perspective in the Renaissance differs from that of the Greeks. For the latter, space is discontinuous and heterogeneous (for Aristotle, but also for Democritus, for whom space is the location of an infinity of indivisible atoms), whereas with Nicholas of Cusa will be born a conception of space formed by the relation between elements which are equally near and distant from the "source of all life." In addition, the pictorial construction of the Greeks corresponded to the organization of their stage, based on a multiplicity of points of view, whereas the painting of the Renaissance will elaborate a centered space. ("Painting is nothing but the intersection of the visual pyramid following a given distance, a fixed center, and a certain lighting."—Alberti.) The center of this space coincides with the eye which Jean Pellerin Viator will so appropriately call the "subject." ("The principal point in perspective should be placed at eye level: this point is called fixed or subject.")[4] Monocular vision, which as Pleynet points out is what the camera has, calls forth a sort of play of "reflection." Based on the principle of a fixed point by reference to which the visualized objects are organized, it specifies in return the position of the "subject,"[5] the very spot it must necessarily occupy.

In focusing it, the optical construct appears to be truly the projection-reflection of a "virtual image" whose hallucinatory reality it creates. It lays out the space of an ideal vision and in this way assures the necessity of a transcendence—metaphorically (by the unknown to which it appeals—here we must recall the structural place occupied by the vanishing point) and metonymically (by the displacement that it seems to carry out: a subject is both "in place of" and "a part for the whole"). Contrary to Chinese and Japanese painting, Western easel painting, presenting as it does a motionless and continuous whole, elaborates a total vision which corresponds to the idealist conception of the fullness and homogenity of "being,"[6] and is, so to speak, representative of this conception. In this sense it contributes in a singularly emphatic way to the ideological function of art, which is to provide the tangible representation of metaphysics. The principle of transcendence which conditions and is conditioned by the perspective construction represented in painting and in the photographic image which copies from it seems to inspire all the idealist paeans to which the cinema has given rise:

This strange mechanism, parodying man's spirit, seems better to accomplish the latter's own tasks. This mimetic play, brother and rival of the intelligence, is, finally, a means of the discovery of truth. (Cohen-Séat)

Far from leading us down the path of determinism, as one could legitimately believe, this art—the most positive of all, insensible to all that is not brute fact, pure appearance— presents us on the contrary the idea of a hierarchical universe, ordered in terms of an ultimate end. Behind what film gives us to see, it is not the existence of atoms that we are led to seek, but rather the existence of an "other world" of phenomena, of a soul or of other spiritual principles. It is in this revelation, above all, of a spiritual presence, that I propose that we seek Poetry. (André Bazin)[7]

Projection: Difference Denied

Nevertheless, whatever the effects proper to optics generally, the movie camera differs from still photography by registering through its mechanical instrumentation a series of images. It might thus seem to counter the unifying and "substantializing" character of the single-perspective image, taking what would seem to be instants of time or slices from "reality" (but always a reality already worked upon, elaborated, selected). This might permit the supposition, especially since the camera moves, of a multiplicity of points of view which would neutralize the fixed position of the eye-subject and even nullify it. But here we must turn to the relation between the succession of images inscribed by the camera and their projection, bypassing momentarily the place occupied by editing, which plays a decisive role in the strategy of the ideology produced.

The projection operation (projector and screen) restores continuity of movement and the temporal dimension to the sequence of static images. The relation between the individual frames and the projection would resemble the relation between points and a curve in geometry. But it is precisely this relation and the restoration of continuity to discontinuous elements which poses a problem. The meaning effect produced does not depend only on the content of the images but also on the material procedures by which an illusion of continuity, dependent on persistence of vision, is restored from discontinuous elements. These separate frames have between them differences that are indispensible for the creation of an illusion of continuity, of a continuous passage (movement, time). But only on one condition can these differences create this illusion: they must be effaced as differences.[7]

Thus on the technical level the question becomes one of the adoption of a very small difference between images, such that each image, in consequence of an organic factor [presumably persistence of vision], is rendered incapable of being seen as such. In this sense we could say that film—and perhaps this instance is exemplary—lives on the denial of difference: difference is necessary for it to live, but it lives on its negation. This is indeed the paradox that emerges if we look directly at a strip of processed film: adjacent images are almost exactly repeated, their divergence being verifiable only by comparison of images at a sufficient distance from each other. We should remember, moreover, the disturbing effects which result during a projection from breakdowns in the recreation of movement, when the spectator is brought abruptly back to discontinuity—that is, to the body, to the technical apparatus which he had *forgotten.*

We might not be far from seeing what is in play on this material basis if we recall that the "language" of the unconscious, as it is found in dreams, slips of the tongue, or hysterical symptoms, manifests itself as continuity destroyed, broken, and as the unexpected surging forth of a marked difference. Couldn't we thus say that cinema reconstructs and forms the mechanical model (with the simplifications that this can entail) of a system of writing *[écriture]* constituted by a material base and a countersystem (ideology, idealism) which uses this system while also concealing it? On the one hand, the optical apparatus and the film permit the marking of difference (but the marking is already negated, we have seen, in the constitution of the perspective image with its mirror effect). On the other hand, the mechanical apparatus both selects the minimal difference and represses it in projection, so that meaning can be constituted; it is at once direction, continuity, movement. The projection mechanism allows the differential elements (the discontinuity inscribed by the camera) to be suppressed, bringing only the relation into play. The individual images as such disappear so that movement and continuity can appear. But movement and continuity are the visible expression (one might even say, the projection) of their relations, derived from the tiny discontinuities between the images. Thus one may presume that what was already at work as the originating basis of the perspective image, namely the eye, the "subject," is put forth, liberated (in the sense that a chemical reaction liberates a substance) by the operation which transforms successive, discrete images (as isolated images they have, strictly speaking, no meaning, or at least no unity of meaning) into continuity, movement, meaning. With continuity restored, both meaning and consciousness are restored.[8]

The Transcendental Subject

Meaning and consciousness, to be sure: at this point we must return to the camera. Its mechanical nature not only permits the shooting of differential images as rapidly as desired but also destines it to change position, to move. Film history shows that as a result of the combined inertia of painting, theater, and photography, it took a certain time to notice the inherent mobility of the cinematic mechanism. The ability to reconstitute movement is after all only a partial, elementary aspect of a more general capability. To seize movement is to become movement, to follow a trajectory is to become trajectory, to choose a direction is to have the possibility of choosing one, to determine a meaning is to give oneself a meaning. In this way the eye–subject, the invisible base of artificial perspective (which in fact only represents a larger effort to produce an ordering, a regulated transcendence) becomes absorbed in, "elevated" to a vaster function, proportional to the movement which it can perform.

And if the eye which moves is no longer fettered by a body, by the laws of matter and time, if there are no more assignable limits to its displacement— conditions fulfilled by the possibilities of shooting and of film—the world will be constituted not only by this eye but for it.[9] The mobility of the camera seems to fulfill the most favorable conditions for the manifestation of the "transcendental subject." There is a phantasmatization of objective reality (images, sounds, colors)—but of an objective reality which, limiting its powers of constraint, seems equally to augment the possibilities or the power of the subject.[10] As it is said of consciousness—and in point of fact we are concerned with nothing less— the image *of* something; it must result from a deliberate act of consciousness *[visée intentionelle]*. "The word intentionality signifies nothing other than this peculiarity that consciousness has of being consciousness *of* something, of carrying in its quality of *ego* its *cogitatum* within itself."[11] In such a definition could perhaps be found the status of the cinematographic image, or rather of its operation, the mode of working which it carries out. For it to be an image of something, it has to constitute this something as meaning. The image seems to reflect the world but solely in the naive inversion of a founding hierarchy: "The domain of natural existence thus has only an authority of the second order, and always presupposes the domain of the transcendental."[12]

The world is no longer only an "open and indeterminate horizon." Limited by the framing, lined up, put at the proper distance, the world offers up an object endowed with meaning, an intentional object, implied by and implying the action of the "subject" which sights it. At the same time that the world's transfer as image seems to accomplish this phenomenological reduction, this putting into parentheses of its real existence (a suspension necessary, we will see, to the formation of the impression of reality) provides a basis for the apodicity[13] of the ego. The multiplicity of aspects of the object in view refers to a synthesizing operation, to the unity of this constituting subject: Husserl speaks of

"aspects," sometimes of "proximity," sometimes of "distance," in variable modes of "here" and "there," as opposed to an absolute here (which is located—for me—in "my own body" which appears to me at the same time), the consciousness of which, though it remains *unperceived,* always accompanies them. [We will see moreover what happens with the body in the mise-en-scène of projection.—J.L.B.] Each "aspect" which the mind grasps, for example, this cube here in the sphere of proximity, is revealed in turn as a unity synthesized from a multiplicity of corresponding modes of presentation. The nearby object may present itself as the same, but under one or another "aspect." There may be variation of visual perspective, but also of "tactile," "acoustic" phenomena, or of other "modes of presentation"[14] as we can observe in directing our attention in the proper direction.[15]

For Husserl, "the original operation [of intentional analysis] is to *unmask the potentialities implied* in the present states of consciousness. And it is by this that will be carried out, from the noematic point of view, the eventual *explication, definition,* and *elucidation* of what is meant by consciousness, that is, its *objective meaning.*"[16] And again in the *Cartesian Meditations:* "A second type of polarization now presents itself to us, another type of synthesis which embraces the particular multiplicities of *cogitationes,* which embraces them all and in a special manner, namely as *cogitationes* of an identical self which, *active* or *passive,* lives in all the lived states of consciousness and which, through them, relates to all objects."[17]

Thus is articulated the relation between the continuity necessary to the constitution of meaning and the "subject" which constitutes this meaning: continuity is an attribute of the subject. It supposes the subject and it circumscribes its place. It appears in the cinema in the two complementary aspects of a "formal" continuity established through a system of negated differences and narrative continuity in the filmic space. The latter, in any case, could not have been conquered without exercising violence to the instrumental base, as can be discovered from most of the texts by filmmakers and critics: the discontinuity that had been effaced at the level of the image could have reappeared on the narrative level, giving rise to effects of rupture disturbing to the spectator (to a *place* which ideology must both conquer and, in the degree that it already dominates it, must also satisfy: fill). "What is important in a film is the feeling of continuity which joins shots and sequences while maintaining unity and cohesion of movements. This continuity was one of the most difficult things to obtain."[18] Pudovkin defined montage as "the art of assembling pieces of film, shot separately, in such a way as to give the spectator the impression of continuous movement." The search for such narrative continuity, so difficult to obtain from the material base, can only be explained by an essential ideological stake projected in this point: it is a question of preserving at any cost the synthetic unity of the locus where meaning originates [the subject]—the constituting transcendental function to which narrative continuity points back as its natural secretion.[19]

The Screen-Mirror: Specularization and Double Identification

But another supplementary operation (made possible by a special technical arrangement) must be added in order that the mechanism thus described can play its role effectively as an ideological machine, so that not only the reworked "objective reality" but also the specific type of identification we have described can be represented.

No doubt the darkened room and the screen bordered with black like a letter of condolence already present privileged conditions of effectiveness—no exchange, no circulation, no communication with any outside. Projection and reflection take place in a closed space, and those who remain there, whether they know it or not (but they do not), find themselves chained, captured, or captivated. (What might one say of the function of the head in this captivation: it suffices to recall that for Bataille materialism makes itself headless—like a wound that bleeds and thus transfuses.) And the mirror, as a reflecting surface, is framed, limited, circumscribed. *An infinite mirror would no longer be a mirror.* The paradoxical nature of the cinematic mirror-screen is without doubt that it reflects *images* but not *"reality"*; the word *reflect,* being transitive, leaves this ambiguity unresolved. In any case this "reality" comes from behind the spectator's head, and if he looked at it directly he would see nothing except the moving beams from an already veiled light source.

The arrangement of the different elements—projector, darkened hall, screen—in addition from reproducing in a striking way the mise-en-scène of Plato's cave (prototypical set for all transcendence and the topological model of idealism,)[20] reconstructs the situation necessary to the release of the "mirror stage" discovered by Lacan. This psychological phase, which occurs between six and eighteen months of age, generates via the mirror image of a unified body the constitution or at least the first sketches of the "I" as an imaginary function. "It is to this unreachable image in the mirror that the specular image gives its garments."[21] But for this imaginary constitution of the self to be possible, there must be—Lacan strongly emphasizes this point—two complementary conditions: immature powers of mobility and a precocious maturation of visual organization (apparent in the first few days of life). If one considers that these two conditions are repeated during cinematographic projection—suspension of mobility and predominance of the visual function—perhaps one could suppose that this is more than a simple analogy. And possibly this very point explains the "impression of reality" so often invoked in connection with the cinema, for which the various explanations proposed seem only to skirt the real problem. In order for this impression to be produced, it would be necessary that the conditions of a formative scene be reproduced. This scene would be repeated and reenacted in such a manner that the imaginary order (activated by a specularization which takes place, everything considered, in reality) fulfills its particular function of occultation or of filling the gap, the split, of the subject on the order of the signifier.[22]

On the other hand, it is to the extent that the child can sustain the look of another in the presence of a third party that he can find the assurance of an identification with the image of his own body. From the very fact that during the mirror stage a dual relationship is established, it constitutes, in conjunction with the formation of the self in the imaginary order, the nexus of secondary identification.[23] The origin of the self, as discovered by Lacan, in pertaining to the imaginary order effectively subverts the "optical machinery" of idealism which the projection room scrupulously reproduces.[24] But it is not as specifically "imaginary," nor as a reproduction of its first configuration, that the self finds a "place" in the cinema. This occurs, rather, as a sort of proof or verification of that function, a solidification through repetition.

The "reality" mimed by the cinema is thus first of all that of a "self." But because the reflected image is not that of the body itself but that of a world already given as meaning, one can distinguish two levels of identification. The first, attached to the image itself, derives from the character portrayed as a center of secondary identifications, carrying an identity which constantly must be seized and reestablished. The second level permits the appearance of the first and places it "in action"—this is the transcendental subject whose place is taken by the camera which constitutes and rules the objects in this "world." Thus the spectator identifies less with what is represented, the spectacle itself, than with what stages the spectacle, makes it seen, obliging him to see what it sees; this is exactly the function taken over by the camera as a sort of relay.[25] Just as the mirror assembles the fragmented body in a sort of imaginary integration of the self, the transcendental self unites the discontinuous fragments of phenomena, of lived experience, into unifying meaning. Through it each fragment assumes meaning by being integrated into an "organic" unity. Between the imaginary gathering of the fragmented body into a unity and the transcendentality of the self, giver of unifying meaning, the current is indefinitely reversible.

The ideological mechanism at work in the cinema seems thus to be concentrated in the relationship between the camera and the subject. The question is whether the former will permit the latter to constitute and seize itself in a particular mode of specular reflection. Ultimately, the forms of narrative adopted, the "contents" of the image, are of little importance so long as an identification remains possible.[26] What emerges here (in outline) is the specific function fulfilled by the cinema as support and instrument of ideology. It constitutes the "subject" by the illusory delimitation of a central location—whether this be that of a god or of any other substitute. It is an apparatus destined to obtain a precise ideological effect, necessary to the dominant ideology: creating a phantasmatization of the subject, it collaborates with a marked efficacy in the maintenance of idealism.

Thus the cinema assumes the role played throughout Western history by various artistic formations. The ideology of representation (as a principal axis orienting the notion of aesthetic "creation") and specularization (which organizes the mise-en-scène required to constitute the transcendental function) form a singularly coherent system in the cinema. Everything happens as if, the subject himself being unable—and for a reason—to account for his own situation, it was necessary to substitute secondary organs, grafted on to replace his own defective ones, instruments or ideological formations capable of filling his function as subject. In fact, this substitution is only possible on the condition that the instrumentation itself be hidden or repressed. Thus disturbing cinematic elements—similar, precisely, to those elements indicating the return of the repressed—signify without fail the arrival of the instrument "in flesh and blood," as in Vertov's *Man With a Movie Camera*. Both specular tranquility and the assurance of one's own identity collapse simultaneously with the revealing of the mechanism, that, is of the inscription of the film work.

The cinema can thus appear as a sort of psychic apparatus of substitution, corresponding to the model defined by the dominant ideology. The system of repression (primarily economic) has as its goal the prevention of deviations and of the active exposure of this "model."[27] Analogously one could say that its "unconscious" is not recognized (we speak of the apparatus and not of the content of films, which have used the unconscious in ways we know all too well). To this unconscious would be attached the mode of production of film, the process of "work" in its multiple determinations, among which must be numbered those depending on instrumentation. This is why reflections on the basic apparatus ought to be possible to integrate into a general theory of the ideology of cinema.

Notes

1. See on this subject Derrida's work "La Scène de l'écriture" in *L'Ecriture et la différence* (Paris: Seuil, 1967).

2. [The term "subject" is used by Baudry and others to mean not the topic of discourse—though this is clearly involved—but rather the perceiving and ordering self, as in our term "subjective"—TRANS.]

3. Obviously we are not speaking here of investment of capital in the process.

4. See L. Brion Guerry, *Jean Pellerin Viator* (Paris: Belles Lettres, 1962.)

5. We understand the term "subject" here as vehicle and as place of intersection of the ideological implications which we are attempting progressively to make clear, and not as the structural function which analytic discourse attempts to locate. It would rather partially take the place of the *ego*, of which we know the deviations seen in the analytic field.

6. The perspective "frame" which will have such an influence on cinematographic shooting has as its role to intensify, to increase the effect of the spectacle, which no divergence may be allowed to split.

7. "We know that the spectator finds it impossible to notice that the images which succeed one another before his eyes were assembled end to end, because the projection of film on the screen offers an impression of continuity although the images which compose it are, in reality, distinct, and are differentiated, moreover, by variations in space and time.

"In a film, there can be hundreds, even thousands of cuts and intervals. But if in the hands of specialists who know the art, the spectacle will not be divulged as such. Only an error or lack of competence will permit them to seize, and this is a disagreeable sensation, the changes of time and place of action." (V.I. Pudovkin, "Le Montage," in *Cinéma d'aujourd'hui et de demain* [Moscow, 1956].)

8. It is thus first at the level of the apparatus that the cinema functions as a language: inscription of discontinuous elements whose effacement in the relationship instituted among them produces meaning.

9. "In the cinema I am simultaneously in this action and *outside* it, in this space and out of this space. Having the power of ubiquity, I am everywhere and nowhere." Jean Mitry, *Esthétique et psychologie du cinéma* [(Paris: Presses Universitaires de France, 1965), p. 179].

10. The cinema manifests in a hallucinatory manner the belief in the omnipotence of thought, described by Freud, which plays so important a role in neurotic defense mechanisms.

11. Husserl, *Les Méditations Cartesiennes* (Paris: Vrin, 1953), p. 28. [Edmund Husserl, *Cartesian Meditations*, trans. Dorion Cairns (The Hague: Nijhoff, 1973), p. 33. There are occasional differences between the French and English versions of Husserl. Where he is quoted, a translation of the French version is used. In subsequent notes, the French citation is followed by the parallel English page number in brackets.—ED.]

12. *Ibid.,* p. 18 [p. 21].

13. ["Apodicity," in phenomenological terminology, indicates something of an irrefutable nature. See Husserl, *Les Méditations Cartesiennes*. Here, Baudry is using the term critically—in a sense *ironically.*—TRANS.]

14. On this point it is true that the camera is revealed as incomplete. But this is only a technical imperfection which, since the birth of cinema, has already in large measure been remedied.

15. *Ibid.,* p. 34, emphasis added [pp. 39–40].

16. *Ibid.,* p. 40 [p. 46].

17. *Ibid.,* p. 56 [p. 66].

18. Mitry, *Esthétique et psychologie*, p. 157.

19. The lens, the "objective," is of course only a particular location of the "subjective." Marked by the idealist opposition interior/exterior, topologically situated at the meeting point of the two, it corresponds, one could say, to the empirical organ of the subjective, to the opening, the fault in the organs of meaning, by which the exterior world may penetrate the interior and assume meaning. "It is the interior which commands," says Bresson. "I know this may seem paradoxical in an art which is all exterior." Also the use of different lenses is already conditioned by camera movement as implication and trajectory of meaning, by this transcendental function which we are attempting to define: it is the possibility of choosing a field as accentuation or modification of the *visée intentionelle*.

No doubt this transcendental function fits without difficulty into the field of psychology. This, moreover, is insisted upon by Husserl himself, who indicates that Brentano's discovery, intentionality, "permits one truly to distinguish the method of a descriptive science of consciousness, as much philosophical and transcendental as psychological."

20. The arrangement of the cave, except that in the cinema it is already doubled in a sort of enclosure in which the camera, the darkened chamber, is enclosed in another darkened chamber, the projection hall.

21. Jacques Lacan, *Ecrits* (Paris: Seuil, 1966). See in particular "Le Stade du miroir comme formateur de la fonction du je."

22. We see that what has been defined as impression of reality refers less to the "reality" than to the apparatus which, although of a hallucinatory order, nonetheless founds this possibility. Reality will never appear except as relative to the images which reflect it, in some way inaugurated by a reflection anterior to itself.

23. We refer here to what Lacan says of identifications in connection with the structure determined by an optical instrument (the mirror), as they are constituted, in the prevailing figuration of the ego, as lines of resistance to the advance of the analytic work.

24. "That the ego be 'in the right' must be avowed, from experience, to be a function of misunderstanding" (Lacan, *Ecrits* p. 637).

25. "That it sustains itself as 'subject' means that language permits it to consider itself as the stagehand or even the director of all the imaginary capturings of which it would otherwise only be the living marionette" *(Ibid.,* p. 637).

26. It is on this point and in terms of the elements which we are trying to put in place that a

discussion of editing could be opened. We will at a later date attempt to make some remarks on this subject.

27. J.-D. Pollet and Phillipe Sollers' *Mediterranée* (1963), which dismantles with exemplary efficiency the "transcendental specularization" which we have attempted to delineate, gives a manifest proof of this point. The film was never able to overcome the economic blockade.

—*translated by Alan Williams*
(translation revised, 1983)

17

Jean-Louis Baudry

The Apparatus: Metapsychological Approaches to the Impression of Reality in the Cinema

One constantly returns to the scene of the cave: real effect or impression of reality. Copy, simulacrum, and even simulacrum of simulacrum. Impression of the real, more-than-the-real? From Plato to Freud, the perspective is reversed; the procedure is inverted—so it seems. The former comes out of the cave, examines what is intelligible, contemplates its source, and, when he goes back, it is to denounce to the prisoners the apparatus which oppresses them, and to persuade them to leave, to get out of that dim space. The latter (on the contrary— no, for it is not a matter of simple opposition, or of a simplifying symmetry) is more interested in making them go back there precisely where they are; where they didn't know how to find themselves, for they thought themselves outside, and it is true they had been contemplating the good, the true, and the beautiful for a long time. But at what price and as a result of what ignorance; failure to recognize or repress, compromise, defense, sublimation? Like Plato, he urges them to consider the apparatus to overcome their resistances, to look a little more closely at what is coming into focus on the screen, the other scene. The other scene? What brings the two together and separates them? For both, as in the theater, a left side, a right side, the master's lodge, the valet's orchestra. But the first scene would seem to be the second's other scene. It is a question of truth in the final analysis, or else: "the failure to recognize has moved to the

Published in *Communications* (1975), no. 23 and translated in *Camera Obscura* (Fall 1976), no. 1, pp. 104–28. Reprinted by permission of the author, and translation used by permission of *Camera Obscura*.

other side." Both distinguish between two scenes, or two places, opposing or confronting one another, one dominating the other. These aren't the same places; they don't respond point by point, although, in many respects, we who come after Freud would not be unjustified in superimposing more or less grossly the solar scene where the philosopher is at first dazzled, blinded by the good, on the scene of the conscious and its well-meaning exploits—we who, as a result of this very discovery of the unconscious, or of the other scene, could be induced to interpret the move, the exit, ascension, an initial blinding of the philosopher in a totally different manner. "Suppose one of them were set free and forced suddenly to stand up, turn his head, and walk with eyes lifted to the light; all these movements would be painful, and he would be too dazzled to make out the objects. . . . And if he were forced to look at the firelight itself, would not his eyes ache, so that he would try to escape and turn back to the things which he could see distinctly?" But the philosopher's cave could certainly not be superimposed onto that other scene, the scene of the unconscious! That remains to be seen. For we are dealing here with an apparatus, with a metaphorical relationship between places or a relationship between metaphorical places, with a topography, the knowledge of which defines for both philosopher and analyst the degree of relationship to truth or to description, or to illusion, and the need for an ethical point of view.

So you see, we return to the real or, for the experiencing subject (I could say, for the subject who is felt or who is acted), the impression of reality. And one could naively wonder why, some two and half thousand years later, it is by means of an optical metaphor—of an optical construct which signals term for term the cinematographic apparatus—that the philosopher exposes man's condition and the distance that separates him from "true reality"; and why it is again precisely by means of an optical metaphor that Freud, at the beginning and at the end of his writings, tries to account for the arrangement of the physical apparatus, for the functioning of the Unconscious and for the rapport/rupture Conscious-Unconscious. Chapter 7 of the *Traumdeutung:*

What is presented to us in these words is the idea of a *psychical locality.* I shall entirely disregard the fact that the mental apparatus with which we are concerned is also known to us in the form of an anatomical preparation, and I shall carefully avoid the temptation to determine psychical locality in an anatomical fashion. I shall remain upon psychological ground, and I propose simply to follow the suggestion that we should picture the instrument which carries out our mental functions as resembling a compound microscope or a photographic apparatus, or something of the kind. On that basis, psychical locality will correspond to a point inside the apparatus at which one of the preliminary stages of an image comes into being. In the microscope and telescope, as we know, these occur in part at ideal points, regions in which no tangible component to the apparatus is situated. I see no necessity to apologize for the imperfections of this or of any similar imagery.[1]

However imperfect this comparison may be, Freud takes it up again forty years later at the very beginning of the *Abriss:* "We admit that psychical life is the function of an apparatus to which we attribute a spatial extension which is made up of several parts. We imagine it like a kind of telescope, or microscope or some similar device." Freud doesn't mention cinema. But this is because cinema is already too technologically determined an apparatus for describing the psychical apparatus as a whole. In 1913, however, Lou Andréas Salomé remarked: "Why is it that cinema has been of no use to us [analysts]? To the numerous arguments that could be advanced to save face for this Cinderella of the artistic conception of art, several psychological considerations should be added. First, that the cinematographic technique is the only one that makes possible a succession of images rapid enough to roughly correspond to our faculty for producing mental images. Furthermore," she concludes, "this provides food for reflection about the impact film could have in the future for our psychical make-up." Clearly Salomé seems to envision a very enigmatic track, unless we have misunderstood her. Does she mean that film may bear some sort of likeness to the psychical apparatus, that, for this reason, it could be of interest to those who, because of its direct relation to their practice, are immediately affected by a theorization of psychical operation linked to the discovery of the Unconscious? And is it not the apparatus, the cinematographic process itself rather than the content of images—that is, the film—which is under scrutiny here? She only points out that there might be correspondences between cinematographic technique and our ability to produce mental images. But there are many aspects of film technique, many different connections, from the recording of the images to their reproduction—an entire process which we have named elsewhere the *basic cinematographic apparatus.* And certainly such a technical construct—if only as examples and metaphor—should have interested Freud, since the major purpose of metapsychological research is to comprehend and to theoretically construct devices capable of recording traces, memory traces, and of restoring them in the form of representation. He admits: the concept of the "magic writing pad" (which he substitutes for the optical metaphor to which he later returns) is missing something: the possibility of restoring inscribed traces by using specific memory mechanisms which are exclusively constituted by living matter but which a certain number of technical inventions of the time already mimic: the phonograph and cinema, precisely. The advantage of the magic writing pad is that since the external surface doesn't retain any trace of the inscriptions, it is best suited to illustrate the system Perception-Conscious; in addition, the waxy substance inside preserves, superimposed and to some extent associated, the different traces which have inscribed themselves throughout time, preserves them from what could be called historical accidents. Obviously, nothing prevents the same thing from applying to the material of the record or to the film stock of the film if not that such reproduction would be confusing and indecipherable to us: the inscription follows other tracks, which are organized according to other principles than those of inanimate matter.

Yet, there is something there which should capture our attention: the double place of the subject (constituted on the one hand by the system perception = Conscious characterized by the transcience, successiveness, and mobility of perceptions and representations; on the other by Unconscious system traces/inscriptions characterized by permanence) finds itself once more within an idealist perspective considerably displaced with respect to the unconscious in Plato. But as we have learned from Marx, there is often a truth hidden from or in idealism, a truth which belongs to materialism, but which materialism can only discover after many detours and delays—a hidden or disguised truth. In Plato, something haunts the subject; something belabors him and determines his condition (could it be the pressure of the "Ideas"?) As for Freud, the subject which Plato describes, the prisoner in the cave, is deceived (this whole theme of the mistaken subject which runs through the history of philosophy!); he is the prey of illusions, and, as for Freud, these illusions are but distortions and symptoms (gradations, the idealist would say—and admit this changes everything) of what is happening somewhere else. Even though Ideas take the place of the Unconscious for him, Plato confronts a problem equivalent to that which at first preoccupies Freud in his metapsychological research and which, precisely, the cave myth is presumed to resolve: the transfer, the access from one place to another, along with the ensuing distortions. Plato's prisoner is the victim of an illusion of reality, that is, of precisely what is known as a hallucination, if one is awake, as a dream, if asleep; he is the prey of an impression, of *an impression of reality*. As I have said, Plato's *topos* does not and could not possibly correspond exactly to Freud's and surely, although it may be interesting to show what displacement occurs from one *topos* to the other (the location of reality for Plato obviously doesn't correspond to what is real for Freud), it is still more important to determine what is at work on the idealist philosopher's discourse unknown to him, the truth which proclaims, very different yet contained within the one he consciously articulates.

As a matter of fact, isn't it curious that Plato, in order to explain the transfer, the access from one place to another and to demonstrate, reveal, and make understood what sort of illusion underlies our direct contact with the real, would imagine or resort to an apparatus that doesn't merely evoke but quite precisely describes in its mode of operation the cinematographic apparatus[2] and the spectator's place in relation to it.

It is worth rereading the description of the cave from this perspective.

First, the space: "a kind of cavernous underground chamber with an entrance open to the light" but too small to light it up. As Plato points out farther on: "a dim space." He emphasizes the effect of the surrounding darkness on the philosopher after his sojourn in the outside world. To his companions he will at first appear blind, his eyesight ruined; and his clumsiness will make them laugh. They will not be able to have confidence in him. In the cave, the prisoner-spectators are seated, still, prisoners because immobilized: unable to move—constraint or paralysis? It is true that they are chained, but, freed, they would still refuse to leave the place where they are; and so obstinately would they resist that they might put to death anyone trying to lead them out. In other words, this first constraint, against their will, this deprivation of movement which was imposed on them initially, this motor inhibition which affected so much their future dispositions, conditions them to the point that they prefer to stay where they are and to perpetuate this immobility rather than leave. Initial constraint which seems in this way to turn itself into a kind of spite or at least to inscribe the compulsion to repeat, the return to a former condition. There are things like that in Plato? It is not unnecessary to insist on this point as we reread the platonic myth from the special perspective of the cinematographic apparatus. Forced immobility is undoubtedly a valuable argument for the demonstration/ description that Plato makes of the human condition: the coincidence of religious and idealist conceptions; but the initial immobility was not invented by Plato; it can also refer to the forced immobility of the child who is without motor resources at birth, and to the forced immobility of the sleeper who we know repeats the postnatal state and even interuterine existence; but this is also the immobility that the visitor to the dim space rediscovers, leaning back into his chair. It might even be added that the spectators' immobility is characteristic of the filmic apparatus as a whole. The prisoner's shackles correspond to an actual reality in the individual's evolution, and Plato even draws the conclusion that it could have an influence on his future behavior, and would be a determining factor in the prisoner's resistance to breaking away from the state of illusion. "He might be required once more to deliver his opinion on those shadows, in competition with the prisoners who had never been released. . . . If they could lay hands on the man who was trying to set them free and lead them up, they would kill him." Does he mean that immobility constitutes a necessary if not sufficient condition for the prisoner's credulity, that it constitutes one of the causes of the state of confusion into which they have been thrown and which makes them take images and shadows for the real? I don't want to stretch Plato's argument too far, even if I am trying to make his myth mean more than it actually says. But note: "In this underground chamber they have been *from childhood,* chained by the leg and also by the neck, so that they cannot move and can see only what is in front of them, because the chains will not let them turn their heads" [my emphasis]. Thus it is their motor paralysis, their inability to move about that, making the reality test impractical for them, reinforces their error and makes them inclined to take for real that which takes its place, perhaps its figuration or its projection onto the wall/screen of the cavern in front of them and from which they cannot detach their eyes and turn away. They are bound, shackled to the screen, tied and related—relation, extension between it and them due to their inability to move in relation to it, the last sight before falling asleep.

Plato says nothing about the quality of the image: is two-dimensional space suited to the representation of depth produced by the images of objects? Admittedly, they are flat shadows, but their movements, crossings over, superimpositions, and displacements allow us perhaps to assume that they are moving along different planes. However, Plato calls the projector to mind. He doesn't feel a need for making use of natural light; but it is also important to him to preserve and protect that light from an impure usage: idealism makes the technician. Plato is satisfied with a fire burning behind them "at some distance higher up." As a necessary precaution, let us examine Plato's accuracy in assembling his apparatus. He is well aware that, placed otherwise, the fire would transmit the reflections of the prisoners themselves most prominently onto the screen. The "operators," the "machinists" are similarly kept out of the prisoners' sight, hidden by "a parapet, like the screen at a puppet-show, which hides the performers while they show their puppets over the top." For, undoubtedly, by associating themselves with the objects that they are moving back and forth before the fire, they would project a heterogeneous image capable of canceling the reality effect they want to produce: they would awake the prisoner's suspicions; they would awake the prisoners.

Here is the strangest thing about the whole apparatus. Instead of projecting images of natural/real objects, of living people, etc. onto the wall/screen of the cave as it would seem only natural to do for simple shadow plays, Plato feels the need, by creating a kind of conversion in the reference to reality, to show the prisoners not direct images and shadows of reality but, even at this point, a simulacrum of it. One might easily recognize the idealist's prudence, the calculated progress of the philosopher who prefers pushing the real back another notch and multiplying the steps leading to it, lest excessive haste lead his listener again to trust his senses too much. In any case, for this reason (or for another), he is led to place and to suppose between the projector, the fire, and the screen something which is itself a mere prop of reality, which is merely its image, its copy, its simulacrum: "figures of men and animals in wood or stone or other materials" suggestive of studio objects of papier mâché decor, were it not for the more striking impression created by their passing in front of the fire like a film.

All that is missing is the sound, in effect much more difficult to reproduce. Not only this: more difficult to copy, to employ like an image in the visible world; as if hearing, as opposed to sight, resisted being caught up in simulacra. Real voices, then, they would emanate from the bearers, the machinists, and the marionette players (a step is skipped in the reference to reality) but nevertheless, given over to the apparatus, integrated with it since it requires a total effect for fear of exposing the illusion. But voice that does not allow representation as do artificial objects—stone and wooden animals, and statues—will still give itself over to the apparatus thanks to its reverberation. "And suppose their prison had an echo from the wall facing them?" "When one of the people crossing behind them spoke, they could only suppose that the sound came from the shadow passing before their eyes." If a link is missing in the chain that connects us back to reality, the apparatus corrects this, by taking over the voice's echo, by integrating into itself these excessively real voices. And it is true that in cinema—as in the case of all talking machines—one does not hear an image of the sounds but the sounds themselves. Even if the procedures for recording the sounds and playing them back deforms them, they are reproduced and not copied. Only their source of emission may partake of illusion; their reality cannot. Hence, no doubt one of the basic reasons for the privileged status of voice in idealist philosophy and in religion: voice does not lend itself to games of illusion, or confusion, between the real and its figurativity (because voice cannot be represented figuratively) to which sight seems particularly liable. Music and singing differ qualitatively from painting in their relation to reality.

As we have seen, Plato constructs an apparatus very much like sound cinema. But, precisely because he has to resort to sound, he anticipates an ambiguity which was to be characteristic of cinema. This ambiguity has to do with the impression of reality: with the means used to create it, and with the confusion and lack of awareness surrounding its origin, from which result the inventions which mark the history of cinema. Plato effectively helps us to recognize this ambiguity. For, on the other hand, he is careful to emphasize the artificial aspect of reproduced reality. It is the apparatus that creates the illusion, and not the degree of fidelity with the Real: here *the prisoners have been chained since childhood,* and it will therefore not be the reproduction of this or that specific aspect of that reality, which they do not know, which will lead them to attribute a greater degree of reality to the illusion to which they are subject (and we have seen that Plato was already careful to insert artifice, and that already what was projected was deception). On the other hand, by introducing voice, by reconstructing a talking machine, by complementing the projection with sound, by illustrating, as it were, the need to affect as many sense faculties as possible, at any rate the two most important, he certainly seems to comply with a necessity to duplicate reality in the most exact manner and to make his artifice as good a likeness as can be made. Plato's myth evidently functions as a metaphor for an analogy on which he himself insists before dealing with the myth: namely that what can be known through the senses is in the same relationship to that which can be known through the intellect as projection in the cave is to experience (that is, to ordinary reality). Besides that, isn't it remarkable that Plato should have been forced to resort to such a procedure and that, in his attempt to explain the position, the locus of that which can be known through the intellect, he was led to take off, so to speak, toward "illusion"; he was led to construct an apparatus which will make it possible, that it is capable of producing a special effect through the impression of reality it communicates to the spectator.

Here I must add something which may be of importance: in the scene taking place inside the cave, voices, words, "[these echoes which] they could only suppose that the sound came from the shadow passing before their eyes," do not have a discursive or conceptual role; they do not communicate a message; they belong to ordinary reality which is as immediate to the prisoners as are images; they cannot be separated from the latter; they are characterized according to the same mode of existence and in effect treated in the same way as words in a dream "fragments of discourse *really* spoken or heard, *detached from their context*" (my emphasis), and functioning like other kinds of dream representation.

But there is another way to state the problem. What desire was aroused, more than two thousand years before the actual invention of cinema, what urge in need of fulfillment would be satisfied by *a montage, rationalized into an idealist perspective precisely in order to show that it rests primarily on an impression of reality?* The impression of reality is central to Plato's demonstration. That his entire argument is developed in order to prove that this impression is deceptive abundantly demonstrates its existence. As we have already noted, something haunts Plato's text: the prisoners' fascination (how better to convey the condition that keeps them chained up, those fetters that prevent them from moving their heads and necks), their reluctance to leave and even their willingness to resort to violence. But isn't it principally the need to construct another scene apart from the world, underground, in short to construct it as if it existed, or as if this construction also satisfied a desire to objectify a similar scene—an apparatus capable precisely of fabricating an impression of reality. This would appear to satisfy and replace the nostalgia for a lost impression which can be seen as running through the idealist movement and eating away at it from inside, and setting it in motion. That the real in Plato's text is at an equal distance from or in a homologous relationship to the "intelligibly real"—the world of Ideas— and "reality-subject"—"the impression of reality" produced by the apparatus in the cave should moreover be sufficient to make us aware of the real meaning of the world of Ideas and of the field of desire on which it has been built (a world which, as we know, "exists outside of time," and which, after numerous encounters, the conscious subject can rediscover in himself).

Cave, grotto, "sort of cavernous chamber underground," people have not failed to see in it a representation of the maternal womb, of the matrix into which we are supposed to wish to return. Granted, but only the place is taken into account by this interpretation and not the apparatus as a whole; and if this apparatus really produces images, it first of all produces an effect of specific subjects—to the extent that a subject is intrinsically part of the apparatus; once the cinema has been technically perfected, it produces this same effect defined by the words "impression of reality" (words that may be confusing but which nevertheless need to be clarified). This impression of reality appears as if—just as if—it were known to Plato. At the very least, it seems that Plato ingeniously attempts and succeeds in fixing up a machine capable of reproducing "something" that he must have known, and that has less to do with its capacity for repeating the real (and this is where the Idealist is of great help to us by sufficiently emphasizing the artifice he employs to make his machine work) than with reproduction and repetition of a particular condition, and the representation of a particular place on which this condition depends.

Of course, from the analytic perspective we have chosen, by asking cinema about the wish it expresses, we are aware of having distorted the allegory of the cave by making it reveal, from a considerable historic distance, the approximate construct of the cinematographic apparatus. In other words, a same apparatus was responsible for the invention of the cinema and was already present in Plato. The text of the cave may well express a desire inherent to a participatory effect deliberately produced, sought for, and expressed by cinema (and the philosopher is first of all a spokesman of desire before becoming its great "channeler, " which shows why it is far from useless to bring an analytic ear to bear on him despite or because of his rationalizations, even though he deny it as tolerable suspicion, even and especially though he complains, rightly from his point of view, of our having distorted his text). We can thus propose that the allegory of the cave is the text of a signifier of desire which haunts the invention of cinema and the history of its invention.

You see why historians of cinema, in order to unearth its first ancestor, never leave off dredging a prehistory which is becoming increasingly cluttered. From the magic lantern to the praxinoscope and the optical theater up to the *camera obscura,* as the booty piles up, the excavations grow: new objects and all kinds of inventions—one can feel the disarray increasing. But if cinema was really the answer to a desire inherent in our psychical structure, how can we date its first beginnings? Would it be too risky to propose that painting, like theater, for lack of suitable technological and economic conditions, were dry runs in the approximation not only of the world of representation but of what might result from a certain aspect of its functioning and which only the cinema is in a position to implement? These attempts have obviously produced their own specificity and their own history, but their existence has at its origin a psychical source equivalent to the one which stimulated the invention of cinema.

It is very possible that there was never any first invention of cinema. Before being the outcome of technical considerations and of a certain state of society's development (necessary to its realization and to its completion), it was primarily the target of a desire which, moreover, its immediate success as well as the interest which its ancestors had aroused has demonstrated clearly enough. A desire, to be sure, a form of lost satisfaction which its apparatus would be aimed at rediscovering in one way or another (even to the point of simulation) and to which the impression of reality would seem to be the key.

I would now like to look more closely at what the impression of reality and the desire objectified in it entails by surveying certain analytical texts.

And since I have already mentioned the cave, "a kind of cavernous underground chamber,"as Plato says, I went back to the *Interpretation of Dreams* and discovered a remark of Freud's that could guide our search. This remark is to be found in the passage dedicated to examples of dream work. Freud examines the kinds of figuration that occur during analysis. After having shown how the treatment gets itself represented, Freud comes to the unconscious. "If the unconscious, insofar as it belongs to waking thought, needs to be represented in dreams, it is represented in them in underground places." Freud adds the following which, because of the above, is very interesting: "Outside of analytic treatment, these representations would have symbolized the woman's body or the womb." If the world of Ideas offers numerous concepts which correspond to those which Freud discovered in the Unconscious (the permanence of traces, the ignorance of time), that is, if the philosophical edifice can be envisaged as a rationalization of the Unconscious's thrust, of its suspected but rejected existence, then we can ask whether it is not the Unconscious or certain of its mechanisms that are figured, that represent themselves in the apparatus of the cave. In any case, paraphrasing Fechner, we could propose that the scene of the cave (and of cinema) is perhaps quite different from that of the activity of representation in a state of wakefulness. In order to learn a little more about that other scene, it might be useful to linger a while before the dream scene.

A parallel between dream and cinema had often been noticed: common sense perceived it right away. The cinematographic projection is reminiscent of dream, would appear to be a kind of dream, really a dream,[3] a parallelism often noticed by the dreamer when, about to describe his dream, he is compelled to say "It was like in a movie. . ." At this point, it seems useful to follow Freud closely in his metaphyschological analysis of dream. Once the role and function of dream as a protector of sleep and as fulfillment of a wish has been recognized as well as its nature and the elaboration of which it is the result, and after the material, the translation of the manifest content into dream thoughts, has been studied, one must still determine the conditions of dream formation, the reasons that give dream a specific qualitative nature in the whole of the psychical life, the specific "dream effect" that it determines. This is the subject of chapter 7 of *The Interpretations of Dreams* and the *Supplement to the Theory of Dreams* fifteen years later. In the latter text, Freud at first seems concerned with understanding why dream manifests itself to the dreamer's consciousness in the form of what might be called the "specific mode of dream," a feature of reality which should more properly belong to the perception of the external world. What are the determining factors of a necessarily metapsychological order, i.e., involving the construction and operation of the psychical apparatus, which makes it possible for dream to pass itself off for reality to the dreamer. Freud begins with sleep: dream is the psychical activity of the dreamer. Sleep, he tells us, "from a somatic viewpoint, is *a revivescence of one's stay in the body of the mother, certain conditions of which it recreates: the rest position, warmth, and isolation which protects him from excitement*" [emphasis added]. This makes possible a first form of regression: *temporal regression,* which follows two paths—regression of the libido back to a previous period of hallucinatory satisfaction of desire; and regression in the development of the self back to a primitive narcissism which results in what has been defined as the totally egotistical nature of dream: *"the person who plays the main part in dream scenes is always the dreamer himself."* Sleep favors the appearance of another form of regression which is extremely important for the manifestation of the dream effect: by deactivating equally the Cs, Pcs, and Ucs systems, i.e., by allowing an easier communication between them, sleep leaves open the regressive path which the cathetic representations will follow as far as perception. *Topical regression* and *temporal regression* combine to reach the edge of dream.

I do not want to insist excessively on Freud's analysis. We need only note that the dream wish is formed from daytime residues in the Preconscious system which are reinforced by drives emanating from the Unconscious. Topical regression first allows the transformation of the dream thoughts into images. It is through the intermediary of regression that word representations belonging to the Preconscious system are translated into thing representations which dominate the Unconscious system.[4] "Thoughts are transposed into images—mostly visual ones—thus the representations of words are reduced to representations of objects corresponding to them as if, throughout the whole system, considerations of representability overwhelmed the whole process." So much so that a dream wish can be turned into a dream fantasy. Once again, it is regression which gives dream its definitive shape. "The completion of the dream process is also marked by the fact that the content of thought, transformed by regression and reshaped into a fantasy of desire, comes into consciousness as a sensory perception and then undergoes the secondary elaboration which affects any perceptual content. We are saying that the dream wish is hallucinated and finds, in the guise of hallucination a belief in the reality of its fulfillment." Dream is "an hallucinatory psychosis of desire"—i.e., a state in which mental perceptions are taken for perceptions of reality. Moreover, Freud hypothesized that the satisfaction resulting from hallucination is a kind of satisfaction which we knew at the beginning of our psychical life when perception and representation could not be differentiated, when the different systems were confused, i.e., when the system of Consciousness-Perception had not differentiated itself. The object of desire (the object of need), if it happens to be lacking, can at this point be hallucinated. It is precisely the repeated failure offered by this form of satisfaction which results in the differentiation between perception and representation through the creation of the reality test. A perception which can be eliminated by an action is recognized as exterior. The reality test is dependent on "motoricity." Once "motoricity" has been interrupted, as during sleep, the reality test can no longer function. The suspension of "motoricity," its being set apart, would indeed favor regression. But it is also because sleep determines a withdrawal of cathexis in the Cs, Ucs, and Pcs systems that the fantasies of the dream wish follow the original path which differentiate them from fantasies produced during the waking state.[5] Like daytime fantasies, they could have become conscious without nevertheless being taken for real or completed; but, having taken the path of regression, not only are they capable of taking over consciousness but, because of the subject's inability to rely upon the reality test, they are marked by the very character of perception and appear as reality. The processes of dream formation succeed well in presenting dream as real.

The transformations accomplished by sleep in the psychical apparatus: withdrawal of cathexis, instability of the different systems, return to narcissism, loss of motoricity (because of the impossibility of applying the reality test), contribute to produce features which are specific to dream: its capacity for figuration, translation of thought into images, reality extended to representations. One might even add that we are dealing with a *more-than-real* in order to differentiate it from the impression of the real which reality produces in the normal waking situation: the more-than-real translating the cohesion of the subject with his perceived representations, the submersion of the subject in his representations, the near impossibility for him to escape their influence and which is dissimilar if not incompatible with the impression resulting from any direct relation to reality. There appears to be an ambiguity in the words poorly expressing the difference between the relationship of the subject to his representations experienced as perceived and his relation to reality.

Dream, Freud also tells us, is a projection, and, in the context in which he uses the word, projection evokes at once the analytic use of the defense mechanism which consists in referring and attributing to the exterior representations and affects which the subject refuses to acknowledge as his own, and it also evokes a distinctly cinematographic use since it involves images which, once projected, come back to the subject as a real perceived from the outside.

That dream is a projection reminiscent of the cinematographic apparatus, is indeed what seems to come out of Lewin's discovery of the *dream screen,* the hypothesis for which was suggested to him by his patients' enigmatic dreams. One young woman's dream, for example: "I had my dream all ready for you, but while I was lying here looking at it, it began to move in circles far from me, wrapped up on itself, again and again, like two acrobats." This dream shows that the screen, which can appear by itself, like a white surface, is not exclusively a representation, a content—in which case it would not be necessary to privilege it among other elements of the dream content; but, rather, it would present itself in all dreams as the indispensable support for the projection of images. It would seem to pertain to the dream apparatus. "The dream screen is a surface on which a dream seems to be projected. It is the 'blank background' (empty basic surface) which is present in dream although it is not necessarily seen; the manifest content of dream ordinarily perceived takes place over it, or in front of it." "Theoretically it can be part of the latent content or of the manifest content, but the distinction is academic. The dream screen is not often noticed by analysts, and, in the practice of dream interpretation, the analyst does not need to deal with it." It is cinema which suggested the term to Lewin because, in the same way as its analog in the cinematographic apparatus, the dream screen is either ignored by the dreamer (the dreaming spectator) or unrelated to the interest resulting from the images and the action.[6] Lewin adds nevertheless (and this remark reminds us of a modern use of the screen in cinema) that in some circumstances, the screen does play a part of its own and becomes discernible. According to Lewin's hypothesis, the dream screen is the dream's hallucinatory representation of the mother's breast on which the child used to fall asleep after nursing. In this way, it expresses a state of complete satisfaction while repeating the original condition of the oral phase in which the body did not have limits of its own, but was extended undifferentiated from the breast. Thus, the dream screen would correspond to the desire to sleep: archetype and prototype of any dream. Lewin adds another hypothesis: the dream itself, the visual representations which are projected upon it, would correspond to the desire to be awake. "A visual dream repeats the child's early impression of being awake. His eyes are open and he sees. For him, to see is to be awake." Actually, Lewin insists on Freud's explanation of the predominance of visual elements in dream: that latent thoughts in a dream are to a large extent shaped by unconscious mnemic traces which can only exist as a visual representation—the repetition of a formal element from the child's earliest experience. It is evident that the dream screen is a residue from the most archaic mnemic traces. But, additionally, and this is at least as important, one might assume that it provides an opening for understanding the dreamer's "primal scene" which establishes itself during the oral phase. The hallucinatory factor, the lack of distinction between representation and perception—representation taken as perception which makes for our belief in the reality of dream—would correspond to the lack of distinction between active and passive, between acting and suffering experience, undifferentiation between the limits of the body (body/breast), between eating and being eaten, etc., characteristics of the oral phase and borne out by the envelopment of the subject by the screen. For the same reasons, we would find ourselves in a position to understand the specific mode in which the dreamer identifies with his dream, a mode which is anterior to the mirror stage, to the formation of the self, and therefore founded on a permeability, a fusion of the interior with the exterior.

On the other hand, if the dream itself, in its visual content, is likely to represent the desire to stay awake, the combination dream screen/projected images would manifest a conflict between contradictory motions, a state in effect of undistinction between a hallucinatory wish, sign of satisfaction, and desire for perception, of contact with the real. It is therefore conceivable that something of a desire in dream unifying perception and representation—whether representation passes itself for perception, in which case we would be closer to hallucination, or whether perception passes itself for perceived representation, i.e., acquires as perception the mode of existence which is proper to hallucination—takes on the character of specific reality which reality does not impart, but which hallucination provokes: *a more-than-real* that dream precisely, considered as apparatus and as the repetition of a particular state which defines the oral phase, would, on its own, be able to bring to it. Dream alone?

Lewin's hypothesis, which complements and extends Freud's ideas on the formation of dream in relation to the feeling of reality which is linked to it, presents, in my opinion, the advantage of offering a kind of formation stage, of dream constitution, which might be construed as operative in the cinema effect.

Impression of reality and that which we have defined as the desire of cinema, as cinema in its general apparatus would recall, would mime a form of archaic satisfaction experienced by the subject by reproducing the scene of it.

Of course, there is no question of identifying mental image, filmic image, mental representation, and cinematographic representation. The fact that the same terms are used, however, does reveal the very workings of desire in cinema i.e., at the same time the desire to rediscover archaic forms of desire which in fact structure any form of desire, and the desire to stage for the subject, to put in the form of representation, what might recall its own operation.

In any case, this deviation through the "metapsychological fiction" of dream could enlighten us about the effect specific to cinema, "the impression of reality," which, as is well known, is different from the usual impression which we receive from reality, but which has precisely this characteristic of being more than real which we have detected in dream.

Actually, cinema is a simulation apparatus. This much was immediately recognized, but, from the positivist viewpoint of scientific rationality which was predominant at the time of its invention, the interest was directed toward the simulation of reality inherent to the moving image with the unexpected effects which could be derived from it, without finding it necessary to examine the fact that the cinematographic apparatus was initially directed toward the subject and that *simulation could be applied to states or subject effects before being directed toward the reproduction of the real*. It is nevertheless curious that in spite of the development of analytic theory, the problem should have remained unsolved or barely considered since that period. Almost exclusively, it is the technique and content of film which have retained attention: characteristics of the image, depth of field, offscreen space, shot, single-shot sequence, montage, etc.; the key to the impression of reality has been sought in the structuring of image and movement, in complete ignorance of the fact that the impression of reality is dependent first of all on a subject effect and that it might be necessary to examine the position of the subject facing the image in order to determine the raison d'être for the cinema effect. Instead of considering cinema as an ideologically neutral apparatus, as it has been rather stupidly called, the impact of which would be entirely determined by the content of the film (a consideration which leaves unsolved the whole question of its persuasive power and of the reason for which it revealed itself to be an instrument particularly well suited to exert ideological influence), in order to explain the cinema effect, it is necessary to consider it from the viewpoint of the apparatus that it constitutes, apparatus which in its totality includes the subject. And first of all, the subject of the unconscious. The difficulties met by the theoreticians of cinema in their attempt to account for the impression of reality are proportionate to the persisting resistance to really recognizing the unconscious. Although nominally accepted, its existence has nevertheless been left out of the theoretical research. If psycho-analysis has finally permeated the content of certain films, as a complement to the classic psychology of character's action and as a new type of narrative spring, it has remained practically absent from the problematics raised by the relation of the projection to the subject. The problem is nevertheless to determine the extent to which the cinematographic apparatus plays an important part in this subject which Lacan after Freud defines as an apparatus,[7] and the way in which the structuring of the unconscious, the modalities of the subject's development throughout the different strata deposited by the various phases of drives, the differentiation between the Cs, Pcs, and Ucs, systems and their relations, the distinction between primary and secondary processes, make it possible to isolate the effect which is specific to cinema.

Consequently, I will only propose several hypotheses.

First of all, that taking into account the darkness of the movie theater, the relative passivity of the situation, the forced immobility of the cine-subject, and the effects which result from the projection of images, moving images, the cinematographic apparatus brings about a state of artificial regression. It artificially leads back to an anterior phase of his development—a phase which is barely hidden, as dream and certain pathological forms of our mental life have shown. It is the desire, unrecognized as such by the subject, to return to this phase, an early state of development with its own forms of satisfaction which may play a determining role in his desire for cinema and the pleasure he finds in it. Return toward a relative narcissism, and even more toward a mode of relating to reality which could be defined as enveloping and in which the separation between one's own body and the exterior world is not well defined. Following this line of reasoning, one may then be able to understand the reasons for the intensity of the subject's attachment to the images and the process of identification created by cinema. A return to a primitive narcissism by the regression of the libido, Freud tells us, noting that the dreamer occupies the entire field of the dream scene; the absence of delimitation of the body; the transfusion of the interior out into the exterior, added Lewin (other works, notably Melanie Klein's could also be mentioned); without excluding other processes of identification which derive from the specular regime of the ego, from its constitution as "Imaginary." These do not, however, strictly pertain to the cinema effect, although the screen, the focalization produced by the basic apparatus, as I indicated in my earlier paper,[8] could effectively produce mirror effects and cause specular phenomena to intervene directly in the viewing experience. In any case, the usual forms of identification, already supported by the apparatus, would be reinforced by a more archaic mode of identification, which has to do with the lack of differentiation between the subject and his environment, a dream scene model which we find in the baby/breast-screen relationship.

In order to understand the particular status of cinema, it is necessary to underline the partial elimination of the reality test. Undoubtedly, the means of cinematographic projection would keep the reality test intact when compared to dreams and hallucination. The subject has always the choice to close his eyes, to withdraw from the spectacle, or to leave, but no more than in dream does he have means to act in any way upon the object of his perception, change his viewpoint as he would like. There is no doubt that in dealing with images, and the unfolding of images, the rhythm of vision and movement are imposed on him in the same way as images in dream and hallucination. His relative motor inhibition which brings him closer to the state of the dreamer, in the same way as the particular status of the reality he perceives (a reality made up of images), would seem to favor the simulation of the regressive state, and would play a determining role in the subject effect of the impression of reality, this more-than-real of the impression of reality, which as we have seen, is characteristic not of the relation of the subject to reality but precisely of dreams and hallucinations.

One must therefore start to analyze the impression of reality by differentiating between perception and representation. The cinematographic apparatus is unique in that *it offers the subject perceptions "of a reality" whose status seems similar to that of representations experienced as perception.* It should also be noted in this connection that if the confusion between representation and perception is characteristic of the primary process which is governed by the pleasure principle, and which is the basic condition for the satisfaction produced by hallucination, the cinematographic apparatus appears to succeed in suspending the secondary process and anything having to do with the principle of reality without eliminating it completely. This would then lead us to propose the following paradoxical formula: the more-than-real, i.e., the specific characteristic (whatever is specific) of what is meant by the expression "impression of reality," consists in keeping apart (toning down, so that they remain present but as background) the secondary process and the reality principle. Perception of the image passing for perception: one might assume that it is precisely here that one might find the key to the impression of reality, that which would at once approximate and differentiate the cinematographic effect and the dream. Return effect, repetition of a phase of the subject's development during which representation and perception were not yet differentiated, and the desire to return to that state along with the kind of satisfaction associated to it, undoubtedly an archetype for all that which seeks to connect with the multiple paths of the subject's desire. It is indeed desire as such, i.e., desire of desire, the nostalgia for a state in which desire has been satisfied through the transfer of a perception to a formation resembling hallucination, which seems to be activated by the cinematographic apparatus. According to Freud: "To desire initially must have been a hallucinatory cathexis of the memory of satisfaction."[9] Survival and insistence of bygone periods, an irrepressible backward movement. Freud never ceased to remind us that in its formal constitution, dream was a vestige of the subject's phylogenetic past, and the expression of a wish to have again the very form of existence associated with this experience. "Dream which fulfills its wish by the short-cut of regression does nothing but conserve a type of primary operation of the psychical apparatus which had been eliminated because of its inefficiency." It is also the same survival and the same wish which are at work in some hallucinatory psychoses. Cinema, like dream, would seem to correspond to a temporary form of regression, but whereas dream, according to Freud, is merely a "normal hallucinatory psychosis," cinema ofers an artificial psychosis without offering the dreamer the possibility of exercising any kind of immediate control. What I am really saying is that for such a regression to be possible, it is necessary for anterior phases to survive, but that it be cathected by a wish, as is proven by the existence of dream. This wish is remarkably precise, and consists in obtaining from reality a position, a condition in which what is perceived would no longer be distinguished from representations. It can be assumed that it is this wish which prepares the long history of cinema: the wish to construct a simulation machine capable of offering the subject perceptions which are really representations mistaken for perceptions. Cinema offers a simulation of regressive movement which is characteristic of dream—the transformation of thoughts by means of figuration. The withdrawal of cathexis of all the systems Cs, Pcs, Ucs, during sleep causes the representations cathected by dream during the dream work to determine a sensory activity; the operation of dream can be crudely represented by a diagram:

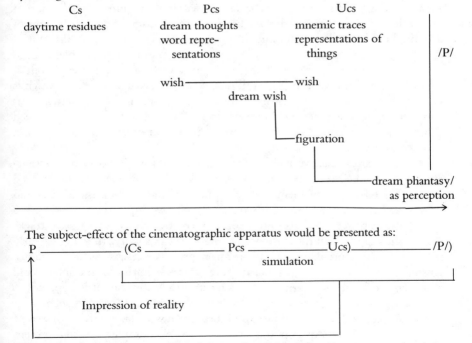

The subject-effect of the cinematographic apparatus would be presented as:

The simulation apparatus therefore consists in transforming a perception into a quasi-hallucination endowed with a reality effect which cannot be compared to that which results from ordinary perception. The cinematographic apparatus reproduces the psychical apparatus during sleep: separation from the outside world, inhibition of motoricity; in sleep, these conditions causing an overcathexis of representation can penetrate the system of perception as sensory stimuli; in cinema, the images perceived (very likely reinforced by the setup of the psychical apparatus) will be overcathected and thus acquire a status which will be the same as that of the sensory images of dream.

One cannot hesitate to insist on the *artificial* character of the cine-subject. It is precisely this artificiality which differentiates it from dream or hallucinations. There is, between cinema and these psychical states, the same distance as between a real object and its simulacrum, with this additional factor that dream and hallucination are already states of simulation (something passing itself off for something else, representation for perception). One might even argue that it is this embedded structure which makes it so difficult to deal with the subject effect. While, in dreams and hallucinations, representations appear in the guise of perceived reality, a real perception takes place in cinema, if not an ordinary perception of reality. It would appear that it is this slight displacement which has misled the theoreticians of cinema, when analyzing the impression of reality. In dream and hallucination, representations are taken as reality in the absence of perception; in cinema, images are taken for reality but require the mediation of perception. This is why, on the one hand, for the realists, cinema is thought of as a duplicate of reality—and on the other cinema is taken as an equivalent of dream—but the comparison stops there, leaving unresolved the problem raised by the impression of reality. It is evident that cinema is not dream: but it reproduces an impression of reality, it unlocks, releases a cinema effect which is comparable to the impression of reality caused by dream. The entire cinematographic apparatus is activated in order to provoke this simulation: it is indeed a simulation of a condition of the subject, a position of the subject, a subject and not reality.

Desire for a real that would have the status of hallucination or of a representation taken for a perception—one might wonder whether cinema is not doubled by another wish, complementary to the one that is at work in the subject and which we have presumed to be at work in Plato's cave apparatus.

For, if dream really opens onto another scene by way of a regressive track, one might suppose that the existence of an unconscious where the subject's early mode of functioning, defined by the primary process, persists, the unconscious, constantly denied, rejected, excluded, never ceases requiring of the subject and proposing to him, by multiple detours (even if only through artistic practice), representations of his own scene. In other words, without his always suspecting it, the subject is induced to produce machines which would not only complement or supplement the workings of the secondary process but which could represent his own overall functioning to him: he is led to produce mechanisms mimicking, simulating the apparatus which is no other than himself. The presence of the unconscious also makes itself felt through the pressure it exerts in seeking to get itself represented by a subject who is still unaware of the fact that he is representing to himself the very scene of the unconscious where he is.

Notes

1. Sigmund Freud, *The Interpretation of Dreams* (New York: Avon, 1965), pp. 574–75.

2. In a general way, we distinguish the *basic cinematographic apparatus [l'appareil de base]*, which concerns the ensemble of the equipment and operations necessary to the production of a film and its projection, from the apparatus *[le dispositif]* discussed in this article, which solely concerns projection and which includes the subject to whom the projection is addressed. Thus the *basic cinematographic apparatus* involves the film stock, the camera, developing, montage considered in its technical aspects, etc., as well as the apparatus *[dispositif]* of projection. The basic cinematographic apparatus is a long way from being the camera by itself, to which some have wanted to say I limit it (one wonders what bad arguments this can serve).

3. A close relationship which has led filmmakers to believe that cinema was the instrument finally suited for the representation of dreams. The failure of their attempt still remains to be understood. Is it not that the representation of dreams in cinema would not function like the representation of dreams in dreams, precisely destroying the impression of reality in the same way as the thought that one is dreaming intervenes in dream as a defense mechanism against the "mashing" desire of dream. The displacement of dream in the projection results unavoidably in sending the spectator back to his consciousness; it imposes a distance which denounces the artifice (and is there anything more ridiculous than those soft focus clouds, supposedly dreamlike representations) and it destroys completely the *impression of reality* which precisely also defines dream.

4. In *The Ego and the Id*, Freud adds comments which allow him to assesrt that "visual thought is closer to the unconscious processes than verbal thought, and older than the latter, from the phylogenetic as well as from the ontogenetic standpoints. Verbal representations all belong to the Pcs, while the unconscious only relies on visual ones."

5. This is why it is not by paying attention to the content of images that one is able to account for the impression of reality but by questioning the apparatus. The differentiation between fantasies and dream is due to the transformation of the psychical apparatus during the transition from the state of being awake to sleep. Sleep will make necessary the work of figuration the economy of which can be created by daytime fantasies; in addition, daytime fantasies do not accompany the belief in reality of the fulfillment which characterizes dream. This is why in attempting to understand the cinema effect—the impression of reality—we have to go through the intermediary of dream and not daytime fantasies.

6. Bertram Lewin, "Sleep, the Mouth and the Dream Screen," *Psychoanalytic Quarterly* (1946), 15:419–43," Inferences from the Dream Screen," *International Journal of Psychoanalysis* (1948), 29:224–431.

7. "The subject is an apparatus. This apparatus is lacunary, and it is within this lacuna that the subject sets up the function of an object as lost object." Jacques Lacan, *Les Quatres Concepts fondamenteux de la psychanalyse* (Paris: Le Seuil, 1973).

8. Jean-Louis Baudry, "Cinéma: Effets idéologiques produits par l'appareil de base," *Cinéthique* (1970) nos. 7–8, pp. 1–8. Published in an English translation by Alan Williams in *Film Quarterly* (Winter 1974–75), 28(2):39–47 [Included in this anthology—ED.]

9. It may seem peculiar that desire which constituted the cine-effect is rooted in the oral structure of the subject. The conditions of projection do evoke the dialectics internal/external,

swallowing/swallowed, eating/being eaten, which is characteristic of what is being structured during the oral phase. But, in the case of the cinematographic situation, the visual orifice has replaced the buccal orifice: the absorption of images is at the same time the absorption of the subject in the image, prepared, predigested by his very entering in the dark theater. The relationship visual orifice/buccal orifice acts at the same time as analogy and differentiation, but also points to the relation of consecution between oral satisfaction, sleep, white screen of the dream on which dream images will be projected, beginning of the dream. On the importance of sight during the oral phase, see Spitz's remarks in *The Yes and the No.* In the same order of ideas, it may be useful to reintroduce Melanie Klein's hypothesis on the oral phase, her extremely complex dialectics between the inside and the outside which refer to reciprocal forms of development.

—*Translated by Jean Andrews and Bertrand Augst*

18

Pascal Bonitzer

The Silences of the Voice
(*A propos* of *Mai 68* by Gudie Lawaetz)

Ah, how repugnant imposing my own thoughts on others is to me!—Nietzsche

The "Minimum of Commentary"

We know that, politically and ideologically, the issue of the *point of view* a film reflects is a crucial question, and often becomes the arena of violent controversy. For example, *Lacombe Lucien* and *The Night Porter* recently gave rise to contradicting interpretations of their ideological content: fascist, progressive, reactionary? Then there was the case of Antonioni's *China*: certain "friends of China" analyzed its point of view as progressive and pro-Chinese, while others (not to mention the Chinese themselves) as anti-Chinese and reactionary. This leads us to questions on three points:

(1) A film produces a *discourse*.

(2) This discourse is, to a greater or lesser extent, *implicit, veiled*.

(3) And it is the *spectators* who, "in the last instance" utter (contradictorily) its truth.

Of course, it is true that the fiction film gives rise to diverse interpretations. Is not ambiguity the element in which all fiction is immersed? But a documen-

Published in *Cahiers du cinéma* (February–March 1975), no. 256, and with revisions in Pascal Bonitzer, *Le Regard et la voix* (Paris: Union Général d'Editions, 1976). Translated here by permission of *Cahiers du Cinéma*.

tary or a montage of documents—on the contrary, isn't its aim to shed light on the real with which it deals? to disengage from that real a readability and hence a point of view? Insofar as it deals with the real, isn't documentary a matter of truth? Camera-views, montage: reality is seized and worked through at a certain angle in order to *render* something on the screen—to the spectators.

It is therefore necessary to envisage the work by which a film organizes its point of view, articulates its discourse. How is it done in the case of a film like *Mai 68*, which is precisely a film that brings together different points of view from divergent political extremes onto the same object? Does this imply that the film in its entirety produces no point of view? But why does this question *have to be asked?*

Mai 68 is connected to a type of film and a type of montage with its own traditions and codes, those of the "free confrontation" (produced essentially by television, but which cinema can take up, as is shown, for example, by the success of *The Sorrow and the Pity*). The free confrontation is that of contradictory images and witnesses, a mise-en-scène of the multiple "facets" of an event by means of interviews and archival documentary footage. (The latter's difference from nature is a sign of the richness of the investigation and of the information and so should be marked: in this case the interviews are shot in color, which has the additional effect of emphasizing the temporal gap 1968–1973, the "receding" of the testimony and of the positions taken.) The lure for the public is that of mastering a dossier—by leafing through it.

A formula credited by Gudie Lawaetz to Sartre rather well summarizes this genre of historical digest, whose success testifies to its seductiveness: *"let the event speak."* This is an interesting formula not only because in it can be read the elision of (the author's) point of view toward the event in question, but also because it displaces this "question of point of view"—which is so important for "politics"—to a problem of *speech*. It is because it is inscribed there that "it speaks,"[1] that the just vision of an event depends on what the latter *says,* that the eye is carried by the voice, and under the circumstances, a voice which, if not silent, is at least *without subject.*

Without subject—this is central to the question. It is true that the event belongs to no one (and this is more true of May 1968 than any other event). Gudie Lawaetz' film shows this well: if it witnesses something, it is the failure of those who appropriate the movement to themselves (see the points of view the film compares, which are all perplexed or worn down). So, is it "the event itself" which actually speaks in this film? Of course not. What speaks is its descent into the past, into journalistic information and into History in the old sense of the word: linear history, flat chronology, trifles of the recent past and the derision of senescence. Of course all the actors of May have aged. Of course the images of May have aged. But what is this? Is this the meaning—this aging, this slackening? It is like the final scene of *Rentrée des usines Wonder,* but taken out of its militant context, for which is substituted an "open ending": *Mai 68* repeats *the end of May.*

This film has the past in its eye. It is indeed a "point of view" which is thus organized, a discourse which is woven in silence. Is it without subject? But this aging, whose image the film offers across its impoverished informative chronology, is indeed that of a subject. Who is this subject? Who if not us, the spectators, in whom "the event speaks" silently. To "let the event speak" is to let it be spoken by the spectators, according to the paths traced in silence by the film and guided by the signposts of montage. It is thus important to analyze the structure, the montage, which conveys the "event" and what historical capacity is distributed to it—here, pretty much that of a *Mirror of History*. It is important to recognize that what speaks in a film is never the "event" (and what is an event, if not a nodal point of redistributed historical intensities?), but rather the subject who is supposed *to know it.*

At stake in this type of film is knowledge. What is desired from it is a knowledge of an object (history, May 1968, etc.), a knowledge that is in some way specifically cinematographic, obtained by the eye and the ear, optical and sound recording, the *scene* which their montage composes.

In this knowledge, it is important to allow the spectator to enjoy—that is, not to take the spectator's place by uttering it. The principle "let the event speak" also signifies *"Let the spectator enjoy (know)."* Of course one can protest that this is a false knowledge, an *impression of knowledge* (in the sense of an "impression of reality") obtained through the specular lure produced by the cinematographic apparatus *[l'appareil];* whereas, in truth, knowledge requires something other than this specular impression, for it only exists as the effect of a labor of inquiry and theoretical elaboration, of placing the object in perspective and investigating its form. Undoubtedly.

But the enjoyment—the *jouissance*[2]—of the spectator? A difficulty arises here, and one which is nodal for a cinema which, more than any other, utters its knowledge. This is the cinema whose principles are opposed to those practiced by Gudie Lawaetz—namely "militant cinema." The latter has often been reproached for ignoring *jouissance* (of the spectators), and to a great extent this reproach is well-grounded. The difficulty thus revolves around a certain number of notions put in play in a specific way by the documentary or the compilation film: *discourse, subject, knowledge, jouissance.* The place of the spectators in the apparatus *[le dispositif]*—their role—is there implicated and acted out.

In the Lawaetz system (which is to say, in a classical system), one sees how *jouissance* under the form (if one likes) of the "impression of knowledge" is put into operation. It is from an *absence* in the body of the film that it is offered to the spectators. This absence is neither that of a discourse nor that of a subject—both of which, as we have seen, can be implicit and veiled, but never lacking. It is the absence of *commentary,* which is to say of a *voice.* More precisely, what is absent is the voice-off, that voice of knowledge *par excellence* in all films, since it resounds from offscreen, in other words from the field of the Other. In this system the concern is to reduce, insofar as possible, not the informative capacity of commentary but its assertive character and, if one likes, its *authoritative* character—that arbitration and arbitrariness of the voice-off which, to the extent that it cannot be localized, can be criticized by nothing and no one. This is a system of "no commentary" or "minimum of commentary." This is, we maintain, a classical system for the documentary, the archival film, and the compilation film. In appearance it is a democratic system: it puts restraints on the arbitrariness of the voice-off, of commentary which does violence to the real and to the spectators (by not allowing them to think about the event). What is this system in reality?

The Voice Which Keeps Its Silence

In *Mai 68,* when Séguy speaks of May, the student movement, and the workers' movement, his words are inflated by his face and have to be evaluated in connection with that face, with that simultaneously embarrassed and cunning air, those fleeting glances, etc.—that collection of traits which, with a light regional accent, connotes the "personality" of a union leader for cinema and television. For the spectators, having the *image* of Séguy (or any politician) imparts a relative critical power. Doubtless, this criticism is greatly limited and very equivocal (how could anyone honestly judge a politics by a physical image of those who reflect it? racism is not far away.) But it is still criticism, and spectators never fail to make more or less use of it. If he speaks facing the camera, one can laugh at what he says or insult him (and this happened in movie theaters of the Latin Quarter when *Mai 68* was shown). Enclosed in the frame of the (large or small) screen and in some way *visibly* calling for our complicity, he is, in a certain fashion, delivered to us. Prisoner of a perceptible appearance, doubly mastered by the lens of the camera and the eye of the spectator, the authority of the voice is thus encountered as being submitted to criticism, or at least to *a* criticism—the most rapid one, that of the look. The image plays the role of fixative for the voice. It restrains the power in it (resonance, amplitude, ambience, its disquieting power.)

It is completely otherwise when the voice absents and uproots itself from the image, and returns to haunt it from outside, from space-off, from off screen. It then secures a hold on the image and, through the latter, on the real which it reflects; and this hold can no longer be countered by an easy criticism from the look. So instead of looking, it is necessary to think—but this is precisely the problem: is there time to do so? Was Merleau-Ponty wrong when he wrote "a film is not thought, it is perceived?"

Voice-off. There are at least two types of voice-off, which refer to at least two types of space-off. Take the case of a narrative fiction such as a detective film, when the voice of a character comes from off screen. Even if there is no reverse shot to suture the gap opened by this voice, we know that it comes from a place homogeneous with that of the scenographic lure offered by the filmic image. This is a homogeneity in accord with realist physical space. Such a voice can be disquieting, as, to a greater or lesser extent, voice-off always is; however, it is so only within the dramatic frame of the fiction, which is to say, in a restricted way. Thus, in *Kiss Me Deadly*, if the criminal whose identity and terrifying secret is sought by Mike Hammer remains off screen until the last sequences, it is unnecessary from the point of view of the detective enigma; for as he himself says, nothing will be learned from his face by the detective (or the spectators). But keeping it off screen (we only see his lower legs and only know him from his blue suede shoes) gives his sentential voice, inflated by mythological comparisons, a much greater disquieting power, the scope of an oracle— somber prophet of the end of the world. And despite that, this voice is submitted to the destiny of the body: the one institution of the narrative to whose law it is submitted renders it decrepit and mortal. It suffices for the subject of this voice to appear in the image (and thus it suffices that he *could* appear there) for it to be no longer anything but the voice of a man, in other words, of any imbecile. Proof? A gunshot, he falls—and with him, but in ridicule, his discourse with its prophetic overtones.

The contrary case is when the voice is inscribed in a space which is not in proper interaction (not homogeneous) with that of the image. This voice introduces a division of the filmic field that is much more enigmatic. In fiction films this division is rare and produces an effect of strangeness (an example of its utilization for this effect of strangeness is Mankiewicz's *A Letter to Three Wives*). But as rare as this is in fiction films, it is common and seems natural in documentaries. And to the extent that this is the case, it makes for no problems in them.

In *Kashima Paradise* the voice-off intervenes with a certain brutality. It forces the image from its discourse of class struggle, and counters naturalness and the perceptibly obvious. But who speaks, and from where and when?

Another practice can be found in *China,* whose commentary is rarefied and barely assertive. Antonioni does not inform the image with any theory (and especially not with Marxist theory), but rather principally with a circle of information about what is not shown, namely the conditions of the filming, the specifics of what is off screen, etc. For example, he describes, off, not what the filmic image reflects—the Chinese peasants are extremely fidgity, clearly uncomfortable with the camera, almost tormented by it—but, *en abime, that which is supposedly seen* by these peasants who are being stalked by the apparatus [*appareil*] (and which is precisely what they avoid looking at): Antonioni himself and his crew, in the disquieting strangeness of their Western disorder (beards, long hair, faded jeans, etc.) But if this permits him, ever so little, to situate himself (unlike the authors of *Kashima*), from where does he get the right, in their place, to speak the look of these peasants? And what effect is he seeking?

The secret power of commentary and voice-off is that these (and other similar) questions *are practically never posed to spectators during the time of projection*. The conventional realist homogeneity of narrative space calls up identification by means of the image, and thus all which intervenes from offscreen immediately causes questioning (at least of an anterior identification by means of the play of the shot/reverse shot, reframings, etc.). At the inverse of such narrative space, in the divided, heterogeneous space of documentary, the voice-off forbids questioning about its enunciator, its place, and its time. The commentary, in informing the image, and the image, in allowing itself to be invested by the commentary, censor such questions.

This is not, one surmises, without ideological implications. The first of these is that the voice-off represents a power, namely the power of the disposition of the image and what it reflects from a place which is absolutely *other* (from that inscribed on the image track)—absolutely other and *absolutely undetermined*. In this sense it is transcendent; hence, incontestable, uncontested, and supposedly knowledgeable. Insofar as it issues from the field of the Other, the voice-off is presumed to know: this is the essence of its power.

Power indeed. For if the voice *knows*, it is inevitably *for* someone, who will not speak. To say it is for someone is to discuss both its addressee and its place. This someone is undoubtedly the spectator, but not only him. In the sequence from *China* cited above, Antonioni (the voice) speaks *from the place* of the Chinese peasants and *addresses* the Western spectators; and the *inverse* is also in operation (for in a certain way the film addresses itself to the Chinese as well, to see how the latter have grasped it; and speaks of China from the place of the spectators, to see precisely the position of Antonioni and of the spectator—privileged). The voice speaks *from the place of the Other,* and this also must be understood in a double sense. It is not charged with manifesting the Other in its radical heterogeneity, but on the contrary with controlling it, with recording it (that is, with suppressing and conserving it), with fixating it by means of knowledge. The power of the voice is a stolen power, stolen from the Other; it is a usurpation.

In his article "Who Says What, but Where and When?" (*Cahiers du cinéma,* no. 250), Serge Daney gives a striking example of the use which Power can make of this appropriated power of the voice-off. It is the daily use which television makes of it:

A short time ago, O.R.T.F. presented a short film on prisons. While the camera fluidly slid along the white walls of a model prison, the commentary-off reprised in *its* way and in its language a certain number of demands and problems posed elsewhere by the prisoners (elsewhere: everywhere, except on television—for example, in the C.A.P.). A "contentist" criticism could satisfy itself with this and see in it, deservedly, the effect— reading through it—of the real struggle of the prisoners, without which television would never have been obliged to make the film. But who does not see a difference in *nature* between a film like this and *Attica?*

For *Attica* speaks with, for, and by means of the voices of the prisoners. It is necessary to note that the film described by Daney is representative of a great deal of news reporting and magazine programs produced by television. Now, what is in operation in that smoothness, that fluidity? First of all the image, that image which shows *nothing* properly speaking (the blank walls of a model prison), only a metonymy (part for whole) of the carceral world, whose pure, abstract presence is made to shine forth by the small screen. This metonymic usage of the image is very frequent in television news. It fills in the hole of real information, the lack of serious inquiry, and functions as a kind of *sign* of information (it is necessary to fill up the image box, to show something). But above all, this radical metonymy, this near-emptiness of the image, makes *the real* shine forth (this paucity of things, these deserted shots, are indications that the camera has *touched* the real, which can, in turn, touch your eyes); and the commentary-off is then able to seize the real. It is the visual and perceivable support of the commentary—if one likes, its flesh. The action of this kind of film is thus a double reduction, a double mastery of the real, which is to say of that which burns (here, not only carceral space, but the entire social crisis which it reveals): mastery by the image, which manifests the real while denying it, and by the voice, which speaks the real while imposing silence on it.

Indeed, what is this voice which "reprised in *its* way and in its language"? Whose way and whose language? But these are precisely the questions which are barred, obscured by space-off. What speaks is the *anonymity* of "public service," of television, of information in general—and, extending the circle of connotations, perhaps the compassionate and grief-stricken Law, Democracy enunciating its wrongs, Man . . . A little of all these silently speak in the anonymity of the voice-off, there vaguely tracing the great veiled and abstract subject in whose name it speaks *[ça parle]*. And this *it* is the homogeneity of the social order, which in reprising "in its way," is straining to reabsorb the heterogeneous, burning discourse of the prisoners.

What the anonymous voice-off of "public service" accomplishes is in fact a double suppression of *the voice of the prisoners*. First, it suppresses their voice by not allowing them to speak, and second by substituting for them. The purpose—television also serves this purpose, and one could demonstrate that a program such as *Dossiers de l'Ecran* has no other rationale—is that the *burning voice* of revolt (and through it the burning fact of revolt) give way to the cold voice of order, normality, and power.

In its function as commentary, the voice-off neither is supposed to be nor can be a burning voice—ephemeral, fragile, troubled by revolts when they have for once managed, at great price, to break through the wall of silence. The atony of commentary recloses that wall.

True, it is not always atonic.

Indeed, this is what leads us back to the stake pointed out by the technique of the "minimum of commentary": the jouissance of the spectator, the right of the latter to knowledge. The submission of the spectator to the master voice indeed has limits. Those limits are encountered when the voice is obviously deceptive—a privilege of the master, but a risky privilege—and when partisan passion is perceived in it. This experience is amusingly illustrated by Chris Marker's short documentary *Letter from Siberia*.

In it the same sequence is seen three times, in continuity, but each time accompanied by different commentaries. The sequence shows workers in an unremarkable Siberian city (Yakutsk) occupied with paving a street; passing through the foreground is an Asiatic whose squinty look crosses the monocular one of the lens. What Chris Marker wishes to demonstrate is that such an image, in itself, is not neutral but is at least ambiguous and is susceptible in its referential function (Siberia, the Soviet Union) to antagonistic, contradictory readings; and that the role of the commentary can be precisely to wrest from the image a strong, univocal meaning (the image opens a field of multiple connotations which the commentary closes in denoting it, in bestowing names on things). Thus, the first commentary for this sequence is a discourse of the sanctimonious Stalinist type: the meaning extorted from the image by this discourse is that of the joyous construction of socialism ("In the joyful spirit of socialist emulation, happy Soviet workers, among them this picturesque denizen of the Arctic reaches, apply themselves to making Yakutsk an even better place to live"). The image track presents the same series of shots and the commentary changes: the voice now extracts from it an eloquent expression of Soviet misery, as would be seen by a professional anticommunist ("Bending to the task like slaves, the miserable Soviet workers, among them this sinister-looking Asiatic, apply themselves to the primitive labor of grading with a drag beam"). For the third and last time, the film returns to the same shots and the end of prosopopoeia: Chris Marker stops parodying the discourse of others—of official joviality or of primitive anti-Sovietism (which, from a certain angle, are the same thing)—and finally enunciates what can be properly said of the material: a commentary which is neither black nor white and which is objective and nuanced ("With courage and tenacity under extremely difficult conditions, Soviet workers, among them this Yakut afflicted with an eye disorder, apply themselves to improving the appearance of their city, which could certainly use it.")[3]

In reading these *(Commentaries* by Chris Marker has been published by Editions de Seuil), one cannot avoid a vague sense of deception the third time the sequence is repeated. Is it a matter of nothing being said? Not completely. To begin with, in its entirety the sequence does say something, but in a negative form: it says that commentary should not do violence to the image. To do violence to the image and to impel its referential reality is to extort a surplus meaning from it, to interdict its ambiguity, to congeal it into a type, symbol, metaphor (paving a street = joyful spirit of socialist emulation; an Asian passing by = yellow peril, etc.). This is what makes for propaganda. The ethic here suggested is close to that professed by André Bazin, when he denounced the rape of the image (of its "ontological realism") by montage, that power of montage to orient the haphazardness of events snared on film toward any meaning (toward a meaning intended a priori). Like Bazin, Marker denounces the reduction of the signifying field opened by the filmic image. He understands it as a terrorist reduction to the benefit of interests exterior to and transcending the cinematographic experience.

In one sense, this is not wrong, but only in one sense. In his brilliant caricature, Marker's critique runs together without distinction the enunciation and the enunciated, voice and meaning. So one cannot avoid the impression that something (in the functioning of commentary) is escaping notice.

There are two aspects of partisan passion: passion and taking sides. It is well-known that passion is blind. It enables one to cast doubt on truth and is the very foundation of one's partiality (retaining the equivocation between partial as meaning in part and partial as meaning biased and unfair). Moreover, it is violent and can settle nothing. (And it is intolerable when it occupies the place of power—"off.") Marker is against this passion and blindness; he does not judge from a position of involvement. But is it necessary always to prefer detached reason, the "scientific" or ironic gaze? Chris Marker poses the question well ("But objectivity isn't exact, either. It does not deform the Siberian reality, but stops its movement for the time of a judgment, and thereby deforms it all the same"). But he responds quickly and vaguely: "What counts is the *élan* and diversity." Another response, which comes closer to what is in the power of the voice, is sketched out in another short documentary which is much older than *Letter from Siberia*: Bunuel's *Las Hurdes [Land Without Bread]*. We will return to this.

What is certain is that the cold voice is imposed (see above) where the accents of passion give birth to mistrust. Ultimately, is this not what Chris Marker is saying in the sequence of *Letter from Siberia*? Isn't he ultimately denouncing not the false character of passionate commentary, but its *inoperative* character? Here we refind the technique of "minimum of commentary." What Chris Marker enunciates is the modern knowledge—Western and bourgeois, if one wishes—of what is the *reserve* of commentary that defines the regime of its mastery, its terrorist opacity. He does not enunciate solely the democratic, liberal ethic of the commentary of political information, but also and perhaps especially, the cynicism of a science, of a mastery of the commentary: it doesn't say too much, it doesn't devour the silent, open meaning of the image, it doesn't counter the "obtuseness," ambiguity, or power of silent assertion of the image. It is a layer protecting the filmic image, lubricating it and not forcing it.

The countertest of this "science" of the commentary is given to us as much by travelogues as by certain militant films, and also by prewar newsreels of the Pathé-Journal type. These experiment with the descent of the voice into falseness and ridiculousness. One laughs, one cries, one doesn't believe one's ears. It is so silly that it is comic, or odious, or both at once. What is evident in this is precisely an accent: the surprising twang, the forced note, the comic rapidity of the voice-off in Pathé newsreels; or the syrupy sentimentality of commentaries in travelogues; or the epic bombast, obligatory class hatred, and insufferable optimism of the commentary in certain militant films. What one hears, then, is something like the *body* of the voice—and its body is its death to meaning. The voice is no longer drawn for us from the image (presuming that the latter is not itself perceived as grotesque and abusive, which happens but in which case the problem is not posed), nor *a fortiori* from the real which is mirrored there. It detaches itself and becomes part of an ensemble which does not hold together. This is what permits aesthetes to love film in spite of itself by finding in it the charm of the old, an aspect of kitsch and nostalgia.

The Voices Which Are Heard

The voice ages. Its signifier (that in it which is heard) "labors." In it is perceived an accent which is not that of a region of geography but rather a region of meaning, the accent of an era, a class, a regime—and this accent neutralizes meaning, defuses the knowledge imposed by that voice. This is why it is necessary for it to speak as little as possible. *No commentary* is the wisdom or the prudence of the master, of power. The voice expounds. It expounds more than the image, for one can play with the image, but then the ridiculous risked is not that of the ultimate, mortal ridiculous—of meaning.

That which has the "right to speech" (in the sense that it has the power to do so) should use it as little as possible. This is a curious rule. Does it hold for all films in the register of the real, of the document and of the documentary? Is it evaded in the limit case (such as *Mai 68)* when commentary is abolished and scansions of montage substitute?

To this second question one can respond that the *accent*—since it is this asperity of the voice which catches critical hearing (as a flood of light can catch the grain of a surface which is the "material" of a painted canvas)—the accent is also perceived, though less directly, beyond the voice in the shocks of montage and the frequency of cuts which are the means by which montage makes discourse. One does not thus escape the hindrances of discourse or truth (even though this is a platitude).

But who is it that is afraid of deception, aging, and dying? Is it everyone? Perhaps everyone, to the extent that, as it is said, *he* aspires to mastery, *he* defends his power, his knowledge, his memory. This is to say to the extent that *he* is *one.*[4] Voice off: the voice of his master. And there can be only one master. This is why, generally in this system, there is only one commentating voice on the sound track (and most of the time it is a man's voice). Sometimes, but more rarely, there are two alternating voices (man, woman) so that the superior unity of discourse arises from their discrete conjugal harmony. But if the voice is found to be geared down and with this the unity of the discourse is found to be broken, the system and its effects change. Space-off then stops being the place of the reserve and the interiority of the voice (that place where it "is heard to speak"); it is itself divided, and from this division takes on the dimension of a scene, is dramatized and is peopled. Something happens there, parallel to the image or interlacing with it, but unfixed from it. The voice is no longer simply planted in the image when there are many voices and they struggle with one another (as in Godard, notably during the period of the "Dziga Vertov Group"), or when they desire and love one another (as in Duras). But what is found to be subverted is the very principle of the documentary, its principle of reality (both as unique and as objective).

To encounter the "body" of the voice (what Barthes calls its grain), this refuse from meaning, is to encounter the subject of the voice with its division, the subject fallen to the rank of object and unmasked: thus, in Chris Marker's exercise "the paranoid anticommunist" and "the jovial Stalinist" were carnival figures. On the one hand meaning is naked, neutralized, laughable ("the emperor has no clothes"); on the other hand, there is its "body," its cadaver: its noise and cacaphony. . . Why is it that when it becomes perceivable, this bursting of the unity of commentary and of voice, this scission of sound and meaning, is accompanied by manifestations of revolt, by laughing and crying in the theaters? Against what is a revolt occurring? Against humbuggery. But this humbuggery does not give rise to a special reaction if it does not claim to dominate with its discourse the real that crosses the image. To recognize the humbuggery in the imperturbable voice-off by laughing is to lift the oppression of the commentary. The laugh explodes, its splits open: it breaks through the voice of the commentator.

If the unity of voice and meaning in the commentary-off defines a regime of mastery or of oppression, it is perhaps starting from its scission that one could begin to define another politics (or erotics) of the voice-off. Something of this order was devised by Buñuel in *Las Hurdes:* the commentary-off is cold, but the image shrieks. Over the image, it cracks, it rots, it cruelly grimaces; and by this, the circumspection, the reserve of the commentary becomes strange, becomes the atony of the disquieting voice, as if the abyss between the silent cry of the image and the discourse of the voice-off were imperceptibly traversed by a silent laugh which belies what this voice says. In the end, this voice is *heard*. Starting from the moment when it is heard, its discourse—which is never that of mastery—is found to be menaced, the function of the commentary is lacking, and that of documentary is placed on trial. What is devised in *Las Hurdes* is a radical testing of the mastery based on the commentary, on imperialism, and on colonialism, which are deep-seated in documentary.

All modern cinema since, let us say, Godard on the one hand and Bresson on the other, is instituted by simultaneously placing on trial the filmic image as a full, centered, and deep image, and the utilization of the voice as homogeneous with and in harmony with the image. It has often been said that what cinematographic modernity puts into play—no matter what claims it uses to promote itself—are effects of rupture, dis-alignings, "noise" in the filmic chain. A tearing in the effect of the real of the image and in the effect of mastery of the voice is brought about. The relation among voice, sound, and silence is transformed and musicalized.

This is what provides the site for limit experiments, such as those in the margin of militant cinema of the "Dziga Vertov Group," or those of Straub or of Duras. Straub is certainly the filmmaker who has played the most richly, musically, and dramatically with plurality, with the capacity of voices in filmic space; it does not always know a lot, but in the end it will be heard.[5] In Duras (who recently declared that she can no longer synchronize—she said *"screw"*— voices into mouths) this is, among other things, an experiment with silence and with the subversion of the voice with silence. This is true from *Destroy, She Said* and *Nathalie Granger* (*Nathalie Granger* is inhabited by silence not in order to reinforce, from an effect of reserve, the power of speech *which is that of man,* but to paralyze and to cast a spell over the latter and to return the voice as lapse, as trouble, as a liberty of the unconscious—*to return the voice to women*) to *Woman of the Ganges* and *India Song* (and perhaps *Vera Baxter*) where the silence of the image provokes the sonic peopling of space-off. Duras thus introduces the spark of desire and sends the question back to the spectators.

But these are fictions, which is to say works supremely unconcerned with that "reflection of the real" by which the truth of a documentary is measured and which imposes on the voice of the latter that specific discretion which is our problem. It would be necessary to discuss militant cinema, where the voice finds itself invested with a precise function which is, moreover, variable. For example, in *Oser lutter* (made in Flins in May–June of 1968 by established militants) there is that confused mixture of voices, over black leader, from which emerges in bits and pieces the "truth" of the struggle: "and above all, no negotiations . . . " To this mixture and burning confusion on the sound track is opposed, as the clarity of revolutionary knowledge, intertitles where that knowledge is all written, white on black. Or in *Shanghai au jour le jour,* there are two voices-off of women in dialogue, but they do not directly comment on the real which the image reflects (as, for example, does Antonioni, discussed above); but rather they comment on the image track and clearly are speaking *in an editing room*. Here there is something which blocks the terrorist indetermination of the voice-off—two women who speak *to one another,* who have a dialogue *before* the images. . .

If, in a general way, the problems here evoked are rarely resolved in an interesting fashion (and rarely even envisaged) by militant cinema, it is never-theless from its place and starting from the problems posed by militant film makers that it is possible to begin to think and to realize a subversion of documentary and of that which secretly operates there: the discourse of power, *the discourse-form of power*. Indeed, militant cinema cannot be something like classical documentary plus rage and great, fine-sounding words. It has to be something else completely, something which organizes otherwise the relation to the real, the look, and the voice.

Here or there, in varying degrees this is being done, for what is called militant cinema never begins except from where classical documentary ends, in that which the latter smothers and erases: the speaking subject. The stake being risked is that of the subject. This is the reason classical documentary represses that stake, most often in the dogmatism of a voice-off without subject. The greatest difficulty in the order of the document and the real which there makes itself known is indeed that of not effacing the subject, the *I* and the *you*. Perhaps this leads toward a new way of approaching the real, a way which is more supple, and also more hazardous, more open to chance. Hazard, discovery—this is the chance of the new.

Hence, militant cinema loves the hazardous. . .

N.B. 1. It will have been understood that commentary is not point of view. Its problem is precisely how to silence a point of view. Not that the commentary exists *before* an organized point of view, which could otherwise say everything. But commentary is not for saying all: its role is to legislate on images of the real, to inject knowledge into them.

Rather, the question of point of view has to do with truth. It is about the way in which a subject is implicated in a process and what emerges from it. In discussing commentary, I have thus spoken of the signifier of the voice. I have placed hardly any emphasis on commentary which is written and which in film is called "intertitles." The procedure of speaking through them has been singularly rare, so that today one barely finds it except in the cinema of Godard and, since May 1968, in a somewhat sophisticated sector of militant cinema: *le Peuple et ses fusils* (distributed commercially), *Oser lutter*. . .

One immediately sees the difference between spoken commentary-off and commentary through intertitles: beyond the necessarily fragmentary, discontinuous, and compiled character of the discourse of "intertitles," in them knowledge is designated as such, which is to say as didacticism. To the interiority of the voice-off is opposed the exteriority of the text presented for reading, which solicits the eye and appeals to the "consciousness" (in the political sense of the word) of the spectators. In comparison to voice-off, intertitles involve a kind of effect of distanciation or—as Philippe Ivernel has proposed to translate the

Brechtian *Verfremdungseffekt*—of "disalienation." This is why it is essentially in militant cinema that intertitles are utilized.

It has to be added that they rarely make for pleasure. They will rather provoke irritation, even hatred. The spectators say they are offended that the dotting of the *i's* is thus placed between the images for them. They would prefer instead to *let the images speak for themselves;* and with the images, the real.

With words and intertitles it [ça] is indeed interposed between the spectators and that which filters the real in the image. This is the appearance. The appearance is not disturbing when you are injected unawares from behind, with the voice-off. But in contrast, when on the screen, that appearance frustrates the eye and provokes resentment (or rather, one's resentment is toward the authors of the film).[6]

N.B. 2. In classical and modern cinema (with the exception of certain underground films), but specifically in documentary, filmic space, and even the ensemble of the cinematic apparatus *[dispositif]*, is polarized by two concurrent orderings—the look and the voice. The look and the voice are not equivalent to image and sound. They are the two complementary and concurrent orderings to which the work of the image track and the sound track (shooting, editing, sound mixing, color and tonal grading of the image, etc.) are submitted. This prevalence of the look and the voice is a relation of the subject's "flickering in eclipses" which regulates the filmic chain (the alternation and disposition of shots: the 30-degree rule, shot/countershot, etc.) and of which the spectator is the support (see Jean-Pierre Oudart, "La Suture" in *Cahiers du cinéma* nos. 210 and 212).[7] This prevalence points toward that which constitutes the spectator as such: spectator of his or her desires (insofar as desires are constituted by the Other). It thus also involves the division, the identificatory alienation of the spectator, in the filmic chain.

Recently the question has been posed whether this "alienation" is irreducible, or whether it is possible to lift it by some perversion of the apparatus *[dispositif]*: for example, by inscribing in the film its own means of production; or by making the screen opaque through the multiplication of iconic or sonic traces to the point of nondifferentiation and unreadability, so that the scene of the phantasm becomes blinding and literally puts the spectator back in his or her place. One can have doubts about the interest of such an operation from the viewpoint of systematicity. It certainly mobilizes the look differently, makes it scan the surface which is the wrong side of the décor, and opens it to other adventures. It is not so certain that the latter would fundamentally be something other than tributaries of "representation"; nor, especially, that they would come socially—on the paths crossed by desire and the social—from a fundamental subversion. Beyond the facile conflicts of imaginary depth and real surface subsists the question of the object: what to do—what is to be done—with the look and the voice?

Notes

1. ["It speaks" is a translation of "ça parle." This is a phrase from Lacanian psychoanalytic thought. "Ça" *(it)* is the French word used to translate the Freudian term *es* (also literally *it)*, which is rendered in English-language usage by the Latin *id*. This is, of course, one of three terms in a famous Freudian psychic topology, along with the ego and superego. In Lacan, the phrase "ça parle" emphasizes that speech is not controlled by the coherent subject *(I, ego)* but something else *(it, id)* which is potentially disordering and disorderly with respect to that subject; language is not a product of reason, but has its roots in the unconscious, the repressed, what is "other" to consciousness.

In this, its first appearance in the article, Bonitzer puts the phrase "it speaks" in quotation marks, which emphasizes the derivation from Lacan. However, there are other times when Bonitzer engages in the ambivalence enabled by the fact that in French a word which can simply mean *it* might also denote the id. Sometimes he chooses to associate the antecedent of *it* with the Freudian id, for example at certain points when the antecedent is the voice-off (speech from elsewhere than the realist space of the image). Since English-language usage maintains the distinction between the two terms, it has not been possible to translate the article's employment of this ambivalence when it occurs. However, where it is especially important to the sense of a sentence, it is noted.—TRANS.]

2. ["Jouissance" is a term notoriously difficult to translate. "Enjoyment" does not capture the full range of intensities covered by the French term. "Pleasure" ignores the distinction—sometimes exploited by theoreticians such as Roland Barthes—between *plaisir* and *jouissance*. Therefore, where it appears in the text, it has been left in French.

What might minimally be said about its significance is first that its meanings can range from enjoying something in the sense of legal possession to pleasure in the sense of sexual climax. In addition, there is a tendency in recent French theoretical formulations to give the term a special, privileged sense. For example, Stephen Heath outlines the distinction in Barthes: "on the one hand a pleasure *(plaisir)* linked to cultural enjoyment and identity, to the cultural enjoyment of identity, to a homogenizing movement of the ego; on the other a radically violent pleasure *(jouissance)* which shatters—dissipates, loses—that cultural identity, that ego." Other thinkers, such as Lacan and Kristeva, have their own special uses of the term which are related but not necessarily identical to that of Barthes. Roland Barthes, *Image-Music-Text,* trans. Stephen Heath (New York: Hill and Wang, 1977), p. 9; cf. Leon S. Roudíez's comments on the term in the introduction to Julia Kristeva, *Desire in Language: A Semiotic Approach to Literature and Art,* ed. Leon S. Roudiez, trans. Thomas Gora, et al. (New York: Columbia University Press, 1980), pp. 15–16.

In Bonitzer's text, the paragraph before the introduction of the noun *jouissance* includes two uses of the verb *jouir,* translated as "enjoy."—TRANS.]

3. It has been pointed out to me that "end of prosopopoeia" is not completely exact. The discourse which Chris Marker opposes to two others (thesis-antithesis-synthesis) may not be an outright caricature; however, neither is it entirely that of Marker, whose dialectic is more subtle. It remains no less true that if "objectivity isn't exact, either" (as all left-intellectuals even sightly tinged by Marxism know), Marker does not say why, or responds to the question obliquely, for want of envisaging wht is arbitrary in discourse-off (he is known, with Rouch, to be one of its most brilliant practitioners). See below.

4. [There is a linguistic play in this paragraph between generalized collective identity and linguistic gender. "Everyone" *(tout le monde)* is a masculine noun phrase, which is usually pronominalized by the impersonal "one" *(on,* often translated into English as "we," but which, interestingly, still takes masculine complements.) In this paragraph it is pronominalized by the masculine *il* ("he").

So in the text when the author writes, for example, that *"he (il)* aspires to mastery," the result is to emphasize, in a somewhat unusual way, the masculine gender of the antecedent "everyone." And, when the author writes "to the extent that *he* is *one,*" the point is not only the pulling together of "everyone" into "one," but also an association of this social homogenization with a hierarchy of gender, because the masculine linguistic gender of "everyone" has been so stressed.— TRANS.]

5. [On the peculiar use of "it" here, see note 1.—TRANS.]

6. Here I think especially of militant cinema and of the Dziga Vertov Group; the earlier films of Godard and *Numero Deux* make use of intertitles and letters in ways which are not reduced to didacticism, but cause fantasies of the unconscious, permutations of language, witticisms, etc. to intervene.

7. [See Kaja Silverman, "Suture," in this volume.—ED.]

—Translated by Philip Rosen
and Marcia Butzel

19

Mary Ann Doane

The Voice in the Cinema:
The Articulation of Body and Space

Synchronization

The silent film is certainly understood, at least retrospectively and even (it is arguable) in its time, as incomplete, as lacking speech. The stylized gestures of the silent cinema, its heavy pantomime, have been defined as a form of compensation for that lack. Hugo Münsterberg wrote, in 1916, "To the actor of the moving pictures. . . the temptation offers itself to overcome the deficiency [the absence of "words and the modulation of the voice"] by a heightening of the gestures and of the facial play, with the result that the emotional expression becomes exaggerated."[1] The absent voice reemerges in gestures and the contortions of the face—it is spread over the body of the actor. The uncanny effect of the silent film in the era of sound is in part linked to the separation, by means of intertitles, of an actor's speech from the image of his/her body.

Consideration of sound in the cinema (in its most historically and institutionally privileged form—that of dialogue or the use of the voice) engenders a network of metaphors whose nodal point appears to be the body. One may readily respond that this is only "natural"—who can conceive of a voice without a body?[2] However, the body reconstituted by the technology and practices of the cinema is a *phantasmatic* body, which offers a support as well as a point of identification for the subject addressed by the film. The purpose of this essay is

Published in *Yale French Studies* (1980), no. 60, pp. 33–50, and reprinted by permission of *Yale French Studies*.

simply to trace some of the ways in which this phantasmatic body acts as a pivot for certain cinematic practices of representation and authorizes and sustains a limited number of relationships between voice and image.

The attributes of this phantasmatic body are first and foremost unity (through the emphasis on a coherence of the senses) and presence-to-itself. The addition of sound to the cinema introduces the possibility of representing a fuller (and organically unified) body, and of confirming the status of speech as an individual property right. The potential number and kinds of articulations between sound and image are reduced by the very name attached to the new heterogeneous medium—the "talkie." Histories of the cinema ascribe the stress on synchroniz-ation to a "public demand": "the public, fascinated by the novelty, wanting to be sure they were hearing what they saw, would have felt that a trick was being played on them if they were not shown the words coming from the lips of the actors."[3] In Lewis Jacobs' account, this fear on the part of the audience of being "cheated" is one of the factors which initially limits the deployment of sonorous material (as well as the mobility of the camera). From this perspective, the use of voice-off or voice over must be a late acquisition, attempted only after a certain "breaking-in" period during which the novelty of the sound film was allowed to wear itself out. But, whatever the fascination of the new medium (or whatever meaning is attached to it by retrospective readings of its prehistory), there is no doubt that synchronization (in the form of "lip-sync") has played a major role in the dominant narrative cinema. Technology standardizes the re-lation through the development of the synchronizer, the Moviola, the flatbed editing table. The mixing apparatus allows a greater control over the establish-ment of relationships between dialogue, music, and sound effects and, in practice, the level of the dialogue generally determines the levels of sound effects and music.[4] Despite a number of experiments with other types of sound/image relationships (those of Clair, Lang, Vigo, and more recently, Godard, Straub, and Duras), synchronous dialogue remains the dominant form of sonorous representation in the cinema.

Yet, even when asynchronous or "wild" sound is utilized, the phantasmatic body's attribute of unity is not lost. It is simply displaced—the body *in* the film becomes the body *of* the film. Its senses work in tandem, for the combination of sound and image is described in terms of "totality" and the "organic."[5] Sound carries with it the potential risk of exposing the material heterogeneity of the medium; attempts to contain that risk surface in the language of the ideology of organic unity. In the discourse of technicians, sound is "married" to the image and, as one sound engineer puts it in an article on post-synchronization, "one of the basic goals of the motion picture industry is to make the screen look alive in the eyes of the audience. . . ."[6]

Concomitant with the demand for a lifelike representation is the desire for "presence," a concept which is not specific to the cinematic sound track but which acts as a standard to measure quality in the sound recording industry as a whole. The term "presence" offers a certain legitimacy to the wish for pure reproduction and becomes a selling point in the construction of sound as a commodity. The television commercial asks whether we can "tell the difference" between the voice of Ella Fitzgerald and that of Memorex (and since our representative in the commercial—the ardent fan—cannot, the only conclusion to be drawn is that owning a Memorex tape is equivalent to having Ella in your living room). Technical advances in sound recording (such as the Dolby system) are aimed at diminishing the noise of the system, concealing the work of the apparatus, and thus reducing the distance perceived between the object and its representation. The maneuvers of the sound recording industry offer evidence which supports Walter Benjamin's thesis linking mechanical reproduction as a phenomenon with contemporary society's destruction of the "aura" (which he defines as "the unique phenomenon of a distance, however close it may be").[7] According to Benjamin,

[the] contemporary decay of the aura. . . rests on two circumstances, both of which are related to the increasing significance of the masses in contemporary life. Namely, the desire of contemporary masses to bring things "closer" spatially and humanly, which is just as ardent as their bent toward overcoming the uniqueness of every reality by accepting its reproduction.[8]

Nevertheless, while the desire to bring things closer is certainly exploited in making sound marketable, the qualities of uniqueness and authenticity are not sacrificed—it is not any voice which the tape brings to the consumer but the voice of Ella Fitzgerald. The voice is not detachable from a body which is quite specific—that of the star. In the cinema, cult value and the "aura" resurface in the star system. In 1930 a writer feels the need to assure audiences that post-synchronization as a technique does not necessarily entail substituting an alien voice for a "real" voice, that the industry does not condone a mismatching of voices and bodies.[9] Thus, the voice serves as a support for the spectator's recognition and his/her identification of, as well as with, the star.

Just as the voice must be anchored by a given body, the body must be anchored in a given space. The phantasmatic visual space which the film constructs is supplemented by techniques designed to spatialize the voice, to localize it, give it depth, and thus lend to the characters the consistency of the real. A concern for room tone, reverberation characteristics, and sound perspective manifests a desire to recreate, as one sound editor describes it, "the bouquet that surrounds the words, the presence of the voice, the way it fits in with the physical environment."[10] The dangers of post-synchronization and looping stem from the fact that the voice is disengaged from its "proper" space (the space conveyed by the visual image) and the credibility of that voice depends upon the technician's ability to return it to the side of its origin. Failure to do so risks exposure of the fact that looping is "narration masking as dialogue."[11] Dialogue is defined, therefore, not simply in terms of the establishment of an I-you relationship but as the necessary spatializing of that relationship. Techniques of sound recording tend to confirm the cinema's function as a mise-en-scène of bodies.

Voice-off and Voiceover

The spatial dimension which monophonic sound is capable of simulating is that of depth—the apparent source of the sound may be moved forward or backward, but the lateral dimension is lacking due to the fact that there is no sideways spread of reverberation or of ambient noise.[12] Nevertheless, sound/image relationships established in the narrative film work to suggest that sound does, indeed, issue from that other dimension. In film theory, this work to provide the effect of a lateral dimension receives recognition in the term "voice-off." "Voice-off" refers to instances in which we hear the voice of a character who is not visible within the frame. Yet the film establishes, by means of previous shots or other contextual determinants, the character's "presence" in the space of the scene, in the diegesis. He/she is "just over there," 'just beyond the frameline," in a space which "exists" but which the camera does not choose to show. The traditional use of voice-off constitutes a denial of the frame as a limit and an affirmation of the unity and homogeneity of the depicted space.

Because it is defined in terms of what is visible within the rectangular space of the screen, the term "voice-off" has been subject to some dispute. Claude Bailblé, for instance, argues that a voice-off must always be a "voice-in" because the literal source of the sound in the theater is always the speaker placed behind the screen.[13] Yet, the space to which the term refers is not that of the theater but the fictional space of the diegesis. Nevertheless, the use of the term is based on the requirement that the two spaces coincide, "overlap" to a certain extent. For the screen limits what *can be seen* of the diegesis (there is always "more" of the diegesis than the camera can cover at any one time). The placement of the speaker behind the screen simply confirms the fact that the cinematic apparatus is designed to promote the impression of a homogeneous space—the senses of the phantasmatic body cannot be split. The screen is the space where the image is deployed, while the theater as a whole is the space of the deployment of sound. Yet, the screen is given precedence over the acoustical space of the theater—the screen is posited as the site of the spectacle's unfolding and all sounds must emanate from it. (Bailblé asks, "What would be, in effect, a voice-off which came from the back of the theater? Poor little screen . . . "[14]—in other words, its effect would be precisely to diminish the epistemological power of the image, to reveal its limitations.)

The hierarchical placement of the visible above the audible, according to

Christian Metz, is not specific to the cinema but a more general cultural production.[15] And the term voice-off merely acts as a reconfirmation of that hierarchy. For it only appears to describe a sound—what it really refers to is the visibility (or lack of visibility) of the source of the sound. Metz argues that sound is never "off." While a visual element specified as "off" actually lacks visibility, a "sound-off" is always audible.

Despite the fact that Metz's argument is valid and we tend to repeat on the level of theory the industry's subordination of sound to image, the term voice-off does name a particular relationship between sound and image—a relationship which has been extremely important historically in diverse film practices. While it is true that sound is almost always discussed with reference to the image, it does not necessarily follow that this automatically makes sound subordinate. From another perspective, it is doubtful that any image (in the sound film) is uninflected by sound. This is crucially so, given the fact that in the dominant narrative cinema, sound extends from beginning to end of the film—sound is never absent (silence is, at the least, room tone). In fact, the lack of any sound whatsoever is taboo in the editing of the sound track.

The point is not that we "need" terms with which to describe, honor, and acknowledge the autonomy of a particular sensory material, but that we must attempt to think the heterogeneity of the cinema. This might be done more fruitfully by means of the concept of space than through the unities of sound and image. In the cinematic situation, three types of space are put into play:

(1) The space of the diegesis. This space has no physical limits; it is not contained or measurable. It is a virtual space constructed by the film and is delineated as having both audible and visible traits (as well as implications that its objects can be touched, smelled, and tasted).

(2) The visible space of the screen as receptor of the image. It is measurable and "contains" the visible signifiers of the film. Strictly speaking, the screen is not audible although the placement of the speaker behind the screen constructs that illusion.

(3) The acoustical space of the theater or auditorium. It might be argued that this space is also visible, but the film cannot visually activate signifiers in this space unless a second projector is used. Again, despite the fact that the speaker is behind the screen and therefore sound appears to be emanating from a focused point, sound is not "framed" in the same way as the image. In a sense, it *envelops* the spectator.

All these are spaces *for the spectator,* but the first is the only space which the characters of the fiction film can acknowledge (for the characters there are no voices-off). Different cinematic modes—documentary, narrative, avant-garde—establish different relationships between the three spaces. The classical narrative film, for instance, works to deny the existence of the last two spaces in order to buttress the credibility (legitimacy) of the first space. If a character looks at and speaks to the spectator, this constitutes an acknowledgment that the character is seen and heard in a radically different space and is therefore generally read as transgressive.

Nothing unites the three spaces but the signifying practice of the film itself, together with the institutionalization of the theater as a type of metaspace which binds together the three spaces, as the *place* where a unified cinematic discourse unfolds. The cinematic institution's stake in this process of unification is apparent. Instances of voice-off in the classical film are particularly interesting examples of the way in which the three spaces undergo an elaborate imbrication. For the phenomenon of the voice-off cannot be understood outside a consideration of the relationships established between the diegesis, the visible space of the screen, *and* the acoustical space of the theater. The place in which the signifier manifests itself is the acoustical space of the theater, but this is the space with which it is least concerned. The voice-off deepens the diegesis, gives it an extent which exceeds that of the image, and thus supports the claim that there is a space in the fictional world which the camera does not register. In its own way, it *accounts for* lost space. The voice-off is a sound which is first and foremost in the service of the film's construction of space and only indirectly in the service of the image. It validates both what the screen reveals of the diegesis and what it conceals.

Nevertheless, the use of the voice-off always entails a risk—that of exposing the material heterogeneity of the cinema. Synchronous sound masks the problem and this at least partially explains its dominance. But the more interesting question, perhaps, is: how can the classical film allow the representation of a voice whose source is not simultaneously represented? As soon as the sound is detached from its source, no longer anchored by a represented body, its potential work as a signifier is revealed. There is always something uncanny about a voice which emanates from a source outside the frame. However, as Pascal Bonitzer points out, the narrative film exploits the marginal anxiety connected with the voice-off by incorporating its disturbing effects within the dramatic framework. Thus, the function of the voice-off (as well as that of the voiceover) becomes extremely important in *film noir.* Bonitzer takes as his example *Kiss Me Deadly,* a *film noir* in which the villain remains out of frame until the last sequences of the film. Maintaining him outside of the field of vision "gives to his sententious voice, swollen by mythological comparisons, a greater power of disturbing, the scope of an oracle—dark prophet of the end of the world. And, in spite of that, his voice is submitted to the destiny of the body. . . a shot, he falls—and with him in ridicule, his discourse with its prophetic accents."[16]

The voice-off is always "submitted to the destiny of the body" because it *belongs* to a character who is confined to the space of the diegesis, if not to the visible space of the screen. Its efficacy rests on the knowledge that the character can easily be made visible by a slight reframing which would reunite the voice and its source. The body acts as an invisible support for the use of both the voiceover during a flashback and the interior monologue as well. Although the voiceover in a flashback effects a temporal dislocation of the voice with respect to the body, the voice is frequently returned to the body as a form of narrative closure. Furthermore, the voiceover very often simply initiates the story and is subsequently superseded by synchronous dialogue, allowing the diegesis to "speak for itself." In *Sunset Boulevard* the convention is taken to its limits: the voiceover narration is, indeed, linked to a body (that of the hero), but it is the body of a dead man.

In the interior monologue, on the other hand, the voice and the body are represented simultaneously, but the voice, far from being an extension of that body, manifests its inner lining. The voice displays what is inaccessible to the image, what exceeds the visible: the "inner life" of the character. The voice here is the privileged mark of interiority, turning the body "inside out."

The voiceover commentary in the documentary, unlike the voice-off, the voiceover during a flashback, or the interior monologue, is, in effect, a *disembodied* voice. While the latter three voices work to affirm the homogeneity and dominance of diegetic space, the voiceover commentary is necessarily presented as outside that space. It is its radical otherness with respect to the diegesis which endows this voice with a certain authority. As a form of direct address, it speaks without mediation to the audience, bypassing the "characters" and establishing a complicity between itself and the spectator—together they understand and thus *place* the image. It is precisely because the voice is not localizable, because it cannot be yoked to a body, that it is capable of interpreting the image, producing its truth. Disembodied, lacking any specification in space or time, the voiceover is, as Bonitzer points out, beyond criticism—it censors the questions "Who is speaking?," "Where?," "In what time?," and "For whom?"

This is not, one suspects, without ideological implications. The first of these implications is that the voice-off[17] represents a power, that of disposing of the image and of what it reflects, from a space absolutely *other* with respect to that inscribed in the image-track. *Absolutely other and absolutely indeterminant.* Because it rises from the field of the Other, the voice-off is assumed to know: this is the essence of its power. . . The power of the voice is a stolen power, a usurpation.[18]

In the history of the documentary, this voice has been for the most part that of the male, and its power resides in the possession of knowledge and in the privileged, unquestioned activity of interpretation. This function of the voice-over has been appropriated by the television documentary and television news programs, in which sound carries the burden of "information" while the impoverished image simply fills the screen. Even when the major voice is explicitly linked with a body (that of the anchorman in television news), this body, in its turn, is situated in the nonspace of the studio. In film, on the other hand, the voiceover is quite often dissociated from any specific figure. The guarantee of knowledge, in such a system, lies in its irreducibility to the spatiotemporal limitations of the body.

The Pleasure of Hearing

The means by which sound is deployed in the cinema inplicate the spectator in a particular textual problematic—they establish certain conditions for understanding which obtain in the "intersubjective relation" between film and spectator. The voiceover commentary and, differently, the interior monologue and voiceover flashback speak more or less *directly* to the spectator, constituting him/her as an empty space to be "filled" with knowledge about events, character psychology, etc. More frequently, in the fiction film, the use of synchronous dialogue and the voice-off presuppose a spectator who *overhears* and, overhearing, is unheard and unseen himself. This activity with respect to the sound track is not unlike the voyeurism often exploited by the cinematic image. In any event, the use of the voice in the cinema appeals to the spectator's desire to hear, or what Lacan refers to as the invocatory drive.

In what does the pleasure of hearing consist? Beyond the added effect of "realism" which sound gives to the cinema, beyond its supplement of meaning anchored by intelligible dialogue, what is the specificity of the pleasure of hearing a voice with its elements escaping a strictly verbal codification—volume, rhythm, timbre, pitch? Psychoanalysis situates pleasure in the divergence between the present experience and the memory of satisfaction: "Between a (more or less inaccessible) memory and a very precise (and localizable) immediacy of perception is opened the gap where pleasure is produced."[19] Memories of the first experiences of the voice, of the hallucinatory satisfaction it offered, circumscribe the pleasure of hearing and ground its relation to the phantasmatic body. This is not simply to situate the experiences of infancy as the sole determinant in a system directly linking cause and effect but to acknowledge that the traces of archaic desires are never annihilated. According to Guy Rosolato, it is "the organization of the fantasm itself which implies a permanence, an insistence of the recall to the origin."[20]

Space, for the child, is defined initially in terms of the audible, not the visible: "It is only in a second phase that the organization of visual space insures the perception of the object as *external*" (p. 80). The first differences are traced along the axis of sound: the voice of the mother, the voice of the father. Furthermore, the voice has a greater command over space than the look—one can hear around corners, through walls. Thus, for the child the voice, even before language, is the instrument of demand. In the construction/hallucination of space and the body's relation to that space, the voice plays a major role. In comparison with sight, as Rosolato points out, the voice is reversible: sound is simultaneously emitted and heard, by the subject himself. As opposed to the situation in seeing, it is as if "an 'acoustical' mirror were always in function. Thus, the images of entry and exit relative to the body are intimately articulated. They can therefore be confounded, inverted, favored one over the other" (p. 79). Because one can hear sounds behind oneself as well as those with sources *inside* the body (sounds of digestion, circulation, respiration, etc.), two sets of terms are placed in opposition: exterior/front/sight and interior/back/hearing. And "hallucinations are determined by an imaginary structuration of the body according to these oppositions . . ." (p. 80). The voice appears to lend itself to hallucination, in particular the hallucination of power over space effected by an extension or restructuration of the body. Thus, as Lacan points out, our mass media and our technology, as mechanical extensions of the body, result in "planeterizing" or "even stratospherizing" the voice.[21]

The voice also traces the forms of unity and separation *between* bodies. The mother's soothing voice, in a particular cultural context, is a major component of the "sonorous envelope" which surrounds the child and is the first model of auditory pleasure. An image of corporeal unity is derived from the realization that the production of sound by the voice and its audition coincide. The imaginary fusion of the child with the mother is supported by the recognition of common traits characterizing the different voices and, more particularly, of their potential for harmony. According to Rosolato, the voice in music makes appeal to the nostalgia for such an imaginary cohesion, for a "veritable incantation" of bodies.

The harmonic and polyphonic unfolding in music can be understood as a succession of tensions and releases, of unifications and divergences between parts which are gradually stacked, opposed in successive chords only to be resolved ultimately into their simplest unity. It is therefore the entire dramatization of separated bodies and their reunion which harmony supports. (p. 82)

Yet, the imaginary unity associated with the earliest experience of the voice is broken by the premonition of difference, division, effected by the intervention of the father whose voice, engaging the desire of the mother, acts as the agent of separation and constitutes the voice of the mother as the irretrievably lost object of desire. The voice in this instance, far from being the narcissistic measure of harmony, is the voice of interdiction. The voice thus understood is an interface of imaginary and symbolic, pulling at once toward the signifying organization of language and its reduction of the range of vocal sounds to those it binds and codifies, and toward original and imaginary attachments, "representable in the fantasm by the body, or by the corporeal mother, the child at her breast" (p. 86).

At the cinema, the sonorous envelope provided by the theatrical space together with techniques employed in the construction of the sound track work to sustain the narcissistic pleasure derived from the image of a certain unity, cohesion, and hence, an identity grounded by the spectator's phantasmatic relation to his/her own body. The aural illusion of position constructed by the approximation of sound perspective and by techniques which spatialize the voice and endow it with "presence" guarantees the singularity and stability of a point of audition, thus holding at bay the potential trauma of dispersal, dismemberment, difference. The subordination of the voice to the screen as the site of the spectacle's unfolding makes vision and hearing work together in manufacturing the "hallucination" of a fully sensory world. Nevertheless, the recorded voice, which presupposes a certain depth, is in contradiction with the flatness of the two-dimensional image. Eisler and Adorno note that the spectator is always aware of this divergence, of the inevitable gap between the represented body and its voice. And for Eisler and Adorno this partially explains the function of film music: first used in the exhibition of silent films to conceal the noise of the projector (to hide from the spectator the "uncanny" fact that his/her pleasure is mediated by a machine), music in the "talkie" takes on the task of closing the gap between voice and body.[22]

If this imaginary harmony is to be maintained, however, the potential aggressivity of the voice (as the instrument of interdiction and the material support of the symptom—hearing voices—in paranoia) must be attenuated. The formal perfection of sound recording in the cinema consists in reducing not only the noise of the apparatus but any "grating" noise which is not "pleasing to the ear." On another level, the aggressivity of the filmic voice can be linked to the fact that sound is directed *at* the spectator—necessitating, in the fiction film, its deflection through dialogue (which the spectator is given only obliquely, to overhear) and, in the documentary, its mediation by the content of the image. In the documentary, however, the voiceover has come to represent an authority and an aggressivity which can no longer be sustained—thus, as Bonitzer points out, the proliferation of new documentaries which reject the absolute of the voiceover and, instead, claim to establish a democratic system, "letting the event speak for itself." Yet, what this type of film actually promotes is the illusion that reality speaks and is not spoken, that the film is not a constructed discourse. In effecting an "impression of knowledge," a knowledge which is given and not produced, the film conceals its own work and posits itself as a voice without a subject.[23] The voice is even more powerful in silence. The solution, then, is not to banish the voice but to construct *another* politics.

The Politics of the Voice

The cinema presents a spectacle composed of disparate elements—images, voices, sound effects, music, writing—which the *mise-en-scène,* in its broadest sense, organizes and aims at the body of the spectator, sensory receptacle of the various stimuli. This is why Lyotard refers to classical *mise-en-scène* (in both the theater and the cinema) as a kind of somatography, or inscription on the body:

The mise-en-scène turns written signifiers into speech, song, and movements executed by bodies capable of moving, singing, speaking; and this transcription is intended for other living bodies—the spectators—capable of being moved by these songs, movements, and words. It is this transcribing on and for bodies, considered as multi-sensory potentialities, which is the work characteristic of the mise-en-scène. Its elementary unity is polyesthetic like the human body: capacity to see, to hear, to touch, to move. . . . The idea of performance. . . even if it remains vague, seems linked to the idea of inscription on the body.[24]

Classical mise-en-scène has a stake in perpetuating the image of unity and identity sustained by this body and in staving off the fear of fragmentation. The different sensory elements work in collusion, and this work denies the material heterogeneity of the "body" of the film. All the signifying strategies for the deployment of the voice discussed earlier are linked with such homogenizing effects: synchronization binds the voice to a body in a unity whose immediacy can only be perceived as a given; the voice-off holds the spectacle to a space—extended but still coherent; and the voiceover commentary places the image by endowing it with a clear intelligibility. In all of this, what must be guarded is a certain "oneness."

This "oneness" is the mark of a mastery and a control and manifests itself most explicitly in the tendency to confine the voiceover commentary in the documentary to a single voice. For, according to Bonitzer, "when one divides that voice or, what amounts to the same things, multiplies it, the system and its effects change. Off-screen space ceases to be that place of reserve and interiority of the voice. . . ."[25] This entails not only or not merely increasing the number of voices but radically changing their relationship to the image, effecting a disjunction between sound and meaning, emphasizing what Barthes refers to as the "grain" of the voice[26] over and against its expressivity or power of representation. In the contemporary cinema, the names which immediately come to mind are those of Godard (who, even in an early film such as *Vivre Sa Vie* which relies heavily upon synchronous sound, resists the homogenizing effects of the traditional use of voice-off by means of a resolute avoidance of the shot/ reverse shot structure—the camera quickly panning to keep the person talking *in frame*) and Straub (for whom the voice and sound in general become the marks of a nonprogressive duration). The image of the body thus obtained is not one of imaginary cohesion but of dispersal, division, fragmentation. Lyotard speaks of the "post-modernist" text which escapes the closure of representation by creating its own addressee, "a disconcerted body, invited to stretch its sensory capacities beyond measure."[27] Such an approach, which takes off from a different image of the body, can be understood as an attempt to forge a politics based on an erotics. Bonitzer uses the two terms interchangeably, claiming that the scission of the voice can contribute to the definition of "another politics (or erotics) of the voice-off."[28] The problem is whether such an erotics, bound to the image of an extended or fragmented body and strongly linked with a particular signifying material, can found a political theory or practice.

There are three major difficulties with the notion of a political erotics of the voice. The first is that, relying as it does on the idea of expanding the range or redefining the power of the senses, and opposing itself to meaning, a political erotics is easily recuperable as a form of romanticism or as a mysticism which effectively skirts problems of epistemology, lodging itself firmly in a mind/ body dualism. Secondly, the overemphasis upon the isolated effectivity of a single signifying material—the voice—risks a crude materialism wherein the physical properties of the medium have the inherent and final power of determining its reading. As Paul Willemen points out, a concentration upon the specificities of the various "technico-sensorial unities" of the cinema often precludes a recognition that the materiality of the signifier is a "second order factor" (with respect to language understood broadly as symbolic system) and tends to reduce a complex heterogeneity to a mere combination of different materials.[29] Yet, a film is not a simple juxtaposition of sensory elements but a discourse, an enunciation. This is not to imply that the isolation and investigation of a single signifying material such as the voice is a fruitless endeavor but that the estabishment of a direct connection between the voice and politics is fraught with difficulties.

Third, the notion of a political erotics of the voice is particularly problematic from a feminist perspective. Over and against the theorization of the look as phallic, as the support of voyeurism and fetishism (a drive and a defense which, in Freud, are linked explicitly with the male),[30] the voice appears to lend itself readily as an alternative to the image, as a potentially viable means whereby the woman can "make herself heard." Luce Irigaray, for instance, claims tht patriarchal culture has a heavier investment in seeing than in hearing.[31] Bonitzer, in the context of defining a political erotics, speaks of "returning the voice to women" as a major component. Nevertheless, it must be remembered that, while psychoanalysis delineates a pre-oedipal scenario in which the voice of the mother dominates, the voice, in psychoanalysis, is also the instrument of interdiction, of the patriarchal order. And to mark the voice as an isolated haven within patriarchy, or as having an essential relation to the woman, is to invoke the specter of feminine specificity, always recuperable as another form of "otherness." A political erotics which posits a new phantasmatic, which relies on images of an "extended" sensory body, is inevitably caught in the double bind which feminism always seems to confront: on the one hand, there is a danger in grounding a politics on a conceptualization of the body because the body has always been *the* site of woman's oppression, posited as the final and undeniable guarantee of a difference and a lack; but, on the other hand, there is a potential gain as well—it is precisely because the body has been a major site of oppression that perhaps it must be the site of the battle to be waged. The supreme achievement of patriarchal ideology is that it has no outside.

In light of the three difficulties outlined above, however, it would seem unwise to base any politics of the voice *solely* on an erotics. The value of thinking the deployment of the voice in the cinema by means of its relation to the body (that of the character, that of the spectator) lies in an understanding of the cinema, from the perspective of a topology, as a series of spaces including that of the spectator—spaces which are often hierarchized or masked, one by the other, in the service of a representational illusion. Nevertheless, whatever the arrangement or interpenetration of the various spaces, they constitute a *place* where signification intrudes. The various techniques and strategies for the deployment of the voice contribute heavily to the definition of the form that "place" takes.

Notes

1. Hugo Munsterberg, *The Film: A Psychological Study* (New York: Dover, 1970), p. 49.

2. Two kinds of "voices without bodies" immediately suggest themselves—one theological the other scientific (two poles which, it might be added, are not ideologically unrelated): (1) the voice of God incarnated in the Word; (2) the artificial voice of a computer. Neither seems to be capable of representation outside a certain anthropomorphism, however. God is pictured, in fact, as having a quite specific body—that of a male patriarchal figure. *Star Wars* and *Battlestar Galactica* illustrate the tendencies toward anthropomorphism in the depiction of computers. In the latter, even a computer (named Cora) deprived of mobility and the simulacrum of a human form, is given a voice which is designed to evoke the image of a sensual female body.

3. Lewis Jacobs, *The Rise of the American Film: A Critical History* (New York: Teachers College Press, 1968), p. 435.

4. For a more detailed discussion of this hierarchy of sounds and of other relevant techniques in the construction of the sound track see M. Doane, "Ideology and the Practices of Sound Editing and Mixing," paper delivered at Milwaukee Conference on the Cinematic Apparatus, February, 1978, published in *The Cinematic Apparatus,* ed. Teresa de Lauretis and Stephan Heath (Bloomington: Indiana University Press; London: Macmillan, 1984).

5. *Ibid.*

6. W. A. Pozner, "Synchronization Techniques," *Journal of the Society of Motion Picture Engineers* (September 1946), 47(3):191.

7. Walter Benjamin, "The Work of Art in the Age of Mechanical Reproduction," in *Illuminations,* ed. Hannah Arendt, trans. Harry Zohn (New York: Schocken, 1969), p. 222.

8. *Ibid.,* p. 223.

9. George Lewin, "Dubbing and Its Relation to Sound Picture Production," *Journal of the Society of Motion Picture Engineers* (January 1931), 16(1):48.

10. Walter Murch, "The Art of the Sound Editor: An Interview with Walter Murch," interview by Larry Sturhahn, *Filmmaker's Newsletter* (December 1974), 8(2):23.

11. *Ibid.*

12. Stereo reduces this problem but does not solve it—the range of perspective effects is still limited. Much of the discussion which follows is based on the use of monophonic sound, but also has implications for stereo. In both mono and stereo, for instance, the location of the speakers is designed to ensure that the audience hears sound "which is roughly coincident with the image." See Alec Nisbett, *The Technique of the Sound Studio* (New York: Focal Press Limited, 1972), pp. 530, 532.

13. C. Bailblé, "Programmation de L'écoute (2)," *Cahiers du cinéma* (October 1978), no. 293, p. 9.

14. *Ibid.* My translation.

15. C. Metz, "Le Perçu et le nommé," in *Essais sémiotiques* (Paris: Klincksieck, 1977), pp. 153–59.

16. Pascal Bonitzer, "Les Silences de la voix," *Cahiers du cinéma* (February–March 1975), no. 256, p. 25. My translation. ["The Silences of the Voice" is included in this anthology—ED.]

17. Bonitzer uses the term "voice-off" in a general sense which includes both voice-off and voiceover, but here he is referring specifically to voiceover commentary.

18. Bonitzer, "Les Silences," p. 26. My translation.

19. Serge Leclaire, *Démasquer le réel*, p. 64, quoted in C. Bailblé, "Programmation de l'écoute (3)," *Cahiers du cinéma* (February 1979), no. 297, p. 46.

20. Guy Rosolato, "La Voix: entre corps et langage," *Revue française de psychoanalyse* (January 1974), 38:83. My translation. My discussion of the pleasure of hearing relies heavily on the work of Rosolato. Further references to this article will appear in parentheses in the text.

21. Jacques Lacan, *The Four Fundamental Concepts of Psycho-Analysis,* ed. Jacques-Alain Miller, trans. Alan Sheridan (London: Hogarth Press and the Institute of Psycho-Analysis, 1977), p. 274.

22. Hanns Eisler, *Composing for the Films* (New York: Oxford University Press, 1947), pp. 75–77.

23. Bonitzer, "Les Silences," pp. 23–24.

24. Jean-François Lyotard, "The Unconscious as Mise-en-scène," in ed. *Performance in Post-modern Culture,* Michel Benamou and Charles Caramello (Madison: Coda Press, 1977), p. 88.

25. Bonitzer, "Les Silences," p. 31.

26. See Roland Barthes, "The Grain of the Voice," in *Image-Music-Text,* ed. trans. Stephen Heath (New York: Hill and Wang, 1977), pp. 179–89.

27. Lyotard, "The Unconscious," p. 96.

28. Bonitzer, "Les Silences," p. 31.

29. Paul Willemen, "Cinema Thoughts," paper delivered at Milwaukee Conference on Cinema and Language, March 1979, pp. 12 and 3. [A version of this paper has since been published as "Cinematic Discourse: The Problem of Inner Speech" in *Cinema and Language,* ed. S. Heath and P. Mellencamp (Frederick MD: University Press of America and American Film Institute, 1983). See pp. 149 and 142–43.—ED.]

30. See Laura Mulvey, "Visual Pleasure and Narrative Cinema," *Screen* (Autumn 1975), 16:6–18 [included in this anthology—ED.] and Stephen Heath, "Sexual Difference and Representation," *Screen* (Autumn 1978), 19:51–112.

31. For a fuller discussion of the relationship some feminists establish between the voice and the woman see Heath, "Sexual Difference," pp. 83–84.

[20]

Jean-François Lyotard
Acinema

The Nihilism of Convened, Conventional Movements

Cinematography is the inscription of movement, a writing with movements—all kinds of movements: for example, in the film shot, those of the actors and other moving objects, those of lights, colors, frame, and lens; in the film sequence, all these again plus the cuts and splices of editing; for the film as a whole, movements of the final script and the spatiotemporal synthesis of the narration (*découpage*). And over or through all these movements are those of the sound and words coming together with them.

Thus there is a crowd (nonetheless, a countable crowd) of elements in motion, a throng of possible moving bodies which are candidates for inscription on film. Learning the techniques of filmmaking involves knowing how to eliminate a large number of these possible movements. It seems that image, sequence, and film must be constituted at the price of these exclusions.

Here arise two questions that are really quite naive considering the deliberations of contemporary cine-critics: *which* movements and moving bodies are these? Why is it necessary to select, sort out, and exclude them?

If no movements are picked out we will accept what is fortuitous, dirty, confused, unsteady, unclear, poorly framed, overexposed . . . For example, suppose you are working on a shot in video, a shot, say, of a gorgeous head of hair à la Renoir; upon viewing it you find that something has come undone: all of a sudden swamps, outlines of incongruous islands, and cliff edges appear,

Published as "L'Acinéma" in *Cinéma: Théorie, lectures* (Paris: Ed. Klincksieck, 1973) and translated in *Wide Angle* (1978), 2(3):53–59. Reprinted by permission of the author, and translation used by permission of The Johns Hopkins University Press.

lurching forth before your startled eyes. A scene from elsewhere, representing nothing identifiable, has been added, a scene not related to the logic of your shot, an undecidable scene, worthless even as an insertion because it will not be repeated and taken up again later. So you cut it out.

We are not demanding a raw cinema, as Dubuffet demanded an *art brut*. We are hardly about to form a club dedicated to the saving of rushes and the rehabilitation of clipped footage. And yet. . . . We observe that if the mistake is eliminated it is because of its incongruity, and to protect the order of the whole (shot and/or sequence and/or film) while banning the intensity it carries. And the order of the whole has its sole object in the functioning of the cinema: that there be order in the movements, that the movements be made in order, that they make order. Writing with movements—cinematography—is thus conceived and practiced as an incessant organizing of movements following the rules of representation for spatial localization, those of narration for the instantiation of language, and those of the form "film music" for the sound track. The so-called impression of reality is a real oppression of orders.

This oppression consists of the enforcement of a nihilism of movements. No movement, arising from any field, is given to the eye/ear of the spectator for what it is: a simple *sterile difference* in an audiovisual field. Instead, every movement put forward *sends back* to something else, is inscribed as a plus or minus on the ledger book which is the film, *is valuable* because it *returns* to something else, because it is thus potential return and profit. The only genuine movement with which the cinema is written is that of value. The law of value (in so-called "political" economy) states that the *object*, in this case the movement, is valuable only insofar as it is exchangeable for other objects and in terms of equal quantities of a definable unity (for example, quantities of money). Therefore, to be valuable the object must move: proceed from other objects ("production" in the narrow sense) and disappear, but on the condition that its *disappearance makes room for still other objects* (consumption). Such a process is not sterile, but productive; it is production in the widest sense.

Pyrotechnics

Let us be certain to distinguish this process from sterile motion. A match once struck is consumed. If you use the match to light the gas that heats the water for the coffee which keeps you alert on your way to work, the consumption is not sterile, for it is a movement belonging to the circuit of capital: merchandise/ match → merchandise/labor power → money/wages → merchandise/match. But when a child strikes the matchhead *to see* what happens—just for the fun of it— he enjoys the movement itself, the changing colors, the light flashing at the height of the blaze, the death of the tiny piece of wood, the hissing of the tiny flame.

He enjoys these sterile differences leading nowhere, these uncompensated losses; what the physicist calls the dissipation of energy.

Intense enjoyment and sexual pleasure (*la jouissance*), insofar as they give rise to perversion and not solely to propagation, are distinguished by this sterility. At the end of *Beyond the Pleasure Principle* Freud cites them as an example of the combination of the life and death instincts. But he is thinking of pleasure obtained through the channels of "normal" genital sexuality: all *jouissance*, including that giving rise to a hysterical attack, or contrariwise, to a perverse scenario, contains the lethal component, but normal pleasure hides it in a movement of return, genital sexuality. Normal genital sexuality leads to child-birth, and the child is the *return* of, or on, its movement. But the motion of pleasure as such, split from the motion of the propagation of the species, would be (whether genital or sexual or neither) that motion which in going beyond the point of no return spills the libidinal forces outside the whole, at the expense of the whole (at the price of the ruin and disintegration of this whole).

In lighting the match the child enjoys this diversion (*détournement*, a word dear to Klossowski) that misspends energy. He produces, in his own movement, a simulacrum of pleasure in its so-called "death instinct" component. Thus if he is assuredly an artist by producing a simulacrum, he is one most of all because this simulacrum is not an object or worth valued for another object. It is not composed with these other objects, compensated for by them, enclosed in a whole ordered by constitutive laws (in a structured group, for example). On the contrary, it is essential that the entire erotic force invested in the simulacrum be promoted, raised, displayed, and burned in vain. It is thus that Adorno said the only truly great art is the making of fireworks: pyrotechnics would simulate perfectly the sterile consumption of energies in jouissance. Joyce grants this privileged position to fireworks in the beach sequence in *Ulysses*. A simulacrum, understood in the sense Klossowski gives it, should not be conceived primarily as belonging to the category of representation, like the representations which imitate pleasure; rather, it is to be conceived as a kinetic problematic, as the paradoxical product of the disorder of the drives, as a composite of decompositions.

The discussion of cinema and representational-narrative art in general begins at this point. Two directions are open to the conception (and production) of an object, and in particular, a cinematographic object, conforming to the pyro-technical imperative. These two seemingly contradictory currents appear to be those attracting whatever is intense in painting today. It is possible that they are also at work in the truly active forms of experimental and underground cinema.

These two poles are immobility and excessive movement. In letting itself be drawn toward these antipodes the cinema insensibly ceases to be an ordering force; it produces true, that is, vain, simulacrums, blissful intensities, instead of productive/consumable objects.

The Movement of Return

Let us back up a bit. What do these movements of return or returned movements have to do with the representational and narrative form of the commercial cinema? We emphasize just how wretched it is to answer this question in terms of a simple superstructural function of an industry, the cinema, the products of which, films, would lull the public consciousness by means of doses of ideology. If film direction is a directing and ordering of movements it is not so by being propaganda (benefiting the bourgeoisie some would say, and the bureaucracy, others would add), but by being a propagation. Just as the libido must renounce its perverse overflow to propagate the species through a normal genital sexuality allowing the constitution of a "sexual body" having that sole end, so the film produced by an artist working in capitalist industry (and all known industry is now capitalist) springs from the effort to eliminate aberrant movements, useless expenditures, differences of pure consumption. This film is composed like a unified and propagating body, a fecund and assembled whole transmitting instead of losing what it carries. The diegesis locks together the synthesis of movements in the temporal order; perspectivist representation does so in the spatial order.

Now, what are these syntheses but the arranging of the cinematographic material following the figure of *return?* We are speaking not only of the requirement of profitability imposed upon the artist by the producer but also of the formal requirements that the artist weighs upon his material. All so-called good form implies the return of sameness, the folding back of diversity upon an identical unity. In painting this may be a plastic rhyme or an equilibrium of colors; in music, the resolution of dissonance by the dominant chord; in architecture, a proportion. Repetition, the principle not only of the metric but even of the rhythmic, if taken in the narrow sense as the repetition of the same (same color, line, angle, chord), is the work of Eros and Apollo disciplining the movements, limiting them to the norms of tolerance characteristic of the system or whole under consideration.

It was an error to accredit Freud with the discovery of the very motion of the drives. Because Freud, in *Beyond the Pleasure Principle,* takes great care to dissociate the repetition of the same, which signals the regime of the life instincts, from the repetition of the other, which can only be other to the first-named repetition. These death drives are just outside the regime delimited by the body or whole considered, and therefore it is impossible to discern *what* is returning, when returning with these drives is the intensity of extreme jouissance and danger that they carry. To the point that it must be asked if indeed any repetition is involved at all, if on the contrary something different returns at each instance, if the *eternal return* of these sterile explosions of libidinal discharge should not be conceived in a wholly different time-space than that of the repetition of the same, as their impossible copresence. Assuredly we find here the insufficiency of *thought,* which must necessarily pass through that sameness which is the concept.

Cinematic movements generally follow the figure of return, that is, of the repetition and propagation of sameness. The scenario or plot, an intrigue and its solution, achieves the same resolution of dissonance as the sonata form in music; its movement of return organizes the affective charges linked to the filmic "signifieds," both connotative and denotative, as Metz would say. In this regard all endings are happy endings, just by being endings, for even if a film finishes with a murder, this too can serve as a final resolution of dissonance. The affective charges carried by every type of cinematographic and filmic "signifier" (lens, framing, cuts, lighting, shooting, etc.) are submitted to the same rule absorbing diversity into unity, the same law of a return of the same after a semblance of difference; a difference that is nothing, in fact, but a detour.

The Instance of Identification

This rule, where it applies, operates principally, we have said, in the form of exclusions and effacements. The exclusion of certain movements is such that the professional filmmakers are not even aware of them; effacements, on the other hand, cannot fail to be noticed by them because a large part of their activity consists of them. Now these effacements and exclusions form the very operation of film directing. In eliminating, before and/or after the shooting, any extreme glare, for example, the director and cameraman condemn the image of film to the sacred task of making itself recognizable to the eye. The image must cast the object or set of objects as the double of a situation that from then on will be supposed real. The image is representational because recognizable, because it addresses itself to the eye's *memory,* to fixed references or identification, references known, but in the sense of "well known," that is, familiar and established. These references are identity measuring the returning and return of movements. They form the instance or group of instances connecting and making them take the form of cycles. Thus all sorts of gaps, jolts, postponements, losses, and confusions can occur, but they no longer act as real diversions or wasteful drifts; when the final count is made they turn out to be nothing but beneficial detours. It is precisely through the return to the ends of identification that cinematographic form, understood as the synthesis of good movement, is articulated following the cyclical organization of capital.

One example chosen from among thousands: in *Joe* (a film built entirely upon the impression of reality) the movement is drastically altered twice: the first time when the father beats to death the hippie who lives with his daughter; the second, when in "mopping up" a hippie commune he unwittingly guns down his own daughter. This last sequence ends with a freeze-frame shot of the bust and face of the daughter who is struck down in full movement. In the first murder we see a hail of fists falling upon the face of the defenseless hippie who quickly loses consciousness. These two effects, the one an immobilization, the other an excess of mobility, are obtained by waiving the rules of representation which demand real motion recorded and projected at 24 frames per second. As a result we could expect a strong affective charge to accompany them, since this greater or lesser perversion of the realistic rhythm responds to the organic rhythm of the intense emotions evoked. And it is indeed produced, but to the benefit, nevertheless, of the filmic totality, and thus, all told, to the benefit of order; both arrhythmias are produced not in some aberrant fashion but at the culminating points in the tragedy of the impossible father/daughter incest underlying the scenario. So while they may upset the representational order, clouding for a few seconds the celluloid's necessary transparency (which is that order's condition), these two affective charges do not fail to suit the narrative order. On the contrary, they mark it with a beautiful melodic curve, the first accelerated murder finding its resolution in the second immobilized murder.

Thus the memory to which films address themselves is *nothing* in itself, just as capital is nothing but an instance of capitalization; it is an instance, a set of empty instances, which in no way operate through their content; *good* form, *good* lighting, *good* editing *good* sound mixing are not good because they conform to perceptual or social reality, but because they are a priori scenographic *operators* which on the contrary determine the objects to be recorded on the screen and in "reality."

Directing: Putting In, and Out, of Scene

Film direction is not an artistic activity; it is a general process touching all fields of activity, a profoundly unconscious process of separation, exclusion, and effacement. In other words, direction is simultaneously executed on two planes, with this being its most enigmatic aspect. On the one hand, this task consists of separating reality on one side and a play space on the other (a "real" or an "unreal"—that which is in the camera's lens): to direct is to institute this limit, this frame, to circumscribe the region of de-responsibility at the heart of a whole which *ideo facto* is posed as responsible (we will call it *nature,* for example, or *society* or *final instance*). Thus between the two regions is established a relation of representation or doubling accompanied necessarily by a relative devaluation of the scene's realities, now only representative of the realities of reality. But on the other hand, and inseparably, in order for the function of representation to be fulfilled, the activity of directing (a placing in and out of scene, as we have just said) must also be an activity which unifies all the movements, those on *both sides* of the frame's limit, imposing here *and* there, in "reality" just as in the real *(réel),* the *same norms,* the same ordering of all drives, excluding, obliterating, effacing them *no less off* the scene than on. The references imposed on the filmic object are imposed just as necessarily on all objects outside the film. Direction first divides—along the axis of representation, and due to the theatrical limit—a reality and its double, and this disjunction constitutes an obvious repression. But also, beyond this representational disjunction and in a "pretheatrical" economic order, it eliminates *all impulsional movement, real or unreal, which will not lend itself to reduplication,* all movement which would escape identification, recognition, and the mnemic fixation. Considered from the angle of this primordial function of an exclusion spreading to the exterior as well as to the interior of the cinematographic playground, film direction acts always as a factor of *libidinal normalization,* and does so independently of all "content," be it as a "violent" as might seem. This normalization consists of the exclusion from the scene of whatever cannot be folded back upon the body of the film, and outside the scene, upon the social body.

The *film,* strange formation reputed to be normal, is no more normal than the *society* or the *organism.* All these so-called objects are the result of the imposition and hope for an accomplished totality. They are supposed to realize the reasonable goal par excellence, the subordination of all partial drives, all sterile and divergent movements, to the unity of an organic body. The film is the organic body of cinematographic movements. It is the ecclesia of images: just as politics is that of the partial social organs. This is why direction, a technique of exclusions and effacements, a political activity par excellence, and political activity, which is direction par excellence, are the religion of the modern irreligion, the ecclesiastic of the secular. The central problem for both is not the representational arrangement and its accompanying question, that of knowing how and what to represent and the definition of good or true representation; the fundamental problem is the exclusion and foreclosure of all that is judged unrepresentable because nonrecurrent.

Thus film acts as the orthopedic mirror analyzed by Lacan in 1949 as constitutive of the imaginary subject or *object a;* that we are dealing with the social body in no way alters its function. But the real problem, missed by Lacan due to his Hegelianism, is to know why the drives spread about the polymorphous body *must have* an object where they can unite. That the imperative of unification is given as hypothesis in a philosophy of "consciousness" is betrayed by the very term "consciousness," but for a "thought" of the unconscious (of which the form related most to pyrotechnics would be the economy sketched here and there in Freud's writings), the question of the production of unity, even an imaginary unity, can no longer fail to be posed in all its opacity. We will no longer have to pretend to understand how the subject's unity is constituted from his image in the mirror. We will have to ask ourselves how and why the *specular wall* in general, and thus the cinema screen in particular, can become a privileged place for the libidinal cathexis; why and how the drives come to take their place on the film *(pellicule,* or *petite peau),* opposing it to themselves as the place of their inscription, and what is more, as the support that the filmic operation in all its aspects will efface. A libidinal economy of the cinema should theoretically construct the operators which exclude aberrations from the social and organic bodies and channel the drives into this apparatus. It is not clear that narcissism or masochism are the proper operators: they carry a tone of subjectivity (of the theory of Self) that is probably still much too strong.

The Tableau Vivant

The acinema, we have said, would be situated at the two poles of the cinema taken as a writing of movements: thus, extreme immobilization and extreme mobilization. It is only for *thought* that these two modes are incompatible. In a libidinal economy they are, on the contrary, necessarily associated; stupefaction, terror, anger, hate, pleasure—all the intensities—are always displacements in place. We should read the term *emotion* as a *motion* moving toward its own exhaustion, an immobilizing motion, an immobilized mobilization. The representational arts offer two symmetrical examples of these intensities, one where immobility appears: the tableau vivant; another where agitation appears: lyric abstraction.

Presently there exists in Sweden an institution called the *posering*, a name derived from the *pose* solicited by portrait photographers: young girls rent their services to these special houses, services which consist of assuming, clothed or unclothed, the poses desired by the client. It is against the rules of these houses (which are not houses of prostitution) for the clients to touch the models in any way. We would say that this institution is made to order for the phantasmatic of Klossowski, knowing as we do the importance he accords to the tableau vivant as the near perfect simulacrum of fantasy in all its paradoxical intensity. But it must be seen how the paradox is distributed in this case: the immobilization seems to touch only the erotic object, while the subject is found overtaken by the liveliest agitation.

But things are probably not as simple as they might seem. Rather, we must understand this arrangement as a demarcation on both bodies, that of model and client, of the regions of extreme erotic intensification, a demarcation performed by one of them, the client, whose integrity reputedly remains intact. We see the proximity such a formulation has to the Sadean problematic of jouissance. We must note, given what concerns us here, that the tableau vivant in general, if it holds a certain libidinal potential, does so because it brings the theatrical and economic orders into communication; because it uses "whole persons" as detached erotic regions to which the spectator's impulses are connected. (We must be suspicious of summing this up too quickly as a simple voyeurism). We must sense the price, beyond price, as Klossowski admirably explains, that the organic body, the pretended unity of the pretended subject, must pay so that the pleasure will burst forth in its irreversible sterility. This is the same price that the cinema should pay if it goes to the first of its extremes, immobilization: because this latter (which is not simply immobility) means that it would be necessary to endlessly undo the conventional synthesis that normally all cinematographic movements proliferate. Instead of good, unifying, and reasonable forms proposed for identification, the image would give rise to the most intense agitation through its fascinating paralysis. We could already find many underground and experimental films illustrating this direction of immobilization. Here we should begin the discussion of a matter of singular importance: if you read Sade or Klossowski, the paradox of immobilization is seen to be clearly distributed along the representational axis. The object, the victim, the prostitute, takes the pose, offering his or her self as a detached region, but *at the same time giving way and humiliating this whole person.* The allusion to this latter is an indispensable factor in the intensification, since it indicates the inestimable price of diverting the drives in order to achieve perverse pleasure. Thus representation is essential to this phantasmatic; that is, it is essential that the spectator be offered instances of identification, recognizable forms, all in all, matter for the memory: for it is at the price, we repeat, of going beyond this and disfiguring the order of propagation that the intense emotion is felt. It follows that the simulacrum's support, be it the writer's descriptive syntax, the film of Pierre Zucca whose photographs illustrate(?) Klossowski's *La Monnaie Vivante,* the paper on which Klossowski himself sketches—it follows that the support itself must not submit to any noticeable perversion in order that the perversion attack only what is supported, the representation of the victim: the support is held in insensibility or unconsciousness. From here springs Klossowski's active militancy in favor of representational plastics and his anathema for abstract painting.

Abstraction

But what occurs if, on the contrary, it is the support itself that is touched by perverse hands? Then the film, movements, lightings, and focus refuse to produce the recognizable image of a victim or immobile model, taking on themselves the price of agitation and libidinal expense and leaving it no longer to the fantasized body. All lyric abstraction in painting maintains such a shift. It implies a polarization no longer toward the immobility of the model but toward the mobility of the support. This mobility is quite the contrary of cinematographic movement; it arises from any process which undoes the beautiful forms suggested by this latter, from any process which to a greater or lesser degree works on and distorts these forms. It blocks the synthesis of identification and thwarts the mnemic instances. It can thus go far toward achieving an *atarxy* of the iconic constituents, but this is still to be understood as a mobilization of the support. This way of frustrating the beautiful movement *by means of the support* must not be confused with that working through a paralyzing attack on the victim who serves as motif. The model is no longer needed, for the relation to the body of the client/spectator is completely displaced.

How is jouissance instantiated by a large canvas by Pollock or Rothko or by a study by Richter, Baruchello, or Eggeling? If there is no longer a reference to the loss of the unified body due to the model's immobilization and its diversion to the ends of partial discharge, just how inestimable must be the disposition the client/spectator can have; the represented ceases to be the libidinal object while the screen itself, in all its most formal aspects, takes its place. The film strip is no longer abolished (made transparent) for the benefit of this or that flesh, for it offers itself as the flesh posing itself. But from what unified body is it torn so that the spectator may enjoy, so that it seems to him to be beyond all price? Before the minute thrills which hem the contact regions adjoining the chromatic sands of a Rothko canvas, or before the almost imperceptible movements of the little objects or organs of Pol Bury, it is at the price of renouncing his own bodily totality and synthesis of movements making it exist that the spectator experiences intense pleasure: these objects demand the paralysis not of the object/model but of the "subject" client, the decomposition of his own organism. The channels of passage and libidinal discharge are restricted to very small partial regions (eye–cortex), and almost the whole body is neutralized in a tension blocking all escape of drives from passages other than those necessary to the detection of very fine differences. It is the same, though following other modalities, with the effects of the excess of movement in Pollock's paintings or with Thompson's manipulation of the lens. Abstract cinema, like abstract painting, in rendering the support opaque reverses the arrangement, making the client a victim. It is the same again though differently in the almost imperceptible movements of the Nō theater.

The question, which must be recognized as being crucial to our time because it is that of the staging of scene and society, follows: is it necessary for the victim to be in the scene for the pleasure to be intense? If the victim is the client, if in the scene is only film screen, canvas, the support, do we lose to this arrangement all the intensity of the sterile discharge? And if so, must we then renounce the hope of finishing with the illusion, not only the cinematographic illusion but also the social and political illusions? Are they not really illusions then? Or is believing so the illusion? Must the return of extreme intensities be founded on at least this empty permanence, on the phantom of the organic body or subject which is the proper noun, and at the same time that they cannot really accomplish this unity? This foundation, this love, how does it differ from that anchorage in nothing which founds capital?

Note

These reflections would not have been possible without the practical and theoretical work accomplished for several years by and with Dominique Avron, Claudine Eizykman, and Guy Fihman.

—translated by Paisley N. Livingston,
in collaboration with the author

21

Teresa de Lauretis
Through the Looking-Glass

To undertake the study of the cinematic apparatus as a social technology, "a relation of the technical and the social as cinema," implies, beyond a critical displacement of concepts central to the discourse on cinema, the posing of the facts of cinema and its conditions of possibility from a different "point of theoretical-discursive articulation"; it also opens up, in the process of that displacement, other critical spaces in which the political instances of feminism and the relation of history and practice can effectively be posed.

Insofar as the cinematic apparatus operates in history, is traversed by and in turn produces ideological effects in social practice, the current debate on representation, identification, subjectivity, gender, and sexual difference not only occupies a critical space within a historical materialist theory of the cinema but directly invests its basic premises. A social being, woman is constructed through effects of language and representation; just as the spectator is the term of the moving series of filmic images, taken up and moved along successive positions of meaning, a woman, or a man, is not an undivided identity, a stable unity of "consciousness," but the term of a shifting series of ideological positions. Put another way, the social being is constructed day by day as the point of articulation of ideological formations, an always provisional encounter of subject and codes

This article was originally a response to the conference on "The Cinematic Apparatus" held in February, 1978, by the Center for Twentieth-Century Studies of the University of Wisconsin, Milwaukee. It was published in *The Cinematic Apparatus,* ed. Teresa de Lauretis and Stephen Heath (London: Macmillan, and New York: St. Martin's Press, 1980). It is reprinted here by permission of the author. A modified version is now included in Teresa de Lauretis, *Alice Doesn't: Feminism, Semiotics, Cinema* (Bloomington: Indiana University Press, and London: Macmillan, 1984).

at the historical (therefore changing) intersection of social formations and her or his personal history; while codes and social formations define positions of meaning, the individual reworks those positions into a personal, subjective construction. A social technology, a textual machine of representation—cinema, for example—is the semiotic apparatus in which the encounter takes place and the individual is addressed as subject; cinema is at once a material apparatus and a "signifying practice" in which the subject is implicated, constructed, but not exhausted. Obviously, then, woman is addressed by cinema and by film, as is man; yet the different modes of that address are far from obvious (and to understand them, to describe their functioning as ideological effects in subject construction is perhaps the main critical task confronting cinematic and semiotic theory).

As the sum of one's experiences as spectator in the socially determined situations of viewing, and in the relations of institutional discourses to the economics of film production, the dominant cinema specifies "woman" in a particular social and natural order, sets her up in certain positions of meaning, fixes her in a certain identification. Represented as the negative term of sexual differentiation, spectacle/fetish or specular image, in any case obscene, "woman" is constituted as the ground of representation and its stability, the looking-glass held up to man; but, as historical individual, the woman viewer is also positioned in the films of classical cinema as spectator/subject and thus doubly bound to that very representation which calls on her directly, engages her desire, elicits her pleasure, frames her identification, and makes her complicit in the production of (her) woman-ness. On this crucial relation of "woman" as constituted in representation to women as historical subjects depend at once the development of a feminist critique and the possibility of a materialist semiotic theory of subjectivity and culture.

It is therefore not simple numerical evidence (women hold up half of the sky) that forces a theory of the cinematic apparatus to hear the questions of women, but their direct critical incidence on its conditions of possibility. It is because this theory is posed in history and articulated in historically specific discourses and practices—semiotics, psychoanalysis, technology—that it cannot disengage itself from the trouble caused by woman, the problems she poses in *its* discursive operations; while those discourses have traditionally assigned to her a position of nonsubject, the latter determines, grounds, and supports the very concept of subject and the theoretical discourse itself. In this paper I will examine certain problematic assumptions and contradictions concealed in that discourse which have hindered and restrained the radical possibilities of cinematic theory even as they provided its initial impulse.

Two major conceptual models are involved in the current development of a theory of the cinema, from classical semiology to the more recent metapsychological studies, and in its formulation of concepts of signification, symbolic exchange, language, subject, unconscious, and so forth: a structural-linguistic model (cinema as "language," as a formal system, a structural organization of codes functioning according to a logic internal to the system) and a dynamic, psychoanalytic model (cinema as production of meaning, of imaginary, of unconscious, for a subject). In both cases, cinema being an apparatus of social representation, assumptions are made, whether implicitly (in the former model) or explicitly (in the latter), as to the conditions and modes of representation and address; those assumptions hinge on sexual difference and the relation of woman to sexuality.

Since Freud imposed the question of sexuality as an area of vital concern to both individual and social development, sexual difference has been taken up and dealt with, in one way or another, by any theorization of cultural processes. In the two models under consideration, the relation of woman to sexuality is either reduced and assimilated to, or contained within, masculine sexuality. But whereas the structural-linguistic model, whose theoretical object is the formal organization of signifiers, assumes sexual difference as a preestablished, stable semantic content (the signified in the cinematic sign), the psychoanalytic model theorizes it in an ambiguous and circular way: on the one hand, sexual difference is a meaning-effect produced in representation; on the other, paradoxically, it is the very support of representation. Both models, however, contain certain contradictions which are produced textually and are thus historically verifiable, for they can be located in the theoretical discourses and in the practices that motivate them.[1] For example, the equation woman: representation (woman as sign, woman as the phallus) and sexual difference: value founded in nature (woman as object of exchange, woman as the Real, as Truth) is not the formula of a naively or malignantly posited equivalence, but the end result of a series of ideological operations that run through an entire theoretical-discursive tradition. It is in these operations that a theory of the cinema must interrogate its models, as it interrogates the operations of the cinematic apparatus.

Excluding any consideration of address and of the social differentiation of spectators, excluding, therefore, the whole problematic of ideology and the subject's construction in it, the structural-linguistic model assumes sexual differentiation as simple complementarity within a "species," as biological fact rather than sociocultural process. That assumption, only implicit in this model of the cinematic apparatus, is fully explicit in Claude Lévi-Strauss' theory of kinship, which, together with Saussurian linguistics, constitutes the historical basis for the development of classical semiology. In the real world, says Lévi-Strauss, women are human beings (that is, like men), but their *social* function is that of chattels, objects, whose regulated possession and exchange among men ensures and maintains social order; and this is so universally because the incest prohibition, the historical event instituting culture, is found in all human societies. Although marriage regulations vary greatly throughout world societies, their underlying rules, kinship structures, are found to be identical *"by treating* marriage regulations and kinship systems *as a kind of language."*[2] Having adopted the analytical method of structural linguistics in "treating" kinship, Lévi-Strauss then says that women are signs, words spoken and "exchanged" by men in social communication; but "in contrast to words, which *have wholly become* signs, woman *has remained* at once sign and value."[3] Women, therefore, are objects whose value is founded in nature ("valuables *par excellence*" as bearers of children, food gatherers, etc.); at the same time, they are signs in social communication established through kinship systems.

The confusion or assimilation of the notion of sign (which Lévi-Strauss takes from Saussure and transposes to the ethnological domain) with the notion of exchange (which he takes from Marx, collapsing use value and exchange value) is not a chance one; it comes from an intellectual tradition, a set of discourses which for centuries has sought to unify cultural processes, to explain "economically" as many diverse phenomena as possible, to totalize the real and, either as a humanism or as imperialism, to control it. In positing exchange as a theoretical abstraction, a structure, and therefore "not itself constitutive of the subordination of women," Lévi-Strauss overlooks the fact that "the terms or items of exchange must *already* be constituted, in a hierarchy of value," which means that women's economic value must be "predicated on a pre-given sexual division which must already be social."[4] Such remarkable oversight may have occurred, I suggest, because the Saussurian model defines value entirely as a differential, systematic relation; but when he states that women are also persons, that is, contribute to the wealth of a culture (his humanistic appeal), then he is invoking a Marxian notion of use value—woman as labor power and/or concealed labor. Hence the confusion between woman as object of exchange, bearer of economic, i.e., positive value, and woman as sign, bearer of semiotic, i.e., negative value, of difference.

The universalizing project of Lévi-Strauss, to conflate the economic and the semiotic orders into a unified theory of culture, *depends on* his positing woman as the functional opposite of subject (man), which automatically excludes the possibility of women's social role as subjects and producers of culture. It is not merely that in the real world women are held in the mute position of chattels; it is his own theory of kinship, his conceptualization of the social, that inscribes them in a discourse where they are doubly negated as subjects: first because they are vehicles of men's communication, second because their sexuality is not cultural but "natural," childbearing being a purely economic fact, a capacity for production such as that of a machine. Desire, like symbolization, is a property of men:

The emergence of symbolic thought must have required that women, like words, should be things that were exchanged. In this new case, indeed, this was the only means of overcoming the contradiction by which the same woman was seen under two incompatible aspects: on the one hand, as the object of personal desire, thus exciting sexual and proprietorial instincts; and on the other, as the subject *[sic]* of the desire of others, and seen as such, i.e. as the means of binding others through alliance with them.[5]

I have stressed the work of Lévi-Strauss because of its often underestimated influence on current neo-Freudian thought and, consequently, on the psychoanalytic model recently assumed by film theory. If we reread the passage just quoted from *The Elementary Structures of Kinship* (1947) or, even more to the point, the essay on "The Effectiveness of Symbols" (1949, reprinted in the first volume of *Structural Anthropology*) in the light of Jacques Lacan's work, we can see how the latter's linguistic conception of the unconscious as *locus* of the discourse of the other must pass through Lévi-Strauss's formulation of the unconscious as the organ of the symbolic function: no longer located in the individual psyche, as it was for Freud, the unconscious is a structuring process, the universal articulatory mechanism of the "human mind," the structural condition of all symbolization.[6] In the shift in focus onto the subject consists Lacan's originality vis-à-vis Lévi-Strauss; the Oedipal law, as the point of entry of the subject into language, is the condition—a structural condition—of its interminable rite of passage through culture. But, as noted by Gayle Rubin, a same conceptual set underlies both theories:

> In one sense, the Oedipal complex is an expression of the circulation of the phallus in intrafamily exchange, an inversion of the circulation of women in interfamily exchange. . . . the phallus passes through the medium of women from one man to another—from father to son, from mother's brother to sister's son, and so forth. In this family *Kula* ring, women go one way, the phallus the other. It is where we aren't. In this sense, the phallus is more than a feature which distinguishes the sexes; it is the embodiment of the male status, to which men accede, and in which certain rights inhere—among them, the right to a woman. It is an expression of the transmission of male dominance. It passes through women and settles upon men. The tracks which it leaves include gender identity, the division of the sexes.[7]

The psychoanalytic model recently assumed by film theory, in acknowledging subjectivity as a construction in language, articulates it in process (drive, desire, symbolization) which depend on the crucial instance of castration and are thus finally possible only for the male: "The interdiction against autoerotism, bearing on *a particular organ,* which for that very reason *acquires the value of an ultimate (or first) symbol of lack (manque),* has the impact of pivotal experience."[8] There is no doubt as to which particular organ is meant: the penis/phallus, symbol of lack and signifier of desire. Despite repeated statements by Lacan(ians) that the phallus is not the penis, the context of the terms I have emphasized in the quotation (there are others, similarly ambivalent) makes it clear that desire and signification are defined ultimately as a masculine process, inscribed in the male body, since they are dependent on the initial—and *pivotal*—experiencing of one's penis, on having a penis. In his discussion of *Encore,* Lacan's 1972/1973 seminar devoted to Freud's question "What does the woman want?," Heath remarks on Lacan's "certainty in a representation and its vision"—Bernini's statue of Saint Teresa as the visible evidence of the *jouissance* of the woman:

> where the conception of the symbolic as movement and production of difference, as

chain of signifiers in which the subject is effected in division, should forbid the notion of some presence from which difference is then derived; Lacan instates the visible as the condition of symbolic functioning, with the phallus the standard of visibility required: seeing is from the male organ.

Against the effective implications of the psychoanalytic theory he himself developed, Lacan "runs analysis back into biology and myth," reinstating sexual reality as nature, as origin and condition of the symbolic: "The constant limit of the theory is the phallus, the phallic function, and the theorization of that limit is constantly eluded, held off, for example, by collapsing castration into a scenario of vision"; thus, in the supposedly crucial distinction between penis and phallus, "Lacan is often no further than the limits of pure analogical rationalization."[9]

Concepts such as voyeurism, fetishism, or the imaginary signifier, however appropriate they may seem to describe the operations of dominant cinema, however apparently convergent—precisely because convergent?—with its historical development as an apparatus of social reproduction, are directly implicated in a discourse which circumscribes woman in the sexual, binds her (in) sexuality, makes her the absolute representation, the phallic scenario. It is then the case that the ideological effects produced in and by those concepts, that discourse, perform, as dominant cinema does, a political function in the service of cultural domination including, but not limited to, the sexual exploitation of women and the repression or containment of their sexuality.

Consider a recent discussion of the pornographic film by Yann Lardeau in *Cahiers du cinéma*. The pornographic film is said relentlessly to repropose sexuality as the field of knowledge and power, power in the uncovering of truth ("the naked woman has always been, in our society, the allegorical representation of Truth"). The closeup is its operation of truth, the camera constantly closing in on the woman's sex, exhibiting it as object of desire and definitive place of *jouissance* only in order to ward off castration, "to keep the subject from his own lack": "Too heavily marked as a term—always susceptible of castration—the phallus is unrepresentable. . . . The porno film is constructed on the *disavowal of castration,* and *its operation of truth is a fetishistic operation*."[10] The cinema, for Lardeau, is *pour cause* pornography's privileged mode of expression. The fragmentation and fabrication of the female body, the play of skin and makeup, nudity and dress, the constant recombination of organs as equivalent terms of a combinatory are but the repetition, inside the erotic scene, of the operations and techniques of the apparatus—fragmentation of the scene by camera movements, construction of the representational space by depth of field, diffraction of light and color effects, in short, the process of fabrication of the film from *découpage* to montage. "It all happens as if the porno film were putting cinema on trial;" hence the final message of the film: *"it is cinema itself, as a medium, which is pornographic."*

Dissociated, isolated (autonomised) from the body by the closeup, circumscribed in its genital materiality (reified), [the sex] can then freely circulate outside the subject—as commodities circulate in exchange independently of the producers or as the linguistic sign circulates as value independent of the speakers. Free circulation of goods, persons and messages in capitalism—this is the liberation effected by the close-up, sex delivered into pure abstraction.[11]

This indictment of cinema and sexuality in capitalism as apparatuses for the reproduction of alienated social relations is doubtless acceptable at first. But two objections eventually take shape, one from the other. First: as the explicit reference to the models discussed earlier is posed in terms critical of the linguistic model alone, while the Lacanian view of subject processes is simply assumed, uncritically, Lardeau's analysis cannot but duplicate the single, masculine perspective inherent in a phallic conception of sexuality; consequently, it reaffirms woman as representation and reproposes woman as scene, rather than subject, of sexuality. Second: however acceptable it may have seemed, the proposition that cinema is pornographic and fetishistic resolves itself in the closure of syllogism; begging its question and unable to question its premise, such a critique is unable to engage social practice and historical change.

But, it may be counterobjected, the pornographic film is just *that* kind of social practice; it addresses, is made for men only. Consider, then, the classical Hollywood narrative fiction film, even the subgenre of the "woman's film."

Think again of *Letter from an Unknown Woman* and its arresting gaze on the illuminated body of Lisa/Joan Fontaine, the film the theatre of that. . . . With the apparatus securing its ground, the narrative plays, that is, on castration known and denied, a movement of difference in the symbolic, the lost object, and the conversion of that movement into the terms of a fixed memory, a construction of the imaginary, the object—and with it the mastery, the unity of the subject—regained.[12]

Again and again narrative film has been exposed as the production of a drama of vision, a memory spectacle, an image of the woman as beauty, desired and untouchable, desired *as* remembered; and the operations of the apparatus deployed in that production—economy of repetition, rhymes, relay of looks, sound-image matches—toward the achieved coherence of a "narrative space" which holds, binds, entertains the spectator at the apex of the representational triangle as the subject of vision.[13] Not only in the pornographic film, then, but in the "woman's film" as well is cinema's obscenity the form of its expression and of its content.

The paradox of this condition of cinema is nowhere more evident than in those films which openly pose the question of sexuality and representation in political terms, films like Pasolini's *Salò,* Cavani's *Night Porter,* or Oshima's *Empire of the Senses.* It is in such films that the difficulties in current theorization appear most evident and a radical reformulation of the questions of enunciation, address, and subject processes most urgent. For example, in contrast with the classic narrative film and its production of a fixed subject–vision, Heath asks us to look at Oshima's film as the film of the uncertainty of vision, "a film working on a problem"—"the problem of 'seeing' for the spectator."

Empire of the Senses is crossed by that possibility of a nothing seen, which is its very trouble of representation, but that possibility is not posed, as it were, from some outside; on the contrary, it is produced as a contradiction within the given system of representation, the given machine.[14]

By shifting to, and forcing on, the spectator the question of "the relations of the sexual and the political in cinema," by marking out the difficulties—perhaps the impossibility—posed by their articulation in representation, the film includes the spectator's view as divided ("the splitting of the seen"), disturbs the coherence of identification, addresses a subject in division. Thus, it is compellingly argued, the struggle is still with representation, not outside or against it; a struggle in the discourse of the film and on the film.

It is not by chance that women's critical attention to the cinema most often insists on the notions of representation and identification, the terms in which are articulated the social construction of sexual difference and the place of woman, at once image and viewer, spectacle and spectator, in that construction:

One of the most basic connections between women's experience in this culture and women's experience in film is precisely the relationship of spectator and spectacle. Since women are spectacles in their everyday lives, there's something about coming to terms with film from the perspective of what it means to be an object of spectacle and what it means to be a spectator that is really coming to terms with how that relationship exists both up on the screen and in everyday life.[15]

In the psychoanalytic view of film as imaginary signifier, representation and identification are processes referred to a masculine subject, predicated on and predicating a subject of phallic desire, dependent on castration as the constitutive instance of the subject; that is to say, they are *subject* processes only *insofar as* they are inscribed in a phallic order. And woman, in a phallic order, is at once the mirror and the screen—image, ground, and support—of *this* subject's projection and identification: "the spectator *identifies with himself*, with himself as pure act of perception"; "as he identifies with himself as look, the spectator can do no other than identify with the camera."[16] Image and representation, woman is "cinema's object of desire," "the sole imaginary" of the film, " 'sole' in the sense that any difference is caught up in that structured disposition, that fixed relation in which the film is centered and held."[17]

What this theory of the apparatus cannot countenance, given its phallic premise, is the possibility of a different relation of woman as spectator-viewer to the filmic image, of different values and meaning-effects being produced for her, producing her, in identification and representation, as subject; in short, the possibility of other subject processes obtaining in that relation. This is the context of the debate, in avant-garde film practice and theory, around narrative and abstract representation, illusionist vs. structural-materialist film (see the essay by Peter Gidal); and in the apparent incompatibility of the latter with feminist instances is the reason for seeking alternative models or economies of desire (see Maureen Turim's essay and the discussion following her and Gidal's papers). This is the context and the main area of feminist intervention (see the essay by Jacqueline Rose).[18]

According to Mulvey, the woman is not visible in the audience which is perceived as male; according to Johnston, the woman is not visible on the screen.. . . . How does one formulate an understanding of a structure that insists on our absence even in the face of our presence? What is there in a film with which a woman viewer identifies? How can the contradictions be used as a critique? And how do all these factors influence what one makes as a woman filmmmmaker, or specifically as a feminist filmmaker?[19]

"A film working on a problem". This must be, provisionally, the task of the critical discourse as well: to oppose the simply totalizing closure of final state-ments (cinema is pornographic, cinema is voyeurist, cinema is the imaginary, the dream machine in Plato's cave, and so on), to seek out contradictions, heterogeneity, ruptures in the fabric of representation so thinly stretched—if powerful—to contain excess, division, difference, resistance; to open up critical spaces in the seamless narrative space constructed by dominant cinema *and* by dominant discourses (psychoanalysis, certainly, but also the discourse on tech-nology as autonomous instance, or the notion of a total manipulation of the public sphere, the exploitation of cinema, by purely economic interests, etc.); finally, to displace those discourses from where they obliterate the claims of other social instances, erase the insistence of practice in history.

   This is the critical work already undertaken, in and out of the institutional margins, by feminist filmmakers, writers, teachers, and by people alerted to the women's movement's singular potential for social transformation by the very effort of containment and recuperation massively deployed by institutions such as cinema. The proliferation of liberal discourses on "the role of women in. . ." corresponds to the revival of the "woman's film" in the seventies and to the "images of women" approach to film encouraged by the media and the pub-lishing industry. Thus, instead of the films of Dorothy Arzner or Marguerite Duras, of Chantal Akerman or Jackie Raynal, we must see *Three Women, An Unmarried Woman, A Woman Under the Influence, Swept Away, Coma,* and we look at ourselves *Looking for Mr. Goodbar* or at *The Eyes of Laura Mars*—films which restabilize "woman" as representation, reassuring the men in the audience and offering to women spectators a new and improved, yet so familiar and equally reassuring, mirror, mirror on the wall.. . .[20] If the cinema and the other media have become, as Rosalind Coward has argued, a "forum for competing definitions" of woman's sexuality, of woman as a sexually defined being, and if the female body—more publicly admitted than before, emphatically displayed—"is a site of particular significance in a struggle of representations which guar-antee particular ideologies,"[21] it is not enough merely to accuse all institutions and all representation of being reactionary. Women live in those institutions, participate in the social construction of reality; and women are not essentially other, possessed of a "true nature" or existing outside of the social relations and representations in which they are produced as women and which they also (re)produce, as subjects, in practice. For this reason, not our participation but our active resistance is required.

The struggle bears precisely on the critique of this alleged nature of woman— the "riddle of the nature of femininity" for which Freud found an appropriately novelistic phrase, a good movie title, "the dark continent"—a critique to be carried on in different discursive registers, as many and as different as are the social apparatuses of representation, including the discourse on cinema and the conceptual models it implicitly or explicitly assumes. It is indeed the pressure of a feminist critique that has challenged psychoanalysis's ideology of mastery and the operations of its Oedipal logic in narrative film;[22] that has, on the other hand, singled out, in the web of its semiotic processes, the breaking points, the areas of rupture and excess, the limits of the system;[23] or that has turned dominant discourse inside out (and shown that it can be done) by subverting its enunciation, unearthing the archaeological stratifications on which it is built, radically altering the meaning-effect of its representation. Thus Luce Irigaray, in "The Blind Spot of an Ancient Dream of Symmetry," rewrites Freud's essay on "Femininity" inscribing her own critical voice into his tightly woven argumentation and creating an effect of distance, like a discordant echo, which ruptures the coherence of address, divides meaning, and continually dislocates the reader in that division.[24] Those different discursive strategies are forms of cultural resistance, each with a use value for particular, not universal, situations of practice; in affirming the historical existence of irreducible contradictions for women in language, they also challenge theory in its own terms, the terms of a semiotic space constructed in language, its power based on social validation and well-tested strategies of enunciation and address.

I have argued that a theory of cinema as a relation of the technical and the social can be developed only with a constant, critical attention to its discursive operations and from the awareness of their present inadequacy. I now want to suggest that the questions of representation and subject processes should be posed from a less rigid, less static or unified notion of meaning than is instated by an exclusive emphasis on the signifier and by a view of signification as always already determined in a fixed order of language. As one way of mapping the terrain in which meanings are produced, I suggest, it may be useful to reconsider the notion of code, somewhat emarginated by current film studies after its heyday in Metzian semiology, and importantly redefined in Umberto Eco's *A Theory of Semiotics*. In the systemic formulation of classical semiology, a code was construed to be a system of oppositional values (Saussure's *langue,* for example, or Metz's code of cinematic punctuation) regardless or upstream of the meanings produced contextually in enunciation and reception; in other words, "meanings" (Saussure's signifieds) were supposed to be subsumed in, and in a stable relationship to, the respective "signs" (Saussure's signifiers). So defined, a code could be envisaged and described like a structure, independently of any communicative purpose and apart from an actual process of signification. For Eco, on the contrary, a code is always a significant and communicational framework linking combinatorial elements (on the expression plane) with semantic elements (on the content plane) or with behavioral responses; and a sign is not a fixed semiotic entity but a "sign-function," the mutual and transitory correlation of two 'functives,' the elements of the correlation: a sign-vehicle (expression, the physical component of the sign) and a "cultural unit" (content, meaning), the latter being a unit in a semantic system of oppositional values. In the historical process, "the same functive can also enter into another correlation, thus becoming a different functive and so giving rise to a new sign-function."[25] As socially established, operational rules that *generate* signs (whereas in classical semiology codes *organize* signs), the codes are historically related to the modes of sign production; it follows that the codes change whenever new or different contents are culturally assigned to the same sign vehicle or whenever new sign vehicles are produced. In this manner a new text, a different interpretation of a text—any new practice of discourse—sets up a different configuration of content, other cultural meanings that in turn transform the codes and rearrange the semantic universe of the society that produces it.

Going back to the cinema, the avant-garde, theoretical dilemma about the politics of abstract vs. "anthropomorphic" forms of representation can be rephrased as follows: what must come first, a change in the form and matter of expression (the structural-materialist position), or a change in the form and matter of content (a position argued by some feminists and suggested in Mulvey and Wollen's *Riddles of the Sphinx)?* If the signifier alone is at work in signification, the answer can only be one, taking us back around the mulberry bush of the argument, to the inevitability of women's oppression, at least in cinema; here artistic practice and social practice must part their ways ("what does one make as a woman filmmaker?"). If both functives of the sign-function, the content of the representation and its expression, its representing, are involved in signification, there is no specific answer—each can affect and effect the other, and artistic practice can become, for women, a practice of social change.

Ironically, and in spite of its disinterest in "the subject of semiosis," a semiotics of the modes of sign production may serve to pose the question of subjectivity in historical terms, to approach the subject through the operations (the modes of sign production) of the material, technological, cultural apparatuses that construct it. Again ironically, in view of the alleged feminine discomfort with technology, it is by posing cinema as a social technology (as a process characterized by the interplay of the social and the technological in the production of signs and meanings for and by a subject who is their term of reference and constant intersection) that one can pose, one cannot in fact *but* pose, the radical questions of feminism; for the latter invest the basic premise of a materialist theory of the cinema, and inform the very possibility of its development. Hence the important stakes that a feminist critique and film theory have in one another, and their belligerent relationship in this book as elsewhere.

Notes

1. "Motivate" here is to be understood not as intentionality or design on the part of individuals who promote those discourses, but rather in the sense in which Marx describes the social determinations by which the capitalist, for example, is not a "bad" person but a function in a specific system of social relations.

2. C. Lévi-Strauss, *Structural Anthropology* (Harmondsworth: Penguin, 1972) p. 61; my emphasis.

3. C. Lévi-Strauss, *The Elementary Structures of Kinship* (London: Eyre and Spottiswoode, 1969) p. 496.

4. Elizabeth Cowie, "Woman as Sign," *m/f* (1978), no. 1, pp. 52 and 57.

5. *The Elementary Structures of Kinship*, p. 496. This passage is echoed in the following, by J. Lacan. "In the Real, women—with all due deference to them—serve as objects for the exchanges ordered by the elementary structures of kinship. These exchanges are perpetuated in the Imaginary, whenever the opportunity offers itself, whereas what is transmitted in parallel fashion in the Symbolic order is the phallus." *Ecrits* (Paris: Seuil, 1966), p. 565, quoted by Anthony Wilden, *System and Structure* (London: Tavistock, 1972), p. 292. Wilden's book develops the argument that both Lacan and Lévi-Strauss operate a confusion in logical typing between discursive orders; see in particular the chapter entitled "The Critique of Phallocentrism."

6. "The unconscious ceases to be the ultimate haven of individual peculiarities—the repository of a unique history which makes each of us an irreplaceable being. It is reducible to a function—the symbolic function, which no doubt is specifically human, and which is carried out according to the same laws among all men, and actually corresponds to the aggregate of these laws . . . As the organ of a specific function, the unconscious merely imposes structural laws upon inarticulated elements which originate elsewhere—impulses, emotions, representations, and memories. We might say, therefore, that the preconscious is the individual lexicon where each of us accumulates the vocabulary of his personal history, but that this vocabulary becomes significant, for us and for others, only to the extent that the unconscious structures it according to its laws and thus transforms it into language." *Structural Anthropology*, pp. 202–3. In this essay, entitled "The Effectiveness of Symbols," Lévi-Strauss describes a Cuna incantation to facilitate childbirth performed by the shaman. The same metaphors return in the language of Lacan's description of the *fort-da* game, establishing a double link in the chain of psychoanalytic discourse: "It is with his object [the spool, the object little a] that the infant leaps the boundaries of his domain transformed into holes, shafts, and with which he commences his incantation." J. Lacan, *Le Séminaire IX*, quoted by Constance Penley, "The Avant-Garde and its Imaginary," *Camera Obscura* (Fall 1977), no. 2, p. 30.

7. G. Rubin, "The Traffic in Women: Notes on the "Political Economy' of Sex," in *Toward an Anthropology of Women*, ed. Rayna R. Reiter (New York: Monthly Review Press, 1975), pp. 191–2.

8. J. Lacan, "Pour une logique du phantasme," *Scilicet* (1970), nos. 2–3, p. 259, quoted by John Brenkman, "The Other and the One: Psycho-analysis, Reading, the *Symposium*," *Yale French Studies* (1977), nos. 55–56, p. 441.

9. S. Heath, "Difference," *Screen* (Autumn 1978), 19(3):52, 54, 66. See also L. Irigaray's

critique of this seminar in "Cosi fan tutti," in *Ce Sexe qui n' en est pas un* (Paris: Minuit, 1977), pp. 84–101.

10. Y. Lardeau, "Le sexe froid (du porno au delà)," *Cahiers du cinéma* (June 1978), no. 289, pp. 49, 52, and 61.

11. *Ibid.*, pp. 51, 54.

12. S. Heath, "The Question Oshima," *Wide Angle* (1977), 2(1):55.

13. See, for example, S. Heath, "Narrative Space," *Screen* (Autumn 1976), 17(3):68–112. [included in this anthology—ED.].

14. Postscript to "The Question Oshima" reprinted in Paul Willemen, ed., *Ophuls* (London: British Film Institute 1978), p. 87. The thought is further developed in the following passage: "The order of the look in the work of the film is neither the thematics of voyeurism (note already the displacement of the look's subject from men to women) nor the binding structure of a classic narrative disposition (where character look is an element at once of the form of content, the definition of the action in the movement of looks exchanged, and of the form of expression, the composition of the images and their arrangment together, their 'match'). Its register is not that of 'out of frame', the '*hors-champ*' to be recaptured in the film by the spatially suturing process of 'folding over' of which field/reverse-field is the most obvious device, but that of the edging of every frame, of every shot, towards a *problem* of 'seeing' *for the spectator*." "The Question Oshima," p. 51.

15. Judith Mayne, in "Women and Film: A Discussion of Feminist Aesthetics," *New German Critique* (Winter 1978), no. 13, p. 86.

16. Christian Metz, "The Imaginary Signifier," *Screen* (Summer 1975), 16(2):51 and 52 [excerpt included in this anthology—ED.].

17. S. Heath, "Questions of Property," *Ciné-tracts* (Spring–Summer 1978), 1(4):6.

18. See Peter Gidal, "Technology and Ideology in/through/and Avant-Garde Film: An Instance," Maureen Turim, "The Place of Visual Illusions," and Jacqueline Rose, "The Cinematic Apparatus: Problems in Current Theory," all included in *The Cinematic Apparatus*, ed. Teresa de Lauretis and Stephen Heath (London: Macmillan, and New York: St. Martin's, 1980).

19. Ruby Rich, in Mayne, "Women and Film," p. 87. Rich here refers to Laura Mulvey, "Visual Pleasure and Narrative Cinema," *Screen* (Autumn 1975), 16(3):6–18 [included in this anthology—ED.] and to Pam Cook and Claire Johnston, "The Place of Women in the Cinema of Raoul Walsh," in *Raoul Walsh*, ed. Phil Hardy (Edinburgh: Edinburgh Film Festival, 1974), pp. 93–109.

20. A small example of how the industry accommodates culture-specific variations: the titling of *An Unmarried Woman* in France is *Une Femme libre* (A Free Woman) and in Italy *Una Donna tutta sola* (A Woman All Alone), the reference to legal status changing to heavily connoted references to sexual aggressivity and social jeopardy.

21. R. Coward, " 'Sexual Liberation' and the Family," *m/f* (1978), no. 1, p. 17.

22. For example, Mulvey's "Visual Pleasure and Narrative Cinema."

23. Ann Kaplan, ed., *Women in Film Noir* (London: British Film Institute, 1978); Patricia Mellencamp, "Spectacle and Spectator: Looking Through the American Musical Comedy," *Ciné-tracts* (Summer 1977), no. 2, pp. 27–35.

24. L. Irigaray, *Speculum, de l'autre femme* (Paris: Minuit, 1974), pp. 7–162. On filmic enunciation see the short pieces on *Jeanne Dielman, La Femme du Gange,* and *What Maisie Knew,* by, respectively, Janet Bergstrom, Elisabeth Lyon, and Constance Penley in *Camera Obscura* (Fall 1977), no. 2, pp. 114–36.

25. U. Eco, *A Theory of Semiotics* (Bloomington: Indiana University Press, and London: Macmillan, 1976), p. 49.

Part Four

Textuality as Ideology

Introduction

It should by now be clear that the place of cinema in sociocultural formations, and particularly in the advanced capitalist formations, was of special interest to major film-theoretical impulses of the 1970s. The ideological and/or political placing of cinema in general and of specific films has been consistently evident in this volume.

The interrelationships among questions of structure, textuality, pleasure, position, and social order can probably be approached most rapidly by reference to the example of feminist film theory (thought the resolutions of the theoretical problems posed by those interrelationships are by no means so quickly achieved). Especially since Laura Mulvey's "Visual Pleasure and Narrative Cinema" became a central, if sometimes controversial, document of film theory in the 1970s, it has not been difficult to understand why the textual position posited by a film for its spectating subject, insofar as it is sexually differentiated, bears close study for its relation to social hierarchy. Additionally, there have been a number of other (though not opposed) angles from which to view the relation of film to ideology in terms of subject position. For example, we have seen that Colin MacCabe's Lacanian analysis of the classical text has as its goal a political-ideological evaluation of narrative structures in terms of their subject effects. And in "The Ideological Effects of the Basic Cinematographic Apparatus," Jean-Louis Baudry argued for the close fit of a transcendental subject implied by the apparatus with certain tendencies in phenomenological (i.e., idealist) philosophy. The list of such examples could be a lengthy one.

If this entire volume is penetrated by concepts of ideology, it follows that a large number of its selections could be included in a section on ideology and cinema. As a conclusion, then, part 4 does not separate itself from the other parts by its topic. Instead, it presents a number of additional articles which formulate varying analyses about cinema as ideology, but with an awareness of the kinds of arguments already encountered in previous parts of this anthology. What we might note in introducing it is precisely this variety.

In the introduction to part 2 there was some attention to the importance attributed to representational systems in Althusserian theories of ideology. Such theories deal with ideology not only as the recirculation of concepts, notions, myths, etc. useful to the maintenance of the social formation, but also and simultaneously as the definition of positionalities for social agents. On that account, the stuff of ideology is representational systems which are integral components of societal organization.

While this kind of social theory supplies important general premises for the social study of textuality, these remain only general premises. Fundamental to any conceptualization of cinema as ideology is the question of how one relates textual operations (and/or apparatuses supporting those operations) to social formations. Specific notions of textual operations are therefore required. On what levels, then, should textual procedures, filmic specificity, cinematic signifying systematicity, cinematic excess, etc., be questioned for ideological affiliations?

One level might clearly be very specific in historical terms (e.g., is a classical film made in 1939, such as *Young Mr. Lincoln,* pro-Democrat or pro-Republican, for socioeconomic reform or against it?). Or such interrogations might be performed on a historically very general level (to what extent do the graphic procedures subtending a classical film participate in a long-range, large-scale implementation of the bourgeois norms of representation and subjectivity that can be traced back to the Renaissance, and what is the specific, distinctive role of cinema in that project?). Another level of ideological analysis is one often associated with a vulgar Marxism, which would treat any text as caused directly, immediately, and readably by its social determinants; so that it becomes relatively easy to demonstrate that a given film's mode of existence and ideological operations are unified around its social purpose, which is ultimately to embody either "false consciousness" or "true consciousness." Or instead, it might be argued that a film's ideological ambitions (which, for example, can have to do with repressing social contradiction) can place textual pressure on a film, a pressure which has the potential to split its totalizing textual facade; so that to read a film ideologically is not simply to find a social determination around which the film can be unified, but is rather to interrogate the evidence of heterogeneity, of "troubles" on the textual "surface" which are symptoms of underlying social determinations of textuality.

If differing views of textuality are among the stakes of differing approaches to ideology, it is clear that film theory of the 1970s tended much more toward this last view of textual complicity and complexity than toward the vulgar Marxist pole. But there is also another stake in the exploration of film and textuality: given these conceptions of textual operations, how are we to analyze film history? Implicitly, the question of the historical—of the diachronic relation of stasis and transformation—haunts the political impulse of such film theory and requires explicit theoretical engagement.

This part begins with Stephen Heath's "Narrative Space," a synthetic essay which here represents a large-scale approach to issues of ideology and signification. Heath summarizes and/or assumes many of the conceptions previously presented in this volume, such as the psychoanalytic-semiotic problematics of subject-positioning and the cinematic apparatus. In the context of the theorization of the subject, he links the norms of spatial construction in narrative cinema to perspectival representation, which he considers a predominantly cultural product with a genealogy in Renaissance painting. Throughout the essay, there is an emphasis on a dialectic between the representational effort to position, and the representational excesses and lacks which the former must constantly encounter and process. His account of the operations of norms of cinematic signification is balanced by a consideration of various theoretical and practical proposals for alternative kinds of filmmaking.

"Technique and Ideology: Camera, Perspective, Depth of Field" was a series written by Jean-Louis Comolli on ideology, technique, and the writing of film history. Two installments from this series are reprinted here. Comolli's argument is based on a theoretical critique of theorists and historians. His series is intended as a radical challenge to "technicist" views of the history of cinematic technology and style, and to their study isolated from conceptualizing their place in the social whole. Because of the complexity of textual and technical determinations, Comolli's argument is also a general provocation with respect to the writing of history as a linear chain of events. His agenda remains a landmark challenge to film historians.

A much more focused attention to ideology is embodied in the analysis of "John Ford's *Young Mr. Lincoln*" by the editors of *Cahiers du cinéma*. This widely cited article employs Lacanian terminology, less for an analysis of subject-positioning than as a means of approaching and describing the excesses, heterogeneities, and contradictions which they find on the textual surface. Despite the psychoanalytic terminology, the purpose is ideological analysis. The goal is to read such "troubles" for the film's textual economy as a surface manifestation of the engagement of cinematic textuality with sociohistoric determinations: that is, to relate textual procedures to a given, ideologically specific enterprise.

Given the dominance of the classical cinema, explored in such different ways by Heath, Comolli, and the editors of *Cahiers du cinéma,* the conceptualization of alternative practices and opposition remains open to significant discussion. Heath argues for the centrality of narrative as a terrain of struggle. Noël Burch is not so certain that narrative is as central to film's ideological effects (including subject-positioning). In "Primitivism and the Avant-Gardes: A Dialectical Approach," an essay which ranges widely over the history of filmmaking, Burch expores two nonclassical traditions, those of the avant-gardes and those of so-called primitive cinema. He investigates the nuances of the similarities and differences between the two from a definite political-ideological perspective.

Such large-scale approaches to the history of filmic signification as those of Heath, Comolli, and Burch make the development of the classical system of signification and its modes of spectatorial positioning one of the central items for film-historical inquiry. Thus, Burch posits the conflict of "Primitive Cinema" and what he calls an "Institutional mode of representation" that has since dominated filmmaking. In "Film Body: An Implantation of Perversions," Linda Williams explores what Burch would regard as the "preinstitutional" cinema of Georges Méliès and the protocinema of Edweard Muybridge. She finds a mobilization of the human body which prefigures the fascination of the classical cinema with sexual difference. On the one hand, her argument might seem to support Comolli's case for the ideological penetration of technique by ideology (especially since, as she points out, Muybridge's work found its justifications as a scientific endeavor); on the other hand, her conclusion—that even this early the cinema was already fully implicated in a discourse of fascination with the body and sexual differentiation—raises important questions concerning the conceptualization of transitions in the history of cinematic signification (what changed with the development of classical cinema, Burch's Institutional mode of representation, etc.?)

From Williams' examination of some of the earliest moments of film history, we go to Thomas Elsaesser's consideration of some of the most recent in the cinema of Rainer Werner Fassbinder and other filmmakers associated with the New German Cinema. Elsaesser explores the problem of historicizing conceptualizations of subjective engagement with cinema. He not only proposes that it is possible to see the New German Cinema as existing through a historically specific mode of constructing subjects (authorial as well as spectatorial). He also suggests that the *theorization* of constructions of subjectivity must itself be read as historical symptom. As the final selection in this volume, Elsaesser's essay does not reject this work in any simple way, for issues of structure, signification, identification, and subject remain crucial for him. Rather, what Elsaesser seeks is to develop this work in complex, dialectical, self-critical ways, in directions which can lead theory toward a genuine historical understanding.

Stephen Heath
Narrative Space

"It is precise that 'events *take place*' "—Michael Snow

At a climactic point in Hitchcock's *Suspicion,* Lina (Joan Fontaine) receives a visit from two police inspectors come to inform her of the death of a friend in circumstances which cannot but increase her fears concerning the probity—the rectitude—of her husband Johnnie (Cary Grant). The scene finds its center in a painting: the massive portrait of Lina's father which bears with all its Oedipal weight on the whole action of the film—this woman held under the eye of the father (the name as crushing as the image: General *MacLaidlaw*), sexuality in place as transgression ("Lina will never marry, she's not the marrying sort. . . Lina has intellect and a fine solid character," declares the General early on in the film), as radically "impossible" (leaving her father for Johnnie, Lina is henceforth racked by doubt, a suspicion that is irresolvable, for her and the film)—and before which she now positions herself to read the newspaper report of the friend's death and to gather strength enough to face the scrutiny of the law, the look relayed from portrait to police and to portrait again (stills 1, 2, 3, 4). Thus centered, the scene is set out according to that unity so characteristic of classical cinema in its narrative spectacle: the new arrives—the visit, the death, the doubt augmented—and the action is continued, pushed forward, but within a movement of rhyme and balance, of sustained coherence: on either side of what Lina is here given to see (the insert "Stop Press" report for which she puts on her

Published in *Screen* (Autumn 1976), 17:19–75, and included with minor revisions in the author's *Questions of Cinema* (London: Macmillan, 1981, and Bloomington: Indiana University Press, 1981). Reprinted by permission of the Society for Education in Film and Television and the author.

glasses, catching up one of the basic figures of the film, and which we share from her reading, as previously we share the photo of Johnnie in the society magazine or his telegram on the eve of the Hunt Ball), from the entry of the two inspectors back to their departure at the end of the scene, a perfectly symmetrical patterning builds up and pieces together the space in which the action can take place, the space which is itself part of that action in its economy, its intelligibility, its own legality.

Consider simply in this respect, across the scene, the shots at the start and close of the visit (still 5, 6). The coherence is clear—the end comes round to the beginning, one shot echoing the other in the resolution of rhyme—at the same time that the distance traveled forward in the scene is registered, space redefined in the light of the dramatization effected—alone, diminished by the high angle, Lina is helplessly entangled in the network of shadows, enmeshed in "the spider's web" of her doubt (the image is common in critical discussions of the film). Moreover, the first shot itself is immediately and dramatically exhaustible in its situation in the film: the maid, Ethel, announces the visitors and functions globally as a comic turn—"Oh! Mr Aysgarth! What will my young man think!"—in what is, after all, a Hollywood version of England in the 1930s; the dog, another turn, is an impetuous present from Johnnie to Lina; the house is an example of Johnnie's profuse irresponsibility ("Johnnie, you're a baby," comments Lina, dumbfounded, when he shows her the house after the honeymoon). Everything is placed, there is nothing out of line. And yet, something does jar, already, in this first shot. The composition is faultless, the framing describes the theatricality of the inspectors' entry (the ring at the door, the interruption, the unknown), with the columns, steps, and walls providing a stage effect, the characters are centered, perspective is sharp: the image is in every sense clearly directed. But not quite. Out of the action, breaking the clarity of direction, obstinately turned away, one of the inspectors is pulling to the left, gazing abruptly at something hidden from us, without reason in this scene.

If a painting stands straight at the center of the scene, the look that holds Lina's reception of the news, that organizes the scene itself, it goes askew at the edges of the beginning and end, instants indeed of another painting. What occupies Benson, the gazing inspector, lost in a kind of fascinated panic, is precisely this other painting, hung on the side wall behind the column by the front door and with a little—repeated—scene of its own within the larger scene in which it is somehow included (stills 7, 8, 9, 10 and 11, 12, 13). At the beginning, just after Lina asks the maid to show the inspectors in, there is a shot of the latter still waiting by the front door but from an angle that now reveals the post-cubist, Picasso-like painting[1] that is the object of Benson's gaze (still 7); the next shot cuts in closer to give the painting in detail while Benson cranes forward to see it (still 8), a brief piano phrase totally different from the expressive orchestrations elsewhere dominant emerging on the sound track; cut back to the angle and distance of the previous shot as the maid comes to take the

1

5

2

6

3

7

4

8

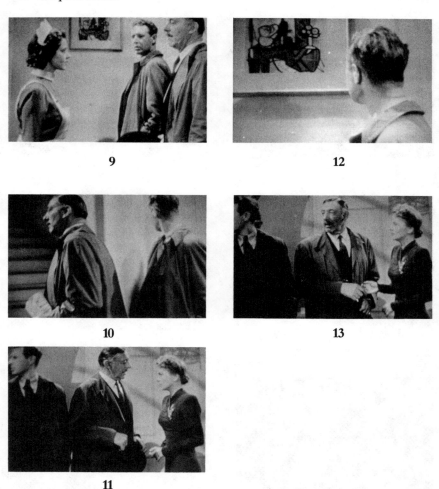

9

12

10

13

11

inspectors in to her mistress, Benson turning round with a look of shock on his face (still 9) and then back to the painting again before following the maid and his colleague, continuing nevertheless to throw backward glances at the painting (still 10). Similarly at the end of the scene: Lina accompanies the inspectors to the door and, while she and the other inspector, Hodgson, are exchanging a few words, Benson once more pulls to the very edge of the frame, toward the disconcerting painting (still 11); cut to a shot of him craning, with the brief piano phrase, exactly parallel to the one at the beginning (still 12, cf. still 8); cut back to the medium three-shot, Benson totally disframed, Hodgson having literally to order him back into the scene, into the action (still 13).

The play here is complex: this other painting has no reason, is "useless" (isolated, without resonance over the film, marked off by the piano phrase and by the fact of its link with Benson who remains more or less apart in the main substance of the scene, out of frame and with only one line of any significance), beyond the limits of the film; and yet it arrives in the film, set into the rhyming balance of the scene, serving to demonstrate the rectitude of the portrait, the true painting at the center of the scene, utterly in frame in the film's action. A "Hitchcock joke"? Perhaps. But a joke that *tells* in a film that hesitates so finely in its enclosure of space, the terms of its points of view. Organized from Lina's point of view (insofar as we have the scenes that she has with respect to her husband, never seeing him separately in a way that might decide the sense of his actions, break the doubt) but under the inspection of an eye (the portrait its mirror) that gives the theater of the suspicion, the setting of Lina's career, the film as story is easy in its ambiguity: no matter if Johnnie is crooked or not, the picture—from portrait to film—is straight, receivable, readable, psychologically and dramatically; Lina's character, her doubt, our experience of that are in place and it is this place that is important, that is the *film's* reason. Hence, however, a problem of *ending* (it is contingently interesting in this connection that Hitchcock had an alternative ending, that an attempt was made by cutting to produce a version that would eliminate any equivocation as to Cary Grant-as-Johnnie's honesty, that there were difficulties). Lina and Johnnie struggle in the car, Johnnie explains, Lina's doubt is resolved, the car U-turns to take them back together. The unity of the place—containing transgression and sexuality and doubt and guilt, the whole family romance—splits, the perspective now lost, the picture of ambiguity broken in the absolute-since-here-arbitrary "banality" of the enforced happy ending (the constraint of "Cary Grant") which brings back, as its contradiction, the memory of the "original" struggle outside the church when, in an abrupt moment of violence, Lina is suddenly somewhere else, fighting off Johnnie in the distance of a shot and a space (a windswept empty wasteland in the middle of an English village hitherto and thereafter presented with all the cosy sporting bucolicness one might expect) that is never finally recaptured in— *for*—the film, remains left over within it, a kind of missing spectacle. Benson's painting too—"his" insofar as it catches him out in his gaze—has its effect as missing spectacle: problem of point of view, different framing, disturbance of the law and its inspectoring eye, interruption of the homogeneity of the narrative economy, it is somewhere else again, another scene, another story, another space.

Snow's stress: events take place. What, then, is this "taking place" in film? *Suspicion* suggests such a question, its action so tightly dependent on the construction and holding of place, its references to painting in the course of that construction and holding, its points of joke or difficulty, excess or otherness. A question that is today posed with insistence, practically and critically, in filmmaking and film theory. Annette Michelson, for instance, describing the achievement of the work of Snow himself, writes that he "has redefined filmic space as that of action," has refound "the tension of narrative" in "the tracing of spatiotemporal *données*."[2] Snow's example, which is indeed crucial in this respect, can serve here as a simple reminder of the importance of a whole number of differing explorations in independent cinema of space and time, narrative and place. Equally, attention has been directed in film theory to "spatial and temporal articulations," to "kinds of space" and their narrative determinations or disruptions. The basic text of such an attention is Noël Burch's *Theory of Film Practice*,[3] and something of its implications—its positions—can be seen in the work on Ozu Yasujiro by Edward Branigan, David Bordwell, and Kristin Thompson; work which hinges on the demonstration of a certain "foregrounding" of space in Ozu's films and on the argument that this foregrounding confirms Ozu as a "modernist" filmmaker: "the modernity of Ozu's work involves the use of specific spatial devices which challenge the supremacy of narrative causality"; "space, constructed alongside and sometimes against the cause/effect sequence, becomes 'foregrounded' to a degree that renders it at times the primary structural level of the film"; "it is this foregrounding of the spatial code in Ozu's films that justifies us in classifying Ozu as a 'modernist' film-maker,"[4] work which in its example in the field of theory again underlines the insistent actuality of the question of space in film and the "taking place" of events.

If that same question were posed to the start of cinema's history, the answer would come easily enough, without problem: the space of film is the space of reality, film's ambition and triumph is "to reproduce life" (Louis Lumière); "nature caught in the act," as a spectator put it after one of the first Cinématographe showings in the Grand Café, while another extolled the finding at last of the "universal language," "la langue universelle est trouvée!"[5] As its source and authority (its very "author"), the universal language has no less than the universe itself, the world embraced by the eye of the camera and delivered over on screen, the world in views (films are listed as *vues* in early French catalogues). The long-shot is there in classical narrative cinema as it subsequently develops as the constant figure of this embracing and authoritative vision, providing the conventional close to a film, the final word of its reality.

That reality, the match of film and world, is a matter of representation, and representation is in turn a matter of discourse, of the organization of the images, the definition of the "views," their construction. It is the discursive operations that decide the work of a film and ultimately determine the scope of the analogical incidence of the images; in this sense at least, film is a series of languages, a history of codes. The universalist temptation, of course, is exactly the grounding in analogy: film works with photographs and, in the technological, economic, and ideological conjuncture of the birth and exploitation of cinema, the photograph is given as the very standard of the reproduction of the real ("photographic realism"). Scientifically, the addition of movement to the photograph to give a picture of life as we see it in the hustle and bustle of the arrival of the train at La Ciotat could be regarded as without interest; illusion is not analysis: Marey, the chronophotographer, has no time for the cinema in the development of which he nevertheless plays a part. Ideologically, the addition of movement (as later the addition of sound to the moving picture) is the possibility of the investment of the photograph as currency of the real in systems of representation that can engage that reality and the guarantee of its vision in a constant—industrial— production of meanings and entertainment within the terms of those meanings.

Meaning, entertainment, vision: film produced as the realization of a coherent and positioned space, and as that realization *in movement,* positioning, cohering, binding in. The passage from views to the process of vision is essentially that of the coding of relations of mobility and continuity. Early film space tends simply to the tableauesque, the set of fixed-camera frontal scenes linked as a story ("The Original Comedy Chase/The Most Familiar and Laughable Incident in the Whole List of Childhood Tales/Shown in Eight Snappy Scenes').[6] Evidently, the tableau has its structure of representation, but that structure misses the subject in the very moment of the movement it now offers: the spectator is placed in respect of the scene but the movement is potentially and perpetually excessive. To link scenes as story is not yet to contain that excess in the achievement of a homogeneously continuous space, the spectator cut in as subject precisely to a process of vision, a positioning and positioned movement. It is here that we touch on the history of cinema in its development of codes and systems: beneath that, on the fact of cinema as order of space and time: "film is not a sum of images but a temporal form"; "movement is not just perceived in itself but localized in space . . . the spectator is not just responsive to what is moving but also to what stays in place and the perception of movement supposes fixed frames."[7] Such phenomenological descriptions insist on the interlocking spatiotemporality of film and suggest in their turn something of the general area of the problems of film in this connection, those problems that are currently and rightly important. Bearing in mind the particular points of the emergence of that current importance, the aim in what follows will be to provide a descriptive and theoretical context for understanding the debate and to indicate, in so doing, certain critical conclusions with regard to film as "narrative space."

Photography and cinema share the camera. Photography is a mode of projecting and fixing solids on a plane surface, of producing images; cinema uses the images produced by photography to reproduce movement, the motion *of* the flow of the images playing on various optical phenomena (phi-effect, retinal persistence) to create the illusion of a single movement *in* the images, an image of movement. Phenomenologically, the result is characterized as "neither absolutely two-dimensional nor absolutely three-dimensional, but something between."[8] The "something between" is the habitual response to the famous "impression of reality" in cinema and it is this impression, this reality that are of concern here in their implications for a consideration of space in film.

Stress has been laid in recent work on the situation of cinema in terms of a development of codes of figuration inherited from the Quattrocento, notably codes of perspective. The focus of attention thus defined is, exactly, the camera: "a camera productive of a perspective code directly constructed on the model of the scientific perspective of Quattrocento" (Marcelin Pleynet);[9] the stress, in other words, is on the camera as machine for the reproduction of objects (of solids) in the form of images realized according to the laws of the rectilinear propagation of light rays, which laws constitute the perspective effect. In this connection, there are already a number of remarks and clarifications to be made, remarks that will bear on Quattrocento perspective, the photograph, and cinema, and in that order.

The perspective system introduced in the early years of the fifteenth century in Italy (developing above all from Florence) is that of *central projection:* "It is the art of depicting three-dimensional objects upon a plane surface in such a manner that the picture *may* affect the eye of an observer in the same way as the natural objects themselves. . . . A perfectly deceptive illusion can be obtained only on *two conditions:* (a) the spectator shall use only one eye, (b) this eye has to be placed in the central point of perspective (or, at least, quite near to this point)."[10] The component elements of that account should be noted: the possible exact match for the eye of picture and object, the deceptive illusion; the center of the illusion, the eye in place. What is fundamental is the idea of the spectator at a window, an *aperta finestra* that gives a view on the world—framed, centered, harmonious (the *istoria*). Alberti, in his treatise *Della Pittura* written circa 1435, talks of the picture plane as of a pane of glass on which the world in view can be traced: "Painters should only seek to present the form of things seen on this plane as if it were of transparent glass. Thus the visual pyramid could pass through it, placed at a definite distance with definite lights and a definite position of center in space and a definite place in respect to the observer."[11] The cost of such fixed centrality is the marginal distortion which ensues when the observer's eye is not correctly in position in the center of the perspective projection but pulls to the edge (like Benson's gaze in *Suspicion,* which then receives the shock of another—confusing—painting). Anamorphosis is the recognition and exploitation of the possibilities of this distortion; playing between "appearance" and "reality," it situates the center of the projection of the painting (or of a single element, as in Holbein's *"The Ambassadors"* in the National Gallery) obliquely to the side, the sense of the painting—its representation—only falling into place (exactly) once the position has been found. Galileo abhorred these perversions of the "normal" view into a turmoil of lines and colors ("una confusa e inordinata mescolanza di linee e di colori"[12]) but, developed in the course of the sixteenth century and particularly appreciated in the following two centuries, they can be seen as a constant triumph of central perspective, a kind of playful liberation from its constraints that remains nevertheless entirely dependent on its system, a ceaseless confirmation of the importance of center and position. What must be more crucially emphasized is that the ideal of a steady position, of a unique embracing center, to which Galileo refers and to which anamorphosis pays its peculiar homage, is precisely that: a powerful ideal. To say this is not simply to acknowledge that the practice of painting from the Quattrocento on is far from a strict adherence to the perspective system but demonstrates a whole variety of "accommodations" (in certain paintings, for example, buildings will be drawn with one center according to central perspective while a separate center will then be chosen for each set of human figures); it is also to suggest that there is a real utopiansim at work, the construction of a code—in every sense a *vision*— projected onto a reality to be gained in all its hoped-for clarity much more than onto some naturally given reality; a suggestion that merely repeats the conclusions of Francastel in his study of the birth of Quattrocento space: "It was a question for a society in process of total transformation of a space in accordance with its actions and its dreams. . . . It is men who create the space in which they move and express themselves. Spaces are born and die like societies; they live, they have a history. In the fifteenth century, the human societies of Western Europe organized, in the material and intellectual senses of the term, a space completely different from that of the preceding generations; with their technical superiority, they progressively imposed that space over the planet."[13] For five centuries men and women exist at ease in that space; the Quattrocento system provides a practical representation of the world which in time appears so natural as to offer its real representation, the immediate translation of reality in itself.

The conception of the Quattrocento system is that of a scenographic space, space set out as spectacle for the eye of a spectator. Eye and knowledge come together; subject, object and the distance of the steady observation that allows the one to master the other; the scene with its strength of geometry and optics. Of that projected utopia, the camera is the culminating realization (the *camera obscura,* described by Giambattista della Porta in 1589 in a treatise on optics, commands attention in the wake of the spread of the Quattrocento system); the images it furnishes become, precisely, the currency of that vision, that space: "Strong as the mathematical convention of perspective had become in picture making before the pervasion of photography, that event definitely clamped it on our vision and our beliefs about 'real' shapes, etc. The public has come to believe that geometrical perspective, so long as it does not involve unfamiliar points of view, is 'true,' just as a long time ago it believed that the old geometry of Euclid was 'the truth' "; "Every day we see photographs which are central perspective images. If another system were applied to the art of painting one could believe that one was living in a bilingual country."[14] Insofar as it is grounded in the photograph, cinema will contribute to the circulation of this currency, will bring with it monocular perspective, the positioning of the spectator/subject in an identification with the camera as the point of a sure and centrally embracing view (Metz draws further conclusions from this identification in his essay "The Imaginary Signifier").[15]

"Our field of vision is full of solid objects but our eye (like the camera) sees this field from only one station point at a given moment. . . . "[16] The comparison of eye and camera in the interests of showing their similarity has come to seem irresistible: our eye like the camera, with its stationary point, its lens, its surface on which the image is captured, and so on. In fact, of course, any modern scientific description of the eye will go on to indicate the limits of the comparison. Our eye is never seized by some static spectacle, is never some motionless recorder; not only is our vision anyway binocular, but one eye alone sees in time: constant scanning movements to bring the different parts of whatever is observed to the fovea, movements necessary in order that the receptive cells produce fresh neuroelectric impulses, immediate activity of memory inasmuch as there is no brute vision to be isolated from the visual experience of the individual inevitably engaged in a specific sociohistorical situation. In a real sense, the ideological force of the photograph has been to "ignore" this in its presentation as a coherent image of vision, an image that then carries over into a suggestion of the world as a kind of sum total of possible photographs, a spectacle to be recorded in its essence in an instantaneous objectification for the eye (it would be worth considering the ideological determinations and resonances of the development and commercialization of polaroid photography); a world, that is, conceived outside process and practice, empirical scene of the confirmed and central master spectator, serenely "present" in tranquil rectilinearity (a curvilinear perspective, for which arguments of "optical realism" can be adduced if need be, comfortably rejected as out of true, as "wrong").

Cinema is involved with photograph and camera, its principal matter of expression that of moving photographic images ("principal" as we know it in its history), its prime achievement that of the creation of the "impression of reality"—"neither absolutely two-dimensional nor absolutely three-dimensional, but something between." The latter description reads in many ways like an account of the effect of depth of field which gives very much the possibility of a cued construction of space in accordance with the Quattrocento system. Yet cinema can also use in one and the same film quite other projections (lenses with long focal length, for example), projections which approximate more or less, but differently, to the perspective model; simply, angles and distances change, the center shifts its points. It may well be that classically cinema acquires "the mobility of the eye" while preserving the contained and delimited visual field on which "correct" perspectives depend, but the mobility is nevertheless difficult: movement of figures "in" film, camera movement, movement from shot to shot; the first gives at once a means of creating perspective (the movements of the figures in a shot can "bring out" the space, show relative positions, suggest depth) and a problem of "composition" (film is said to destroy the "ordinary laws" of pictorial organization because of its moving figures which capture attention against all else); the second equally produces problems of composition and, though often motivated in the manuals by some extension of the eye-camera comparison (the camera executes the same movements as the head; horizontal panning is turning the head, etc.), is strictly regulated in the interests of the maintenance of scenographic space (the version of space, indeed, which determines the justifying comparison); the third, again apt to receive the comparative motivation ("Insofar as the film is photographic and reproduces movement, it can give us a life-like semblance of what we see, insofar as it employs editing, it can exactly reproduce the *manner* in which we normally see it"[17]), effectively indicates the filmic nature of film space, film as constantly the construction of a space (thus Branigan will conclude that "that space exists only at twenty-four frames per second"[18]). The ideal of space remains that of photographic vision, which brings with it the concern to sustain the camera as eye; in the sense of the detached, untroubled eye discussed earlier, an eye free from the body, outside process, purely looking (no matter, finally, if the falsity of eye-camera comparison be admitted since it can be retrieved with a confirming twist: the eye in cinema is the *perfect* eye, the steady and ubiquitous control of the scene passed from director to spectator by virtue of the cinematic apparatus: "The director's aim is to give an *ideal* picture of the scene, in each case placing his camera in such a position that it records most effectively the particular piece of action or detail which is dramatically significant. He becomes, as it were, a ubiquitous observer, giving the audience at each moment of the action the best possible viewpoint.")[19] The ideal, however, is a construction, the mobility acquired is still not easy, the shifting center needs to be settled along the film in its making scenes, its taking place; space will be difficult.

To put it another way: mobility is exactly what is *possible* in film, complicit—the possibility of holding film within a certain vision, thereby "perfected"—and radical—the possibility of film disturbing that vision, with which nonetheless it is immediately involved, historically, industrially, ideologically. Cinema is not simply and specifically ideological "in itself"; but it is developed in the context of concrete and specific ideological determinations which inform as well the "technical" as the "commercial" or "artistic" sides of that development. For Marey, cinema did nothing "to rid the eye of any of its illusions" since set up precisely to play on the illusions of a conventional vision, to "reproduce life" as Lumière put it; for Vertov, cinema could be made to challenge that vision by constructions of dissociations in time and space that would produce the contradictions of the alignment of camera-eye and human eye in order to displace the subject-eye of the sociohistorical individual into an operative—transforming—relation to reality. Film is dominantly articulated in the interests of the "theatrical cinema" Vertov sought to shatter, the world of the scene and the stasis of its relations of vision; but Brecht, and Benjamin with him, will see in the very fact of the succession of film images a certain contradiction to be exploited against that theater, for a different vision, a different space. In its developments and possibilities, its constraints and disruptions, it is the whole question of space in film that must now be examined further.

The examination of space in film may be divided for the moment into two: the

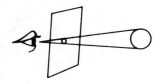

examination of space "in frame," of the space determined by the frame, held within its limits; the examination of space "out of frame," the space beyond the limits of the frame, there in its absence and given back, as it were, in the editing of shot with shot or in camera movement with its reframings. The division can be maintained long enough to allow an order for the remarks that follow, remarks which will finally suggest more clearly its inadequacy.

Screen, frame: Notions of screen and frame are fundamental in the elaboration of the perspective system. Leonardo da Vinci writes: "Perspective is nothing else than seeing a place (or objects) behind a pane of glass, quite transparent, on the surface of which the objects behind that glass are drawn. These can be traced in pyramids to the point in the eye, and these pyramids are intersected on the glass pane."[20] The pane is at once a frame, the frame of a window, and a screen, the area of projection on which what is seen can be traced and fixed; from the Quattrocento on, the "pane" delimits and holds a view, the painter's canvas as a screen situated between eye and object, point of interception of the light rays (see figure). It is worth noting, indeed, in Renaissance (and post-Renaissance) painting the powerful attraction of the window as theme, the fascination with the rectangle of tamed light, the luminously defined space of vision. In Ghirlandaio's *Vecchio e bambino* (Louvre, Paris), Titian's *Isabel di Portogallo* (Prado, Madrid) or Dürer's *Selbstbildnis* (Prado), for example, a window opens to the right, behind the figure portrayed, on to the perspective of a distant horizon; the figure placed almost as by a cinema screen, the sudden illumination of another view, a frame of light to which we are invited to attend. More important, however, is to grasp the very idea of the frame as fully historical in the developments it is given. Before the fifteenth century, frames hardly exist, other than as the specific architectural setting that is to be decorated (wall, altarpiece, or whatever); it is during that century that frames begin to have an independent reality, this concomitant with the growth of the notion itself of "a painting" (the first instance of the use of the word "frame" in an artistic sense recorded by the *Oxford English Dictionary* is *c.* 1600). The new frame is symmetrical (the centered rectangle, clearly "composable") and inevitable (the Quattrocento system cannot be realized without it, it becomes a reflex of "natural" composition). Significantly, it brings with it the easel (first recorded instance *c.* 1634—"a frame or easel called by artists"), "significantly" because the easel is precisely dependent on the idea of "a painting" as single, central view. The painter stands as spectator in front of his easel (in this history it is men who are the professionals of painting, the authoritative gaze), capturing on the canvas screen the scene behind onto which it gives and which it sets as such: no longer englobed in the area of the painting (dome or arch or ceiling), the painter is definitely upright, an eye on the world, an eye that stations itself, with the easel carried from place to place, much like a tripod. Easel painting, that is, established along with perspective system and camera obscura (the latter itself rapidly becomes a portable apparatus for the mobile painter), is a step in the direction of the camera, a camera that will provide screen and frame and the image reflected, fixed, painted with light: a camera that will culminate this whole vision.

"Frame" describes the material unit of film ("the single transparent photograph in a series of such photographs printed on a length of cinematographic film," "twenty-four frames a second") and, equally, the film image in its setting, the delimitation of the image on screen (in Arnheim's *Film as Art,* for example, "frame" and "delimitation" are assumed as synonymous). Framing, determining and laying out the frame, is quickly seen as a fundamental cinematic act, the moment of the very "rightness" of the image: "framing, that is to say, bringing the image to the place it must occupy," a definition taken from a manual for teachers written in the 1920s.[21] Quickly too, and in consequence, it becomes the object of an aesthetic attention concerned to pose decisively the problems of the composition of the frame, of what Eisenstein calls "mise en cadre."

"There it is, our 1.33 to 1 rectangle, it will tolerate precious little tampering with at all" (Hollis Frampton).[22] The compositional rectangle is there, carried through into cinema; space is structured within its frame, areas are assigned position in relation to its edges. In a sense, moreover, the constraint of the rectangle is even greater in cinema than in painting: in the latter, its proportions are relatively free; in the former, they are limited to a standard aspect ratio (Frampton's 1.33 to 1 rectangle, the aptly named "academy frame") or, as now, to a very small number of ratios,[23] with techniques such as masking the sides of the frame to change the size of the rectangle in general disfavor. Hence the rectangle must be mastered—"Maîtriser le rectangle," the title of one of the key sections in a modern manual for young people. Hence the rules for mastery, rules which come straight from the Quattrocento system, its balanced vision and the composition of the clarity thus decided; so, from the same modern manual: "To consider the rectangle as a surface crossed by lines of force. . . and with strong points (the points of intersection of those lines) is to guarantee it a solid base structure and to refuse the notion of it as a sort of visual hold-all"; "If, therefore, we have to place an actor in this rectangle, one of the best places will be that which follows one of the lines of force in question. And the face, 'strong point' of the human person, will be placed at one of the strong points of the rectangle"; "A second character will naturally be placed at one of the strong points . . ."; "Let us quickly note when we come to 'landscapes' how inharmonious is a division of the surface which does not correspond to the famous 'third' and how placing the horizon midway in the frame is only apparently logical."[24] In cinema, however, these rules also have their "excess," there is always a further court of appeal—life itself, the very aim of cinema: "But cinema is life, is movement. The cinéaste must not fall into the traps of a plastic aesthetic. Failure to remember the rules of framing will often bring agreeable surprises, for it is not without truth that the world is already, in itself, harmonious."[25]

If life enters cinema as movement, that movement brings with it nevertheless its problems of composition in frame, as was mentioned earlier in the discussion of perspective. In fact, composition will organize the frame in function of the human figures in their actions; what enters cinema is a logic of movement and it is this logic that centers the frame. Frame space, in other words, is constructed as narrative space. It is narrative significance that at any moment sets the space of the frame to be followed and "read," and that determines the development of the filmic cues in their contributions to the definition of space in frame (focus pull, for example, or backlighting). Narrative contains the mobility that could threaten the clarity of vision in a constant renewal of perspective; space becomes place—narrrative as the taking place of film—in a movement which is no more than the fulfillment of the Renaissance impetus, an impetus that a De Kooning can describe as follows: "It was up to the artist to measure out the exact space for a person to die in or to be dead already. The exactness of the space was determined or, rather inspired by whatever reason the person was dying or being killed for. The space thus measured out on the original plane of the canvas surface became a 'place' somewhere on the floor."[26] What is crucial is the conversion of seen into scene, the holding of signifier on signified: the frame, composed, centered, narrated, is the point of that conversion.

Cinema as "life in its truth as scene," the frame as the instance of such a vision. Metz talks here of the regime "of the primal scene and the keyhole": "the rectangular screen permits every type of fetishism, all the effects of 'just-before,' since it places at exactly the height it wants the sharp vibrant bar which stops the seen. . . ."[27] The fascination of the scene is there, and from the beginnings of cinema with its tableaux, its dramatic masks (including the keyhole-shaped matte; as in *A Search for Evidence,* AM & B 1903), its occasional thematic directness (in *Gay Shoe Clerk,* Edison Co. 1903, which involves a flirtatious shoe clerk, an attractive young lady, and her chaperone armed with an umbrella, a cut-in closeup shows the young lady's ankle with the clerk's hand gripping her foot into the shoe);[28] the fetishism is there, with the edge, the limit, the setting, the careful place, and from Alberti on—witness that whole series of machines and devices for the production of a certain distance of image, a sure illusion of scrutiny. Simply, the "just-before" in film is spatially moving, the itinerary of a fixity perpetually gained, and the frame stands—acts—in relation to that.

As for the screen, it receives and gives the frame; its flatness halts the image and lays the base of that triangle for which the spectator's eye provides the apex.

Doubtless there is a sheer pleasure for the position of the eye in the very fact of the projection of the frames onto and from the screen, in their "hitting the screen";[29] a space is established with no "behind" (it is important that the Lumière brothers should set the screen as they do in the Grand Café and not with the audience on either side of a translucent screen, that cinema architecture should take its forms in consequence, that there should be no feeling of machinery to the side of or beyond the screen, that the screen should be one of the most stable elements in cinema's history), a pure expanse that can be invested with depth. The screen, that is, is at once ground, the surface that supports the projected images, and background, its surface caught up in the cone of light to give the frame of the image. Ground and background are one in the alignment of frame and screen, the "on screen in frame" that is the basis of the spatial articulations a film will make, the start of its composition.[30]

Psychoanalysis, it may be briefly added, has come to stress the dream as itself projected on a screen: the *dream screen,* blank surface present in dreams though mostly "unseen," covered over by the manifest content of the projected dream; a screen that represents the breast (infinitely extensive center of the baby's visual space) and then also sleep (the desire for sleep) as an original ground of pleasure "before" difference, "before" identity, "before" symbolization.[31] In cinema, the images pass (twenty-four per second), the screen remains; covered but there, specified—the images of this or that film—but the same—the satisfying projection of a basic oneness. The force of this relation, however, must be understood: it is the passing of the images that produces the constancy of the screen; without those images the screen is "empty," with them it is an impression, a surface/ground that the film and the spectator find as the frames hit the screen, that they find intact, safely *in* the background (revealing and disturbing moment when a character in a film throws something, as is said, "at the screen").[32]

Movement, transitions. From the very first, as though of right, human figures enter film, spilling out of the train, leaving the factory or the photographic congress, *moving*—this is the movies, these are moving pictures. The figures move in the frame, they come and go, and there is then need to change the frame, reframing with a camera movement or moving to another shot. The transitions thus effected pose acutely the problem of the filmic construction of space, of achieving a coherence of place and positioning the spectator as the unified and unifying subject of its vision. It is this process of construction, indeed, which is often regarded as the power of cinema and as defining the overall reality of film as that of a kind of generalized "trick effect": "if several successive images represent a space under different angles, the spectator, victim of the 'trick effect,' spontaneously perceives the space as unitary. . . ."[33]

Early films are typically organized as a series of fixed scenes, with a strict unity of time and place. The example was cited above of *Tom, Tom, the Piper's Son* which tells the well-known story in "eight snappy scenes," simply joined the one after the other as so many tableaux. The actions of the characters in frame, as though on a stage, make out the sense of the image, center the eye in paths of reading, but within the limits of the distance of the fixed frontal view which creates difficulties of effectively maintaining such a centered perception given the continual wealth of movements and details potentially offered by the photographic image (Ken Jacobs in his film of the same title minutely explores the surface of *Tom, Tom, the Piper's Son,* refilming from the screen and finding in so doing not just "other" actions but also "central" actions not easily grasped or possibly even missed in the original—as, for instance, the handkerchief stealing in the opening shot). Those difficulties, in the context of its commercial exploitation, are fundamental for cinema's development. The center is the movement, not movements but the logic of a consequent and temporally coherent action. The vision of the image is its narrative clarity and that clarity hangs on the negation of space for place, the constant realization of center in function of narrative purpose, narrative movement: "Negatively, the space is presented so as not to distract attention from the dominant actions: positively, the space is 'used up' by the presentation of narratively important settings, character traits ('psychology'), or other causal agents."[34] Specific spatial cues—importantly, among others, those depending on camera movement and editing—will be established and used accordingly, centering the flow of the images, taking place.

Which is to say, of course, that the tableaux space of the early films is intolerable in its particular fixity, must be broken up in the interests of the unity of action and place and subject view as that unity is conceived from the narrative models of the novelistic that cinema is dominantly exploited to relay and extend. Burch puts it well: "It was necessary to be able to film objects or people close up—to isolate a face, a hand, an accessory (as the discourse of the novel does)— but avoiding any disorientation of the spectator in respect of his or her own 'reasoned' analysis of the spatial continuum. . . ."[35] The need is to cut up and then join together in a kind of spatial *Aufhebung* that decides a superior unity, the binding of the spectator in the space of the film, the space it realizes. In the late 1930s and early 1940s, the average shot length of a full-length Hollywood film has been estimated at about 9–10 seconds,[36] but that fragmentation is the condition of a fundamental continuity.

"There are no jerks in time or space in real life. Time and space are continuous. Not so in film. The period of time that is being photographed may be interrupted at any point. One scene may be immediately followed by another that takes place at a totally different time. And the continuity of space may be broken in the same manner."[37] Why is it, Arnheim goes on to ask, that the "juggling with space" possible in film (and including the breaking of a single "real life" space into "several successive images . . . under different angles") does not cause discomfort? The answer refers back to the "something between" status of film previously mentioned: "Film gives simultaneously the efffect of an actual happening and of a picture. A result of the 'pictureness' of film is, then, that a sequence of scenes that are diverse in time and space is not felt as arbitrary. . . . If film photographs gave a very strong spatial impression, montage probably would be impossible. It is the partial unreality of the film picture that makes it possible."[38] The emphasis on the "pictureness" of the image is crucial here (there would be problems of cutting for spatial unity with holography): the space constructed in film is exactly *a filmic construction*. Thus Mitry, for example, will write that shots are like "cells," "distinct spaces the succession of which, however, reconstitutes a homogeneous space, but a space *unlike* that from which these elements were subtracted."[39]

The conception at work in such descriptions can be seen (even if in this or that writer that conception may be inflected "aesthetically," turned in the direction of film as "art"). The filmic construction of space is recognized in its difference but that difference is the term of an ultimate similarity (indeed, a final "illusion"); the space is "unlike" but at the same time "reconstitutes," using elements lifted from real space. In fact, we are back in the realm of "composition," where composition is now the laying out of a succession of images in order to give the picture, to produce the implication of a coherent ("real") space; in short, to create continuity.

The compositional rules for spatial clarity and continuity are sufficiently well known not to need extended discussion at this stage; it will be enough merely to stress one or two of their determinations. Firstly, the establishment of fixed patterns of clarity for the variation of scale of shot in a scene: there are "normal ways" of organizing dialogue scenes, action scenes, and so on;[40] these systems allowing for a certain free play—"exceptions"—within their overall structure in the interests of "dramatic effect" ("In the normal way, it is almost certainly better to cut the scenes as we have indicated, but . . . there may be exceptions when the rules need to be modified to convey certain dramatic effects").[41] What may be remembered above all in this context is the extreme importance attached to providing an overall view, literally the "master shot" that will allow the scene to be dominated in the course of its reconstitution narratively as dramatic unity ("Even where a sequence starts on a detail, it is important that the whole setting should be shown at some stage").[42] Take the beginning of *Jaws:* a beach party with the camera tracking slowly right along the line of the faces of the participants until it stops on a young man looking off; eyeline cut to a young woman who is thus revealed as the object of his gaze; cut to a high-angle shot onto the party that shows its general space, its situation, before the start of the action with the run down to the ocean and the first shark attack—the shot serves, that is, as a kind of master fold in the sequence, setting it correctly in place. Second, the establishment of the 180-degree and 30-degree rules. The former matches screen space and narrative space (the space represented in the articulation of the images), ground and background; with its help, "one will always find the same characters in the same parts of the screen."[43] The 180-degree line that the camera is forbidden to cross answers exactly to the 180-degree line of the screen behind which the spectator cannot and must not go, in front of which he or she is placed within the triangle of representation, the space of the image projected, that is repeated in the very terms of the fiction of the imaged space. As for the latter, a "quick, simple rule that issues directly from the necessities of cinematic fragmentation" and that avoids the "disagreeable sensation" of a "jump in space,"[44] it is finally nothing other than a specific perspective rule for a smooth line of direction in film, for the achievement of a smooth line in from shot to shot. Third and last, following on from those more particular remarks, the establishment generally as a powerful evidence, as a natural basis, of the idea of continuity as smoothness in transitions: the rules of the filmic construction of space on screen (master shot, 180-degree and 30-degree rules, matching on action, eyeline matching, field/reverse field, etc.) background the image flow into a unified subject-space, immediately and fully continuous, reconstitutive: "Making a smooth cut means joining two shots in such a way that the transition does not create a noticeable jerk and the spectator's illusion of seeing a continuous piece of action is not interrupted."[45]

Continuity in these terms is also decisive with regard to transitions and changes of frame effected by camera movement. "Imperceptible" reframing movements, more definite pans, and tracking shots are developed in the interests of the narrative composition of space in relation to the actions of the characters;[46] here, too, rules are elaborated accordingly, the camera having, for instance, to impregnate space with the anticipation of action: "if the actor is accompanied by a movement of the camera, more 'room' must be left in front of him or her than behind, so as to figure sensorially the space to be crossed."[47] In this respect, it is worth bearing in mind the extent to which the sequence-shot-with-deep-focus long take valued by Bazin in his account of "the evolution of cinematic language" can stay within such a conception of space. The narrative of a Welles or a Wyler in Bazin's account is carried through in a manner that retains the particular effects to be derived from "the unity of the image in time and space," a manner that refinds and draws out the essential "realism" of cinema; a realism in which space is all important: "the cinematographic image can be emptied of all reality save one—the reality of space."[48] The space of *Citizen Kane* or *The Best Years of Our Lives* is still entirely dramatic, however; heightened indeed in its drama: as was suggested earlier, deep focus allows composition for a high degree of perspective ("depth of field" exactly), and this can be increased over the long take with its potential definition of a complex action in a single shot, its filling out of movements and positions in a temporally visible demonstration of space as narrative place.[49] It should anyway be noted that the average shot length overall of *Citizen Kane* is 12 seconds, "about average for its period,"[50] and it remains true that classically continuity is built on fragmentation rather than the long take—on a segmentation for recomposition that can bind the spectator in the strong articulations of the unity it seeks to create. Elsewhere, Bazin was to refer to the version of the spatial realism he ontologically cherished provided by Italian Neorealism; a version that might show the possibilities of the long take away from an absorbed dramatic space; and so, by contrast, the force of the classical continuity in that dependence on segmentation/articulation and its effective inclusion of the longer take within its terms of spatial construction.

Those terms, as they have been described here, are the terms of a constant welding together: screen and frame, ground and background, surface and depth, the whole setting of movements and transitions, the implication of space and spectator in the taking place of film as narrative. The classical *economy* of film is its organization thus as organic unity, and the *form* of that economy is narrative, the *narrativization* of film. Narrative, as it were, determines the film which is contained in its process in that determination, this "bind" being itself a process—precisely the narrativization. The narration is to be held on the narrated, the enunciation on the enounced; filmic procedures are to be held as narrative instances (very much as "cues"), exhaustively, without gap or contradiction. What is sometimes vaguely referred to as "transparency" has its meaning in this narrativization: the proposal of a discourse that disavows its operations and positions in the name of a signified that it proposes as its preexistent justification. "Transparency," moreover, is entirely misleading insofar as it implies that narrativization has necessarily to do with some simple "invisibility" (anyway impossible—no one has yet seen a signified without a signifier). The narration may well be given as visible in its filmic procedures; what is crucial is that it be given as visible *for the narrated* and that the spectator be caught up in the play of *that* process, that the *address* of the film be clear. (Does anyone who has watched, say, *The Big Sleep* seriously believe that a central part of Hollywood films, differently defined from genre to genre, was not the address of a process with a movement of play and that that was not a central part of their pleasure?)

Within this narrativization of film, the role of the character-look has been fundamental for the welding of a spatial unity of narrative implication. In so many senses, every film is a veritable drama of vision, and this drama has thematically and symptomatically "returned" in film since the very beginning: from the fascination of the magnifying glass in *Grandma's Reading Glass* to Lina's shortsightedness in *Suspicion* to the windscreen and rearview mirror of *Taxi Driver*, from the keyhole of *A Search for Evidence* to the images that flicker reflected over Brody's glasses in *Jaws* as he turns the pages of the book on sharks, finding the images of the film to come and which he will close as he closes the book; not to mention the extended dramatizations such as *Rear Window* or *Peeping Tom*. How to make sense in film if not through vision, film with its founding ideology of vision as truth? The drama of vision in the film returns the drama of vision of the film: the spectator will be bound to the film as spectacle as the world of the film is itself revealed as spectacle on the basis of a narrative organization of look and point of view that moves space into place through the image flow; the character, figure of the look, is a kind of perspective within the perspective system, regulating the world, orientating space, providing directions—and for the spectator.

Film works at a loss, the loss of the divisions, the discontinuities, the absences that structure it—as, for example, the "outside" of the frame, offscreen space, the *hors-champ*. Such absence is the final tragedy of a Bazin, who wants to believe in cinema as a global consciousness of reality, an illimitation of picture frame and theater scene—"The screen is not a frame like that of a picture, but a mask which allows us to see a part of the event only. When a person leaves the field of the camera, we recognize that he or she is out of the field of vision, though continuing to exist identically in another part of the scene which is hidden from us. The screen has no wings . . ."[51]—but who can only inspect the damage of "camera angles or prejudices,"[52] acknowledge nonetheless the frame, the scene, the mask, the hidden, the absent. The sequence-shot-with-deep-focus long take functions as a utopia in this context—the ideal of a kind of "full angle," without prejudices, but hence too without cinema; the ideal recognized in *Bicycle Thieves,* "*plus de cinéma.*"[53]

Burch writes that "off-screen space has only an intermittent or, rather, *fluctuating* existence during any film, and structuring this fluctuation can become a powerful tool in a filmmaker's hands."[54] The term "fluctuation" is excellent, yet it must be seen that the work of classical continuity is not to hide or ignore offscreen space but, on the contrary, to contain it, to regularize its fluctuation in a constant movement of reappropriation. It is this movement that defines the rules of continuity and the fiction of space they serve to construct, the whole functioning according to a kind of metonymic lock in which offscreen space becomes onscreen space and is replaced in turn by the space it holds off, each joining over the next. The join is conventional and ruthlessly selective (it generally leaves out of account, for example, the space that might be supposed to be masked at the top and bottom of the frame, concentrating much more on the space at the sides of the frame or on that "in front," "behind the camera," as in variations of field/reverse field), and demands that the offscreen space recaptured must be "called for," must be "logically consequential," must arrive as "answer," "fulfillment of promise," or whatever (and not as difference or contradiction)—must be narrativized. Classical continuity, in other words, is an order of the pregnancy of space in frame; one of the narrative acts of a film is the creation of space,[55] but what gives the moving space its coherence in time, decides the metonymy as a "taking place," is here "the narrative itself," and above all as it crystallizes round character as look and point of view. The fundamental role of these is exactly their pivotal use as a mode of organization and organicization, the joining of a film's constructions, the stitching together of the overlaying metonymies.

"If in the left of the frame an actor in close-up is looking off right, he has an empty space in front of him; if the following shot shows an empty space to the left and an object situated to the right, then the actor's look appears to cross an orientated, rectilinear, thus logical space: it seems to bear with precision on the object. One has an eye-line match."[56] The look, that is, joins form of expression—the composition of the images and their disposition in relation to one another—and form of content—the definition of the action of the film in the movement of looks, exchanges, objects seen, and so on. Point of view develops on the basis of this joining operation of the look, the camera taking the position of a character in order to show the spectator what he or she sees.[57] Playing on the assumption of point of view, a film has an evident means of placing its space, of giving it immediate and holding significance; Burch talks of the establishment of an organization founded on the "traditional dichotomy between the 'subjective camera' (which 'places the spectator in the position of a character') and the 'objective camera' (which makes the spectator the ideal, immaterial 'voyeur' of a profilmic pseudo-reality)."[58]

This account, however, requires clarification. The point-of-view shot is "subjective" in that it assumes the position of a subject-character, but to refer to that assumption in terms of "subjective camera" or "subjective image" can lead to misunderstanding with regard to the functioning of point of view. Subjective images can be many things; Mitry, for example, classifies them into five major categories: "the purely mental image (more or less impracticable in the cinema); the truly subjective or analytical image (i.e. what is looked at without the person looking), which is practicable in small doses; the semi-subjective or associated image (i.e. the person looking + what is looked at, which is in fact looked at from the viewpoint of the person looking), the most generalizable formula; the complete sequence given over to the imaginary, which does not raise special problems; and finally the memory image, which is in principle simply a variety of the mental image but, when presented in the form of a flash-back with commentary, allows for a specific filmic treatment which is far more successful than in the case of other mental images."[59] The point-of-view shot includes "the semi-subjective or associated image" (its general mode) and "the truly subjective or analytical image" (its pure mode, as it were) in that classification but not necessarily any of the other categories (a memory sequence, for instance, need not contain any point-of-view shots); what is "subjective" in the point-of-view shot is its spatial positioning (its place), not the image or the camera.

To stress this is to stress a crucial factor in the exploitation of the film image and its relation to point-of-view organization. Within the terms of that organization, a true subjective image would effectively need to mark its subjectivity *in the image itself.* Examples are common: the blurred image of Gutman in *The Maltese Falcon* is the subjective image of the drugged Spade; the blurring of focus marks the subjectivity of the image, exclusively Spade's, and the spectator is set not simply *with* Spade but as Spade. They are also limited, since they depend exactly on some recognizable—marking—distortion of the "normal" image, a narratively motivated aberration of vision of some kind or another (the character is drugged, intoxicated, shortsighted, terrified . . . down to he or she running, with hand-held effects of the image "jogging," or even walking, with regular speed of camera movement forward matched on a shot that effectively establishes the character as in the process of walking; the latter represents the lowest limit on the scale, since the camera movement is there a weak subjective marking of the image which itself remains more or less "normal"—except, of course, and hence this limit position of the banal action of walking, that the normal image is precisely static, that movement in a central perspective system can quickly become a problem of vision). The implication of this, of course, is then the strength of the unmarked image as a constant third person—the vision of picture and scene, the Quattrocento view, Burch's "voyeur" position—*which is generally continued within point-of-view shots themselves;* the point-of-view shot is marked as subjective in its emplacement but the resulting image is still finally (or rather firstly) objective, the objective sight of what is seen from the subject position assumed. Indicatively enough, the general mode of the point-of-view shot is the shot which shows both what is looked at and the person looking. Instances of the pure shot, showing what is looked at without the person looking, however, are equally conclusive. Take the shot in *Suspicion* of the telegram that Lina receives from Johnnie to tell her of his intention to attend the Hunt Ball: the telegram is clearly shown from Lina's reading position and the end of the shot—the end of the reading—is marked by her putting down her glasses onto the telegram lying on a table, the glasses thus coming down into frame; the position of the shot is marked as subjective with Lina but the image nevertheless continues to be objective, "the real case" for the narrative.[60]

Point of view, that is, depends on an overlaying of first and third person modes. There is no radical dichotomy between subjective point-of-view shots and objective non-point-of-view shots; the latter mode is the continual basis over which the former can run in its particular organization of space, its disposition of the images. The structure of the photographic image—with its vision, its scene, its distance, its normality—is to the film somewhat as language is to the novel: the grounds of its representations, which representations can include the creation of an acknowledged movement of point of view. This is the sense of the spectator identification with the camera that is so often remarked upon (Benjamin: "the audience's identification with the actor is really an identification with the camera"; Metz: "the spectator can do no other than identify with the camera").[61] The spectator must *see*, and this structuring vision is the condition of the possibility of the disposition of the images via the relay of character look and viewpoint which pulls together vision and narrative. Emphasis was laid earlier on the structures of the structuring vision that found cinema; what is emphasized now is the dependence of our very notion of point of view on those structures; dependence at once insofar as the whole Quattrocento system is built on the establishment of point of view, the central position of the eye, and insofar as the mode of representation thus defined brings with it fixity and movement in a systematic complicity of interaction—brings with it, that is, the "objective" and the "subjective," the "third person" and the "first person," the view and its partial points, and finds this drama of vision as the resolving action of its narratives.

Identification with the camera, seeing, the "ideal picture" of the scene: "the usual scene in a classical film is narrated as if from the point of view of an observer capable of moving about the room."[62] Such movement may be given in editing or by camera movement within a shot, and the importance accruing to some master view that will define the space of the mobility has been noted. Movement, in fact, will be treated as a supplement to produce precisely the "ideal *picture*" (going to the movies is going to the pictures): on the basis of the vision of the photographic image, that is, it will provide the "total" point of view of an observer capable of moving about the room without changing anything of the terms of the vision, the scene laid out for the central observer (and spectator); every shot or reframing adds a difference, but that difference is always the same image, with the organization—the continuity, the rules, the matches, the pyramid structures—constantly doing the sum of the *scene*.

That said, it remains no less true, as has again been noted and as will become important later on, that movement represents a potentially radical disturbance of the smooth stability of the scenographic vision (hence the need for a systematic organization to contain it). Such a disturbance, however, is not as simple as is sometimes suggested, and it is necessary briefly to consider at this stage two instances of disturbance as they are conventionally described; both bear on the mobility of the camera.

The first is that of what Branigan characterizes as the impossible place: "To the extent that the camera is located in an 'impossible' place, the narration questions its own origin, that is, suggests a shift in narration."[63] "Impossible," of course, is here decided in respect of the "possible" positions of the observer moving about, the disturbance involved seen as a disjunction of the unity of narration and narrated, enunciation and enounced. Thus defined, impossible places are certainly utilized in classical narrative cinema, with examples ranging from the relatively weak to the relatively strong. At one end of the range, the weak examples would be any high or low angles that are not motivated as the point of view of a character; or, indeed, any high or low angles that, while so motivated, are nevertheless sufficiently divergent from the assumed normal upright observing position as to be experienced as in some sense "impossible" in their peculiarity (the most celebrated—and complex—example is the dead-man-in-the-coffin point of view in *Vampyr*).[64] At the other end, the strong examples—those intended by Branigan—can be illustrated by a description of two shots from *Killer's Kiss*: (1) as Davey, the boxer-hero, is seen stooping to feed his goldfish, there is a cut to a shot through the bowl, from the other side, of his face peering in as the feed drops down; since the bowl is on a table against a wall, the place taken by the camera is not possible; (2) Rappello, the dance-hall owner, furious at being left by the heroine, is drinking in a back room, its walls covered with posters and prints; a closeup of a print showing two men leering from a window is followed by a shot of Rappello who throws his drink at the camera ("at the screen"!); a crack appears as the drink runs down a plate of glass; impossibly, the shot was from "in" the print. The second—and related— instance of disturbance is that of the development of camera movement as a kind of autonomous figure; what Burch calls "the camera designated as an 'omnipotent and omniscient' (i.e. manipulative and pre-cognitive) presence."[65] This presence too is utilized in classical narrative cinema, and weak and strong examples can once more be indicated. In *Taxi Driver*, Travis Bickle is seen phoning Betsy after the porno–film fiasco; as he stands talking into the pay phone, fixed on a wall inside a building, the camera tracks right and stops to frame a long empty corridor leading out to the street; when Travis finishes his call, he walks into frame and exits via the corridor. The tracking movement designates the camera with a certain autonomy—there is an effect of a casual decision to go somewhere else, off to the side of the narrative—but the example is ultimately weak: the corridor is eventually brought into the action with Travis' exit and, more important, it has its rhyming and thematic resonances—the corridors in the rooming house used by Iris, the marked existential atmosphere of isolation, nothingness, etc. Stronger examples are provided in the work of an Ophuls or a Welles—the spectacular tracking shot at the start of *Touch of Evil* or the intense mobility in many of the shots at the end of that same film.

These two instances of disturbance have been characterized here in their existence in established cinema simply to make one or two points directly in the context of the present account. Thus, the examples given of autonomy of camera movement are all clearly operating in terms of "style" (Welles, Ophuls, the tics of a new American commercial cinema that has learnt a consciousness of style). The crucial factor is not the valuation of camera movement, autonomous or not, but the point at which a certain work on the camera in movement produces the normality of the third person objective basis as itself a construction, gives it as role or fiction, and breaks the balance of the point-of-view system. Similarly, the examples of the impossible place from *Killer's Kiss*, which also have their reality as stylistic marking in the film, are without critically disruptive extension in themselves, are simply tricks (in the sense of spatial prestidigitations): the impossible place is entirely possible if held within a system that defines it *as such*, that it confirms in its signified exceptionality. The felt element of trick, moreover, raises the general point of the realization of film as process. It is too readily assumed that the operation—the determination, the effect, the pleasure— of classical cinema lies in the attempt at an invisibility of process, the intended transparency of a kind of absolute "realism" from which all signs of production have been effaced. The actual case is much more complex and subtle, and much more telling. Classical cinema does not efface the signs of production, it contains them, according to the narrativization described above. It is that process that is the action of the film for the spectator—what counts is as much the representation as the represented, is as much the production as the product. Nor is there anything surprising in this: film is not a static and isolated object but a series of relations with the spectator it imagines, plays, and sets as subject in its movement. The process of film is then perfectly available to certain terms of excess—those of that movement in its subject openings, its energetic controls. "Style" is one area of such controlled excess, as again, more powerfully, are genres in their specific version of process. The musical is an obvious and extreme example with its systematic "freedom" of space—crane choreography—and its shifting balances of narrative and spectacle; but an example that should not be allowed to mask the fundamental importance of the experience of process in other genres and in the basic order of classical cinema on which the various genres are grounded. Which is to say, finally, the radical disturbance is not to be linked to the mere autonomization of a formal element such as camera movement; on the contrary, it can only be effectively grasped as a work that operates at the expense of the classical suppositions of "form" and "content" in cinema, posing not autonomies but contradictions in the process of film and its narrative-subject binding.

The construction of space as a term of that binding in classical cinema is its implication for the spectator in the taking place of film as narrative; implication-process of a constant refinding—space regulated, orientated, continued, reconstituted. The use of look and point-of-view structures—exemplarily, the field/reverse field figure (not necessarily dependent, of course, on point-of-view shots)[66]—is fundamental to this process that has been described in terms of *suture*, a stitching or tying as in the surgical joining of the lips of a wound.[67] In its movement, its framings, its cuts, its intermittences, the film ceaselessly poses an absence, a lack, which is ceaselessly recaptured for—one needs to be able to say "forin"—the film, that process binding the spectator as subject in the realization of the film's space.

In psychoanalysis, "suture" refers to the relation of the individual as subject to the chain of its discourse where it figures missing in the guise of a stand-in; the subject is an effect of the signifier in which it is represented, stood in for, taken place (the signifier is the narration of the subject).[68] Ideological representation turns on—supports itself from—this "initial" production of the subject in the symbolic order (hence the crucial role of psychoanalysis, as potential science of the construction of the subject, with historical materialism), directs it as a set of images and fixed positions, metonymy stopped into fictions of coherence. What must be emphasized, however, is that stopping—the functioning of suture in image, frame, narrative, etc.—is exactly a *process:* it counters a productivity, an excess, that it states and restates in the very moment of containing in the interests of coherence—thus the film frame, for example, exceeded from within by the outside it delimits and poses and has ceaselessly to recapture (with post-Quattrocento painting itself, images are multiplied and the conditions are laid for a certain mechanical reproduction that the photograph will fulfill, the multiplication now massive, with image machines a normal appendage of the subject). The process never ends, is always *going on;* the construction-reconstruction has always to be renewed; machines, cinema included, are there for that—and their ideological operation is not only in the images but in the suture.

The film poses an image, not immediate or neutral,[69] but posed, framed and centered. Perspective-system images bind the spectator in place, the suturing central position that is the sense of the image, that sets its scene (in place, the spectator *completes* the image as its subject). Film too, but it also moves in all sort of ways and directions, flows with energies, is potentially a veritable festival of affects. Placed, that movement is all the value of film in its development and exploitation: reproduction of life and the engagement of the spectator in the process of that reproduction as articulation of coherence. What moves in film, finally, is the spectator, immobile in front of the screen. Film is the regulation of that movement, the individual as subject held in a shifting and placing of desire, energy, contradiction, in a perpetual retotalization of the imaginary (the set scene of image and subject). This is the investment of film in narrativization; and crucially for a coherent space, the unity of place for vision.

Once again, however, the investment is in the process. Space comes in place through procedures such as look and point-of-view structures, and the spectator with it as subject in its realization. A reverse shot folds over the shot it joins and is joined in turn by the reverse it positions; a shot of a person looking is succeeded by a shot of the object looked at which is succeeded in turn by a shot of the person looking to confirm the object as seen; and so on, in a number of multiple imbrications. *Fields* are made, *moving* fields, and the process includes not just the completions but the definitions of absence for completion. The suturing operation is in the process, the give and take of absence and presence, the play of negativity and negation, flow and bind. Narrativization, with its continuity, closes, and is that movement of closure that shifts the spectator as subject in its terms: the spectator is the *point* of the film's spatial relations—the turn, say, of shot to reverse shot—their subject-passage (point-of-view organization, more-over, doubles over that passage in its third/first person layerings). Narrativization is scene and movement, movement and scene, the reconstruction of the subject in the pleasure of that balance (with genres as specific instances of equilibrium)—*for* homogeneity, containment. What is foreclosed in the process is not its production—often signified as such, from genre instances down to this or that "impossible" shot—but the terms of the unity of that production (narration on narrated, enunciation on enounced), the other scene of its vision of the subject, the outside—heterogeneity, contradiction, history—of its coherent address.

The role of look and point of view for the holding organization of space has been heavily stressed; the whole weight of the remarks made has been on the image and on the laying out of the images in film. It is important, however, not to overlook in this context the role played by sound. Hence one or two indications here concerning sound and film's narrative of space, indications all the more necessary in that they bear on the problem of address.

The equivalent of the look in its direction of the image track is the voice in its direction of the sound track. Significantly, there is much less play of process practicable with the latter in classical cinema than with the former; the sound track is hierarchically subservient to the image track and its pivot is the voice as the presence of character in frame, a supplement to the dramatization of space, along with accompanying "sound effects." Vertov's loathed "theatrical cinema" is confirmed in its domination with the arrival of sound and the narrative forms of cinema develop in respect of that theatricality (the truth of the common reference to "novels dramatized for the screen"). In fact, the regime of sound as voice in the cinema is that of the "safe place": either in the narrative in its "scenes," as with the normal fiction film, or in the discourse that accompanies the images to declare their meaning, as with the documentary film which remains marginal in commercial cinema. The safe place is carefully preserved in fiction films. Voice and sound are diegetic (with music following the images as an element of dramatic heightening), generally "on screen" but equally defined in their contiguity to the field in frame when "off screen"; voiceover is limited to certain conventional uses (as, for example, the direction of memory sequences, a kind of documentary of the past of a life within the film) which effectively forbid any discrepancy—any different activity—between sound and image tracks (Malick is even reputed to have had trouble in getting Holly's narration in *Badlands* accepted). The stress is everywhere on the unity of sound and image and the voice is the point of that unity: at once subservient to the images and entirely dominant in the dramatic space it opens in them—the film stops when the drama the voices carry in the image ends, when there are no more words, only "The End."

In this context, against that unity, it is worth recalling briefly the insistent emphases of Straub and Huillet in their work on the "directness" of sound: "Space-off exists. Which is what one discovers when one shoots with sound and what those who shoot without cannot know. And they are wrong to do so, because they go against the essence of cinema. They have the impression that they are only photographing what they have in front of the camera; but that is not true, one also photographs what one has behind and around the frame."[70] Straub and Huillet disrupt by reference to an extreme of "truth" (often linked, as here, to a Bazin-like reference to "the essence of cinema"). Dominant and subservient, the voice drama in the fiction film can be dubbed after the shooting, added on to an image track which, as script, it was anyway controlling (in Italy, where Straub and Huillet work, dubbing is standard practice). Neither dominant nor subservient, sound (which includes a veritable work on the grain of the voice itself, the material rhythms of its existence in language—*Othon, History*

Lessons, Moses and Aaron) in Straub and Huillet *gives space,* not as coherence but as contradiction, heterogeneity, outside (the extreme of "truth" thus leading away from Bazin): "Shooting with direct sound, one cannot cheat with space: one must respect it, and, in respecting it, one offers the spectator the possibility of reconstructing it, because a film is made of 'extracts' of time and space. One can also not respect the space one films, but one must then offer the spectator the possibility of understanding why one did not respect it. . . . "[71] It is the coherence of the *fiction* that falls: the fiction film disrespects space in order to construct a unity that will bind spectator and film in its fiction; where a Godard breaks space, fragments and sets up oppositions in the interests of analysis ("analysis with image and sound"), Straub and Huillet film a unity, sound and image, in and off, that will never "make a scene"; in both cases, the address is complex, in process, no longer the single and central vision but a certain freedom of contradictions.[72]

What has been described here is the whole context of the importance of work and reflection on space in film, the whole context of its actuality; Burch, for instance, as filmmaker and theorist, can say that "we are just beginning to realize that the formal organization of shot transitions and 'matches' in the strict sense of the word is the essential cinematic task."[73] What must now be considered are some of the terms in which that actuality has been articulated and, critically, something of the implications of those terms; the examples will be limited, the final argument more general.

It is hardly necessary to underline the extent to which American independent cinema set about destroying the narrative frame in the interests of the action of the film as flow of images (flashes of movement and energy, sheets of rhythmic multiplicity), the perpetual action of an eye for which every object, in Brakhage's words, is "a new adventure of perception," an eye in panic and fascination (like that of Hitchcock's Benson in front of the troubling picture). There is a sense of redoing the history of cinema again, from zero; hence, in part and at the same time, the interest accorded to experimental directions indicated and lost in the early moments of that history (including those of "cubist cinema;" Benson's painting has its specific resonances here and in the radical separation from Quattrocento space that cubism represents)[74] or even to the interrogation of its initial productions (as Jacobs explores and extends *Tom, Tom, the Piper's Son,* finding and creating fresh spaces on screen).

Evidently, the practice of American independent cinema is not to be limited to the simple desire for the capture of the present—the presence—of a pheno-menologico–romantic visionary consciousness, what P. Adams Sitney calls "the cinematic reproduction of the human mind." At a time when that cinema already has its own history—from *Meshes of the Afternoon* to *Zorns Lemma,* the field covered by Sitney's book[75]—the very problems of screen and frame, movement

and framing, and their narrative-spatial determinations are of increasing concern—and this without being reducible to a category of the "structural film"
type. In Frampton's *Poetic Justice,* nothing but a table with a cup of coffee, a
cactus, and in the middle a pile of sheets of paper; silently, the sheets follow one
another to the top of the pile and we read—fragments seized at the whim of
the succession—the scenario of a film; a rubber glove rests on the last page. In
J. J. Murphy's *Print Generation,* a sequence of images is passed through a series
of "generations" until it arrives at a printing close to the "normal" from which
it is run back down to the initial state of luminous abstraction. Two quite
different films, but both engaging problems of narrative and frame: in the one,
the image is fixed in the frame of a written narrative which makes this film
which exceeds it, vacillation of reading the film (where is the point of view to
be held?), each viewing varied against the fixity of the image (and not more
complete); in the other, the film as the action of a technical process, the image
narrated, scales of readings in that action (suspense of the point of recognition
of the image), the screen in dots, impressions/pulsations of new spaces.

Those examples were minor, cited as such and a little at random. The films
of Michael Snow, on the contrary, are a major example, quite different but again
finding their particular force in this connection, with respect to space in film.
Wavelength gives the economy of the formal explorations of the "structural film"
in a radical work on the problems of the spaces of narrative and the narratives
of space. The famous forty-five minute zoom constructs the filmed room (the
New York loft) into a *crossing,* a time of continuously jerky spaces—the superimposition of fixed images, the unsteadiness of the regulation of the zoom, the
human events that arrive in its path. It is a matter of narrating in the time of
the film the space covered, of making that crossing of space—with its frames
(the play of the windows onto the street, the photograph picked out on the wall,
the events themselves—so many quotations of actions, of commonplaces) and
its framings (the changing focal length of the zoom)—the scene of a veritably
filmic action, a process without any *single* view. In *La Région centrale,* the program
of 360-degree rotations works at the loss of any perspective frame, as a kind of
speed-jubilation of a time of space (landscape as movement, movement as
landscape), an impossibly uncentered narrative in which the apparatus (the
camera), sole "character" in the film, serves to disjoin the subject-eye, to open
gaps between sight and seen, overturning the technological "yield" of cinema.

What remains is the difficulty of sound as the address of voice. *Rameau's
Nephew by Diderot (thanx to Dennis Young) by Wilma Schoen* is conceived as a
"real 'talking picture' " (hence the title, Rameau's nephew as the irruption of the
body/voice onto the scene of philosophy) and over its twenty-four sections—
so many sketches and gags—explores "image-sound relationships" in the cinema
in a way that often connects with the spatial preoccupations to be found in, say,
Wavelength and *La Région centrale.* The result is something akin to an indefatigably
prolonged version of Godard's *Le gai savoir,* but lacking the political insistence

of any analysis as text; the film talks, jokes, accumulates, overlays, reverses, confuses and tricks as though empty of any reflective contradiction. Its work, as it were, fails to *carry,* in the sense in which the crucial filmic-narrative concerns of the previous films might have led one to expect, fails to transform—and to transform politically—the cinematic relations of form and content, and the setting of narrative accordingly.

Burch's arguments in *Theory of Film Practice* come together as a central plea— developed via terms such as "dialectical," "organic," "structural," these terms tending to synonymity—for the poetic function of film, "conflictual organization" as "unity through diversity": "Although film remains largely an imperfect means of communication, it is none the less possible to foresee a time when it will become a totally immanent object where semantic function will be intimately joined with its plastic function to create a *poetic function.*"[76] The analysis of spatial tensions and movements is made in this context and *Theory of Film Practice* finally falls within a range of writing on film that would also include, for instance, the work of Arnheim; Burch introduces structural conflict with dialectical relationship, disorientation with dynamic organicism, the ultimate concern always composition, film as *art.* It is easy enough, moreover, to transpose such a concern, with its brand of phenomenological formalism, into notions of "deconstruction" as a formal crisis of codes. Indicating the importance of deconstruction in an interview in 1973 ("I should say right now that this concept of deconstruction is something which is quite important to me"), Burch continues: "let's leave the word deconstruction for the moment because it's a more modern word than the actual origin of this concept, which can be traced back to the Prague school and to Jakobson and Mukařovský and work in semiotics which involves the concept that there is an aesthetic message (I'm using the word now in the specifically semiotic sense) if you like, produced through the subversion, through the breaking down of, through creating a crisis in what we call the dominant codes of representation in a given medium. This language can be extended to practically anything."[77] What is emerging is a potentially critical idea of deconstruction covered by its simple articulation as a poetics, this latter being its history in Burch's work. Thus a description of *Man with a Movie Camera* as deconstruction film will read exactly as a transposition of the definition of the poetic function of film, the totally immanent object found in *Theory of Film Practice,* with Jakobson precisely as an underlying presence for both: "But it was only with Dziga Vertov's *Man with a Movie Camera* (1929) that the work of paradigmatic deconstruction of the illusionist codes gave rise to the constitution of a comprehensive dialetic, informing the totality of the work along the syntagmatic axis."[78]

Something of the problems of a formal idea of deconstruction can be seen in the Thompson and Bordwell and the Branigan texts on Ozu. What those texts suggest is a modernity of Ozu's films based on a foregrounding—here too, it is worth noting the reference made to concepts derived from literary formalism—of space that challenges the supremacy of narrative causality. In fact, there are two components in the argument developed. The first concerns the demonstration of a certain autonomy of space: "Ozu's films include not only the spaces between points but also space *before* and *after* actions occur there . . ."; "Ozu's cutaways and transitions usually present spaces distinct from the characters' personal projects . . . at the most radical level, in presenting space empty of character—spaces around characters, locales seen before characters arrive or after they leave, or even spaces which they never traverse—Ozu's films displace the illusion of narrative presence and plenitude."[79] The second concerns the description of a 360-degree shooting space: "If Hollywood builds upon spatial patterns bounded by 180 degrees and 30 degrees, Ozu's films use limits of 360 degrees and 90 degrees."[80]

These two components are related in their demonstration of the importance of space in Ozu but can at the same time be differentiated a little in a way that will help focus the problems of that demonstration. Thus, the analysis of the 360-degree shooting space is very much the analysis of a closed system: "Ozu's scenic space is systematically built up, modified by subtle repetitions and variations within the limits he has set for himself."[81] That system is effectively different from that of Hollywood (where 360-degree movements are very conventionally and narratively limited—the slow pan at the beginning of the drive in *Red River*), which it can serve to contrast, but the question of its effective functioning, its critical activity, *in the films* is not posed. Indeed, certain formulations imply 360-degree space in Ozu as a formal accompaniment to a content that in itself and in its other devices is very close to Hollywood: "Once this pattern of circular space is established, Ozu's films use the same devices Hollywood does, but without the axis of action."[82] The description of the autonomy tends to avoid consideration of its activity outside of formal limits. More radical in a sense is the account of a presence of space based specifically on terms of autonomy, the space that is there, distinct, before and after; this insofar as it suggests an exploration of the tensions between surface and place, screen and frame, economy of the film and economy of narrative. When followed through into the discussion of graphic matches, however, the tensions are once again shown as subdued in a formal independence (near to an art of composition): "Such graphic play is central to Ozu's modernity because the screen surface itself and the configurations that traverse it are treated as independent of the scenographic space of the narrative."[83] Spatial nuances are set up as graphic matches in the systematic and repetitious space of the films, but what are the critical tensions of this autonomy in the *action* of the films?

In this respect, the description of the "most transgressive transition," the baseball-game transition in *An Autumn Afternoon,* is significantly weak: "Ozu's transition goes first to the place the character is *not,* then to the place where he actually is. This sequence is one of the culminations of Ozu's exercises in moving through spaces between scenes independently of any narrative demands."[84] Nothing in the description suggests more than an "exercise"; the transition goes not so much to the place the character is not as to the place *he should have been,* a projected space (Kawai insists that he is going to the game), exactly a simple *place;* certainly there is a play of difficulty in finding the men, but that play—irony and revelation (so Kawai didn't go. . .)—is not transgressive of the terms of the narrative in the terms of the narration it gives. And to pose such a transgressive activity involves an analysis directed not to a unity of dominants and overtones but to the bindings of those terms, to the modes of address of film in its subject-vision relations in narrative space, to the contradictions they contain.

Frames hit the screen in succession, figures pass across screen through the frames, the camera tracks, pans, reframes, shots replace and—according to the rules—continue one another. Film is the production not just of a negation but equally, simultaneously, of a negativity, the excessive foundation of the process itself, of the very movement of the spectator as subject in the film; which movement is stopped in the negation and its centering positions, the constant phasing in of subject vision ("this but not that" as the sense of the image in flow). Such a negativity is the *disphasure* of the subject in process, the fading, the "flickering of eclipses" or "time between" that the classical narrative film seeks to contain in *its* process, film aiming thus to *entertain* the subject (etymologically, "entertainment" is a holding-in and a maintenance—the subject occupied in time). Narrativization is then the term of film's entertaining: process and process contained, subject bound in that process and its directions of meaning. The ideological operation lies in the balance, in the capture and regulation of energy; film circulates—rhythms, spaces, surfaces, moments, multiple intensities of signification—and narrativization entertains the subject—on screen, in frame—in exact turnings of difference and repetition, semiotic and suture, negativity and negation; in short, the spectator is *moved,* and *related* as subject in the process and images of that movement. The spatial organization of film as it has been described here in the overall context of its various articulations is crucial to this moving relation, to the whole address of film: film makes spaces, takes place as narrative, and the subject too, set—sutured—in the conversion of the one to the other.

In his essay on "Le Cinéma et la nouvelle psychologie," Merleau-Ponty writes that "the aspect of the world would be transformed if we succeeded in seeing as *things* the intervals between things."[85] The formulation can now be recast: the relations of the subject set by film—its vision, its address—would be radically transformed if the intervals of its production were opened in their negativity, if the fictions of the closure of those intervals were discontinued, found in all the contradictions of their activity. Take the second of the five sections of *Penthesilea* in which Wollen traces a complex itinerary round the sun-and-shadow-strewn house, the camera accompanying, leaving, rejoining him, fixing for itself—in its own time—the memory-cards of the discourse he delivers. A certain influence from films of Snow is clear but difficult: a theoretical narrative of the space of the film—Wollen here "speaks" his and Mulvey's film—within a constant dis-framing of the time of that narrative, the shifting choreography of discourse to space in the wake of the camera. The camera has an "autonomy"—dancing high-angle circles round a tabletop, for instance—but that autonomy is given in its history: its history in the sequence, where it slips from classical subordi-nation of movement to character into a rediscovery of the space of the initial subordination through new variations of movement along its path; its history in cinema, Wollen's discourse involving reflection on film space and spaces; its history in this film, which plays systematically across its sections on movement and fixity, scene and space and distance. The autonomy, moreover, is at every moment taken up elsewhere, divided in its articulations within the political action of the film which is itself, exactly, a series of actions, of histories—the women's struggle, Penthesilea, the Amazons, Kleist and psychoanalysis, func-tions of myth and questions posed to "feminine" myths, to images, to cinema, and to this film with respect to those myths—that includes the action and the history of the camera spacing as a critical term in its reflection—finding the cards, for example, and indicating the problems of voice and image and movement and their material force: what is a film that speaks, speaks politically? How is the point to be arrived at from which such a question can be formulated in film? Hence, indeed, the importance of the final section of *Penthesilea* with its four screens on screen, the film remembered in their separation and relation and working over, the film repeated differently again in this critical inflection of its present struggle: this woman who now faces the camera with the problem of speech, these images, these words and sounds, this film in the intervals of struggle, with the narrative space of the film extended plurally to a movement of spaces and the contradictions of their intersection. *Penthesilea,* finally, marks a recognition, and across the unity of the conventional opposition in film, that to fight for a revolutionary content is also to fight for a revolution of form, but that—in a dialectic which defines the work of a specific signifying practice—the content ceaselessly "goes beyond" (Marx's insistence at the start of *The Eighteenth Brumaire)* and that a *political* struggle is to be carried through in the articulations of "form" and "content" at every point of that process.

Which is where it becomes possible to say that the narrative space of film is today not simply a theoretical and practical actuality but is a crucial and political avant-garde problem in a way which offers perspectives on the existing terms of that actuality. Deconstruction is quickly the impasse of formal device, an aesthetics of transgression when the need is an activity of transformation, and a politically consequent materialism in film is not to be expressed as veering contact past internal content in order to proceed with "film as film"[86] but rather as a work on the constructions and relations of meaning and subject in a specific signifying practice in a given sociohistorical situation, a work that is then much less on "codes" than on the operations of narrativization. At its most effectively critical, moreover, that work may well bear little resemblance to what in the given situation is officially acknowledged and defined as "avant-garde"; in particular, and in the context of the whole account offered here of film and space, it may well involve an action at the limits of narrative within the narrative film, at the limits of its fictions of unity.

This, to take an example chosen since Japanese films are often used as a contrasting frame of reference in the formal deconstruction arguments, is the radical importance of several of the films of Oshima Nagisa. The *intensity* of Oshima's work lies in a "going beyond" of content that constantly breaks available articulations of "form" and "content" and poses the film in the hollow of those breaks. The films have an immediate presence of narrative articulation but that presence in each case presents the absence of another film the discourse of which, punctuating this film and its space, finds its determinations, its contradictions, its negativity. Split *in* the narrativization, the films are thus out of true with—out of "the truth" of—any single address: the subject divided in complexes of representation and their contradictory relations.

In *Death by Hanging,* the prisoner refuses to die and the hanging fails: R The Korean (Yun Yun-do), R worker, as the court verdict begins, cannot be hanged again until he is "conscious," "himself," fully identical with "the real R" ("he must realize his guilt is being justly punished"); the officials busy themselves in efforts to restore R, their R, the legal R, and the film builds its immediate narrative round those efforts, organized into sections announced by written titles, stages in the problem of R's identity and identification. At one point, the action leaves the carefully and theatrically structured confines of the execution chamber and moves outside, still in the interests of the memory of R that must be reawakened in R; the sequence finds shantytown, riverbank, station, alleyway, bridge, ice-cream parlor, and school, where the Education Officer (Watanabe Fumio) becomes carried away in his demonstration of the murder of the woman on the roof. One or two remarks must suffice to suggest the difficult space of this sequence.

The first is general: throughout the sequence R is accompanied by a voice, that of the Education Officer who recounts and enacts R's story, where he should be in the space in frame, specifying its place; the Education Officer's voice is literally "all over the place"—R sits down by the river, the Education Officer joins him to tell what his feelings must have been and must be (since in this acting out R has to be made to coincide exactly with the repeated story); R telephones at the station, the Education Officer, out of frame, calls instructions. Simply, R is never quite there, in the place assigned; the events take place without him and the space-place conversion is troubled in that absence; another film is possible, but only in the hollow of this film, dialectically in its contradiction. R

14

17

15

18

16

19

has neither voice nor look: voices are given—that of the Education Officer but also that of the Sister figure (Koyama Akiko) with a direct militant account of R's acts—and R can come to accept (being R for the sake of all Rs, a certain reality in the Sister) and look (into camera, framed in closeup against the Japanese-flag motif at the start of the final—acceptance—section); something remains over, however, something that Oshima's films constantly attempt to articulate as a new content (in Marx's sense of a content that goes beyond) in the exploration of the political relations of the subject and the subjective relations of the political. In that double and simultaneous movement lies a utopianism that is equally constant, the utopianism of another space (remember the utopianism of the perspective system and its centered subject), a radically transformed subjectivity (often formulated by Oshima in terms of the imaginary as in excess

20

22

21

of existing definitions of reality and struggle which it sees as both necessary and as alienating in those definitions—the whole play between R and the Sister figure, between the original news story of the Korean, the reactions to the story in contemporary Japan, and Oshima's film). The work of Oshima is political and obliquely political, a return of the one on the other through questions posed to meanings, images, fictions of unity, the questions of subject relations and transformations.

The second remark is particular: a quotation from within the sequence as a kind of coda. R is never quite there, in the place assigned. R is seen coming along the riverbank followed by the compact group of uniformed officials, the Education Officer on a bicycle narrating the story, R eventually bringing the group to a halt by sitting down (stills 14, 15); the Education Officer sits down in his turn by the side of R, the camera having been repositioned to hold the two men in left profile in near shot but still facing in the direction from which the group arrived, and R turns to look back over his right shoulder (still 16); a cat is revealed as the object of R's gaze by a straightforward transition answering to the orientation of space established by that gaze in the previous shot (still 17); R is now seen from a position behind him and the Education Officer, R continuing to look back (still 18); the cat (still 19); R in closeup is seen looking, the camera here positioned to his right (still 20); the cat (still 21); a long-shot from behind the cat which shows the group of officials, the Education Officer's bicycle, R sitting looking, and the Education Officer stretched out beside him in a line across the frame from left to right, with the bridge beyond in the background and the cat in the center foreground (still 22); the shots are linked by cuts and the camera is fixed in every shot. The composition is evident, both in frame and in the development of the shots together, the last shot reversing the direction and the positions in frame—note the group of officials—of the first; in three shots, punctuated by the cat shots, the camera moves a half circle round R, enacting a little narrative on its own, and of R on his own, taken away from the Education Officer, more and more distant from the story relayed by his voice until the separation of the closeup. What then breaks the R/cat exchange, gives the distancing of R one more turn and brings it back against the overall space and movement of this sequence within a sequence, is the final longshot: the match of look and object is interrupted by a shot that catches the cat itself as look in another direction; in front of R in frame, with R and along the line of his look, the cat gazes off into camera, to something never seen, abruptly absent. The place of the camera, moreover, is impossible: object of R's gaze, the cat is seen against a little "wall" of concrete blocks; gazing, the cat is seen free in its space, from behind the blocks which seem to have vanished. In its composed lines—from cat to R, from bicycle wheel to the middle of the bridge—the shot offers a perfect perspective, but a perspective that runs short in the completion it seeks, the scene opened out—intervaled—in its focus of address, a sudden pull to the relations of space, to the elements therein, to the places they take, and for whom (as Oshima's voice over at the close of the film turns its action to the audience—"and you too, and you too, and you too. . .").

From Benson's painting to this cat, glimpsed by R and pulled out of his gaze, framed elsewhere. Thus pulled, thus framed, the cat says something important that has been the whole insistence here: events take place, a place for some one, and the need is to pose the question of that "one" and its narrative terms of film space.

Notes

1. See Picasso's *Nature morte au pichet, bol et fruit,* 1931.

2. Annette Michelson, "Toward Snow," *Artforum* (June 1971), p. 32; reprinted in Peter Gidal, ed., *Structural Film Anthology* (London: British Film Institute, 1976), p. 41.

3. Noël Burch, *Theory of Film Practice* (London: Secker and Warburg, 1973); first published in French as *Praxis du cinéma* (Paris: Gallimard, 1969).

4. Kristin Thompson and David Bordwell, "Space and Narrative in the Films of Ozu," *Screen* (Summer 1976), 17(2):42, 45; Edward Branigan, "The Space of *Equinox Flower,*" *ibid.* p. 104.

5. See Georges Sadoul, *Histoire générale du cinéma* (Paris: Denoel, 1963), 1:288, 290.

6. American Mutoscope and Biograph Company *Bulletin* account of *Tom, Tom, the Piper's Son,* made in 1905; see Kemp R. Niver, *The First Twenty Years: A Segment of Film History* (Los Angeles and Berkeley: University of California Press, 1968), p. 88.

7. M. Merleau-Ponty, "Le Cinéma et la nouvelle psychologie," in *Sens et non-sens* (Paris:

Gallimard, 1948), p. 110; P. Francastel, "Espace et illusion," *Revue internationale de filmologie* (1948), 2(5):66.

8. R. Arnheim, *Film as Art* (London: Faber, 1969), p. 20.

9. See M. Pleynet, interview (with Gérard Leblanc), *Cinéthique* (1969), no. 3.

10. G. Ten Doesschate, *Perspective: Fundamentals, Controversials, History* (Nieuwkoop: B. de Graaf, 1964), pp. 6–7.

11. Leon Battista Alberti, *On Painting* (New Haven and London: Yale University Press, 1966), p. 51.

12. Galileo, *Opere*, ed. A. Favaro (Florence: Edizione nazionale, 1890–1909), 9:129.

[A recent book by Ernest B. Gilman, *The Curious Perspective: Literary and Pictorial Wit in the Seventeenth Century* (New Haven and London: Yale University Press, 1978), stresses—as in effect does Galileo—a parodic, almost subversive implication of the use of anamorphosis: "Although the curious perspective system would have been impossible without the achievement of a systematic linear perspective in the earlier Renaissance, its effect was to parody, question, and even undermine the central cognitive assumption behind perspective representation" (p. 233). It remains, however, that the "wit" of anamorphosis is constantly a reference to a rational and stable system that it assumes in the very moment it parodies or questions and is thus always available as a final image of order; as witness the idea of anamorphosis in a passage from Leibniz on universal harmony quoted by Gilman (p. 97). "It is as in the inventions of perspective, where certain lovely drawings appear only as confusion, until one finds their true point of view or sees them by means of a certain glass or mirror.. . . . Thus the apparent deformities of our little world come together as beauties in the greater world, and there is nothing opposed to the unity of a universally perfect principle." What is clear and important is that the Renaissance perspective system opens the way to an assurance and a trap for the look, the vision of the subject, to an *illusion* of *reality*, in the play of which two terms a whole problematic of representation is established—a problematic in which cinema is engaged, *moves.*—S.H.]

13. P. Francastel, *Etudes de sociologie de l'art* (Paris: Denoël, 1970), pp. 136–37.

14. W. M. Ivins, *Art and Geometry* (New York: Dover, 1964), p. 108; Ten Doesschate, *Perspective*, p. 157.

15. C. Metz, "Le Signifiant imaginaire," *Communications* (1975), 23:35–137; translation, "The Imaginary Signifier," *Screen* (Summer 1975) 16(2):52–54 [Excerpt included in this anthology—ED.].

16. Arnheim, *Film as Art*, p. 18.

17. E. Lindgren, *The Art of the Film* (London: Allen and Unwin, 1948), p. 54.

18. Branigan, "The Space of *Equinox Flower*," p. 104.

19. K. Reisz and G. Millar, *The Technique of Film Editing* (New York and London: Hastings House, 1968), p. 215.

20. J. P. Richter, ed., *The Literary Works of Leonardo da Vinci* (London: Oxford University Press, 1939), 1:150. The figure is Leonardo's own, *ibid.*

[Leonardo was much exercised by difficulties in the match between the Albertian perspective system and visual appearances, exploring elsewhere the possibility of an alternative system based on a spherical optics; see J. White, *The Birth and Rebirth of Pictorial Space* (Boston: Boston Book and Art Shop, 1967) pp. 207–15.—S.H.]

21. E. Reboul, *Le Cinéma scolaire et éducateur* (Paris: Presses Universitaires de France, 1926).

22. Hollis Frampton, interview with Simon Field and Peter Sainsbury, *Afterimage* (Autumn 1972), no. 4, p. 65.

23. Frampton writes elsewhere: "The film frame is a rectangle, rather anonymous in its proportions, that has been fiddled with recently in the interests of publicising, so far as I can see, nothing much more interesting than the notions of an unbroken and boundless horizon. The wide screen glorifies, it would seem, frontiers long gone: the landscapes of the American corn-flats and the Soviet steppes; it is accommodating to the human body only when that body is lying in state. Eisenstein once proposed that the frame be condensed into a 'dynamic' square,

which is as close to a circle as a rectangle can get, but his arguments failed to prosper." Hollis Frampton, "The Withering Away of the State of Art," *Artforum* (December 1974), p. 53.

24. *Apprendre le cinéma,* special issue of *Image et son* (May 1966), no. 194 bis, pp. 119, 121.

25. *Ibid.,* p. 123.

26. Quoted by Rosalind Krauss in "A View of Modernism," *Artforum* (September 1972), p. 50. Krauss comments: "Perspective is the visual correlate of causality that one thing follows the next in space according to rule. . . . perspective space carried with it the meaning of narrative: a succession of events leading up to and away from this moment; and within that temporal succession—given as a spatial analogue—was secreted the 'meaning' of both that space and those events."

27. C. Metz, "Histoire/Discours," in *Langue, discours, société,* ed. J. Kristeva, J.-C. Milner, and N. Ruwet (Paris: Seuil, 1975), p. 304; translation, "History/Discourse," *Edinburgh '76 Magazine* (1976), p. 23.

28. A still from the shot can be found in Niver, *First Twenty Years,* p. 36.

29. "There must be a lot of essential pleasure just in the films when they hit the screen—I heard this expression yesterday, 'to hit the screen,' that's fantastic in English. Hit the screen—this is really what the frames do. The projected frames hit the screen." Peter Kubelka, interview with Jonas Mekas in Gidal, *Structural Film Anthology,* p. 102.

30. It can be noted that much independent film work has been concerned with experiencing dislocations of screen and frame; Sharits, for example, writes: "When a film 'loses its loop' it allows us to see a blurred strip of jerking frames; this is quite natural and quite compelling subject material. When this non-framed condition is intentionally induced, a procedure I am currently exploring, it could be thought of as 'anti-framing.' " Paul Sharits, "Words per Page," *Afterimage* (Autumn 1972), no. 4, p. 40. For an attempt by a filmmaker to provide a theoretical formulation of such dislocation using the notion of a "second screen" (in fact, the frame on screen in a narrative coherence of ground/background) that independent cinema will destroy ("in independent cinema, there is no second screen"), see Claudine Eizykman, *La Jouissance-cinéma* (Paris: Bourgois, 1976) esp. pp. 147–51.

31. B. D. Lewin, "Sleep, the Mouth, and the Dream Screen," *Psychoanalytic Quarterly* (1946), 15:419–34.

32. Discussion of screen and dream screen is suggested at the close of a recent article by Guy Rosolato, "Souvenir-écran," *Communications* (1975), no. 23, pp. 86–87. See also my "Screen Images, Film Memory," *Edinburgh '76 Magaine* (1976), pp. 33–42.

33. C. Metz, *Essais sur la signification au cinéma* (Paris: Klincksieck, 1972), 2:189.

34. Thompson and Bordwell, "Space and Narrative in the Films of Ozu," p. 42. For an initial discussion of procedures of image centering ("specification procedures"), see my "Film and System: Terms of Analysis" part II, *Screen* (Summer 1975), 16(2):99–100.

35. Noël Burch, "De *Mabuse à M:* le travail de Fritz Lang," in *Cinéma: Théorie, Lectures,* special issue of the *Revue e'Esthétique* (Paris: Klincksieck, 1973), p. 229.

36. See Barry Salt, "Statistical Style Analysis of Motion Pictures," *Film Quarterly* (Fall 1974), pp. 13–22.

37. Arnheim, *Film as Art,* p. 27.

38. *Ibid.,* p. 32.

39. J. Mitry, *Esthétique et psychologie de cinéma* (Paris: Editions Universitaires, 1965) 2:10.

40. Branigan, "The Space of *Equinox Flower,*" p. 75 gives the schema of the inverted pyramid structure characteristic of classical Hollywood film: "1. Establishing Shot (a major variant: we see a detail of the scene, then pull back or cut to the establishing shot) 2. Long Shot (master shot) 3. Medium Two-Shot 4. Reverse Angles (over-the-shoulder shots) 5. alternating Medium Close-ups 6. Cut-away (or Insert) 7. alternating Medium Close-ups 8. Re-establishing Shot (usually a reverse angle or two-shot)."

41. Reisz and Millar, *Technique of Film Editing,* pp. 224–25.

42. *Ibid.,* p. 225–26.

43. *Apprendre le cinéma*, p. 142.

44. *Ibid.*, p. 151.

45. Reisz and Millar, *Technique of Film Editing*, p. 216. To emphasize the reality of this smoothness as construction rather than "reflection," it can be noted that the Navajo Indians studied by Worth and Adair, though capable of producing the "correct" continuity (for example, by matching on action), were very far from the "rules" in their films, articulating another system of space as an area of action (in which "jumps" from the standpoint of the vision of the rules becomes essential continuities); see Sol Worth and John Adair, *Through Navajo Eyes* (Bloomington: Indiana University Press, 1972), p. 174 and stills 22–35, 35–40.

46. Barry Salt has pointed to the importance of the outdoor-action subject film (notably the western) historically in this development; "The Early Development of Film Form," *Film Form* (Spring 1976), no. 1, pp. 97–98.

47. *Apprendre le cinéma*, p. 125 ("an orientated empty space is a promise").

48. André Bazin, *What Is Cinema?* (Los Angeles and Berkeley: University of California Press, 1967), 1:108.

49. Which is not, of course, to say that deep focus must necessarily be used in this way; for analysis of "a refusal of perspective within depth of field," see Cl. Bailblé, M. Marie, and M.-C. Ropars, *Muriel* (Paris: Galilée, 1974), pp. 128–36.

50. Salt, "Statistical Style Analysis," p. 20.

51. André Bazin, *Qu'est-ce que le cinéma?* (Paris: Cerf, 1959), 2:100.

52. Bazin, *Qu'est-ce que le cinéma?* (Paris: Cerf, 1962), 4:57.

53. *Ibid.*, p. 59. For discussion of Bazin on Neorealism, see Christopher William's article of that title in *Screen* (Winter 1973–74), 14(4):61–68.

54. Burch, *Theory of Film Practice*, p. 21.

55. Branigan, "The Space of *Equinox Flower*," p. 103.

56. *Apprendre le cinéma*, p. 148.

57. For a detailed analysis of the point-of-view shot, see Edward Branigan, "Formal Permutations of the Point-of-View Shot," *Screen* (Autumn 1975), 16(3):54–64.

58. Noël Burch and Jorge Dana, "Propositions," *Afterimage* (Spring 1974), no. 5, p. 45.

59. As summarized by Metz in his "Current Problems in Film Theory," *Screen* (Spring–Summer 1973), 14(1–2):49.

60. In fact, and not suprisingly, the less narratively "metonymical" and the more "metaphorical" what is looked at in the pure point-of-view shot is (without the marking of image distortion), the nearer such a shot will come to subjectivizing the image. Released from prison at the beginning of *High Sierra*, Roy Earle is shown walking through a park, breathing the air of freedom; shots of him looking up are followed by shots of treetops against the sky, with a certain effect of subjectivization insofar as the treetops against the sky are outside the immediate scope of the movement of the narrative and, objectively useless (unlike Lina's telegram in *Suspicion*), belong only for Roy's character (he was born of a modest farming family and is not the hardened criminal his reputation would have him be).

61. Walter Benjamin, *Illuminations* (London: Fontana, 1970), p. 230; C. Metz, "Le Signifiant imaginaire," p. 35; translation, p. 52.

62. Edward Branigan, "Narration and Subjectivity in Cinema," mimeographed (University of Wisconsin at Madison, 1975), p. 24.

63. *Ibid.*

64. Discussed by R. Barthes, "Diderot, Brecht, Eisenstein," *Screen* (Summer 1974), 15(2):38 [included in this anthology—ED.]; Branigan, "Formal Permutations," p. 57; and M. Nash, "*Vampyr* and the Fantastic," *Screen* (Autumn 1976) 17(3):32–33, 54–60.

65. Burch and Dana, "Propositions," p. 45.

66. Salt distinguishes three varieties of field/reverse field and assigns an order and approximate dates for their respective appearances: "It is necessary to distinguish between different varieties of angle—reverse-angle cuts; the cut from a watcher to his point of view

was the first to appear; the cut from one long shot of a scene to another more or less oppositely angled long shot, which must have happened somewhat later—the first example that can be quoted is in *Røverens Brud* (Viggo Larsen, 1907); and the cut between just-off-the-eye-line angle—reverse-angle shots of two people interacting—the earliest example that can be quoted occurs in *The Loafer* (Essanay, 1911). "The Early Development of Film Form," p. 98.

67. For details of the introduction and various accounts of suture, see "On Suture," in Stephen Heath, *Questions of Cinema* (London: Macmillan, and Bloomington: Indiana University Press, 1981), pp. 86–101.

68. See J.-A. Miller, "La Suture," *Cahiers pour l'analyse* (1966), no. 1, pp. 37–49; translation, "Suture," *Screen* (Winter 1977–78), 18(4):24–34.

69. "Another characteristic of the film image is its neutrality"; *Encyclopaedia Britannica* (Macropaedia, 1974), 12:498.

70. "Entretien avec Jean-Marie Straub et Danièle Huillet," *Cahiers du cinéma* (August–September 1970), no. 223, p. 54.

71. "Sur le son (entretian avec Jean-Marie Straub et Danièle Huillet)," *Cahiers du cinéma* (October–November 1975), no. 260–61, p. 49.

72. No mention has been made in this section of the difficult problem of the verbal organization of the image according to "inner speech"; see Paul Willemen, "Reflections on Eikhenbaum's Concept of Internal Speech," *Screen* (Winter 1974–75), 15(4):59–70; and Stephen Heath, "Language, Sight, and Sound," in *Questions of Cinema*, pp. 204–17. Worth and Adair, *Through Navajo Eyes*, p. 130, note examples of Navajo Indians who judged certain *silent* films incomprehensible because "in English."

73. Burch, *Theory of Film Practice*, p. 11.

74. Cubism as "construction of deformable and varied worlds, subject to non-Euclidean but extremely topological notions of proximity and separation, succession and surrounding, envelopment and continuity, independently of any fixed schema and of any metrical scale of measurement," Francastel, *Etudes de sociologie de l'art* p. 142; see, in the same volume, the chapter entitled "Destruction d'un espace plastique," pp. 191–252.

75. P. Adams Sitney, *Visionary Film* (New York and London: Oxford University Press, 1974).

76. Burch, *Theory of Film Practice*, p. 12; in her "Introduction," Annette Michelson writes: "his voice puts forth a claim for total structural rigor and authenticity" (p. xv). It should be noted: first, that the remarks made here consider only the implications of Burch's arguments and do not touch on the value of his working out of those arguments; second, that Burch himself, in the "preface" to this English version of his initially French publication (pp. xvi–xx), is retrospectively critical of the book, though within limits which actually close the distance from it he now asserts and bring the intended criticism very near to the formulations of the original.

77. "Beyond *Theory of Film Practice*: An Interview with Noel Burch," *Women and Film,* (1974) no. 5–6, p. 22.

78. Burch and Dana, "Propositions," p. 44.
Jakobson: "The poetic function projects the principle of equivalence from the axis of selection into the axis of combination." "Linguistics and Poetics," in *Style in Language* ed. T. A. Sebeok (Cambridge, Mass.: MIT Press, 1960) p. 358.

79. Thompson and Bordwell, "Space and Narrative in the Films of Ozu," pp. 52, 54.

80. *Ibid.,* p. 58

81. *Ibid.*

82. *Ibid.,* p. 60.

83. *Ibid.,* p. 70.

84. *Ibid.,* p. 51; full details of the transition discussed here can be found on this same page. [Thompson and Bordwell have since returned to the terms of their account of Ozu's "modernism," taking up points made here; see Kristin Thompson, "Notes on the Spatial

System of Ozu's Early Films," *Wide Angle* (1977), 1(4):8–17, esp. pp. 8–9; David Bordwell, "Our Dream Cinema: Western Historiography and the Japanese Film," *Film Reader* (1979), no. 4, pp. 45–62, (esp. p. 54)—S.H.]

85. Merleau-Ponty, "Le Cinéma et la nouvelle psychologie," p. 98.

86. "The structural/materialist film must minimize the content in its over-powering, imagistically seductive sense, in an attempt to get through this miasmic area of 'experience' and proceed with film as film. Devices such as loops or seeming loops, as well as a whole series of technical possibilities, can, carefully constructed to operate in the correct manner, serve to veer the point of contact with the film past internal content. The content thus serves as a function upon which, time and time again, a filmmaker works to bring forth the filmic event." Peter Gidal, "Theory and Definition of Structural/Materialist Film," *Studio International* (November–December 1975), p. 189; reprinted in *Structural Film Anthology,* p. 2.

23

Jean-Louis Comolli
Technique and Ideology:
Camera, Perspective, Depth
of Field [Parts 3 and 4]

EDITOR'S NOTE: *What follows are two installments from a series by Jean-Louis Comolli on questions of technology, ideology, and historiography published intermittently in* Cahiers du cinéma *during 1971 and 1972. In installments which preceded the two included here, Comolli establishes his own approach through critiques of Jean-Patrick Lebel's arguments in* Cinéma et idéologie *(Paris: Ed. Sociales, 1971); of André Bazin; and of the critiques of Bazin made by Jean Mitry and by some of the theorists and critics whose work had recently appeared in the journal* Cinéthique. *(A translation of Comolli's first installment has been published in* Film Reader *[1977] no. 2.)*

Against Lebel, Comolli attacks the idea that cinematic technology is ideologically neutral because the apparatus is based on scientific principles. From a consideration of the prehistory of cinema and its "origins" (a notion which he calls into question), Comolli argues that cinema, even in its technology, is part of the complex of determinations which makes up the social whole, and that it responds to economic and ideological demands. This is the broad view which he develops in his critiques of Bazin, Mitry, and the Cinéthique *writers. The "natural" "realism" of the film image is in fact the result of codification processes. A key indicator of this purported "realism" of the image is the illusion of depth, so Comolli takes that as his privileged examples of a technique. As an important object of study, deep focus must be interrogated not as a "natural" tendency of*

Published as "II. Profondeur de champ: la double scène (suite): (Notes pour une histoire matérialiste. . . suite)" in *Cahiers du cinéma* (August–September 1971), no. 231 pp. 42–49; and "La profondeur de champ 'primitive' " in *Cahiers du cinéma* (November 1971) no. 233, pp. 40–45. Reprinted and translation used by permission of the British Film Institute.

cinema, but as a symptom, both in the discourses of theoreticians and historians and in filmmaking practices. On the other hand, Mitry's limited critique of Bazin is said to miss the crucial function of the spectator, which is precisely to deny the otherness of the image that Mitry emphasizes, and thus to disavow certain of the differences between image and reality established by Mitry.

Comolli suggests that a materialist history of the cinema would require sensitivity to the complexity and diffuseness of determinations. It would require a new way of reading films, film theories, film histories—and film history. (His references are to the conceptualization of Louis Althusser on "symptomatic readings" in Reading Capital *[Paris: Maspero, 1968; trans. London: New Left Books, 1970], and to the theoretical approach of Julia Kristeva, cited below.) Comolli calls for a historical work which refuses to postulate linear causality as its fundamental organizing principle; which constructs the theoretical status of its objects (such as "the" cinema or deep focus) rather than just taking them as givens; and which takes its objects of study in terms of their (potentially shifting) positions within systems of representation, or signifying practices—which means attention to the constitutive impregnation of cinema by codes that are not specifically cinematic. Such a materialist history would not, for example, study the "story" of deep focus—the who, when, and where of its supposed "first" uses and the line of uses which followed necessarily and solely from these; nor would it outline cinema's purported "progress" toward greater and greater technical and therefore referential perfection. Rather, a materialist history would study "the convergences and divergences, breaks and reinforcements which characterize the inscription of deep focus into this historical context," a context which is never separable from the ideological requirements, contestations, and contradictions of the social whole.*

Part 3
Depth of Field: The Double Scene

(Notes Toward a Materialist History of the Cinema, Continued)

I will now try to apply along two main axes the general principles for the conditions of a materialist approach to the history of the cinema.[1] Firstly, what it is that drives all current "histories of the cinema" (all empiricist in method, and idealist in the concept of cinema which activates them and which they inscribe: as we shall see, what has been said of Bazin in fact applies as much to

Mitry as to Deslandes) to go on endlessly and systematically cataloguing the long series of "first times," that chain of "inaugurations" of technical devices and stylistic figures by this or that film. They adopt the empirical object "cinema" without troubling to construct its theory, and proceed to exhaust themselves in an obsessive re-marking of its proliferation of "births" (seen as automatic in the absence of theory); in other words, they seek to establish its "origin," which can only prove to be dispersed. This should of course seriously shake the very notion of an "origin," but these histories hasten to slide over and confine the damage by making the dispersal itself the justification for their basic eclecticism.[2]

The second axis along which I will test the notions put forward so far will proceed inversely. Its point of departure will be the theoretical implications of the object depth of field. It will be remembered that this study designated depth of field as one of the scenes for an operational analysis of the connections between cinematic technique and its economic and ideological determinations. On the one hand we will examine the historical inscription of deep focus, which means looking closely at the varied and uneven effects of the different (economic, ideological, and technological) factors which produce this inscription—its modes, curve, and pattern which explain why deep focus is used occasionally in some instances, systematically in others, why it is brought forward or re-pressed on the scene of filmic signifiers.

On the other hand, we will at the same time consider the "solutions" which idealist history and aesthetics (Bazin, Mitry) have contributed to the conflicts revealed by such an analysis. What we intend therefore is a rereading of the idealist discourse from the standpoint of the main area it represses—that complex of economic, political, and ideological determinants which shatter any notion of "the aesthetic evolution of the cinema" (any claim for complete autonomy for the aesthetic process). Since this is, in fact, the mainstay of idealist criticism, it is clear why it wants no part of such an argument.

On this basis we will bring into play the *specific* contradictions of the concept of signifying practice in its application to the cinema. This will be, notably, the unremitting division (antagonistic contradiction) between two categories of film. The first is the general mass of films which, whether "art" films or not, are held by idealist discourse on however frail a pretext to incarnate "the cinema" (the effect of "mass medium," and of the generation of "waves" of filmmaking is precisely what guarantees the eclecticism already mentioned). In the final analysis these are simply the endless modulations and repetitions of cinematic discourse as communication, representation, and univocal sense—whose exposure by theory is therefore essential. They are the innumerable realizations of the cinema as an ideological instrument, a vector and disseminator of ideological representations where the subject of ideology (the spectator of the spectacle) cannot fail to identify himself since what is involved is always the communication of "A Meaning ever present to itself in the presence of the Subject." (In fact, this describes the way the system of "transparency" *functions:* denying the work of differences, work as difference, meaning as work, in order to postulate meaning as an [intersubjective] exchange: the sign as money.)

In the second category of films (or practices), on the other hand, the status of meaning is modified by the work in the signifier. In this sense they may be called films of *rupture* after the work of Julia Kristeva.[3] Kristeva has referred to this work in the signifier as "always a *surplus* which exceeds the laws of ordinary communication";[4] it also sets signifying processes in action on the "other scene of *signifiance*"[5]—that of the production of meaning (as opposed to the re-presentation of A Meaning); and as work, it represents a break with "the ideology of signification" insofar as that "censors the problematic of work." In these terms the work in the signifier therefore constitutes that *text* from which the ideological inscription of those films can be reformulated and recast. Above all it can give rise to an *other cinema object,* one which would not always be assigned the same, sole—ideological—function (expressing, representing, specularizing, spectacularizing, changelessly distracting, tirelessly reconducting).[6] Instead, as a signifying practice, it would both be and reintegrate into ideology the "network of differences which characterize and/or combine with the mutations of different historical blocs."[7]

Constructing the theory of this new cinema object—the "cine-signifier"— would also mean putting a definitive end to the linear (literary) model of the "histories of the cinema." More precisely, it would mean "destroying the conceptual mechanism which installs historical linearity and reading in its place a *stratified history;* that is, a history characterized by discontinuous temporality, which is recursive, dialectical, and not reducible to a single meaning, but rather is made up of types of *signifying practices* whose plural series has neither origin nor end. Thus another history will be outlined, which underpins linear history; a recursively stratified history of *signifiances* where communicative language and its underlying ideology (sociological, historicist, or subjectivist) represent only its superficial facet. This is the role played by the text in all present-day society, required of it unconsciously, and prohibited or obstructed in *practice.*"[8]

Whatever the difficulties of this work (and they are great) it is no longer possible to maintain the history and the theory of cinema in separate watertight compartments: the new cinema object displaces the classifications and orderings set up at various times by historians and aestheticians, and the action of displacement informs both the practice and the theory. The new cinema object defines itself within this displacement and it can be read in the recasting of the relations of the different signifying practices to each other and to the social whole. But the theory of the new cinema object, which in establishing itself gives the first impulse to this displacement, is also constantly produced, informed, and recast by it.

Thus, a little of this dialectic will be put into play in what follows, at the modest level of a number of film techniques where are produced, perhaps more readably than elsewhere, the conjunction and conflicts of economic pressures, ideological obfuscations (masking/recuperation), scientific knowledge, "influences" of other signifying practices, relations of production, signifying work, the thrust of *signifiance,* which is never fully abolished even if it is repressed or "forbidden"—in short, cinematic technique as a double scene of practice and signifying.

"For the First Time. . ."

The considerable frequency with which the *fixed syntagm* "for the first time" recurs in existing "histories of the cinema" offers itself as a symptom for a reading of these histories. Beyond the issues with which polemics between film "historians" are exclusively concerned—i.e., the accuracy of the facts and recollections they record, the number and detail of the references provided—this reading would also have to take into account the system by which these histories are written, the rhetoric and terminology which governs them, the ideas which program them and for which they are the scene.

The decisive operation in these histories seems inevitably to be the selection and review of the greatest possible number of technical, stylistic, and formal innovations, each of which is presented (and researched) as the initiator of a succession of aesthetic developments (the "progress" of a "language"). And the culmination of the process is the cinema practiced at the time that the given historian writes, when it is discovered in its final and *perfected* form.

In other words, by an effect of inversion and misrecognition proper to ideological inscription, the cinematic practice contemporary with the historian is seen to program, determine, and originate as veritable source the historian's research into the "sources" and "origins" of that practice. Thus he hypostasizes what is here and now as the "reality" of cinema and the truth of that practice; for, since it is contemporary to the historian, he is implicated in it, and his own practice is necessarily articulated with it. In the name of a temporary and particular film practice held illusorily as knowledge of the cinema object, the historian catalogues masses of signs of forerunners of this practice. This serves to *authenticate* the moment of a practice in which he himself is implicated, that is, to *legitimize* a particular *experience.* And thus (on the model of "In the beginning" of all religious and cultural myths of origins), he transports back to cinematic ancient times, its prehistory and early history, as many of the characteristic traits of today's practice as possible. By thus finding their origin (their foundation: their law), these are constituted in a chain with a beginning, a development, and an ending; in other words, with a *logic* and a history that are *autonomous,* marginal to the determinations of the social whole.

The cataloguing and multiplication of origins thus act as *proofs* of this autonomy: the necessary usage of the expression "for the first time" *guarantees* the cogency of all the "next times," and especially the features of the cinematic practice of the moment, the "this time": the "First" at the same time valorizes, inscribes, comprehends, and bears all the rest. The eclecticism of contemporary cinema (the apparently equal status and "value" of its products, their "richness" and "diversity") is thereby condoned by a comparable eclecticism in its beginnings (there is no form which doesn't have its mold, its "original" somewhere in the beginnings of cinema), and this is all the more readily possible since the latter is a rigorous copy and retrospective projection of the former.

Thus it is indeed an ideological discourse about (notably) the ideological place of cinematographic technique which the fixed syntagm "for the first time" incessantly maintains.

A point already mentioned needs to be stressed here. In these articles we have systematically opposed two different historical approaches, and the radical distinction between them has to be kept in view, even though they both establish cinema's historical scene from its scene in the present. The first approach, criticized here, is characterized by its retrospective eclecticism. When faced with the mass of traits which together present themselves as constituting the "cinema," it is incapable of theorizing and sorting out principal contradictions from surface effects: it makes no distinction between those contradictions in film practice which are related to the contradictions of the social whole, the forces of production and the relations of production, and the secondary contradictions which come into play as derivation and occultation. It fails to separate the lines of force of the text from supplementary aesthetic effects. Instead, it unifies and brings together on the same level under the label "cinema" everything that empirically presents itself as such. The question of relevance in relation to this jumble of notations and signals is suppressed. The task is cataloguing these various manifestations and producing their "birth certificates" for history, making the mere historical record the condition as well as the justification for their present existence.

The historical scene is therefore only a double, the copy which conforms to the contemporary scene. This is not at all the case for the second approach outlined in "Notes for a materialist history of the cinema" (a previous installment in this series; *Cahiers du cinéma*, no. 230, p. 57), as "eminently critical, i.e., recursive" and constituting "the past from the lines of force of the present." This approach would begin by exposing the principal contradictions of the present moment in cinematic practice to take up again and reactivate the cinema as (and upon) the scene of its principal determinations. This would be done by bringing to the forefront the forces which the effect/function of the first approach is to drown in the mass of films. The second approach therefore cannot be envisaged outside the continuous intervention of theory on the scene of history, whereby the latter ceases to be restricted to an accumulation of "historical data," but breaks up on several levels where the articulations, interactions, and contradictions of the processes of production are in play.

The opposite of this necessity to incorporate history and theory is seen in Mitry's work, with its academic division into *History of the Cinema* on the one hand, and *Aesthetics and Psychology of the Cinema* on the other. Obviously these two pendant texts can only function by reference to each other. But since what regulates these cross-references is never determined—i.e., the definition of the history-theory relationship—they establish themselves according to the principle of a crisscrossing volley between history and aesthetics. At each difficulty, the one throws back to the other the "ball" of present practice as explanation.

Symptomatic of this to-ing and fro-ing in the ideological series of "first times," for example, is the difficulty Mitry has in settling the origin of the "first closeup."

If what is meant by "closeup" is a simple enlargement effect, its use is as old as cinema itself. The so-called "big heads" which loomed up in the midst of a series of uniform long-shots had already appeared in the films of Méliès *circa* 1901, and the fire alarm which appears in *The Life of an American Fireman* is doubtless the first closeup of an object recorded on film. But the "big heads" whose sudden appearance provoked a surprise effect derived far more from the "animated portrait" than from cinematic expression. It is only with montage, as we have seen, that shots take on meaning in relation to each other [*sic; anything else would be astonishing*—J.-L. C.]. These shots, almost all of which were discovered, experimented with, and applied by Griffith in numerous little films made in 1909 and 1910, were only brought together, organized, and structured into a coherent whole from 1911 and 1912. To say therefore that Griffith was the first to use the closeup doesn't mean that the enlargement effect was not used before him, but that he was the first to make it a means of expression by raising it to the level of a *sign*. One would look in vain in any film—even those of Griffith before 1911—for closeups used other than for descriptive ends. The closeup as we know it [?] only made its appearance in 1913, notably in *Judith of Bethulia*.[9]

This passage alone raises a number of questions:

(1) What is the relevance of the hierarchy implied by Mitry between "big heads" provoking "a surprise effect," closeups of objects, "closeups used for descriptive ends," and finally "enlargement effects raised to the level of a *sign*"? Couldn't each of these empirical categories also cover the rest? What, for instance, prevents the "big heads" from both "provoking a surprise effect" and rising to the level of a "sign"?

(2) If the problem is deciding on the "first closeup," why bring in criteria of "content" (i.e., the role of these closeups in the production of meaning) and oppose the simple "descriptive" closeups to those which are "expressive" (inasmuch as it would be difficult to argue that descriptive closeups—like that of the fire alarm—are totally devoid of dramatic effect, denoting without connoting).[10] Either the scale of the shot is important, or else, if its plastic and dramatic value is also important, mustn't one abandon the attempt to fix on "the first closeup"?

(3) What must we ultimately understand by "the closeup as we know it"? The least one can say is that "we" don't "know" a single variety, but a thousand, an infinite number, including of course the "big heads" which are still in use, and "shots used for descriptive ends."

Mitry therefore has no basis for opposing with any pertinence the "simple enlargement effect" to "a means of expression raised to the level of a sign," since the closeup-sign necessarily produces an "enlargement effect" (otherwise, no closeup) and all "enlargement effects" can also have the value of a "sign" and arise from an "expression." No basis, that is, other than the theoretical lack which makes him take a particular customary usage (the closeup "as we know it"), a certain "norm" at the time he was writing, as law and truth, because it constitutes the empirical mean for the films of the time—a mean which assures Griffith's aptitude as "experimenter" and his aesthetic rather than historical primacy. To pursue this particular instance further: the closeups of Hollywood stars no more "descend" from the closeups of Griffith's actors than they do from the "animated portraits" of Demeny (1891). We know they were due to the contractual conditions imposed by the star system: the number and kinds of closeups were prescribed even before shooting began, and before the film narrative was completely fleshed out.

No necessary equivalence links the closeups of 1913 to those of 1960 because the relevant element of opposition is not the parameter of enlargement in shots but the network of differences between the forces which determine two moments of film practice. These differences specifically preclude constituting "closeups" (or traveling shots, etc.) into an ahistorical chain and collapsing them all onto the same level. Founding thus the "closeup as we know it," Mitry effaces the scene of contradictions where the conditions of cinematographic *significance* are played out and erects instead a series of autonomous processes; these techniques, once "invented," systematized, and enthroned by some pioneer (whose practice for this very reason is not necessarily connected to that of later filmmakers), forever remain what they were on first appearance, available once and for all, usable universally and out of time—abstract molds whose nature, function, and meaning do not change (recognizable in this argument is the action of consensus which supports Lebel's technicians' discourse).

The necessary precedence of a theoretical definition of the closeup over the question of its first historical appearance is glaringly obvious here ("if one understands by 'closeup'. . . the closeup as we know it"). Unless we undertake this work of definition within the analysis of history itself, we will, like Mitry, remain imprisoned by the empirical notion of "closeup" which opens out into an intellectual flux: it never achieves the rigor of a concept because it claims to embrace and cover all closeups simply by describing their empirical existence in films already there, where each case is in fact necessarily different. Taking as a point of departure this extremely problematic—because extremely vast— "closeup as we know it" to establish its "first" inscription into history can only lead to the discovery of *more* than one—as many as one likes (in proportion to the initial grab bag): in fact, as many "as we know" empirically.

What Mitry's text demonstrates unwittingly (for to make it explicit would destroy his plan to establish the "first times") is that until a concept of the closeup has been constructed, there can be no "first" closeup since all closeups are in some sense "first";[11] Mitry's argument in fact makes plain the bankruptcy of the very "notion" of closeup which sustains it. We are thus led to question this notion of closeup as it circulates in technical and critical discourse, there "by right," unquestioned, presented as a "unit of language," whereas no closeup is inscribed as such in film texts. Not only are all closeups inscribed as a network of signifiers, a complex system, but they are also held in signifying chains which comprehend, traverse, and structure them. For example, if when he opposes the "closeup as a simple enlargement effect" to the "closeup sign," Mitry means that Griffith's closeups have a more essential function in the production of meaning than they could have in the films of Méliès (which has yet to be demonstrated), the response would be that the process of production of meaning as a whole has quite a different status in Griffith, and that isolating the "notion" of closeup to bring into play not the parameter of enlargement but the textual differences leads to an aporia. For either the closeup is always a closeup, or else what constitutes the closeup is its insertion into a signifying process, in which case the closeup cannot be isolated in a relevant way, and its "notion" produces no knowledge of its status in the functioning of film. This procedure seems, in an unconsidered (but "natural") way, to deport the "notion" of closeup from the technical practice of film production, where it is an operational index, into that of film criticism and theory, where it acts as a *false abstraction*. Precisely because it is so convenient (so easily "naturalized" into the technical-critical language), does it not mask more than it reveals of the signifying work? By abstracting, for example, the "enlargement" scale[12] as a syntactical category of "cinematic language," does technical-critical discourse produce anything besides a formalist grid aimed at concealing, fixing, and finally ousting the problematic of the signifying production; that is, doesn't it carefully maintain a mystification around the mechanisms of this production which serves to preserve the autonomy (magical power) of technique?

From this angle we need to take up the whole of Mitry's text (no doubt the most exemplary, since it attempts and fails to formulate the aesthetics-history relationship) to study systematically the status of each of the basic terms of the technical discourse in the chain of "first times": "shots," "traveling shots," "long-shots," "decor," "montage" (instructive, for instance, is his ordering of the first films to establish a narrative continuity through montage), etc. The fact that technical terminology has at all costs to be stamped with its origin is an admission of its inadequacy in the field of criticism and theory in the form in which it has been institutionalized.[13]

In fact the fetishization of "the first time" (in addition to its ideological connotations: the cult of the exploit, of the unique; everything that bourgeois ideology attaches to origin and the original as a manifestation of primacy and purity, etc.) is aimed in the case of technical devices at keeping them apart from the forces which determine them, that is, the processes in which they are held; they can therefore be presented in their totality and for all time as a chronolgical and logical linear succession, since in each case a first appearance can be marked *outside* any problematic of signifying production (i.e., the ideologies and the economies where this production is articulated) and outside the cultural codes and the signifying system which governed its status in the particular film in which it emerged "for the first time." (In other words emergence *[émergement]* = *émargement*—placing in the margin a signature which appropriates and reduces to itself the whole signfying process. To take an example from Mitry: *"Mary Jane's Mishap* [G. A. Smith, 1902]: for the first time, the idea of continuity in the cinema.") And clearly Lebel (knowingly or not) rests his claim for technique as autonomous and always open to but empty of signifying on the separation which the Histories and the Aesthetics of the cinema make between technical and signifying processes.

As soon as one interprets a technical process "for its own sake" (i.e., "the first traveling shot in the history of the cinema") by cutting it off from the signifying practice where it is not just a factor but an *effect* (i.e., not jut a "form" which "takes on" or "gives" a meaning, but itself already a meaning, a signifier activated as a signified on the other scene of film, its outside: history, economy, ideology)—it becomes an ahistorical empirical object. With a few minor adjustments (technical perfecting) it can wander from film to film, always already there and always identical to itself ("a closeup of the boss and a closeup of the worker are both a closeup"). It has this possibility in spite of and in order to *mask* the system of differences into which it is necessarily inscribed, including the contradictions between one fiction and another, one practice and another, as well as the contradictions of interests and ideologies with which the cinema is practiced and whose positive and negative marks it bears. On this "common basis" of historical, critical, and aesthetic discourses a technical scene is erected which dominates the scene of *signifiance*—since a closeup from *Jeanne d'Arc* and a closeup from *Battleship Potemkin* both refer back to the "first close-up in cinema." In other words, the discourse which proclaims technique as always open to but empty of signifying and ideologically "neutral" itself began by disassociating technique from the signifying production. *Formalist* from the beginning, it can not fail to find in its path anything besides "formal" techniques, "neutral" and "universal" forms.

Part 4
"Primitive" Depth of Field

In the case of "deep focus"[14]—as with the "closeup" (or any other term from the practice and metalanguage of technique)—it is not possible to postulate a continuous chain of connections running through the history of the cinema. And the history of "deep focus," like that of the "closeup," cannot be constructed without bringing into play a system of determinations which *are not exclusively technical*. They are rather economic and ideological, and as such they break down the boundaries of the specifically cinematic field, extending and therefore transforming it with a series of additional areas; they bring the field of cinema to bear on other scenes and integrate these other scenes into that of the cinema. They break apart the fiction of an autonomous history of the cinema—that is, of "styles and techniques." They produce the complex relationships which link the field and history of the cinema to other fields and other histories.

In the particular case of deep focus, therefore, an analysis of these economic and ideological determinations will allow us to assess the way that codes which are themselves not specifically cinematic (in this case pictorial, theatrical, and photographic), regulate the functions—i.e., *meanings*—assumed by deep focus in the process of production of meanings in film; and to assess the economic/ ideological forces which bring pressure to bear for or against the effects of this regulation and these codes. Historian-aestheticians like Mitry and theoreticians like Bazin succumbed to the attractions of the view which sees the film text and the evolution of film language as determined by technical progress (the gradual development and improvement of the means). That is, they fell prey to the idea of a "treasure house" of technique whch filmmakers could draw on "freely," according to the stylistic effects they were after; or of the technical processes as a "reserve" held somewhere independent of systems of meaning (histories, codes, ideologies), and "ready" to intervene in signifying production. To succumb to such a view they had to see the technical system in its entirety as so "natural" and so "self-generating" that the question of its utility (what is it used for?) was completely obscured by that of its utilization (how is it used?). The naturalization of the metalanguage of technique into the metalanguage of criticism and the automatic and unreasoned identification of technical devices and their actions with the "figures" of "film language" (or what Christian Metz has more rigorously called "the minimal units of signification specific to cinematic codes")[15] is precisely what constitutes the immediate problem for a materialist theory of the cinema which is not content with "the facts," nor with remaining at the level of empiricism.

A semiology of cinematographic "figures" which would fail to question the applicability of terms "consecrated by use" in identifying these "figures" also fails to deconstruct the strata of history, ideology, and code in these "terms/ figures." Such a semiology, in short, would give credence to the notion that "cinematographic language" is but one with the metalanguage of technique, the latter itself considered homologous to the metalanguage of criticism. These failures would mean missing the distinct specificity of the three levels, and the play of their gaps and contradictions. This is the direction which Christian Metz has taken in his latest work, and Pascal Bonitzer has also initiated such a deconstruction.[16] I also intend to intervene in a more detailed way on this problem and to comment on some of Metz's analyses in the third part of this article (in addition to my preceding chapter on "first times"). For it seems clear that what anchors the idea of technique as neutral (i.e., as a "pool") is the "naturalized" and unthought absorption of "cinematic language" into the metalanguage of technique, and of the latter into the metalanguage of criticism. (This idea is still very dominant today, and Lebel's book seems intent on prolonging that dominance.) The technical ideology insists on setting technical practice apart from the systems of meaning, presenting it instead as the cause producing effects of meaning in a film text, and not as itself produced, itself an effect of meaning in the signifying systems, histories, and ideologies which determine it. This technical ideology in my view draws its strength of conviction from the (distant) bearing of "science" on the technical practices that produce film. For criticism, this "science" has guaranteed the intrinsic validity of these practices and favored the unquestioned and unmodified importation of their basic terms into the metalanguage of criticism.

It is indeed about "strength of conviction" and "naturalness"—and, a corollary, about the blind spots of theoreticians—that we have to speak. Mitry, for example, raises the fact that deep focus—used almost continuously in the early years of the cinema—disappeared from the scene of film signifiers for some twenty years (with a few particular exceptions, namely certain of Renoir's films), but offers only strictly technical motivations for its shelving. Mitry thus installs technique as the deciding factor, establishing a closed and autonomous circuit where the fluctuations of technique would only be determined by other fluctuations of technique. We, on the other hand, will study the specific historical nature of deep focus as the scene of determinations which are not exclusively technical—that is, a scene of technical determinations themselves overdetermined economically and ideologically. This will give us a measure of the relative status of technical practice in the context of the other practices which articulate it; we will be able to look at the way the latter determine technical practice, thereby inscribing it into a system of meanings in which technical practice itself is made to signify. At the same time we will be able to formulate theoretically the *work* of the technical device deep focus, i.e., the *relationship*—in a particular film text or body of films—between the signifying function of deep focus and the codified signified which it inscribes there as part of, and in addition to, its signifying function: this relationship can be one of doubling or of contradiction.

From the very first films produced, the cinematic image was "naturally" a deep focus image. The majority of the films of Lumière and his cameramen (cf. *L'Arrivée d'un train en gare*) demonstrate deep focus as a constituent element of the image. Mitry provides a number of other examples, including *Attack on a Chinese Mission* (Williamson, 1900) which I cite here because it also takes its place in Mitry's chain of "first times" and recalls how Mitry is constrained by his system to introduce other than purely technical criteria into his genealogy of technical innovations: "Because he was filming in natural surroundings, Williamson, liberated from the constraints of the studio and the scenic conditions it imposed, was able to make his actors move freely. . . . They not only moved laterally in the frame, but also through depth. In *Attack on a Chinese Mission* the officer who arrives at the end of the garden to sweep a girl into his saddle, leaps straight at the spectator. We have already seen this effect produced by Lumière in *L'Arrivée d'un train en gare,* but there it was a question of *documentary filming, real movement shot by the cameraman, not a movement specifically composed for the camera*" (my emphasis).[17]

In fact, it's most often in exterior filming that the field achieves depth in this period. The reason is indisputably of a technical order: the lenses used before 1915 were, Mitry stresses, "uniquely f35 and f50"[18]—"medium" focal lengths which had to be stopped down in order to produce an image in depth, and therefore needed a great deal of light, more readily and economically obtainable outside than in the studio.

What we have to ask ourselves, therefore, is precisely why only these "medium" focal lengths were used during the first twenty years of cinema. I see no more pertinent reason than the fact that they restored the spatial relationships which corresponded to "normal vision" and that they therefore played their role in the production of the impression of reality to which the cinematograph owed its success. These lenses themselves were thus dictated by the codes of analogy and realism (other codes corresponding to other social demands would have produced other types of lenses). The depth of field which they allowed was thus also what authorized them, was the basis for their utilization and existence. It wasn't therefore just a supplementary effect whose use could be passed up as a matter of indifference. On the contrary, it was what *had* to be obtained, and it had been necessary to strive for its production. The ideological instrument cinema was made as a gamble and staked itself completely on the desire to identify, duplicate, and recognize "life" in visual forms, that is, on a relationship of identity between the cinematic image and "life itself." (Cf. the fantastic efforts made for decades by hundreds of inventors in quest of "total cinema"—the complete illusion and duplication of life, including sound, color, relief, etc.)

The ideological instrument cinema couldn't therefore have neglected the production of effects of relief and depth and failed to put into operation the patented technique which produced them. These effects strive to integrate into the image a vanishing perspective on the one hand, and, on the other, the movement of people and things along retreating lines (e.g., the train at La Ciotat station). (And the latter effect is one which photography, and painting *a fortiori,* could not provide, which is why the most perfect *trompe l'oeil,* meticulously constructed according to the laws of perspective, is, as Paulhan observed,[19] incapable of deceiving the eye.) The two effects are related: for characters to be able to move "perpendicularly" on the screen requires their being reached by light, requires depth and stratified planes—in short the code of artificial perspective. Furthermore, often in studio filming, where space was relatively tight and lighting inadequate, background was in fact provided by *trompe l'oeil* canvasses which, while they couldn't enable the movement of people in depth, did on the other hand show perspective.

We know what perspective brought with it, and therefore what deep focus brought into the film image as its constituent codes: namely, the pictorial and theatrical codes of classic Western representation. Méliès, that specialist in "illusion" and the studio film, as early as 1897 characterized his "studio" in Montreuil as "in a word, the combination of a giant photographic workshop and a theater stage."[20] And no more exact indication is needed of the double background on which the cinematic image emerged—not fortuitously, but explicitly and deliberately. Deep focus is more than just the mark of the primitive cinematic image's submission to the codes of representation and the histories and ideologies which necessarily determine and operate these codes (and Lebel can't eliminate the fact that these histories and ideologies are caught in the rise and domination of the capitalist bourgeoisie and its ideology). In more general terms, it is a sign that the ideological instrument cinema is itself produced within these codes and by these systems of representation, completing, perfecting, and surpassing them. There is nothing accidental or specifically technical in the fact that the cinematic image claims depth from the first; not only does depth dictate and inform the image, but the possibility of its restoration dictates the optical instruments which produce the image. Contrary to what the technicians seem to believe, the restoration of movement and depth are not the effects of the camera, but the camera is the effect—the solution—to the problem of their restoration.

If depth of field is thus one of the principle determining factors regulating the cinematic image (and the apparatus), it is astonishing that its almost total eclipse for fifteen to twenty years hasn't presented more of a problem for the historian-aestheticians who, like Mitry and Bazin, draw attention to this fact. The former, as we shall see, limits the analysis of the problem to purely technical difficulties, though in other parts of his *Aesthetics* he nevertheless stresses the perspective-movement link in the production of a third dimension in the cinema. This presents no problem to Mitry precisely because for him all the technical processes are equal in right and in history, equivalent to and substitutable for each other without any consequences except those reflected in the effects of meaning which the filmmaker seeks to produce. The "freedom to choose" from this panoply of technical processes which he postulates for the contemporary filmmaker (the filmmaker out of time) is extended metonymically to those processes themselves, whose essence is thus the ability to be freely chosen—the sole reservation being the technically impossible. In other words, we have a series of more or less interchangeable accessories of more or less recent date whose "fashion" may or may not catch on. But deep focus was not "modish" in 1896—it was one of the credibility factors in the film image (like, even if not quite for the same reason, the faithful reproduction of movements and figurative analogy). And in order to account for the effacement of deep focus we need to consider not just the

"delays" in the development of techniques, but the transformation of the conditions of this credibility—the displacement of the codes of cinematic verisimilitude, the levels of fictional logic (narrative codes), psychological
verisimilitude, and the impression of homogeneity and continuity (the consistent
space-time relations of classical drama). For the technical "delays" are not accidental, they are themselves involved in and effects of this displacement or
replacement of codes.

It would seem no less surprising (at least if one remains at the level of technical
causes) that a process which reigned "naturally" over the greater part of films
shot between 1895 and 1925[21] could disappear or fall into disuse for so long
without filmmakers (apart from a few, including Renoir) showing the slightest
concern. "Primitive" deep focus had been "given" to them in combination with
the film image (at least in exterior shooting). It therefore presented no problem
(unless one should want to annul it, but that would imply some reflection on its
effects, an understanding of its code, and as far as I know, no signs of this
manifested themselves during the period in question), and we could argue that
the codes it inscribes had been "internalized" by filmmakers and spectators alike.
It was not just that the film image seemed to tend "spontaneously" and naturally
toward depth. Many filmmakers played its game and worked to reinforce its
effect through a "mise-en-scène in depth." Apart from Williamson, Mitry cites
Stroheim, Feuillade's *Fantomas* (1913), and Griffith's *Intolerance* (1916). One could
add at least Stiller, Lubitsch, and Lang. What reversal took place to enable
Brunius to write in 1936:

In summer 1936 I was working with Jean Renoir on the preparations for the filming of
his *A Day in the Country* and we decided that scenes could be developed between people
more than ten metres or so from each other in depth. But it was only with the greatest
difficulty that we were able to procure old lenses, considered fossils—a few Zeiss and a
3.5 Bosch and Lomb. . . . [22]

This is Mitry's explanation:

One might ask oneself why, with rare exceptions (notably Stroheim), "depth" was
abandoned between 1925 and 1940 in favor of intensive fragmentation. Some attribute
it to fashion, others[23] to the influence of the Soviet cinema. While neither are entirely
wrong, these are not the reasons, nor are they connected with the almost exclusive use
of lenses with large apertures. Or, more exactly, the use of large apertures was itself the
consequence of something else, since to get depth one only had to stop down more. But
to get equivalent photographic quality, more light was needed. Nothing was simpler
before 1925: the use of orthochromatic film permitted lighting with arc lamps, whose
capacity for illumination was considerable; their number and power could just be increased. But beginning in 1925 panchromatic film came into general use and upset the
situation altogether. Panchromatic film was sensitive to red and to all visible light (as the
name indicates), but unevenly so, and this meant that arc lamps, whose spectrum tended
towards violet and coincided precisely with the least sensitive area of the film, could no
longer be used. Incandescent lighting was therefore resorted to. But these lamps were

not powerful enough, and, on the other hand, the first panchromatic emulsions were far less sensitive than existing emulsions. Consequently, in order for there to be adequate light, one had to "open up" the lens more rather than stop it down. Hence, the utilization of lenses with large apertures (and the consequent loss of depth); hence, the "narrowing" of the fields; and hence, the necessarily greater fragmentation. That this became a method of work normalized by routine, a mode rather than "modish," is undoubtedly true, but his so-called "cause" was never more than a consequence. A minimum of technical knowledge would have saved our theoreticians [the reference, no doubt, is to Bazin] a lot of unnecessary effort.[24]

A fine example of the technicist discourse (the final statement must have provoked laughter in the studios); the least of its weaknesses is that it resolves one difficulty by substituting *several others*.

First, the technical difficulties: it's worth pausing over these for a moment (and Mitry lists them for us), since the retracing of the (endless) chain of "technical causes" which pass the responsibility back from one to another reveals a number of *nontechnical* determinants—which it is precisely the function of this criss-crossing of "technical causes" to mask. Mitry assures us that everything stems from the "general acceptance of panchromatic film in the years after 1925." Perhaps. But to produce this as a weighty piece of evidence and immediately slide to the inadaptability of the system of lighting to the spectrum of this emulsion is exactly *not to say* what necessity is implied in this "general acceptance," what (new) functions the new film stock came to fulfill that the old one could not. It is to conjure away the question of what demanded the replacement of an emulsion in universal use, and which (if we take Mitry's word for it) was not all that mediocre, by another which, again according to Mitry, was at the outset far from its equal.

Now as far as we know, it isn't in the logic of technique, nor in the logic of the film industry (already highly structured and well-equipped in 1925) to adopt (or impose) a new product which in its early stages poses more problems than the old and therefore implies the expense of adaptation (modification of systems of lighting, lenses, etc.) *without finding something to its advantage and profit somewhere*.

And the first of these advantages is that the panchromatic film is *more sensitive* than orthochromatic, since as Mitry himself points out, even if the consequences are not followed up in his work—it is, "as its name indicates. . . sensitive to all visible light," while orthochromatic film is only sensitive to the radiations of blue and violet.

The *Dictionnaire du Cinéma*[25] describes the gain:

with orthochromatic film the various tones composing a face were unevenly transcribed into black and white. To compensate for this, actors were made up in blue and ochre. . . . In 1927 the first panchromatic emulsions were launched on the film market and the range of sensitivity was considerably enlarged. Makeup returned to almost normal colors.

The image obtained in black and white was called panchromatic, i.e., it reproduced the intensity of the normal tones within a considerably extended range of gray, black, and white.

It is not just a question of a gain in the sensitivity of the film stock, but a gain in the *faithfulness* "to natural colors"—*a gain in realism*. The film image refined and perfected its "rendering," and entered into renewed competition with the quality of the photographic image which had been using panchromatic emulsion for a long time. The reason for this "technical advance" is not purely technical (but ideological); it is not so much the greater sensitivity to light which counts as the ability "to make things more real." The hard and contrasted image of the early cinema no longer satisfied the codes of photographic realism which had been transformed and refined by the growth of photography. My view is that in the production of "realistic effects," the importance of depth (perspective) lessened with the extension of the range of tones and colors. But this is not all.

We can agree with Mitry that during the few (two or three) years of transition from orthochromatic to panchromatic film, the (bad because unadapted) conditions for the use of the new emulsion prevented a full exploitation of its greater sensitivity. But this doubly affects Mitry's argument.

First, because this necessary exploratory period was only very provisional (otherwise it would have compromised the industry itself); panchromatic film was soon perfected (in 1931 Kodak launched the supersensitive Eastman color); and an antidote was found to the arc lamp's tendency toward violet (the addition of salts—fluorides of calcium, barium, and chromium—to the carbons). One wouldn't think that a difficulty as ephemeral and as soluble as this could have seriously prohibited work with deep focus or "broken the habit of its use." One might suppose that an industry capable of shedding its skin (not just from orthochromatic to panchromatic, but from silent to sound) and of overcoming the inconveniences of these transformations could also, had it wished—i.e., if the demand had existed and exerted a pressure—obtain both a panchromatic image and deep focus without too much difficulty (the one only temporarily excluding the other). While it had been really necessary to change the emulsion, apparently no pressure was exerted to preserve deep focus. The fault in Mitry's argument (and the sense in which it is technicist) is that it explains technical transformations through other technical transformations, never for a moment considering that these transformations do not come about "freely," that they bring into play economic forces and forces of work, in short, economically and socially programed demands. There is no "technical heaven" where one method is exchangeable for another.

Second, Mitry's argument is affected because the argument limits itself according to the requirements of its cause to studio filming alone (where, of course, the power of the lamps and the sensitivity of the film is determining), "forgetting" that filmmakers went out to shoot on location in the years immediately after 1925, as they did later on. Here, all the technical difficulties ceased (panchromatic film was, moreover, more sensitive than orthochromatic), and deep focus, which was given from the start, could not therefore have posed a problem. Yet from this point until *Citizen Kane,* when it was seen again, it was *generally* reduced to the status of an additional "décor" effect in the landscapes of westerns and adventure films—in other words to being a *code* of the landscape in long-shot, the very code of filmed "nature" itself. One can go further: difficult to avoid, depth of field was on the whole not exploited and remained residual. It is this "dis-affectation," which was not always linked to a material impossibility, that must be interrogated.

In fact, in classical Hollywood cinema this residual decorative status belongs not so much to "natural" depth of field as to landscape, to nature itself. The dominance of studio filming (tied to practico-economic reasons, but also historical ones—the heritage of silent film—and ideological ones—concern for "technical perfection"), even for the majority of "exterior scenes," codified the representation of nature in genre cinema. The role of landscape was reduced to that of 'décor'—the decorative background, the painted canvas inherited from the theater and convenient for the cutting-up/assemblage operations[26] of the psychological dramas which the many silent films had brought to the screen (even if only as burlesques, as in *Our Hospitality* and most of Keaton, and the films of Lloyd and Langdon). To send a second crew to get some of the Grand Canyon's "sights" was to confirm the "truth" of the painted canvasses by duplicating the code, pictorializing natural landscapes in "decor-fashion." The determination absent from Mitry's discourse is that of the ideology of studio shooting, of the (interior/exterior) representation of space it produced.

Notes

1. See *Cahiers du cinéma,* nos. 229 (May 1971) and 230 (July 1971) for the first two parts of this text.

2. It will be observed that what happened for the "prehistory" of the cinema, the period of its invention, happens again for its "history" proper. We saw, in fact ("Birth = *différance*," *Cahiers du cinéma* (May 1971), no. 229, p. 9) how the quest for (the myth of) an origin was shattered by its encounter with the multiplicity of "inaugural inventions," and how it was exhausted in an attempt to establish the numerous acts of a dispersed production, irreducible to *single* logic, into a single causal chain (a progression). The histories of the cinema *would like* to find their object had an *origin* and a *unity,* in fact that it conformed to their concern for autonomy and linearity. Instead they find it dispersed, contradictory, never completely there; they refuse to analyze this birth and this history as *difference* and *différance* and strive pathetically through their discourse to patch up the breaches which specifically preclude *that* discourse; they make themselves the scene of contradictions which explode all possibility of a single scene of operation. That is, their discourse produces a "dream" object: "the invention of the cinema" or "the cinema," the absence of which object they imperturbably deny and about which they imperturbably comment. It is therefore the method which needs to be changed. The complexity of determinations and the

multiplicity of scenes where production is in play, whether this be technical, "aesthetic," or signifying production, can only be thought through the Marxist science of history.

[EDITOR'S NOTE: A comment on a term used here might be helpful for understanding Comolli's project. *Différance* is a neologism developed by Jacques Derrida. The French verb *différer* means both to differ and to defer. *Différance* is an invented noun form marking the combination of the two senses in a single word. This term is part of a complex philosophical argument which includes the notion that a neologism is necessary to point toward—though it can never adequately name or signify—the principle underlying the differentiated structure of language as well as that which drives language and knowledge toward an impression of adequacy or "presence."

Here we may say very briefly that, for Derrida, something which manifests a meaning or identity can never be fully present in its manifestation; it is always mediated. Hence, any manifestation or experience is always *different* from what it "professes" to be, and an experience of its full presence is "always already" *deferred*. As Derrida's translator Gayatri Chakravorty Spivak puts it, "*differance*—being the structure (a structure never quite there, never by us perceived, itself deferred and different) of our psyche—is also the structure of 'presence,' a term itself under erasure. For *differance*, producing the differential structure of our hold on 'presence,' never produces presence as such."

Comolli mobilizes Derrida's term as part of his critique of film scholars who, explicity or implicitly, see the historian's task as devising an account of "firsts." For example, Comolli attacks the illusion that if one can name the first time cinema appeared, one has focused on the generative identity of cinema itself. Comolli wishes to stress the discursive and differential character both of the historian's task and of historical "material" itself. Instead of assuming a punctual, unified source of all cinema history ("the" "birth" of cinema), Comolli argues for the dispersed quality of historical phenomena and events. In previous installments, Comolli argued that if one searches for the birth of cinema, one will continually find side paths, a complex of events, factors, and determinations not reducible to a single, unified origin. Hence, for the historian the birth of cinema should be constantly found in difference and as deferred; therefore "birth = *différance*."

Derrida's essay "Differance" is in his *Speech and Phenomena, and other essays on Husserl's Theory of Signs*, trans. David B. Allison (Evanston: Northwestern University Press, 1973). See the translator's preface in Jacques Derrida, *Of Grammatology*, trans. Gayatri Chakravorty Spivak (Baltimore: Johns Hopkins University Press, 1976), *passim* and pp. xliii–xliv.]

3. See Julia Kristeva, *Sémeiotikè: Recherches pour une Sémanalyse* (Paris: Seuil, 1969); "Littérature, Sémiotique, Marxisme," interview with Christine Glucksmann and Jean Peytard, *Nouvelle Critique* (November 1970), no. 38; and "Pratique analytique, pratique révolutionnaire," *Cinéthique* (1971), no. 9–10.

4. Kristeva, *Sémiotikè*, p. 16.

5. [*Signifiance* is a special term introduced by Julia Kristeva. It is equivalent neither to signifier *(signifiant)* nor signifed *(signifié)* nor significance. Kristeva explains *signifiance* is a force subtending all signification, but which is exploited especially by modernist texts. As Comolli indicates, these underlying processes of signification are what produce the possibility of meaning. Therefore, in any instance of signification the existence of *signifiance* may be more heavily or less heavily marked (which can serve as an account of the relations between classical and modernist textuality).

But if *signifiance* is the underlying processes which enable meaning, this is precisely why it is in some sense other than and outside meaning. In Kristeva, it has a number of associations: with *work* on the signifier (rather than deemphasizing the characteristics of the signifier in order to stress the signified/meaning), with textual excess, with psychoanalytic conceptualization of the drives and the unconscious. It designates a certain "alterity," something beyond meaning in the very processes that produce "communication." Comolli's use of the concept of *signifiance* allies itself with his use of the concept of *différance*: they both function in his argument to signal a resistance to any quick unification of history or films around meaning ("the" meaning of history,

440 Jean-Louis Comolli

or films taken solely from the perspective of their "meanings"); and both terms support a dialectic between meaning and/or signifying system on the one hand, and the nonspeakable processs and forces underlying discursive "surfaces" that produce those surfaces on the other.

Since *signifiance* both is necessary to "ordinary communication," and is there repressed, it can provide the basis for kinds of "countersignification," where its existence would be figured. Furthermore, as Comolli will argue, one can construct a history of *signifiances*—the various modes of repressing *signifiance* and/or figuring and exploiting it at different times and places.

Comolli's reference is to Kristeva's essay "La Texte et sa science" in her collection *Sémiotikè*. In that essay, pp. 8–12 provide a general, schematic introduction to the concept of *signifiance* on which this note has drawn.—ED.]

6. "The dialectical distinction signifier/ideology is all the more important when the problem is constructing the theory of a concrete signifying practice—for example, the cinema. Substituting ideology for the signifier is in this case not just a theoretical error; it leads to a blockage of the *work* that is properly cinematic, replacing it with discourses on its ideological *function*." Kristeva, "Pratique analytique, pratique révolutionnaire," p. 72. This observation, which is published in *Cinéthique* nos. 9–10, seems also to be *aimed* at *Cinéthique* 9–10 where the flattening of the signifier under ideology takes the form of law. A reading of our editorial statement "Cinéma/idéologie/critique," in *Cahiers du cinéma*, no. 216, p. 13b, will show that our position does not date from today; the paragraph referred to also situates "films of *rupture*."

[This editorial, "Cinema/Ideology/Criticism," was translated in *Screen* (1971) vol. 12, no. 1 and reprinted in John Ellis, ed., *Screen Reader 1* (London: Society for Education in Film and Television, 1977)—TRANS..]

7. Kristeva, *Sémioitikè* p. 11.

8. *Ibid.*, p. 13.

9. J. Mitry, *Esthétique et psychologie du cinéma*, 2 vols. Paris: (Ed. Universitaires, 1963 and 1965), 1:162, 163.

[At the time Comolli's series appeared, only the first two volumes of Jean Mitry's *Histoire du cinéma: Art et industrie* (Paris: Ed. Universitaires, 1967 and 1969) had been completed. Comolli's remarks on Mitry's *Histoire* seem to be based on volume 1 (subtitled 1895–1914).—ED.]

10. Which Mitry doesn't fail to observe *elsewhere*, in passages of both the *Aesthetic* and the *History:* "for the first time a closeup (showing the fire alarm) took on dramatic meaning. This was no longer the simple enlargement of a detail, but the enhancement of an object on which the resolution of the drama depended" (Mitry, *Esthétique*, 1:274). This formula is repeated almost word for word in his *Histoire*, 1:235: "The closeup of the fire alarm, although isolated, is no longer a simple enlargement of a detail, but the enhancement of an object on which the resolution of the drama depends." This kind of contradiction between the two observations quoted and the passage analyzed above is not to be read as an "error" but as the logic of the system: to meet demands of a new "first time," each new "first closeup" (Griffith's, for example) relegates the preceding one to a lower rank.

11. Thus in his *History*, Mitry is constantly forced by his system to name ever-new particularizations of the "first closeup." For example: "Smith was also the first to combine the effects of lighting with his closeups" (*Histoire*, 1:227).

12. See on this point Pascal Bonitzer, "'Realité de la dénotation," *Cahiers du cinéma* (May 1971), no. 229, pp. 39–41, esp. note 1.

13. In addition to what has been said on the "closeup," we will limit ourselves to a relatively simple example of the "first traveling shot," leaving open to later work the important problematic of the "first montage." We read in Mitry's *Histoire*, 1:113:

. . . Promio, profiting from a stay in Italy, had the idea of mounting his camera on a gondola. The viewpoint was "fixed" as always until 1909, but the displacement of the gondola recorded wide panoramic views such that *The Grand Canal of Venice* (1897) was the first "traveling" shot ever realized. Proud of his discovery,

Promio then fixed his camera on a variety of moving objects such as a train carriage, the bridge of a liner, and the Mont Blanc chair lift.

A response to which comes in the *Histoire* (1:151):

The *traveling shot* can be understood in a variety of ways. It may be a question of filming in movement, i.e., recording a landscape from a moving train, a vehicle, a chair lift, etc., where the camera remains stationary and moves with the moving object on which it is situated [?]. This kind of "traveling shot" is as old as the cinema itself *(The Grand Canal of Venice,* filmed by Promio in 1899 *[sic]).* What is understood more generally by this term is the "dollying" of the camera on a platform mounted on rails or on wheels. The camera thus advances in concert with, for example, two people walking along a road, but with a movement independent of them. That is, it can either precede them and allow itself to be overtaken, so as to show them at closer range, or inversely it can follow and gain on them. Or again, it can follow them laterally. This traveling shot according with the displacement of actors was used for the first time by Griffith in 1909. The closed-circuit traveling shot [?] in a fixed group of people, where the camera seizes on the actions of some of the characters of the drama or "figures" the displacement of any of them, is much more recent. . . . It was used for the first time in 1925 by Murnau in *The Last Laugh.*

But on 1:407 of the *Histoire* we already have this contradictory "precision":

In *The Massacre* (Griffith, 1912), for the first ever, large-scale *descriptive* [?] traveling shots, following characters, situating locations, presenting events (with a camera mounted on a dolly three years before Patrone's famous "carello").

The height of confusion is reached in Mitry's note to this last passage.

In his *Histoire général du cinéma* (Paris Denoël, vol. 3, p. 83), G. Sadoul contests the originality of these traveling shots: "It's worth recalling," he notes at the bottom of the page, "that the first examples we know of traveling shots predate *The Massacre* by more than ten years." We would like to know what traveling shots he has in mind. Obviously he is thinking of *The Grand Canal of Venice.* But are these really travelling shots? . . . A fixed shot from a moving element—train, car, etc.—records only the displacement of the landscape and is not properly speaking a traveling shot, any more than is the dollying forward of the camera toward a black background in *L'Homme a la tête de Caoutchouc* (Méliés, 1902), which aimed not at bringing the head *closer,* but at its *enlargement.* Apart from these examples and their analogies *(The Great Train Robbery,* etc.), there was *no* traveling shot in any film before 1912, the first having been produced as we said by Griffith in *The Sands of Dee* (1912).

Without dwelling on the contradictions between the dates given (ludicrous nevertheless for a historian who claims to be settling "first times": does the "descriptive traveling shot following the characters" date from 1909 or did it appear "for the first time in the world" in 1912?), let's look at those which bear on the definition of the very processes of the "traveling shot." There is cause for astonishment in the radical distinction which Mitry makes between the "fixed camera mounted on a moving element," and the camera "dollied" on "a platform mounted on rails or on wheels": of course the moving object supporting the camera is not of the same order, but in both cases the latter is displaced in the same way and the shot produced by this displacement is of the same type, whether the displacement is that of a gondola, a train, a dolly, etc. Whatever the mobile support which carries it, the camera is not "fixed," and the shot which it records is defined as being in movement. The concern for technical precision which found this distinction (train/dolly) cannot itself guarantee the slightest technical and/or stylistic difference between the takes effected by one or the other means, both of which are mobile in any case. Thus, in this opposition Mitry is putting determinants other than the specifically technical ones into operation: the fact, for example, that in *The Grand Canal* there is neither the fiction nor the characters which are in play in the films of Griffith. Once again (see above on the closeup) the relevant criteria which decide technical primacy are not themselves technical, which simultaneously manifests both the conceptual inadequacy of technical terms and the dependence of technical processes on the signifying chains and on the narrative codes in which they take part. Note again how specious is the distinction operating between the traveling shot which "advances" and the traveling shot which "enlarges": all dollying forward both brings the camera closer to its subject and makes it enlarge within the frame. It is not clear therefore what would prevent *L'Homme à la tête de Caoutchouc* (also) being credited with a "first traveling shot," except that Mitry again interposes—without saying it and undoubtedly without realizing it—the precise context of the production of the particular traveling shot: trick effect in Méliès, narrative effect in Griffith.

14. See the beginning of the text in *Cahiers du cinéma,* nos. 229 (May 1971), 230 (July 1971), 231 (August–September 1971).

15. Christian Metz, *Langage et cinéma* (Paris: Larousse, 1971) and particularly the chapter "Tendance pansémique de certaines figures" (pp. 98–103) to which I shall return subsequently.

16. Metz, *Langage et cinéma;* Pascal Bonitzer, three articles in *Cahiers du cinéma:* "'Réalité de la denotation"; "Le Gros Orteil" (October 1971) no. 232; and "Fétchisme du plan" in this issue [(November 1971), no. 233]. Metz's concern to unravel the overabounding terminological and conceptual confusions in critical and theoretical metalanguage invites one to extend the concern to technical metalanguage.

17. Mitry, *Esthétique,* 1:273.

18. *Ibid.,* p. 149.

19. Paulhan, *La Peinture Cubiste* (Denoël-Gonthier, Médiations), p. 86.

20. Quoted by Jean Vivié, *Historique et développement de la technique cinematographique* (B. P. I.), p. 64. This work does not come near to carrying out the program inscribed by its title. It is symptomatic that no "history of cinematographic technique" exists, at least none in French. There are practical manuals and glosses on the fabrication of the "first" equipment, but outside this mythical past and this present of practice (and even the future of "progress"), the technicians have no history.

21. This date is the one given by Mitry. It's not the only one, as we shall see. Brunius, agreeing with Bessy and Chardans' *Dictionary* [see note 25—ED.] gives 1927 (the sound film). There may well be a relationship (direct or indirect) between the disappearance of depth of field and the coming of sound.

22. Quoted in *La Revue de cinéma* (January 1947), no. 4, p. 24. (The question of depth of field recurs all through this issue.) Quotations drawn from J. B. Brunius' *Photographie et photographie de cinéma* (Arts et Métiers graphiques, 1938).

23. One wonders who: if the date of change is indeed around 1925, "the influence of Soviet cinema" could not possibly have been strong.

24. Mitry, *Esthétique,* 2:41.

25. By Maurice Bessy and J.-L. Chardans (Pauvert): the only dictionary in which there are some technical details and a little technical history. *L'Encyclopaedie Universalis,* in the chapter "Technique d'un cinema," gives the title "Emulsions" to a paragraph which treats only the format of films.

26. ["Cutting-up/assemblage operations" is a rendering of Comolli's term *découpement.* There seems to be no English term which captures the implications of the French. Briefly, a possible sense of the verb *découper* is not only to cut into pieces, but also to carve out. Thus one of Comolli's points is that the psychological dramas in silent film involve a "carving out," whereby the mot pertinent elements of the psychological drama occur in the foreground and are played out against the scenic background. (This can be quite evident for some films in the use of process shots.)

But for cinema the noun *découpage* has specialized meanings. To begin with, it is rooted in the verb *couper,* to cut, which as in English can denote the activity of editing a film. However, *découpage* itself means something like the English terms "shooting script," "storyboard," or "shot breakdown." In addition, in his *Theory of Film Practice,* trans. Helen R. Lane (New York: Praeger,

1973), Noël Burch glosses the French term, pointing out some of its further potential not captured in English renderings. As Burch puts it on p. 4:

Formally, a film consists of a succession of fragments excerpted from a spatial and temporal continuum. *Découpage* in its [further] meaning refers to what results when the spatial fragments, or, more accurately, the succession of spatial fragments excerpted in the shooting process, converge with the temporal fragments whose duration may be roughly determined during the shooting, but whose final duration is established only on the editing table.

Thus, the noun *découpage* implies the synthetic organizational structure underlying and governing the spatiotemporal composition of a film—the specific mode by which a film cuts up and joins together time and space.

It seems, then, that with the term *découpement* Comolli is not solely highlighting the codified and organized stratification and sectioning ("cutting-up/assemblage") of the dramatic scene in terms of the *spatial* organization of a given *frame*. In addition, he is simultaneously (if somewhat implicitly) indicating that that this "synchronic" construction of space is tied to the *temporal* organization of spatial fragments ("cutting-up/assemblage") in the classical cinematic system of signification. That is, Comolli suggests that relations of temporal fragments (often highlighted in discussions of editing) are tied to another axis of the partitioning of space, one which (for the period he is interested in) gives much emphasis to the organization of depth planes; and that the history of the classical cinematic construction of space is to be theorized along both these axes. Their mobilization as part of the heritage of the "psychological drama" of the silent period provides one avenue of thinking through their interrelation. Perhaps it is to emphasize his doubled use of the term that Comolli uses *découpement* rather than the more usual *découpage* here.—ED.]

—Translated by Diana Matias.
Revisions in translation by Marcia Butzel and Philip Rosen

24

A collective text by the Editors of Cahiers du Cinéma
John Ford's *Young Mr Lincoln*

Lincoln is not the product of popular revolution: the banal game of universal suffrage, ignorant of the great historical tasks that must be achieved, has raised him to the top, him, a plebeian, a self-made man who rose from being a stonebreaker to being the Senator for Illinois, a man lacking intellectual brilliance, without any greatness of character, with no exceptional value, because he is an average, well-meaning man.—Marx and Engels[1]

At one point in our interview, Mr. Ford was talking about a cut sequence from *Young Mr Lincoln,* and he described Lincoln as a shabby figure, riding into town on a mule, stopping to gaze at a theater poster. "The poor ape," he said, "wishing he had enough money to see Hamlet." Reading over the edited version of the interview it was one of the few things Ford asked me to change; he said he didn't much like "the idea of calling Mr Lincoln a poor ape."—John Ford[2]

Young Mr Lincoln: American film by John Ford. *Script:* Lamar Trotti. *Photography:* Bert Glennon. *Music:* Alfred Newman *Art direction:* Richard Day, Mark Lee Kirk. *Set decorations:* Thomas Little. *Editor:* Walter Thompson. *Costume:* Royer. *Sound assistant:* Robert Parrish. *Cast:* Henry Fonda (Abraham Lincoln), Alice Brady (Abigail Clay), Arleen Whelan (Hannah Clay), Marjorie Weaver (Mary Todd), Eddie Collins (Efe Turner), Pauline Moore (Ann Rutledge), Ward Bond (J. Palmer Cass), Richard Cromwell (Matt Clay), Donald Meek (John Felder), Judith Dickens (Carrie Sue), Eddie Quillan (Adam Clay), Spencer Charters (Judge Herbert A. Bell), Milburn Stone (Stephen A. Douglas), Cliff Clark (Sheriff Billings), Robert Lowery (juror), Charles Tannen (Ninian Edwards), Francis Ford (Sam Boone), Fred Kohler, Jr. (Scrub White), Kay Linaker (Mrs. Edwards), Russel Simpson (Woolridge), Charles Halton (Hawthorne), Clarence Wilson (Dr. Mason), Edwin Maxwell (John T. Stuart), Robert Homans (Mr. Clay), Jack Kelly (Matt Clay boy), Dickie Jones (Adam Clay boy), Harry Tyler (barber), Louis Mason (clerk), Jack Pennick (Big Buck), Steven Randall (juror), Paul Burns, Frank Orth, George Chandler,

Published as "Young Mr. Lincoln, texte collectif" in *Cahiers du cinéma* (August 1970), no. 223 and translated in *Screen* (Autumn 1972), 13:5–44. Reprinted by permission of *Cahiers du cinéma,* and translation used by permission of the Society for Education in Film and Television.

Dave Morris, Dorothy Vaughan, Virginia Brissac, Elizabeth Jones. *Producer:* Kenneth Macgowan. *Executive producer:* Darryl F. Zanuck. *Production:* Cosmopolitan/Twentieth Century Fox, 1939. *Distribution:* Associated Cinemas. Length: 101min.

1.

This text inaugurates a series of studies the need for which was indicated in the editorial of issue no. 218. We must now specify the objects and method of this work, and the origin of its necessity which has hitherto been merely affirmed.

1. Object: A certain number of "classic" films, which today are *readable* (and therefore, anticipating our definition of method we will designate this work as one of reading) insofar as we can distinguish the historicity of their inscription:[3] the relation of these films to the codes (social, cultural. . .) for which they are a site of intersection, and to other films, themselves held in an intertextual space; therefore, the relation of these films to the ideology which they convey, a particular "phase" which they represent, and to the events (present, past, historical, mythical, fictional) which they aimed to represent.

For convenience we will retain the term "classic" (though obviously in the course of these studies we will have to examine, and perhaps even challenge it, in order finally to construct its theory). The term is convenient in that it roughly designates a cinema which has been described as based on analogical representation and linear narrative ("transparency" and "presence") and is therefore apparently completely held within the "system" which subtends and unifies these concepts. It has obviously been possible to consider the Hollywood cinema as a model of such "classicism" insofar as its reception has been totally dictated by this system—and limited to a kind of nonreading of the films assured by thier apparent nonwriting, which was seen as the very essence of their mastery.

2. Our work will therefore be a *reading* in the sense of a *rescanning* of these films. That is, to define it negatively first: (a) it will not be (yet another) commentary. The function of the commentary is to distill an ideally constituted sense presented as the object's ultimate meaning (which however remains elusive indefinitely, given the infinite possibilities of talking about film): a wandering and prolific pseudoreading which misses the reality of the inscription, and substitutes for it a discourse consisting of a simple ideological delineation of what appear(s) to be the main statement(s) of the film at a given moment.

(b) Nor will it be a new *interpretation,* i.e., the translation of what is supposed to be already in the film into a critical system (metalanguage) where the interpreter has the kind of absolute knowledge of the exegetist blind to the (historical) ideological determination of his practice and his object–pretext, when he is not a hermeneute à la Viridiana slotting things into a preordained structure.

(c) Nor will this be a dissection of an object conceived of as a closed structure, the cataloguing of progressively smaller and more "discrete" units; in other words, an inventory of the elements which ignores their predestination for the filmmaker's writing project and, having added a portion of intelligibility to the initial object, claims to deconstruct, then reconstruct that object, without taking any account of the dynamic of the inscription. Not, therefore, a mechanistic structural reading.

(d) Nor finally will it be a demystification in the sense where it is enough to relocate the film within its historical determinations, "reveal" its assumptions, declare its problematic and its aesthetic prejudices and criticize its statement in the name of a mechanically applied materialist knowledge, in order to see its collapse and feel no more needs to be said. This amounts to throwing the baby out with the bathwater without getting wet. To be more precise, it would be disposing of the film in a moralist way, with an argument which separates the "good" from the "bad," and evading any effective reading of it. (An effective reading can only be such by returning on its own deciphering operation and by integrating its functioning into the text it produces, which is something quite different from brandishing a method—even if it is Marxist-Leninist—and leaving it at that.)

It is worth recalling that the external and mechanistic application of possibly even rigorously constructed concepts has always tried to pass for the exercise of a theoretical practice: and—though this has long been established—that an artistic product cannot be linked to its sociohistorical context according to a linear, expressive, direct causality (unless one falls into a reductionist historical determinism), but that it has a complex, mediated, and *decentered* relationship with this context, which has to be rigorously specified (which is why it is simplistic to discard "classic" Hollywood cinema on the pretext that since it is part of the capitalist system it can only reflect it). Walter Benjamin has insisted strongly on the necessity to consider literary work (but similarly any art product) not as a reflection of the relations of production, but as having a place *within* these relations (obviously he was talking of progressive works, past, present, and to come; but a materialist reading of art products which appear to lack any intentional critical dimension concerning capitalist relations of production must do the same thing. We will return later at greater length to this basic notion of "the author as producer"). In this respect we must once again quote Macherey's theses on literary production (in particular those concerning the Leninist corrections to Trotsky and Plekhanov's simplistic positions on Tolstoy) and Badiou's concerning the autonomy of the aesthetic process and the complex relation historical truth/ideologies/author (as place and not as "internalization")/work.

And that, given this, denouncing ideological assumptions and ideological production, and designating them as falsification and error, has never sufficed to ensure that those who operated the critique themselves produced truth. Nor what's more has it sufficed to bring out the truth about the very things they are opposing. It is therefore absurd to demand that a film account for what it doesn't say about the positions and the knowledge which form the basis from which it is being questioned; and it is too easy (but of what use?) to "deconstruct" it in the name of this same knowledge (in this case, the science of historical materialism which has to be practiced an active method and not used as a guarantee). Lest we be accused of dishonesty, let us make it clear that the points made in paragraph (d) refer to the most extreme positions within *Cinéthique*.

3. At this point we seem to have come up against a contradiction: we are not content to demand that a film justify itself vis-à-vis its context, and at the same time we refuse to look for "depth," to go from the "literal meaning" to some "secret meaning"; we are not content with what it says (what it intends to say). This is only an apparent contradiction. What will be attempted here through a rescansion of these films in a process of active reading, is to make them say what they have to say *within* what they leave unsaid, to reveal their constituent lacks; these are neither faults in the work (since these films, as Jean-Pierre Oudart has clearly demonstrated—see the preceding issue—are the work of extremely skilled filmmakers) nor a deception on the part of the author (for why should he practice deception?); they are *structuring absences,* always displaced—an overdetermination which is the only possible basis from which these discourses could be realized, the unsaid included in the said and necessary to its constitution. In short, to use Althusser's expression—"the internal shadows of exclusion."

The films we will be studying do not need filling out, they do not demand a teleological reading, nor do we require them to account for their *external* shadows (except purely and simply to dismiss them); all that is involved is traversing their statement to locate what sets it in place, to double their writing with an active reading to reveal what is already there, but silent (see the notion of *palimpsest* in Barthes and Daney), to make them say not only "what this says, but what it doesn't say because it doesn't want to say it" (J. A. Miller, and we would add: what, while intending to leave unsaid, it is nevertheless obliged to say).

4. What is the use of such a work? We would be obliged if the reader didn't envisage this as a "Hollywood revisited." Anyone so tempted is advised to give up the reading with the very next paragraph. To the rest we say: that the structuring absences mentioned above and the establishment of an ersatz which this dictates have some connection with the sexual *other scene,* and that "other other scene" which is politics; that the double repression—politics and eroticism—which our reading will bring out (a repression which cannot be indicated once and for all and left at that but rather has to be written into the constantly renewed process of its repression) allows the answer to be deduced; and this is an answer whose very question would not have been possible without the two

discourses of overdetermination, the Marxist and the Freudian. This is why we will not choose films for their value as "eternal masterpieces" but rather because the negatory force of their writing provides enough *scope* for a reading—because they can be rewritten.

2. Hollywood in 1938–1939

One of the consequences of the 1929 economic crisis was that the major banking groups (Morgan, Rockefeller, DuPont, Hearst, General Motors, etc.) strengthened their grip on the Hollywood firms which were having problems (weakened by the talkies' "new patents war").

As early as 1935, the five Major Companies (Paramount, Warner, MGM, Fox, RKO) and the three Minor (Universal, Columbia, United Artists) were totally controlled by bankers and financiers, often directly linked to one company or another. Big business' grip on Hollywood had already translated itself (aside from economic management and the ideological orientation of the American cinema) into the regrouping of the eight companies in the MPPA (Motion Pictures Producers Association) and the creation of a central system of self-censorship (the Hays code—the American bank is known to be puritanical: the major shareholder of the Metropolitan in New York, Morgan, exercise a real censorship on its programs).

It was precisely in 1935 that, under the aegis of the Chase National Bank, William Fox's Fox (founded in 1914) merged with Darryl F. Zanuck's 20th Century Productions, to form 20th Century Fox, where Zanuck became vice-president and took control.

During the same period, and mainly in 1937–1938 the American cinemas suffered from a very serious drop in box-office receipts (this is first attributed to the consequences of the recession, then, with the situation getting worse, to lack of regeneration of Hollywood's stock of stars); the bank's boards, very worried, ordered a *maximum reduction in costs of production.* This national marketing crisis (in a field in which Hollywood films previously covered their entire costs, foreign sales being mainly a source of profits) was made even worse by the reduced income from foreign sales; this was due to the political situation in Europe, the gradual closure of the German and Italian markets to American films, and the currency blockade set up by these two countries.

3. The USA in 1938–1939

In 1932, in the middle of the economic crisis, the Democrat Roosevelt became President, succeeding the Republican Hoover whose policies, both economic (favorable to the trusts, deflationist) and social (leaving local groups and charitable organizations to deal with unemployment: see *Mr. Deeds Goes to Town,* Capra) had been incapable of avoiding the crisis and also of suppressing its effects. Roosevelt's policies were the opposite; federal intervention in the whole country's economic and social life, states as private powers (New Deal); establishment of federal intervention and public works agencies, impinging on the rights and areas previously reserved to state legislature and private companies; a controlled economy, social budget, etc.: so many measures which encountered violent opposition from the Republicans and big business. In 1935 they succeeded: the Supreme Court declares Roosevelt's federal economic intervention agencies to be unconstitutional (because they interfere with the rights of the states). But Roosevelt's second victory in 1936 smashed these maneuvers, and the Supreme Court, threatened with reform, ended up by recognizing the New Deal's social policies and (among others) the right to unionize.

At the level of the structures of American society, the crisis and its remedies have caused the strengthening of the federal state and increased its control over the individual states and the Trust's policies: by its "conditional subsidies," its nationwide economic programs, its social regulations, the federal government took control of vast areas which had previously depended only on the authority of the states and on the interests of free enterprise. In 1937, "the dualist" interpretation of the tenth amendment to the Constitution—which forbade any federal intervention in the economic and social policies of the states (their private domain)—was abrogated by the Supreme Court from its judgments. This strengthening of federal power at all levels had the effect of *increasing the President's power.*

But, as early as 1937, a new economic crisis emerged: economic activity dropped by 37 percent compared to 1929, the number of unemployed was again over 10 million in 1938, and despite the refloating of major public works, stayed at 9 million in 1939 (see *The Grapes of Wrath*). The war (arms industries becoming predominant in the economy) was to help end the new crisis by allowing full employment. . .

Federal centralism, isolationism, economic reorganization (including Hollywood), strengthening of the Democrat-Republican opposition, new threats of internal and international crisis, crisis and restrictions in Hollywood itself; such is the fairly gloomy context of the *Young Mr. Lincoln* (1939) undertaking.

It is no doubt difficult, but necessary, to attempt to estimate the total and respective importance of these factors to the project and the ideological "message" of the film. In Hollywood, more than anywhere else the cinema is not "innocent." Creditor of the capitalist system, subject to its constraints, its crises, its contradictions, the American cinema, the main instrument of the ideological superstructure, is heavily determined at every level of its existence. As a product of the capitalist sytem and of its ideology, its role is in turn to reproduce the one and thereby to help the survival of the other. Each film, however, is inserted into this circuit according to its specificity, and there has been no analysis if one is content to say that each Hollywood film confirms and spreads the ideology of American capitalism: it is the precise articulations (rarely the same from one film to the next) of the film and of the ideology which must be studied (see 1).

4. Fox and Zanuck

20th Century Fox (which produced *Young Mr Lincoln*), because of its links with big business, also supports the Republican Party. From its inception the Republican Party has been the party of the "Great Families." Associated with (and an instrument of) industrial development, it rapidly became the "party of big business" and follows its social and economic directives: protectionism to assist industry, anti-unionist struggle, moral reaction, and racism (directed against immigrants and blacks—whom the party had fleetingly championed in Lincoln's time: but it is common knowledge that this was due once again to economic reasons and to pressures from religious groups, groups which fifty years later were to lead a campaign against everything that is "un-American").

In power from 1928 to 1932 with Hoover as President, the Republican Party is financed by some of Hollywood's masters (Rockefeller, Dupont de Nemours, General Motors, etc). At the elections in 1928 87 percent of the people listed in *Who's Who in America* supported Hoover. He has put the underwriters of capital at key posts in the administration: the Secretary of the Treasury is none other than Mellon, the richest man in the world (take an example of his policies: he brings down the income tax ceiling from 65 percent in 1919 to 50 percent in 1921, and 26 percent in 1929).

Forced by Roosevelt to make a number of concessions, American big business goes to war against the New Deal as soon as the immediate effects of the depression decrease (for example, the private electricity companies withdraw their advertising—which, in the USA is equivalent to a death sentence—from the newspapers which support Roosevelt and his Tennessee Valley Authority) and they do everything in their power to win the 1940 election.

All this allows us to assume that in 1938–1939, Fox, managed by the (also) Republican Zanuck, participated in its own way in the Republican offensive by producing a film on the legendary character Lincoln. Of all the Republican Presidents, he is not only the most famous, but on the whole the only one capable of attracting mass support, because of his humble origins, his simplicity, his righteousness, his historical role, and the legendary aspects of his career and his death.

This choice is, no doubt, all the less fortuitous on the part of Fox (which—through Zanuck and the contracted producer Kenneth Macgowan—is as usual responsible for taking the initiative in the project, and not Ford) that during the preceding season, the Democrat Sherwood's play "Abe Lincoln in Illinois" had been a great success on Broadway. With very likely the simultaneous concern to anticipate the adaptations planned in Hollywood of Sherwood's play (John Cromwell's film with Raymond Massey came out the same year and, unlike Ford's, was very successful), and to reverse the impact of the play and of Lincoln's myth in favor of the Republicans, Zanuck immediately put *Young Mr. Lincoln* into production—it would, however, be wrong to exaggerate the film's political determinism which cannot, under any circumstances, be seen, in contrast, for example, to Zanuck's personal productions, *The Grapes of Wrath,* or *Wilson,* as promoting the company's line.

Producer Kenneth Macgowan's past is that of a famous theater man. Along with Robert Edmond Jones and Eugene O'Neill, he has been manager of the Provincetown Playhouse; they had had a considerable influence on American theater. A friend of Ford's, whom he met at RKO during the period of *The Informer,* he moved over to Fox in 1935 (there he produced *Four Men and a Prayer* among others) and became the man responsible for historical biographies which constitute the core of the company's productions.

Young Mr. Lincoln is far from being one of Fox's most important productions in 1939, but this film was shot in particularly favorable conditions; it is one of the few cases in which the original undertaking was least distorted, at least at the production stage: of thirty films produced by Macgowan in the eight years he spent at Fox (1935–1943) this is one of the only two which were written by only one scriptwriter (Lamar Trotti) (the other being *The Return of Frank James,* written by S. M. Hellman). Another thing to remark on: these two scripts were written in close collaboration with the directors, who were, therefore, involved at a very early stage instead of being chosen at the last minute, as is the custom, even at Fox (the "directors studio"). Ford even says of the script: "We wrote it together" (with L. Trotti), a rare if not exceptional statement coming from him.

Lamar Trotti had already written two comedies on old America for Ford (of the species known as "Americana"), *Judge Priest* and *Steamboat Round the Bend,* before specializing in historical films with Fox (such as *Drums Along the Mohawk,* directed by Ford after *Young Mr. Lincoln*).

The background to a whole section of the script is the obsession with lynching and legality which is so strong in the thirties' cinema, because of the increase in expeditve justice (lynching), the consequences of gangsterism, the rebirth of terrorist organizations such as the KKK (see Lang's *Fury,* Mervyn LeRoy's *They Won't Forget,* Archie Mayo's *Black Legion*). Trotti, a Southerner (he was born in Atlanta and had been a crime reporter before editing a local Hearst paper), combined one of Lincoln's most famous anecdotes with a memory from his youth. "When Trotti was a reporter in Georgia he had covered the trial of two young men accused of murder at which their mother, the only witness, would not tell which son had committed the crime. Both were hanged" (Robert G. Dickson, "Kenneth Macgowan" in *Films in Review,* Ootober 1963). In Lincoln's story, a witness stated having seen, in the moonlight, an acquaintance of Lincoln's (Duff Armstrong) participate in a murder. Using an almanac as evidence, Lincoln argued that the night was too dark for the witness to have seen anything and thus obtained Armstrong's acquittal with this plea.

5. Ford and Lincoln

Ford had already spent the greater part of his career with Fox: he made thirty-eight movies between 1920 and 1935! Since Zanuck's takeover, he had made four movies in two years, the first in 1936, *The Prisoner of Shark Island* ("I haven't killed Lincoln"). Thus it was to one of the company's older and more trustworthy directors that the project was entrusted. The same year, again with Zanuck, Ford shot *Drums Along the Mohawk* (whose ideological orientation is glaringly obvious: the struggle of the pioneers, side by side with Washington and the *Whigs* against the English in alliance with the Indians) and in 1940 *The Grapes of Wrath* which paints a very gloomy portrait of the America of 1938–1939. Despite the fact that he calls himself apolitical we know that Ford in any case greatly admires Lincoln as a historical figure and as a person: Ford too claims humble peasant origins—but this closeness with Lincoln as a man is, however, moderated by the fact that Ford is also, if not primarily, Irish and Catholic.

In 1924 already, in *The Iron Horse,* Lincoln appears as favoring the construction of the intercontinental railway (industry and unification); at the beginning of *The Prisoner of Shark Island* we see Lincoln requesting "Dixie" from an orchestra after the Civil War (this is the tune which he "already" plays in *Young Mr. Lincoln):* symbolically, the emphasis is put on Lincoln's unifying, nonvindictive side and his deep Southern sympathies by means of the hymn of the Confederacy; in *Sergeant Rutledge* (1960) he is evoked by the blacks as their Savior, the antislavery aspect; in *How the West Was Won* (1962) the strategist is presented; finally in *Cheyenne Autumn* (1964), a cornered politician turns to a portrait of Lincoln, presented as the model for the resolution of any crisis.

Each of these films thus concentrates on a particular aspect either of Lincoln's synthetic personality or of his complex historical role; he thus appears to be a sort of universal referent which can be activated in all situations. As long as Lincoln appears in Ford's fiction as a myth, a figure of reference, a symbol of America, his intervention is natural, apparently in complete harmony with Ford's morality and ideology; the situation is different in a film like *Young Mr. Lincoln* where he becomes the protagonist of the fiction. We will see that he can only be inscribed as a Fordian character at the expense of a number of distortions and reciprocal assaults (by him on the course of fiction and by fiction on his historical truth).

6. Ideological Undertaking

What is the subject of *Young Mr Lincoln?* Ostensibly and textually it is "Lincoln's youth" (on the classic cultural model—"Apprenticeship and Travels"). In fact—through the expedient of a simple chronicle of events presented (through the presence and actualization effect specific to classic cinema) as if they were taking place for the first time under our eyes—it is the *reformulation* of the historical figure of Lincoln on the level of the myth and the eternal.

This ideological project may appear to be clear and simple—of the edifying and apologetic type. Of course, if one considers its statement alone, extracting it as a *separable ideological statement* disconnected from the complex network of determinations through which it is realized and inscribed—through which it possibly even criticises itself—then it is easy to operate an illusory deconstruction of the film through a reading of the demystificatory type (see 1). Our work, on the contrary, will consist in activating this network in its complexity, where philosophical assumptions (idealism, theologism), political determinations (republicanism, capitalism) and the relatively autonomous aesthetic process (characters, cinematic *signifiers,* narrative mode) specific to Ford's writing intervene simultaneously. If our work, which will necessarily be held to the linear sequentiality of the discourse, should isolate the orders of determination interlocking in the film, it will always be in the perspective of their relations: it therefore demands a recurrent reading, on all levels.

7. Methodology

Young Mr. Lincoln, like the vast majority of Hollywood films, follows linear and chronological narrative, in which events appear to follow each other according to a certain "natural" sequence and logic. Thus two options were open to us: either, in discussing each of the determining moments, to simultaneously refer to all the scenes involved; or to present each scene in its fictional chronological *order* and discuss the different determining moments, emphasizing in each case what we believe to be the main determinant (the key signification), and indicating the secondary determinants, which may in turn become the main determinant in other scenes. The first method thus sets up the film as the object of a reading (a text) and then supposedly takes up the totality of its overdetermination networks simultaneously, *without taking account of the repressive operation* which, in each scene, determines the realization of a key signification; while the second method *bases itself on the key signification of each scene,* in order to understand the scriptural operation (overdetermination and repression) which has set it up.

The first method has the drawback of turning the film into a text which is *readable a priori;* the second has the advantage of making the reading itself participate in the *film's process of becoming-a-text,* and of authorizing such a reading only by what authorizes it in each successive moment of the film. We have therefore chosen the latter method. The fact that the course of our reading will be modeled on the "cutting" of the film into sequences is absolutely intentional, but the work will involve breaking down the closures of the individual scenes by setting them in action with each other and *in* each other.

8. The Poem

After the credits (and in the same graphic style: i.e., engraved in marble) there is a poem which consists of a number of questions which "if she were to come back on earth," Lincoln's mother would ask, concerning the destiny of her son.

(a) Let us simply observe for the moment that the figure of the mother is inscribed from the start, and that it is an absent Mother, already dead, a symbolic figure who will only later make her full impact.

(b) The enumeration of questions, on the other hand, programs the development of the film by designating Lincoln's problematic as being that of a choice: the interrogative form of this poem, like a matrix, generates the binary sytem (the necessity to choose between two careers, two pies, two plaintiffs, two defendants, etc.) according to which the fiction is organized (see 14).

(c) In fact, the main function of the poem, which pretends that the questions posed therein haven't yet been answered (whereas they are only the simulation of questions, since they presume the spectator's knowledge of Lincoln's *historical character),* is to set up the dualist nature of film and to initiate the process of a double reading. By inviting the spectator to ask himself "questions" to which he already has the answers, the poem induces him to look at history—something which, for him, has already happened—as if it were "still to happen." Similarly by on the one hand playing on a fictional structure of the "chronicle" type ("natural" juxtaposition and succession of events, as if they were not dictated by any determinism or directed toward a necessary end), and on the other hand by contriving, in the scenes where a crucial choice must be made by the character, a margin of *feigned indecisiveness* (as if the game had not already been played, Lincoln had not entered history, and as if he was taking every one of his decisions on the spot, in the present), the film thus effects *naturalization* of the Lincolnian myth (which already exists as such in the mind of the spectator).

The retroactive action of the spectator's knowledge of the myth on the chronicle of events and the naturalist rewriting of the myth in the divisions of this chronicle thus impose a reading in the future perfect. "What is realized in my story is not the past definite of what once was since it is no more, nor the perfect of what has been in what I am, but the future perfect of what I will have been for what I am in the process of becoming" (Lacan).

A classic *ideological* operation manifests itself here, normally, through questions asked after the event whose answer, which has already been given, is the very condition for the existence of the question.

9. The Electoral Speech

First scene. A politician dressed in townclothes (John T. Stuart, later to become Lincoln's associate in Springfield) addresses a few farmers. He denounces the corrupt politicians who are in power and Andrew Jackson, President of the USA; he then introduces the local candidate whom he is sponsoring: young Lincoln. The first shot, in which we see Lincoln, shows him sitting on a barrel leaning backwards in shirtsleeves, wearing heavy boots (one recognizes the classic casualness of Ford's hero, who has returned and/or is above everything). In the next shot, addressing the audience of farmers, Lincoln in a friendly tone (but not without a hint of nervousness) declares: "My politics are short and sweet like your ladies' dances; I am in favor of a National Bank and for everybody's participation in wealth." His first words are "You all know who I am, plain Abraham Lincoln"—this is meant not only for the spectators in the film, who are anyway absent from the screen, but also to involve the spectator of the movie, brought into the cinematic space; thus this treatment in the future perfect is immediately confirmed (see 8).

This program is that of the Whig party, at that time in opposition. It is in essence the program of nascent American capitalism: protectionism to favor national industrial production, National Bank to favor the circulation of capital in all the states. The first point traditionally has a place in the program of the Republican Party (it is thus easily recognizable to the spectator of 1939); the second calls to mind a point in history: while in power before 1830, the Whigs had created a National Bank (helping industrial development in the North) whose powers Jackson, who succeeded them, attempted to weaken: the defense of this bank was thus one of the demands of the Whigs, who later became Republicans.

(a) The specifically *political* notations which introduce the film have the obvious function of presenting Lincoln as the candidate (that is, in the future perfect, the President, the champion) of the Republicans.

(b) But the scorn which is immediately shown toward the "corrupt politicians" and the strength in the contrast of Lincoln's program which is simple as "a dance" have the effect of introducing him (and the Republicans in his wake) as the opposition and the remedy to such "politics." Furthermore, we will see later that it is not only his opponents' politics which are "corrupt" but all politics, condemned in the name of morality (the figure of Lincoln will be contrasted with that of his opponent Douglas, with that of the prosecutor, as the defender of Justice versus the politicians, the Uncompromising versus the manipulators).

This disparagement of politics carries and confirms the *idealist* project of the film (see 4 and 6): moral virtues are worth more than political guile, the Spirit more than the Word (cf. 4, 6, 8). (Likewise, politics appears again, later, as the object of discussion among drunks—quarrel between J.P. Cass and his acolyte—or of socialite conversation: carriage scene between Mary Todd and Douglas).

But what is most significant here is that the points of the electoral program are the *only indications* of a *positive relation* between Lincoln and politics, all others being negative (separating Lincoln from the mass of "politicians").

(c) We may be surprised that a film on Lincoln's youth could thus empty out the truly political dimension from the career of the future President. This massive omission is too useful to the film's ideological purpose to be fortuitous. By playing once again on the spectator's knowledge of Lincoln's political and historical role it is possible to establish the idea that these were founded on and validated by a Morality superior to all politics (and could thus be neglected in favor of their Cause) and that Lincoln always draws his prestige and his strength from an intimate relationship with Law, from a (natural and/or divine) knowledge of Good and Evil. Lincoln *starts* with politics but soon rises to the moral level, divine right, which for an idealist discourse originates and valorizes all politics. Indeed, the first scene of the film already shows Lincoln as a political candidate without providing any information either on what may have brought him to this stage: *concealment* of *origins* (both his personal—family—origins and those of his political knowledge, however basic: that is "his education") which establishes the mythical nature of the character; or on the results of this electoral campaign (we know that he was defeated, and that the Republicans' failure resulted in the shelving of the National Bank, among other things): as if they were in fact of no importance in the light of the already evident significance of fate and the myth. Lincoln's character makes all politics appear trivial.

But this very *repression* of politics, on which the ideological undertaking of the film is based, is itself a *direct result* of political assumptions (the eternal false idealist debate between morality and politics: Descartes versus Machiavelli); and at the level of its reception by the spectator, this repression is not without consequences of an equally political nature. We know that the ideology of American Capitalism (and the Republican Party which traditionally represents it) is to assert its divine right, to conceptualize it in terms of permanence, naturalism, and even biology (cf. Benjamin Franklin's famous formula: "Remember that money has genital potency and fecundity") and to extol it as a universal Good and Power. The enterprise consisting of the concealment of politics (of social relations in America, of Lincoln's career) under the idealist mask of Morality has the effect of regilding the cause of Capital with the gold of myth, by manifesting the "spirituality" in which American Capitalism believes it finds its origins and sees its eternal justification. The seeds of Lincoln's future were already sown in his youth—the future of America (its eternal values) is already written into Lincoln's moral virtues, which include the Republican Party and Capitalism.

(d) Finally, with the total suppression of Lincoln's political dimension, his main historicopolitical characteristic disappears from the scene of the film: i.e. his struggle against the slaver states. Indeed, neither in the initial political sequence nor in the rest of the film is this dominant characteristic of his history, of his legend even, indicated, whereas it is mainly to it that Lincoln owes his being inscribed into American history more than any other President (Republican or otherwise).

Strangely enough, only one allusion is made to slavery (this exception has the value of a signal): Lincoln explains to the defendants' family that he had to leave his native state since "with all the slaves coming in, white folks just had a hard time making a living." The fact that this comment emphasizes the economic aspects of the problem at the expense of its moral and humanitarian aspects would appear to contradict the points outlined above (primary of morality over politics) if Lincoln had not spoken these words in a scene (see 19) where he puts himself in the imaginary role of the son of the poor farmer family. He recalls his own origins as a poor white who, like everyone else, suffered from unemployment. The accent is thus put on the economic problem, i.e. the problem of the whites, not the blacks.

The *not-said* here, this exclusion from the scene of the film of Lincoln's most notable political dimension, can also not be fortuitous (the "omission" would be enormous!), it too must have *political significance.*

On the one hand, it was indeed necessary to present Lincoln as the unifier, the harmonizer, and not the divider of America (this is why he likes playing "Dixie": he is a Southerner). On the other hand, we know that the Republican Party, abolitionist by economic opportunism, after the Civil War rapidly reappeared as more or less racist and segregationist. (Already, Lincoln was in favor of a progressive emancipation of the blacks, which would only slowly give them equal rights with the whites). He never concealed the restrictions he asked for concerning the integration of blacks. Considering the political impact that the film could have in the context described above (see 3, 4), it would have been in bad taste on both these accounts to insist on Lincoln's liberating role.

This feature is thus silenced, excluded from the hero's youth, as if it had not appeared until later, when all the legendary figure's other features are given by the film as present from the outset and are given value by this predestination.

The shelving of this dimension (the Civil War) which is directly responsible for the Lincolnian Legend thus allows a political use of this legend and at the same time, by castrating Lincoln of his historicopolitical dimension, reinforces the idealization of the myth.

But the exclusion of this dominant sign from Lincoln's politics is also possible because *all the others* are rapidly pushed out (except for the brief positive and negative notations mentioned above, which in any case are in play as *indicators—* of the general repression of politics, and of stamping of the Republican cause by the seal of the Myth) and because this fact places the film immediately on the purely ideological plane (Lincoln's ahistorical dimension, his symbolic value).

Thus what *projects the political meaning* of the film is not a directly political discourse: it is a *moralizing discourse.* History, almost totally reduced to the time scale of the myth with neither past nor future, can thus at best only survive in the film in the form of a *specific repetition:* on the teleological model of history as a continuous and linear development of a preexisting *seed,* of the future contained in the past (anticipation, predestination). Everything is there, all the features and characters of the historical scene are in their place (Mary Todd who will become Lincoln's wife, Douglas whom he will beat at the presidential elections, etc, right up to Lincoln's death: in a scene which Fox cut, before the film was first released, one could see Lincoln stop in front of a theater presenting Hamlet and facing one of the [Booth family] troupe of actors—his future murderer), the problematic of deciding (see 14) and of unifying is already posed . . . The only missing thing is the main historical feature, this being the one on which the myth was first constructed.

But such repression is possible (acceptable by the spectator) only inasmuch as the film plays on what is *already known* about Lincoln, treating it as if it were a factor of *nonrecognition* and at the limit, a not-known (at least, something that nobody wants to know anymore, which for having been known is all the more easily forgotten): it is the already constituted force of the myth which allows not only its reproduction but also its reorientation. It is the universal knowledge of Lincoln's fate which allows, while restating it, the omission of parts of it. For the problem here is not to build a myth but to negotiate its realization and even more to rid it of its historical roots in order to liberate its universal and eternal meaning. "Told," Lincoln's youth is in fact *rewritten* by what has to filter through the Lincolnian myth. The film establishes not only Lincoln's total predestination (teleological axis) but also that *only that to which he has been shown to be predestined* deserves immortality (theological axis). A double operation of addition and subtraction at the end of which the historical axis, having been abolished and mythified, returns cleansed of all impurities and thus recuperable to the service not just of Morality but of the morality reasserted by capitalist ideology. Morality not only rejects politics and surpasses history; it also rewrites them.

10. The Book

Lincoln's electoral speech seems to open up a fiction: electoral campaign, elections . . . A problem is presented, which we have the right to expect to see solved, but which in fact will not be solved. To use the Barthesian formula, we have the elements of a hermeneutic chain: enigma (will he or won't he be elected?) and nonresolution. This chain is abandoned by the use of an abrupt fictional displacement: the arrival of the family of farmers. Lincoln is called away to help them. This family comprises the father, the mother, and two twelve-year-old boys. They want to buy some material from Lincoln, thus informing us of his occupation: he is a shopkeeper. But the family has no money: Lincoln offers them credit, and confronted by the mother's embarrassment, argues that he himself has acquired his shop on credit. The situation is resolved by the use of barter: the family owns a barrel full of old books (left behind by the grandfather). Delighted at the mere mention of a book (legendary thirst for reading) Lincoln respectfully takes one out of the barrel: *as if by chance,* it is Blackstone's *Commentaries.* He dusts the book, opens it, reads, realizes that it is about Law (he says: "Law"), and is delighted that the book is in good condition (the Law is indestructible).

(a) It's a *family* (see 19) of pioneers who are *passing through* that give Lincoln the opportunity of coming in contact with Law: emphasis on the luck–predestination connection as well as on the fact that *even without knowing it* it is the humble who transmit Law (religiously kept by the family as legacy from the ancestor). On the other hand, we have here a classic Fordian fictional feature (apart from the family as a displaced center): meeting and exchange between two groups whose paths need not have crossed (a new fictional sequence is born from this very meeting; it is first presented as a suspension and simple digressive delay of the main narrative axis, later it constitutes itself as being central, until another sequence arises, functioning in the same mode, Ford's total fiction existing finally only as an articulation of successive digressions).

(b) Lincoln makes a brief but precise speech in praise of credit: "I give you credit"—"I don't like credit" (says the farmer-woman incarnating the dignity of the poor)—"I myself bought my shop on credit": when one is aware of the role played by the extension of credit in the 1929 crisis, this kind of publicity slogan uttered by an American hero (who later, with ever increasing emphasis, will be the Righteous man) tends to appear as a form of exorcism: without credit, the development of capital is impossible; in a period of recession (1935–1940) when unemployment is high and wages have gone down, the maintenance of the level of consumption is the only thing which allows industry to carry on.

(c) The fact that Law is acquired by barter introduces a circuit of debt and repayments which is to run through the film (see 23).

(d) The principal function of this sequence is to introduce a number of constituent elements of the symbolic scene from which the film is to proceed, by *varying* and activating it (in this sense it is the true expository scene of the fiction, the first scene becoming pretextual and possibly even *extratextual*): the book and the Law, the Family and the Son, exchange and debt, predestination . . . This *setting up* of the fictional matrix means *putting aside* the first sequence (political speech): a simple digression, first believed to be temporary, but then seen to be in fact the first step in the operation of the repression of politics by morality which will continue through the whole film (see 9).

11. Nature, Law, Woman

Third sequence: lying in the grass under a tree, near a river, Lincoln is reading Blackstone's *Commentaries.* He summarizes its theories in a few sentences: "The right to acquire and hold property . . . the right to life and reputation . . . and

wrongs are a violation of those rights. . . . that's all there is to it: right and wrong
. . ." A young woman appears and expresses surprise that he should lie down
while reading. He gets up and answers: "When I'm lying down, my mind's
standing up, when I'm standing up, my mind lies down." They walk along the
river discussing Lincoln's ambitions and culture (poets, Shakespeare, and now
Law). They stop and while she is talking he starts to stare at her and tells her
that he thinks she is beautiful. This declaration of love continues for a few
moments, centered on the question of those who do and those who don't like
redheads, then the young girl leaves the scene (the frame, the shot). Alone,
Lincoln approaches the river and throws a stone into it. Close up of the ripples
on the water.

(a) The first anecdotic signified of the scene refers to Lincoln's legend: like any
layman in law in the States at that time, Lincoln discovers Law in Blackstone.
His *Commentaries* were young America's legal Bible, and they largely inspired
the 1787 constitution. They are, in fact, no more than a summary and a confused
vulgarization of eighteenth century English law. The second anecdotic signified
(again made explicit in the following scene) is Lincoln's first acknowledged love
affair, his relationship with Ann Rutledge—presented in the legend and the film
as the ideal wife (who shares similar tastes) whom he will never meet again.

(b) Centered on Lincoln, the scene presents the relationship Law-Woman-
Nature which will be articulated according to a system of complementarity and
of substitution/replacement.

It is in nature that Lincoln communes with Law:

It is at the moment of this communion that he meets Woman: the relationship
Lincoln-Woman replaces the relationship Lincoln-Law, since Woman simultaneously interrupts Lincoln's reading of the book by her arrival and marks her
appreciation of Lincoln's knowledge and encourages him in his vocation as man
of knowledge and Law.

The declaration of love is made according to the classic (banal) cultural analogy
Nature-Woman, in Nature (on the bank of a river). But above all the promotion
of the river to the status of the woman corresponds to the Woman's (the wife's)
disappearance from the sequence (which in the fiction turns out to be definitive);
this promotion is signaled by the throwing of the stone (see 18).

Just as culturally determined and codified as the relationship Nature-Woman,
the equivalence Nature-Law is here underlined precisely by the fact that the Law
book is Blackstone, for whom all forms of Law (the laws of gravitation as well
as those which regulate society) grow from a natural Law which is none other
than God's law. In the final analysis, this supreme law separates Good from Evil,
and is indeed called upon to legislate on the soundness of other human laws (the
spirit against the word, see 6, 7, 9). Consequence: the acquisition and the defense
of property are here presented as being based on the natural, indeed, on the
divine (cf. the ideology of capitalism, 4, 9).

12. The Tomb, the Bet

The ripples caused by the stone falling in the river dissolve into ice breaking up on the same river, as a transition between the scenes. A "dramatic" music underlines this passage. Lincoln arrives near a tomb covered in snow, near the river, at the spot where the preceding scene took place. Ann Rutledge's name can be read on the marble stone. Lincoln places a bunch of flowers on the tomb, while soliloquizing on the return of spring ("the woods are already full of them too, the snow when it's drifting . . . . ice breaking up . . . . coming of the spring"). He says he is still hesitant on the path to follow: whether to stay in the village or to follow Ann's advice, go to town and choose a legal career. He picks up a twig of dead wood: if it falls toward Ann, he will choose law, if not, he will stay in the village. The twig falls on Ann's side. Lincoln, kneeling down, says: "Well, Ann, you win, it's the Law" and after a moment of silence, "I wonder if I could have tipped it your way just a little."

(a) The dissolve, which links the scene of the declaration of love (see 11) to that of the loved one's tomb, gives the impression that the transition from one to the other follows the same time scale as the transition from summer to spring (the breaking ice) according to a symbolic (classic) opposition of the seasons: life/death (and resurrection). There is at the same time a smooth (continuous) succession from one season to the other, and a brutal contrast (Ann alive in one shot, dead in the next) between the two scenes. The effect of temporal continuity reinforces the violence of the contrast (the fictional shock) between life and death.

This process of temporal sequence and continuity (which is specific to great classical cinema) has in fact the function of absorbing referential time by juxtaposing and connecting two events (romance, death) separated by what will appear only later (at his arrival in Springfield) to be an interval of many years. This elimination has the effect of presenting Lincoln's first decisive choice (to become a lawyer) as if it had been neither thought out nor elaborated, nor rational; it *denies him the time of reflection,* it abolishes all *work.* Thus, once again, following the film's general strategy, it submits the hero to predestination, by reducing referential time to cinematic time: new *coup de force* by the film.

(b) Lincoln's definitive acceptance of Law is thus, once again, made under Woman's direct influence (we have seen in 11 the nature of her relationship with Law and Nature) and is in phase with the awakening of nature. But despite the fact that this decision is inevitable, both because of the logic of the symbolic axis Woman-Nature-Law and because of the spectator's knowledge of Lincoln's fate, the film skillfully creates suspense, pretending that luck could change the course of events. As with Hitchcock, with whom suspense, far from being weakened by our knowledge of the outcome, is increased at each viewing by this knowledge, the tension built up in this scene, far from being compromised by our knowledge of Lincoln's future (perfect), is increased by it. The film's supreme guile then consists in reintroducing—deceptively—at the very end of the scene the indication of intention, a voluntary choice on Lincoln's part ("I wonder if I could have tipped it your way just a little"), which is in fact no more than a feigned delegation of power: as if Lincoln's already-accomplished destiny were referring to him to decide its path, following Spinoza's principle of *verum index sui,* of truth as indicator of itself, the *self-determination of an already determined figure.*

13. The Plaintiffs

Lincoln's arrival in Springfield. He sets himself up as a solicitor. Two Mormon farmers consult him, intending to take legal action. One owes the other money and the second has satisfied himself by violently beating up the first; therefore the first is claiming damages of an amount roughly equivalent to his debt. Having read the two plaintiffs' statements, Lincoln informs them of the quasi equivalence of their respective debts, the difference being equal to his bill; faced with their hesitation he threatens the use of force, if they don't accept his compromise. The farmers agree to pay him, and one of them tries to give him a fake coin. Lincoln first notices this by the sound it produces, then by biting the coin, and the scene ends on Lincoln's very insistent stare fixed on the forger.

(a) Lincoln's first legal act in the film is the solution of an extremely commonplace case. In fact, this anecdote, which introduces the viewer to the violence of social relations in Lincoln's period, indicates his legal function, which throughout the film is to repress violence even, as a final resort, by the use of a specifically legal violence (incarnated in Lincoln's physical strength but most of the time simply manifested by a verbal threat).

(b) The scene insists on Lincoln's supreme *cleverness,* in resolving any situation, the Law being able to decide either by taking one side against the other, or as here, by craftily restoring the balance between the two sides of the scales. This second solution is obviously preferred by the film because it emphasizes Lincoln's legendary unifying role.

(c) Lincoln knows about money; he is not interested in its origin (credit, exchange, debt form, a circle) but it has a ring, a consistency, a value. It is precisely about a money swindle that Lincoln's *castrating power* (see 16 and 22) is manifested for the first time, as an empty, icy, terrifying stare and his speed at hitting his opponents where it hurts, characteristics which will constitute the terrifying dimension of Lincoln's figure accentuated from scene to scene. Here for the first time the supreme process of Law eclipses the anecdotal character of Lincoln.

It will be observed that this terrifying dimension widely exceeds all the connotative signifieds (whether psychological—"I'm a farmer too, you can't fool me," or moral—reprobation, or situational, etc.) which could be applied to it. The irreducible character of Lincoln's castrating figure will persist throughout the film, transcending, altering the ideological discourse.

14. The Celebrations

It is in order to take part in the Independence Day celebrations that Lincoln is in such a hurry to conclude the quarrel between the farmers. This celebration is made up of a number of episodes, announced in a program, the order of which we will follow: (a) a parade (in which Lincoln meets Douglas, his opponent, and Mary Todd, his future wife); (b) a pie judging contest in which Lincoln is the judge (and during which the family from the first scene reappear); (c) a Tug of War (across a pond) in which Lincoln takes part (and in the course of which there is an incident between the family and two roughnecks); (d) a rail splitting contest (longitudinal section of a tree trunk) which Lincoln wins; (e) the burning of tar barrels.

(a) Lincoln is confronted by a historical evocation of America: the local militias parade past him, followed by the veterans of the war against Spain, and finally the survivors of the War of Independence, whom Lincoln salutes by removing his top hat. But Lincoln's slightly ridiculous solemnity is underlined on the one hand by the other spectators' joyful exuberance, and on the other by a succession of grotesque incidents, coupled with the veterans' shabby appearance, very much in the Fordian tradition.

(b) The principle of Justice (whether or not to choose) is here realized through a series of derivatives which exhaust all its modalities: either Lincoln literally splits a rail in two, and thus separates himself from, places himself above his opponents (adventitious meaning: affirmation of the physical strength of literally his cutting edge); or he doesn't hesitate to give *his* side, that is the right side, a helping hand, to help it win (by tying the rope to a horse-drawn cart): Law represented by its ideal figure has every right: just as it doesn't hesitate to use force (see 13, 16) so it doesn't shrink before the use of cunning and deception; a deception whose scandalous aspect is masked by the triviality of the stake, and the "Fordian gag" aspect of the action. Finally, more subtly, faced with the undecidable character of a situation (the ethic, or gastronomic, impossibility of preferring the product of one cook to that of another) the fiction itself must, by abandoning the scene, censor the moment of choice and not show Lincoln making an impossible choice, both for the sake of the scene and for that of the myth.

(c) The celebration sequence is made up of a series of fictionally autonomous *sketches* which are in fact determined by the necessity of presenting a certain number of Lincoln's features. This mode of narration continues and stresses that of the preceding scenes: namely a succession of sequences whose length can vary but which are all subject to the *unity of action*. Indeed each of them establishes a situation, presents, develops, and syntagmatically encloses an action (whether this latter is resolved in terms of the diegesis or not: nothing said of the consequences of the electoral speech, no decision about the pies). (Insofar as it closes a scene only, the closure does not preclude the later reinvestment of any one of the elements which the scene has elevated to the status of a signifier: for example, the Law book or the Mother).

In fact it is at the moment of its greatest systematization (a series of headings) that this mode of narration is *infiltrated by the first elements of a new narrative principle* (that of the detective story enigma and its solution: a hermeneutic chain which articulates all the following sequences). Indeed, during the different episodes of the celebration, characters who will all play a more or less important role in the problem are present: Douglas and Mary Todd, the Clay family, the two bad boys, and a few extras who will reappear at the lynching and the trial. This new narrative device is reinforced (at the end of the celebration) by a scene (between Carrie Sue and her fiancé, Matt, the younger Clay son) which seems to reproduce Hollywood's most banal clichés (chatter of lovers, discussion of the future: how many children); in fact it is important insofar as it is the first scene from which Lincoln is physically absent. He is, however, constantly mentioned: first, indirectly, by Carrie Sue, who is very excited by the celebration and makes her fiancé promise to bring her back every year (what can be here taken as a simple whim, the manifestation of innocent joy and desire—the innocence briefly unmasked when she tells Matt she wishes "we was married right now. . ."—will be revealed and accentuated in all the scenes where Carrie Sue is present as the systematic denial of the violent erotic attraction provoked— not in her alone—by Lincoln (cf. the direction indicated by the film in 19, where Lincoln identifies her with Ann Rutledge); then, directly, by the fiancé who says: "I wish it was going to be that fella' splitting them rails again," taking it on himself to formulate on her behalf *what she cannot say.*

15. The Murder

The new plot, which this scene develops and which is to dominate the rest of the film, started, as we noted with the appearance of a number of elements which disturb the course of the celebration and its narrative presentation; the deputy sheriff (Scrub White) and his friend (J. Palmer Cass), somewhat worked up and high, pester Adam's (one of the Clay sons) wife. A fight breaks out, and is stopped by the mother's (Abigail Clay) intervention. This forgotten quarrel brutally reemerges during the final act of the celebration: the burning of the tar barrels. The two brothers and Scrub White start fighting again, this results in the death of the latter.

We have purposely not described the scene here; it is literally *indescribable,* insofar as it is the realization—through the succession and length of the shots, abrupt changes of angle, play on distance, the reactions and the behavior of the participants, the successive arrival of witnesses—of an amazing system of *deception* which affects all the characters implicated in the event, and blinds them as well as the spectator. The radical difference between Ford's procedure here, and other films of the enigma type, is that the latter, in order to be able to function and permit a solution to the enigma, must at first give the spectator only scraps of knowledge and deprive him of a number of clues, the revelation of which, after the event, will provide the solution to the plot; whereas here, on the contrary, everything is given, present but undecipherable, and it can only be deciphered at the second, *informed,* look.

The system of deception here set up is effective because *it develops as the scene progresses:* all the characters are caught up in it and duped, thus making it more powerful; and the spectator witnessing these successive mystifications and called upon to agree with all is thus the most deceived.

But we must also note that the effect of the deception continues and is *legitimized* by the substitution of a deceptive question: *which of the two brothers killed him?* for the real question, who killed him? The former question implies that the latter has already been answered, thus (successfully) suppressing the first: it will only be brought back by Lincoln (see 22).

All the different characters of the scene—*among them the spectator*—have either an active or a passive relationship to the deception—either way strengthening its influence. The spectator, who will be completely duped, is the initial witness of the fight: for him a perfectly plausible causal chain is constituted (except for one thing which we will specify): a cause of death: the shot; an effect: the wounded man's moans as he lies on the ground; reactions of the guilty: the two brothers, frightened, take refuge near their mother who has just arrived. There is only one element to contradict this causal chain: before hearing the shot, we see Scrub White's arm, which holds the weapon, turned away. But this element of confusion (Scrub White appearing to be seriously wounded by his own weapon when it was pointed elsewhere) far from invalidates this first setting up of the deception; on the contrary it provokes distraction, thus permitting the intervention of a new factor (Cass's arrival) to pass almost unnoticed: the wounded man's death throes at this point can easily be accommodated by a classic typology: dying-in-one's-best-friend's-arms.

Cass, arriving during this break in attention, kneels down by his friend, placing himself *between him and the spectator* (longshot). He gets up in a *closeup* shot, holding a bloody knife (a weapon which had not been previously seen); a shot which *independently of this drama* (as in Kuleshov's experiment) *is classically a shot of the guilty* (which is indeed what Cass is, since it is he who gave his friend this fatal knife wound, but we will only learn this at the end of the movie, *even though all this has already been shown—but rendered not-readable).*

The two sons Adam and Matt behave, even before Cass's arrival (ever since the shot was fired) like guilty men. Cass saying "He's dead" confirms them in this guilt; each one believes the other to be guilty but takes responsibility for the crime to protect his brother.

The mother intervenes when the shot is fired, and seeing a man aground and her two sons alive but frightened, enters into the system of deception in her turn, believing them to be guilty. This feeling is strengthened when Cass gets up showing the knife, a knife which she recognizes, believing then that she knows which of her two sons is guilty. But since they both accuse themselves, she plays the game and refuses to say which one she believes to be guilty (refusing to sacrifice one for the sake of the other). This refusal reinforces the deception because it accepts the displacement of the question: the mother thinks she keeps a secret, but it is the wrong one.

The spectator in his turn accepts this second causal chain: since the victim has been murdered with a knife by one of the two brothers, the gunshot from now on appears to him as a trivial episode, even a digression.

Thus what is happening here is precisely the cinematic questioning of direct vision, of perception insofar as it conceals the structure. The work that needs to be done to make the scene legible is not a search for hidden meanings but the bringing to light of the *meaning which is already there:* which is why paradoxically, it is our type of reading (see 1) of the film *in its entirety* which is called for and justified by this central scene.

This sequence and the preceding one (dialogue between the lovers) constitute, as we have already said, *a new fiction, from which Lincoln is absent.* He only comes into it when everything is decided (the crime committed, the accused taken away by the sheriff): neither actor, nor witness, *a priori* uninvolved in the problem, he *has no knowledge of it.* This is a necessary condition, in terms of Lincoln's mythical role, for the truth to emerge by magical rather than scientific means: to solve this crime story situation Lincoln will use means very different from those of an inquiry along ordinary thriller lines.

16. The Lynching

(a) Introduced at the end of the celebration by the burning of the barrels (a commonplace episode in American celebrations, but here dramatically emphasized by the double fictional and historical context: KKK/fascist *auto-da-fés),* the cycle of violence (fight, crime) will culminate with the lynching. (The scene thereby acquires extra political significance because in the years 1925–1935 a large number of lynchings took place in the USA—see films from that period, e.g., *Fury).* This violence carries with it an acceleration of the narrative: between the moment when the defendants are taken away and the one when the lynching starts, there are only a few seconds, the time of a reframing; during this time Lincoln offers his legal services to the mother. She asks who he is, since she doesn't recognize him as the man who once gave her credit (this is not without importance; see the circulation of the debts, 19) whereas he has just recognized her as the woman who gave him the Book. He answers, after a pause, "I'm your lawyer, ma'am."

(b) Inside the prison, under attack from the lynchers, there is a violent contrast between the understandable nervousness of the defendants and the sheriff and the unjustifiable panic of Cass (who has just been promoted deputy sheriff); for the second time—and here again in a nonreadable way—the film exposes Cass as the culprit, i.e., as the man who is afraid of being lynched.

(c) Lincoln's action, insofar as he represents the Law, can only be the, if necessary violent, prohibition of any nonlegal violence. Since the whole film is meant to manifest Lincoln's absolute superiority to all those who surround him, the scene of the lynching provides the opportunity for a masterly demonstration of it in a number of set scenes, each new stage of his victory increasing his castrating violence; this is inversely proportional to the expenditure of physical violence (since, in the ideological discourse, Law must have power insofar as it is legitimized by its own statement, not through physical strength, which is used as a last resort and often simply as a verbal threat). Here the escalation of legal repression is effected in many stages: (1) alone, Lincoln physically repels the lynchers' assault (courage and physical strength); (2) he incites one of the leaders to single combat, this the man evades (verbal threat based on knowledge of the opponent's weakness); (3) he defuses the crowd's anger by a cunning speech (so cunning, that the mother, not knowing *who he is*—i.e., in the fiction a good man, and in the myth President Lincoln—takes his speech literally and is very disturbed, before *believing* in him); he is also humorous (shifting to another level: complicity/familiarity with the crowd); (4) he throws back on the crowd the threat of its own violence by showing it that each one of them one way or the other, could be lynched (intimidation producing terror); (5) addressing one individual among the lynchers, whom he knows to be a religious man, he threatens him with retribution in the name of the Bible (ultimate recourse to divine writing as an instance of the Law). Lincoln's castrating triumph is sanctioned in the film itself not only by the subsiding of the crowd's anger, but very precisely by the lowering of the tree trunk, which on Lincoln's order is dropped by the lynchers—who are dispersing. (Note that it is with this same tree trunk that the lynchers attempted to break open the prison door, protected by Lincoln's body.)

17. The Dance

Invited by Mary Todd to a dance (the invitation card, congratulating him on his attitude in this "recent deplorable uprising," says "My sister invites you. . .": here again, denial of desire), Lincoln, abandoning his boots, vigorously shines his black high-button shoes, and with the same unusual concern to be smart cuts his hair (see the anecdote told by Eisenstein about the new President moving to Washington: "he went as far as cleaning his own boots. Somebody said: *Gentlemen never clean their boots—And whose boots do real gentlemen clean?")* The dance is in full swing, elegant and very genteel. Lincoln enters the lobby and is immediately surrounded by elderly gentlemen whom he entertains with funny stories (which we cannot hear). He is asked about his family ("Are you by any chance a member of the well-known Lincoln family from Massachusetts?"— "I'd say the evidence is against it if they own land"). Mary Todd responds absentmindedly to Douglas' advances; she is only interested in Lincoln. She goes to him and demands that he ask her to dance. He replies that he would very much like to dance with her, but warns her that he is a very poor dancer. He follows her to the middle of the dance floor, they start to dance a kind of waltz, then a polka, which Mary Todd suddenly interrupts and drags Lincoln to the balcony.

(a) The dance sequence is more or less compulsory in Ford's films. These dances almost always have the function first of setting up and ordering a ritual *miming ideal harmony* which in fact is far from regulating the relations of the social group; then later, to disturb, unmask, and destroy this simulation of harmony by the intervention of a foreign element. Here Lincoln's social heterogeneity gives place to the realization of his symbolic otherness (figure of the Law): this involves him (socially and sexually) in a seduction relationship which simultaneously *integrates and excludes him;* this causes a confusion which is not resolved dramatically, unlike what takes place in other Ford films (cf. the dance in *Two Rode Together, Fort Apache* for example).

(b) The scandal of Lincoln's difference is even more noticeable to the spectators than to the characters of the scene. First it is apparent at the *physical* level, his shape, size, gait, rigidity, his undertaker look (Lincoln's mythical costume), then, while he is dancing, in the lack of coordination and rhythm in his movements. On the other hand, the social difference (made clear in the scene where Lincoln is dressing for the dance), emphasized by the question about his family, is immediately defused of any political significance and deflected into an amiable originality (it is out of the question according to the film's ideological system that his class origins should play anything but a positive role).

(c) But it is at the symbolic level that the scandal is most apparent. In terms of the logic of castration, Lincoln's status, whereas it is realized in the lynching scene in its active form (castrating action), figures here in the passive form: that of *inversion* (the fact that these two dimensions—the action of castrating/being castrated—belong together will be made obvious in the balcony scene). Indeed, Mary Todd fully takes the initiative. First she expresses her resentment at Lincoln's coldness (in her conversation with Douglas); then she accuses Lincoln of not making the first move and demands that he dance with her; finally she brings the dance to a sudden halt and drags him out to the balcony. Thus if the dance scene signifies the hero's social recognition (reward), the dance with Mary Todd puts him into a real castration, the retroactive effect of the lynching scene (which already implied it logically, writing it into the unconscious of Ford's text). There the castrating action was made on the basis of a castration which becomes effective in the dance scene, and particularly in the balcony scene.

18. The Balcony

As soon as he is on the balcony, Lincoln is enchanted by the river. Mary Todd waits for a moment for Lincoln to speak or show some interest in her. Then she draws aside, leaving him alone in front of the river.

(a) Dance, balcony, river, moonlight, couple: all these elements create a romantic, intimate, sentimental atmosphere. The scene, however, mercilessly destroys this atmosphere (whose physical signifieds could be already read as more fantastic than romantic) to introduce the dimension of the Sacred.

(b) The transfer from one dimension to the other is effected by Lincoln's enchantment with the river: the commonplace accessory of the "romantic scene" is shifted to an other scene and is at the same time the agent of this shift. An other scene (from which Mary Todd, having no place, withdraws) in which a process of displacement-condensation takes place so that the river simultaneously evokes the first woman Lincoln loved (Ann Rutledge)—an evocation here emptied of any nostalgic or sentimental character—and (see 11) the relationship Nature-Woman-Law. The river is here the ratification of Lincoln's contract with Law. Lincoln, faced with his fate, accepts it; the classic moment of any mythological story, where the hero sees his future written and accepts its revelation (the balcony, also a typical accessory of romantic love scenes, is here promoted, by Lincoln's gesture and the camera angle, to the anticipated role of the presidential balcony). Correlatively Lincoln's renunciation of pleasure is written here: from now on Ann Rutledge's death must be read as the real origin both of his castration and of his identification with the Law; and the "inversion" of the dance scene as well as its relation to the lynching scene take on their true meaning: Lincoln does not have the phallus, he is the phallus (see Lacan *"La signification du phallus"*).

19. The Family

Immediately after the lynching Lincoln accompanies the mother (Mrs. Clay) and her two daughters-in-law back to their wagon. He tells her "My mother would be just about your age if she were alive, you know she used to look a lot like you." After the scene of the balcony and before the opening of the trial, he goes to visit the family. On his way to the Clay farm, as he passes the river again, his companion tells him, "I've never known a fella look at a river like you do; fella would think it was a pretty girl the way you carry on" (see 11, 18).

(a) The scene in the farm yard acts as a reminder: Lincoln fantasizes himself in the role of son of the family. First, by chopping wood (see 14), he evokes the time when this was his daily task—and compares himself to the son of the family. Then, one by one all the elements of the scene remind him of his house, his garden, his trees, the members of his family; he himself asserts the sequence of these equivalences: Mrs. Clay = his mother, Sarah = his dead sister, whose name was also Sarah; Carrie Sue = Ann Rutledge; and even the dish which is being cooked is his favorite dish: turnips. This insistant parallelism between the Lincoln family and the Clay family is carried through to the *absence* of the father: total exclusion in the case of Lincoln's father who is not even mentioned; the disappearance from the fiction of Mr. Clay (present in the first scene) is explained by an "accident." The rejection of the Name of the Father logically corresponds to Lincoln's identification with the Law (his installation in the place of the great Other) which can neither guarantee itself nor originate itself through any other law than itself. We can here diagnose the *paranoia* which governs the symbolics of the film.

This reliving of memories also has the function of stressing Lincoln's social origins (see 9).

(b) This climate of nostalgic effusion—unique in the film—is brutally interrupted by one of Lincoln's fixed stares which can from now on be understood as the mark of his possession by Law. Giving up the role of son, he becomes inquisitor, interrupts the mother by asking her persistently which of her two sons is guilty. Terrified, she refuses to answer (as she had done earlier in front of the sheriff, and will do later in front of the prosecutor). Her consternation affects Lincoln and makes him immediately cast off this attitude of investigator; he gives up both trying to discover the mother's secret (but it is a useless secret) and to separate the two sons (for the problematic of one or the other, he substitutes that of all or nothing) and once again symbolically takes their place beside the mother. Let us add that the film firmly avoids a possibility which could have been exploited: namely that the question of the choice between the two sons might upset Lincoln himself, make him doubt or worry for a moment: Lincoln is totally ignorant of the *lamma sabbachtani*.

(c) But this scene has the simultaneous function of continuing the circuit of debt and gift which links and will continue to link Lincoln and the mother, and of providing it with an *origin:* fictionally introduced by the exchange—unequal in Lincoln's favor—of the material for the Book (see 10). It seems at the symbolic level to go back to the time when the child "used to stretch out while my mother read to me"; the situation is here reversed since Mrs. Clay can't read and it is Lincoln—still paying off this debt of which Mrs. Clay is unaware—who reads her the letter from her sons (note the way in which he pronounces the first words of this letter: "Dear Ma.").

The origin of Lincoln's knowledge is here given for the second time (see 11) as being feminine-maternal; the same equivalence Woman-Nature-(Mother)-Law is once again posed, the identification of Lincoln to the Law being related to the preliminary identification of the Law with Nature and Woman-Wife-Mother; the debt contracted by Lincoln toward his mother (she teaches him to read) as well as Mrs. Clay (she gives the Book) and Ann Rutledge (she pushes him toward knowledge) can only be "paid back" by his assumption of this mission, and his incarnation of the Law. Let us not insist on the assumptions behind this series (see 6), but notice that the circulation of the debt and its resolution are here enriched with an extra indicator: to answer, under the mother's dictation, the sons' letter, Lincoln asks Sarah for some paper, and she gives him an almanac. Thus it is from the same family that Law and Truth originate: through the Book (the carrier of the Law) and the almanac: first used as a support for writing (letter from the mother to the imprisoned sons), it will reveal the truth when *exhibited by Lincoln* (see 22). It carries the solution to the enigma, it is the sign of Truth.

20. The Trial

(a) The trial, a classic feature of Hollywood cinema, represents the staging of American legalist ideology and constitutes a microcosm of the social whole (sample of the different social strata represented by this or that type, this or that "silhouette"); confidence in the forms of legality is based precisely on this representativeness of the trial; it is America itself which constitutes the Jury, and who cannot be wrong, so that the Truth cannot fail to manifest itself by the end of the proceedings (carried out according to an almost ritualized alternation of comic and tragic moments). We have here a slight departure from this traditional trial, since the question is not to prove the culpability or the innocence of a defendant, but to *choose* (according to the principle of alternatives which has regulated the whole film) between two defendants. But here, as everywhere else, the constraints of the film's ideological strategy will compel Lincoln to *choose not to choose,* either (see 13) by deciding to reestablish the balance between the two parties, or (see 14) by indefinitely postponing the choice, or even, in the trial, by positively refusing to decide, thus trying to save both brothers, be it at the risk of losing both; all things which label and confirm Lincoln as a unifier and not a divider.

(b) During the different stages of the trial, Lincoln appears successively (1) As the weigher of souls: he quickly estimates the moral value of the members of the jury (and he does this according to norms which escape common understanding, even conventional morality: he accepts a man who drinks, lynches, loafs about, because by admitting to these faults, he manifests his deeper honesty). (2) As entertainer of the crowd (jokes, little stories, etc. . . . .) which put him in contrast with the prosecutor, a starchy man of mean appearance. (3) As manifesting his castrating power over Cass, whom he immediately attacks without apparent reasons: intimidation, vicious interrogation, and totally displaced onomastic play on words, thundering looks: all these things imply a premonition of Cass's guilt on Lincoln's part, which is not to be backed up by any knowledge but is nonetheless the Truth. For throughout the film Lincoln relates not to knowledge, but to Truth (= Law). (4) As the spirit opposed to the word, the natural and/or divine Law to social Laws which are their more or less perfect transcription (he interrupts the prosecutor's cross-examination of the mother by telling him "I may not know so much of Law, Mr. Prosecutor, but I know what's right and what's wrong"). (5) As the righteous against the corridor filibusterer, morality against politics (i.e. his political opponent Douglas' asides with the prosecutor and with Cass).

(c) But this first day of the trial ends in a defeat for Lincoln, brought about by a sensational development: Cass's second testimony. From humanitarian concern, to save at least one of the two defendants he goes back on the first evidence he gave, and claims to have been an eyewitness of the murder (thanks to the moonlight) and points out the murderer: the elder of the two brothers. In the hermeneutic chain ("which one has killed?") this reversal of the situation introduces a deceptive answer. A new question is thus posed: how will Lincoln sort this one out, not only to win the trial but also to remain faithful to his refusal to choose?

21. The Night

(a) As before any "great crisis" in Hollywood cinema, there is a pause: the scene of the family vigil in the prison—whose function, in very classically codified form, is to instill a sense of expectancy allowing a dramatic resurgence. Here the demands of this code (tension–relaxation–tension) are precisely fulfilled: no information is given which makes the drama progress (the family's communion in song replacing/forbidding all explanatory dialogue); it is a "precarious situation lived through with serenity." But the lack of any allusion on the part of the other members of the family to the guilt of the elder brother is itself sufficient to ratify Cass's accusations against him; the fact that it is not questioned—as if it presented no problem—seems to authenticate it.

In the duration of the scene, its adherence to the code seems perfect and even excessive: the convention is accepted and pushed to its extreme by the Fordian inscription (for everything which delineates the family group in Ford is grafted here), even to bestowing its character of strangeness on the scene (static frame, scenes shot from the front, strong light-dark contrasts, position of the characters, choir). But this adherence on repeated reading is revealed to be a deception. When we know that the real culprit is neither of the brothers, the absence of any discussion between them or with their family has the effect of a real *coup de force* at the price of which the miraculous dimension of Lincoln's revelation of the Truth is made possible. The scene is thus regulated—with great skill—by *the necessity of making the code* (the waiting period in which the group communes in silence or song—when words are useless, even improper) *responsible for the censorship of any information* about the defendants' innocence. If the scene is silent, it is because anything that might be intimated would inevitably have lifted the deception from the enigma and ruined the magic of Lincoln's act.

(b) The second part of this night of vigil starts, concerning Lincoln, on the same model: the hero's solitude and meditation before the decisive test. Lincoln is in his rocking chair by his office window, playing the Jew's harp. This isolation signifying his defeat is strengthened by two events: (1) Douglas and Mary Todd go past his window in a carriage; they both look at him condescendingly; Mary Todd turns away and says to Douglas: "You were discussing your political plans Mr. Douglas, please go on." (2) The judge appears in Lincoln's office and, arguing from his long experience, suggests a double compromise: to get help the next day from a more experienced lawyer (he suggests Douglas) and to agree to plead guilty to save the other brother. Lincoln categorically refuses: "I'm not the sort of fella who can just swap horses in the middle of the stream."

In (1) the change in size between the first long-shot of the carriage and the closeup when Mary Todd speaks, a trick of the direction which eliminates the "real" distance by changing the axis (high angle shot) and the width of the shot so that Lincoln appears to be right above the carriage, and Mary Todd's words cannot then fail to reach him, thanks to this unrealistic proximity—compel the viewer to interpret them as being addressed not to Douglas (Lincoln's eternal contrast) but to Lincoln, and their political contents *standing* for an erotic content. "You were discussing your political plans Mr. Douglas, please go on" can be read as "I couldn't possibly do so with you Lincoln, *nor make love*" at a time when everything in Mary Todd's behavior, look, and gestures points to her obvious spite, and to her speech as a denial of her desire. In the film's other scenes the repression taking place alternately between the erotic and the political (Law as repressed desire and as natural/divine morality) becomes here, in a single sentence, the repression of the erotic by the political.

In (2) Lincoln's paranoid features are confirmed: his refusal of all help, of any compromise, his hallucinatory faith in his own power, his certainty of being Chosen, his rigidity, the holding out to the bitter end.

22. Victory

Second day of the trial. Lincoln calls the main prosecution witness Cass back to the witness box, and by his questions makes him *repeat* his statement of the previous day point by point: it was in fact thanks to the full moon that he was able to witness the scene; it is to save one of the two brothers that he has gone back on his first statement. Mary Todd, like the rest of the public, doesn't see the point of Lincoln's insistence to have things which are already known repeated. Lincoln pretends to let Cass go again, and just as he is about to leave the well of the Court, he suddenly asks him "What d'you have against Scrub White, what did you kill him for?" Pulling the almanac out of his hat he thrusts it forward, saying: "Look at page 12: see what it says about the moon; it says it was in its first quarter and set at 10.21 PM, forty minutes before the murder" and, addressing Cass, "You lied about this point, you lied about the rest." From this point onward Lincoln harasses Cass with questions until, collapsing, in a broken, shrill voice, he confesses: "I didn't mean to kill him. . . ." The confession obtained, Lincoln casually turns away from his victim and, addressing the prosecutor: "Your witness," while Cass's former supporters surround him threateningly.

(a) The almanac: a *signifier* first present in the scenes where the mother asks Lincoln to write to her imprisoned sons for her (see 19), as a simple support for writing, reappears on the first day of the trial (where it is on Lincoln's table, near his hat), then in the night scene where Lincoln is fingering it with apparent casualness. It is finally produced as *sign* of the Truth at the end of the second day of the trial, when Lincoln pulls it out of his hat like a conjuror.

We have here the typical example of a signifier running through the film without a signified, representing nothing, acquiring the status of a sign under Lincoln's revelation (the almanac representing proof of the truth for everyone) *but without ever having been an indicator.* Thus the thriller process of deduction is *completely eliminated* in favor of a scriptural logic which demands that such a signifier be produced as a veiled term whose very concealment and sudden final revelation would constitute a mise-en-scène inseparable from the meaning it induces, the mark of the unconscious determination of its writing into Ford's text. Veiled first in the extent to which it realizes the operation of repression of (erotic/criminal) violence in the fiction, whose return is effected according to a rhetoric of negation, and second because its only *place* is that of a term whose sole function is to effect a mediation (between the criminal and the crime, between the mother and the sons), it is thereby doomed to disappearance as it is produced and to be included/excluded from the propositions in which it is actualized, by the very fact that it determines the production of their meaning; this is so to the extent to which the *signifier* of truth must remain veiled as long as truth is not stated, since at no moment is it presented as a clue (which would imply a work, the exercise of a knowledge, even a manipulation, which is not the case here). Lincoln's powers are thus not presented as the exercise of the art of detective deduction, but as a paranoid interpretation which short-circuits its process. Thus the proof of the crime seems to be materialized by the mere faculty which Lincoln has of producing the signifier as the concrete result of his omnipotent powers of Revelation.

But the manifestation of this omnipotence at the end of the film, made necessary by the ideological project (Lincoln, a mythical hero representing Law and guarantor of Truth), takes place at the end of the series of relations of copresence between Lincoln and the almanac (three scenes where it is present without Lincoln knowing what to do with it in terms of the truth) and in such an unlikely and arbitrary (magical) way that it can be read in the following ways: (1) effectively as omnipotence, (2) as a pure fictional *coup de force* implying an imposition of Ford's writing on Lincoln's character (Lincoln's omnipotence is then *controlled and limited* by Ford's omnipotence, the latter not adopting the best possible viewpoint on his character, which would have been to show him as himself having the revelation of the Truth and not merely as its agent) and (3) as Lincoln's *impotence* insofar as he appears subject to the power of the signifier (the almanac) and in a position of radical nonrecognition regarding it, such that one can just as well say that the truth revolves around Lincoln (and not Lincoln around the truth), and that it is not Lincoln who uses the signifier to manifest the truth, but the signifier which uses Lincoln as mediator to accede to the status of the sign of truth. Two and 3 (one specific to the film's writing, the other to its reading: but as we have stated in the introduction, we do not hesitate to force the text, even to rewrite it, insofar as the film only constitutes itself as a text by integration of the reader's knowledge) *manifest a distortion of the ideological project by the writing of the film.*

(b) Once the truth is revealed, Lincoln harasses Cass with brutal questions until he obtains his confession. (1) Lincoln must obtain from the culprit the confirmation of what he has just stated to be truth; on the one hand to finalize the fiction (save the two brothers, solve the mystery: but at the same time, this solution is the admission that the enigma was in fact a mere deception set up by the film); and on the other hand to be confirmed in the eyes of the other characters as possessor of the truth (if it is in fact enough for the spectator—who knows who Lincoln is—to see him reveal the truth to believe it, the characters of the fiction, his enemies, those who have witnessed his failure of the previous day, etc. . . . cannot be so easily satisfied with his word). (2) Lincoln's insistence and violence at this moment can read, first, as the classic harshness of rampant Justice, but mainly as the culmination of Lincoln's castrating power (see 16), which is attested by the fact that Cass, around whom the whole film has accumulated the clichés of hypervirility, collapses in tears when he confesses, crying like a child. (3) This excessive violence of the characterization of Lincoln in the writing of the film, which is motivated neither by the needs of Lincoln's cause (he could triumph without terror) nor by those of the fiction (Cass could confess without resisting), shows an imbalance with the idealized figure of Lincoln: even if this violence in the writing implies no intentional criticism of the character Lincoln, it makes visible—by its own scriptural excesses—the truly repressive dimension of the figure which this writing dictates, and deroutes what could have been edifying or hagiographic in the ideological project of the film.

23. "Toward His Destiny"

After his victory, Lincoln leaves the court alone. Four people are waiting for him, among them Mary Todd and Douglas. She congratulates him, looking at him seductively. Douglas then comes to shake his hand: "I give you my sincere promise never to make the mistake of underrating you again." Lincoln replies: "Neither of us will underrate each other again." He is about to go but is called back: "The town's waiting." He moves toward the door, fully lit, and the crowd can be heard applauding offscreen.

(a) Victorious, Lincoln is *recognized* by those who doubted him: this type of scene (recognition of the hero) belongs to a very classic register. But the way the scene is filmed, the camera at a slightly low angle shot, disposition of the groups, Lincoln's rather weary solemnity, the tone in which he is called ("the town's waiting"), and chiefly, when he goes to the threshold, his entry into a beam of violent light, the frontal low angle shot when he faces the crowd whom he greets by removing his hat, the very harsh lighting of the end of this scene, all set this sequence in a very specifically theatrical dimension: congratulations backstage after the performance, recall to the stage of the prima donna. But the fact that, by spatial displacement, this *encore* takes place not in the court in front of the spectators of the trial but on another stage (the street, the town, the country) and in front of a crowd *which is not shown* (which is no longer only the inhabitants of Springfield but of America) retroactively shows the performance of the trial (definitely given as theatrical by the entrances, the recalls, the repeats, the attitude of the spectators, the wings, etc.) to be a simple rehearsal (provincial tour) and what is to follow on the other stage (which the whole film has played on as something having already happened which no one could be ignorant of) will be the real performance (national tour); and the *encore* is, in fact, the true entrance on the stage of the legend. At the moment when he is *discovered* (intercepted) by the others as Lincoln, and stripped of his character, he can only act it out, play his own role. This interception is very precisely indicated in the film by the violent call of the brilliant light: the reference to German expressionism (even to horror films: *Nosferatu)*—much admired by Ford, as we well know—is therefore compulsory at this point.

(b) Preceding the film's last shots, which will only serve to heighten this tragic dimension, we have the scene of farewell to the Clays; like all other scenes with the family (as a function of its status in relation to Lincoln) it is treated in an intimate, familiar way, without solemnity. A scene in which the fiction will terminate the double circuit of the symbolic debt linking Lincoln to Mrs. Clay and of the desire which drives Carrie Sue (as we have seen, she is a substitute for Ann Rutledge) toward a Lincoln who can no longer love her; first the mother insists on paying Lincoln and gives him a few coins which he accepts, saying: "Thank you ma'am it's mighty generous of you"; then Carrie Sue leaps to his neck and kisses him, saying: "I reckon I'd just about die if I didn't kiss you Mr.

Lincoln." This confirms everything in Carrie Sue's attitude, which already exceeded the simple feeling of gratitude toward Lincoln, showing her to be driven by the desire which throughout the film, makes her "play" around him, thus allowing her kiss to be read as a form of "acting out," a substitute for orgasm.

(c) Final scene: Lincoln takes leave of his companion (who is simultaneously a classic theatrical confidant and a sort of Sancho Panza, who is at his side in a number of scenes in the film) by telling him "I think I might go on apiece. . . . maybe to the top of that hill." The confidant goes out of frame. A storm threatens. Lincoln is slowly climbing the hill. A last shot shows him facing the camera, with a vacant look, while threatening clouds cross the background and the "Battle Hymn of the Republic" begins to be heard. Lincoln leaves the frame. Rain begins to fall violently and continues into the final shot of the film (his statue at the Capitol) while music intensifies.

Here again, it is the excesses of Ford's writing (accumulation of signs of the tragic, of ascent: hill—mythical reference—storm, lightning, rain, wind, thunder, etc.) which by overlaying all the clichés, underlines the monstrous character of the figure of Lincoln: he leaves the frame and the film (like *Nosferatu*) as if it had become impossible for him to be filmed any longer; *he is an intolerable figure,* not because he has become too big for any film on account of the ideological project but rather because the constraints and violences of Ford's writing, having exploited this figure for their own ends and manifested its excessive and monstrous dimensions, have no further use for it and so return it to the museum.

24. Work of the Film

With the fiction reaching saturation point here, what culminates in the final sequence is nothing other than the effects of meaning, rescanned by our reading through the film as a whole, taken to their extreme. That is: the unexpected results (which are also contrary in relation to the ideological project) produced by the inscription—rather than flat illustration—of this project within a cinematic texture and its treatment by a writing which, in order to carry through the project successfully, maximizing its value *and only that* (it's obvious that Ford takes practically no distance in relation to the figure and the ideology of Lincoln) is led to: such distortions (the setting up of a system of deception); such omissions (all those scenes necessary in the logic of the crime thriller but whose presence could have lessened the miraculous dimension of Lincoln's omnipotence: the confrontation with the accused, the least one could expect of a lawyer); such accentuations (the dramatization of the final scenes); such scriptural violence (be it for the repression of violence—the lynching, the trial); such a systematization of determination and election (throughout a film which at the same time wants to play on a certain suspense and free choice without which the fiction could neither develop nor capture interest); in short to such a *work* that today simply delimiting its operation and the series of means it puts into action allows us to see the price at which such a film could be made, the effort and detours demanded to carry the project through.

And which Jean-Pierre Oudart in the following conclusion, the point of departure of our study, cannot but repeat.

25. Violence and Law

I. A discourse on the Law produced in a society which can only represent it as the statement and practice of a moralist prohibition of all violence, Ford's film could only reassert all the idealist representations which have been given it. Thus it is not very difficult to extract from it an ideological statement which seems to valorize in all innocence the ascetic rigor of its agent, making it into the unalterable value which circulates throughout the film from scene to scene; it is also easy to observe that this cliché, presented as such in the film and systematically accentuated, is not there merely to ensure the acceptability of the Fordian inscription. Without this cliché which provides the fiction with a kind of metonymic continuity (the same constantly reasserted figure)—whose necessity is moreover overdetermined, its function being more than simply setting up a character whose "idealism" can most conveniently be signified by the external signs of the very puritan sense of election—the film would appear, in fact does appear in spite of it, to be a text of disquieting unintelligibility; through its constant disconnections, it places us in a forced position for the reading and in fact its comprehension demands.

(1) That one first take no account of this at once insistent and fixed statement;

(2) That one listens carefully to what is stated in the succession of so obviously "Fordian" scenes which support this statement, and in the relations between the figures, all more or less part of the Fordian fiction, which constitute these scenes;

(3) That one tries to determine how all these are involved; i.e., to discover what the operation by which Ford inscribes this character into his fiction consists of, insofar as, despite appearances, it is not superimposed on Ford's "world," does not traverse it like a foreign body, but finds through this inscription into his fiction a designated place as representative of his Law; for the filmmaker promotes the character to the role to which his (legendary) historical referent destines him only at the price of his subjection to the (Fordian) fictional logic. This determined his entry there in advance insofar as his role was already written and his place already set out in Ford's fiction. The work of Ford's *écriture* only becomes apparent in this film through the problem involved in producing the character in this role, in that he took a place which was already occupied.

II. It is the character of the mother that incarnates the idealized figure of Ideal Law in Ford's fiction. Moreover, it is often, as in *Young Mr. Lincoln,* the widowed mother, guardian of the deceased father's law. It is for her that the men (the regiment) sacrifice the cause of their desire, and under her presidency that the Fordian celebration takes place; this in fact consists in a simulacrum of sexual relations from which all effective desire is banned. But it is in the constantly renewed relationship of this group with another (the Indians), in the dualism of Ford's universe that the inscription of the structural imperative of Law which dictates the deferment of desire and imposes exchange and alliance is realized in violence, guided by the mediating action of the hero (often a bastard), who is placed at its intersection.

III. In *Young Mr. Lincoln* one of the results of using a single character for both roles is that he will have both their functions, which will inevitably create, by their interference and their incompatibility (insofar as one secures the taboo on the violence of desire, the other is agent of its inscription), disturbances, actions which oppose the order of Ford's world, and it is remarkable that each comical effect always shows them up (there is no film in which laughter is so precisely a sign of a constant disorder of the universe). The compression of their functions will in fact be used only on the one level of the castration of the character (signified at the ideological level by its puritan cliché, and at the same time written, in the unconscious of the text, as the effect of the fictional logic on the structural determination of the character) and of his castrating action, in a fiction ruled by Ideal Law alone since the dualism of Ford's world is abandoned in favor of the mass-individual opposition. (In fact the political conflict intervenes only as a secondary determination of the fiction and literally only acts backstage). In fact, we see that:

(1) The character's calling originates in his renouncing the pleasures of love, and it is strengthened because he resists its attraction: Lincoln becomes so well integrated in the fiction and is so vigilant against the violences and plots which take place there only because he refuses to give in to the advances constantly made to him by women, affected by a charm which is due only to the prestige of his castration.

(2) This extreme postponement of the hero's desire soon becomes meaningful, since it permits him to become the restorer of Ideal Law, whose order has been perturbed by a crime which the Mother has not been able to prevent but which she will attempt to stifle.

This shows that:

(1) The puritan cliché which Ford emphasizes has the very precise function of promoting the character to his role as mediator, insofar as the pleasure which he rejects allows him to thwart any attempt at sexual and political corruption; it thus simultaneously guarantees the credibility of the figure of Lincoln and the position of the character as the figure of Ideal Law in Ford's fiction. At the obvious price of installing him within a castration, whose comical aspects Ford uses sufficiently to indicate how indifferent he is to producing an edifying figure,

and how much more attentive he is to the disturbing results of its presence in the fiction: for example, in the dance scene in which his character perturbs the harmony, where the agent of Law behaves like a killjoy, thus making visible what the harmony of the Fordian celebration would conceal.

(2) The fact that the character literally takes the place of the Mother, i.e., takes on simultaneously her ideal position and her function (since he assumes responsibility for her children and promises to feed them well in the new home which the prison becomes), gives rise to a curious transformation of the figure, as this repetition of roles is effected under the sign of a secret which the Mother must (believes she does) keep to try to prevent any violence—even, inconceivably, that of the Ideal Law which she incarnates—against her children; and by thus incubating the crime she projects her role into a quasi-erotic (almost Hitchcockian) dimension never presented as such by Ford, since usually the fiction protects her from any relationship with the crime (since it is part of her function to be ignorant of violence). This is comically reintroduced in the final scene of the trial, when the real proof (an almanac on a sheet of which should have been written the letter of love which Lincoln was planning to write for her, only to lull her attention and extract confessions from her) is pulled out of Lincoln's hat; it was necessary for the reestablishment of Law that by the end of the trial a signifier (the proof of the crime) be produced whose very occultation renders it erotic; and that it must be necessarily be produced by the figure of Law to fit into the fictional logic, since it is from this ideal Law that originated the cancellation of the criminal act in the fiction, the statement of the taboo on violence (on pleasure), the position of the Mother as the figure of forbidden violence (pleasure), the possession of the phallus by this figure (as a signifier of this pleasure), and the production of the proof of the crime as if it were a phallic signifier obviously proceeding from the same statement. In such fictions this usually means either that the weapon, the trace of the crime, acts like a letter which Law must decipher, since its very proscription has written it, or that the confession be produced by the criminal as a return of the repressed in an erotic form. The two results are here compressed, Law producing the proof of the crime (the writing which reveals the murderer) as if it were a phallic object which Ford's comedy presents like the rabbit pulled out of the conjuror's hat; the improbable levity with which Ford brings the trial to its close really can only be read as a masking effect which conceals to the end the "human" context, thus allowing the logic of the inscription to produce this gag as its ultimate effect, a final consequence of Lincoln's reenactment of the Mother's role, a fantastic return of the mask.

IV. The fact that the overdetermination of this inscription of the Lincoln figure, as agent of the Law, in Ford's fiction by all the idealized representations of Law and its effects produced by the bourgeoisie, far from having been erased by Ford, has been declared by his writing and emphasized by his comedy shows

what a strange ideological balancing act the filmmaker has insisted on performing, and what strange scriptural incongruities he has insisted on exploiting; to
the extent that by the fictional constraints he gave himself, by giving up the
usual bisection of his fiction and the sometimes truly epic inscription of Law
thereby articulated (which recalls Eisenstein in *The General Line*), he could only
produce the Law as a pure prohibition of violence, whose result is only a
permanent indictment of the castrating effects of its discourse. Indeed, to what
is the action of his character reduced if not hitting his opponents at their weakest
point—weaknesses which Ford always perversely presents as being capable of
provoking a deadly laughter? So that the sole but extreme violence of the film
consists of verbal repression of violence which, in certain scenes (the unsuccessful
lynching), is indicated as really being a death sentence, a mortal interdict which
has no equivalent except maybe in Lang and which shows the distance Ford, or
rather his writing, keeps between himself and the idealist propositions which he
uses.

V. For, with a kind of absolute indifference to the reception given to his stylistic
effects, the filmmaker ends by practicing stubbornly a scriptural perversion
which is implied by the fact that, paradoxically, in a film meant to be the
Apology of the Word, the last word is always given to the iconic signifier,
entrusted by Ford with the production of the determining effects of meaning.
And as in this film what is to be signified is always either the (erotic, social,
ideological) separation of the hero relative to his surroundings, or the immeas-
urable distance between him and his actions, or the absence of any common
denominator between the results he obtains and the means he uses, and those
obtained by his opponents (insofar as he holds the privilege of the castrating
speech), Ford succeeds, by the economy of means which he uses to that effect—
his style forbidding him the use of effects of implicit valorization of the character
which he could have drawn from an "interiorized" writing—in simultaneously
producing the same signifier in completely different statements (for example, in
the moonlight scene, where the moonlight on the river indicates at the same
time the attempted seduction, the past idyll, and the hero's "idealist" vocation);
or even in renewing the same effect of meaning in totally different contexts (the
same spatial disconnections of the character used in the dance scene and the
murder scene). So that the intention of always making sense, of closing the door
to any implicit effect of meaning, of constantly reasserting these same meanings,
in fact results—since to produce them the filmmaker always actualizes the same
signifiers, sets up the same stylistic effects—in constantly undermining them,
turning them into parodies of themselves. (With Ford parody always proceeds
from a denunciation of the writing by its own effects). The film's ideological
project thus finds itself led astray by the worst means it could have been given
to realize itself (Ford's style, the inflexible logic of his fiction) mainly to the benefit
of a properly scriptural projection (obtained not by the valorization after the

event of previously constituted effects of meaning but proceeding directly from the inscription, produced anew and resolved in each scene, of the character in Ford's fiction) of the effects of the repression of violence: a violence whose repression, written thus, turns into exorcism and gives to its signifiers, in the murder and the lynching scenes, a fantastic contrast which contributes considerably to the subversion of the deceptively calm surface of the text.

Notes

1. Friedrich Engels and Karl Marx, *Die Presse,* October 12, 1862.
2. Peter Bogdanovich, *John Ford* (London: Studio Vista, 1967).
3. This usage of inscription *(l'inscription)* refers to work done by Jacques Derrida on the concept of *écriture* in *Théorie d'ensemble* (Collection Tel Quel, 1968) [. . . .] *Cahiers'* point here is that all individual texts are part of and inscribe themselves into one historically determined "text" *(l'histoire textuelle)* within which they are produced; a reading of the individual text therefore requires examining both its dynamic relationship with this general text and the relationship between the general text and specific historical events. [Note by editors of *Screen*]

—Translated by Helen Lackner
and Diana Matias

25

Noël Burch

Primitivism and the Avant-Gardes: A Dialectical Approach

In 1899, Jules-Etienne Marey, physiologist and inventor of what had potentially been the first motion picture camera, wrote in a preface to a book on "animated photographs":

What such pictures show, after all, our eye could have seen directly. They add nothing to our ocular powers, they remove none of our illusions. Now the true character of scientific method is to remedy the inadequacies of our senses or correct their errors. In order to achieve this, chronophotography must renounce showing things as they really are.

And Marey concluded this veritable credo of anti-illusionism by asserting that the only techniques of motion synthesis that could possibly interest science were those which enabled us to slow down or speed up the appearance of reality.[1]

Twenty-five years later, Dziga Vertov wrote:

What am I to do with my camera? What is its role in the offensive I am launching against the visible world?

I think of the Camera Eye. . . I abolish the customary sixteen frames-per-second. . . high speed cinematography, . . . frame-by-frame animation and many other techniques . . . become commonplace.

The Camera Eye must be understood as "that which cannot be seen by the human eye, as the microscope and telescope of time. . ."

The Camera Eye is the possibility of making visible the invisible, of bringing light into darkness, of revealing what is hidden. . . of turning the lie into truth.[2]

This article was originally presented in slightly different form as a lecture at the Whitney Museum of American Art on November 18, 1979, as part of a series of lectures and films entitled "Researches and Investigations into Film: Its Origins and the Avant-Garde," organized by John G. Hanhardt, curator of video and film at the Whitney. It is published here for the first time.

And now here is another echo, spanning, this time, a period of over sixty years. In 1904, future pioneer producer Fred J. Balshofer was working for the Shields Lantern Slide Company in New York City. In his memoirs, he recalls the following anecdote:

I timidly suggested to Shields the possibility of making moving pictures as well as lantern slides. Shields was a stubborn, pompous man and in his typical sarcastic manner, said: "Making moving pictures? Why those flickering things hurt your eyes. They're just a passing fancy."[3]

In 1966, Jonas Mekas interviewed Tony Conrad, maker of *The Flicker:*

CONRAD:. . . The patterns that I selected to use in *The Flicker* are an extension of the usual stroboscope techniques into a much more complex system. *The Flicker* employs harmonic relations, speeds, pulses and patterns different from those used until now.

(At this point in our conversation, James Mullins, the manager of the Cinematheque, where *The Flicker* was screened, walked in.)

JONAS MEKAS: What was the effect of the film on you? You saw it twice.

JAMES MULLINS: It gave me headaches.[4]

What these two sets of anecdotes have in common is their ambivalence. Neither can be said to express a true equivalence—either between the thinking of the conservative, middle-class scientist whose mechanistic materialism goes straight back to Descartes and a Communist filmmaker deeply committed to dialectical and historical materialism; or between the effect of scintillation due to a technological "blind spot" of the early cinema (the failure to discover that flicker could be eliminated by the simple expedient of the double-action shutter) and that which was deliberately produced by a sophisticated filmmaker using single-frame exposures of a kind unthinkable until at least the nineteen-twenties.

Yet at the same time, there is no doubt in my mind that such encounters—and there have been many—are meaningful, that they can clarify our thinking, not only about the Primitive Cinema—and precinema—but also about the various avant-gardes, provided we avoid simplistic conflations, provided we are careful to hold on to both ends of the chain, as the French working class colloquially expresses its grasp of Marx's dialectics.

It is no exaggeration to say that Marey, on the brink of inventing the cinema, and in spite of his belated and half-hearted attempt to emulate Edison, actually did refuse to accomplish the decisive step. The attitude behind this behavior, expressed in the above quotation and shared implicitly by Muybridge, explicitly by Albert Londe, was derived from a scientist functionalism which inclined him to see the synthesis of movement as a gross redundancy from his cognitive point of view. Yet Marey's science was far from innocent: he himself advocated applying the results of his studies of human locomotion to the rationalization of the burdens of Monsieur Thiers' foot soldiers, and his analyses of work motion may be seen as one source of Taylorism, that technology by which capital sought and still seeks to make the worker an appendage to his or her machine. Vertov, of course, made no pretense of being a scientist in the usual sense; yet, perhaps because Marxism is also a rationalism, his project does have that one point of tangency with Marey's, the preeminence of the cognitive over the analogical model.

What, however, can possibly link these two other facts: that on the one hand in the 1960s a handful of middle-class connoisseurs successfully combatted headache and eyestrain to achieve, no doubt, an "expanded vision," an attentiveness to the marginal functionings of their own optic system under stimulation and that, on the other, the large plebeian audience of the first ten years of motion pictures put up with a flicker that their social "betters" regarded as such intolerable discomfort that it contributed to their staying away in droves from the places where films were shown . . . those smoke-filled, rowdy places frequented exclusively in those days by a class of people for whom motion pictures were cheaper than an evening at the gin mill and no doubt somewhat less uncomfortable than a day spent in the racket and stench of the factory or sweatshop?

In any but a purely contingent sense, there would seem to be no link at all here, and in fact any attempt to establish one might seem at best ahistoric, at worst grotesque. Yet I have come to regard this encounter as an emblem of the contradictory relationships between the cinema of the Primitive Era and the avant-gardes of later periods. For the elimination of flicker and the trembling image, fairly complete after 1909 it seems, was a crucial moment in the realization of the conditions for the emergence of a system of representation complying with the norms of the bourgeois novel, painting, and the theater . . . and for the recruitment of an audience which would include various strata of the bourgeoisie. When the successive modernist movements set about extending, pragmatically or systematically, their "deconstructive" critiques of those representational norms to the realm of film, it was inevitable that sooner or later the flicker should reappear, valued now for both its synesthetic and its "self-reflexive" potentials.

While such correspondences, then, are never entirely fortuitous, we must, it seems to me, consider them with the greatest caution. For while it is no doubt the experience of the avant-gardes—and particularly those of the sixties, in both Europe and the United States—which has made it possible for us today simply to *read* many of the phenomena encountered in the earliest films, that experience has also led, for want of an understanding of the historical context, for want too of any coherent theoretical framework, to highly abusive assumptions of many kinds.

I will cite only two, sufficiently remote that evoking them will perhaps not be too embarrassing to their authors. Early in the sixties, a well-known scholar of the American film actually had the naiveté to suggest that the celebrated narrative anomaly found in Porter's *Life of an American Fireman*—the same action shown twice under different angles—was in some way a prefiguration of the labyrinthian textuality of *Last Year at Marienbad*. Later in the sixties, a distinguished archivist, who certainly should have known better, authenticated what appears to be the prodigiously "modern" editing of a 1907 bicycle farce included in the Paper Print Collection of the Library of Congress. Yet a perusal of other films deposited by the same firm (the Selig Polyscope Company) clearly shows that those daringly elliptical match-cuts, worthy of Eisenstein at the very least, are due simply to the fact that the producers deemed it necessary to supply only fragments of their films for copyright purposes.

Such confusions should make us leery whenever we encounter an effect of familiarity in a historical context which is in fact only deceptively close: these seventy-five years of cinema history are to be equated in my view with 700 years of literary or theatrical history, and the "logic" which governed the productions of Pathé or Biograph before 1905 is in many respects more contemporary with that of *The Romance of the Rose* or *Le Jeu de Robin et de Marion* than with *Major Barbara* or *L'Assommoir.*

The otherness of the Primitive Cinema—and I am referring precisely to that which is recognized by a generation of critics, historians, and filmmakers weaned on the radical modernism of the last three decades—this otherness is, in fact, twofold. Let us first consider the Primitive Mode of Representation proper, derived without doubt from a number of models that were socially important at the turn of the century—the picture postcard, the vaudeville and melodrama stages, the circus, the Wild West show, the comic strip, etc.—but which cannot be said to be a literal or monolithic translation of any of these. By the time it reached maturity, by the time it began gradually to give way to the Institutional Mode of Representation that was to supersede it, the Primitive Mode was undeniably *stabilized,* having acquired a degree of specificity as high as that which the Institutional Mode itself was one day to achieve. The Primitive Mode was initiated as much by W.K.L. Dickson as by Louis Lumière, and was kept alive in its purest form until 1912 by Georges Méliès. However, it continued to haunt the cinema of France until the end of the silent era and left visible traces in many American films until at least 1920.

In its most characteristic guise, the Primitive Mode has, I believe, four primary traits. The first is well known: the *autarky* and *unicity* of each frame. Any given tableau will remain unchanged in its framing throughout its passage on the screen and from one appearance to the next (in the event of a recurring set or location); it is complete unto itself and never "communicates" with any other. In other words, the successive spaces depicted are presumed to occupy a common diegetic framework, but that is all: their spatio-temporal connections remain fundamentally unspecified.

The second primary trait which I distinguish may be called the *noncentered quality* of the image, and it must be considered under two separate aspects: on the one hand, the entire frame is a possible playing area. The areas close to the edges of the frame are as likely to be the site of vital action as those more centrally located. Concurrently, it is often difficult for the eye—at least it is for our eye—to locate the narratively significant center of the diegetic action—and there are times when none actually exists at all, when the entire image is being offered simultaneously to our gaze. The most famous films of Louis Lumière come to mind here, of couse *(Workers Leaving a Factory, Arrival of a Train at La Ciotat)* but also countless tableaux of narrative films as well.

Next, there is the crucial matter of camera distance. In the great majority of films made before 1906 (though not in all, and I shall return to this point), shot size approximated what we would call today the medium long-shot. That is to say, a standing character seldom occupied more than two-thirds of the height of the screen and often much less. The consequences of this were several, but they may, I believe, be summed up as producing an overall effect of *exteriority*. The lack of any significant facial detail in such shots inevitably rendered the characters' presence solely *behavioral:* one saw what they *did,* but there was absolutely no sense of that psychological interiority characteristic, for example, of the classical novel, except when such interiority was grossly exteriorized through a markedly calligraphic pantomime, which deprived it of any "naturalness." The Primitive Cinema at its most characteristic is ab-psychological. Characters lack that internal "presence" which was guaranteed, on the bourgeois stage, by the voice (with the help, from a gallery seat, of a strong pair of opera glasses), in the bourgeois novel by such strategies as the omniscience of a demiurgical narrator. Moreover their external presence was comparatively weak as well: spectators remained far more *apart* from those tiny silhouettes than from the characters on any stage, whose actual, physical presence could be verified by countless details addressing nearly all the senses (besides the visual perception of color and depth, we may mention the sounds of footsteps on the planks or of swirling gowns, the odor of greasepaint, tobacco, or perfume).

Maxim Gorki, in an article written upon first seeing the Lumière Cinématographe at the Nizhni-Novgorod fair in 1896, expressed eloquently the alienation which the spectator accustomed to the bourgeois stage and novel almost certainly must have experienced to some degree when confronted with those images:

Before you a life is surging, a life deprived of words and shorn of the living spectrum of colours—the grey, the soundless, the bleak and dismal life.

It is terrifying to see, but it is the movement of shadows, only of shadows . . . you feel as though Merlin's vicious trick is being enacted before you. As though he had bewitched the entire street, had compressed its many-storied buildings from roof-tops to foundations to yard-like size. He dwarfed the people in corresponding proportions, robbing them of the power of speech and scraping together all the pigment of earth and sky into a monotonous grey colour.[5]

Significantly, the film from that first Lumière program which seemed most "alive" to the great Naturalist writer was *Baby's Breakfast.* And while he not unexpectedly addresses his remarks to the iconography of the film alone—the couple "are so charming, gay and happy and the baby is so amusing"—we cannot fail to note that this film was the only close shot on the program. And in this connection, I wish to stress that *Baby's Breakfast* was not to remain an isolated instance in the primitive cinema. Contrary to popular belief, this shot—and other similar ones produced by Dickson—inaugurated an important minor genre which was to last for nearly ten years, a presentational medium closeup—or closeup—of one or two (generally well-known) actors mugging into the camera or even—in the Gaumont *Phonoscènes,* for example—singing or reciting comic monologues in very approximate synchronism with a tiny cylinder phonograph. These shots, which undoubtedly introduced *the presence of the persona* into the primitive cinema program and later, through the related practice of the emblematic closeup, into individual films, may be said to have fulfilled symbolically, at the level of the primitive cinema as a whole, a role prefiguring that of the interpolated closeup in the nascent Institutional Mode of Representation after around 1910.

The fourth major trait of the Primitive Mode as I perceive it may be designated by the somewhat barbarous term of *nonclosure.* Consider one of the latest and most accomplished examples I know in the American cinema of the purely primitive film: the 1905 Biograph *Kentucky Feud,* which is thought to have been directed by Billy Bitzer, soon to become Griffith's precious collaborator. This film refers to a feud which actually took place in Kentucky and which has come down to us through a celebrated ballad. However, the film's mode of fictionalization has little to do with that of, let us say, *All the President's Men.* Instead, it is assumed that the audience is familiar with the broad lines of the events described, and the successive tableaux seem conceived more like *hors-textes* or tabloid newspaper engravings. They are illustrations for a narrative which is elsewhere, and not self-contained scenes in the usual sense. Moreover, the function of the intertitles bears careful consideration here, exemplifying as it does the fundamental nonlinearity of many primitive narrative procedures. Indeed, here as in so many films of the period (and the films which Griffith directed six or seven years later for that same Biograph Company still retain this trait), the titles preempt, as it were, the strictly narrative dimension of the images, destroying any sense of suspense, balking for the moment any formation of the bi-univocally concatenated narrative chain that ultimately was to characterize the Institutional Mode.

Of course, in one sense, this description of the narrative process that was at work here is incomplete, as was my description—and one's experience—of the topologically acentric primitive tableau. For we must never forget that in what may have been a majority of cases by this time, and certainly in a great many, the presentation of a film was accompanied by some sort of verbal commentary in the theater, delivered by the so-called lecturer. And however much these "lectures" varied in quality and efficacy, it seems fairly certain today that their chief aim was to linearize the visual signifiers—in other words, to tell the audience where to look and when—and to operate some sort of closure—in other words, in this case, to give the audience background material they might not have known. Yet at the same time that the lecturer represented a concerted attempt to overcome certain "inadequacies" of the Primitive Mode, and to help new middle-class patrons decipher a medium to which they were unaccustomed, he or she was part of a general exhibition situation which continued to stress the priority of the actual spectatorial space-time over the illusory space-time of the film; we know that besides the lecturer's comments, off-color jokes, etc., there was always a more or less irrelevant piano player, constant comings and goings among the patrons, and, in New York City at least, it seems that the nickelodeon doors were generally left open during the performance. Clearly this was a far cry from the rapt attention devoted to silent films in film societies and Cinematheques today, but was strangely close to the atmosphere that reigns in a Forty-second Street flea-house during a kung fu movie.

Now before going on to describe a very different aspect of the "otherness" of primitive cinema, I would like to open a brief parenthesis concerning terminology. It seems to me that the films of the primitive era suggest why the category of "narrative film" is powerless to define in any essential way the films produced within the Institution. *Kentucky Feud* can hardly be described as non-narrative, yet I am sure most of us would agree that the experience of watching it is about as far from that which is ours watching a full-fledged institutional film as is the experience of watching, say, Ernie Gehr's *Reverberation*. Not, I hasten to add, that I regard these as equivalent experiences; however, they do help us to define the boundaries of a centered, linear, closured, Institutional experience which is absolutely not coextensive with the space of narrative (most classical documentaries are less "narrative" than *Kentucky Feud,* and yet are an integral part of the Institution). The very meaning of the term "narrative" for some of those who adopt a critical stance toward whatever in their minds it may cover, is even further clouded for me when I recall that a well-known American film artist recently presented one of his works to a London audience with the precautionary statement that it contained "narrative elements." These turned out to be a strip of film apparently slipping past the camera lens and on which there were dark, blurred photograms showing what might have been a woman's face. My preference for the term Institutional Mode of Representation to designate the basic framework within which mainstream cinema has evolved during the last fifty years has, I feel, if no other merit, that of avoiding such tendentious confusions.[6]

The pressures, economic, ideological, and cultural, that were eventually to create, first in the United States, then throughout the Western world, the conditions for the triumph of the Institutional Mode exerted themselves on the cinema as soon as it was born. The Primitive Mode, as a consequence, never existed in a vacuum. It was challenged from the outset by that aspiration to analog representation that is so deep-rooted in Western culture, which throughout the nineteenth century was so closely associated with the development of photography, and which further manifested itself in such peripheral but significant phenomena as the Diorama, the stereoscope, and the British temperance movement's photographic lantern shows known as "life models." The Primitive Era was essentially contradictory, it was the scene of a constant confrontation. On the one hand we have the analog aspiration, exemplified in Edison's sensationalist declarations about the canned operas of the future, and in the couplets about "man's victory over death" intoned by French newspapers after the premiere of Lumière's films at the Grand Café. On the other hand are the attitudes about representation which stemmed both from certain popular art forms and from the scientistic ideology upheld by a number of pioneers. Marey's out-and-out anti-illusionism was one instance of this attitude and Louis Lumière's personal commitment to the "raw document," his indifference to mise-en-scène, was another.

Actually, the most spectacular and most "obvious" evidence of the drive toward the perfect analog is to be found in the constant presence on the motion picture market, between 1894 and the First World War, of systems designed to endow those silent pictures with the Logos—with a Soul, as some have put it—in other words with lip-synch sound. From the Edison Company's Kinetophone of 1894, whose earphones and eyepiece prefigure, over and beyond the clatter of the penny arcade and the nickelodeon, the sensorial isolation of the thirties picture palace, to the vastly improved machine bearing the same name that was placed on the market in 1911 but which failed, like all its rivals, for want of adequate amplification, a really impressive number of synch sound systems appeared and disappeared during that twenty-year period. The Gaumont Chronophone, already mentioned, had a considerable commercial success, and the several hundred *Phonoscènes* directed by Alice Guy figured on the programs of theaters in France and elsewhere for over half a decade, in alternation with silent films. It is significant, of course, that all these efforts (as well as those which involved the "dubbing" of films during the projection by actors hidden behind the screen) had ceased completely by the eve of the Great War, when the Institutional Mode with its interpolated closeups and spoken titles was beginning to assert itself in the films of Reginald Barker, the Ince brothers, De Mille, and others.

Far more exotic, however, are the traces left by attempts to transform films *visually* in such a way as to overcome the exteriority, the lack of presence from which the primitive cinema, judged by the criteria of late nineteenth-century naturalism, was felt to suffer so severely. One of the most spectacular of these was the Cinéorama, presented by the French engineer Grimoin-Sanson at the 1900 Paris Exposition. This was a technically successful attempt to create a single, unbroken, circular image, filmed by twelve synchronized cameras and projected on the inside of a dome-like screen by twelve projectors placed beneath a platform which held the audience. This ingenuous attempt to *surround* the audience, to *enfold* them in an image which still otherwise cleaved to the distant exteriority of the Lumière model can, of course, only have heightened the topological dispersion of the primitive tableau (where were you supposed to look now?), and this experiment objectively retarded the historical movement toward spectatorial identification with an ubiquitous camera, that linchpin of the Institutional Mode.

The American equivalent of the Cinéorama was Hale's Tours. Here we are no longer dealing with an eccentric parapraxis—a term which can aptly describe many of the contradictory experiments of the age—but with an astute commercial venture, however extravagant it may appear today. Hale's Tours were permanent cinemas which flourished in the United States between 1904 and 1912 and which were more or less elaborately fitted out inside to resemble Pullman coaches. Sitting in the seats as if they were passengers in a moving train, patrons watched films that had been taken from the cow-catchers of moving trains or trolley-cars. This *strategy of penetration* no doubt conferred upon the Lumière model an effect of presence which it hitherto had lacked, but such exhibitions were necessarily limited to documents of a very particular sort, and the only immediate impact of Hale's Tours was to establish the need for fixed exhibition centers for films. Yet for me, Hale's Tours are above all emblematic of a tendency which marked the first decade of cinema and which consisted in interventions from outside the film, interventions in spectatorial space, destined to achieve a goal which history was to show could only be achieved, on the contrary, by blotting out spectatorial space.

The director whose work perhaps best embodies the contradictory "otherness" of the Primitive Era is Edwin S. Porter. The anomalous character of so many of the major experiments (and here I use this word advisedly) which he produced for the Edison Company between 1900 and 1906 was always due to the conflict between the Primitive Mode as I have described and illustrated it and the drive to overcome its "shortcomings," to achieve the interiorized presence of the future institution.

I shall cite only two examples here, chosen for what might seem to be their direct relevance to our subject. The celebrated *Great Train Robbery* was taxed by Sidney Peterson,[7] among other spokespersons of the American avant-garde, with being the Original Sin of the motion picture, as incarnating the precise moment when the Primitive Paradise was lost, when that evil object "narrative film" reared its ugly head. Paradoxically, this view was also shared by chauvinistic historians of mainstream film (such as Lewis Jacobs), for whom Porter was indeed the inventor of all the basic elements of "motion picture grammar." However, when the smoke of such special pleading has cleared, the film can be seen for what it is: a significant moment in the ongoing, historically inevitable process of the expansion of diegetic space-time beyond the confines of the primitive tableau. It was certainly not the first film to attempt what semiology has dubbed the alternating syntagma, and its famous chase sequence was only one of the first of its kind—both had appeared earlier in the work of the British pioneers. However, it was certainly one of the earliest attempts in the USA at a *developed form* using these linearizing figures, key harbingers of the future Institutional Mode.

At the same time, however, this film remains wholly within the Primitive Mode in at least one essential respect: for every tableau, the camera is still placed at a considerable distance from the action, and the lens used is such that the characters are often no taller than a quarter of the height of the screen, with their faces only barely readable. Despite, then, the extension and linearization of diegetic space-time, perceptual exteriority is maintained throughout and character presence is still minimal. However, this film—and in this respect it may have been a "first"—also displays a peculiarly acute awareness of this lack, an awareness expressed in the famous medium closeup showing Barnes, the outlaw chief, shooting into the camera. This shot, as is well known, was not actually incorporated into the film itself but delivered to exhibitors as a separate roll which they could splice onto the beginning or the end of the film, whichever they chose.

Now, at this simple statement of fact, our minds may begin to wander. We think of rare and relatively recent experiments in the film-mobile, such as *Chelsea Girls,* we think of aleatoric music, etc. But before indulging in such extrapolations, it is important to understand exactly what sort of object we are dealing with here. At a time when spectatorial identification with the camera and hence the possibility of camera ubiquity within the profilmic space of the primary tableau was still far in the future, despite isolated experiments in England and even the USA (including one by Porter himself, oddly enough), this shot is a particular kind of anaphore of the interpolated closeup. It brings to the film as a whole the dimension of individual presence, but cannot as yet "penetrate" the diegesis proper and must be content to wander about at the periphery, to be placed indiscriminately at the beginning or end of the film, at the discretion of exhibitors, that is to say, at random. Excluded from the film by the taboo still surrounding unicity of viewpoint, this "emblematic" closeup not only introduces the dimension of presence in this overall manner but also provides an early attempt to encapsulate the "essence" of the film, to provide a "treasure" which each spectator could carry home. Here is another anaphore of an Institutional strategy par excellence, essential to the constitution of the film as a consumer product. In this double capacity, the emblematic closeup became quite widespread over the next five or six years, chiefly in the USA but also in Europe.

The mobility of the closeup appended to *The Great Train Robbery* is thus seen not to be simply an instance of Primitive "freedom" (though it is true that similar "editorial responsibilities" were sometimes left to the exhibitors). It was the contradictory symptom of a historical blind spot on the one hand, and a relentless ideological undercurrent on the other. And while this instance of the "openness" of the primitive film clearly finds an objective echo in the occasional film-mobile of our time, one wonders if reflection on the organic relationship of this "wandering closeup" to the history of the Institution might not give rise, in our time indeed, to a more consequential exploration of aleatoric film forms.

No doubt the most celebrated anomaly in the work of Porter occurs in his film *The Life of an American Fireman* (1903). In the form in which the film was deposited at the Library of Congress in 1903, the rescue of the woman and child by a fireman is shown *twice,* from two different "points of view"—one (dieget-ically) inside the room where the victims are trapped, and one from outside. We see the same action successively. Now it is well known, I believe, that for many years this film was in fact shown in a different version.

On the strength of the fantasies of a film historian, themselves based on an ambivalence in the Edison catalogue, the two shots of the firemen fighting the fire were actually intercut, in such a way that they carried perfect continuity in the modern Institutional sense. As recently as last year, a professor of film history at a midwestern university taught students that Porter had "invented" cross-cutting, on the evidence of a print of that "improved" version, distributed for many years by the Museum of Modern Art, and which is still in the archives of his department. Yet today there is absolutely no question that the former version is the one shown to audiences in 1903, since only recently a contemporary show-print was discovered in the state of Maine which confirms the evidence of the copyright version in the Paper Print Collection of the Library of Congress.

This tampering is not simply one more example of the sloppiness of classical film history. It has, I believe, several important lessons to teach us. In the first place, it was done during a period—the 1930s—when the Institutional norms were so interiorized, so completely naturalized among all those who made or looked at films, that it must have been considered absolutely inconceivable that anyone could ever have exhibited or anyone else ever have "consumed" such an object, and the film has always been known to have had considerable success in its day. In the second place, as I have indicated, there appears to be just motivation for this tampering in the Edison catalogue's description of the fire-fighting scene *as if the action were in fact shown only once.* There is mention of a dissolve from inside the house to outside, but the fact that in the film the action begins all over again in the exterior shot is completely censored in the catalogue.

Now my work on the Primitive Era as a whole inclines me to see this discrepancy between film and catalogue as a perfect expression of the contra-diction between the historical pressures toward linearization and camera ubiquity on the one hand, and the exteriority of the Subject built into the primitive relation between spectator and screen image on the other. As our tamperers clearly sensed, we have here indeed a very early anaphore of camera ubiquity, a gesture toward a type of match-cutting which in fact would not even begin to come into use for another decade in the cinema, but which corresponded so easily and naturally to the most commonplace novelistic procedure—"Quickly the fireman climbed the ladder, *semi-colon,* inside the room he saw the inanimate woman on the bed"—*that it could be formulated on paper when it could not be on film*. Within the archetypal filmic situation of the time, frontality, exteriority, and, ultimately, the spectator's presumed consciousness of being seated in front of a screen, in an auditorium, in a single place, were generally regarded, at least by those who made production decisions, as overriding still the need simultaneously felt to linearize the narrative elements, a need expressed here in all the preceding shots. In short, rightly or wrongly, it was judged that this repeated action was less perturbing than any editing figure which posited an imaginary transportation in space. It was, implicitly at least, considered easier to say in effect to the audience: "Let's look at all that again from another angle" than to say: "Let's look at what happens next from a new angle."

I know of no example in primitive cinema where "time reversal" as radical as this occurs again. However, other, shorter overlaps do occur in a few American films and in those of Méliès, for example. Moreover, a film like *The Story the Biograph Told* (1905) admirably dramatizes the taboo surrounding camera ubiquity with an elaborate narrative apparatus whose sole purpose is to accomplish a 90-degree shot-change, a figure which as far as I can judge was not to be generalized until the end of the First World War. And the existence of this taboo is what authorizes me, I feel, to speak of the "price" that Porter paid for challenging it in his *Fireman* as a kind of parapraxis or failed act in the Freudian sense but with a "collective unconscious" replacing the individual.

This film by Porter also gives us a further clue as to the underlying nature of the many encounters between strategies employed by this or that modernist movement and certain of these primitive parapraxes. Let us consider the overlap match-cutting in certain films of Eisenstein (the most famous example here would no doubt be the raising of the bridges in *October*). It is clear that it has nothing in common, contextually or conceptually, with the "time reversal" in *The Life of an American Fireman* (or such little-known films as *Next!* or *The Policeman's Little Run,* both from 1902, in which the overlaps are of a much narrower ambit). Yet the Eisensteinian strategy is, at one level, the *negative* of the primitive parapraxis. The latter is a contradiction characteristic of an era we may regard as "preseamless," while Eisenstein's dialectic between the visual expression of a temporal "impossibility" and the common-sense notion of the linear flow of time is, among other things, a critique, implicitly at least, of *that same seamlessness*. Moreover, if my reading of the narrative anomaly in *The Life of an American Fireman* is a historically relevant hypothesis (it can never be more than that, since even if producers' or director's rationale were conscious, it is no doubt buried forever with them), then there is an encounter also at the level of the "positioning of the audience" implicit in the two procedures. The resolution of the Eisensteinian conflict, the acceptance of the time reversals by the spectators of *October*, is a specifically cultural act today—once it may also have been a political act—but it is hard to believe that the primitive spectators, to the extent that they were following *The Fireman* at all, did not also need to make some kind of conscious mental adjustment to the fact that they were seeing the same narrative fragment twice.

Here, however, I am treading on dangerous ground, which can in particular lead so easily to such myths as the Lost Paradise of the Primitive Cinema. I must stress immediately that a parallel such as this is of theoretical interest only. It says little if anything about film history as it was lived by those who made it (behind the cameras or sitting in halls before screens). It is in fact only from the point of view of a working theory of the Institutional Mode and its genealogy that any meaningful correlation can be established between processes which to all intents and purposes took place on different planets. And I should add that to my knowledge, none of these parapraxic anomalies was ever consciously emulated. There have, however, in the history of what has been called avant-garde or perhaps radical filmmaking, been a number of more or less concerted "revivals" of this or that aspect of the Primitive Mode proper.

Without doubt, the first of these efforts was *The Cabinet of Doctor Caligari.* Although it has not been fashionable in avant-garde circles in the U.S.A. to do so, I continue to regard *Caligari* as a film of considerable importance, and in particular as the first significant modernist film. It seems to me not at all accidental that the epithet which certain modernist critics have used to dismiss this film from the Pantheon of the avant-garde was "theatrical." This, after all, is the same epithet with which classical film history has dismissed the primitive cinema—motion pictures "begin" with Smith, Porter, Griffith, with the premises of the Institutional Mode, while the primitive cinema is merely an "imitation" of the theater, the history of the early cinema is reducible to the history of the "shaking off" of the theatrical influence, etc. *ad nauseum.* What such pronouncements have always carefully censored is that the theater which indeed had a deep impact on the earliest cinema was not the legitimate stage of the middle classes at all, but melodrama, vaudeville, Grand Guignol, and other plebeian forms; and that when cinema at last "became a language and an art" as the saying usually goes, it was through the constitution of a mode of representation which reproduced, albeit with specific original means, the underlying project of the bourgeois ("legitimate"!) stage.

Nor was it by accident that it was a film issued directly from the Expressionist movement which should have been the first to effect a deliberate, sweeping "return" to some of the major gestures of the Primitive Mode. Expressionism, after all, in its critique of all the manifestations of Naturalism, had for nearly two decades been keenly attentive to "primitive" art of all kinds: the sculptures of Africa and the folk woodcuts of Germany, as well as the creations of mental patients and children. I have no evidence that the collective effort which produced *Caligari* was actually informed by any awareness (or remembrance) of the forms of the Primitive Era. However, here I feel we can all agree that the encounter is striking in its scope. Let me simply point up its chief traits.

Caligari was produced in 1919, at a time when Institutional editing had become a universal aspiration, although mastery of it varied from country to country. Yet here we are dealing with a film consisting almost solely of a series of frontally shot, autonomous tableaux from which intrasequential editing is almost excluded. The autonomy of the successive tableaux is stressed by articulations that are strongly disjunctive, either through sharp graphic contrasts or through elaborately hesitant irises. Moreover, on the occasional instances when there is a shot change within a tableau, disjunctiveness is similarly stressed—by graphic contrast, notably through the use of vignettes—to a point that we usually feel these "match-cuts" to be as ragged as those in, say, the films Sigmund Lubin was making around 1906.

However, it seems to me that *Caligari* engages most resolutely with the historical process of constitution of the Institutional Mode in the matter of what I now see as the homogenization of pictorial space. Until around 1912 and even afterward in France, the cinema was characterized by a sharp division between two types of pictorial space. One type, exemplified by so many Lumière films, derives most immediately, I believe, from the scenic picture postcard, so much in vogue in the late nineteenth century. It is a model associated in the cinema for over a decade with outdoor shots almost exclusively, and involves a very strong emphasis on linear perspective and the rendering of haptic space in accordance with the model provided by the painting of the Renaissance. However, and contrary to a rather persistent myth (albeit of relatively recent origin), as soon as films began to contain both interior and exterior scenes, there coexisted with this model, and often within the same film, a pictorial approach which on the contrary emphasizes the picture plane. This is done through a number of strategies, some of which seem due to contingency (e.g., small studios, low budgets) while others seem quite deliberate. The role of contingency—massive at this time yet never, I feel, historically meaningless—is illustrated by an anecdote recorded by Georges Sadoul. One of Ferdinand Zecca's many tasks when he became the principal director for Pathé was to paint scenery. He was not good at it. One day, having set out to paint a backdrop meant to represent a cobbled street in perspective, he wound up with what looked like nothing so much as a pile of rocks. Always able to cope with a emergency, Zecca hung a sign over the canvas flat: "Men working: detour."[8]

A British film by a populist filmmaker, himself of plebeian origins, the remarkable William Haggar, demonstrates vividly the contrast between the two modes of pictorial representation which characterized the era. *The Life of Charles Peace* depicts with bold, simple strokes the career of a famous robber and murderer of the day. During the early sequences, shot mostly in studio, each autonomous tableau is filmed against a backdrop that is blatantly and schematically flat, with, for example, wall beams merely outlined with white paint on a canvas flat. In the latter part of the film, a chase, that typically primitive mode of narrative concatenation, is shown in a series of shots which, on the contrary, make systematic and equally typical use of deep space (in fact, one of them reproduces the by then archetypal frame of Lumière's *Arrival of a Train*).

It has not, I believe, been widely recognized that in this matter of the pictorial representation of space on the screen, those whose historical mission was the constitution of the Institutional Mode had a double task to perform. On the one hand, they had to bring depth and volume to the interior scenes of the Primitive cinema—and to overcome the tendency, very evident with Griffith in particular, to flatten even exterior images through a rigidly level camera attitude and frames decentered toward their lower edge. This transformation was achieved through innovations in camera attitude and set design, as well as the development of electric lighting which made it possible to introduce the codes of classical painting into cinematography. At the same time, through a variety of means which also included camera placement along with the choice and handling of lenses and, of course, the development of editing, they had to reduce that depth of field which, in the Lumière model, produced such a strongly dispersed, decentered image. This homogenization of pictorial screen space, conferring on closeups and long-shots alike a similar look of controlled haptic depth, was not fully achieved in the United States until the end of the First World War, in France a few years later.

Here, *Caligari's* relationship to the cinema of previous years is not simply at the level of mimetics, conscious or unconscious. Here the film actually puts the elements of a historical process to work within its own singular system. We are dealing with a precocious example of "epistemological creation" in the film medium.

The imagery in *Caligari* continually plays upon a carefully contrived ambiguity. The film's famous graphic style presents each shot as a stylized, flat renndition of deep space, with dramatic obliques so avowedly plastic, so artificially "depth-producing" that they immediately conjure up the tactile surface of the engraver's page somewhat in the manner of Méliès. Yet at the same time, the movement of the actors within these frames is systematically perpendicular to the picture plane, in a way reminiscent of Primitive deep-field blocking. The same images thus seem simultaneously to produce two historical types of pictorial space, superimposed one upon the other.

This issue of haptic space has, of course, been at the center of many important films of recent years—those of Godard and Snow, as well as Dreyer's *Gertrud*, come immediately to mind. But what seems to me so striking about *Caligari* is that through these multiple references to the issue as it historically evolved, the film offers an almost unique commentary on the constitution of the Institutional Mode as a visual system.

It is clear from much modern critical work, however, that no purely visual model can satisfactorily account for the Institutional Mode. The issues involved can be indicated by juxtaposing Cocteau's *Blood of a Poet* and a 1902 Biograph called *A Search for Evidence*, in which a woman and a private detective peer through a series of hotel-room keyholes affording the audience a suggestion of picturesque scenes . . . until the unfaithful husband and his mistress are confounded at last.

A Search for Evidence was by no means an unusual film for its day. We know that during the Primitive Era, when copyright was either nonexistent or virtually impossible to enforce, especially from one country to another, there was an extraordinary *circulation of signs*. It is no exaggeration to say that for a time film images were public property. This is a situation difficult to imagine today and it invariably arouses the righteous indignation of classical historians, always quick to denounce plagiarism when in fact they are peering into a kind of historical enclave in which, for a combination of ideological and economic reasons, the bourgeois concept of property took several years to establish the hegemony which it exerted over every other human endeavour throughout the Western world.

Here I might point out that while I personally know of no such avowed intertextuality among avant-garde artists in the USA or Western Europe—these tend on the contrary to jealously safeguard the principles of artistic property— I did see in London this year an example from Yugoslavia which deserves mention and reflection. Ivan Ladislav Galeta's *Two Times in One Space* (1972) is a two-projector, single-screen performance of an interesting single-shot slice-of-life exercise, directed three years earlier by a mainstream director. A ten-second lag between the superimposed pictures and the sound tracks heard through separate speakers adds a new dimension to the original film without ever impinging decisively on its visual and narrative impact. I am not sure that it is completely by accident that such an experiment should come to us from a Socialist country, where the concept of property in general is under reconsideration.

I have no idea which was the first version of the archetypal keyhole film, actually more developed in a *Search for Evidence* than in the standard model, which was totally devoid of narrative structure and simply showed scenes viewed through a keyhole by a peeping maid or bathboy. I am not even sure where the genre originated, though I suspect that it was in France

Now it is my contention that the Primitive Cinema acted out, in naive, overt fashion, many essential gestures which would eventually become consubstantial with the very morphology of the Insitutional Mode, which would become submerged in what we call "film language" to such an extent as to be completely interiorized by makers and spectators alike. The gesture of voyeurism is indubitably one of these.

The earliest voyeur scenes, however, do not follow the model of *A Search for Evidence* but rather that of Léar's famous film, *The Bride Retires* of 1897. In that purely Primitive model, the voyeur is at all times copresent on the screen with the object of his gaze—invariably a woman undressing. The shift from this first type of representation to the keyhole types involves a curious change of emphasis, for while overt voyeurism is still at the forefront of the action, curiously enough it is the *process* of voyeuristic desire, rather than its object, which is exhibited. Destined, it seems, for a larger audience, these films rarely show women undressing, but rather a series of incongruous vignettes such as those seen in *A Search for Evidence*. More important, however, this evolution clearly introduces the earliest mode of spectatorial identification with the camera, a phenomenon which was to be at the center of the diegetic process of Institutional Cinema. The keyhole film, I should add, was not the only manifestation of the new voyeurism: there also appeared films with telescopes (and these, it is true, were often pointed at women), magnifying glasses, and even microscopes, but the principle was always the same. Through the alternation of views of the watcher and the watched, spectators were given their first, very simple lesson in camera ubiquity, in identifying with the camera, since the voyeur on the screen is the spectator's obvious surrogate.

It has been pointed out (by Charles Musser, I believe) that the spectators of the earliest keyhole films were often peering through a hole themselves, since they were patrons of the kinetoscope or, later, the mutoscope. But of course this technology was itself by no means "innocent," especially if we remember the analogical dreams that haunted the West Orange Laboratory where the kinetoscope was born. The fulfillment of the ideal of analog representation through moving photographs would absolutely require a certain positioning, a certain centering of the spectatorial subject. The peephole film was the first step in this process.

What has this to do with Cocteau's work? In a lecture which Jean Cocteau delivered in 1932 on the occasion of a presentation of *Blood of a Poet*, he said: "I used to think that. . . films weary us with shots taken from below or above. I wanted to shoot my films from the front, artlessly."[9] This is already enough to indicate that to some degree Cocteau was consciously thinking of the early cinema when he devised his pioneering film. I believe he may have been the first modernist film maker to have turned deliberately to primitive strategies as an "antidote" to those of the Institution. After all, has he not often discussed the slowness and distinctive syntax of his films by contrasting them to what are, in effect, the practices of the Institutional Mode of Production?[10]

I have little doubt that when Cocteau conceived the sequence of l'Hotel des Folies Dramatiques in *Blood of a Poet* he was remembering, consciously or unconsciously, the many keyhole films he must almost certainly have seen as a child (the children of the French bourgeoisie, along with their grandmothers or nannies, were almost the only middle-class spectators which the French cinema had for many years). When one reflects on the crucial articulation which the keyhole film represents in the genealogy of the Institutional Mode and on the central role that the voyeuristic position was to play in the established mode itself, it becomes difficult to dismiss this as a chance remembrance. Especially when one further observes that this sequence, which aligns apparently disconnected fantasies in the best Primitive manner, also contains an explicit allusion to a type of Primitive trick-film which, though perhaps not as commonplace as the peephole film, was in its way equally significant.

In a Pathé film from around 1902, an "Ingenious Soubrette" hangs pictures on a wall by apparently crawling up it. The trick, of course—hardly one at all for the modern eye, accustomed as it is to camera ubiquity—consisted merely in placing the camera perpendicular to a horizontal set which looked as if it must be perpendicular to the ground (here the wall of a set suggesting an eighteenth-century drawing room was painted to resemble the roof of the Pathé studio). The overwhelming dominance of frontality and unicity of viewpoint in the Primitive Era must have made such tricks totally effective illusions, even when there was only a black backdrop lying beneath an actor rolling about on the studio floor (as in another Pathé film of 1903, *The Devil's Dance*).

Now Cocteau uses the same device twice in this sequence, first in the shots of the poet in the hallway, where the effect is to show the actor struggling against invisible forces, and again, in more elaborate form (the camera is upside down, but the principle is the same) inside the room marked "Flying Lessons," when the little girl is seen inching her way up the wall and across the ceiling. It is difficult not to be impressed by this association in a single sequence of two overt allusions to such central—and ultimately related—issues of early cinema development: the historical resistance to the abandoning of frontality in favor of camera ubiquity, and spectatorial identification with the camera.

It will perhaps seem incongruous that I have decided to dwell for so long on two modernist films that were made fifty years ago and more, when it is clear that these instances are singularly isolated in their period when compared with what appear to be the numerous and widespread correlations with the Primitive Cinema among modernist films of Europe and the USA since the late fifties.

However, it seemed important in this context to give ourselves some perspective on these matters, to stress that the otherness of preinstitutional cinema was a natural pole of attraction for even the earliest modernist contestations of the institution. And perhaps it was also useful to remind ourselves that until 1930 the impact of primitive cinema could still be direct, through personal memory, through traces still found in the cinema of France, in particular, while today we are dealing with the coincidence of apparently fortuitous encounters or with the consciously assumed shock of rediscovery and recognition. Moreover—and this is no doubt of great significance—the aspect of the Primitive Cinema which we may say has had the most "success" among modernist filmmakers of this generation (and I say this even of those who may never have seen a film made before 1920) is one which never remotely interested any filmmaker at all, I believe, until the painter Andy Warhol turned to film (although I am, of course, confining my frame of reference to the cinema of the West: films from the Japanese thirties would belie this statement). I am referring to what I will call here the Primitive camera stare, epitomized in the films of

Lumière and his cameramen but evinced in the fictional primitive film as well (see *Kentucky Feud*).

To what extent is P. Adams Sitney's recognition of Lumière as a distant "precursor" of the so-called structural film—from Warhol to Gehr, let us say— the recognition in fact of a larger affiliation between the Primitive Mode proper and what is still today, I take it, the dominant attitude in the avant-garde film?

It was the successive reductions of the major traits of the Primitive Mode— the autarky and the acentric quality of its image, the exteriority of the spectatorial subject and the nonclosure of the filmic commodity—which in my view made possible the constitution of an Institutional Mode founded on the indefinite extensibility of diegetic space-time, on the centered organization of the image (and later of sound), on camera identification and the presence of the filmic persona, and on the closure of the film as a consumable, throwaway product.

Now it is not difficult to demonstrate, in the light of these mutually exclusive models, that many of the major gestures of today's modernist cinema—and I do mean the gestures, not necessarily the work—have been objectively aimed at *reversing* the changes that took place after 1905.

The Warhol camera—which, in *Chelsea Girls*, typically remains staring into space, unable or unwilling to move, when a character goes out of shot, gets involved in some tussle on the stairs, and finally returns only after a long absence—is behaving after all like the camera of Méliès which Georges Sadoul likened to the eye of "that gentleman in the stalls who never once thought of getting a closer look at the leading lady's smile or following her into the dining room when she left the parlour."[11]

When Barry Gerson says of his films "one part of the image is no more important than another part—the forms operate together—what is occurring on the left edge of the screen lives because of what occurs on the right edge, top edge, middle, etc.,"[12] how can we fail to think of the acentric primitive image and the topological reading which it required?

And here is a really juicy example: Michael Snow's *A Casing Shelved* is, of course, actually a single-color slide with an hour-long magnetic tape, but I share the view that in our context it is equivalent to a film performance, with "the artist's voice, taped, . . . cataloguing the objects, bringing them into our view, directing the spectator's eye in a reading of the image"[13] as Annette Michelson has described it. Here, the encounter with the Primitive model is spectacular, since the projected image of objects on shelves forcefully inscribes—though with very different means, of course—the Primitive exteriority of the spectatorial subject, while the artist's voice on tape reading that image, organizing those apparently disparate, "meaningless" objects into autobiographical narrative, recapitulates almost literally the primitive lecturer's contradictory gesture, both linearizing and distancing.

The films mentioned here are limit instances. But their chief privative traits serve to define a space within which has evolved much of the significant modernist filmmaking in the USA and Europe over the past fifteen or twenty years. However, having marked this clear affinity with the Primitive Mode, what, I wonder, have I said about these films? Have I not simply said what they are not . . . and discovered that what they are *not,* the Primitive Cinema was *not* also, and for good reason? Have I not simply constructed a tautology which in itself says nothing about, for example, the elaborate and comprehensive work of testing the limits of diegesis that is to be found in the work of Michael Snow? Or about the contradictory ideological implications of role-playing in Warhol? Or about the significant role of the new drug culture in the emergence of an audience for these films, if not in the films themselves?

But perhaps the word "tautology" is too severe. Perhaps I have simply defined in the most general terms possible (or shall I say pertinent) the conceptual framework which so much of the recent avant-garde has laid out for itself, a framework which not too surprisingly appears to be definable in terms of the "interface" between the Primitive and Institutional Modes. But the limitations of this "discovery" must be clearly perceived, in order for the usefulness of such insight, to theoreticians and filmmakers, to be able to grow.

Personally, I know of only three modernist films which, in recognition of this affinity, have explicitly engaged with Primitive Cinema.

In *After Lumière,* Malcolm LeGrice stages a series of black and white variations on *L'Arroseur Arrosé.* seemingly stressing the mechanical, exterior nature of narrative in that archetypal film-gag. The ensuing shift to a color shot of a woman playing the piano music which has accompanied the previous variations opens up an interesting reflection on the role of music in bridging the gap between spectatorial and diegetic space in early film history.

Both Ken Jacobs and Ernie Gehr have engaged directly with Primitive films as "found objects" which can be said to have stimulated the sense of recognition in question here. Jacob's choice of *Tom, Tom, the Piper's Son,* a film from the mature Primitive era (1905) is of considerable interest from my heuristic viewpoint. The film's rigorous respect of the "rule'" that all the characters must enter and leave a shot before it may end, originally a sign of the chase film's attachment to the autarky of the Lumière tableau, was ambivalent at this late date, and verged, I believe, on parody. The film's stiff frontality, and highly mechanized gags, appear almost as a last, half-sophisticated indulgence in the "child's play" of the Primitive Era before Biograph was to get down to the serious business that began with Griffith. It is, of course, with the future course of film history that Ken Jacobs' work on this film engages directly, through his refilming procedures. The opening shot of the film, so typically primitive in that its narrative substance is totally unreadable for the modern eye at first viewing, is analyzed in a way evocative—though only evocative— of the linearizing editing procedures of the institution, so that it becomes readable on second viewing. Here, I feel, is a wonderful example of a combination of work and play on the materials of a crucial historical process.

In contrast to the complexity of Jacobs' film—addressed as much, I realize, to the synchronic paradigm of film production as to the diachronic—Ernie Gehr's more recent *Eureka,* by its very simplicity, points up admirably the ambivalence and indeed certain illusory aspects of the parallel between the Primitive and the modernist. This film, which Gehr painstakingly stretched to many times its original length, again by a process of refilming, was, in all likelihood, made to be shown in the mock Pullman coaches of Hale's Tours, already described. It was shot from the front of a Market Street cable car in San Francisco and shows the long approach to the Ferry Building. As I have indicated, its existence corresponds to a need felt at the time to create the conditions for *penetration* into the motion picture image a good ten years before this could be achieved by editing and camera placement, and by the establishment of theaters which were simply dark, quiet, and comfortable enough to create the conditions for a symbolical voyage, rather than a simulated one.

Gehr was actually extracting the main visual component—the film—from a context which can be described as a form of synesthetic illusionism—in some instances, fans blew air and even smoke through coaches which swayed and creaked like a real train. In his appropriation, Gehr takes images which, though they follow the Lumière model, were no longer viewed as were the original Lumière films, but were experienced as part of a physical environment—and proceeds, indeed, to reverse a historical process, restoring to those images that alienness which Gorki had felt ten years earlier. In fact, as we watch, or try to watch, that swarming uncentered, "unreadable" frame, we seem to hear Gorki's voice: "This is not life, but its shadow, this is not movement but its soundless spectre."[14] And of course, for modern anti-illusionism such a statement is not a lament.

Now, as Peter Wollen had occasion to point out a number of years ago,[15] there have been, in the sixties and seventies, two avant-gardes, the one resolutely placing itself outside the Institution—and largely outside history—in a resolutely "anti-narrative" perspective, the other working on the fringes of the Institution, in both the aesthetic and economic sense, addressing itself to the Institution explicitly—and often, as well, to the social system which fostered its growth and maintains its power. This other avant-garde, mainly European, has incorporated into its critical arsenal strategies which clearly hark back to the Primitive era. I should say that in my opinion these instances on the whole reflect a much higher degree of historical responsibility than any such in the American film, where the work, with all its enormous artistic importance usually seems to have taken place somewhere in the Platonic firmament of Form and Perception.

Jean-Luc Godard's use of frontality—in the sense both of setting his camera up perpendicularly, to a wall, for example, and of having his actors play to the camera—has been much discussed. I simply wish to stress here that this encounter is far from being historically uninformed, as is evidenced by the scene in one of his most radically frontal films, *La Chinoise,* where the characters discuss the respective roles in film history of Méliès and Lumière.

But I would like to mention three other, lesser known instances, from France,

Spain and Belgium, where the issues implicit in the confrontation between the Primitive and Institutional Modes play, it seems to me, a central role.

Jackie Raynal's *Deux Fois,* which has been extensively analyzed by the *Camera Obscura* Collective,[16] is in my view an important meditation on several important aspects of Institutional Representation. Its almost literal use of the Lumière model (long, uncentered Barcelona street scenes, in particular, all the more panoramic as they are filmed in Cinemascope) provide a kind of point zero from which such elementary but primary issues as the extension of diegetic space-time and the exchanges of the gaze can be explored.

In the Spanish filmmaker Paulino Viota's still unknown *Contactos,* which I continue to regard as one of the most important European films of the past decade, Primitive stare is conscripted into a representational and narrative system based upon a radical decentering. For example, an exchange of a few words between two revolutionary activists working in a restaurant is buried, as it were, in the comings and goings of waiters and waitresses through the kitchen door, as the camera stares at this uncentered work activity for several minutes on end.

As for Chantal Ackerman's masterful meditation on a woman's alienation, *Jeanne Dielman . . .,* it may be said to be an almost systematic tribute to the primitive stare, reproduced often with extraordinary fidelity under its two major aspects: the medium long-shot, filmed from a position rigorously perpendicular to a wall, and the frontal medium closeup of a person seated behind a table, facing the camera, "doing something" (whether it was the Lumière's baby eating breakfast or Dranhem kneading dough and reciting his monologue, *The Baker*). Furthermore, Ackerman studiously avoids any direct matching, inconceivable in the Primitive Cinema, indispensable to the principle of camera ubiquity in the Institution. The association of these attitudes produces one of the most distanced narrative films of recent years, recreating to a large extent the conditions of exteriority of the Primitive Mode (the sparseness of speech seems to be a further contributing factor here), positioning the spectator once again in his or her seat, hardly able because hardly enabled to embark upon that imaginary journey through diegetic space-time to which we are so accustomed, obliged ultimately to reflect on what is seen rather than merely experience it.

To conclude: it may have seemed at certain times that my presentation was overly polemical. This is because I feel that there has been a tendency in the past—and perhaps not only in the past—to oversimplify the significance of our responses to those strange objects happily encountered in some archive and "signed" Lumière, Méliès or Zecca—though never, perhaps, was the concept of authorship so irrelevant to an understanding of films than with those of the Primitive Era. The tendency in particular to regard the Primitive Cinema as a Lost Paradise wherein "our" values thrived before being squelched by the Demon Narrative has helped at times to reinforce a dichotomous, indeed Manichean view of film history and film aesthetics which has only served to cloud our understanding of the filmic experience in our society, determined essentially, after all, by fifty years' experience of the Institutional Mode of Representation: the Institution is in us and we are in it, and it has been the scene of practices of immense importance, both artistic and societal.

This dichotomous ideology—the Institution as bad object, primitivism and modernism as good object—has also given rise to the idea that film history might have been—i.e., should have been—different somehow, and that the Muses were only waiting for the New American Cinema to come along and set cinema back on the path of adventure from which it had veered when the shadow of Griffith fell upon it. I am afraid I can only qualify such a viewpoint as childish.

As for the theoretician wishing to elucidate the Institutional experience, to clarify its origins, its growth, and its transformations, and the relationships of all these to the contest for social control in our societies, it appears necessary to deal with early cinema as both a metadiscourse about filmic process—and here the perspective offered by modernism is of value—but also in terms of its actual insertion into history, no matter how many unanswered, and perhaps unanswerable questions such an approach may raise. As I said earlier, it is indispensable at least to try to hold on to both ends of the chain.

Notes

1. Marey, preface to Trutat, *Les Photographies animée* (Paris, 1899).
2. Vertov, *Articles, journaux, projects* (Paris: UGE, 1972), pp. 61–62.
3. Fred J. Balshofer and Arthur C. Miller, *One Reel a Week* (Berkeley: University of California Press, 1967), p. 3.
4. *Village Voice,* March 24, 1966, p. 13.
5. Quoted in Jay Leyda, *Kino* (London: Allen and Unwin, 1973), p. 408.
6. A comprehensive survey of even the visual dimension of my theory of the institutional mode and its development over the thirty-five years that preceded the coming of sound lies outside the scope of this article, although I will be led to evoke certain aspects of it. See my forthcoming book *La Lucarne de L'Infini.*
7. In P. Adam Sitney, ed., *Film Culture Reader* (New York: Praeger, 1970), p. 402.
8. George Sadoul, *Histoire générale du cinéma,* (Paris: Denoël, 1973), 2:187.
9. *The Blood of a Poet, a film by Jean Cocteau,* trans. Lily Pons (New York: Bodley Press, 1949), p. 52.
10. For example, see "Cocteau on the Film" in *Film: An Anthology,* ed. Daniel Talbot (Berkeley: University of Calfornia Press, 1970), pp. 216–24, esp. pp. 216–18, 221; and Cocteau's comments on "The Rules" of filmmaking such as editing restrictions, excerpt from *Entretiens autour du cinématographe* in René Gilson, *Jean Cocteau: An Investigation into his Films and Philosophy,* trans. Ciba Vaughn (New York: Crown, 1969), pp. 112–13.
11. Sadoul, *Histoire générale,* 2:141.
12. *Film Culture* (1977), nos. 3–4, p. 115.
13. Annette Michelson, "Towards Snow," *Artforum,* July 1971.
14. Leyda, *Kino,* p. 407.

15. Peter Wollen, "Godard and Counter-Cinema: *Vent d'est*," *Afterimage* (1972), no. 4 [Included in this anthology. See also Peter Wollen, "The Two Avant-Gardes," *Studio International*, December 1975. Since Noël Burch's lecture was written, both of these have been reprinted in the collection of Peter Wollen's writings, *Readings and Writing: Semiotic Counter-Strategies* (London: New Left Books and Verso, 1982).—ED.]

16. *Camera Obscura* (Fall 1976), no. 1.

26

Linda Williams
Film Body: An Implantation
of Perversions

In the first volume of *The History of Sexuality,* Michel Foucault writes that ever since the seventeenth century there has been in the West an increasing intensi-fication of the body both as object of knowledge and element in the relations of power.[1] This intensification has emerged in a proliferation of discourses of sexuality which have produced a whole range of sexual behavior now categorized as perverse. For Foucault this "implantation of perversions" is the result of the encroachment of power on bodies and their pleasures.

The implantation of perversions is an instrument-effect: it is through the isolation, intensification, and consolidation of peripheral sexualities that the relations of power to sex and pleasure branched out and multiplied, measured the body, and penetrated modes of conduct. And accompanying this encroachment of powers, scattered sexualities rigi-dified, became stuck to an age, a place, a type of practice. A proliferation of sexualities through the extension of power; an optimization of the power to which each of these local sexualities gave a surface of intervention: this concatenation, particularly since the nineteenth century, has been ensured and relayed by the countless economic interests which, with the help of medicine, psychiatry, prostitution, and pornography, have tapped into both this analytical multiplication of pleasure and this optimization of the power that controls it. Pleasure and power do not cancel or turn back against one another; they seek out, overlap, and reinforce one another. They are linked together by complex mechanisms and devices of excitation and incitement.[2]

Foucault's argument offers a significant challenge to the commonly held notion that sex exists autonomously in nature, independent of any discourse on

Published in *Ciné-Tracts* (Winter 1981), no. 12, pp. 19–35, and reprinted here, slightly revised, by permission of the author.

it and as a natural challenge to a power which either pretends it does not exist or prohibits it. He argues instead that sex is a fictitious causal principle that allows us to evade the true relation of power to sexuality. Thus we do not escape social determination when we have recourse to the supposedly natural pleasures of the body, since the particular forms these pleasures take are themselves produced by the needs of power.

Psychoanalysis has been a major force in the deployment of a sexuality that has intensified the body as a site of knowledge and power, making this body the major arena for the discovery of the nonexistent "truth" of sex. But nowhere has the deployment of sexuality, and its attendant implantation of perversions, been more evident than in the visible intensification of the body that came about with the invention of cinema. This invention itself grew out of a scientific discourse on the body in the work of Muybridge and Marey whose "chrono-photography" attempted to document the previously unobserved facts of its movements. And yet, this very machinery of observation and measurement turns out to be, even at this early stage, less an impartial instrument than a crucial mechanism in the power established over that body, constituting it as an object or subject of desire, offering up an image of the body *as mechanism* that is in many ways a reflection of the mechanical nature of the medium itself.

The Film Body and the Body of the Spectator

In his essay on "The Apparatus" Jean Louis Baudry argues that the cinematic apparatus—considered not just as the film itself but the technical specificity of the entire cinematic process and its ideological effects—brings about a state of regression and narcissism in the spectator. Baudry suggests that this regression imitates an original condition of unity with the body of the mother. In this original state of plenitude, before the separation of the subject's body from everything else in the world, the images produced by dreams and hallucinations are taken as real perceptions. Baudry suggests that the cinematic apparatus imitates aspects of this original condition of unity by placing the film spectator before "representations experienced as perceptions" similar to those of dreams and hallucinations. Thus the cinema recreates a form of lost satisfaction from a time when desire could be immediately satisfied through the transfer of the memory of a perception to the form of hallucination.[3]

In other words, according to Baudry, the very formation of the cinematic apparatus responds to a desire to figure a unity and coherence in the spectator that has long since been lost in the spectator–subject's entrance into the symbolic of difference. But if the "invention" of the cinema corresponds to a desire to figure a lost unity in the body of the spectator–subject, what is the effect of this invention on the primary object of this spectator–subject's vision: the human body figured in the film?

To a certain extent we know what the status of this body becomes as a relay to the body of the spectator within the already formulated institution of classical narrative films and their system of "suture."[4] To a certain extent we also know how these films constitute the male viewer within the film as surrogate for the look of the male spectator and the female body as site of the spectacle.[5] But we know much less about the position of these male and female bodies in the "prehistoric" and "primitive" stages of the evolution of the cinema, before codes of narrative, editing, and mise-en-scène were fully established. I hope to show that those "film bodies," like the apparatus itself, operate to restore a lost unity in the spectator–subject. But I also hope to show that this unity is a more specific and perverse response to the threat of disunity posed by the visible "presence" of the body on the screen—that in fact, there exists, at the very moment of the emergence of a "simulation machine"[6] capable of figuring the human body in a dreamlike "representation mistaken for a perception," a dramatic restaging within this representation of the male child's traumatic discovery of, and subsequent mastery over, sexual difference.

Both Eadweard Muybridge and Georges Méliès, two child-men whose work, in different ways and at different times, was formative of the institution and apparatus of cinema, privilege the body as pure object of truth in their work. For Muybridge this truth is scientific—a matter of isolating the essential. He strips the body of clothes to better reveal its musculature and movement. He isolates it against a bare background or grid to measure it, and he tailors his frame to accommodate the body's full extension in size. For Méliès, on the other hand, the truth of the body is both magical and mysterious. He complicates and clutters his bodies with a vast array of costumes, mechanized scenery, and gadgets of all sorts, and he situates all this within a rudimentary diegesis. But for both men the naked body of the woman, whether boldly and repeatedly figured by Muybridge as in the plate from *The Human Figure in Motion*[7] (fig. 1), or briefly and coyly glimpsed as in a still from Méliès *After the Ball*[8] (fig. 2), poses a problem of sexual difference which it then becomes the work of the incipient forms of narrative and mise-en-scène to overcome.

Eadweard Muybridge

As early as 1880 Muybridge had illustrated his lectures on animal locomotion with the aid of his own "zoopraxiscope"—a circular glass plate that could mount up to 200 transparencies which, when revolved, could project a short sequence of movement. These projections of movement sequences, like the printed plates of *Animal Location*—his vast study of both human and animal movement published in 1887—repeated very short motions from side, front, and rear points of view. Both the published photo sequences and the projected movements of these sequences mounted in the zoopraxiscope portray an image of

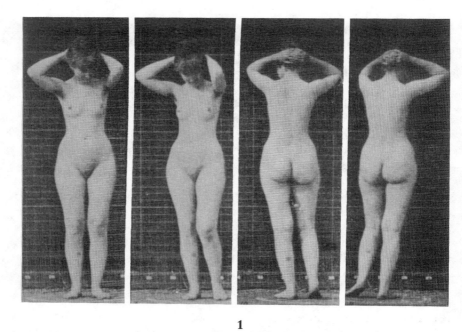

1

2

3

the body as a repeatable mechanism. This body mechanism is controlled in the published work by a whole battery of machines (Muybridge employed as many as 48 cameras in a single setup) capable of arresting movement for further scrutiny; and it is controlled in the zoopraxiscope by a mechanism capable of reconstructing this movement as illusion. Thus with Muybridge we encounter the very moment at which the representation of the discontinuous fragments of the still photograph begins to be reconstituted as a perception (Baudry's "representation mistaken for a perception") of continuous motion.

What is striking, however, is that with this mastery of the illusion of motion, with this near restoration of the whole body in its full perceptual force, come, in Muybridge's studies of the human body, gratuitous fantasization and iconization of the bodies of women that have no parallel in the representation of the male. And this is so in spite of the enormously simplified decor and relative absence of clothing of all his subjects.

In *The Human Figure in Motion* Muybridge divides his subjects into three categories: men, women, and children. In each category, sequences of movements are arranged to reveal a progression from simple to more complex motions. The male figures progress, for example, through various forms of walking (fig. 3), running, and jumping to more complex tasks such as throwing and catching, kicking, boxing, and wrestling, and finally to the performance of "Various Trades" such as carpentry (fig. 4) and hod carrying.

Women's bodies are put through a similar progression of activities designed to reveal movement in more typically "feminine" contexts. For example, we see many sequences of women walking but only one that shows a woman running. In place of the "Throwing and Catching" activities for men, we have women

4

more sedately "Picking Up and Putting Down" to which a very brief section on throwing has been added. On the other hand, there are many variations on the comparatively passive postures of standing, sitting, and kneeling.

Some of the movements and gestures in the women's section—walking, running, jumping—parallel those of the men. Yet even here there is a tendency to add a superfluous detail to the woman's movements—details which tend to mark her as more embedded within a socially prescribed system of objects and gestures than her male counterparts. For example, the sequence of a woman walking (fig. 5) adds the inexplicable, and rather coy, detail of having her walk with her hand to her mouth, thus lending an air of mystery, an extra mark of difference which far exceeds the obvious anatomical difference between the male and female. Or, in the single instance in which a woman runs (fig. 6), her run is again differentiated from the male's by the gesture of grasping her left breast with her right hand. Although one could presume that this is to keep her breast from bouncing, the narcissism of the gesture is unmistakable, especially since it has no parallel among the similarly bouncing male genitals.

A frequent feature of the various male activities is some kind of simple prop that is either carried or manipulated to facilitate different muscular and kinetic activities: dumbbells, boulders, baseballs; the equipment of various combat sports such as swords for fencing; and the tools of the "Various Trades" such as spades, saws, and hammers. (Many male activities show men lifting, throwing, balancing, and carrying a simple round boulder.) But when the women's gestures include props, these props are always very specific objects, never simple weights that can be reused in a variety of situations. Lifting or carrying activities for women employ two types of baskets carried on the head, a jug of water, a

5

6

7

bucket of water, and a basin of water—all of which engage the woman in specific activities of washing, watering, or giving to drink.

Although these props serve the ostensible purpose of eliciting certain kinds of motor activities, and although we do encounter *some* equally specific props for men as well, the props associated with women's bodies are never just devices to elicit movement. They are always something more, investing the woman's body with an iconographic, or even diegetic, surplus of meaning. For example, when a woman lies down on a blanket placed on the ground in an activity that is identical to the series entitled "Man Lying Down" (fig. 7), she does not *only* lie down. She is provided with a narrative reason for doing so and the extra prop that goes with it: she lies down in order to read a newspaper (fig. 8). In other variations of lying down that have no male equivalent, the woman lies down in a hammock and, finally, in a bed complete with sheets and pillows (fig. 9). The latter offers the bizarre sight of covering up the woman's nudity. It is

8

9

complemented, in the final plate of the women's section, by the reverse spectacle of uncovering her nudity as the woman gets out of this same bed (fig. 10).

It does not seem entirely accidental that Muybridge concludes his section on women with this particular prop which, in addition to its obvious sexual use, entirely covers and then uncovers the very body which the motion study seeks to reveal.[9] A similar game of peek-a-boo is played with a variety of materials or garments which partially cover—and in that covering seem to reveal all the more—the woman's body. We see this in the sequence entitled "Woman Walking Downstairs Throwing Scarf over Shoulders" (fig. 11), which covers her body only to uncover it again (fig. 12, 13). Thus the women are consistently provided with an extra prop which overdetermines their difference from the male. This overdetermination of difference also extends to such propless activities as walk-

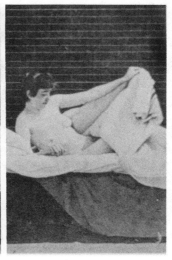

10

11

12

13

ing and running or, strikingly, in a sequence in which the gratuitous gesture of difference, blowing a kiss, entirely defines her as a flirtatious being (fig. 14).

An even greater surplus of erotic meaning runs through the group of photos which show two women in the same frame. These sequences are paralleled in the male section by such two-person activities as boxing, fencing, and wrestling which show the men performing a limited repertoire of combat sports. It would

14

15

be absurd to expect women of the period to engage in similar sports. But it is interesting that even though Muybridge makes no attempt to imitate with women the motor activities of these male combat sports, he nevertheless does attempt to create activities that women can perform together. Since he must often invent these activities, it is not surprising that we find in them extreme instances of what can already be termed a cinematic mise-en-scène.

In one almost comically incongruous "scene," an ambulant naked woman serves a cup of coffee to another seated woman who drinks it and hands it back. In another (fig. 15), a woman stands on a chair and pours a bucket of water over another woman seated in a large basin. This second woman reacts, as if surprised by the coldness of the water, by jumping out of the basin and running away. In both examples Muybridge has directed his female figures in what are very nearly dramatic scenes of domestic interaction taking place in a minimally defined dining room and bathroom. These scenes have a much greater degree of diegetic illusion than the less spatially situated, more purely motor activities of the men.

But even more erotically charged are the scenes in which two women perform an atypical series of movements, as when two women dance together, or the sequence entitled "Woman Turning and Holding Water Jug for Kneeling Companion" (fig. 16). This sequence depicts the unlikely situation of a woman pouring water into the mouth of another from a large and unwieldy jug, with the added detail that she appears to spill a little water. Here, the unconventionality of the activity invests the scene with an enigmatic eroticism: why are these women playing with this large jug and what is the nature of their relationship? The two women are defined as "companions"; none of the two-person male activities offers a similar description of the nature of the relationship between them. Another enigmatic scene, entitled "Woman Sitting Down in Chair Held by Companion, Smoking Cigarette" (fig. 17)—the very length of these titles indicates their increased narrativity—shows a standing woman leaning against the back of the chair of her "seated companion" gazing down on her almost longingly.

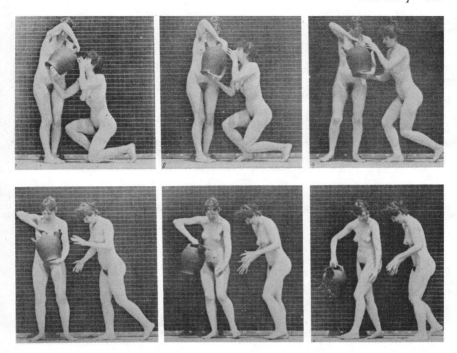

16

The cigarette in this last sequence offers a powerful connotation of both loose morals and, for the period, masculinity, both of which lend overtones to the scene which are completely unequaled in the comparable male activities of boxing or wrestling. For even though these male activities involve body contact, their purposeful and conventional nature does not allow the same erotic invest-ment. The cigarette is yet another of the many gratuitious details which perv-

17

18

ersely fetishize the woman's body But it does so with some insistence, as in an equally unmotivated, extravagantly lascivious "pose" of a single woman (fig. 18), or in a twosome in which both women smoke while walking arm in arm (fig. 19).[10]

Of course, one could try to explain all these props and poses by the fact that most of the women Muybridge used for his photos were professional artist's models, while the male "performers" were everyday people whose movements were linked to their activities in real life, e.g., the University of Penensylvania's "professor of physical culture," two "instructors at the Fencing and Sparing Club," etc. But all this really explains is the significant fact that even in the prehistory of cinema, at a time when the cinema was much more a document of reality than a narrative art, women were already fictionalized, already playing assumed roles, already *not there* as themselves.[11]

Robert Taft, who wrote the introduction to the current edition of *The Human Figure in Motion,* tries to explain the need for professional female models by the fact that many of the women were required to appear nude.[12] But even allowing for the fact that it was more risqué for a Victorian woman to pose nude than for Victorian male and thus the need for professional models, we cannot use this same reasoning to account for the fact that the women are both categorically

19

20

and numerically *more* nude than the men. Of the fourteen classes of human and animal subjects photographed by Muybridge during his stay at the University of Pennsylvania, the first three are of men in three stages of undress listed as (1) "draped," (2) "pelvis cloth"—a kind of jock strap—and (3) "nude." Thus the women's intermediate level of undress, transparent drapery and seminude, does not perform the same function of covering the genitals as the male "pelvis cloth." In fact, it does quite the reverse, draping the female body with a transparent veil (fig. 20) or partial garment which, like the bedcovers, scarf, or dress, only calls attention to her nudity all the more. These transparent and partial clothes offer a variation on what Roland Barthes has described as the erotic function of all revealing clothes: the "staging of an appearance as disappearance."[13]

The contradictory nature of the gesture which discloses the "truth" of the woman's body at the same time that it attempts to hide it is common to almost all the surplus props and gestures throughout these photo sequences, revealing the unmistakable structure of the fetish. In its classic Freudian definition, the fetish is any object which acts as a substitute for the penis, allowing the male to continue to believe in the myth of the female phallus so as not to have to confront the threat of castration which underlies the fact of sexual difference.[14] These erotically charged substitutes often cover or connect with the part of the female body thought to have undergone castration to preserve the illusion—the perverse male fantasy—of a female phallus. Freud calls these substitutes a "disavowal" but he also notes that it is in the very nature of this disavowal[15] to perpetuate beliefs that have been abandoned, thus paradoxically reasserting the very same fears it is intended to allay.

If Muybridge's photos of naked women insist on their nakedness at the same time that they also attempt to disavow it, if, in a sense, he always gives us more to see—more of her body, more of her gestures, and more objects which decorate or situate her in a prototypical narrative—this could be because of the male fear that this "more" is really less, that women pose the terrifying threat of "lack." The obsessive gaze at the naked female body attempts to reassure itself in the very sight (and site) of this "lack" by the fetish substitutes which endow her with a surplus of male-generated erotic meaning. By denying the woman any existence apart from the marks of difference, Muybridge exerts a form of mastery over that difference. But the very nature of the fetish disavowal also assures that the woman is defined entirely in terms that will perpetuate the nagging fear of the lack she represents. Her body can never by anything more than the two poles of this contradiction.

In this Freudian reading, the woman's body is reduced to the pure expression of desires produced in the male unconscious. But as Foucault notes, since it is law that constructs both desire and the lack upon which it is based, "where there is desire, the power relation is already present."[16] In other words, we find in the work of Muybridge, long before the evolution of the cores of either the primitive or the classical illusionist cinemas, at the very inception of the basic apparatus itself, a patriarchal power which places the woman's body within a perversely fetishized structure. The cinematic apparatus thus becomes, even at this early stage, an instrument in the "implantation of perversion" whose first effect is to deny the very existence of women.

We have seen that the "presence" of the woman's body on the screen generates a fetish response on the part of the male image-producer to restore the unity which this body appears to lack. This fetishization operates on the level of the cinematic signified. But as Christian Metz has shown, another form of fetishization exists on the level of the cinematic signifier. This too is structured upon a similar process of disavowal. However, this disavowal is of the illusory nature of the signifier itself. In other words, part of our pleasure in cinema derives from the contradiction between our belief in the perceptual truth of the image and our simultaneous knowledge that it is only imaginary—the discrepancy between the perceived illusion of presence created by the image and the actual absence of the object replaced by the image. As Metz writes:

The cinema fetishist is the person who is enchanted by what the machine is capable of, at the *theatre of shadows* as such. For the establishment of his full potency of cinematic enjoyment *(jouissance)* he must think at every moment (and above all simultaneously) of the force of presence the film has and of the absence on which this force is constructed . . . his pleasure lodges in the gap between the two.[17]

The fetishist's pleasure in the holding of two contradictory beliefs is doubly inscribed in the early invention of the cinematic apparatus: (1) on the level of its signified when it first comes to represent women's bodies, forever arresting the look at this body with a look at the fetish which disavows the very perception of which the machine is capable, and (2) on the level of the signifier. Here it is significant that the fetish pleasure is strongest at the moment the "theater of shadows" first emerges, when audiences—like the audiences who first viewed the projection of moving bodies by Muybridge's zoopraxiscope—are still capable of amazement at the magical abilities of the machine itself. Muybridge's apparatus, present and visible in the space of projection, hand operated by its own inventor, thus revealed more acutely than the later invention of the projector the magical power to create an illusion of motion from a succession of stills. Even though this illusion would be perfected in Lumiére and Edison's later invention of celluloid film and the resulting ability to film and project much longer sequences of motion, at no time would the fetish pleasure of the signifier alone be so pronounced, until, that is, George Mélies—that other original fetishist of the early cinema—found new ways to amaze his audiences at the capabilities of the machine.

Georges Méliès

For Muybridge the pleasure in the cinematic signifier lodged in the ability of the projection machine to produce an illusion of movement. He himself stood outside this machine as its operator. Méliès, however, redoubles and refines this pleasure in the cinematic signifier by placing his own body within the machine, casting himself in the role of the magician–scientist–jester–Mephisto who manipulates its magic. Thus he makes a spectacle of his own perverse pleasure in the tricks of which his personal "theater of shadows" is capable. In film after film Méliès obsessively repeats the same game, playing, like the fetishist, upon the contradictory knowledge of presence and absence, making the game of presence and absence the very source of his own and the spectator's pleasure, while privileging his pleasure over that of the spectator insofar as he alone, as filmmaker *behind* the scene and as magician *on* the scene, penetrates more deeply its contradictory nature. As typified by a frame from the 1902 film, *The Devil and the Statue* (fig. 21), his mugging delight in the game of illusion is clearly visible in each role he assumes.

But if Méliès refines and increases the fetishistic pleasure in the cinematic signifier, he also refines and increases a similar pleasure in the cinematic signified of the human body. As with Muybridge, the primary impetus behind Méliès' manipulation of the body is, once again, the need to master the threat of difference posed by the naked female form. And if for Muybridge this fetishization of the women's body begins to produce a level of diegetic illusion and mise-en-scène that far exceeds the levels called for in his motion studies, then a similar fetishization, running rampant in Méliès, produces even more elaborate forms of diegesis and mise-en-scène.

Long before Méliès had discovered the illusory powers of cinema, he was already engaged in an obsessive pursuit of mastery over the human body. From 1885 to 1888, before purchasing the theater of the magician Robert-Houdin, Méliès constructed a number of robots in imitation of Robert-Houdin's own work.[18] These mechanical simulations of the human body allowed their inventor-operator complete control over their appearance and movements.

(There is a fascinating parallel here, not only between the mechanical simulation of the human body constructed in the robot and the later simulation of

21

22

23

that body afforded by the cinema, but also in the manner of Méliès' mastery of both. According to Méliès' own account, he had seen robots on the stage of the Robert-Houdin theater and had proceeded to imitate them without any prior understanding of their mechanism.[19] Thus he reinvented an invention whose trick was the simulation of the human body. This simulation of a simulation was then repeated ten years later in 1895 when, after failing to purchase the new invention of the cinématographe from Auguste Lumière after an evening showing at the Grand Café, Méliès proceeded to reinvent it as well. Thus Méliès seems to have been fated to repeat the invention/construction of machines capable of ever more perfect and lifelike simulations of the human body, *and* to repeat this construction through a process that was itself a simulation of an already existing mechanism.)

From the first trick of assembling a simulation of the whole body out of mechanical parts to the further trick of making the imaginary bodies projected on a screen appear and disappear, Méliès perfects his mastery over the threatening presence of the actual body, investing his pleasure in an infinitely repeatable *trucage*. This *trucage* offers two related forms of mastery over the threat of castration posed by the illusory presence of the woman's body made possible by the cinema : on the one hand, the drama of dismemberment[20] and reintegration performed on all bodies, and on the other hand the celebration of the fetish function of the apparatus itself, particularly in its ability to reproduce an image of the woman's body.

A 1903 film entitled *Extraordinary Illusions (Illusions funambulesques)*[21] is a typical example of mastery over dismemberment and of particular interest because it combines cinematic *trucage* with Méliès original obsession with the mechanized limbs of a robot. The film shows Méliès as conjurer removing from a shallow box, obviously incapable of holding what emerges from it, a pair of legs, a dummy's torso, and finally a head. He assembles these pieces into the body of a mechanical woman who becomes animated enough to turn her head to give the conjurer a kiss. He then tosses this mannequin into the air. Upon landing on the other side of the stage, she changes into a flesh-and-blood woman. The rest of the film shows the conjurer trying with some difficulty to maintain this apparition—the woman has a disturbing tendency to change into a chef with a saucepan—but not without a further variation on the theme of dismemberment and reintegration in which the woman is tied up in a large cloth which explodes into fragments of paper whose pieces again reform the woman. Finally, when the woman turns into a chef once again, the conjurer rips the chef to pieces and gradually vanishes himself.

Many of Méliès' early films (1898–1903) have similar rudimentary narratives based on variations of this drama of the dismemberment and reintegration of both male and female bodies. As early as 1898 *The Famous Box Trick (Illusions fantasmagorique)* shows Méliès, again as conjurer, making another magic box appear from which emerges a little boy. The body of the boy is first conjured up, cut in two by the magician's wand, then restored to its original wholeness by the creation of two boys who begin to fight among themselves. Only after the drama of morcellation and restoration does a final transformation, causing the boys to vanish, bring an end to the conflict.

Frequently this drama of morcellation takes place on the body of the magician-conjurer himself. In *The Melomaniac (Le Mélomane,* 1903) Méliès, plays a magical music teacher who gives a music lesson using a string of five telegraph wires as his staff. To obtain notes he tears off his own head and throws it up on the staff. Since his head always grows back he is able to musically notate a performance of "God Save the King" sung by the infinitely replenishable supply of heads (fig. 22).

The Melomaniac is in many ways a refinement of the earlier *The Four Trouble-some Heads (L'Homme de têtes,* 1898) in which the magician alternately removes and regrows his own head until the group of removed heads begin to annoy him with their singing. He then makes two of them disappear and tosses the third into the air to land on top of and merge with his current head. In both these films the magician stages the morcellation of his own body with the aid of a cinematic trick; he then restores his unity with another trick to become a virtuoso performer of the drama of dismemberment and integration.[22]

In those films in which morcellation of the body is not followed by reintegration, we often find that the body undergoing morcellation can be regarded as a threat to another character who functions as a more sympathetic prototype of a hero. In these films two male protagonists engage in a crude Oedipal drama ending in the dismemberment of one of them and the triumph of the other. Occasionally a woman figures as prize or cause of the conflict. In *The Man with the Rubber Head (L'Homme à la tête de caoutchouc,* 1902) a conflict between a chemist and his assistant ends when the assistant inflates the head of the chemist to the point of explosion. In true comic Oedipal wish-fulfillment it is frequently the younger of the two men who succeeds in dismembering the older one, as also in *The Cook's Revenge (La Vengence du gâte-sauce,* 1900). In this film a kitchen boy steals a kiss from a chambermaid, is caught by his boss, but then decapitates this boss in the ensuing chase. The film ends with the kitchen boy using the headless body of the boss as a broom to continue his work.

In all the above films we encounter a specific use of cinematic magic first to assert and then to disavow an original "lack." Even when women's bodies do not appear at all (as in *The Four Troublesome Heads* and *The Famous Box Trick),* the threat of castration posed by their bodies seems to underlie the pattern of each scenario.

In a recent *Film Quarterly* article entitled "The Lady Vanishes: Women, Magic, and the Movies," Lucy Fischer argues that the primary function of women's bodies in Méliès' films—and in many other "trick" films of the period—is to disappear.[23] Fischer takes Méliès' 1906 film *The Vanishing Lady* as a paradigm for the magical treatment of women throughout the period. In this first use of a cinematic "substitution trick," a magician, played as always by Méliès, covers the body of a seated woman with a piece of cloth. When he removes the cloth not only has the lady disappeared but in her place is a skeleton.

Fisher is quite right to stress the significance of a magic which exerts power over women's bodies, decorporealizing and reducing them to the status of a decorative object. But it is simply not accurate to privilege the disappearance of women in Méliès' films, any more than it would be accurate to privilege her magical appearance. In fact, there are probably an equal number of magical appearances and disappearances of men in these films, or of any object for that matter, since the staging of appearance and disappearance is the primary way Méliès exercises the illusory power of his simulation machine.

Fischer's ultimate point is not only that Méliès' magic makes women disappear but that often in the process this magic acts out a drama of male envy of the female procreative power, "giving birth" to all manner of animals and objects. This latter idea is tempting in its opposition to the patriarchal notion of a female "lack,"[24] and the somewhat shaky Freudian construct of "penis envy" which sometimes accompanies it. Fischer actually reverses the process to suggest that a kind of "womb envy" is at work. But again I fear that there is not enough evidence from the films. More important than the vanishing act, more important than the imitation of procreative powers, is the construction of a scenario which gives the magician–filmmaker power over *all* the bodies in his domain, allowing him not simply to conjure away the woman but symbolically to reenact, and thus master through obsessive repetition, the problem of difference, the threat of disunity and dismemberment posed by the woman's body. Like the child's symbolic restaging of the problem of his mother's absence in the game of *fort!/ da!*, making her disappear so that she may again, this time as a result of his *own* manipulation, reappear,[25] Méliès scenarios of fetishistic disavowal announce his own role as magician/auteur/metteur-en-scène with great flourish.

Significantly, these flourishes radically exclude his own body from the voyeuristic regime that Méliès, more than any other early master of film, inaugurates. In all the early films over which Méliès presides as magician (or as some thinly disguised variant), the magician usually enters the scene, bows directly to the audience, begins an act containing many hand flourishes which call attention to the magic performed, and finally bows again before exiting. No one else in the film is allowed this knowledge of the existence of the film audience. Although it is possible to attribute these flourishes to the conventions of stage magic reigning at the time, it seems significant that even after the magician disappears from his films, Méliès retains characters, like Mephistopheles in *The Damnation of Faust* or the witch in *The Kingdom of the Fairies,* who carry on the function of the magician. If Méliès persists in this acknowledgment of the distance separating audience and scene, even going against all the emerging codes of cinematic illusion to do so, and if, at the same time, he animates this scene with a multitude of characters who do not seem to be aware that they are on a scene, he does so in order to share with the audience his perverse pleasure in a visible mise-en-scène. Like the proverbial dirty old man who delights in showing his obscene pictures to others, part of his pleasure is in watching us watch. But for Méliès this pleasure is further enhanced by the inclusion in his own pictures of the fetish machine that tames the threat of the female body.

It is striking, for example, just how many of Méliès' films, especially his later ones, revolve around the functioning of an elaborate machine that is operated and manufactured by the fictional surrogate of the original magician. These machines, whether the clocks of the 1889 *Cinderella* or the rocket ship of *A Trip to the Moon* (1902), are often associated with or adorned by the multiplying bodies of beautiful women in scant attire. The proliferation of the machines themselves—the many fantastic vehicles, futuristic laboratories, even mechanized monsters such as the giant in *The Conquest of the Pole* (1912)—are obvious ways in which Méliès celebrates and makes visible the primary invisible machinery of the cinema itself. A great many of the machines featured in these films are, in fact, optical devices: telescopes in *A Trip to the Moon* and *The Merry Frolics of Satan* (1906) (fig. 23), a fantastic camera in *Long Distance Wireless Photography* (1908), a magic lantern that turns out to be a motion picture projector in *The Magic Lantern* (1903). These devices allow their operator and the film spectator a privileged view of women's bodies, variously producing, reproducing, or voyeuristically spying upon them.

In *Long Distance Wireless Photography* Méliès plays the Marconi-like inventor of a magical camera capable of projecting life-size moving images of whatever

24

is placed before it. This fantasy on the potential of the recently invented telegraph is an uncanny anticipation of the not yet invented marvel of television. Méliès, the inventor-operator, shows off the capabilities of his machine to an elderly couple in his laboratory. He first reproduces a life-size image of three identically dressed women take from a small photograph (fig. 24), then "televises" the movements of a live model.

In both cases Méliès celebrates the power of the apparatus to frame, tame, and reduce the flesh and blood woman to the status of a two-dimensional image. In the first case it may even be significant that the live model is dispensed with entirely as Méliès creates a life-size enlargement of what is already only a two-dimensional image of women's bodies. In the second case, a live model is present but a comic discrepancy between the seductive movements of the "televised" image and the less seductive behavior of the original model suggests a preference for the image over the less obliging reality of the original model.

Thus Méliès celebrates within the primary image machine of his own cinema a secondary image machine that is capable, like the first, of reproducing an image of women's bodies to the voyeuristic measure of male desire. The apparatus which makes possible "long distance wireless photography" packages the real-life bodies of women into safely proffered cheesecake tableaux. Individual female bodies become the simple stereotypes of femaleness which uniformly differ from the male.[26] As figure 24 amply reveals, Méliès' own pleasure is that of the

25

purveyor of images who delights in watching others watch. The "Others" who watch in this case are the elderly couple, the in-the-laboratory audience of the film's scientific demonstration. Like the doubling of the cinematic apparatus itself, this within-the-film audience duplicates the voyeuristic structure of the relationship of primary audience to filmed image.

In *A Spiritualistic Photographer* (1903), Méliès reverses the above process to bring the two dimensional photograph of a woman back to life. He performs a similar trick with the figure of the queen on a life-size playing card in the 1905 film *The Living Playing Cards*. In all these films the device of the frame within the frame alerts us to the fact that everything we see, particularly the body of the woman, has been animated and produced by a voyeuristic, optical machine which safely situates the female object of desire at a distance and on a different plane from the male voyeur. Thus the image machine itself, through contiguous association with the woman's body and through its ability to reproduce that body as an image which disavows its inherent threat of lack, becomes the fetish-object par excellence of all Méliès films.

Perhaps the most complex illustration of the inscription of women's bodies within the voyeuristic and fetishistic regime of cinema occurs in Méliès' 1903 film *The Magic Lantern*. In a children's playroom two clowns, a Pulcinella and a Pierrot, build a giant magic lantern to which they attach a lens. When they place a burning torch in it, it projects a series of circularly framed moving images upon the wall of the playroom. The progression of these images is significant: a static landscape is followed by closeups of a man and a woman in eighteenth-century wigs flirting with one another against the background of the same landscape (fig. 25); finally we see the clowns themselves projected in closeup upon the wall. With this progression Méliès demonstrates the power of his toy which, like the machine in *Long Distance Wireless Photography*, is once again a metaphor for the cinematic apparatus. Thus we discover the ability of this apparatus to (1) document external reality (the landscape) (2) represent a fictional world (the characters in eighteenth-century dress), and (3) confuse the categories of real and imaginary in a gesture of reflexivity (the projection of the clowns from the "real" world into the fictional space on the wall).

After this brief anticipation of the entire history of film art, the two clowns become curious about the internal workings of the machine producing this magic (or perhaps they are like the naive spectator who suspects that the machine itself houses the people and objects it produces). They dismantle the box to discover that it contains a whole bevy of beauties attired in long dresses and hats who do a little dance in front of the dismantled machine. This process of dismantling is repeated several times to yield a pair of women in clown suits who do another dance, exit, and then perform two more choruses of dances, this time dressed in scanty tutus.

The two clowns interrupt the dancers to battle with one another center stage. Soldiers with drawn sabers arrive to restore order. They march around the two clowns and force them to climb into the magic lantern. When the soldiers reopen the box, the clowns have been transformed into a single giant jack-in-the-box Pulcinella capable of extending itself to a height twice that of a normal human. As this jack-in-the-box moves up and down, the soldiers continue to brandish their sabers in a circle around it. Finally, the soldiers exit and all the women dancers do a circular dance around the alternating elongations and retractions of the jack-in-the-box.

Once again Méliès plays with the contrast between a two-dimensional framed image and three-dimensional reality. And once again this contrast suggests a metaphor for the machine's ability to produce women's bodies. But while Lucy Fischer emphasizes the envious male's appropriation of female procreative powers in the construction of this machine that gives "birth" to women, I would stress instead that this spewing forth of identical female bodies only calls attention even more to the status of these bodies as totally mastered, infinitely reproducible *images* whose potential threat of castration has been disavowed by the fetish object of the machine with which they are associated. In other words, not only can this image machine be construed as a metaphor for the womb, but also and more powerfully, it can be construed as a metaphor for the penis—in particular since, as we have seen, the fetish object is itself a stand-in for the fantasy of the maternal penis.[27] In the *Magic Lantern* this fantasy penis emerges first in the proliferating bodies of the women produced by the machine and second in the phallic protrusion of the jack-in-the-box. In fact, the shift from soldiers brandishing their sabers at this jack-in-the-box to the final dance of the women around it would seem to offer yet another variation of the drama of threatened dismemberment and integration. There is probably no greater illustration of the centrality of this fetish object in all of Méliès' work than this dance of worship around the undulating phallus at the center of this giant magic lantern.

Conclusion: The Perverse Implantation

In the prehistoric cinema of Muybridge and in the primitive cinema of Méliès, the unprecedented illusion of presence of the film body acutely posed the problem of sexual difference to the male image-maker. Of course painting and photography had long since set precedents for the eroticization and objectification of women's bodies.[28] In many ways Muybridge simply follows these precedents. What is particularly striking in Muybridge, however, is the extent to which a supposedly *scientific* study of the human body elicits the surplus aesthetic qualities of incipient diegesis and mise-en-scène in the treatment of his women subjects alone. It is as if the unprecedented perceptual reality of the female body made possible by the emerging cinematic apparatus necessitated a counterbalancing fictionalization even more powerful than what could already be found in the arts of painting and still photography.

Thus what began as a scientific impulse to measure and record the "truth" of the human body, quickly became a powerful fantasization of the body of the woman aimed at mastering the threat posed by her body. This surplus of male-generated erotic meaning works to deny the woman any meaning apart from her marks of difference from the male. As we have seen, Méliès complicates and refines this mastery over the threat of castration through the drama of dismemberment and reintegration performed on all bodies and through the celebration of the fetish function of the cinematic apparatus.

So if, as Baudry suggests, the cinematic apparatus in general affords the simulation of a lost unity with the body of the mother, then we find that some of the earliest representations of the female body within this apparatus aim at a more specific restoration of unity in the fetishistic disavowal of castration. But if the woman's body generates a surplus aestheticism designed to disavow difference, this surplus also severely limits the meaning of this body to the two contradictory poles of the assertion and denial of sexual difference. Like the fetish which it in some ways becomes, the woman's body arrests the male's gaze just short of the site of difference. Caught between these two poles of the fetish structure of disavowal, the woman's body is perversely trapped with the contradictory assertion and denial of the fear of castration. Thus the cinema became, even before its full "invention," one more discourse of sexuality, one more form of the "implantation of perversions" extending power over the body.[29]

Notes

1. Michel Foucault, *The History of Sexuality,* trans. Robert Hurley (New York: Pantheon Books, 1978), P. 107. Published in French as *La Volonté de savoir* (Paris: Gallimard, 1976).

2. Foucault, *History of Sexuality,* p. 48.

3. Jean Louis Baudry, "The Apparatus,"*Camera Obscura* (Fall 1976), no. 1, pp. 97–126. Translated into English by Jean Andrews and Bertrand Augst [included in this anthology—ED.].

4. As applied to film, the term "suture" implies the process by which the spectator as subject fills in the discontinuities and absences of a cinematic discourse which proceeds by cuts, framings, and the fundamental absence of the signifier itself. The term derives from Jacques-Alain Miller's discussion of Lacan's "logic of the signifier." In Miller's extention of Lacanian theory, suture describes the way the "I" created by language is both a division and a joining. Divisions of the "I" are overcome by the imaginary projections of a unitary ego to produce the fiction of the subject. In a similar way, the spectator/subject of the cinema overcomes the disunity of the cinematic discourse. See Miller, "Suture" (elements of the logic of the signifier)," and Jean-Pierre Oudart, "Cinema and Suture," both in *Screen* (Winter–Spring 1977–1978), 18:24–47. [Cf. Kaja Silverman, "Suture," in this anthology—ED.]

5. See Laura Mulvey, "Visual Pleasure and the Narrative Cinema," *Screen* (Autumn 1975), 16:6–18 [included in this anthology—ED.]

6. See Baudry, "The Apparatus," p. 122.

7. Eadweard Muybridge, *The Human Figure in Motion* (New York; Dover, 1955). This is the latter of the two abridgments Muybridge made of his vast and very expensive original 1887 work, *Animal Locomotion. Animal Locomotion* is an eleven-folio volume of some 20,000 photos of animals and humans in movement. Muybridge later abridged this work into two smaller volumes: *Animals in Motion,* published in 1899, and *The Human Figure in Motion,* published in 1901. All the photo sequences reproduced here are from this latter work. In a longer study (the book in progress entitled *Film Bodies*) I discuss the complete *Animal Locomotion.*

8. *After the Ball* (1897) stars Méliès' mistress and future wife, Jehanne d'Alcy. It is cited as one of a group of "stag films" by Méliès in Paul Hammond's *Marvelous Méliès* (New York: St. Martin's Press, 1975), p. 113. A more recent and thorough study of Méliès is John Frazer's *Artificially Arranged Scenes* (Boston: G. K. Hall, 1974). Frazer's book contains excellent synopses of all Méliès' extant films. Other studies include: Georges Sadoul, *Georges Méliès* (Paris: Seghers, 1961) and Maurice Bessy and Lo Duca, *Georges Méliès Mage* (Paris: Pauvert, 1961).

9. Nor does it seem entirely accidental that Muybridge concludes the male section with what could be taken as a complementary metaphor of male ejaculation; a man with rifle falling prone on the ground and firing. The point, however, is that while the activity with the rifle reveals the male body in movement, the activity with the bed both conceals and reveals the female body in an erotically charged state of relative stasis.

10. See Lucy Fischer's analysis of a similarly masculine use of a cigarette in the Edison 1905 short *A Pipe Dream.* This film shows a woman who smokes playing with a miniature man in her hand. Lucy Fischer, "The Lady Vanishes: Women, Magic, and the Movies," *Film Quarterly* (Fall 1979), pp. 32–33.

11. Claire Johnston, writing with reference to an earlier article by Laura Mulvey, has proclaimed the basic feminist criticism of the representation of women in film: "woman as woman" is never present. She simply comes to represent the male phallus. "Women's Cinema as Counter Cinema," in *Notes on Women's Cinema,* ed. Claire Johnston, *Screen* Pamphlet 2 (London: Society for Education in Film and Television, 1973, rpt. 1975).

12. Robert Taft, "An introduction: Eadweard Muybridge and His Work," in *The Human Figure in Motion,* p. x.

13. Roland Barthes, *The Pleasure of the Text,* trans. Richard Miller (New York: Hill and Wang, 1975), p. 10.

14. Sigmund Freud, "Fetishism," in *Standard Edition of the Complete Psychological Works,* vol. 21 (London: Hogarth Press, 1968).

15. Octave Mannoni, in his book *Clefs pour l'imaginaire ou l'autre scène* (Paris: Seuil, 1969), pp. 9–34, has emphasized the contradictory nature of this form of belief that knows itself to be false, calling it the process of "je sais bien, mais quand même. . ." (I know very well, but all the same . . .).

16. Foucault, *History of Sexuality,* p. 81.

17. Metz, "The Imaginary Signifier," trans. Ben Brewster, *Screen* (Summer 1975), 16:72 [excerpts included in this anthology—ED.].

18. According to a letter from Méliès published in Georges Sadoul's *Georges Méliès,* p. 127.

19. *Ibid.*

20. In his *Film Biographies* (Berkeley: Turtle Island, 1977), Stan Brakhage has much to say about Méliès' trauma of dismemberment: "Young George. . . completely overwhelmed, torn to pieces before what-we-would-call his 'birth'—begins as a child to invent a spirit-of-himself which will revenge him . . . a hero who will FREE the wickedly enchanted—or otherwise destroyed—pieces of his actual being, cause the monsters to dis-gorge the parts of his actuality; and young George, perhaps later then, begins to imagine a heroine who will restore him, a woman who will sew together or otherwise re-member his actual being" (p. 17). Although I cannot agree with this attribution of dismemberment to "young George's" fetus, or to the supposition that a woman would "re-member" his being—quite the reverse seems to be the case in both instances—Brakhage does correctly identify the primary concerns of much of Méliès' cinema.

21. Frazer, *Artificially Arranged Scenes,* p. 127, lists this as the correct title of the film. There are, however, some super 8mm. prints bearing the title *The Magic Box*.

22. An even more threatening version of this same drama occurs in the 1902 film *Up-to-Date Surgery,* in which a doctor diagnoses indigestion in a patient, performs an operation that cuts the patient up into many pieces, reassembles these pieces in the wrong order, then finally in the right order.

23. Fischer, "The Lady Vanishes," p. 30.

24. This apprehension of a female "lack" does not mean that such a lack really exists. It is a male fantasy which has been instrumental in the implantation of perversion within the cinema.

25. Sigmund Freud, *Beyond the Pleasure Principle* (New York: Bantam, 1959), pp. 32–35.

26. It is interesting to compare, in this connection, the enormous differentiation in the costumes of the male characters in all Méliès' films to the near uniformity of dress among the females; e.g., the scant sailor suits of the women who help the scientists board the rocket ship in *A Trip to the Moon,* or the similar uniforms of the women in *The Kingdom of the Fairies*.

27. Freud, "Fetishism," *Standard Edition,* 21:153.

28. See John Berger, *Ways of Seeing* (New York: Penguin Books and the British Broadcasting Corporation, 1973).

29. I would like to thank Patricia Mellencamp and Stephen Heath for suggesting the "Film Body" portion of this title and the general topic of the presence of the human figure in film. I am also indebted to Virgil Grillo and Betty Theoteokatos of the University of Colorado for helping me to reproduce the Muybridge plates and to Andrew Lovinescu of the University of Wisconsin, Milwaukee for "transforming" the slides into photographs for the original publication of this article.

27

Thomas Elsaesser
Primary Identification and the
Historical Subject:
Fassbinder and Germany

The entire cinematographic appartatus is aimed at provoking . . . a subject-effect and not a reality-effect.—J. L. Baudry

Film Studies returns to the question of identification[1] in the cinema, which used to be one of the main concerns of mass-media studies in forties and fifties, with a symptomatic ambivalence. American social psychologists like Martha Wolfenstein and Nathan Leites[2]—indebted to Siegfried Kracauer and, at one remove, the Institute for Social Research—represented the very type of approach from which film theory dissociated itself in order to establish a "theory of the visible." And yet, by a completely different route, Baudry and Metz seem to confirm a fundamental insight of media psychology: the cinema as an institution confines the spectator in an illusory identity, by a play of self-images. But whereas media psychology sees these self-images as social roles, for Baudry they are structures of cognition.

Two kinds of determinism seem to be implied in the perspectives opened up by Baudry's description of the "apparatus": a historical one, where the development of optics and the technology of mechanical reproduction produce the

First published in *Ciné-Tracts* (Fall 1980), no. 11, pp. 43–52, and portions incorporated in the author's book *The Historical Imaginary* (London: Methuen, forthcoming). Reprinted by permission of the author and Methuen.

cinema, as a specific visual organization of the subject, and an ontogenetic one, where the cinema imitates the very structure of the human psyche and the formation of the ego. The "apparatus" seems to be locked into a kind of teleology, in which the illusionist cinema, the viewing situation, and the spectator's psyche combine in the concrete realization of a fantasy that characterizes "Western man" and his philosophical efforts toward self-cognition.

While in Baudry's writing, one can still make out a historical argument which, however remotely, underpins his ideas about the condition of a contemporary epistemology, Metz has used Baudry in "The Imaginary Signifier" in order to establish a classification system rather than an ambivalently evolutionary ontology. With this, the historical determinants seem to be entirely displaced toward other parts of the "institution cinema," and the question of identification—in the concept of primary identification—is recast significantly, so as to make as clear a distinction as possible between his work and work concerned with role definition, stereotyping, and role projection.

Metz's and Baudry's arguments have several important implications for film studies. For instance, part of the aim of auteur or genre studies and close textual analysis has been to identify levels of coherence in a film or a body of films. In the light of "The Imaginary Signifier" one might be better advised to speak of a "coherence-effect," and to call the very attempt to establish coherence a displaced subject-effect. The task of analysis or interpretation comes to an end at precisely the point where the spectator-critic has objectified his or her subjectivity, by phantasmatizing an author, a genre, or any other category, to act as a substitute for the "transcendental subject" that Baudry talks about. The perversity of this conclusion can only be mitigated, it seems, if one reminds oneself that Metz's distinction between primary and secondary identification is a procedural one, defining a certain logic operation. Or as Alan Williams put it: "The first and most fundamental level of meaning in cinema is . . . that of the coherence of each film's overall surrogate 'subject.'"[3] This leaves open the possibility that the surrogate subject is differently constituted from film to film.

The more immediately apparent consequence of accepting Metz's position affects independent or avant-garde filmmaking practice.[4] Baudry's argument implicitly and explicitly designates the cinema as "idealist" in the philosophical sense, not because of a specific historical or ideological practice, such as Hollywood classical narrative, but by its "basic cinematographic apparatus." An unbridgeable subject/object division renders the object forever unknowable, and consciousness grasps the outer world only in terms of its own unconscious/linguistic structure. The cinema, in this respect, is an apparatus constructed by a Kantian epistemologist. Metz's distinction of primary identification amplifies this point. The filmic signifier is an imaginary one because perception in the cinema always involves between spectator and image the presence of a third term which is hidden: the camera. It is the repression of this absence and deferment in the act of perception that turns the subject–object relation into an

imaginary one. Primary identification designates the unperceived and unrecognized mirroring effect that such a constellation produces for the viewer, with
the consequence that all possible identifications with the characters in particular
are modeled on and circumscribed by a structure of narcissism which inflects the
viewer-screen relationship at any given moment.

Perception in the cinema is voyeuristic not because of any particular kinds of
representations or points of view. It is not the implied hidden spectator which a
scene sometimes addresses, but the always hidden camera which the scene cannot
exist without that turns all object relations in the cinema into fetishistic ones.
They hold the subject in a position of miscognition or self-estrangement, regardless of whether the film in question is representational or not, avant-garde
or narrative-illusionist. A film either fetishizes the characters or it fetishizes the
apparatus. According to Metz, there is no escape from this closed circle.[5] In this
respect, the cinema is indeed an "invention without a future" because it systematically ties the spectator to a regressive state, in an endless circuit of substitution
and fetishization.

Such pessimism has been questioned, not least because it seems to invalidate
the political and cognitive aims of radical avant-garde filmmaking. Suspecting
a logical flaw, Geoffrey Nowell-Smith[6] has challenged Metz's distinction, by
arguing that it is difficult to see how one can talk about primary and secondary
identification, if one means by this an anteriority, in a process that is essentially
simultaneous and dynamic. Consequently, Nowell-Smith wants to argue that
"pure specularity," the transformation of Freud's secondary narcissism into the
imaginary reintegration of the subject's self-image, is an abstraction, and no
more than a misleading theoretical construct. In any concrete act of viewing,
the spectator is involved in identifications which are "primary" and "secondary"
at the same time (if only by the metonymization of shots), and every fragmentation, be it montage, point-of-view shots, or any other principle of alternation
breaks down primary identification.

The very fact that something is posited as primary should make us instantly suspicious.
To say something is primary is simply to locate it further back in the psychic apparatus.
It does not, or should not, invite any conclusions about its efficacy. I would argue,
therefore, that the so-called secondary identifications do tend to break down the pure
specularity of the screen/spectator relation in itself and to displace it onto relations which
are more properly intra-textual, relations to the spectator posited from within the image
and in the movement from shot to shot.[7]

Metz might well reply that he is not talking about a perceptual anteriority but
a conceptual a priori, and that he is not interested in concrete acts of viewing as
much as in a classification of distinct categories. However, much of Metz's
argument is buttressed by Baudry's essays, whose Platonic ontology of the
cinema is historicized only at the price of turning it into a negative teleology.
At times, it appears that Metz accepts or is indifferent to the suggestion that the

cinema is inescapably idealist. Confronted with the question whether "primary identification" is coextensive with the cinematic apparatus as analyzed by Baudry, and to that extent unaffected by textual or historical production, Metz conceded, without much enthusiasm or conviction, that conceivably, if the nature of the family were to change radically, so might the cinematic apparatus.[8]

Film Studies has responded to these problems not only by a renewed interest in theory. Equally significant is the attention given to alternative or deviating practices in the history of cinema regarding the relationship of spectator to film, and the kind of "materialism" or "specularization" which it undergoes. The Japanese cinema (Ozu, Oshima, Mizoguchi) has become a privileged area for such investigations, in terms of narrative space, point-of-view shots, or culturally different codes of representation and identification.[9] This paper is an attempt to isolate another deviating practice, within the European context, which has developed as closely as the Japanese cinema in a reciprocity and rivalry with the "dominant" practice of classical narrative. The recent German cinema seems to me to represent both a confirmation of Baudry's and Metz's arguments and at the same time offers a textual practice which might make apparent a dimension elided or repressed in "The Imaginary Signifier." In particular, I am wondering whether the mirroring effect of cinema, the specularization of all subject–object relations, their rigid division (which is the "other scene" of primary identification), and the return of a transcendental subject may not point to internalized social relations whose dynamic has been blocked, a blockage that Metz and Baudry have theorized and systematized.

In choosing the films of Fassbinder, I am guided by the fact that his work has given rise to the most widespread discussions about spectator-positioning and types of identification/distanciation. Thus, a certain familiarity can be assumed for the terms of the argument and the examples cited.

Most of Fassbinder's films are centered on interpersonal relationships and problems of sexual and social identity, in a way that is recognizable from classical Hollywood cinema; and yet, even on casual inspection, his work seems to confirm quite strongly a heavy investment in vision itself, and a concentration on glance/glance, point-of-view shots, and seemingly unmotivated camera movements that foreground the processes of filmic signification. Accordingly, one finds two Fassbinders in the critical literature: (1) the German director who wants to make Hollywood pictures and whose audience-effects keep a balance between recognition and identification through genre-formulae and the use of stars, while at the same time distancing the spectator, placing him/her elsewhere through stylization and artifice. Tony Rayns, for instance, sums up some of these points when he argues that "Sirk taught Fassbinder how to handle genre, which became an important facet of his audience-getting strategies."[10] (2) The modernist Fassbinder, whose work is self-reflexive even to the point of formalism, and whose deconstruction of narrative involves him in fetishizing the apparatus. Cathy Johnson writes:

Fassbinder's highly visible cinematic signifier points to a fetishization of cinematic technique. Because all fetishism is an attempt to return to the unity of the mirror stage, one suspects Fassbinder of indulging in the very pleasure he withholds from his audience. Fassbinder is finally a director who approaches the Imaginary by means of a powerful attachment to and manipulation of cinematic technique as technique, while simultaneously barring entry to those of his audience who seek the Imaginary in the invisible cinematic signifier.[11]

I think one needs to argue that these positions contradict each other only insofar as they see audience-getting and audience-frustrating as opposite aspects of a basically unproblematic category, namely the spectator. It seems to me that Fassbinder's highly systematic textuality is not so much a fetishization of technique as the result of inscribing in his films and addressing a historical subject and a subjectivity formed by specific social relations. What is historical, for instance, in films like *Despair, The Marriage of Maria Braun,* or *Germany in Autumn* is the subject as much as the subject matter.

In West Germany, the "spectator" is a problematic category first of all in a sociological sense. Given that most film production is state and TV-financed, the audience does not recruit itself through box-office mechanisms but via diverse cultural and institutional mediations. And yet, filmmakers want to create an audience for themselves, not only by being active in restructuring the distribution and exhibition machine of cinema but also by trying to bind potential audiences to the pleasure and habit of "going to the cinema." Paradoxically, however, the most common form of binding in the commercial cinema, through character identification, is almost completely and consistently avoided by directors like Fassbinder, Herzog, Wenders, Syberberg, or Kluge as if somehow in the absence of a genre tradition, or an indigenous commercial cinema, audiences needed to be addressed at a different level.

It has been argued that the German cinema, and Fassbinder in particular, show in this respect the influence of Brecht: characters do not embody their parts but enact roles. But it seems to me that the viewer-film relation and the relation of the characters to the fiction which they enact is considerably more complex. In one sense, the two structures mirror each other infinitely and indefinitely, yet, as I shall argue, there is built into them an asymmetry, an instability that brings the relations constantly into crisis. Where Fassbinder seems to differ from both classical narrative and from modernist, deconstructive cinema is in his attitude to voyeurism and fascination. It is rarely fetishized in the form of action or spectacle, and does not seem to derive from primal scene or castration fantasies, as in the suspense or horror genre. Yet neither is it ascetically banished, not even in the long frontal takes of the early films. Instead, the awareness of watching marks both the entry point of the spectator into the text and the manner in which characters interact and experience social reality. One is tempted to say that in Fassbinder's films all human relations, all bodily contact, all power structures and social hierarchies, all forms of communication and action manifest themselves and ultimately regulate themselves along the single axis of seeing and being seen. It is a cinema in which all possible subject matter seems to suffer the movement between fascination and exhibitionism, of who controls, contains, places whom through the gaze or the willingness to become the object of the gaze. It is as if all secondary identifications were collapsed into primary identification, and the act of seeing itself the center of the narrative.

Faithful to a persistent Romantic tradition, German directors seem to be preoccupied with questions of identity, subjectivity, estrangment. Foundlings, orphans, abandoned children, social and sexual outsiders wherever one looks. Yet narrativization of these quests for identity are almost never coded in the classical tradition of conflict, enigma, complication, resolution. Instead of (Oedipal) drama, there is discontinuity, tableau, apparent randomness and fortuity in the sequence of events. One might say that in Fassbinder, but it is also true of Wenders and Herzog, there is a preference for paratactic sequencing, with little interest in action montage. Identity is a movement, an unstable structure of vanishing points, encounters, vistas, and absences. It appears negatively, as nostalgia, deprivation, lack of motivation, loss. Characters only know they exist by the negative emotion of anxiety—the word that in the German cinema has become a cliché; *Angst vor der Angst,* the title of one of Fassbinder's films, and also an important line in both *Alice in the Cities* and *The American Friend.* As in *Die Angst des Tormann's beim Elfmeter,* it almost graphically marks the place, the position where the ego, the self, ought to be, or used to be, but isn't. It is the empty center, the intermittent, negative reference point which primarily affects the protagonists, but which in another movement is also the empty place of the spectator; and one of the most striking characteristics of the films of Wenders, Fassbinder, and Herzog are the ingenious strategies employed to render the position of the camera both unlocalizable and omnipresent, decentered and palpably absent.

"I would like to be what someone else once was" is the sentence uttered by Kaspar Hauser, the foundling, when he was first discovered standing in the town square. The historical phrase appears in Herzog's *Enigma of Kaspar Hauser* as "I want to be a horseman like my father once was." As an attempt to formulate one's identity, such a project is symptomatic in its contradiction and impossibility. It tries to inscribe an Oedipal supercession in a temporal-historical succession: I/someone else, I/my father is the unthinkable equation, immersed in the Heraclitean flux of identity, difference, deferment. In Wim Wenders' *Alice in the Cities,* the same impossibility articulates itself in terms peculiar to the cinema. Traveling through America in search of himself, the hero takes pictures with his Polaroid. But by the time he looks at them, they never show *what* he saw *when* he saw it. Delay and difference as functions of an identity mediated by the presence/absence of the camera. Visiting a former girlfriend in New York, the hero has to agree with her when she says: "You only take pictures so you can prove to yourself that you exist at all." The cinema as mirror confirming an illusory identity, in the form of a double matrix of estrangement. Film and subjectivity find a common denominator in the German word *Einstellung,* whose polysemic etymology is often drawn on by Wenders in his writings. In filmmaking, the term applies both to the type of shot (i.e., the distance of camera from object) and the take itself (e.g., a long take). But outside filmmaking it means "attitude, perspective, moral point of view," and is literally derived from "finding oneself or putting oneself in a particular place." Language here anticipates the image of a spatial and specular relation, which only the cinema can fully realize.

In Fassbinder's *Merchant of Four Seasons,* Hans, the hero—another outcast seeking an identity by trying to take the place where someone else once was—explains how he lost his job: "The police had to sack me from the force for what I did. If I couldn't see that, then I wouldn't have been a good policeman. And I was a good policeman. So they had to fire me." Such double binds, where identity is coextensive with its simultaneous denial, fatally flaw all attempts at reintegration in Fassbinder, and they form the basis for a structure of self-estrangement that in other films appears as a social problem before it becomes a definition of cinema. In Margareta von Trotta's film, *Sisters, or the Balance of Happiness* one finds the line: "It's not me that needs you, it's you who needs me needing you." The story concerns a woman who systematically tries to turn her younger sister into a double and idealized self-image of herself, until the weaker one commits suicide in order to punish the stronger one. As a symptom of the split subject, the configuration described here has much in common with recent trends in the commercial cinema, especially as reflected in sci-fi and horror thrillers. To find the same material in the German cinema reminds one of its origins in German Romanticism and Expressionist cinema. The situation where a character seeks out or encounters an Other, only to put himself in their place and from that place (that *Einstellung*) turn them into an idealized, loved, and hated self-image, is of course the constellation of the Double, analyzed by Freud in terms of castration anxiety and secondary narcissism. If one can agree that, especially in the light of Metz's and Baudry's use of Lacan's mirror phase, the problematic of Other and Double has emerged as the cinematic structure *par excellence,* then its predominance as the cinematic theme *par excellence* of German films seems to demand further exploration. In classical narrative, the double and the split subject make up the repressed structure of primary identification. It appears that in the German films, because this structure is actually represented on screen, it points to a repression elsewhere, which in turn might serve to "deconstruct" primary identification.

Fassbinder's filmic output is instructive in that a certain line of development becomes clear in retrospect. What gives the impression of continuity despite the change of genres—gangster parody, melodrama, international art film—is that an obsession with mirroring, doubling, illusory self-images evolves from being a generalized cinematic theme to becoming a specifically German theme, or at any rate, the occasion for historicizing the obsession.

In the early gangster films *(Gods of the Plague, American Soldier)* the heroes' desire does not revolve around the acquisition of money or women but is a completely narcissistic desire to play their roles "correctly." Both men and women have a conception of themselves where their behavior is defined by how they wish to appear in the eyes of others: as gangsters, pimps, tough guys, prostitutes, femmes fatales. They play the roles with such deadly seriousness because it is the only way they know how to impose an identity on aimless, impermanent lives. What authenticates these roles is the cinema itself, because it provides a reality more real, but it is a reality only because it implies spectators. The characters in *Katzelmacher* are passive not because they are marginals, and spectators of life. Their endless waiting wants to attract someone to play the spectator, who would confirm them as subjects, by displaying the sort of behavior that would conform to the reactions they expect to elicit. The audience is inscribed as voyeurs, but only because the characters are so manifestly exhibitionist. Substantiality is denied to both characters and audience, they derealize each other, as all relations polarize themselves in terms of seeing and being seen. Except that to this negative sense of identity corresponds an idealism as radical as that of Baudry's "apparatus": to be, in Fassbinder, is to be perceived, *esse est percipi*. To the imaginary plenitude of classical narrative, Fassbinder answers by showing the imaginary always constructing itself anew.

The sociological name for this imaginary is conformism. The melodramas seem to offer a social critique of pressures to conform and the narrow roles that prejudice tolerates. But what if conformism was merely the moral abstraction applied to certain object relations under the regime of the gaze? An example from *Fear Eats the Soul* might illustrate the problem. Ali and Emmi suffer from social ostracism because of a liaison that is considered a breach of decorum. But the way it presents itself is as a contradiction: the couple cannot be "seen together," because there is no social space (work, leisure, family) in which they are not objects of extremely aggressive, hostile, disapproving gazes (neighbors, shopkeepers, bartenders). Yet conversely, they discover that they cannot exist without being seen by others, for when they are alone, the mutually sustaining gaze is not enough to confer or confirm a sense of identity. Love at home or even sex is incapable of providing the pleasure that being looked at by others gives.

The final scene resolves the contradiction. At the hospital where Ali is recovering from an ulcer, a doctor keeps a benevolent eye on the happily reunited couple. It is a look which only we, as spectators, can see, in a mirror placed on a parallel plane to the camera. The need which is also an impossibility of being perceived by others and nonetheless remain a subject produces both the sickness and the cure (in this case, a wish-fulfilling regression to a mother-son, nurse-invalid relationship under the eyes of an institutionally benevolent, sanitized father figure). Only the spectator, however, can read it as such, because the mirror inscribes the audience as another, this time "knowing" gaze.

It is a configuration strongly reminiscent of *Petra von Kant*. As the drama of double and Other unfolds between Petra and Karin, the spectator becomes ever more aware of Marlene as his/her double within the film. Instead of adopting the classical narrative system of delegating, circulating, and exchanging the spectator's look, via camera position, characters' points of view, and glance-off, Fassbinder here "embodies" the spectator's gaze and thus locates it, fixes it. Marlene's shadowy presence in the background seems to give her secret knowledge and powers of mastery. Yet this other character, virtually outside or at the edge of the fiction, is offered to the spectator not as a figure of projection, merely as an increasingly uncanny awareness of a double. But to perceive this means also to perceive that Marlene only *appears* to be the puppeteer who holds the strings to the mechanism called Petra von Kant. As soon as we recognize our double, we become aware of the camera, and in an attempt to gain control over the film, phantasmatize an author, a coherent point of view, a transcendental subject. We are plunged into the abyss of the *en abyme* costruction: Marlene is inscribed in another structure, that of the camera and its point of view, which in turn stands apart from the structure in which the spectator tries to find an imaginary identity. *Petra von Kant* is dedicated to "him who here becomes Marlene": who, among the audience, realizing that the dedication addresses them, would *want* to become Marlene?

Fassbinder's characters endlessly try to place themselves or arrange others in a configuration that allows them to reexperience the mirror phase, but precisely because the characters enact this ritual of miscognition and dis-placement, the spectator is not permitted to participate in it. Explicitly, this is the subject of *Despair,* in which the central character, attempting to escape from a particular sexual, economic, and political identity, chooses as his double a perfect stranger, projecting on him the idealized nonself, the Other he wishes to be. When this surrogate structure collapses, the hero addresses the audience by a look into the camera, saying: "don't look at the camera—I am coming out." If in Metz's term, the screen becomes a mirror without reflection, in Fassbinder's films we see characters act before a mirror, but this mirror is not the screen, except insofar as it coincides with the place where the camera once was. A dimension of time, of delay and absence is inscribed, in such an insistent way as to make it impossible for the spectators to use the screen as the mirror of primary cinematic identification.

Instead, one constantly tries to imagine as filled the absence that provokes the characters' self-display. The paradox which I have been trying to describe is that in Fassbinder's films the protagonists' exhibitionism is only partly motivated by the action, however theatrical, and does not mesh with the spectators' voyeurism, because another, more urgent gaze is already negatively present in the film. Another Fassbinder film in which this absent gaze is both named and erased is *The Marriage of Maria Braun*. Hermann, Maria's husband, has a role similar to that of Marlene in *Petra von Kant*. His disappearance, coinciding with the fall of

Hitler, becomes a necessary condition for the fiction to continue. The *idée fixe* of true love, on which Maria bases her career, is only disturbed by the periodic return of the husband, from the war, from prison, from making his fortune in Canada. It is for him that she does what she does, but only on condition that his place remains empty—reduced to the sign where someone once was. Absence turns her object-choice into an infatuation, which—expelled and phantasmatized into an *idée fixe*—becomes a transcendental but alienated self-image. Maria represses the return of the source of idealization, thereby also repressing the knowledge of the source of her economic wealth. Her life and identity appear under the sign of a marriage whose consummation is forever postponed and deferred.

The apparent perfunctoriness and lack of plausibility that strike one so disagreeably about motive and motivation in characters like Maria or the hero of *Despair* render palpable that not only is the visual space centered elsewhere, but so is the narrative. The characters, motivated by attracting a confirming gaze and simultaneously repressing it, display a symptomatically "paranoid" behavior. An ambiguity arises from the fact that the split corresponds to a repressed desire, where the anxiety of knowing oneself to be observed or under surveillance is overlaid by the pleasure of knowing oneself looked at and looked after: Fassbinder's cinema focuses on the pleasure of exhibitionism, not voyeurism.

Increasingly, and explicitly, this exhibitionism is identified with German fascism. In *Despair*, for instance, Nazism appears as both the reverse side and the complementary aspect of the protagonist's dilemma: to escape the sexual and social demands made on him, Hermann's personality splits into a paranoid and a narcissistic self, and he dresses up in someone else's clothes. Meanwhile, in the subplot, the personality split is metonymically related to economics, the change from small-enterprise capitalism to monopoly capitalism, and the proletarianization of the middle classes, who believe in the world-Jewish-Bolshevik conspiracy as a way of relieving anxiety about the future. The white-collar supervisor Muller, who works in Hermann's family firm, resolves *his* identity crisis also by dressing up: one morning he appears at the office wearing the brownshirt uniform of the SA. The exhibitionist-narcissist of practically all of Fassbinder's films here assumes a particular historical subjectivity: that of the German petit-bourgeois, identifying himself with the State, and making a public spectacle of his good behavior and conformism. Compared to Muller, Hermann's paranoia is sanity itself, and to narcissism as repressed paranoia in Hermann corresponds exhibitionist aggression in Muller. Conformism appears as the social side of the Imaginary which breaks down and constructs itself always anew in Fassbinder's films. To vary Brecht's poem *The Mask of Evil,* one might say that Fassbinder's films, optimistically, show how painful and difficult it is to fit in, to conform.

The structures of self-estrangement, of mirroring and miscognition, of positionality and identification with the Other, the double binds, structures that have habitually been interpreted as coinciding with the construction of the basic cinematic apparatus: might they not here be equally amenable to a historical reading? For instance, in terms of fascism, or more generally, as the need even today of binding a petit-bourgeois audience in the "social imaginary" of secondary narcissism. What, Fassbinder seems to ask, was fascism for the German middle and working-class which supported Hitler? We know what it was for Jews, for those actively persecuted by the regime, for the exiles. But for the apolitical Germans who stayed behind? Might not the pleasure of fascism, its fascination have been less the sadism and brutality of SS officers than the pleasure of being seen, of placing oneself in view of the all-seeing eye of the State? Fascism in its Imaginary encouraged a moral exhibitionism, as it encouraged denunciation and mutual surveillance. Hitler appealed to the *Volk* but always by picturing the German nation, standing there, observed by "the eye of the world." The massive specularization of public and private life, diagnosed perhaps too cryptically by Walter Benjamin as the "aestheticization of politics": might it not have helped to institutionalize the structure of "to be is to be perceived" that Fassbinder's cinema problematizes? But what produces this social imaginary, once one conceives of the Imaginary outside cinema or the individual psyche? And conversely, what or whom does the cinema serve by reproducing in its apparatus socially paranoid and narcissist behavior?

Such questions raise the political context in which Fassbinder works, what is usually referred to as the "repressive climate," the "counterrevolution" that has taken over in West Germany. As the government perfected its law-and-order state in overreaction to terrorist acts and political kidnapping, the experience of the semipoliticized student movement and many of the intellectuals was a massive flight into paranoia. In the face of a bureaucratic surveillance system every more ubiquitous, Fassbinder toys with another response: an act of terroist exhibitionism which turns the machinery of surveillance—including the cinema—into an occasion for self-display. For in his contribution to the omnibus film *Germany in Autumn,* he quite explicitly enacts the breakdown of authority, the paranoid narcissistic split whch he sees as the subjective dimension of an objectively fascist society. In this film—structured around the question of the right to mourn and to bury one's dead, of letters sent by dead fathers to their sons, of sons of the Fatherland forced by the state to commit suicide, so their bodies can return home for a hero's funeral, of children who kill father figures and father substitutes, and then commit suicide inside state prisons—Fassbinder concentrates singlemindedly on himself. Naked, in frontal view, close to the camera, he shows himself falling to pieces under the pressure of police sirens, house searches, and a virtual news blackout in the media. During the days of Mogadishu, when German soldiers carried out an Entebbe style raid to recapture a hijacked plane, he enacts a spectacle of seedy, flamboyant paranoia: that of a left-wing, homosexual, drug-taking artist and filmmaker (the Jew of the seventies?) hiding out in his apartment, while his mother explains to him the virtues of conformism in times of political crisis and why she wishes the state were ruled by a benevolent dictator whom everyone could love. Fassbinder makes the connection between paranoia and narcissistic object choice by a double metaphor, boldly cutting from his mother saying that she wished Hitler back to himself helplessly embracing his homosexual lover, as they roll on the floor, just as in *Despair* the employee Muller puts on a Nazi uniform, while Hermann goes off in search of a double.

What becomes problematic for Fassbinder is ultimately the question of sexual and social roles, and the impossibility of deriving stable role models from a "normal" Oedipal development. In the absence of constructing identity within the family (Fassbinder always demonstrates the violence and double binds that families impose on their members), the need to be perceived, to be confirmed, becomes paramount as the structure that regulates and at the same time disturbs the articulations of subjectivity. This means that the cinema, spectacle, the street, as places where the look is symbolically traded, become privileged spaces that actually structure identity outside the family, and in effect *replace* the family as an identity-generating institution. A film like *The Marriage of Maria Braun* on one level depicts a socialization process that enforces identity not through Oedipal conflict, substituting an object choice to escape the threat of castration, but through a structure modeled on the reaction formation to the loss of a particularly extreme substitution of the ego by an object. And under these conditions, the individual's most satisfying experience of subjectivity may be paradoxically as an exhibitionist, a conformist, in the experience of the self as object, not for anyone in particular but under the gaze of the Other—be it history, destiny, the moral imperative, the community, peer groups: anyone who can be imagined as a spectator. What may once have been the place of the Father, the Law, Authority and its castrating gaze,[12] here manifests itself as the desire to identify with a lost object, the benevolent eye of the "mother" as we know it from the mirror phase, It would therefore be wrong to say that the palpaple absence of the camera marks necessarily the place of the Father.

Conformism became, after World War II, one of the central preoccupations of American schools of sociology and ego psychology. David Riesman's idea of "inner-directed–other directed" *(The Lonely Crowd)*, Erik Erikson's "approval/ disapproval by a significant other," Melanie Klein's "good/bad object" in various ways all used Freud's papers on narcissism or his *Mass Psychology and the Ego* to conceptualize changes in social behavior in the face of a weakening family structure. In Germany, two books by the director of the Sigmund Freud Institute in Frankfurt, Alexander Mitscherlich, discuss the social psychology of German fascism and the post–WW II reconstruction period. In *Society Without the Father,* for instance, Mitscherlich argues that fascism, in its appeal to Germans of all classes, represents a regressive solution to the "fatherlessness . . . in a world in which the division of labour has been extended to the exercise of authority."[13]

Instead of assuming that Hitler figured as the Father, one has to imagine him fulfilling the role of a substitute for the primary love object:

[The mass leader], surprising as it may seem, . . . is much more like the image of a primitive mother-goddess. He acts as if he were superior to conscience, and demands a regressive obedience and the begging behaviour that belongs to the behaviour pattern of a child in the pre-Oedipal state. . . . The ties to the Führer, in spite of all the protestations of eternal loyalty, never reached the level (ie Oedipal) so rich in conflict, where the conscience is formed and ties with it are established.[14]

According to Mitscherlich, this helps to explain why Hitler vanished so quickly from the minds of Germans after 1945 and why the collapse of the Third Reich did not provoke the kinds of reactions of conscience, of guilt and remorse that 'the world' had expected. In *The Inability to Mourn* he writes:

Thus, the choice of Hitler as the love object took place on a narcissistic basis; that is to say, on a basis of self-love. . . The possibility of any dissociation from the object is lost; the person is in the truest sense of the term "under alien control". . . After this symbolic state has been dissolved, the millions of subjects released from its spell will remember it all the less clearly because they never assimilated the leader into their ego as one does the model of an admired teacher, for instance but instead surrendered their own ego in favour of the object. . . . Thus, the inability to mourn was preceded by a way of loving that was less intent on sharing in the feelings of the other person than on confirming one's own self-esteem. Susceptibility to this form of love is one of the German people's collective character traits. The structure of the love-relation of the Germans to their ideals, or the the various human incarnations of those ideals, seems to us to underlie a long history of misfortune. . . . Germans vacillate all too often between arrogance and self-abasement. But their self-abasement bears the marks not so much of humility, as of melancholy. . . .[15]

The West German economic miracle was sustained psychologically by defense mechanisms. The work ethic, ideologies of effort, the performance principle took on such ferocious proportions because of the "self-hatred of melancholia."[16] Why did West Germans rebuild such a conservative and conformist society? Democracy came to them imposed from without, and once again "under alien control," they reconstructed their Imaginary in the image of American consumer capitalism. In parabolic fashion, this is the story of *The Marriage of Maria Braun,* whose heroine's ambiguous strength lies precisely in her "inability to mourn." Benevolent eyes, such as those of Chancellors Adenauer or Schmidt, gaze in ghostly fashion out of portraits whose frame once contained that of Hitler.

To support a film analysis, however cursory, with such metapsychological observations courts many risks: can complex social and historical developments be reduced to and modeled on psychoanalytical concepts derived from clinical practice with individuals? Are generalizations about the national character not bound to remain at best abstractions, at worst mystifications that involve a mysteriously collective unconscious? Implicitly analogizing capitalism and the family structure as Mitscherlich does runs counter to the work, say, of R. D. Laing, or Bateson, where it is the family that becomes the place of contradictions specifically produced by capitalism. More serious still is the danger of collapsing a particular form of textual production, such as the cinema, with a naive reflection theory, so favored by sociologists of film or literature.

What is different between the Freud of Riesman, Erikson, Klein on the one hand, and that of Lacan, Metz, or Baudry on the other, is that the latter emphasize over and over again the specularity of relations which for the former are some-how substantial, physical, like the symptoms displayed by Freud's hysterical patients. Lacan's insistence on the image, the eye, in the deformation of the self—however incomplete this would be without his notion of textuality—shows the extent to which he has in fact read Freud in the light of concrete historical and social changes. Conversely, what separates Fassbinder from Mitscherlich, and what makes me risk speaking of a "social imaginary" without fear of getting it confused with some "collective unconscious" is Fassbinder's commitment to the primacy of vision and the representation of interaction and action in terms of fascination and specular relations.

If fascism is then only the historical name given to the specularization of social, sexual, and political life, then the concepts of Freudian psychoanalysis can indeed be pertinent, once Lacan has taught us how to read them. But by the same token, it suggests itself that Metz's primary identification partakes, as a theoretical construct or a descriptive category, in a historical development: call it, for the sake of the argument, the specularization of consciousness and social production—which his categories do not adequately reflect. In particular, to talk about primary and secondary identification as if it were a closed system risks conflating important distinctions, and, in the case of Fassbinder, and other "de-viant" cinematic practices, tends to institutionalize a deconstructive, overly the-oretical reading, where a historical reading might also be essential.

This said, it can be argued that in the case of the New German Cinema, we may actually have an interesting example of a productive misreading. One of the problems of the New German Cinema is that it is only slowly and against much resistance finding the audience inscribed in its texts—German intellectuals and the middle class. The major successes have been in the capitals of Western Europe and on American university campuses, i.e., with an audience who, ignoring the peculiar historical inscriptions that the texts might carry, have been happy to appropriate the films on the basis precisely of a familiarity with models of narrative deconstruction, modernist self-reflexivity, whether of the kind typical for certain European films or of the critical readings that film scholars have produced for the classical Hollywood narrative. In turn, the popularity which the films of Fassbinder, Herzog, Wenders have achieved abroad, and above all the critical attention given to them by magazines, at conferences, or in seminars, have, in a considerable way, strengthened their directors' chances of gaining more financial support in their own country from the government. This repeats the structure (on the level of production) which I tried to indicate is present in the texts themselves: the Germans are beginning to love their own cinema because it has been endorsed, confirmed, and benevolently looked at by someone else: for the German cinema to exist, it first had to be seen by non-Germans. It enacts, as a national cinema, now in explicitly economic and cultural terms, yet another form of self-estranged exhibitionism.

Notes

1. The reader is asked to forgive a rather large assumption made here. In the context of the conference it was necessary to presuppose the audience's familiarity with three essays that discuss (primary/secondary) identification, the "apparatus," and "subject-effect": Jean Louis Baudry, "Ideological Effects of the Basic Cinematographic Apparatus," *Film Quarterly* (Winter 1974–1975), vol. 28, no. 2; Christian Metz, "The Imaginary Signifier," *Screen* (1975), vol. 16, no. 2; Jean Louis Baudry, "The Apparatus," *Camera Obscura* (1976), vol. 1, no. 1. [All are included in this anthology—ED.]

2. Martha Wolfenstein and Nathan Leites, *Movies—A Psychological Study* (New York: Atheneum, 1970).

3. Alan Williams, *Max Ophuls and the Cinema of Desire* (New York, 1980).

4. See Constance Penley, "The Avant-garde and its Imaginary," *Camera Obscura* (1977), vol. 1, no. 2.

5. See interview with Christian Metz, *Discourse* (1979), no. 1.

6. Geoffrey Nowell-Smith, "A Note on History—Discourse," *Edinburgh Magazine* (1978), no. 1, pp. 26–32.

7. *Ibid.,* p. 31

8. Interview, *Discourse* (1979), no. 1.

9. See, for instance, Kristin Thompson and David Bordwell, "Space and Narrative in the Films of Ozu," *Screen* (1976), vol. 17, no. 2; Edward Branigan, "Formal Permutations of the Point of View Shot," *Screen* (1975), vol. 16, no. 3; Stephen Heath, "Narrative Space," *Screen* (1976), vol. 17, no. 3 [included in this anthology—ED.]; Noel Burch, *To the Distant Observer* (Berkeley: University of California Press, 1979).

10. Tony Rayns, ed., *Fassbinder* (London: British Film Institute, 1980), p. 4.

11. Cathy Johnson, "The Bitter Tears of Petra von Kant," *Wide Angle* (1980), vol. 3, no. 4.

12. See *Cahiers du cinéma's* reading of "Young Mr. Lincoln," *Screen* (1972), vol. 13, no. 3 [included in this anthology—ED.].

13. Alexander Mitscherlich, *Society Without the Father* (London: Tavistock 1969), p. 283.

14. *Ibid.,* p. 284.

15. Alexander Mitscherlich, *The Inability to Mourn* (1975), pp. 60–61, 63–64.

16. *Ibid.,* p. 63.